DINOSAURS
THE ENCYCLOPEDIA
Supplement 1

by Donald F. Glut

Foreword by RALPH E. MOLNAR,
PH.D., QUEENSLAND MUSEUM

McFarland & Company, Inc., Publishers
Jefferson, North Carolina, and London

To the
Society of Vertebrate Paleontology
and all its members
who have helped me so much over the years

Library of Congress Cataloguing-in-Publication Data

Glut, Donald F.
Dinosaurs: the encyclopedia : supplement one / by Donald F. Glut :
foreword by Ralph E. Molnar.
p.   cm.
Includes bibliographical references and index.
ISBN 0-7864-0591-0 (library binding : 50# alkaline paper) ∞
1. Dinosaurs — Encyclopedias.   I. Title.
QE862.D5G652   2000
567.9'1'03 — dc20   95-47668
CIP

British Library Cataloguing-in-Publication data are available

Manufactured in the United States of America

*McFarland & Company, Inc., Publishers
Box 611, Jefferson, North Carolina 28640
www.mcfarlandpub.com*

Acknowledgments

I thank the following vertebrate paleontologists for their critical review of selected sections of the manuscript, for their invaluable criticisms, suggestions, and other comments, and for generally improving the text: (For theropods) Ralph E. Molnar of the Queensland Museum, Queensland, Australia; (prosauropods) Peter M. Galton, University of Bridgeport; (sauropods) John S. McIntosh, formerly of Wesleyan University, Middletown, Connecticut; (thyreophorans) Kenneth Carpenter, of the Denver Museum of Natural History; (miscellaneous ornithischians) Hans-Dieter Sues of the Royal Ontario Museum, Toronto; (hadrosaurs) Michael K. Brett-Surman of the National Museum of Natural History, Smithsonian Institution, Washington, D.C., also my chief scientific advisor, who reviewed the entire work and made myriad suggestions for improving the manuscript; and (ceratopsians) Peter Dodson of the School of Veterinary Medicine, University of Pennsylvania, Philadelphia.

Thanks to the following vertebrate paleontologists, who sent me journals, reprints of articles, personal communications, and illustrations, or otherwise contributed to this first supplement to the 1997 *Encyclopedia:*

John R. Bolt, John J. Flynn and William F. Simpson, The Field Museum; Daniel J. Chure, Dinosaur National Monument; Walter P. Coombs, Jr., Department of Biology, Western New England College; Rodolfo A. Coria, Museo Mun Carmen Funes; Philip J. Currie, Royal Tyrrell Museum of Palaeontology; James O. Farlow, Department of Geosciences, Indiana-Purdue University at Fort Wayne; Mark B. Goodwin and Robert A. Long, University of California Museum of Paleontology, Berkeley; James I. Kirkland, Dinamation International Society; Giuseppe Leonardi, Conselho Nacional de Desenvolvimento Cientico e Tecnologico (CNPQ); James H. Madsen, Jr.,

DINOLAB; José Luis Sanz, Ciudad Universitaria de Cantoblanco, Madrid, Spain; Paul C. Sereno, Department of Anatomy, University of Chicago; Robert M. Sullivan, Paleontology and Geology, State Museum of Pennsylvania; and Matt Wedel.

Thanks to the following "paleo-artists" who contributed dinosaur illustrations (and who retain all copyrights and any other rights to their respective illustrations, whether explicitly stated or not) to this volume: Allen A. Debus (Hell Creek Productions and *Dinosaur World*); Brian Franczak; David Krentz; Gregory S. Paul; Michael W. Skrepnick; William Stout; and Robert F. Walters.

Also, thanks to Nina Cummings of The Field Museum; Stephen A. and Sylvia J. Czerkas, The Dinosaur Museum; The Dinosaur Society; Randy Epstein; Tracy L. Ford ("Dino Hunter"); my mother, Julia Glut; Don Lessem, Dinosaur Productions; Mike Fredericks, *Prehistoric Times*; Chris Mays and Michael Converse, Dinamation International Corp.; Mary Jean and Tosh Odano, Valley Anatomical Preparations; George Olshevsky, Publications Requiring Research; the Society of Vertebrate Paleontology; Susan Shaffer; Pete Von Sholly, Fossil Records; and Donald L. Wolberg, The Academy of Natural Sciences of Philadelphia. I apologize to any person or institution I may have missed.

As before, I have done my best to credit all illustrations and to obtain permissions for their use in this book, if permissions are so required. Copyrights for photographs (except for those privately taken, such as the ones shot by the author) and drawings of specimens, whether stated or not, are assumed to be held by the institution housing those specimens or by the publications in which those pictures initially appeared.

Foreword

One of the exciting things about science is that there is always something new. New discoveries are made, new information comes to light. The study of dinosaurs is no exception. Although dinosaurs, in the popular sense of the word (excluding birds), have been extinct these last 65 million years, there is still much more to learn about them. We tend to think that the past is dead, and we need only consult the record — be it our memories, written documents, or fossils — to know just what happened. Historians know how far they can — and cannot — trust the written word. And even our own memories are not completely reliable. Who has not sometimes disagreed with someone about the details of a shared past experience? Fossils do not lie, but they do require interpretation. There are always more, and new, fossils to be found, and these shed new light on old interpretations, sometimes casting doubt, but other times adding support.

Dinosaurs: The Encyclopedia is the reference work that interested laymen and amateur paleontologists always assumed existed, but which did not until Don Glut wrote it. It lists every known dinosaur, diagnoses the genera and species (where recent diagnoses are available), and illustrates some skeletal elements pertaining to almost all the dinosaurs. It is the kind of book that researchers working in taxonomy make up for themselves in their notebooks, with the aid of a photocopier and a good library. Now one can save the time and copying charges and just buy the book.

A lot of new information has been accumulated about dinosaurs in the past few years. It has been estimated that since 1970 there have been five times as many people working on dinosaurs as there were in all the years prior to that time. This has resulted in the proverbial "explosion" of information. New specimens of known dinosaurs, and new

kinds of dinosaurs, have added to our understanding of how dinosaurs lived and evolved. Specimens of small theropods (*Scipionyx* and *Sinosauropteryx*) have been found that preserve some of the visceral organs, and one of these (*Sinosauropteryx*) has rows of fine, branching filaments projecting from the skin, to form some kind of (still poorly understood) covering. Theropod embryos (presumably *Megalosaurus*) have been found in eggs in Portugal, and new dromaeosaurs from Mongolia have provided yet more evidence of the relationship between birds and theropods. Even though dinosaurs have been long gone — in body if not in spirit — we are still learning new things about them, and finding new kinds.

And when it comes to books about dinosaurs, this means that updates are necessary. The old knowledge is not necessarily wrong, but it must be viewed in a different light. Don Glut's *Dinosaurs: The Encyclopedia* provided a benchmark for all the dinosaurs named and described through 1996. In the following two years, new dinosaurs, like *Siluosaurus*, *Gojirasaurus*, *Archaeoceratops*, and *Megaraptor* have been found. In order to keep us abreast of these new developments, this supplement to that encyclopedia has been written.

The research that went into *Dinosaurs: The Encyclopedia* made it a necessary reference book for anyone learning about, interested in, or working with dinosaurs. This new volume is intended to meet the same standards and to carry forward the information provided there, in the light of these new discoveries.

RALPH E. MOLNAR, PH.D.
Queensland Museum

Composite skeleton (AMNH 460, 222, 339, and 592) of *Apatosaurus excelsus* in the American Museum of Natural History's Hall of Saurischian Dinosaurs. The specimen, recovered in the late 1890s, is historically significant as the first large dinosaur skeleton ever mounted for public display (in 1905) and is the heaviest dinosaur specimen in the museum's collection. It was remounted in the 1990s with a cast of the correct skull (former skull based on *Camarasaurus*), reconfigured ankle bones, additional neck and tail vertebrae (increasing the length from about 21 to over 25 meters), and with its tail off the ground. Photograph by the author, courtesy American Museum of Natural History.

Table of Contents

Preface

The book *Dinosaurs: The Encyclopedia* (McFarland & Company, 1997) was a compendium of data about dinosaurs based upon the original research of professional paleontologists as published in the literature (mostly in peer-reviewed articles appearing in scientific journals).

With that project (hereafter generally referred to in the abbreviated form *D:TE*), my intent was not to publish a substitute for the literature, nor was that book used for formal taxonomic purposes; rather, it was intended to serve as a handy reference tool for both professional paleontologists and students while also offering less technical information of interest to the amateur paleontologist, the dinosaur enthusiast or "buff," or the casual reader. Ambitious amateurs were given the opportunity and encouragement to tackle the more difficult parts of the book by utilizing the glossary, and seeking out the original cited references as listed in the bibliography.

Paleontology is a science in which there is constant change, based upon new fossil discoveries and fresh interpretations of previously studied fossil material. Unlike mathematics, history, and so many other disciplines with the suffix "-ology," much that pertains to this field is not locked down forever. That is why, as several vertebrate paleontologists have made clear to me, while mathematicians "prove" things, paleontologists "suggest," "propose," "hypothesize," "postulate," "demonstrate," and so forth. Indeed, this perpetual state of flux — along with the uncertainties, challenges, and creative ideas resulting from it — is one of the major appeals of this science.

However, the fact that there always seems to be something new in a science dealing with life forms so old creates both excitement and frustration for all authors who try to keep their reference books current. This is the curse known in the publishing world as "lead time" or "lag time" — that is, the length of time, usually spanning many months and sometimes even years, between a book's officially going into production (after which many changes, corrections, and updates are no longer possible to make for a variety of reasons, with those that are possible being quite costly) and its actual release to the consumer.

Especially frustrating to the writer impassioned with the subject of dinosaurs is the reality that new information about these animals continues to be published in the paleontological literature or made public in the news media and popular press. Unfortunately, sometimes the most interesting, spectacular, and important new data — such as the discovery in Mongolia of additional skeletons of *Oviraptor* found in a brooding posture atop their nests, in Spain of *Pelecanimimus* and in Italy of *Scipionyx* with internal soft tissues preserved, and in China of *Caudipteryx*, *Protarchaeopteryx*, and *Sinosauropteryx* with preserved feather impressions or feather-like structures; (see respective entries) — become known or available to an author too late for inclusion.

Another problem in keeping a book such as this "current" is the fact that much new information about dinosaurs, although known to the author, cannot ethically be incorporated into the text until the scientist working on that particular topic officially publishes his or her findings. This entire process can take years to reach completion, involving such realities as the time and money required in collecting a fossil, preparing it, studying it, then writing the paper in which the new data are revealed, waiting for the paper to be peer reviewed, awaiting its acceptance by a journal, and finally its publication, taking into consideration the journal's waiting list for papers and its own "lead time."

It may not be inaccurate to state that most books written about dinosaurs, whether technical, popular, or semipopular, and no matter how correct and current they are at the time of writing or final editing, are at least in some ways dated by the time they reach their readership. However, with so many new discoveries being made, and with so much fresh information about dinosaurs regularly appearing in the paleontological literature, it can be as exciting a learning experience for the writer to digest it all as it is to the eventual reader.

Attempting to keep a work the size of *D:TE* current through a potentially unending series of revised editions would be impractical for a number of reasons. These include the cost problems that would be heaped upon the publisher as well as the author; the financial burden imposed upon the reader attempting to keep current with the subject matter by purchasing subsequent updated editions; technical problems involving art direction and recompositing; and the inevitable size of some future edition that could be simply too big for the hands of any *Homo sapiens* to handle.

The plan to keep this project current is to maintain the encyclopedia as originally published, not changing its content (which would remain, as we might symbolically

Preface

Fanciful life restoration of the horned dinosaur *Agathaumas*, painted in 1895 by Charles R. Knight under the direction of paleontologist Edward Drinker Cope (see *Agathaumas* and *Monoclonius* entries, *D:TE*). This genus is known from very incomplete fossil remains lacking the skull, some details of this restoration having been based upon *?Monoclonius sphenocerus* (then thought to be another species of *Agathaumas*).

Courtesy Department of Library Services, American Museum of Natural History (neg. #322527).

say, carved in stone). That volume will remain a foundation upon which future publications could build, as new information surfaced, became available, and was assessed. All additions, corrections, revisions, and other changes could then be dealt with in an open-ended series of irregularly published supplementary volumes. These subsequent books would then ensure that this project would always be reasonably — while allowing for the dreaded lead time, during which editorial alterations would no longer be possible — up to date. Utilizing this plan, new ideas and theories will doubtlessly sometimes contradict those discussed in *D:TE* or earlier supplements; in some instances, however, the originals could prove to be correct after all.

The present *Supplement 1* is the first in that intended series. Between its covers are well over a dozen new dinosaurian genera and even more new species. There is no doubt that some of the information contained in these pages will also become dated or found to be incorrect, perhaps even before this volume's publication. Future corrections and updates will then be dealt with in those proposed follow up volumes.

Again, I invite the reader to point out to me (via McFarland & Company) any errors or omissions in the text so that they can be properly dealt with in a future supplement.

It must be noted that *D:TE* included much material — including background information, definitions of taxa above the genus level, pictures, *etc.* — that is not repeated in this supplement. Doing so would have been redundant, but more importantly, would have resulted in a new book perhaps as large as, if not larger than, the original. Therefore, regarding such encountered obstacles as undefined terms or the lack of a particular illustration, I suggest that the reader consult the original volume. Regarding material found in that first book, the reader will be directed to see *D:TE*; all references not so designated concern the present volume.

For the record, most additions, corrections, and other changes to this supplement ceased on August 25, 1998.

As in *D:TE*, life restorations of dinosaurs are featured in the "Genera" chapter of this book *only* if, in my opinion, the fossil material pertaining to a particular genus is sufficient to allow a reasonably accurate illustration.

(Unfortunately, this attitude will not always satisfy the cravings of some of the more avid and less technically minded dinosaur fans who might prefer seeing a picture of "every kind of dinosaur" no matter how scrappy the fossil materials representing those genera may be.)

Creating and then publishing (as do so many popular books about extinct animals) such fanciful life restorations provides no useful information to either the scientist or the lay person. Furthermore, these reconstructions only contribute misinformation and promulgate confusion in our interpretation of dinosaurs. Even more, they can also provide fuel for the antiscience sentiments and paranoia that still somehow manage to plague our modern world. Indeed, beautifully rendered life restorations, whether paintings or sculptures, based upon dinosaurian genera known from only a paucity of fossil remains, can and sometimes do impart to the public the false notion that scientists, as a group, are out to deceive or "trick" them for some unfathomable (to this writer) reason.

Therefore, following the policy established in my original encyclopedia, out-of-date or otherwise incorrect restorations (*e.g.,* world's fair exhibit figures, artwork by Charles R. Knight, *etc.*) are included herein only for their historical or aesthetic interest, or to illustrate an idea or theory discussed in the text; most of these are used only when a more accurate restoration is also available, reproduced either in this book or in *D:TE*; and none of these restorations appears in the section on dinosaurian genera.

New life restorations of dinosaurs appearing in this volume have been kindly supplied by artists whom I regard as among the best of a still relatively small but growing community of people who combine true art with scientific accuracy (see acknowledgments).

DONALD F. GLUT
Burbank, California

I: Introduction

Dinosaurs continue to be a prime subject of research among vertebrate paleontologists, as well as a topic of interest for the public.

Although these extinct animals always seem to be popular with the public, their appeal, over more recent years, has notably increased. Some almost impossible to pronounce (and even more difficult to spell) dinosaur names have become household words, while dinosaur imagery has found its way into virtually every aspect of our culture.

For well over a century, the impression by the world-at-large of what dinosaurs (as well as other extinct animals) were like in life were those created by artist Charles R. Knight (1874–1953) (see Massey-Czerkas and Glut 1982; see also *D:TE* for selected reproductions), who made a long and prosperous career out of restoring animals that had long ago vanished from the Earth. Knight's drawings, paintings, and sculptures were the first to depict these erstwhile animals and their environments both artistically and realistically, and in a modern sense. Unlike the fanciful recreations of "prehistoric animals" and "antediluvian monsters" created by artists that preceeded him (see Benjamin Waterhouse Hawkins' models in *D:TE*; McCarthy and Gilbert 1994; also, Colbert 1997 for an overview of the evolving images of dinosaurs in art), Knight's had a basis in scientific reality.

Knight based his restorations upon the paleontological information available to him at the time, always working from the hard fossil evidence and under the guidance of some of the world's most renowned paleontologists (*e.g.*, Edward Drinker Cope and Henry Fairfield Osborn). Also, Knight had an extensive knowledge of living animals, which he applied to his restorations. When gaps needed to be filled in and the fossil record could not do that job, Knight's own educated guesses often sufficed.

For many decades, it was through Charles R. Knight's perceptive and intuitive eyes that the world viewed dinosaurs and other animals long extinct. His visions became our own, his works constituting the standard or common denominator for the depiction of animals none of us could ever see alive. Put into the perspective of the time they were created and what scientific data were available to him, Knight's works can indeed be considered paleontologically correct. They also remain valid as fine art. However, by today's standards, Knight's works have become dated, based as they were on earlier conceptions of what dinosaurs were, how they appeared in life, and how they behaved. (For example, contrary to the images conveyed through Knight's works, we now know that dinosaurs were not slow-moving and sluggish beasts, that they did not drag their tails, and that the huge sauropods were not water-bound.)

Today, we know that dinosaurs were far more

Small "cartoon" painted by Charles R. Knight done prior to his 1931 oil mural (see *D:TE* for reproduction) depicting dinosaurs of the Late Cretaceous of western Canada: (left to right) *Corythosaurus casuarius, Parasaurolophus walkeri* group, armored *"Palaeoscincus" costatus* (based on *Edmontonia rugosidens*), *Struthiomimus altus* pair, and *Edmontosaurus regalis* group.

Courtesy The Field Museum (neg. #66247).

"Cartoon" of *Stegosaurus stenops* painted by Charles R. Knight in 1928 prior to his mural (circa 1928–31; see *D:TE*), a restoration now thought somewhat inaccurate based on what is today known about this plated dinosaur.

interesting creatures than even a visionary such as Knight ever imagined — and the facts about these animals are, at last, getting out to an interested and receptive public. More recently, technical articles reporting new discoveries of dinosaur fossils, naming and describing new dinosaurian genera and species, revising dinosaurian systematics, offering new theories regarding possible behavior, and discussing other topics pertaining to these fascinating animals, once relatively rare in the paleontological literature, have become common.

Our knowledge about dinosaurs is enriched on a daily basis, while many of the new and sometimes revolutionary ideas about these animals introduced within the past couple of decades are now being seriously contested.

Increased dinosaur research has resulted, in part,

through substantial funding arranged by organizations like the Dinamation International Society (originally a part of the Dinamation International Corporation, founded in 1983 by president Chris Mays, but now an independent entity) and The Dinosaur Society (founded in 1991 by writer Don Lessem). The latter (see Lessem 1997) is an international, not-for-profit organization dedicated to furthering paleontological education and research. The Dinosaur Society has provided grants on a worldwide basis for research in the dinosaur sciences, published technical and popular works, arranged special traveling dinosaur exhibits (such as "The Dinosaurs of *Jurassic Park*"), approved various dinosaur-related products, and has underwritten dinosaur-related articles appearing in the *Journal of Vertebrate Paleontology*, the official publication of the Society of Vertebrate Paleontology (publication costs for journal articles often paid for by the authors themselves). In 1996, The Dinosaur Society joined forces with the Society of Vertebrate Paleontology (SVP) and The Palaeontological Society in a mutual philosophical and scientific commitment "to developing responsible policies and legislation to protect fossils on public lands from commercial exploitation."* In 1998, The Dinosaur Society was undergoing financial reorganization.

Dinosaurs and the Public

As scientists continue to sort out and interpret the information gleaned from dinosaur remains and traces, the public also reaps some of that information (albeit often the more sensational or controversial new ideas) through such outlets as newspaper and magazine articles, popular books, radio and television news and information programs, video documentaries, and other sources. Dinosaur toys and models, though usually inaccurate (see Paul 1997), never cease to be popular and are collected by many adults as well as the children at which most of these items are generally targeted.

Obviously, the public craves viewing dinosaurs, not only as fossil remains displayed in museums, but as these animals appeared in life and in full size.

The first permanent display of such creatures were those unveiled in 1852 on the old Crystal Palace grounds in Sydenham, London. The figures, largely based upon a paucity of fossil specimens, and therefore incorporating as much imagination as science, were created by artist Benjamin Waterhouse Hawkins, based on the ideas of scientist Richard Owen (see *D:TE*; Glut 1980; McCarthy and Gilbert 1994). The hollow animals were built over iron frameworks utilizing brick, cement, and plaster. Maintained and repainted regularly by the Greater London Council, they can still be viewed today, preserved as the perfect example of the world's earliest interpretations of dinosaurs.

Future such parks were rather slow in coming, the next being the permanent display erected circa 1909 at Carl Hagenbeck's Tiergarten at Stellingen, near Hamburg, Germany. Part of this zoo was set aside for a suite of figures of dinosaurs and other

---

*Society of Vertebrate Paleontology News Bulletin, *Number 168, October, 1996, p. 9.*

Hypothetical restoration of *Iguanodon*, the second dinosaurian genus to be named and described by sculptor Benjamin Waterhouse Hawkins under the supervision of anatomist and pioneer paleontologist Richard Owen for the Crystal Palace grounds in Sydenham, London. Although the vegetation has changed much in this May 1984 picture, the "life-sized" figures in this display have remained constant since they were constructed in 1853.

Mesozoic reptiles sculpted by Josef Franz Pallenberg. In 1935, the Calgary Zoo opened to the public its own new Prehistoric Park, inspired by Hagenbeck's, to which it has continued to add new figures of dinosaurs and other extinct animals for more than half a century. The first permanent display of full-scale dinosaur figures in the United States, Dinosaur Park, can still be visited on a hilltop overlooking Rapid City, South Dakota. Dinosaur Park was established during the middle 1930s and featured a group of concrete models made by local sculptor Emmett A. Sullivan.

In later years, with dinosaurs becoming ever more popular with the public thanks in part to the exposure they would enjoy in the various media, the concept of the dinosaur park would truly proliferate. Indeed, by the 1980s, similar parks of various quality could be found throughout the world.

The desire by the public to see dinosaurs not only in full size but also moving, as if alive, was orig-inally satisfied by the makers of the mechanical creatures that appeared at such events as world's fairs, including the 1933-34 Chicago World's Fair, and the 1964-65 New York World's Fair. At the former world's fair, nonjaded visitors were treated to the then state-of-the-art wonders of life-sized mechanical prehis-toric creatures in both "The World a Million Years Ago" exhibit, presented by Messmore and Damon (which produced the world's first mechanical di-nosaur, an *Apatosaurus*, for exhibition as early as 1919), and the "Sinclair Dinosaur Exhibit," courtesy of the Sinclair Refining Company (which had used dinosaurs in their advertising since 1930; see anonymous 1966). For the latter fair's "Sinclair Dinoland" exhibit, sculp-tor Louis Paul Jonas created a suite of full-scale di-nosaur figures, some of them mechanically animated, that can still be seen today, either the originals or copies of them, in parks and tourist spots in various parts of the world (see Glut 1980).

Courtesy Browarny Photographs, Ltd. (neg. #10-170-1).

Full-scale model of *Al-losaurus fragilis* as it origi-nally appeared in the Juras-sic section of the Calgary Zoological Society's di-nosaur park, the first such "permanent" outdoor ex-hibit in North America. This and other figures were removed during the late 1970s when the park was renovated and updated.

Courtesy Travel Division, South Dakota Department of Highways, Pierre, South Dakota.

Tyrannosaurus rex and *Triceratops horridus* at Dinosaur Park (the first permanent display of such figures in the United States) atop Skyline Drive in Rapid City, South Dakota. The figures, sculpted by Emmett A. Sullivan, were based on a mural painted by Charles R. Knight for the Field Museum of Natural History, and also on the figures at the "Sinclair Dinosaur Exhibit," Chicago World's Fair (1933-34).

Photograph by Larry Williams.

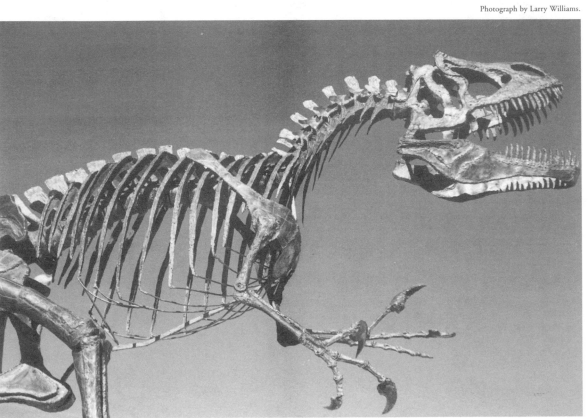

A unique modern full-scale dinosaur sculpture — a steel *Allosaurus* skeleton made in 1997 by Larry Williams for the Wyoming Dinosaur Center, Thermopolis, Wyoming.

In more recent years, companies such as Kokoro Company, Ltd., in Japan and, most prominently, Dinamation International Corporation,* the latter based in Irvine, California, have met the public's desire to be in the presence of life-sized and also moving dinosaurs, ensuring that the information conveyed by their figures is mostly correct and up to date. Both companies produce and distribute a line of scientifically accurate robotic dinosaurs (as well as other

Courtesy Francis B. Messmore, Messmore and Damon.

Mechanical *Triceratops horridus* and *Tyrannosaurus rex* figures designed by P. G. Alen (based on a mural by Charles R. Knight; see *D:TE*) as they appeared in the "Sinclair Dinosaur Exhibit," Chicago World's Fair (1933-34).

See Callison (1997) for detailed information on how Dinamation's robotic creatures are designed, manufactured, and operated, with particular emphasis on the relatively new genus Utahraptor; also see Utahraptor entries, D:TE and this volume.

This diminutive *Apatosaurus* was one of many mechanical creatures inhabiting "The World a Million Years Ago," Messmore and Damon's popular attraction that played in various locations in the United States from 1933 to 1972.

Courtesy Chicago Historical Society.

extinct creatures) which are very popular attractions at the museums, schools, shopping malls, and other places where they are exhibited throughout the world. The Kokoro and Dinamation International figures are designed under the supervision of prominent vertebrate paleontologists — John R. Horner for the former, George Callison, James I. Kirkland, and Robert T. Bakker for the latter — to ensure the accuracy of their figures.

Perhaps the public's greatest exposure to "live" dinosaurs, in recent years, came not from museums but from popular media. Michael Crichton's *Jurassic Park* (1990), a cautionary science-fiction novel about cloning dinosaurs, sold as a major Hollywood property even before the book's publication, became an almost instant national best-seller. Though the novel

and subsequent motion picture based on it were speculative fiction, their scientist characters (one of them based upon paleontologist John R. Horner) brought to mainstream readers some of the more recent findings and theories about dinosaurs, while adding the much-promoted yet often misused word "Jurassic" and the suffix "raptor" (actually an ornithological term) to our mainstream vocabulary.

The movie version of *Jurassic Park* (released by Universal in 1993), directed by Steven Spielberg, brought Crichton's concepts to the screen via some ground-breaking special-effects techniques (created by Stan Winston and Industrial Light and Magic). Unlike the vast majority of Hollywood dinosaur movies, *Jurassic Park* attempted to present dinosaurs more realistically, and as animals instead of monsters

A *Deinonychus antirrhopus* group feast on *Tenontosaurus tilletti* as the pterosaur *Pteranodon ingens* watches. Robotic creatures designed, built, and exhibited worldwide by Dinamation International Corporation, Irvine, California.

(although for artistic reasons, some liberties were taken with scientific accuracy).

The filmed version of Crichton's story was seen by a vast audience and quickly became the most profitable dinosaur movie in the history of the industry. It inspired a sequel, *The Lost World: Jurassic Park* (1997), which, in turn, had been based in part on *The Lost World*, a followup novel by Crichton.

Museums and Publications

Museums, themselves often relics of some earlier time and outmoded scientific thought, have also done much, in recent years, to bring new ideas about dinosaurs to the general public. During the 1980s and 1990s, a number of museums have renovated and updated their fossil halls, some of these having remained virtually unchanged for nearly a century, to reflect current paleontological knowledge and theories. Such renovations include the removal of outdated artwork, dioramas, charts, and other sources of information, and also the costly dismantling and remounting — in new and often more dynamic poses — of skeletons that had stood silent and unmoving for the public to marvel at and study since the late 1800s or early 1900s.

Among those grand institutions that have, at considerable effort and expense, relatively recently so modernized are the Yale Peabody Museum of Natural History, the Denver Museum of Natural History, the Natural History Museum of Los Angeles County, and The Field Museum (see the booklet *Chicago's Dinosaurs*, published in 1994; also Danis 1997*a*, 1997*b*).

The Academy of Natural Sciences of Philadelphia, which fully renovated their dinosaur hall in 1984 — with the old and also newly acquired skeletons mounted correctly by paleontologist Kenneth Carpenter (see Carpenter 1997*b*, 1997*c* for information regarding the correct ways of mounting dinosaur skeletons for exhibit, explaining his work done for the Denver and Philadelphia museums, and also the Museum of the Rockies) — undertook another major reworking of the gallery in the late 1990s. This latest variation, called the "Discovering Dinosaurs" exhibition (Fretz 1998), opened in 1998 with the new designation Dinosaur Hall (see Wolf 1998). Among the Academy's prized new exhibits in this hall was a cast of the skeleton, produced by Valley Anatomical Preparations, of the gigantic Argentinian theropod *Giganotosaurus carolinii*.

One of The Field Museum's innovations for its new exhibition was the first-time mounting, by Prehistoric Animal Structures, Inc., of East Coulee, Canada, of the holotype skeleton of the crested duckbilled dinosaur *Parasaurolophus cyrtocristatus* (Danis 1997*a*; see also *D:TE* for photograph). The bones were

mounted with no restoration and no alterations within a structure designed to suggest the animal's shape, and secured by a lockpin system that allowed every element to be easily removed for study without the need for tools.

Perhaps the most ambitious of all such renovations were those undertaken by the American Museum of Natural History (see Dingus, Gaffney, Norell and Sampson 1995; Dingus 1996), which reorganized its two classic dinosaur halls, the so-called Brontosaur Hall (also known by such names as the Hall of Early Dinosaurs and Jurassic Hall) and Tyrannosaur Hall (also Hall of Late Dinosaurs and Cretaceous Hall).

Like the fossil galleries of most museums, those at the American Museum had been traditionally arranged according to their geological sequence and had remained virtually unchanged since the early 1950s, when they were last renovated under the direction of the museum's then Curator of Fossil Reptiles and Amphibians, Edwin H. Colbert (1953). The American Museum closed these hallowed galleries to the public in 1991, began the long work of renovation the following year, and reopened the newly designed galleries in 1995.

As the American Museum of Natural History had played a key role in the development of a method of scientific analysis for determining evolutionary relationships called cladistics (see *D:TE*), the halls were now arranged along modern cladistic lines and appropriately renamed the Hall of Saurischian Dinosaurs and Hall of Ornithischian Dinosaurs. State-of-the-art technology, video programs, special effects, and hands-on exhibits utilized by the above mentioned museums have made dinosaurs and paleontology more accessible and comprehensible to the non-scientists visiting their halls. (As of 1998 there were also plans to renovate the Carnegie Museum of Natural History in Pittsburgh, Pennsylvania.)

In addition to changes in the look and presentation of museum galleries, much correct information about dinosaurs in particular and paleontology in general, in past years largely accessible only to the professional researcher, has been made available to the public thanks to the increasing number of dinosaur scientists producing handsomely packaged books for a lay (yet willing to learn) audience.

Two such books were issued within a month of each other in a single year, 1997 — *Encyclopedia of Dinosaurs*, edited by vertebrate paleontologists Philip J. Currie and Kevin Padian, and *The Complete Dinosaur*, edited by vertebrate paleontologists James O. Farlow and Michael K. Brett-Surman. Both books comprised numerous in-depth articles, written by a grouping of the world's leading dinosaur experts on a level that was not, for the most part, overly technical.

These books were soon followed that same year by *Dinofest*™ *International: Proceedings of a Symposium Held at Arizona State University*, edited by paleontologists Donald L. Wolberg, Edmund Stump, and Gary Rosenberg, and containing numerous articles about dinosaurs and related topics, most of them of a technical nature. For dinosaur-related topics discussed in a depth beyond the scope of the present book, I refer the reader without hesitation to any or all three of these excellent volumes.

Although we know more today about dinosaurs than ever before, it is ironic that the more we learn, the more we realize how much about them yet remains to be learned.

As pointed out by Dodson (1990*a*) in a paper attempting to estimate the total number of dinosaurian genera that may actually have existed, our knowledge about dinosaurs is "hampered by archaic taxonomy, imprecise biostratigraphy, and imperfect preservation that bias our understanding of dinosaur diversity." Using a model of increasing dinosaur diversity and a bottleneck model to compensate for biases in the preserved fossil record, Dodson noted that new genera had been introduced between 1970 and 1988 at the rate of more than six per year, bringing the total number of valid genera up to 285 (circa 1990; the current total is more than 300). (Applying that rate to the *D:TE* project, it may be predicted that approximately seven new genera will appear for every year separating one supplement from the next.)

Dodson estimated the total number of dinosaurian genera to have been 900 to 1,200, this number representing about 75 percent more of the probably valid genera than is currently known from the fossil record.

In a similar paper published seven years later, Holmes and Dodson (1997) noted that about 51 new dinosaurian genera (most of them theropods) had been named and described between 1989 and 1995, thereby increasing the total number of known valid genera to about 336. Most of these new dinosaurian genera had been discovered in the United States, Mongolia, and China, with Canada, England, and Argentina trailing behind them, a significant trend being "the discovery of dinosaurs of Early Cretaceous age and the exploitation of certain geographic areas previously poorly known or underrepresented, including Europe, Africa, Southeast Asia, Australia, and Antarctica." Holmes and Dodson, after discussing such topics as the number of paleontologists who have

The American Museum of Natural History's cladistically arranged Hall of Saurischian Dinosaurs, which opened in 1995, dominated by skeletons of (left) *Tyrannosaurus rex* (AMNH 5027) and (right) *Apatosaurus excelsus* (composite: AMNH 460, 222, 339, and 592), remounted between 1992–94 to reflect modern paleontological ideas.

named and described new dinosaurian taxa, concluded with this statement: "Even in the United States, the number of prospective sites exceeds the number of qualified workers. No end is in sight, and there is no reason why any child fascinated by dinosaurs today cannot be a major explorer and contributor to dinosaur science 20 years from now."

Some of the more recent dinosaur discoveries and ideas about dinosaurs are discussed in the text of this book. The sections that follow include information about dinosaurs, most of which was acquired by the present writer after *D:TE* went to press. As in that first book, most of this information originally appeared in the paleontological literature; and some was based on studies yet in their early stages and published as "abstracts" of longer articles (presumably to appear in some journal or symposium volume at some later date), usually delivered orally at annual meetings of the SVP, or at symposia such as those held at the highly attended Dinofest™ (established by vertebrate paleontologist Donald L. Wolberg) events. However, as stressed by paleontologist Ralph E. Molnar (personal communication, 1997), many research results presented in such preliminary reports "never see the light of publication, because they turn out to be wrong or dubious," and the research involved cannot be evaluated until a full paper is published.

For information mentioned herein but not otherwise discussed in this text, please consult the original volume.

The Mesozoic Era

The dinosaurs reigned on this planet during most of a geologic expanse of time that has been named the Mesozoic Era (approximately 248 to 65 million years ago). The Mesozoic is subdivided into three "periods": the Triassic (245 to 208 million years ago, in the latter part of which the earliest dinosaurs appeared); the Jurassic (208 to 145.6 million years ago); and the Cretaceous (145.6 to 65 million years ago). Each of these periods, then, is further divided into various "stages," designated by such (always capitalized) adjectives as "Early" and "Late." In turn, each stage is subdivided into various "ages," such as "Maastrichtian" and "Norian," which can also be modified by such (noncapitalized) adjectives as "early" and "late."

Thus far, no dinosaurs are known to predate the Late Triassic epoch. (The Mesozoic Era and its divisions are discussed in *D:TE*.)

For a convenient reference, a basic breakdown of the Mesozoic Era follows. As is customary (*e.g.*, Weishampel, Dodson and Osmólska 1990), the three periods of the Mesozoic are arranged in descending

Courtesy G. Leonardi.

A record of a living dinosaur from the Early Cretaceous period: Fossil trackway made by an iguanodontid ornithischian preserved in Brazil (width of an individual footprint is 35–40 centimeters).

order from Cretaceous to Triassic. In turn, the various levels within each period are also arranged in descending order (revised geologic time scales adapted by Farlow 1997 from Gradstein, Agterberg, Ogg, Hardenbol, van Veen, Thierry and Huang 1994):

Cretaceous

LATE
MAASTRICHTIAN (71 to 65 million years ago)
CAMPANIAN (83 to 71 million years ago)
SANTONIAN (86 to 83 million years ago)
CONIACIAN (89 to 86 million years ago)
TURONIAN (93 to 89 million years ago)
CENOMANIAN (99 to 93 million years ago)

EARLY
ALBIAN (112 to 99 million years ago)
APTIAN (121 to 112 million years ago)
BARREMIAN (127 to 121 million years ago)
HAUTERIVIAN (132 to 127 million years ago)
VALANGINIAN (137 to 132 million years ago)
BERRIASIAN (144 to 137 million years ago)

Jurassic

LATE
TITHONIAN/PORTLADIAN (151 to 144 million years ago)
KIMMERIDGIAN (154 to 151 million years ago)
OXFORDIAN (159 to 154 million years ago)

MIDDLE
CALLOVIAN (164 to 159 million years ago)
BATHONIAN (168 to 164 million years ago)
BAJOCIAN (177 to 168 million years ago)
AALENIAN (180 to 177 million years ago)

EARLY
TOARCIAN (190 to 180 million years ago)
PLIENSBACHIAN (195 to 190 million years ago)
SINEMURIAN (202 to 195 million years ago)
HETTANGIAN (206 to 202 million years ago)

Triassic

LATE
"RHAETIAN" (210 to 206 million years ago)
NORIAN (221 to 210 million years ago)
CARNIAN (227 to 221 million years ago)

MIDDLE
LADINIAN (234 to 227 million years ago)
ANISIAN (242 to 234 million years ago)

EARLY
OLENEKIAN (245 to 242 million years ago)
INDUAN (248 to 245 million years ago)

New Discoveries, Ideas and Studies

In the past few years, dinosaur remains have continued to be found, collected, prepared, and studied at a remarkable rate. Work on some of this fossil material, as of this writing, remains in the early stages of research, and may eventually be formally described as new genera or species.

Much interest has been focused in recent years on the behavior of dinosaurs. A new insight into the possible lifestyle of at least some (unidentified) kinds of dinosaurs resulted from the discovery of well-preserved dinosaur nests in the Arenisca de Arén Formation Late Cretaceous (Maastrichtian) in the southern Pyrénées, Bastús, Lleida, Spain. As reported by Sanz, Moratalla, Diaz-Molina, López-Martínez, Kälin and Vianey-Liaud (1995), the nests, containing fossil eggshell fragments, were found mainly at the top of the formation in red sandstone 2 meters thick; underlying this red layer is sandstone exhibiting wave-induced sedimentary structures suggesting a near-shore environment.

(Other material recovered from this site include large bone fragments, tiny smashed bones apparently belonging to young dinosaurs, an incomplete skeleton of a small lizard, and land snails.)

A total of 14 nests were found at the site, each preserving from one to seven eggs (most nests having only two or three), and representing portions of nests deposited in a hole dug in the sand. The nests are closely spaced but do not overlap, their generally good state of preservation and lack of destruction possibly

Introduction

Once rare among fossil finds, dinosaur eggs are now relatively common. The first eggs identified as those of dinosaurs were incorrectly believed to belong to the primitive ceratopsian *Protoceratops andrewsi* (see *D:TE*). This painting by Chicago Natural History museum staff artist Maidi Wiebe portrays *P. andrewsi* in an unlikely bipedal pose apparently caring for its nest. The concept of dinosaurian parental care was not taken seriously until the late 1970s.

implying some degree of territorial behavior. The short distances between the nests could be explained by a high population density or a scarcity of favorable substratum. Most of the preserved eggshell sections exhibit subcircular contours. As some of the nests (and bone fragments) are well preserved, Sanz *et al.* interpreted them as having been destroyed by such animal activities as nesting and trampling, with nesting apparently having taken place during a short period of time "in the unconsolidated sands of the beach ridge."

As calculated by Sanz *et al.*, up to 300,000 eggs (each egg having an assumed 20-centimeter diameter) are present at this site in a rock volume of about 12,000 meters, the eggshell material amounting to about 5 percent of the total rock volume. This suggested to the authors that the nests and eggs represent "a nesting ground, and that the dinosaurs may have returned to this same area during several reproductive seasons."

Sanz *et al.* concluded that the "Bastús site is the result of the nesting behaviour of a dinosaur population living very near the sea shore and may represent a local example of a widespread phenomenon in the Upper Cretaceous of the south-central Pyrenees." The authors also noted that dinosaurian remains reported previously from marine sediments, and seemingly suggesting a marine habitat for some kinds of dinosaurs, had generally been later interpreted as those that had been washed out to sea.

A spectacular discovery of dinosaur fossils was reported via various information agencies—including radio news programs—in September and October, 1998, just as this supplement was going to press. The find, made in 1995 in Kila Kila, Bolivia, southeast of La Paz, included the largest dinosaur footprint site yet discovered (measuring approximately a thousand feet in length), representing such groups as theropods and ornithopods, and also at least two new dinosaurian species. The locality was worked by a team led by Swiss paleontologist Christian Meyer, with work concluding in 1998. At least 50 tracksites were found in the area, including those at Cal Orcko and one near the town of Sucre.

The site near Sucre is the largest dinosaur footprint site yet found anywhere in the world; that at Cal Orcko includes some 3,000 footprints contributing to 250 different trackways.

According to David Keremba, president of the Paleontology Society of the San Francisco Xavier University, as reported by Reuters (October 7, 1998), the largest (and square-shaped) tracks found were made by a very large quadrupedal dinosaur that must have measured up to 66 feet in length, with a pelvis at least three feet in width. These prints apparently represent a new species possibly indigenous to Kila Kila.

Saurischians

The Saurischia—the group of so-called "lizard-hipped" dinosaurs (see *D:TE*; also "Systematics" chapter, this volume)—include the only known carnivorous dinosaurs (theropods), as well as the largest of dinosaurs (sauropodomorphs).

THEROPODS

The carnivorous dinosaurs, or those belonging to the Theropoda, remain among some of the most interesting to scientists and laymen alike, and much research continues to reveal more about this large group.

A new theropod belonging to the relatively primitive group "Ceratosauridae" was announced in a preliminary report by Tykoski (1997). This theropod is known from hundreds of postcranial elements collected during the late 1970s by crews from the Museum of Northern Arizona and Museum of Comparative Zoology from the Kayenta Formation of Northern Arizona. The small size of these specimens originally led workers to assume that they represented juvenile individuals of some known species.

More recently, however, closer examination of these specimens revealed that many displayed features associated with later ontogenetic stages. As observed by Tykoski, these features include the following: Fusion of sacral centra, neural spines, ribs, and transverse processes; fusion of pelvic bones to one another; total closure of sutures between neural arches and vertebral centra; unification of astragalus and calcaneum; fusion of resulting astragalocalcaneum to distal tibia; and complete fusion between scapula and coracoid.

According to Tykoski, the above features suggest that these specimens represent adult and not juvenile individuals. As the largest of these elements are less than one-half the size of comparable elements belonging to other known "ceratosaurids" which show similar degress of skeletal ossification, Tykoski was unable to refer these specimens to any previously described "ceratosaurid" species.

Although Tykoski had not yet determined if these remains possess any characters diagnostic beyond the level of "Ceratosauria," this discovery, the author noted, is significant in increasing what is known of theropod diversity in the Early Jurassic.

The front limbs in "ceratosaurs," and also those of other kinds of carnivorous dinosaurs came under the scrutiny of Holtz (1995*a*) in a preliminary study on the adaptive trends in major subgroups of theropods and related taxa. Holtz found that the manus of coelophysoids (and also of herrerasaurids, a group of yet more primitive theropods) was capable of hyperextensions. This capability, according to Holtz, "may have served to enhance the raking effects of the claws or may indicate that these forms may have occasionally used a quadrupedal stance."

Holtz also noted that the forelimb and manual mobility (not the manus itself) of neoceratosaurs are reduced relative to all other theropods excluding tyrannosaurids and, therefore, were probably not used in predations, while the forelimb in basal tetanurines ("megalosaurs") and true carnosaurs was most likely the main predatory weapon.

New "ceratosaurian" taxa continue to be discovered. Bonaparte (1996*b*), in a review of Cretaceous tetrapods of Argentina, briefly reported on a possible "ceratosaur" taxon known from the distal portion of a third metatarsal, with distal, lateral, and medial areas preserved, recovered from the Rayoso Formation (Aptian), Quili Malal, Neuquén Province. The specimen is currently in the private collection of a Mr. Melo, a farmer at Quili Malal. According to Bonaparte, the size of this specimen indicates a rather large animal.

Molnar, Lopez Angriman and Gasparini (1996) reported a new taxon distinguished as the first Cretaceous theropod and also the oldest Cretaceous tetrapod yet found in Antarctica. The specimen (MLP 89-XII-1-1) was discovered in summer 1988 by Alejandro Lopez Angriman in the Upper Cretaceous (Coniacian–Santonian; see Buatois and Lopez Angriman 1992), middle section of the Hidden Lake Formation, north of Col Crane, near Cape Lachman, northwestern James Ross Island. It consists of the distal end (measuring 40 centimeters long, probably 10 to 15% of the entire length) of a left tibia. Associated with this specimen were the fossilized remains of logs and various trace fossils.

According to Molnar *et al.*, the specimen resembles in general form the corresponding part of the tibia in the "megalosaurids" *Megalosaurus bucklandii* and *Poekilopleuron bucklandii*, and the allosaurid *Piatnitzkysaurus floresi*, all of which are Middle Jurassic forms, and also the Early Cretaceous (Albian) species *Erectopus superbus*. This suggested to the authors "that the Hidden Lake theropod represents a lineage probably derived from relatively plesiomorphic megalosaur or primitive allosauroid (but not sinraptorid) stock, unrelated to the lineages culminating in the more or less contemporaneous arctometatarsalians," this lineage, with its less advanced distal tibial structure, persisting in the Antarctic.

Assuming that the Hidden Lake theropod was at an adult stage of maturity when it died, Molnar *et al.* (1996) projected that it had a length of 3 to 3.5 meters (over 10 to almost 12 feet), if more gracile, or 2.5 to 3 meters (about 8.4 to 10 feet), if more robust. At either size, this dinosaur was relatively small, comparable to a large *Coelophysis*. In fact, this was probably too small, according to the authors, for the dinosaur to have been ectothermic and live under a climate below 15 degrees centigrade (see Molnar and Wiffen 1994). This also implied a rather mild climate for at least some areas of James Ross Island during Coniacian–Santonian times.

Bakker (1996) has informally referred to a new and as yet undescribed "megalosaurid," apparently to be named "Brontoraptor," from the basal Talking Rocks member of the Morrison Formation (Upper Jurassic, Kimmeridgian–Tithonian) at Como Bluff, Wyoming (see Breithaupt 1997 for a detailed report on the early history of this, one of the world's first major dinosaur localities). According to Bakker, this genus is more advanced than *Torvosaurus* "in having squared-off iliac outlines and lower pelvic bones with large accessory outline."

In a preliminary report based upon theropod specimens collected at Como Bluff, Wyoming, Bakker (1997*a*) found the "Megalosauridae" to be the oldest family of top predators and the one exhibiting the widest adaptive breadth. According to Bakker, different "megalosaurid" species differ from one another dramatically in such features as body form, the ratio of leg length to torso length, and the degree of pelvic fenestration. Also, the history of this family parallels that of the "Cetiosauridae" and Brachiosauridae (see "Systematics" chapter), the oldest sauropod families, all of them showing increase in size before the disappearance of these taxa some two million years before the end of the Jurassic period.

Bakker (1997*a*) found the Allosauridae to be the youngest clade among the Como Bluff fauna, its members showing only modest diversity in body shape. Allosaurid species are separated from one another mostly in features of the jaw joints, jaw depth, and ear region, the postcrania of these taxa only rarely showing diagnostic differences. Body size in allosaurids increases 100 percent following the extinction of "megalosaurids," this consequently suggesting to Bakker release from competition with that group and co-evolution with large camarasaurid sauropods. Bakker (1997*a*) further pointed out that all "megalosaurids" and the most specialized allosaurids were extinct by the end of the Jurassic, and that only generalized allosaurids survived into the Cretaceous.

Coria and Currie (1997) reported a new theropod discovered in a quarry at the locality of Cortaderas, in the Río Limay Formation (Upper Cretaceous), south of Plaza Huincul, Nequén, Argentina. The specimen represents the second theropod recorded from the Huincul member; these taxa, in addition to a new iguanodontid and the sauropod *Argentinosaurus,* making up one of the more diverse faunas from the Neuquén Group.

As noted by Coria and Currie, the material collected at the time of their initial report include an isolated maxillary tooth, a surangular, caudal vertebra, manual ungual, acetabular region of an ilium, pubis, proximal part of an ischium, femora, tibiae, a fibula, metatarsal, and numerous pedal phalanges, with fossil material yet to be recovered. In their preliminary description of this material, Coria and Currie noted that the dental morphology is suggestive of carcharodontosaurids, while some femoral features (*e.g.*, deep sulcus, dorsally oriented femoral head) are also present in *Giganotosaurus*.

As this specimen is distinct from *Giganotosaurus* and an unpublished 5-meter abelisaurid from Neuquén in both size and ontogenetic stage of development, Coria and Currie proposed that it represents a new taxon that may allow the authors "to evaluate the phylogenetic relationship between abelisaurids, carcharodontosaurids, and other carnosaurs."

Chure, Manabe, Tanimoto and Tomida (1998) briefly described, in a preliminary report, an "unusual theropod tooth" that had been collected in 1990 from the Upper Formation (Late Cretaceous: upper Cenomanian) of the Mifune Group, near Amagimi Dam, at Tashiro, Mifune-cho, Kamimasuki-Gun, Kunamoto Prefecture, Japan. Though presently indeterminate, the find represents one of the relatively small number of dinosaurs known from Japan, implying a greater diversity in the Mifune theropod fauna than was earlier suspected.

Chure *et al.* described this tooth as follows: Crown bladelike, measuring 50 millimeters in height and, at the base, 9 millimeters in width; posterior margin rising vertically with but a slight curvature near the tip; anterior and posterior serrations small (15 serrations per 5 millimeters); arcuate enamel wrinkles along the lingual and labial surfaces of both margins, these ridges sweeping down and away from the serrations, separated by shallow grooves, and fading away from the crown margin, ridges becoming fainter towards the tip, ending before the tip.

Although enamel ridges are also known in teeth of the allosauroid *Carcharodontosaurus*, Chure *et al.* pointed out that the tooth crown shape in that genus is quite different, with the wrinkles running across the side of the tooth. Other teeth known from the Mifune Group, the authors noted, do not show such wrinkles.

In an abstract, Naish (1998c) reported that undescribed materials now indicate that several theropods — some of them even larger than the well known genera *Neovenator* ("an allosaur with a puffin-shaped snout"; see entry) and *Baryonyx*— were present in Wealden faunas, some of them comparable with the highly diverse faunas of the Late Jurassic of North America.

Naish (1998a), in another abstract, briefly reported on a robust partial right tibia (BMNH R9385) belonging to an unnamed and undescribed, medium-sized theropod recovered from Wealden rocks of Hastings (Sussex). This specimen measures 16 centimeters in length as preserved, with an estimated complete length of 24 centimeters, indicating an animal about the size of the North American genus *Deinonychus*. Diagnostic features are not evident, although the tibia clearly does not belong to *Neovenator*. As Naish observed, the most potentially interesting features of this specimen are markings suggesting bite marks of another theropod. This, according to Naish (1998c), constitutes the first reported instance of theropod tooth marks on a bone of a Wealden theropod.

In another abstract, Naish (1998b) reported that a small (123 millimeters in length) femur (MIWG 6214) belonging to a previously unknown Wealden theropod dinosaur was found in 1986 on the Isle of Wight. The specimen represents a juvenile individual, as evidenced by the degree of pitting on the femoral head and lesser trochanter. It "is remarkable in possessing an extremely long and low lesser trochanter that is clearly not of the 'wing-like' morphology characteristic of tetanuran theropods." Certain primitive characters otherwise known only in Late Triassic and Early Jurassic taxa indicate that MIWG 6214 pertains to a late-surviving member of a clade believed to be extinct (*i.e.,* "a Lazarus taxon").

Makovicky (1997) described a new (unnamed) small coelurosaurian theropod from the Morrison Formation (Upper Jurassic) of Como Bluff, Albany County, Wyoming. The dinosaur is represented by probable fifth and probable fourth cervical vertebrae (YPM 1996 and YPM 1997, respectively), possibly belonging to the same individual. Marsh (1897) originally referred these remains to his new genus *Coelurus* (see entry, *D:TE*), the type material of which had been collected from a different quarry than that which yielded the above two specimens.

In reexamining YPM 1996 and YPM 1997, Makovicky found that these two vertebrae can be distinguished from corresponding elements of other small theropods by the following three autapomorphies: 1. Anterior intercentral articulation moderately convex, intercentral articular facet offset from centrum by distinct rim; 2. longitudinal ridge extending from each parapophysis posteriorly, tapering distally; and 3. depression located on posterior face of each parapophysis.

Makovicky observed the following coelurosaurian synapomorphies in the above specimens: 1. Anterior cervical vertebrae having wide and low anterior intercentral articulation; 2. cervical prezygapophyses anteroventrally inclined; and the following synapomorphies with manuraptorans (spelling corrected by Charig and Milner 1997 from "maniraptoran"; see "Systematics" section) more derived than *Coelurus*: 1. Anterior cervical zygapophyses large relative to intercentral articulation; and 2. neural spines low, axially short.

As noted by Makovicky, the opisthocoelous nature of YPM 1996 and 1997 is unusual for a coelurosaur, the only other known form displaying this feature being the Wealden species *Calamospondylus oweni*. Furthermore, the intercentral-articulation morphology in the two cervical vertebrae is unique among the Coelurosauria, thereby representing another diagnostic feature of this new taxon.

Ideas about the possible feeding techniques employed by the coelurosaurian group Tyrannosauridae

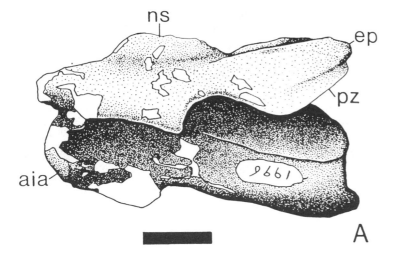

ns

ep

pz

aia

9661

A

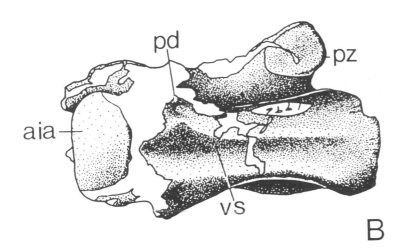

pd

pz

aia

vs

B

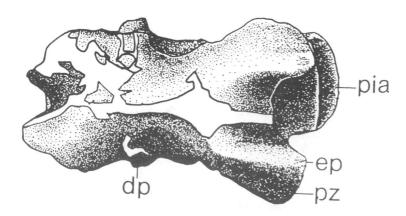

pia

pd

ep

dp

pz

Fifth cervical vertebra (YPM 1996) of a new (unnamed) coelurosaurian theropod from Como Bluff, Wyoming, in A. lateral, B. ventral, and C. dorsal views. Scale = 1 cm. (After Makovicky 1997.)

were offered in various studies of tyrannosaurid teeth.

Brandvold (1996), in a preliminary report based upon a study of Campanian-age shed tyrannosaurid teeth, showed that these teeth exhibit breakage and wear from pressure on their tips, this consequently suggesting that repeated striking of the bone occurred during feeding. As observed by Brandvold, the "wear ranges from fresh breaks without subsequent wear, to teeth that were broken and worn smooth, to nearly rounded off stubs." The fresh break was indicated by spiral fracturing that would occur only in very fresh dentin, evidenced by similar fractures wherein the broken surfaces had been rounded by wear. This kind of fracture would most easily be made by direct pressure of the tooth tip with a solid material such as bone; the later rounding would indicate repeated contact with the bone.

Brandvold postulated that tooth breakage was less likely if a tooth were hammered into bone by repeated bites (as opposed to one massive bite), allowing the dissipation of stresses occurring in the tooth while crushing bone, this technique being comparable to using an air scribe instead of a hammer and chisel.

Jacobsen (1996) reported on the possible biting strategies of tyrannosaurids, based on a study of wear patterns found on 706 teeth gathered from the Dinosaur Park Formation of Alberta, Canada. Of this total, 383 teeth either had wear facets or were broken. Of those teeth, 49 percent had anterior wear facets, 29 percent were broken, 25 percent had lingual wear facets, 20 percent posterior wear facets, and 4 percent labial wear facets. Some teeth had more than one wear facet.

As Jacobsen noted, the location of the main wear facet shows that the tooth row was positioned perpendicular to the longitudinal axis of the bone into which it was biting. "This assumes that the tip of the tooth was the first to contact bone, and the stronger curvature of the tip of the tooth brought the anterior edge into contact with bone during a bite." Jacobsen states if the biting force was greater than the strength of the tooth, either 1. the tooth tip broke off in a characteristic chip shape, or 2. the tooth broke off nearer the root. Jacobsen's conclusions were supported by a correlation with the morphology of theropod tooth marks found on prey bones (see *Tyrannosaurus* entry.)

Senter (1998), in a brief report on the configuration of jaw adductors and possible biting style in tyrannosaurids, noted that a theropod jaw adductor plus the mandible constitutes a third-degree lever. Two basic configurations were apparent in tyrannosaurids for this mechanism implying two different feeding strategies:

1. In order for a tyrannosaurid's jaws to clamp onto and then hold its prey with maximum efficiency, the muscles must point upwards (this configuration typical for noncoelurosaurian theropods).

2. For the tyrannosaurid to execute a "hit and run" (or bite and release) attack, accommodating forward-bolting prey or tearing off a piece of its victim's flesh without dislocating its own jaws, the muscles must point backwards (the typical coelurosaurian configuration). With this configuration, the jaw adductors maximize resistance to anterior motion of the mandible.

Photograph by the author, courtesy Royal Tyrrell Museum/Alberta Community Development.

Skeleton of *Gorgosaurus libratus.* Recent studies of the teeth of such dinosaurs are leading to new conclusions regarding tyrannosaurid biting strategies.

The jaw adductors of adult tyrannosaurids pointed upwards, indicating that adults were "oral clampers" that held their prey still in order to avoid dislocation of their jaws. On the other hand, the jaws of juveniles exhibit rearward-pointing muscles. These configurations suggested to Senter that juveniles attacked their prey predaciously, while adults were more suited for feeding upon carion and small prey. This further suggested to the author that tyrannosaurid tooth marks found on the bones of large animals were probably produced during scavenging rather than predation.

Another report regarding teeth and theropod feeding methods was made by Brandvold and Brandvold (1996), based upon scavenged bones of the hadrosaur *Maiasaura* (as well as remains of turtles, fishes, and theropods, including a tooth of the carnivorous dinosaur *Saurornitholestes langstoni*) from the Jones' site, Two Medicine Formation (Campanian) of north-central Montana. Bite marks on the hadrosaur remains also indicate crushing by repeated hammering of teeth against bone.

Brandvold and Brandvold also briefly mentioned a trampled ornithomimid tail found at this sight, evidence interpreted by them as possibly "representing the trimming of a food item"; and two examples of short vertebral sections perhaps representing trimming of a food item by tearing, apparently performed by holding the item down with one foot, then utilizing teeth, jaws, and neck to tear the item in the fashion of some birds of prey.

Among more recently recovered theropod specimens is an incomplete partially prepared sacrum, mentioned by Frey and Martill (1995), from the Santana Formation in Brazil. The specimen was interpreted by them, on the basis of the presence of pleurocoels, as possibly belonging to an oviraptorosaurid theropod. However, according to the authors, and also to Kellner (1996) in a review of Brazilian dinosaurs, this assessment should be regarded with caution, as the Oviraptorosauridae is a very specialized group otherwise known only in Asia and North America (Barsbold, Maryańska and Osmólska 1990).

In reporting various fossil remains from the El Pelillal locality, Cerro del Pueblo Formation (Late Cretaceous, Campanian), Coahuila, Mexico, Rodriguez de la Rosa (1996) announced the finding of "a new troodontid represented by a II-2 toe phalanx that differs from that of other troodontids in being slender." From the same locality, Rodriguez de la Rosa also reported a possible dromaeosaurid, hadrosaurid (represented by an isolated tooth), pterosaur, crocodilian, chelonian, fish, plant fossils, and coprolites.

Manning, Joysey and Cruickshank (1997)—in a summary of recent research into especially well-preserved embryos in a series of fossil eggs collected during the early 1900s from the Nanchao Formation, Nanyang Valley, near Xinye, Henan Province, People's Republic of China—identified these specimens as belonging to the theropod family Therizinosauridae and egg family Dendroolithidae. The eggs are spherical in shape and generally about 90 millimeters in diameter (or approximately the size of a grapefruit). Some eggs included remains of an almost-hatchling and also several embryos displaying earlier stages of development. Jaws were found with teeth *in situ*, and soft tissues observed by the authors included cartilege, skin, and muscle. Most of the embryos were not preserved as entire skeletons, some having decomposed before drying out and consequently becoming disarranged, some apparently having been gnawed or reduced to bone chips. Several eggs contain numerous small oval-shaped structures closely matching the fecal pellets of

Introduction

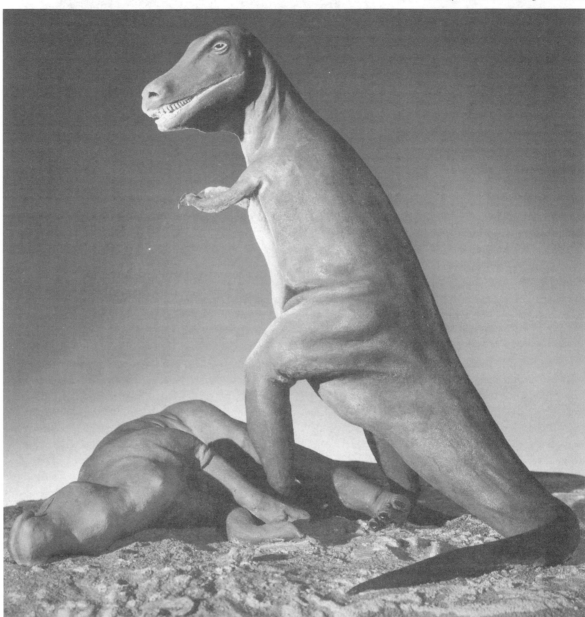

Were tyrannosaurids active predators or scavengers? This sculpture by Maidi Wiebe depicts what was originally identified as the tyrannosaurid *Gorgosaurus libratus* (but is probably *Daspletosaurus*; see entry) posed over the hadrosaurid *Lambeosaurus lambei*, these models based on skeletons as originally mounted in 1956. The tableau portrays the carnivore having found the recently dead herbivore: "While the predator was looking it over, something disturbed him: he has reared up, startled" (Zangerl 1956).

insect larvae, this being evidence as to what may have fed upon the embryos. Some eggs were found with apparent yolk preserved.

Manning *et al.* noted that the embryos in these eggs are close to the genus *Erlikosaurus*, but added that a final identification for them has yet to be worked out. The authors further noted that this "is one of the few cases where an egg parataxon can be confidently correlated with its body fossil."

De Klerk, Forster, Ross, Sampson and Chinsamy (1997) reported the discovery of the well-preserved, virtually complete skeleton of a new, small (length of ulna = 4.2 centimeters) manuraptoran theropod, found in 1996 in the Kirkwood Formation (Lower Cretaceous), Algoa Basin, South Africa, a locality pre-

viously known only for poor dinosaurian material. In a preliminary description of this specimen, De Klerk *et al.* stated that the pes is extremely elongate, and that the manus is reduced to three digits and is more than twice the length of the forearm, these and other features identifying the theropod as a manuraptoran. Discovery of this specimen is significant in establishing the first record of the Manuraptora in Africa.

Le Loeuff and Buffetaut (1996) reported new dromaeosaurid material found at three Late Cretaceous localities in southern France. The type and referred specimens (the collected material including a sacrum with five fused vertebrae, dorsal vertebrae, and an odd humerus with strongly developed medial

tubercle) represent a new genus and species of dromaeosaurid. This material was recovered from two
late Campanian to early Maastrichtian localities of
Provence, in southeastern France (other vertebrates
from these localities including titanosaurid sauropods,
nonhadrosaurid ornithopods, ankylosaurs, birds, crocodilians, and chelonians). Two dromaeosaurid vertebrae (also many hadrosaur and pterosaur elements)
were found in a third late Maastrichtian locality in the
Corbiere area (in southwestern France).

According to Le Loeuff and Buffetaut, dromaeosaurids were survivors of Euramerica (a Late
Jurassic–Early Cretaceous land mass uniting Europe
and North America) that evolved in Europe. Also, the
occurrence in Europe of West-Gondwanan theropods
such as *Tarascosaurus* indicate faunal exchanges between the European archipelago and Africa during the
Late Cretaceous.

Artist Tracy L. Ford (1997, 1998*a*) questioned the
restoration of theropods in general with "lizard lips,"
noting that carnivorous dinosaurs are usually depicted
in life restorations with teeth covered when their
mouths are closed. The idea that theropods possessed
lizard-like lips was earlier popularized by Bakker
(1986) in his successful book *The Dinosaur Heresies*,
built on the presence of foramina that run the lengths
of the dentary, premaxilla, and maxillary edges with
a slight bevel near the teeth.

Lizards, Ford pointed out, have oral glands —
which secrete mucus and other fluids that facilitate
the swallowing of food — between the skull and skin
and also inside the skull. Skin forms over these labial
glands to become something akin to lips. Archosaurs,
not possessing such glands, therefore do not have
"lips," Ford argued.

Disagreeing with Bakker's interpretation, Ford
also denied that theropods could have had lips based
on the way the lower jaws of these dinosaurs fit inside
the upper jaw; the thickness and length of the "over-
bite" teeth; the large gap between dentary and premaxilla; and the observation that, if theropods had
lips, "they would have bitten through the lower lips
when they closed their mouths."

PROSAUROPODS

A possible prosauropod — one of the group of
herbivorous saurischians belonging to the assemblage
Sauropodomorpha, and including some of the first
very large dinosaurs, was announced by Raath (1996)
in a paper recounting the earliest record of African
dinosaurs. The ?prosauropod remains consist of a
fragmentary femur, discovered along with rhynchosaur fossils at a Late Triassic site in the Dande
Communal Lands, in the Cabora Basin of the central
Zambezi Valley, in Zimbabwe.

The specimen was identified as a prosauropod
by Raath, possessing as it does the crestlike fourth
trochanter characteristic of the Prosauropoda. Though
regarded as adult based on the degree of ossification
of scars of minor surface features, the specimen represents a form considerably smaller than most known
African prosauropods (*e.g.*, *Euskelosaurus* and *Massospondylus*).

Raath noted that, if this bone does, in fact, represent a prosauropod, it establishes the presence of
this group of dinosaurs in South Africa when the
Dande beds were laid down. (At the same time that
he reported this specimen, Raath also identified tridactyl tracks, preserved along the banks of the Pot
River in the underlying Molteno Formation, near the
town of Maclear, as theropod.)

The dinosaurian fauna at this site predates that
found in rocks of the overlying lower Elliot Formation (see Olsen and Galton 1984) of the Stormberg
Group in South Africa, the latter and its equivalents
having been generally thought of as the oldest dinosaur-bearing formations in that part of the continent.

Regarding other early possible prosauropods,
Galton and Walker (1996*a*, 1996*b*) reassessed Middle
Triassic fossil material collected during the late 1830s
by Dr. G. Lloyd of Leamington from the Coton End
Quarry, Warwick, and from the Bromsgrove Sandstone Formation of Leamington, Warwickshire, central Midlands of England, and originally regarded as
belonging to the Prosauropoda. The material includes
a tooth (BCM Ca 7448) from Leamington, and the
posterior end of a large left ilium (WM Gz 4713), a
partial posterior cervical vertebra (BMNH R2628),
and several teeth (WM Gz 8, 954, 956, 957, 969, and
973) from Warwick. Huene (1907–08) had described
some of the postcranial remains from Warwick as
?*Thecodontosaurus antiquus*. Walker (1969) later referred most of the postcranial fossils (right ilium WM
Gz 3, WM Gz 4713, as well as other remains) from
the central Midlands of England belonging to ?*Thecodontosaurus* to an unnamed group within the
rauisuchian family Poposauridae. Subsequently, Galton (1985*a*; see Galton and Walker 1996*a* for formal
description) referred this material to the new genus
and species *Bromsgroeveia walkeri*, representing the
earliest record of the Poposauridae from the Middle
Triassic of England.

Galton and Walker (1996*b*) found the tooth from
Leamington, and the partial ilium and those teeth not
referred to *B. walkeri* from Warwick, also to be nondinosaurian and, noting that they compared quite favorably to corresponding remains of parasuchian phytosaurs, referred these specimens to the Parasuchia.
According to Galton and Walker (1996*b*), the partial

vertebra, though comparing closely to the anterior end of a prosauropod vertebra, displays no synapomorphies to identify it as a sauropodomorph or even a dinosaur, and can only be diagnosed to the level of Dinosauriformes (=*Marasuchus* plus Dinosauria).

The prosauropod genus *Azendohsaurus* (see *D:TE*), regarded by Galton (1990*b*) as belonging to the prosauropod family Thecodontosauridae and by Gauffre (1993*a*) as Prosauropoda *incertae sedis*, was accepted as a thecodontosaurid by Galton and Walker (1996*b*).

Galton (1998) reported that a tooth (figured by Cuny and Ramboer 1991), collected from the Norian of Saint-Nicholas-de-Port (Meurthe-et-Moselle), Lorraine, France, may represent a sauropod-like prosauropod (with unworn teeth similar to *Plateosaurus*) or the earliest record of the Sauropoda (so distinct from *Plateosaurus* teeth). If belonging to a prosauropod, the tooth is quite unusual in showing two well-marked surfaces formed by tooth-to-tooth wear. The tooth somewhat resembles a maxillary tooth of the sauropod *Brachiosaurus*.

SAUROPODS

Sauropods—sauropodomorphs include in their number the most gigantic of dinosaurs—continue to be studied, although much of what is known about these fascinating saurischians has been learned from only sketchy fossil evidence.

In a review of the global fossil record of the Sauropoda, Hunt, Lockley, Lucas and Meyer (1994) pointed out that only about five of 90 valid sauropod genera are known from complete skeletons (McIntosh 1992), and that only 11 genera are known from reasonably complete skulls (Olshevsky 1993).

Camarasaurus supremus, one of the few sauropod taxa known from relatively complete skeletons and skulls.

Courtesy Royal Tyrrell Museum/Alberta Community Development.

According to Hunt *et al.*, confusion of genus and species level taxonomy of these giant dinosaurs is mostly the result of their size and their susceptibility to taphonomic factors; and a carcass the size of a sauropod's "is not easily moved into a sedimentary environment where depositional rates are high, and it takes unusually rapid sedimentation to bury such a cadaver to protect it from weathering and scavengers." The relatively small and delicately constructed skulls possessed by sauropods "were easily damaged physically by weathering, erosion and scavengers and were more transportable than the other skeletal elements." Adding to the taxonomic difficulties is the problem that many sauropod taxa, based on teeth or fragmentary remains, cannot be distinguished from each other; also, as pointed out by Russell and Zheng (1993), convergence (or parallelism) are common within the Sauropoda.

The first record of a sauropod dinosaur from the Republic of Georgia, Europe, was reported by Gabunia, Mchedlidze, Chkhikvadze and Lucas (1998). The sauropod is represented by a nearly complete, relatively large caudal centrum (IPGAN D-6), broken so that it is missing both anterior and posterior zygapophyses, and measuring 116 millimeters in length. The specimen was discovered by Sh. Chalauri, a geologist from the Caucasian Institute of Mineral Raw Materials (Tbilisi), in Upper Jurassic (Oxfordian age, based on fossil foraminas and corals; see Bendukidze 1964, Todria 1976) strata in the canyon of the Aapsta River, in the Gudautha Region, Abkhaziya, western Georgia. It was identified by the authors as belonging to the "Diplodocinae" (see "Systematics" chapter) based on the presence of a small pleurocoel and slightly procoelous centrum (McIntosh 1990*b*). Although the specimen bears a striking resemblance to caudal vertebrae of *Apatosaurus louisae*, especially in its V-shaped cross-section, Gabunia *et al.* found the specimen to be indeterminate at the genus level. The authors noted that the fossil is significant in 1. greatly expanding the paleobiogeographic distribution of the "Diplodocinae," 2. its direct correlation to the Marine Jurassic timescale (thereby constituting one of the most exactly dated Jurassic "diplodocines"), and 3. indicating the possibility of other Jurassic dinosaurs being present in Georgia.

Britt, Stadtman, Scheetz and McIntosh (1997) reported and very briefly described two distinct moderate-sized sauropod taxa—a camarasaurid and a titanosaurid—from the Dalton Wells Quarry, Early Cretaceous Cedar Mountain Formation, Utah.

The camarasaurid taxon is represented by five crania, one of which is articulated with camarasaurid cervical vertebrae. Elements identified by Britt *et al.* as camarasaurid include cervical vertebrae having bifid neural spines, dorsal vertebrae with thin laminae and opisthocoelous centra. Cranial characters include prominent supraoccipital boss, deep sulcus between basal tubera of basioccipital and basispheroid, and moderately short and thin basipterygoid processes. The teeth are large, a crown measuring 50 by 30 millimeters, spatulate, and have a massive labial ridge.

The titanosaurid was identified by Britt *et al.* by strongly procoelous proximal caudal centra with the other caudals moderately procoelous. As described by these authors, the cervical vertebrae have nonbifid neural spines and broad lateral fossae. Dorsal vertebra centra are long and opisthocoelous, and have high neural arches and short neural spines. The sternal plates are subrectangular in shape and over twice as wide as they are long. Cranial characters observed by Britt *et al.* include low (or absent) supraoccipital boss, lack of sulcus between basal tubera of basioccipital and basisphenoid, and basipterygoid with thick base. According to the authors, this taxon is closer to *Haplocanthosaurus* than to the Brachiosauridae (see "Systematics" chapter).

The first (tentative) record of the Titanosauridae — a large complete claw (IVPP V. 11122) collected in 1993 during the Sino-Japanese Silk Road Dinosaur Expedition from the Shisanjiangfang Formation (Upper Cretaceous) of Shashan County, in the Turpan Basin, Xinjiang, China (Dong 1997*f*) — was reported by Dong (1997*h*) in a major publication about this project. The tongue-shaped claw measures 16.2 centimeters (more than 6 inches) in length and 11.3 centimeters (about 4.25 inches) in width. According to Dong (1997*h*), it is distinct from those of all known sauropods from the Middle to Upper Jurassic.

Kellner and Campos (1997), in an abstract, reported remains of titanosaurids collected from Upper Cretaceous sedimentary rocks of the Bauru Group, especially in the Peirópolis and Galga localities in the State of Minas Gerais, and Presidente Prudente in the State of Saõ Paulo, Brazil. The material recovered from these localities includes several postcranial specimens and teeth. Preservation varies with these fossils, with most remains showing little or no distortion.

As noted by Kellner and Campos, most of these remains were found in conglomeratic sandstones, in some places forming bonebeds, at the Peirópolis locality, where seven sites have yielded most Brazilian titanosaurid remains. Most of the elements were isolated, though some vertebrae were found in articulation. Material recovered includes three incomplete pelves of about equal size (sacrum length of 57–61 centimeters; maximum width of 104–108 centimeters between ilia). Every sacrum found includes six vertebrae, with five fused to the ilia, the first vertebra (an incorporated dorsal) having a short rib that borders the cranial margin of the ilia. The last sacral centrum in two of the pelves is convex, while in another specimen this vertebra is slightly concave. This feature, along with other as yet undisclosed differences observed in the presacral vertebrae, suggests to the authors that two distinct titanosaurid taxa are present in the Bauru Group.

In a subsequent abstract, Campos and Kellner (1998) briefly described two titanosaurid pelves from "Caieira," a Peirópolis bonebed site from which most of the dinosaurian fossils have been collected. The first of these specimens, excavated in 1955, includes an ilium articulated with a sacrum and several dorsal vertebrae. Recovered in 1959, the second specimen comprises both ilia articulated with a sacrum. Sacra measure 57 and 61 centimeters in length, respectively, the maximum width between ilia being 104 and 108 centimeters. Each sacrum comprises six vertebrae, with five fused to the ilia. The first specimen incorporates a dorsal vertebra having a short rib that borders the cranial margin of the ilia; neural spines in this specimen are united by rodlike structures, showing that fusion of the neural spines was occurring.

According to Campos and Kellner, the centrum of the last sacral vertebra is the most distinguishing feature of both specimens. In one, this centrum is convex, in the second it is slightly concave, the latter showing that the first caudal of that specimen was biconvex. Along with other unstated anatomical features of the presacral vertebrae, these differences indicated to the authors the presence of at least two distinct titanosaurid taxa at the "Caieira" site.

Kellner and Azevedo (1998), in another abstract, reported on a partially articulated incomplete titanosaurid skeleton (MN 4111-V) representing a new taxon, discovered in the "Sitio Myzobushi," near the city of Álvarez Machado in Saõ Paulo, this specimen constituting the most complete sauropod material belonging to a single individual yet found in Brazil. The specimen, preserved in a mudstone, was collected by a crew directed by Fausto L. de Souza Cunha (Museu Nacional/UFRJ). To date of this writing, 42 vertebrae (dorsals, sacrals, and caudals, some of them articulated), both humeri, an incomplete scapula, both tibiae, a few ribs, a pelvis including an ilium and incomplete ischia, and some unidentified elements have been recovered.

Kellner and Azevedo briefly described this titanosaurid as follows: Dorsal vertebrae opisthocoelian, exhibiting a well-developed pleurocoel in middle part of centrum; no evidence of hyposphene-hypantrum; caudal vertebrae procoelic, the more anterior caudals having relatively well-developed protuberances on ventral side of posterior part of centrum; posterior caudals tending to be proportionally more elongated, with low neural spines; prezygapophyses comparatively short, horizontal; neural arches cranially displaced; most caudals showing lateral protuberance near connection with centrum; humerus with well-developed, inward-curving deltopectoral crest; pronounced concavity in dorsal surface near distal end of humerus, this being more developed than in other known titanosaurids; tibia very compressed lateromedially, possessing well-marked depression on lateral surface near proximal articulation.

Preliminary comparisons by Kellner and Azevedo with other titanosaurids revealed that MN 4111-V differs in a number of ways from these taxa (indicating that the new specimen represents a new taxon): Caudal vertebrae procoelous, with lower neural spines than in *Andesaurus*; tibia more compressed laterally, with smaller cranial projection than in *Titanosaurus*; caudal prezygapophyses shorter, more horizontal than in *Aeolosaurus*; tibia relatively longer and thinner, with less expanded caudal projection of proximal articulation, than in *Saltasaurus*; scapula comparatively longer, deltopectoral crest of humerus more inclined and inwardly displaced, than in *Neuquensaurus*.

Dodson, Krause, Forster, Sampson and Ravoavy (1997) reported the collection in 1996 of three isolated and eight associated osteoderms from the (?Campanian) Maevarano Formation of the Mahajanga Basin in Madagascar, this discovery thereby confirming and extending the observations published a century ago by Depéret (1896) that titanosaurid sauropods such as *Titanosaurus madagascarensis* were armored.

As briefly described by Dodson *et al.*, all of these specimens have a coarse, fibrous, and porous texture. One osteoderm (measuring 17 by 15.5 by 6.5 centimeters) is robust, biconvex, subcircular in dorsal view, and has two parasagittal ridges and tapered edges. A second specimen (measuring 12 by 9 by 6.5 centimeters) is ovoid in shape, has steep edges, and lacks ridges. A small specimen (length of 5 centimeters) is pyramidal in shape. The osteoderms preserved in a cluster have the form of irregular nodules, the largest in this grouping measuring 6 by 4 by 3 centimeters. Several of these osteoderms possess large vascular foramina and crossing fibers on their undersides.

As titanosaurs are the most commonly known dinosaurs from the Late Cretaceous of Madagascar, and because titanosaur osteoderms are rare, Dodson *et al.* speculated that, at least in Madagascar, such sauropods were only sparsely armored.

Discovery in 1995 of a diplodocid caudal vertebra was reported by De Klerk *et al.* (1997) from the Early Cretaceous Kirkwood Formation, Algoa Basin, South Africa. According to the authors, this find extends the Diplodocidae into southern Africa during the Cretaceous period.

In a preliminary report on the feeding habits of various kinds of sauropods, Chatterjee and Zheng (1997) noted that two different styles of feeding strategies may be reflected in these dinosaurs by differences "in tooth morphology, occlusion pattern, placement of external naris, attitude of quadrate, and neck curvature."

According to these authors, skulls of basal sauropods (*e.g.*, *Shunosaurus* and *Camarasaurus*) exhibit the following features: Large, lateral nasal openings; spatulate teeth; high dental count; parabolic dental arcade; quadrate moderately inclined (less than 120 degrees); long mandibular ramus; ossified jaw symphysis. These dinosaurs developed a shearing, orthal (or up-and-down) jaw action suited to hard and resistant food (*e.g.*, conifer twigs and cones). With powerful front limbs and long, vertically oriented necks, these animals were, according to Chatterjee and Zheng, "high browsers, searching the upper reaches of trees for food."

Skulls of more advanced sauropods (*e.g.*, *Apatosaurus* and *Diplodocus*), Chatterjee and Zheng noted, show the following: Median confluent naris on top of skull roof; weak, peglike teeth; reduced dental count; rectangular dental arcade; quadrate highly inclined (more than 140 degrees); short mandibular ramus; ossified jaw symphysis. Their incisiform, peglike teeth were suited to cropping soft vegetation by tooth-to-tooth contact. The essentially orthal jaw action included a small component of propalinal (forward and backward) motion. The high position of the nostrils and horizontal orientation of the neck are apparently adaptations for acquiring aquatic food from river banks without interruption for breathing. For the above reasons, Chatterjee and Zheng concluded that these sauropods "were low browsers and probably fed upon soft, aquatic vegetation."

New studies have been made regarding the flexibility of the necks of different kinds of sauropods. In a popular article directed toward a young readership, Batten (1997) briefly recounted an experiment (the results of which have not been formally published) by Kenneth Carpenter of the Denver Museum of Natural History to test flexibility in the neck of *Diplodocus*. According to this article, Carpenter laid out the cervical vertebrae of *Diplodocus* on the museum floor, then moved them into various positions. Carpenter found that the neck of this genus had only limited movement, which included the capability to swing around beside the body, and could not curve back over its body as depicted in a number of life restoration.

Stevens and Parrish (1997) began a formal study (using techniques first announced at the annual meeting of the Society of Vertebrate Paleontology in 1996) comparing the form and function of the neck in different kinds of diplodocid sauropods. Utilizing three-dimensional computer-graphics software, Stevens and Parrish generated articulated models of the diplodocids *Diplodocus carnegii* and *Apatosaurus louisae*. Particular attention was focused upon rendering the osteology of the necks with accuracy.

The completed models allowed Stevens and Parrish to explore the maximum ranges of movement as permitted by osteological constraints. Critical to the total flexibility of the neck—indeed, of that of any tetrapod—"is the geometry of the paired zygapophyseal joints and their placement to the center of rotation of the intervertebral joint." Neck mobility of the sauropod models was found to be substantially affected by comparatively subtle differences in the size and location of the articular facets of the zygapophyses.

Based on measurements taken from specimens including mounted skeletons, Stevens and Parrish could model the "neutral pose" (*i.e.,* one centering prezygapophyses over postzygapophyses throughout length of neck), "extremes of mediolateral and dorsoventral flexion, and the range and extent of compound movements such as torsion." It was believed that this study would revise traditional views on neck posture in these dinosaurs, refine geometric estimates of their feeding envelopes, suggest peculiarities of bending to achieve extremes of flexture, and demonstrate the possibilities, based on osteology, for extraordinary ventrification, the latter consistent with the idea of tripodal feeding (see *D:TE, e.g.,* entries for *Apatosaurus, Barosaurus, Brachiosaurus,* and *Diplodocus,* for pro and con arguments regarding sauropods rearing up bipedally).

Although the findings of Stevens and Parrish have not, to date of this writing, been published in a technical journal, they were presented in the form of a "poster," complete with copies of their computer simulations of sauropod skeletons, during the annual SVP meeting in 1997 and in an article written by Carl Zimmer (1997) appearing in the popular magazine *Discovery.*

According to Zimmer's piece, Stevens and Parrish found, at least from results of their work thus far, that *Apatosaurus* and *Diplodocus,* diplodocids closely related to one another, exhibit very different neck morphology: The "neutral poses" of the necks are somewhat the same, tilted downward rather than gently sloping upward as usually depicted in life restorations and mounted skeletons. In the case of *Apatosaurus,* the head would normally have been held just a few feet off the ground, while in *Diplodocus* the head would have usually hung down only inches above the ground. Regarding mobility, *Apatosaurus* was

found to have a remarkably flexible neck, capable of raising the head some 17 feet into the air, move the head to either side, bend in a "U" shape to face backwards, and twist into a forward-directed "S." The neck of *Diplodocus* was less flexible, capable of raising the head just 12 feet above ground level, and bending only about seven feet to the right or left.

In examining other kinds of sauropods, Stevens and Parrish found that the Chinese genus *Euhelopus* had an extremely flexible neck, capable of turning in three-quarters of a circle and almost touch its ribs with its snout. *Camarasaurus,* which has a relatively short and stocky neck, could hold its neck almost vertically, a rare pose for sauropods. *Brachiosaurus,* according to the cyber images, normally held its neck at about 20 degrees over horizontal, its head some 18 feet above the ground. Its very long neck seems capable of moving just nine feet to the right or left.

These findings suggest different feeding strategies for different kinds of sauropods, offering a possible answer to the question of how such similar and gigantic forms of herbivorous tetrapods were able to occupy the same territory and survive. Sauropods could have divided up their ecosystems partly by the different ways in which they maneuvered their heads. *Brachiosaurus* probably primarily fed on higher-growing vegetation; *Apatosaurus* could have maneuvered its head to feed on a greater variety of plants; and *Diplodocus* may have normally fed, like a grazing cow, on ground-level vegetation.

According to Zimmer's article, one of the most unusual results of this computer study is the extent to which some sauropod necks could reach downwards, particularly the diplodocids *Apatosaurus* and *Diplodocus.* In the case of these two genera, the necks could be bent so that their heads could reach a point in space considerably below ground level. Stevens and Parrish offered two possible explanations for this finding: Perhaps the necks required such flexibility during their embryonic stages while still in the nest; or possibly they permitted the animals to feed from dry land upon underwater plants, their high-located nostrils allowing them to breath while they ate.

Not all new ideas regarding sauropods have sprung exclusively from the paleontology field, however. As also recounted in Zimmer's article, physicist Nathan P. Myhrvold (see also Myhrvold and Currie 1998), utilizing sophisticated computer softwear and also hands-on tests performed with a bullwhip, made some tantalizing speculations regarding such whips and their analogy to the supposed "whiplash" tails in diplodocids (see also *Diplodocus* entry). Myrhvold found that, by flicking the handle of the bullwhip, he created an energy wave that traveled down the whip's length, moving faster as the whip tapered toward its

Introduction

end and eventually reaching a speed of some 787 miles per hour. The wave exceeded the speed of sound as it reached the tip, the "crack" of the whip actually being a small sonic boom.

Creating a computer-generated simulation of the tail of the mounted skeleton (CM 3018) of *Apatosaurus louisae* on display at the Carnegie Museum of Natural History (see *D:TE* for photograph), Myrhvold discovered that, using only a small amount of energy, the tail of this diplodocid could be driven above the speed of sound to produce a whiplike "crack" sound. Although "whiplash" tails in diplodocids have generally been interpreted as defensive weapons used primarily against predators (see *Diplodocus* entry, *D:TE* and this volume), Myhrvold found that notion to be unrealistic, pointing out that the tips of the tail, where most of the energy would have been released, were too slender to have caused much damage, except to the sauropod itself. Myhrvold speculated that these tails may rather have had some significance relating to sexual selection; perhaps loud "cracks" were produced by males to attract females, or were made by dueling males competing with one another for females. According to the brief report by Myhrvold and Currie, the "cracks" may also have been used in defense against theropods. "Similarity in tail structure," Myhrvold and Currie stated, "suggests this was feasible for other diplodocids, and possibly for unrelated sauropods like *Mamenchisaurus* and the dicraeosaurids."

According to Myhrvold and Currie, comparisons of the tails in these sauropods with the club-bearing tails of sauropods *Omeisaurus tianfuensis* and *Shunosaurus lii* reveal that "the diplodocid whiplash tail was not well adapted as a direct-impact weapon, bringing the tail-as-weapon hypothesis into doubt."

Kaye (1998) offered a new theory regarding the fusion of midcaudal vertebrae in the tails of *Diplodocus*, *Apatosaurus*, and *Camarasaurus*. Noting that a variety of extant animals utilize a lateral tail motion as part of their natural gait, Kaye examined the lateral swing dynamics and resulting kinetic energy profile along the tail in these kinds of dinosaurs.

As pointed out by Kaye, the sauropod tail is not a smooth tapering organ, but one that reduces in stages that are defined by the changing morphology of the transverse processes and chevrons of the caudal vertebrae. The mass of the tail, therefore, decreases distally as the speed of lateral motion increases. Employing a formula utilizing "tail mass as estimated from diameter times velocity along many points on the swinging tail produces kinetic energy profile." Kaye found that this profile is not constant, but rather "peaks in different areas along the length, closely corresponding to the observed points of fusion." This section, therefore, would become less flexible, as the vertebral fusion would dissipate energy further up and down the tail and smooth out the energy profile.

Testing this theory further, Kaye constructed a mechanical model that indicated a higher flex angle in the same central area of the tail. Correlating peak energy with location of caudal fusion suggested to the author a believable mechanical basis for this trait in sauropods. Dinosaurs lacking fused vertebrae were found by Kaye to show a smooth energy distribution in that region of the tail.

Pagnac and Chure (1997) briefly reported on various sauropod specimens recently found in the Morrison Formation (Upper Jurassic) of Dinosaur National Monument, Utah. Among these remains was a pair, preserved in life position, of isolated triangular sternal plates (elements often found but rarely in articulation) that compare better with those of *Diplodocus* than *Barosaurus* or *Apatosaurus*. As the authors noted, there is a wider gap between these bones than previously reported, this suggesting that a significant amount of cartilage was present between the plates.

Seven scattered and presumably posterior sauropod gastralia, probably belonging to a single individual, were also reported, these, despite the many sauropod specimens recovered at the Monument, remaining the only gastralia yet found in the quarry. Also, Pagnac and Chure reported an articulated forelimb belonging to *Camarasaurus*, this being one of the few instances in which a sauropod calcaneum has been preserved in life position.

In an effort to facilitate identification at the genus level of isolated sauropod bones, Curtice, Foster and Wilhite (1997) undertook a statistical analysis of limb bones incorporating 506 elements pertaining to 40 sauropod taxa and belonging primarily to five genera (*Apatosaurus*, *Barosaurus*, *Brachiosaurus*, *Camarasaurus*, and *Diplodocus*). Variables considered in this study included maximum length of the bones, minimum circumference, and proximal, mid-, and distal shaft widths. Data resulting from this study were then subjected to discriminant, principal component, regression, ANOVA (software analysis of variance), and nonparametric analyses.

Though limited by a small sample size for most taxa and broad within-genus variation, Curtice *et al.* were able to observe the following trends from this study: Juvenile elements almost always have a higher robusticity index than in adults; most gracile of all sauropod humeri belong to *Brachiosaurus*; the femur (AMNH 5764) of *Amphicoelias altus* is not significantly

Courtesy José Luis Sanz.

Insights regarding the behavior of dinosaurs can be gleaned from the interpretation of ichnites, or fossil footprints, such as the sauropod prints in this trackway from Portugal.

different from those of *Barosaurus* or *Diplodocus* (suggesting that femoral ratios used to differentiate these taxa from each other are problematic); bimodal distributions among tibiae of *Apatosaurus* and *Diplodocus* suggest possible species or dimorphic differences; the radius and ulna of *Barosaurus* are more gracile than those of *Diplodocus*, complete statistical separation occurring between these genera. However, despite the above findings, the authors cautioned, most sauropod limb bones are indistinguishable to generic level based only on measurements.

In the past, studies of sauropod feet have resulted in interpretations that the manus and pes had little or no significant functions to their being used for digging or even as weapons. Recently, Bonnan (1997) reported on a preliminary study on the functional biology of the manus and pes in sauropods, emphasizing the salient differences in the structure of front and hind feet of these dinosaurs (*i.e.,* manus entirely digitigrade, characterized by five tightly interlocking metacarpals, pollex claw, reduced phalanges, and two carpals; pes semiplantigrade, characterized by five interlocking metatarsals, 3–4 large claws, two tarsals).

From an examination and measurement of the foot bones in five sauropod genera—*Apatosaurus, Barosaurus, Camarasaurus, Diplodocus,* and *Haplocanthosaurus*—Bonnan found evidence suggesting the following: 1. Robustness of the metacarpal (minimum circumference/length ratio) can vary among families, with metacarpal IV apparently more robust in camarasaurids, I and V apparently more so in *Apatosaurus* and *Barosaurus*, these differences possibly indicative of alternative use of the manus among sauropod families; 2. robustness of the metatarsals is similar in all of the examined sauropod families; 3. in *Apatosaurus, Camarasaurus,* and *Diplodocus,* the large articular surface of the astragalus, plus the large proximal articular surface of the metatarsals, suggest at least a modicum of hinge-like mobility at the ankle, perhaps required for plantarflexion of the hind foot during

Cotype (CM 94) *in situ* hind foot of the sauropod *Diplodocus carnegii.*

Courtesy The Field Museum (neg. #GEO81855).

locomotion; and 4. the relatively small number of bones in the feet may be reflective of historical constraints rather than reduced agility of the feet.

Gale (1997) made a study of sauropod lung ventilation and the problems of breathing through a very long neck. As explained by Gale in a preliminary report: The lungs in living terrestrial animals are positioned near the heart and distant from air vents located in the head. The trachea connecting the head vents and the lungs acts as "dead space" by not permitting the transfer of gas to the blood. The size of the conducting airway has significant influence on the oxygen content of air delivered to the lungs. Following expiration, oxygen-depleted "used air" fills the trachea, which returns to the lungs at the start of inspiration, followed by inhaled "fresh" air, the entire volume of inhaled air getting distributed between trachea and lung. The more fresh air remaining in the "dead space," the less is received by the lungs. If a neck is too long and the "dead space" of the trachea exceeds the tidal volume of inhaled air, fresh air cannot reach the lung and the entering air is depleted of oxygen.

Applying the above to long-necked sauropods, Gale pointed out that the additional "dead space" of an elongated trachea in these dinosaurs could be reduced by narrowing it, though this would have significantly increased the resistance to airway friction and the work of breathing. Increasing the amount of air taken in might have compensated for the excessive "dead space," although increasing breath size during rest encroaches upon exercise capacity. Large lungs could have increased both resting and exercise performance, but would also have necessitated redesign of the whole animal. Gale suggested that a more reasonable solution to the above problem would be "to reduce dead space by positioning the air vent in the neck, near to the lungs."

Ornithischians

All known members of the very diverse group known as Ornithischia (or "bird-hipped" dinosaurs) were herbivorous. Barrett (1997) offered a preliminary report on the correlated progression and the evolution of herbivory in dinosaurs including ornithischians and sauropodomorph saurischians, based upon the examination of the feeding mechanisms of a wide variety of taxa. This data was then integrated with current phylogenetic analyses of the major dinosaurian clades to document the distribution of features (*e.g.*, horny beak, tooth morphology, and large abdominal cavity) associated with herbivory.

Barrett found that 1. feeding mechanisms in plant-eating dinosaurs become more complex in more derived members of any individual clade; 2.

feeding systems may be considered to be "character-complexes" that came together gradually resulting from the elaboration of existing features; and 3. changes in feeding-system components "facilitated the development of other features in these complexes and may be explained as a consequence of correlated progression."

Papp (1997) questioned the almost universally accepted (and virtually untested) idea that ornithischian dinosaurs possessed muscular cheeks (or buccal recesses), also pointing out that this assumption "has been regarded as an intrinsic part of the masticatory apparatus, and even has been proposed to be the key innovation allowing the radiation of ornithischians and the subsequent extinction of the prosauropods."

As noted by Papp, the key evidence for cheeks in ornithischians has focused upon "a lateral space partially enclosed by shelves of the dentary and maxilla with the dentition inset instead of marginal"; also, horizontal ridges on the maxilla and dentary have been interpreted as places of attachments for cheek muscles. Among extant animals, only mammals possess cheeks, while birds and crocodilians, the closest living relatives of dinosaurs, do not.

After dissection and CT scanning of various mammals, Papp found "that the osteological correlates of mammalian cheeks are generally dissimilar to those proposed for ornithischians," these findings suggesting that the inference of cheeks in these dinosaurs is problematic, and that "caution should be exercised when making functional inferences that are dependent on the presence of cheeks."

EARLY ORNITHISCHIANS

Heckert, Lucas and Hunt (1997) pointed out that the Late Triassic primitive ornithischians "*Tecovasaurus murryi* and *Revueltosaurus callenderi*— to date, the only Triassic ornithischians known from more than one locality — occur stratigraphically superposed at several localities in the Chinle Group in Texas, New Mexico, and Arizona."

T. murryi has been found at the type locality in the Tecovas Formation in Crosby County, Texas, the *Placerias* quarry in the Blue Water Creek Formation of eastern Arizona, and probably the Blue Water Creek Formation near Fort Wingate, New Mexico (these localities all in strata producing a vertebrate fossil assemblage typical of the Adamanian [latest Carnian age] land vertebrate faunachron).

R. callenderi occurs in the Bull Canyon Formation of eastern New Mexico, also the Painted Desert Member of the Petrified Forest Formation, in the Petrified Forest National Park in eastern Arizona (these localities in strata assigned to the "Revueltian" [early to middle Norian] land vertebrate faunachron based upon tetrapod fossils including aetosaurs and phytosaurs).

Heckbert *et al.* suggested that *Tecovasaurus* be accepted as an additional index taxon of the Adamanian land vertebrate faunachrona and *Revueltosaurus* for the "Revueltian," thereby establishing the first use of dinosaurian genera as biostratigraphic indicators in the Upper Triassic, indices that should be useful in studies of Chinle Group microvertebrates.

THYREOPHORANS

The Stegosaurs, a group of plated dinosaurs belonging to the larger group Thyreophora (an assemblage of armored dinosaurs), remain one of the more poorly represented ornithischian groups in terms of numbers of individual genera and species. New taxa, however, continue to be found and collected.

The first report of stegosaurian remains found in Argentina was published by Bonaparte (1996*b*), who announced the recovery of a specimen (MACN-N 43) comprising an incomplete posterior cervical centrum, ?seventh cervical centrum, and a middle-anterior caudal centrum with the base of the transverse processes, collected in 1985 by José F. Bonaparte and Martin Vince from the La Amarga Formation (Early Cretaceous, Hauterivian; Bonaparte used the former, mostly abandoned, North American geologist's stratigraphic designation "Neocomian") of Neuquén Province. Bonaparte (1996*b*) described but did not name this material, observing that the cervical vertebra is quite similar to that of the Late Jurassic, East African genus *Kentrosaurus*, though the cervicals of that taxon are about 30 percent more elongated, this implying that the neck of the South American form is relatively shorter. Furthermore, Bonaparte speculated that the stegosaur from Argentina was approximately the same size as the African genus.

Regarding a taxon originally described as an Indian stegosaur, Chatterjee and Rudra (1996) visited the site (*Kossmaticeras theobaldianum* Zone, Trichinopoly Group) which yielded the only remains thus far collected of *Dravidosaurus blandordi* (see *Dravidosaurus* entry, *D:TE*), there finding only fragmentary material belonging to plesiosaurs. Reexamining the holotype (GSI SR PAL 1, a fragmentary skeleton) of this type species, Chatterjee and Rudra found nothing pertaining to the supposed stegosaurian plates and skull as claimed by this species' authors, Yadagiri and Ayyasami (1979). Instead, they found "highly weathered limb and girdle elements that may belong to plesiosaurs."

A new genus of primitive stegosaurid stegosaur was briefly reported by Carpenter and Miles (1997) from the Upper Jurassic Morrison Formation near Buffalo, Wyoming. The specimen is represented by an almost complete skull and most of the postcranial skeleton, the latter missing the pectoral girdle, forelimbs, and hind limbs.

Cranial features observed by Carpenter and Miles in this specimen include the following: Length to width ratio intermediate between the North American *Stegosaurus stenops* and Chinese *Huayangosaurus taibaii*; cranium domed (not flat as in other stegosaurs); cranial openings large (as in *H. taibaii*); cheek teeth large relative to size of skull (premaxillae unknown); mandibles quite deep. Postcranial features include: More cervical vertebrae and fewer dorsals than in other stegosaurs; middorsal neural arches low (as in *H. taibaii* or *Dacentrurus*; not tall as in *S. stenops* and *S. armatus*); cervical ribs expanded distally, anterior caudal neural spines not bifurcated as in *S. stenops*; ilia strongly divergent; distal end of pubis expanded (as in *H. taibaii* and *Dacentrurus*); of known armor, cervical plates oval in shape, wider than tall (taller than wide, often tapering, in other stegosaurs); four tail spikes (as in *S. stenops*).

According to Carpenter and Miles' preliminary analysis, this genus is more primitive than *S. armatus* and *S. stenops*, but more advanced than *H. taibaii*; its closest sister group could be *Dacentrurus*, from the Upper Jurassic of England.

Ankylosaurs, the more advanced thyreophorans — and the "armored tanks" of the dinosaur world — have fared better than their more primitive relatives, the stegosaurs, in terms of the number of new specimens found.

The largest number of ankylosaurian individuals yet recovered from the eastern North America land mass during the Late Cretaceous was reported by Lamb (1996). The find comprises remains of from three to possibly six ankylosaurs from the late Santonian–early Campanian of Alabama. As with all ankylosaurs found in Alabama to date, these specimens represent extremely young animals, this ontogenetic factor possibly precluding generic identification.

According to Lamb, most of these specimens cannot be identified even at the family level. However, one specimen (RMM 1224) can be referred to the Nodosauridae by possession of the following nodosaurid features: Fluting of teeth coincident with notches between cusps; teeth with well-developed basal cingulum; ventrally deflected occipital condyle set off on short neck; and narrow, curved scapula.

Features conflicting with assigment of this specimen to the Nodosauridae (*e.g.*, nonspherical occipital condyle seemingly comprising basioccipital and exoccipitals, which contributed to dorsolateral border of occipital condyle) may be attributable to ontogeny, as RMM 1224 represents a very young individual.

New information concerning the first ankylosaurian remains found on the continent of Antarctica (Olivero, Gasparini, Rinaldi and Scasso 1991) was

Skeleton of *Huayangosaurus taibaii* mounted at Dino-fest™ in 1998. Kenneth Carpenter and C. A. Miles will name and describe a new stegosaur that seems to be intermediate between this primitive Chinese species and the more advanced North American species *Stegosaurus stenops*.

Photograph by the author.

published by Gasparini, Pereda-Suberbiola and Molnar (1996), after preparation of the matrix in which the fossils were imbedded. The material (MLP 86-X-28-1) was discovered by geologists E. Olivero and R. Scasso and excavated in January 1986 during fieldwork by the Instituto Antártico Argentino from massive green silty sandstones at Santa Marta Cove, in the Gamma Member of the Santa Marta Formation (Upper Cretaceous, Campanian), lowermost part of the Marambio Group, in the northern part of James Ross Island on the northeast coast of the Antarctic Peninsula (Gasparini, Olivero, Scasso and Rinaldi 1987; Olivero *et al.*). The specimen includes a lower jaw, teeth, vertebrae (cervical, dorsal, ?sacral, and caudal), ribs, parts of the scapula, parts of the ilium, autopodial bones, and armor, most of these elements being fragmentary and shattered by frost action.

Preliminary descriptions of some of this material had already been published by Gasparini *et al.* (1987) and Olivero *et al.* With the newly prepared elements, Gasparini *et al.* (1996) were able to describe in detail the lower jaw, teeth, scapula, ilium, metapodials, phalanges, and armor.

Originally, Gasparini *et al.* (1987) tentatively assigned this specimen to the ankylosaurian family Ankylosauridae, based on possession of the following characters: Skull co-ossifications with lateral projec-

tions; teeth with cingula; and a tail club (although K. Carpenter, personal communication 1997, doubts the presence of a club). Having redescribed the teeth of this specimen, Gasparini *et al.* (1996), found them to appear more likely nodosaurid, possessing characters (conspicuous basal cingulum, cingulum higher on lingual face, grooves on crown generally better developed) cited by Coombs and Maryańska (1990) as useful in differentiating nodosaurids from ankylosaurids. For the present, then, Gasparini *et al.* (1996) referred MLP 86-X-28-1 to Nodosauridae [an indeterminate nodosaurid] this material being too fragmentary for generic or specific identification, and too sparse to define with certainty regarding its affinities.

All of these remains could belong to the same

Tooth (MLP 86-X-28-1) of ankylosaur from James Ross Island, Antarctic Peninsula, in lingual, distal, labial, and mesial views. Scale = 5 mm. (After Gasparini, Pereda-Suberbiola and Molnar 1996.)

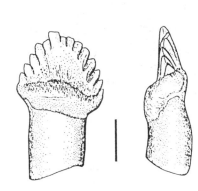
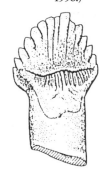

Introduction

animal, as reported earlier (E. Olivero, personal communication to Gasparini *et al.* 1996), though, according to Gasparini *et al.* (1996), size differences between the bones might suggest two distinct and rather small individuals. Supporting the latter interpretation, the neural arches are fused to the centra, suggesting an adult animal, while the scapula and coracoid (not found) were not fused, suggesting immaturity. On the other hand, both of these conditions are present in the articulated holotype skeleton (QM F18101) of the small Australian nodosaurid *Minmi*; and fusion of scapula to coracoid does not occur in adult *Hylaeosaurus* (Pareda-Suberbiola).

As concluded by Gasparini *et al.* (1996), most of the ankylosaurian remains from James Ross Island can tentatively be regarded as representing an immature individual measuring only from 3 to 4 meters (more than 10 to less than 14 feet) in length.

Gasparini *et al.* (1996) explained the presence of ankylosaurs in Antarctica during the Late Cretaceous as resulting from dispersal from the northern continents into southern Gondwana (see also Gasparini *et al.* 1987; Olivero *et al.* 1991), this time passage taking into consideration two hypotheses: 1. An earlier migration of ankylosaurs taking place during the Late Jurassic or Early Cretaceous, with nodosaurids dispersing to the Antarctic Peninsula by way of Africa or South America, or 2. a migration via South America during the Late Cretaceous.

According to Gasparini *et al.* (1996), the presence of an ankylosaur on the Antarctic Peninsula is also of interest in that this is one of the rare occurrences of such dinosaurs in high latitudes (about 64 degrees south; see Zinsmeister 1987), with independent evidence of a diversified flora suggesting a somewhat mild climate and relatively high humidity in the area where MLP 86-X-28-1 was found (Baldoni 1992). Also, these ankylosaurian remains were collected from shal-

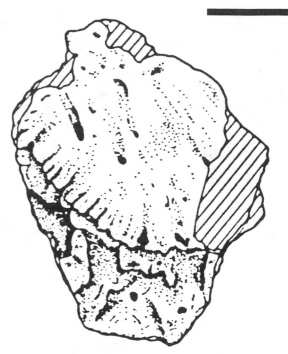

Dermal plate (MLP 86-X-28-1) of ankylosaur from James Ross Island, Antarctic Peninsula. Scale = 20 mm. (After Gasparini, Pereda-Suberbiola and Molnar 1996).

low marine deposits. That nodosaurids (but not certain ankylosaurids) are known from high paleolatitudes and nodosaurid (but never ankylosaurid) specimens are typically found in marine formations may constitute indirect evidence further supporting affinities of the Antarctic ankylosaur with the Nodosauridae.

Other Gondwanan ankylosaurian material was reported by Chatterjee and Rudra (1996). These remains, recently recovered from the Upper Cretaceous (Maastrichtian) Raiholi site, Lameta Group, India, include isolated vertebrae, a scapulocoracoid, humerus, femur, and a few pieces of armor (*e.g.*, hollow lateral spikes and solid dorsal scutes). They are to be described in the future, presumably by both Chatterjee and Rudra.

The first ankylosaur — indeed, the first unquestionable armored ornithischian of any sort — documented in South America was reported and described by Salgado and Coria (1996). The dinosaur is represented by a small (25.5 centimeters in length) right femur (MPCA-SM-1) from the Upper Cretaceous Allen Formation (Campanian–Maastrichtian; Powell 1986) of Salitral Moreno, south of General Roca, Rio Negro Province, Patagonia, Argentina, a locality previously known mostly for titanosaurid sauropods and hadrosaurs (Powell 1986; Salgado and Coria 1993).

The specimen resembles femora of both stegosaurs and nodosaurid ankylosaurs in the plesiomorphic condition of a proximally-located fourth trochanter. The size more suggests the European nodosaurid

Latex cast of three articulated vertebrae (MLP 86-X-28-1) of ankylosaur from James Ross Island, Antarctic Peninsula, right lateral view. Scale = 20 mm. (After Gasparini, Pereda-Suberbiola and Molnar 1996).

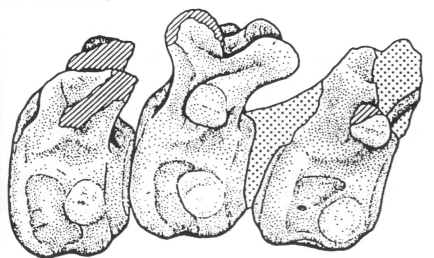

Struthiosaurus than larger North American ankylosaurids like *Edmontonia* and *Panoplosaurus*. For these
reasons, Salgado and Coria regarded MPCA-SM-1 as
probably belonging to the Nodosauridae.

Ford (1998*b*) may name and describe a nodosaurid specimen discovered by Bradford Rey in
1985 while monitoring a construction site in the Late
Cretaceous (Late Campanian) of Carlsbad, San Diego
County, California. The skeleton, which has since its
discovery been housed at the San Diego Museum of
Natural History, had been determined by paleontologists Walter P. Coombs, Jr., and Thomas Demere as
nondiagnostic at the genus level. Included in the specimen are a sacrum, ribs, partial scapula, ilia, ?ischium,
humerus, parts of a radius, ulnae, femora, tibiae,
fibulae, several different kinds of scutes, and various
indeterminate bones.

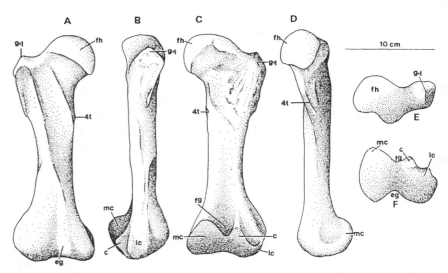

Ankylosaurian femur (MPCA-SM-1), in A. anterior, B. lateral, C. posterior, D. medial, E.
proximal, and F. distal views, this specimen constituting remains of the first armored ornithischian to be found in South America. (After Salgado and Coria 1996).

PRIMITIVE ORNITHOPODS

The oldest ornithishian remains known from the
Pacific Slope of North America — in fact, 20–30 million years older than any known dinosaur from that
region — were described (but not named) by Hilton,
DeCourten, Murphy, Rodda and Embree (1997). As
reported by Hilton *et al.*, the fragmentary but well-
preserved specimen consists of an almost complete
lower left hind limb (SC geological collections) recovered from the Chickabally Member of the Lower
Cretaceous (late Aptian, documented by the association of ammonites) Budden Canyon Formation (Mur-

phy, Peterson and Rodda 1964) in western Shasta
County, California (Murphy, Rodda and Morton
1969). Though disarticulated, the elements comprising the specimen were found in close association with
one another in two adjacent limestone concretions
within the marine mudstone and siltstone that make
up most of the upper Chickabally Member. Individual elements of this specimen include a complete left
tibia (SC VRO4A), almost complete left fibula (SC
VRO4B), three complete metatarsals (SC VRO4C,
D, and G), and three complete phalanges (SC VRO4E,

Skeleton (AMNH 28496,
cast by paleontologist
Stephen Hutt, Museum Isle
of Wight Geology) of the
hypsilophodontid orntitho-
pod *Hypsilophodon foxii*.
Richard P. Hilton, Frank L.
DeCourten, Michael A.
Murphy, Peter U. Rodda,
and Patrick G. Embree have
described a new and
slightly larger primitive ornithischian found in California.

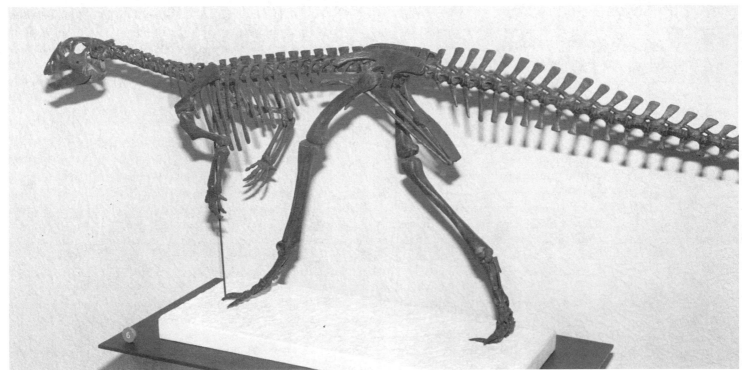

Photograph by the author, courtesy American Museum of Natural History.

F, and H). Found in association with this specimen were fossils including ammonites, bivalves, fragments of wood, and other plant fossils.

According to Hilton *et al.*, the specimen seems to belong to a small member of the quite diverse group Ornithopoda, having a relatively slender tibia (measuring 239 millimeters in length) intermediate in size between that of the hypsilophodontids *Hypsilophodon* and larger *Parksosaurus*.

In comparing the California specimen with other primitive ornithopods, Hilton *et al.* found that it resembles most closely *Hypsilophodon* and *Parksosaurus* in the moderately robust metatarsals. However, as the classification of hypsilophodontids at both family and genus levels requires data on certain cranial features and characters of the axial skeleton, the specimen could not be referred with certainty to the Hypsilophodontidae. It could, according to the authors, represent a new taxon.

Hilton *et al.* pointed out that the features of the hind limb and foot of this Early Cretaceous ornithopod do not precisely conform with those of any other known Early Cretaceous taxa from the North American interior. Also noted was the fact that certain Late Cretaceous dinosaurs known from the Pacific Coast are distinct from forms of about equal age found elsewhere on the continent (see Morris 1973; Molnar 1974). Consequently, Hilton *et al.* suggested the possibility that the northern California ornithopod might "belong to a unique and endemic coastal fauna, differing in taxonomic composition and adaptive specializations from contemporaneous faunas in the Western Interior of North America."

Maxwell, Hallas and Horner (1997) announced in a preliminary report the discovery, in the Cloverly Formation (Lower Cretaceous; Aptian–Albian) in south-central Montana, of fossil remains including rare neonate skeletal material pertaining to a probable hypsilophodontid ornithopod. These remains include a pedal phalanx and ungual and are similar, the authors observed, to those of *Orodromeus*, but significantly different from *Camptosaurus*, *Zephyrosaurus*, and *Tenontosaurus*.

(From this same site, Maxwell *et al.* also announced the recovery of additional fossil vertebrate material, including two new varieties of dinosaurian eggshell having surface ornamentation differing markedly from that previously reported and establishing the number of known, distinct types of Cloverly eggshell at five; teeth belonging to a sauropod dinosaur, one tooth representing a quite young individual; remains of three theropods, including *Deinonychus*, and the nodosaurid ankylosaur *Sauropelta*; also, various nondinosaurian vertebrate bones, teeth, and coprolites.)

Choo (1997), in an informal report on Australian dinosaurs, mentioned a new and as yet undescribed hypsilophodontid found at Dinosaur Cove, a fossil site of Albian age in the Otway Group of Victoria. This new genus — an animal approximately 1.3 meters in length — will probably be named "Qantassaurus" (in honor of QANTAS Airlines, an acronym for Queensland and Northern Territory Air Service, the company which provided air transportation for the "Great Russian Dinosaurs Exhibition" when it toured Australia), founded upon a partial articulated skeleton including hind limbs, the pelvis, and some caudal vertebrae. According to Choo, the left tibia of this dinosaur is about 2 centimeters shorter than the right tibia and is also approximately four times thicker at its proximal end, this severe deformation probably being the result of the bone disease osteomyelitis. If that assessment is correct, the specimen displays the earliest known occurrence of this disease.

Rich (1998), in an abstract reporting on the Hypsilophodontidae as represented in southeastern Australia, pointed out that two distinct hypsilophodontid femoral morphologies and three different tooth patterns are known from Early Aptian to Early Albian localities on that continent. Most femora have been referred to *Fulgurotherium australe*, three of these (Albian) having a very distinct morphology, with virtually identical femora of *F. australe* occurring in both Aptian and Albian sites. Most teeth — including the holotype of *Atlascoposaurus loadsi* — have one form. The fact that most femora are referred to one taxon and most teeth to the other implied to Rich that they could represent a single taxon. "Ironically," Rich added, "that they span the time from the Early Aptian to Early Albian coupled with the variation in the morphology of the femora, is suggestive that more than one species may prove to be within the teeth and femora assigned to *A. loadsi* and *F. australe*, respectively."

IGUANODONTS

De Klerk *et al.* (1997) reported a new taxon belonging to the more advanced ornithopod group Iguanodontia, represented by disarticulated elements from at least a half dozen small (length of largest femur = 5.5 centimeters) and apparently juvenile individuals, found in 1995 in the Early Cretaceous Kirkwood Formation, Algoa Basin, South Africa. Derived iguanodontian characters identified in these bones by De Klerk *et al.* include a hatchet-shaped sternal plate and loss of subsidiary ridges on teeth.

Moratalla, Sanz and Jiménez (1994) reported iguanodontids represented by fossil footprints found at a tracksite in Lower Cretaceous (Wealden) deposits of the Urbion Group, in the Western Cameros Basin in Regumiel de la Sierra township, province of Burgos, in north-central Spain. Observed at this site were eight trackways and several isolated tracks. All footprints are tridactyl, and also included among them are tracks of a theropod.

According to Moratalla *et al.*, one trackway at this site—very similar to a Lower Cretaceous trackway found at La Magdalena, province of La Rioja, Spain—suggests the presence of a very large and different kind of iguanodontid possessing a graviportal foot. If *Iguanodon bernissartensis* is regarded as the more graviportal of the known Lower Cretaceous iguanodontid taxa, then these tracks could have been made by an unknown ornithopod possessing a more compact foot based upon the following assumptions: 1. Same phalangeal formula (0, 3, 4, 5, 0); 2. first phalanx would be shorter, more similar to intermediate phalanges; 3. ungual phalanx would be quite short, wide, distally rounded, probably similar to that of a hadrosaur; and 4. metatarsals would be shorter, wider, but without plantigrade support. Therefore, this unknown iguanodontid probably was more graviportal than *I. bernissartensis*.

HADROSAURS

Evidence of some of the earliest known members of the most advanced iguanodontian group, the Hadrosauridae (or duckbilled dinosaurs), has surfaced in the past few years.

The almost complete skull of a primitive hadrosaur, as yet neither named nor formally described, was collected from the Cenomanian Woodbine Formation of northeast Texas and briefly reported by Head (1996). This find constitutes the oldest known definitive hadrosaur from eastern North America.

According to Head, the specimen displays "a mixture of derived hadrosaurian and generalized iguanodontid characters": (hadrosaurid) premaxillae forming expanded rostral bill; wide diastema between predentary and dentary tooth battery; small maxillary teeth; and (iguanodontid) retention of jugal-ectopterygoid articulation and surangular foramen; quadrate massive, with poorly differentiated mandibular condyles.

The most striking features observed are the massive, expanded dentary and ventrally deflected muzzle. Head placed this specimen at the basal position within Hadrosauridae, postulating "that the suggested Turonian origin and radiation of hadrosaurs from western Asia may have occurred earlier elsewhere."

The first record of the Hadrosauridae in south-central Alaska, "adding a new high latitude locality for dinosaurs and the only association of dinosaurs in Alaska which can be attributed to a single animal," was reported by Pasch (1997) in an issue of *The Di-*

Courtesy José Luis Sanz.

Trackway at La Magdalena, La Rioja, Spain, representing a large graviportal iguanodontid.

nosaur Report (a publication of The Dinosaur Society). The hadrosaur specimen—comprising more than 70 postcranial elements—was recovered over a period of three years from the (Turonian) Matanuska Formation of the Talkeetna Mountains. Remains collected include most of the limb bones, numerous vertebral centra, a partial pectoral girdle, and fragments of ribs. The remains were found at a marine site while Anne D. Pasch and other workers were searching for ammonites and bivalves.

Based on its size and comparison with those of other hadrosaurs, the Alaskan specimen seems to represent a juvenile. According to Pasch, this duckbilled dinosaur differs from geologically younger North American forms in having more elongated tail vertebrae and a somewhat different shaped deltopectoral crest of the humerus. Puncture marks indicate that the carcass had been scavenged on the sea floor, where the hadrosaur had sunk to be preserved in the ancient mud. At the site, the discovery of shark teeth, scales, jaw fragments, and also teeth from a bony fish may provide a clue as to the type of creature that scavenged the hadrosaur bones, although none of the teeth found to date of this writing match the size or shape of the punctures. (In a subsequent 1998 popular article written for the publication *Dinosaur World*, Pasch revealed that the discovery of this hadrosaurid specimen was made by 12-year-old Lizzie Williams, and that it has been nicknamed "Lizzie" in her honor.)

Ryan, Currie, Gardner and Lavigne (1997) announced the discovery of a new microvertebrate fossil site occurring as an isolated outcrop in the Horseshoe Canyon Formation (early Maastrichtian), in the Drumheller Valley badlands, in south-central Alberta, representing deposition on a waterlogged coastal plain some 100 kilometers west of the Western Interior Seaway. Most of the material collected at this locality pertains to embryonic and hatchling remains of unknown species of hadrosaurids, suggesting a nearby nesting site. The discovery is significant in being the first occurrence of baby dinosaurs from this formation, and also the geologically youngest occurrence of baby dinosaurs in Canada. According to Ryan *et al.*, the next most common taxon from this locality is the small theropod *Troodon*, represented by numerous teeth (usually extremely rare in Late Cretaceous sites in Alberta), their large number suggesting a nonrandom association with the hadrosaurids, perhaps indicative of predation. Other remains found at this site include teeth referred to the theropods *Ricardoestesia*

sp., *Saurornitholestes* sp., *Paronychodon* sp., rare fragmentary remains of a large indeterminate theropod (cf. *Albertosaurus*), and fossils belonging to an indeterminate ankylosaurian and ceratopsian.

CERATOPSIANS

In past years, "protoceratopsians" (see "Systematics" chapter) — primitive members of the Neoceratopsia, a major group of horned dinosaurs within the Ceratopsia — have been known in North America only in the early Maastrichtian of Montana (*Montanoceratops*) and the late Maastrichtian of Alberta and Wyoming (*Leptoceratops*); and protoceratopsid remains have been found in microvertebrate assemblages from the Santonian (Milk River Formation) and Maastrichtian (Scollard Formation) of Alberta.

Recently, however, Ryan and Currie (1996) announced in a preliminary report the first occurrence of a "protoceratopsian" from the late Campanian Dinosaur Park Formation of Alberta. Ryan and Currie reported that "protoceratopsians" at that locality are represented by a left dentary missing the caudal margin and coronoid process, with 15 preserved alveoli, with some *in situ* teeth. As briefly described by Ryan and Currie, the dentary is deep and has a curved ventral border resembling that of *Leptoceratops gracilis*. As, despite extensive searching, protoceratopsids have not been found in any of the more than 26 screenwashed microvertebrate sites in the Judith River Group, Ryan and Currie speculated that this group of ceratopsians "may have been almost completely

Photograph by the author, courtesy National Museum of Natural History, Smithsonian Institution.

Albertosaurus

Virtually complete skeletons of the (left) theropod *Gorgosaurus libratus* (USNM 12814), missing only the tail, from Little Sandhill Creek basin, Alberta, Canada, and (right) *Edmontosaurus annectens*, almost complete holotype skeleton (USNM 2414) of *Claosaurus annectens*, from Niobrara County, Wyoming.

ecologically excluded from the wet, coastal environments of these Formations which were preferred by larger ceratopsians."

Ryan and Currie noted that, although "protoceratopsians" are generally thought to have originated in Asia, the presence of this group in the Santonian of North America, rivalling the oldest published records for Asia (*Microceratops*), suggests that these dinosaurs may have originated *in situ* in North America, then dispersed to Asia where they flourished in dry inland environments. Furthermore, the paucity of "protoceratopsian" material in North America may "be attributed to lack of arid and semiarid, eoliandominated environments for these dinosaurs on this continent."

Vickers-Rich and Rich (1997) reported the discovery of neoceratopsian remains found at The Arch, Wonthaggi Formation (Early Cretaceous; Aptian), Strzelecki Group, in southeastern polar Australia. The fossil, an ulna bearing "a remarkable resemblance to that of [the protoceratopsid] *Leptoceratops gracilis* from the latest Cretaceous of Alberta." If this questionable specimen proves to be that of a protoceratopsid, its Early Cretaceous age may imply that horned dinosaurs evolved in Gondwana rather than, as generally believed, in Asia.

Sampson, Ryan and Tanke (1997) published an analysis of the ontogenetic and taxonomic variation in the skulls of ceratopsids belonging to the Centrosaurinae — the subfamily of ceratopsians distinguished by well-developed nasal horncores or bosses, comparatively short brow horncores or bosses, and parietosquamosal frills adorned with various hooks and spikes — based mostly upon several centrosaurine bonebeds, each of which included remains representing a variety of sizes and age classes. The bonebeds utilized in their study, located in late Campanian and early Maastrichtian deposits in Alberta, Canada, and Montana, United States, indicate mass deaths confidently assumed by the authors to represent but a single taxon. Specimens in these bonebeds belong to such taxa as *Centrosaurus apertus*, *Styracosaurus albertensis*, *Einiosaurus procurvicornis*, *Pachyrhinosaurus canadensis*, and "an undescribed species of pachyrhinosaur."

This investigation was made following direct observations and measurements (made to the closest millimeter and repeated three times, averaged when necessary) of fossil remains including more than a thousand ceratopsid cranial elements preserved in the collections of various institutions in North America. The study focused upon these regions of the centrosaurine skull roof—"(1) nasal horncores, (2) supraorbital horncores, (3) frontal fontanelle and supracranial cavities, and (4) parietosquamosal frill." It was

Photograph by the author, courtesy American Museum of Natural History.

Protoceratops andrewsi skeletons (AMNH 6417 and 6467) with nest of eggs (belonging to this or some other dinosaurian species) found in Mongolia. The generally accepted idea that ceratopsians originated in Asia has recently been questioned.

made recognizing two ontogenetic stages in ceratopsids — "(1) fusion of cranial elements, including accessory of dermal elements, and (2) bone surface texture." As no embryonic or hatchlings were known in ceratopsids, those criteria, used to examine relative sexual maturity in extant vertebrates, could not be employed in this study. Yet a fourth stage of ontogeny, old age, could apparently only be recognized by the authors on the basis of several craniofacial features, but could not be verified based on the above two aging techniques.

From this study, Sampson *et al.* (1997) observed that the horns, bosses, and frills of centrosaurines acquired adult morphologies late in ontogeny and only upon reaching or nearing adult body size, while exhibiting a variety of taxonomically distinct features.

Partial skeleton of Leptoceratops gracilis, a primitive ceratopsian from Wyoming. Similar dinosaurs may now be known from both Canada and Australia.

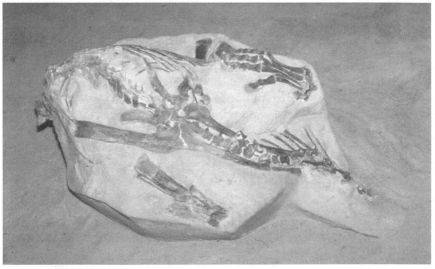

Photograph by the author, courtesy Royal Tyrrell Museum/Alberta Community Development.

Introduction

According to Sampson *et al.*, immature individuals of various centrosaurine taxa display remarkable similarity in horncore morphology. All juveniles and subadults possess transversely-compressed, sagitally-divided nasal horncores that fused, from the tip down, late in ontogeny. The horncore or boss morphology later seen in adult centrosaurines developed as direct outgrowths of the nasal bones and only after the fusion of the nasals.

Brow horns followed a parallel sequence of development, all juveniles and subadults possessing relatively small supraorbital horncores exhibiting only minor differences between some genera. In juveniles, these horncores consist of a long, low rounded process which laterally "tends to be flush with the external surface of the face," while "the medial surface slopes steeply toward the midline," the surface texture of these horncores being finely pitted or usually smooth. The brow horns in subadults are also quite similar across taxa.

A pattern quite similar to that expressed by the horns was observed by Sampson *et al.* in the ontogeny of centrosaurine parietal frills (but not of squamosals). In adult individuals, the median bar of the parietal "is low and rounded dorsally with several variably developed processes that are usually small but attained large size in at least one undescribed species of *Pachyrhinosaurus*"; also, the surface texture of bone in mature individuals varies, but lacks the striations indicative of comparatively rapid growth. In juveniles, the parietals are always thin and fragile, having small to nearly nonexistent fenestrae, a simple scalloped margin without epoccipital processes, a median bar having a saggital ridge, and a predominance of striated or long-grained surface bone texture. However, the parietals of subadult centrosaurines are large, often as big as those in adults, and have well-developed fenestrae, but are otherwise thin and unadorned as in juveniles. Other subadult characters of the parietal frill include "a variable fusion of epoccipitals, when present; a predictable mixture of surface bone morphology, including striated juvenile texture and mottled or rugose adult texture; and variable evidence of the transition to adult parietal processes, particularly those placed most medial and posterior on the parietal, which may show the initial stages of anterodorsally directed growth (*Centrosaurus* and *Styracosaurus*)." During ontogeny, the parietal progressively thickens, especially on the posterior transverse ramus; epoccipitals, often present on the marginal processes in adults, fuse anteriorly from the posterior.

In observing these positive allometric changes manifested in centrosaurine skulls, Sampson *et al.* made the important point that the skulls of juvenile and subadult individuals are "essentially equivalent" at both the generic and specific levels, and are thus difficult if not impossible to distinguish taxonomically. Therefore, some genera, established upon immature specimens at a time when these ontogenetic stages were not yet recognized, are probably, in these authors' opinion, juvenile or subadult individuals of better known adult taxa.

Brachyceratops montanensis (see *Brachyceratops* entry, *D:TE*) is known only from a few juvenile or sub-adult specimens, none of them exhibiting diagnostic characters. Most of these were collected without detailed stratigraphic and geographic data, the type locality occurring relatively close to the bed that yielded *Einiosaurus* and *Achelousaurus*. According to Sampson *et al.*, *Brachyceratops* could represent a juvenile of either of these genera, or some other taxon, although more specimens are required to resolve the issue. *Monoclonius crassus* was regarded as a junior synonym, based on immature specimens, of possibly a number of centrosaurine taxa, probably *Centrosaurus* (see entries, *D:TE* and this volume). Both *B. montanensis* and *M. crassus* were, therefore, regarded by Sampson *et al.* as *nomina dubia*, based upon immature and nondiagnostic remains.

Also, Sampson *et al.* addressed the problem that numerous mature adult centrosaurine skulls (about 25 percent of those examined by these authors) do not have true supraorbital horncores at all, but instead possess low, rounded masses of bone, simple raised ridges, or concavities. As already stated, juveniles do possess brow horncores that developed during ontogeny. Where, then, did these horncores go?

As the authors' pointed out, the brow horn in both the Centrosaurinae and Chasmosaurinae, the other ceratopsid family, does not seem to be a separate ossification of the horncore, but is rather an outgrowth of the postorbital and palpebral bones. Some centrosaurine postorbitals seem to be "morphological intermediates" having well-developed although pitted horncores, these specimens suggesting that, upon reaching full development before death, the horn was resorbed.

Sampson *et al.* offered the following four ways to account possibly for this secondary lack of supraorbital horncores in only some adult centrosaurines: "(1) periodic resorption by regrowth; (2) age-related resorption; (3) periodic loss due to seasonal antler-style of replacement; and (4) pathology, related either to disease or trauma."

Regarding the above, the authors suggested that this horncore resorption might be due to calcium requirements, possibly related to egg-laying in females, but noted that a pattern of sexual dimorphism would then be expected in the presence or absence of brow horns, a pattern that presently cannot be determined.

The horncores may have been lost in aged individuals of both sexes, perhaps from lack of use, and yet many fully mature specimens have well-developed brow horns. The horncores may have been replaced periodically, growing rapidly on a seasonal basis and then being partially lost or resorbed. Regarding pathology due to activity such as head-to-head intraspecific contests involving competition for females or hierarchical disputes, Sampson *et al.* pointed out that several specimens (including *Styracosaurus* specimen CMN [formerly NMC] 344) exhibit symmetrical pits rather than horncores, a rather implausible pattern if pathologic.

A ceratopsid belonging to the subfamily Chasmosaurinae, informally referred to as the "El Picacho ceratopsian," was described by Lehman (1996), based upon fragmentary remains collected from the lower part of the El Picacho Formation (middle–late Maastrichtian [Lancian]), in the valley of San Carlos Creek, west of Sierra Vieja, in Presidio County, West Texas.

Specimens referred to the "El Picacho ceratopsian" include (TMM 42304-1) the posterior part of a braincase and occipital condyle, parts of both squamosals, small fragments of a parietal, parts of coossified nasals, the proximal end of a right humerus, three almost complete dorsal ribs, and many rib fragments, the association of these remains at the recovery site suggesting that they all represent a single individual; (TMM 42535-1) a nearly complete braincase; and (TMM 40814-6) a very large epijugal, all of these remains being compatible in size and form, and from the same general area and stratigraphic horizon. Possibly referrable to this taxon are other remains including a dorsal vertebra (TMM 40814-2). The material was all collected by Jack Wilson and Wann Langston, Jr., for the Texas Memorial Museum during the 1960s; additional specimens were recovered by Thomas M. Lehman in the 1980s.

As Lehman pointed out, the above remains are not sufficient enough to diagnose this new taxon fully, but are enough to establish the presence in the El Picacho Formation of a species not previously known from this region. Although these remains possibly (and maybe probably) represent a new species, key elements were lacking to warrant assigning it a formal name at this point. The long squamosals indicate that this taxon belongs to the Chasmosaurinae.

Pending the possible discovery of new material, Lehman published the following character summary based upon the collected remains: Large chasmosaurine having long (more than 100 centimeters) and thick (up to 4 centimeters) squamosals bearing prominent irregular marginal undulations; nasals without discrete horncore; parietal thin, sheetlike, with large epoccipitals; very large trihedral epijugals; braincase

Monoclonius lowei, CMN 8470 (formerly NMC 8790) holotype skull. Some paleontologists believe this species to belong in the genus *Centrosaurus* (see entry, *D:TE* and this volume); others regard it as a valid taxon. Scale = 12 cm. (After Sternberg 1940.)

with thick lateral walls and large postfrontal foramen.

According to Lehman, the remains indicate that this species is comparable in size to the very large ceratopsians *Torosaurus* and *Pentaceratops*. The squamosals, different in shape and thickness from those in *Triceratops* and *Torosaurus*, are similar to those in *Arrhinoceratops* and *Pentaceratops*; the braincase differs from that of *Pentaceratops* (see Lehman 1993), "the thin plate-like parietal fragments and subdued nasal horncore" suggesting *Arrhinoceratops*; and the El Picacho form differs from *Torosaurus latus*, the only

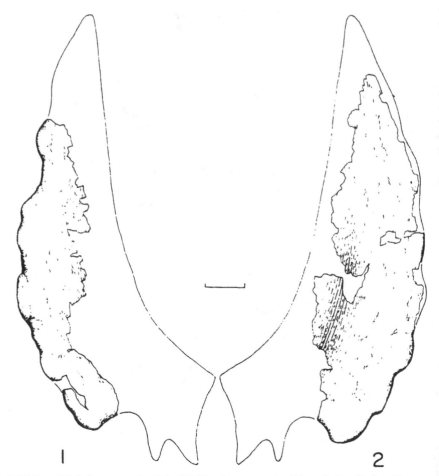

1. Right and 2. left squamosals of the "El Picacho ceratopsian," lateral view. Scale = 10 cm. (After Lehman 1996.)

other contemporaneous Lancian ceratopsian from the American Southwest.

Lehman speculated that other remains reported over the years from Lancian strata of the Southwest may be referable, or at least similar, to the "El Picacho ceratopsian." These include a fragmentary skull (USNM 16577) with very large epijugals, and several parietal fragments, collected from the North Horn Formation of Utah and mentioned by Gilmore (1946b); parts of a postcranial skeleton (TMM 41361) from the Javelina Formation of Texas, described by Lawson (1972); and a squamosal and fragmentary parietal (UNM FKK-035) from the uppermost part of the Kirtland Shale, New Mexico, described by Lehman (1981).

Ectothermy Versus Endothermy

Vertebrate paleontologist Michael Morales, in an abstract delivered verbally at the second Dinofest™ International event, held in 1996 at Arizona State University in Tempe, listed a number of unresolved modern controversies involving dinosaurs. Included on Morales' (1996) list was a question of interest both to the scientist and the general public alike: "Were dinosaurs endothermic ('hot-blooded'), ectothermic ('cold-blooded'), or something else?"

As Morales correctly pointed out, such inquiries — which continue in both the scientific literature and popular media — are largely based on ideas that have been proposed since the early 1970s (the beginning of the so-called "Dinosaur Renaissance"), these illustrating the fact that dinosaur research is "dynamic and often contentious," and that there is yet much to learn about these "wonderful beasts."

Indeed, dinosaurian metabolism remains a controversial issue and a most intriguing topic of research among vertebrate paleontologists (as well as a subject of discussion among nonprofessionals interested in dinosaurs), and one that has prompted numerous and diverse avenues of approach. However, this matter of ectothermy versus endothermy in dinosaurs has not yet, despite often misleading articles to the contrary appearing in the popular press, been unequivocally resolved. Published arguments, offering both pro and con evidence, continue to be strong and often compelling.

The "RT" Controversy

New approaches to attempt solving this problem have surfaced in more recent years. For example, complex respiratory turbinates (or RT)—structures present in the nasal cavities of all extant mammals and birds — have recently been used as criteria for determining whether various extinct animals were warm- or cold-blooded (see D:TE). Indeed, arguments based upon this topic would become quite vocal and even "heated" during the latter 1990s, not only at Society of Vertebrate Paleontology meetings and in the paleontological literature, but also on the Internet.

Ruben, Leitch and Hillenius (1995) posited that respiratory turbinates were probably not present in tyrannosaurid, dromaeosaurid, and ornithomimid theropods (which included the most likely candidates for dinosaurian endothermy) and probably the bird Archaeopteryx. This condition was interpreted by them as direct evidence for ectothermic or near-ectothermic metabolic status in these taxa. Ruben et al. argued that, lacking respiratory turbinates, "unacceptably high rates of respiratory water loss would probably always have posed a chronic obstacle to maintenance of bulk lung ventilation rates consistent with endothermy, or with metabolic rates approaching endothermy" (see D:TE).

Results of a more recent study by Hillenius (1996) seemingly supported the above idea. Hillenius, after performing CT analysis on several dinosaur skulls, was unable to identify evidence of such structures in these skulls, although "ossified elements apparently involved in directing the respiratory airflow onto the turbinate complex" were observed in Late Cretaceous herperornithid birds. Furthermore, Hillenius found that nasal dimensions of several dinosaurian taxa closely match the condition in extant ectotherms, suggesting that it was unlikely that dinosaurs "had room in the nasal cavity for an elaborate respiratory turbinate complex, or possessed expanded ventilation rates."

Favoring the idea that dinosaurs were endothermic animals, Paul (1995), in a preliminary report, challenged the hypothesis of Ruben et al. that respiratory turbinates supposedly constitute the first reliable morphological indicators of high metabolic rates in the fossil record. Paul (1995) cited the following: 1. Absence of RT in whales and some birds (including those with closed external nares), and small, poorly developed RT in some birds and primates (including large-snouted baboons); 2. high rates of respiratory water conservation in birds and mammals with little or no RT; 3. brain-cooling function of RT in animals with large brains; 4. lack of strong correlation or direct causal link between RT and metabolic power production; and 4. low rate of preservation and poor identifiability of RT in fossils, especially when nasal regions differ from those of mammals.

Paul (1995) proposed that, rather than metabolic

Courtesy Milwaukee Public Museum (neg. #425836).

Dinosaurs, such as the herbivorous *Stegosaurus stenops* (left) and carnivorous *Allosaurus fragilis* (right) shown in these diorama models (no longer displayed), were formerly portrayed as sluggish, tail-dragging, and certainly cold-blooded reptiles.

rates, RT may be correlated with brain size, especially in mammals (except very large-brained primates which have their own alternate cooling systems); that in small-brained trachyaerobic tetrapods, RT could range from absent to well-developed; that uncrushed dinosaur nasal cavities have ample space for better developed RT than in reptiles; and that ossified RT structures have been preserved in ankylosaurs.

Bone Histologies

As in the past, bone histologies — studies of the fine structures in bones utilizing microscopic magnification (see *D:TE*) — continue to be used to attempt interpreting aspects of dinosaurian biology, and rapid growth rate has been used as evidence supporting dinosaurian endothermy.

Curry (1996) conducted an histologic study utilizing bones (including transverse sections of mid-diaphysis of radii, ulnae, and scapulae) from early to late diplodocid sauropods collected from the Morrison Formation, Cactus Park Site, Colorado. Curry's analysis indicated the following: Sauropod bone characterized by densely vascularized fibro-lamellar tissue, suggesting rapid primary growth; vascular canals with laminar to plexiform arrangement; two to three Lines of Arrested Growth (LAGs) in external cortices of late juveniles, followed by vascular fibro-lamellar zones; apposition of disorganized periosteal bone [fibrous membrane covering a bone] indicating active deposition at all ontogenetic stages; Haversian bone [or secondary bone, built from structures called secondary osteons], most abundant in older individuals, in perimedullar region of all individuals. These results indicated to Curry that diplodocid bone sustained rapid growth until late juvenile ontogenetic states, the osteogenic pattern observed in these bones resembling closely that of modern artiodactyls. (See also Tkach 1996 and *Dilophosaurus* entry, this volume, for a similar study.)

According to Vickers-Rich and Rich (1997) (see also Vickers-Rich 1998), absences of LAGs in the

Australian hypsilophodontid species *Leaellynasaura amicagraphica* and all other hypsilophodontids, coupled with the enlarged optic lobes in *L. amicagraphica* (see *Leaellynasaura* entry, *D:TE*) but not in lower paleolatitude members of this group, suggest that hypsilophodontids "were preadapted for year around activity and then greater visual acuity when they entered higher latitudes if they in fact first evolved in lower paleolatitudes." Also, half of the approximately dozen taxa known in the southeastern Australian dinosaur assemblage are hypsilophodontids, the diversity of the Hypsilophodontidae in this region suggesting that these animals lived in a particularly suitable habitat.

Robin E. H. Reid (1996), a leading specialist in dinosaur bone histology, published the first part of a planned three-part, comprehensive study of the bone of dinosaurs recovered from the Cleveland-Lloyd Dinosaur Quarry and also other localities. Following "an account of the nature of bone, of various processes and factors that affect it, and the ways in which bone tissues can be classified," those found in dinosaurs were examined.

From this extensive and comprehensive study, it was Reid's opinion that "there is reasonable evidence from bone that [dinosaurs] differed physiologically from all modern reptiles but no certain evidence of how they differed."

First, Reid pointed out that none of the many tissues (including Haversian bone) that are normal constituents of tetrapod bones can be used as criteria to distinguish between ectotherms and endotherms, as all of these tissues occur in both. Both groups exhibit contrasting general styles of bone histology, typical zonal patterns being seen mainly in ectotherms, continuous growth fibro-lamellar bone and extensive Haversian reconstruction observed chiefly in endotherms. However, "exceptions occur in all of these cases, and bones of very small forms often show no hint of different physiologies."

Reid stated that, while modern ectotherms and endotherms display contrasting general styles of bone histology, such a contrast has no importance when it comes to fossils, as there is no way to determine at what stage in physiological evolution the "endothermic" style originated. As an example, Reid mentioned that the earliest synapsids exhibiting endotherm-like bone were primitive therapsids showing no other signs of endothermy, this bone seemingly not marking endothermy, but rather some earlier step in physiological evolution which needed to be taken for endotherms to begin evolving (see Reid 1987).

Though Haversian bone is extensive in some dinosaurs and has been used as evidence of high metabolic rates, Reid listed the following problems involved with that assessment:

1. Haversian bone is not unknown in modern reptiles. Dense Haversian bone in these animals is rare, although Reid (1987) found it to be as extensively developed in the tortoise *Geochelone triserrata* as in humans.

2. Haversian bone, even in endotherms, is mainly a feature of medium-sized and large forms. It is characteristically absent even in the smallest forms despite their high metabolic rates. This implies that size is a factor and discounts a causal connection between levels of Haversian reconstruction and high metabolic levels.

3. Delayed reconstruction in some species discounts a simple relationship between Haversian bone and metabolic levels. Cats, for example, do not start to form Haversian bone until well after sexual maturity, while reconstruction has been seen in the scutes of 6- to 8-year-old alligators whose metabolic rates decrease as they grow.

4. Association of extensive Haversian reconstruction with large sizes implies mechanical stresses produced by heavy weights as a causal factor, particularly in animals that walk upright.

5. Other nonmetabolic factors leading to local Haversian reconstruction can apply to dinosaurs. This includes the radial blocks of dense Haversian bone found under various muscle scars in *Iguanodon* (see Reid 1984).

6. General reconstruction in dinosaurian diaphyses, even in forms as large as *Iguanodon* and *Allosaurus*, can be as total as in some mammals, or as limited as is normal for crocodiles. Reid (1996) noted that this notion conflicts with the idea of weight being a causal factor, except at even larger sizes.

7. Extensive reconstruction in large forms could reflect the effects of size combined with those of mass homeothermy based upon bulk rather than warm-bloodedness.

Fibro-lamellar bone in dinosaurs constitutes evidence showing continuous growth at rates comparable with those of birds and large, rapidly growing mammals; and because such growth is now seen only in warm-blooded animals, it is sometimes used as evidence supporting endothermy in dinosaurs (*e.g.*, Ricqlès 1983). Reid (1996), though finding this idea plausible, found in it two salient problems:

1. Ricqlès first used this argument believing that zonal patterns, typical of ectotherms, do not occur in dinosaurs. Ricqlès abandoned this line of reasoning in favor of the influence of mass effects when examples were found by Reid (1981) in sauropods, zonal bone now known to be common in dinosaurs though less common than nonzonal tissues (Reid 1990).

2. Ricqlès used the term fibro-lamellar only for tissues of this type that formed continuously, but did not apply it to identical tissues formed by crocodiles and turtles during periodic rapid growth, thereby implying that the simple formation of such bone does not require higher rates of metabolism than such animals experience during rapid growth.

To Reid (1996), then, the ability of dinosaurs to grow very large rapidly and continuously, as implied by the presence of nonzonal fibro-lamellar bone, constitutes good evidence that dinosaurs were quite different physiologically from modern reptiles. The only positive inference Reid (1996) could draw from this evidence is that dinosaurs possessed a cardiovascular and hemal system able to support such growth. Reid (1996) further speculated that the circulatory systems of dinosaurs must have kept pace with growth in a way that permitted the basically constant rates of bone formation observed in gigantic forms.

From the above perspective, high circulatory efficiency rather than high metabolic rates may have been the primary basis of rapid continuous growth in dinosaurs. According to Reid (1996), such circulation would probably lead to a rise in metabolic rates to above those of modern reptiles, although how far above he could not predict.

Regarding endothermy in birds and mammals, Reid (1996) cautioned that this involves more than just high metabolic rates; also, it includes the ability to maintain, regardless of bulk and activity, a constant body temperature via exact physiologically controlled balances between heat production and losses. Reid (1996) concluded that there "is no way in which bone histology can show dinosaurs as having this ability."

More recently, Horner (1998) suggested that, of all the arguments used to answer the question "Were dinosaurs warm-blooded or cold-blooded, or maybe even a combination of both?" the last strong lines of data seem to result from bone histology. Horner acknowledged that the "Highly vascularized plexiform, fibro-lamellar tissues replaced by dense Haversian Systems is so similar to the bone patterns of living endotherms it is difficult to envision the animals having been ectotherms," but also noted that "it is the presence of LAGs or rest lines that even the score, for these features are known almost exclusively in ectotherms."

Horner, a specialist in dinosaur eggs, embryos, and baby dinosaurs, pointed out that both highly vascularized plexiform, fibro-lamellar bone, and also the calcified cartilage cones observed in the metaphyseal regions of young dinosaurs, are derived characters shared with birds. Rest lines, on the other hand, are plesiomorphic characters that could reflect ancestry instead of physiology.

Respiration and Other Considerations

Robert T. Bakker remains one of the leading and most vocal champions of the warm-blooded dinosaurs theory. Bakker (1997*b*) added to his ever-increasing body of evidence supporting the hypothesis that dinosaurs were endothermic with his detailed report on abundant shed allosaur teeth. These teeth (representing individuals ranging from hatchlings to adults, and found in association with chewed bones of very large

Since the "Dinosaur Renaissance" beginning in the early 1970s, dinosaurs have been portrayed as active, often agile, and possibly warm-blooded animals, as in this painting by "paleoartist" Gregory S. Paul, depicting a predacious *Allosaurus fragilis* and its prey, the armored *Stegosaurus stenops*.

prey animals) recovered from Nail Quarry, a site in the Morrison Formation at Como Bluff, were collected during excavations by the Dinamation International Society (DIS) and the Tate Museum in Casper, Wyoming.

From analyses of these teeth, Bakker (1997b) extrapolated the following conclusions, explaining most of them in detail: 1. Tiny predatory dinosaurs (teeth identified by James H. Madsen, Jr., a specialist in allosaurs) sometimes fed on gigantic carcasses; 2. very young allosaurs fed upon gigantic bones; 3. baby allosaurs did most of their chewing on large carcasses in lair sites; 4. scavengers from all species except allosaurs were excluded from lairs; 5. adult allosaurs joined baby allosaurs in feeding at lairs; 6. adult allosaurs in groups probably prevented scavengers of every size from interfering with the activities of their babies in their lairs; 7. moving water did not carry in the large carcass parts and concentrate them at Nail Quarry; 8. adult allosaurs dragged in the carcass pieces that were chewed at Nail Quarry and avoided bringing in carcasses of small prey; 9. the allosaurs fed upon large dead carnivores as well as herbivores; and 10. young allosaurs fed upon giant pieces of carcasses, in the presence of the adults, until the young were fully grown.

If Bakker's (1997b) interpretation of this evidence is correct, then adult allosaurs exercised a more sophisticated level of parental care for their young than had previously been suspected. However, this interpretation also has implications germane to the ectothermy versus endothermy controversy. Cold-blooded predatory reptiles like lizards, Bakker (1997b) noted, require a wide size range in prey as the individual animal grows up; warm-blooded predatory mammals, on the other hand, require a much narrower range. Tooth crowns of hatchling allosaurs have the same overall shapes as those of adults, this indicating to Bakker (1997b) "that the hatchlings were feeding on prey tissue of the same general texture and consistency as that fed upon by adults."

Hengst, Alix and Rigby (1996), acknowledging in a brief report that dinosaurs are now portrayed by some modern researchers "as aerobically active, metabolically demanding organisms," pointed out that high requirements of oxygen are necessary for such a lifestyle, and that these needs should be reflected in adaptations for respiration. According to Hengst et al., at least some dinosaurian species probably breathed by rib movements supplemented by movement of gastralia.

By measuring the thoracic geometry of both saurischian and ornithischian dinosaurs, Hengst et al. deduced that breathing improved by approximately 40 percent from Late Triassic to Late Jurassic (no additional change being found during the Cretaceous) times, this change in rib orientation apparently indicating increased aerobic behavior. (The authors studied living alligators to confirm the accuracy of their method of calculating maximal rib movement, and rib-breathing rats to test the ability of rib-breathing to support endothermic metabolism and modest activity.)

In a follow up report, Hengst (1998) found "that costal-vertebral articulation angles establish the direction of rib movement." Comparing North American theropods with those from South America, Hengst discovered that North American forms reached optimal breathing alignment by the Late Jurassic, further change not taking place during the Cretaceous. This suggested "that these angles provide the optimum contribution to breathing for the effort involved." South American (Argentine) forms did not reach this same end point until the "Middle" to Late Cretaceous, this possibly indicating "that selection for greater aerobic capacity may not have been as great as in North American dinosaurs."

Taking another approach to this controversy of endothermy versus ectothermy in dinosaurs, Ruben, Jones, Geist and Hillenius (1997) made a study of the probable lung structure in theropod dinosaurs (see also Jones, Ruben and Geist 1998).

Ruben et al. (1997) and Jones et al. (1998) pointed out that all living reptiles and birds have septate-style lungs. Mammals, on the other hand, possess alveolar-style lungs consisting of millions of tiny, highly vascularized, blind air sacs. This and other attributes of the mammalian lung combine to allow for "facilitating homogeneous maintenance of a constantly refreshed supply of alveolar oxygen as well as continuous elimination of carbon dioxide," and also maintaining "high rates of oxygen consumption during extended periods of intensive activity."

The reptilian lung—analogous to one oversized alveolus of the mammalian lung—has an unmodified bellowslike morphology that restricts the maximum rates of exchange of oxygen and carbon dioxide, and the ability to support high rates of oxygen consumption during exercise. The avian lung, however, has a modified "flow-through" morphology capable of the respiratory gas exchange rates typical of the lungs of active endotherms. Only the types of lungs possessed by mammals and birds, therefore, are capable of oxygen–carbon dioxide exchange rates consistent with endothermy.

According to these authors, skeletal evidence and fossilized soft tissue evidence in theropod specimens shows that many, if not all, of these dinosaurs—like modern crocodiles—possessed reptilian style septate lungs, this evidence including the following: The ribcage-pectoral girdle in theropods displays no indications of skeletomuscular capacity for the inhalatory filling of abdominal air sacs, such modifications not appearing until the Cretaceous in ornithiurine birds.

The preserved visceral cavity in the theropod *Sinosauropteryx* (see entry) shows "complete thoracic-abdominal separation, defined by a remarkably crocodilianlike vertically oriented partition coincident with the apparent dome-shaped anterior surface of the liver." Theropods possess a distinct, relatively vertical, and highly elongate pubis and also well-developed gastralia. According to the authors, theropods then, like crocodiles, most likely "possessed a vertical thoracic-abdominal subdivision of the visceral cavity and relied on a hepatic-piston diaphragm to ventilate a bellowslike septate lung."

Archaeopteryx and most other early birds, the authors noted, also probably had bellowslike septate lungs, as they "possessed a relatively unremarkable ribcage-sternum apparatus" and did not have the skeletomuscular arrangement required for ventilated abdominal air sacs.

The above arrangement made it unlikely, in the opinion of Ruben *et al.* (1997) and Jones *et al.* (1998), that theropods as well as *Archaeopteryx* and other early birds (enantiornithines) had the capacity for the high, exercise-related, oxygen consumption rates that are typical of endotherms, the data therefore suggesting an ectothermic status for these animals.

The authors further suggested that the occurrence of hepatic-piston diaphragmatic lung ventilation in theropod dinosaurs throughout the Mesozoic Era also presents a major obstacle to the commonly held theory that birds are their direct descendants (see section following). The earliest derivation of the avian abdominal air sac or flow-through system from a diaphragm-ventilating ancestor could only have resulted from the unlikely scenario of intense "selection for a diaphragmatic hernia in taxa transitional between theropods and birds." According to Ruben *et al.* (1997) and Jones *et al.* (1998), such a condition would hardly have been of any selective advantage, immediately compromising the entire pulmonary ventilatory apparatus.

In a preliminary report responding to the above studies, Claessens, Perry and Currie (1998) utilized osteology (*e.g.*, shape and volume of the trunk, nature of rib-vertebra interlocking, existence of lung diverticula through pneumaticity of certain skeletal elements, presence of well-developed attachment areas for a diaphragm, *etc.*) and comparative anatomy (analyzing similar structures in phylogenetically closely related extant organisms or in more distant extant fauna) as a basis to reconstruct the possible respiratory apparatus of theropods.

Accepting that theropods should be placed phylogenetically between Aves (see section below) and other Archosauria, Claessens *et al.* noted that birds are unique in their possession of a lung having "discrete groups of diverticula or air-sacs, which are instrumental in generating unidirectional airflow"; and that this kind of "lung construction is technically much more efficient than the bidirectional airflow system employed in reptiles and mammals."

Claessens *et al.* found it likely that the avian-type lung evolved somewhere in the Theropoda-Aves lineage. Like birds, saurischian dinosaurs have some bones that are pneumatic. Theropods possess lung diverticula to varying degree in the axial skeleton, with pneumatization extending in oviraptorosaurs and tyrannosaurids as far back as the sacral and caudal vertebrae. Theropods have ribs possessing well-separated heads that define specific planes of movement. Distinct attachment areas for intercostal muscles are present in more derived theropods. Theropods such as *Velociraptor* possess ribs with uncinate processes, which in birds increase the efficiency of costal breathing. Also, both nonavian theropods and *Archaeopteryx* possess kinetic gastralia that are joined in a characteristic interlocking pattern.

Based on the presence of dorsal diverticula, which invaded the axial skeleton, Claessens *et al.* concluded that "the lungs of theropods must have been attached dorsally. Heterogenously partitioned lungs with extensive sac-like ventral and caudal regions were most probably present. The ribs were adequately built for manipulation of the shape of the thorax. The gastralia prevented paradoxial movement of the viscera in the lung space upon inspiration." Although Claessens *et al.* could not determine the precise extent of lung diverticula formation, the authors speculated that, if "the caudal sac-like lung region had differentiated to form abdominal air-sacs, the kinetic gastralia would have been well suited for ventilating them."

From the morphology of the pelvis, laterally flattened trunk, and extensive pneumatization of bones in theropods, Claessens *et al.* found it unlikely that these dinosaurs possessed a hepatic-piston pump comparable to the system found in modern crocodilians; furthermore, as evident from the similarities in the axial skeletons of advanced theropods and *Archaeopteryx*, unidirectional airflow possibly became established comparatively late during the theropod-avian transition.

Dinosaurs and Birds

Another of Michael Morales' list of dinosaur-related questions was, "Did birds evolve from theropod dinosaurs or from nondinosaurian archosaurs?"

As previously discussed in *D:TE*, much debate has raged in the paleontological literature over the decades regarding the seeming relationships between

Introduction

Holotype (LP-4450-IEI) incomplete skeleton of *Iberomesornis romerali* (Sanz and Bonaparte 1992), an Early Cretaceous (Barremian) nestling bird similar in some ways to both *Archaeopteryx* and modern birds. The specimen was found in the Las Hoyas Konservat-lagerstätte, Serraniá de Cuenca, province of Cuenca, Spain.

birds and dinosaurs, as well as birds and other reptilian groups (*e.g.*, "thecodontians" and crocodilians). Since that book went to press, work has been steadily done concerning these relationships and toward arriving at unequivocal answers to such questions as that posted by Morales, and also to these: 1. Should the Late Jurassic genus *Archaeopteryx*, usually considered to be the first bird, be classified as a dinosaur (in the more "traditional" sense)?; and 2. should modern birds be regarded as living, feathered theropods?

Associations of birds with theropods were already surfacing during the time of earliest discoveries of dinosaur trace (and later bone) fossils, the early to middle nineteenth century. As far back as 1802, a youth named Pliny Moody discovered a stone slab containing five small fossilized three-toed footprints on his father's farm in South Hadley, Massachusetts (see Steinbock 1989). Some seven years later, these birdlike tracks, now believed to be the first authenticated dinosaur footprints ever found, were bought by Dr. Elihu Dwight, who exhibited them as the probable tracks of the raven from Noah's ark (see Hitchcock 1844). In 1841, Professor Edward Hitchcock of Amherst College described this specimen as the new ichnotaxon *Ornithoidichnites fulcicoides* which, he noted, resembled the tracks of the American coot (see also Thulborn 1990).

In later years, other scientists began to notice various anatomical similarities between birds and some

dinosaurs. Most notably, Thomas Henry Huxley (1868), a firm advocate of Charles Darwin and evolutionary theory, noted the rather striking resemblance between *Archaeopteryx* and the tiny theropod *Compsognathus*. Boldly, Huxley originated "the hypothesis that the phylum of the Class of Aves has its foot in the Dinosaurian Reptiles — that these, passing through a series of such modifications as are exhibited in one of their phases by *Compsognathus*, have given rise to [birds]."

Throughout the rest of the nineteenth century and through more than half of the twentieth, observations such as Huxley's went largely disavowed or entirely ignored by the paleontological community (see Feduccia 1980 for details). In fact, only in about the latter half of the twentieth century did scientists again begin to investigate seriously the possible evolutionary connections between theropods and birds.

Supporting the idea that birds *are* dinosaurs (see Thulborn 1985, who proposed that modern birds are "neotenous" dinosaurs, that is, they have retained various juvenile theropod features), many modern vertebrate paleontologists now refer to birds as "theropods," while those dinosaurs traditionally called theropods are also more specifically designated "nonavian" (or "nonavialian") theropods. To emphasize this idea, an exhibit sign displayed in the American Museum of Natural History's cladistically arranged Hall of Saurischian Dinosaurs unequivocally proclaims that "birds are dinosaurs."

Today, most vertebrate paleontologists have come to embrace what became the widespread idea that birds descended from a line of coelurosaurian theropods. Nevertheless, the matter only quite recently seems to have been resolved. Indeed, evidence leading to an apparent conclusion in this matter has been amassing over the last several years at an amazing rate, gradually and successively building up like clues in a piece of detective fiction, in which the last piece of evidence could just be that proverbial and much desired "smoking gun."

Dissenting Opinions

Although the majority of dinosaur researchers have favored the dinosaur-bird relationship, and most of the data seems to support the view that certain theropods are directly ancestral to birds, a relatively small number of workers have continued to disagree with that assessment.

Fossil bird specialist Larry D. Martin has remained one of the relatively few modern dissenting voices, positing that birds had their own lineage separate from that of dinosaurs, deriving not from theropods but, along with dinosaurs, from some earlier archosaurian group. In an abstract, Martin (1995) argued that confusion "of dinosaurs with early birds is based more on a lack of familiarity with avian anatomy than any profound similarity." According to Martin, all known dinosaurs lack a series of features expected to be found in any protobird, including a laterally facing glenoid (allowing the arm to be brought out laterally to form a wing), a dorso-ventrally compressed body that can be flattened for lift in flight, and the ability to climb almost vertical surfaces (this based on the hypothesis that flight apparently originated in an arboreal protobird).

Concerning *Archaeopteryx*, Martin pointed out that at least two *Archaeopteryx* specimens (Eichstätt and Solnhofen) were once identified as the small theropod *Compsognathus*, despite that the latter, known from just a single specimen, is much rarer than the former; that the hands of *Compsognathus* are reduced with "two" shortened fingers (enlarged metacarpal I and two large proximal carpal elements) [note: this feature is now under contention, the hand of *Compsognathus* possibly having three digits rather than two], while those of *Archaeopteryx* have three elongated fingers (small metacarpal I and two large carpal elements); and that *Compsognathus* possesses a diapsid bar separating upper and lower fenestrae, laterally situated coracoids and scapulae with downward facing glenoids, ventrally directed pubis, and ventrally elongated hypophyses, none of these features being present in *Archaeopteryx*.

Ann C. Burke and another fossil bird specialist, Alan Feduccia (1997), addressed another problem regarding the manuses of theropods and birds, indeed one that has been argued about for some century and a half. Acknowledging that, through cladistic analysis, birds have been placed within the Theropoda, the authors noted that a key synapomorphy uniting these two groups is a manus that has been reduced to three digits. In the Theropoda, these digits have been identified as I, II and III, because *Herrerasaurus* and other early theropods show considerable reduction of the fourth and fifth digits. Considering developmental anatomy, if birds evolved directly from theropods, the digits of the avian manus should, therefore, also be I through III. However, debate has continued for decades as to whether the three fingers in a bird's hand are, in fact, I-II-III or, rather, II-III-IV.

Burke and Feduccia's study focused upon the developing manus and pes in a number of amniote (*i.e.,* animals possessing in life a fetal membrane, called "amnion") embryos, including those of various bird species (also a chick), an alligator, and a primitive chelonian (*Chrysemys*). Utilizing Alcian blue photomicrography, the authors showed the quite similar developmental pattern in all three groups of amniotes: Limbs develop from a typical primary axis. Digits form posterior to anterior. In the alligator and turtle, which have five easily identified digits, the fourth digit forms first from this primary axis, apparently continuing a connected axis from the more proximal ulna/ulnare through its distal fourth carpal. The first digit formed in the wing-bud of the chick occupies the same position as the first formed and with the same connections as in the alligator, and must therefore be digit IV. Additional evidence for this identification was based upon serial homology and the similarity of wing-bud and leg-bud, the latter clearly revealing that the first digit to form is the fourth as all five digits are present. Based upon their interpretation, Burke and Fedducia assessed that the digits in the fully developed bird's wing are II through IV, which is problematic for the hypothesis that birds arose from theropods.

The authors' findings again brought to the fore the possibility that birds did not descend from theropods, but instead that theropods and birds, though closely related, descended from a common ancestor. Consequently, the similarities between the forelimbs of theropods and birds may, according to Burke and Feduccia, be the result of homoplasy. However, the authors noted, if a variation of the above pattern could be identified — perhaps with some future discovery of a primary axis running through digit III — then all phylogenetic significance would be erased from the morphological and molecular similarities in the development of amniote limbs, with patterns of limb development consequently jettisoned from phylogeny and accepted as convergence. Burke and Feduccia further pointed out that the theropod hand is indeed unusual, retaining as it does digit I and losing digit IV, while in all other tetrapod groups (*e.g.*, amphibians, lizards, turtles, and mammals) digits I or V are always the first to be lost. The authors offered that the first digit may have evolved by strong selection for use in grasping or raking (as suggested earlier by Sereno and Novas 1992; see also Sereno 1993).

Although the above arguments are certainly not to be ignored, the majority of technical papers published in recent years have supported the dinosaur-to-bird hypothesis.

Archaeopteryx *and the Origins of Flight*

Andrzej Elźanowski and Peter Wellnhofer (1996), also specialists in fossil birds, studied skull features of the so-called "seventh skeleton" (or Munich or Solnhofer Aktien Verein specimen) of *Archaeopteryx*—traditionally and, until only recently (see text on *Rahonavis*, below), generally regarded as the earliest known fossil bird—described by Wellnhofer (1993) as the new species, *A. bavarica*. Thus far, this is the only specimen in which most of the cranial bones are preserved. The authors noted, due to the poor preservation of the skulls of earlier collected *Archaeopteryx* specimens, only superficial cranial features of this genus could previously be determined with certainty, with little being known of the interior of the skull.

From their study of this seventh specimen, Elźanowski and Wellnhofer found that, in contrast to the predominantly reptilian postcranial skeleton of *Archaeopteryx*, the skull exhibits the following distinctively avian traits: Palatine (differing from tetraradiate bone of theropods) with maxillary (=premaxillary) process, and hook-shaped choanal (vomeral) process; long pterygoid wing, "distinctively avian and different from the tetraradiate palatine of archosaurs"; mandible lacking coronoid (suggesting its absence as a separate bone may be an apomorphy of all birds). According to Elźanowski and Wellnhofer, the avian features of the skull, being unrelated to locomotion, demonstrate that *Archaeopteryx* is a bird and not a feathered nonavian archosaur.

The following cranial features were noted by Elźanowski and Wellnhofer as evidence supporting the interpretation of *Archaeopteryx* as the most primitive of unquestionable birds yet known: Interdental plates (a distinctive theropod trait present in most theropods; Currie, Rigby and Sloan 1990; Wellnhofer 1993); ectopterygoid (apparently unique among archosaurs in having much wider than long main plate); prootic with large rostroventral wing (absent in modern birds, but present in some theropods, such as *Syntarsus*, *Velociraptor*, and *Oviraptor*, as well as in some other nontheropod archosaurs) contacting laterosphenoid rostral to trigeminal foramen; and squamosal (as a whole, comparing in detail with that of *Allosaurus*) with postorbital and quadratojugal (descending) processes.

Elźanowski and Wellnhofer added that *Archaeopteryx* is more like certain theropods in the possession of "a strongly curved, hook-shaped jugal process of the ectopterygoid and probably a single vomer." As observed by Elźanowski and Wellnhofer, the skull of *Archaeopteryx* displays a combination of avian and primitive archosaurian characters allowing for an insight into the remodelling of the skull that accompanied the origins of birds, these changes occurring in the palatine, pterygoquadrate articulation (as well as adjacent parts of pterygoid and quadrate), mandible, and interdental plates. The authors concluded that the primitive characters of the skull of *Archaeopteryx* "are perfectly compatible with the theropodan origins of birds (Ostrom 1976[a])," with all of them present in at least some theropods.

Elźanowski and Wellnhofer further stated that *Archaeopteryx* shares with theropods three cranial synapomorphies (single vomer, strong curvature of ectopterygoid hook, and dorsal recess in prootic). Therefore, without a single well-documented skull character shared by *Archaeopteryx* and any other archosaurian group, the cranial morphology of this genus "supports at least the monophyly of theropods and birds."

John H. Ostrom, among the top researchers and theorists regarding the origins of birds and their relationships to theropod dinosaurs—indeed, the first major modern voice to propose these ideas—continues to publish his findings on *Archaeopteryx*. In a paper offering new, innovative speculations as to how avian flight may have originated, Ostrom (1997) gave a compelling argument favoring the relatively—until recently, at least (see below)—unpopular scenario that flight in birds originated from the "ground up" (first proposed by Ostrom 1976c) rather than from the "trees down." The latter, more widely accepted view presupposed the existence of an as yet undiscovered arboreal proto-bird—the so-called "*Proavis*," first imagined by Gerhard Heilmann (1926) in his classic book *The Origin of Birds*—that supposedly first took to the air as a glider incapable of flapping its wings. With seven specimens of *Archaeopteryx* available for study (only five had been collected in 1976), Ostrom (1997) found in this ancient bird what he interpreted to be a semilunate carpal analagous to "the proximal articular surface of the modern avian carpo-metacarpus (trochlea carpalis). This condition would have permitted the wrist of *Archaeopteryx* to flap rapidly. Ostrom (1997) further pointed out that the semilunate carpal has also been identified in various manuraptoran theropods including *Deinonychus* (identified in this genus by Ostrom 1964), *Velociraptor*, *Sinornithoides* and "*Stenonychosaurus*" [=*Troodon*].

In a separate study, Chatterjee (1997; see also *Protoavis* entry), who regards dromaeosaurs (dinosaurs generally believed to be the most closely related to birds) such as *Velociraptor* and *Deinonychus* as constituting the sister group of birds, found the "trees down" scenario as the more acceptable in trying to explain the origins of flight. Chatterjee speculated that birds exist today thanks to various historical evidence: 1. "Ceratosaurs" standing up bipedally with digitigrade pes; 2. brain of ornithomimosaurs growing rapidly; 3. wrist of dromaeosaurs developing swivel joint for tree-climbing; and 4. "proto-avians" developing attempting parachuting and gliding from tree branches.

Ostrom (1997), however, took a stern issue with Chatterjee's claims that a suite of anatomical features (*e.g.*, ossified sternum, enlarged coracoid, rigid tail, and opisthopubic pelvis) "in small dromaeosaur-like 'pro-avians' indicate flying adaptation," further stating that he did "not see those characters as climbing adaptations at all."

Padian (1998*a*), in a preliminary report investigating avian origins and the evolution of flight, boldly stated that there is no longer any "reasonable doubt that birds evolved from and are coelurosaurian dinosaurs," pointing out that more than 130 synapomorphies place them within Archosauria as the sister group to the Dromaeosauridae. According to Padian, the principles of cladistic analysis and homology clearly demonstrate that the fingers of the avian hand are not II-III-IV, but I-II-III; the semilunate carpal present in manuraptoriformes (including birds) is really the fusion of the first and second carpals (see above); and the pretibial bone of birds is homologous to the ascending process of the theropod astragalus. Both the earliest birds and "dromaeosaurs" are found in Late Jurassic deposits, so there is not a 40-million — not even a 20-million — year stratigraphic gap between these two groups. Padian further posited that "Arguments against the origin of birds from Mesozoic theropods are no longer matters of evidence, but of the failure or refusal to use the methods of modern comparative biology."

Regarding the beginnings of flight, Padian pointed out that, although there is no real evidence that bird ancestors could not get into trees, there is also none to support an arboreal origin for avian flight, noting that "there has never been an adequate analysis addressing the morphological regime that simultaneously allowed the encouraged tree-climbing and flapping, as well as more conventional functions such as prey-catching." Padian could find no salient reasons why flight could not have evolved from the ground up in terrestrial cursorial animals, rather than from the trees down, adding that the latter scenario seems the more likely, given the phylogenetic and ecological origins of birds.

A fresh and original (also rather provocative) hypothesis regarding the possible evolution of flight feathers (and related to the ground-up theories of the origins of flight) was offered in a brief report by Hopp and Orsen (1998) (also in a "poster" by Orsen and Hopp 1998), who regarded birds as having descended directly from theropod dinosaurs. As acknowledged by these authors, it is difficult to comprehend how wing feathers developed through short intermediate evolutionary stages before becoming long enough to generate the adequate lift required for flight. Rather than pursuing (as had earlier studies) lines of research based upon the possible uses of feathers in primitive birds like *Archaeopteryx*, Hopp and Orsen (also Orsen and Hopp) proposed a different mechanism—*i.e.*, brooding, or the use of wing feathers to cover protectively eggs or hatchlings—as a selective pressure that possibly originated the process of lengthening the arm and tail feathers.

As observed by these authors, brooding is widespread among diverse groups of modern birds and, as such, suggests that this trait is basal and may have existed in the common ancestor of all birds. The following questions were considered: 1. Is there skeletal fossil evidence to provide insight into the capability of theropod bird ancestors to adopt modern bird brooding postures; 2. could requirements for brooding have driven the evolution of long feathers on the arms of a nonflying bird ancestor; and 3. how ancient might be the trait of feathered-brooding?

In responding to these questions, the authors noted two postural traits that are common among modern brooding birds — squatting with medial placement of the feet, and extension of the forelimbs — which ancient birds and even some of the earliest theropods were capable of assuming. Several nesting specimens of the theropod *Oviraptor* (see entry; also *D:TE*) display an arm position indicating that long feathers on the arms would have improved these dinosaurs' coverage of their eggs (gaps existing in this coverage large enough to allow solar heating, wind cooling, or rain wetting on exposed eggs, these spaces normally covered by wing and tail feathers in modern birds). The latter further suggested a previously unidentified "selective pressure to drive the arm-

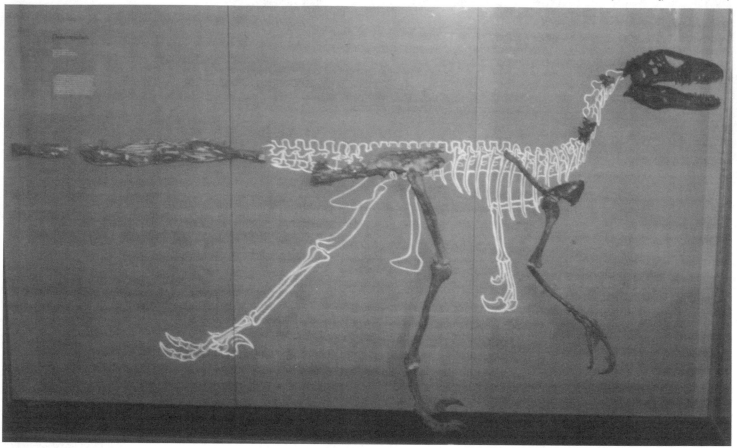

Deinonychus antirrhopus, a quite birdlike nonavian theropod that lived long after *Archaeopteryx*. Partial skeleton (cast of MCZ 4371) discovered by Steven Orzack, collected in July 1974 from the Cloverly Formation (Lower Cretaceous) in southern Montana by a Harvard University expedition led by Farish A. Jenkins.

feather lengthening process through its early phases in which no advantage could be gained for flying or gliding" (Orsen and Hopp). This capability of adopting the brooding postures observed in *Oviraptor*, the authors added, also existed even in the most ancient of theropods.

Hopp and Orsen (also Orsen and Hopp) noted that the use of arm feathers to cover eggs or chicks, by enhancing brooding success, would certainly have been advantageous during every phase of the evolutionary feather-lengthening process. The brooding mechanism, then, could have brought wing feathers to the length observed in *Archaeopteryx*, with flight an additional or secondary adaptation after brooding. The nesting and care of hatchlings may, consequently, have led to the development of long feathers on the arms and tails of nonavian theropod dinosaurs. The authors further speculated that wing feathers may have been an early development in theropod evolution existing in nonavian forms as far back as the Late Triassic, more than 150 million years before *Oviraptor* and 80 million years before *Archaeopteryx*.

The Status of Mononykus

Differences of opinion persist over whether *Mononykus olecranus*, an unusual long-tailed, slender-limbed, single-clawed animal from the Late Cretaceous of Bogin Tsav, Mongolia, first described by Perle, Norell, Chiappe and Clark (1993) as a bird, should retain its systematic position within Aves belonging to the group Metornithes, or be classified as a nonavian theropod.

Chiappe, Norell and Clark (1995, 1996) conducted a cladistic analysis in order to determine the phylogenetic relationships of *Mononykus*, utilizing velociraptorine theropods as outgroups to produce a single most parsimonious cladogram in which the diverse monophyletic group Alvarezsauridae (a clade of Late Cretaceous but primitive birds occurring in central Asia, southern South America, and perhaps North America, including the Mongolian *Mononykus* and Argentine *Patagonykus* and *Alvarezsaurus**) is the

*Bonaparte (1991) first described Alvarezsaurus calvoi, a type species founded on partial skeletal remains collected in 1989 by Jorge O. Calvo, as a theropod of uncertain relationships, yet warranting its own family, Alvarezsauridae (see D:TE).

As envisioned by Bonaparte (1996b), (cont. on page 51)

Photograph by the author, courtesy American Museum of Natural History.

Bird (in the traditional sense) or nonavian theropod? Mounted skeleton (cast of AMNH 28508) of *Mononykus olecranus*, remains of which were first collected in the 1920s by an American Museum of Natural History expedition to Mongolia led by Roy Chapman Andrews.

Alvarezsaurus *superficially resembled Laurasian ornithomimids, but exhibited the following important anatomical differences: Though cervical, dorsal, and sacral vertebrae show general similarities to ornithomimids, caudals, particularly the middle ones, are very low, lack neural spines, are procoelous, and have wing-like processes; sacrum, ilium, and proximal portion of femur suggest similar anatomical arrangement as in the ornithomimids* Gallimimus *and* Struthiomimus, *while morphology of astragalus and calcaneum are quite different, probably with plesiomorphic characters in* Alvarezsaurus; *foot much less derived than in ornithomimids, metatarsal III not reduced proximally, its entire dorsal surface exposed. Bonaparte (1996b) observed that the small pectoral girdle indicates a very reduced forelimb, contrasting with the long forearms of ornithomimids; the pectoral girdle displays various unique characters (e.g., dorsal border nearly straight without acromial expansion); ventral border with marked curvature towards glenoid; and glenoid more posteriorly projected.*

Bonaparte (1996b) concluded that Alvarezsaurus *was probably not a predator, its pedal claws suggesting "that they were not aggressive organs," and that the animal was an herbivore "representing a vicariant adaptive type to the Laurasian ornithomimids, but with a different evolutionary history."*

With the collection of additional materials including remains belonging to the similar taxa Mononykus *and* Patagonykus, *Novas (1996c) found that these three genera comprise a clade of primitive and "bizarre avialan theropods." According to Novas' (1996c) analysis, the Alvarezsauridae is a monophyletic clade of birds as supported by 20 shared synapomorphies. Diagnostic characters surfaced from a cladistic analysis of 74 derived features positioning Alvarezsauridae as the sister group of the bird clade Ornithothoraces.*

This assessment was accepted by other workers, including Chiappe (1996), and Chiappe, Norell and Clark (1996).

sister taxon of all other birds, excluding *Archaeopteryx*.

Chiappe *et al.* (1995, 1996) found the monophyly of Aves (=Avialae sensu Gauthier 1986, defined as "a clade composed of the common ancestor of *Archaeopteryx lithographica* and modern birds [*i.e.*, Neornithes] plus all its descendants") to be supported by seven unambiguous synapomorphies, four of them (tail with fewer than 25 to 26 caudal vertebrae; caudals with short distal prezygapophyses; teeth with unserrated crowns and constriction between crown and base; caudal tympanic recess opening only inside tympatic cavity) present in *Mononykus*.

Six characters (prominent ventral processes on cervico-dorsal vertebrae; sternum of longitudinal rectangular shape; ossified sternal keel; carpometacarpus formed by distal carpals fused to metacarpals; pelvis with prominent antitrochanter; ischium over two-thirds length of pubis) supported the monophyly of Metornithes (Aves exclusive of *Archaeopteryx*), all of them present in *Mononykus*. Six synapomorphies (dorsal vertebrae with wide foramen, vertebral foramen/cranial articular ratio greater than 0.40; lack of contact between ischial terminal processes; laterally projecting fibular tubercle for m. iliofibularis; quadratojugal not contacting squamosal; absence of medial fossa on promixal end of fibula; absence of postorbital-jugal contact), each one present in *Mononykus*, ambiguously diagnose both Aves and Metornithes.

Introduction

Archaeopteryx lithographica, cast (AMNH 5120) of the "Berlin specimen," showing exquisite feather impressions. This specimen, apparently preserving an animal in evolutionary transition from reptile to bird, is regarded by many scientists as the single most important vertebrate fossil ever found.

It was the conclusion of Chiappe *et al.* (1996) that *Mononykus* is a metornithine bird that "presents an intermediate condition between the morphology of nonavian theropods and that of more advanced birds such as Hesperornithiformes or Neornithes."

Chiappe *et al.* (1996) responded to various criticisms by other authors as to their hypothesis of avian relationships for *Mononykus*, noting that those objections were largely built upon arguments lying outside the boundaries of modern systematics and comparative biology. As stated by Chiappe *et al.* (1996), the alternative hypothesis "is based on misleading evolutionary assumptions and 'a priori' speculation" and "is insufficient to authoritatively proclaim that

Mononykus is not avian (or not a bird), without proposing an alternative hypothesis of what it is related to (supported by character evidence)."

Contradicting Martin and Rinaldi (1994) and Martin (1995), Chiappe *et al.* stated that *Mononykus* does possess numerous tiny teeth; a skull that is larger than that shown in the original reconstruction; a tail that is shorter than that of any known nonavian thero-

pod; a well-developed antitrochanter; and that this genus might possess a furcula and free carpals (these elements not preserved in the specimens collected).

In a subsequent paper, Chiappe *et al.* (1998) described the new genus and species *Shuvuuia deserti*, an alvarezsaurid bird closely related to *Mononykus*, represented by material including two beautifully preserved skulls (the first known for the Alvarezsauridae).

Courtesy Sinclair Oil Corporation.

Louis Paul Jonas Studios full-sized statue of the ornithomimid theropod *Struthiomimus altus* made for the "Sinclair Dinoland" exhibit, New York World's Fair (1964), all figures in this display having been designed under the supervision of paleontologists Barnum Brown and John H. Ostrom. Fossil bird specialist Larry D. Martin regards *Mononykus* as an ornithomimid rather than a true avian.

The holotype, catalogued as MGI 100/975, was collected from the Late Cretaceous of the Gobi Desert in Mongolia by joint expeditions of the American Museum of Natural History and the Mongolian Academy of Sciences. According to Chiappe *et al.* (1998), cranial evidence observed in alvarezsaurids further supports the group's close relationships with birds. Skull characters of *Shuvuuia* shared with birds, but not with nonavian theropods, include the following: Absence of postorbital-jugal contact; moveable joint (nonsutured) between quadratojugal and quadrate; separate articulation of quadrate with braincase; and disproportionately large formanen magnum relative to occipital condyle. *Shuvuuia* and *Archaeopteryx* share cranial characters not present in the outgroup Velocoraptorinae, these including the following: Lack of squamosal-quadratojugal contact, coronoid in mandible, presence of triradiate palatine, caudal tympanic recess confluent with columellar recess, and unserrated tooth crowns.

Chiappe *et al.* (1998) noted that, although other authors have suggested that alvarezsaurids are either specialized ornithomimosaurs (Martin and Rinaldi 1994) or another group of nonmanuraptoran theropods altogether (Sereno 1997), cladistic analyses have not yet been published to support such claims; furthermore, those similarities observed between alvarezsaurids and nonmanuraptoran coelurosaurs can be attributed to convergence.

Schweitzer (1998), in a preliminary study of keratin preservation in the fossil record, briefly discussed a *Mononykus* skeleton collected from the Gobi desert. The specimen includes small white fibers preserved in sediments surrounding the skeleton. Localized to the skeleton, these fibers were arrayed in a manner suggesting feathers. According to Schweitzer, "Microscopic and chemical analyses eliminated plant material or fungal hyphae as a source of these fibers." The reactions of various kinds of antibodies with these fibers produced patterns consistent with modern feathers. Schweitzer suggested that data regarding this specimen might provide some insights into the evolutionary process within the bird/dinosaur lineage.

Martin (1997), however, insisted that *M. olecrans* is clearly a theropod, stating that this fact was clouded because previous comparisons have been with "birds and not to the dinosaurs that mimic them." Martin (1997) mused that, "depending on one's cladogram, *Tyrannosaurus* (Thulborn 1984) or *Mononykus* (Perle, Chiappe, Barsbold, Clark and Norell 1994) is closer to birds than is *Archaeopteryx*."

According to Martin's (1997) own analysis of *Mononykus*, this genus shares many derived features with ornithomimid theropods that are not found in birds, these including the following: Absence of clavicles (furcula); absence of free carpals in wrist; extreme enlargement of metacarpal I; direction of elongation of coracoids; shortened ribs (based on published reconstruction); elongated caudal hypopophyses; astragalus forming tibiotarsal contribution to mesotarsal joint (some ratite birds possibly converging on this condition); and middle metatarsal excluded from anteroproximal face of metatarsus complex. Other features shared with ornithomimids (and not characteristic of Mesozoic birds) include: Elongation of postacetabular ilium (also in foot-propelled diving birds); small head; laterally placed coracoid and scapula, with posterior and downwards facing glenoid; and dorsal acetabular shelf (putative antitrochanter) for articulation with femur.

Martin (1997) contended that none of the features in *Mononykus* described as avian are diagnostic of birds or even similar to the avian condition; and noted that the holotype femur of *Elopteryx* and tibiotarsi referred to *Heptasteornis* and *Bradycneme*, two dinosaurian taxa originally described as birds, share derived features with *Mononykus*. Martin (1997) further stated that the general configuration of the shoulder girdle, forelimbs, and hands of *Mononykus* is quite unlike *Archaeopteryx*, but very much like *Compsognathus*.

In a later abstract, Martin and Simmons (1998) regarded *Mononykus* as an ornithomimid that may have stolen other theropods' eggs. McNeil (1998) also regarded *Mononykus* as a nonavian theropod, one that may have used its short, yet strong arms and claws to dig through sand and disturb burrowing animals, including arthropods. "As they scurried across the surface of the ground," McNeil speculated, "flexibility in the long neck of *Mononykus* allowed the arthropods to be snatched and eaten before they could escape."

Additional Osteological Evidence

The clavicle (or "collarbone") and furcula (or "wishbone") are elements present in all birds. Since the latter nineteenth century, it was generally accepted that dinosaurs had lost their clavicles in their evolution. Indeed, the apparent lack of the clavicle and furcula in dinosaurs has been used as negative evidence that led to the removal of dinosaurs from the ancestry of birds, an opinion that prevailed for most of the 1900s. More recently, however, furculae have been reported in a relatively small number of dinosaurs. Identification of the furcula in the manuraptoran theropods *Oviraptor* and *Troodon* constituted evidence that seemed to support a link between nonavian theropods and birds. Recently, furculae have also been identified in *Velociraptor* and *Scipionyx* (see entries), the latter new genus also preserving articulated gastralia and internal organs.

As pointed out by Chure and Madsen (1996*b*), in a preliminary report on the furcula in the carnosaurian family Allosauridae and its implication for determining bird origins, debate goes on about the distribution of this bone in theropods and its confusion with gastralia. Chure and Madsen will later describe a new allosaurid species, known from an almost complete articulated skeleton including a furcula, from the Morrison Formation of Dinosaur National Monument, Jensen, Utah. Preserved in this specimen is the furcula, in contact with both scapulae, and also a complete gastral cuirass (or articulated set of gastralia), these elements allowing comparison between them in a single specimen.

Chure and Madsen observed that the cuirass has no median element, and that the furcula seems to contact the scapula only. The furcula differs from gastral elements "in being a V-shaped medial element, having

Skeleton (ROM 12868) of *Allosaurus fragilis*, a theropod species for which a furcula — a bone present in birds but rarely found in dinosaurs — has recently been identified.

rugose distal ends for contact with the scapulae, lacking grooves for overlap with lateral gastralia, and with a different curvature of the arms." Examination by the authors of various *Allosaurus* specimens revealed the presence of the furcula; furthermore, previously reported *Allosaurus* "gastralia" (figured in Madsen 1976), observed in specimens from the Cleveland-Lloyd Dinosaur Quarry, were reidentified as a growth series of furculae, the only such series known to date in a nonavian theropod.

The discovery of the furcula in another theropod group, the coelurosaurian family Tyrannosauridae, was announced in a preliminary report by Makovicky (1996). Makovicky (1996) identified a furcula in two recently discovered *Gorgosaurus* [="*Albertosaurus*" of his usage] specimens. According to Makovicky (1996), the furcula in this genus is distinguishable from fused anterior gastralia by "smaller size, denser histology, sigmoid curvature, and widened and flattened epicleidea. The ridge corresponds topologically to the hypocleidium of some extant birds, and may be homologous to the latter structure."

In a detailed follow up paper, Makovicky and Currie (1998) identified a furcula in three tyrannosaurid specimens: An almost complete skeleton, with skull, of a juvenile *Albertosaurus sarcophagus* (RTMP 86.64) from the Horseshoe Canyon Formation (Campanian–lower Maastrichtian) in the Red Deer River Valley, near Drumheller, Alberta; the almost complete skeleton (RTMP 91.36.500) of a juvenile *Gorgosaurus libratus* from the Campanian Dinosaur Park Formation of Dinosaur Provincial Park, Alberta; and the skeleton (RTMP 94.12.602) of an adult *G. libratus* from a channel deposit of the Dinosaur Park Formation.

According to Makovicky (1996), and Makovicky and Currie (1998), the small span of this element in tyrannosaurids, as well as in other theropods, imposed restrictions on the width of the ribcage and the orientation of the scapulocoracoids. The coracoids abutted each other on the ventral midline to ensure correct articulation, their mobility restricted by the articulation of the furcula with the acromia anteriorly and sternum posteriorly. From homology tests performed based upon recent ideas of theropod phylogeny, and also based on new information regarding the presence of clavicles in theropods, the authors concluded that the clavicle and furcula also seem to have been primitively present in theropods, also observed by Makovicky and Chure in such taxa as the "ceratosaur" *Segisaurus* (see Camp 1936), oviraptorids (AMNH 6517, IGM 100/30, and IGM 100/42), *Sinornithoides* (IVPP V9612), and an allosaurid (Chure and Madsen 1996*b*). (For the first discovery of a furcula in the Dromaeosauridae, see *Velociraptor* entry.)

The "Half Bird"

Among the most compelling of recent discoveries supporting the theropod-to-bird scenario has been *Unenlagia* (see also below), a new genus that seems to represent a transitional form between *Deinonychus* and *Archaeopteryx*. The type species *Unenlagia* [name meaning "half bird"] *comahuensis* was originally described by Novas and Puerta (1997) as a nonavian manuraptoran theropod belonging to the Deinonychosauria, based on a partial postcranial skeleton (MCF PVPH 78) from the Upper Cretaceous (Turonian–Coniacian) Río Neuquén Formation, of Sierra del Portezuelo, Argentina.

Novas and Puerta diagnosed this new taxon as follows: Neural spines of posterior dorsal and anterior sacral vertebrae tall, almost twice height of centrum; lateral pits deep in base of these neural spines; shaft of scapula twisted; dorsal margin of postacetabular iliac blade inflected. According to these authors' original study of *Unenlagia*, this "half bird" possesses a mixture of features both dinosaurian and avian, and may be one of the bridges to the morphological gap between the Dromaeosauridae and *Archaeopteryx lithographica*. Novas and Puerta described *Unenlagia* as a medium-sized manuraptoran which, if the skeleton were complete, would measure almost 2 meters (nearly 7 feet) in length—about two-thirds the size of the Early Cretaceous dromaeosaurid *Deinonychus*.

Until the discovery of this genus, the dromaeosaurid *Deinonychus* was the dinosaur regarded as having a morphology most closely resembling that of *Archaeopteryx*. Though geologically younger, *Unenlagia* seemed to represent an "intermediate" form more closely related to birds than are dromaeosaurids. Consequently, Novas and Puerta regarded *Unenlagia* as a relic descendant of a theropod group that was present before the line leading to *Archaeopteryx* and true birds.

Novas and Puerta observed the following in *Unenlagia*: Scapula strap-like in dorsal view and curved in lateral view, closely resembling that of *Archaeopteryx*; acromion of scapula triangular in side view and sharply projected anteroventrally, as in *Archaeopteryx*; humeral articulation laterally oriented as in birds; ischium possessing triangular obturator process, a feature found in most advanced coelurosaurs; however, dorsal edge of ischium showing prominent proximodorsal process separated from ischiadic antitrochanter by deep notch, a feature until now unique to *Archaeopteryx* and other birds. The ilium has both well-developed fossa for m. cuppedicus found in Coelurosauria (including basal birds), but also an extensive inner wall to the hip socket as in

Photograph by the author, courtesy Royal Tyrrell Museum/Alberta Community Development.

Skeleton of *Gorgosaurus libratus*, another theropod for which a furcula has been identified. The skeleton is posed over bones of the horned dinosaur *Centrosaurus.*

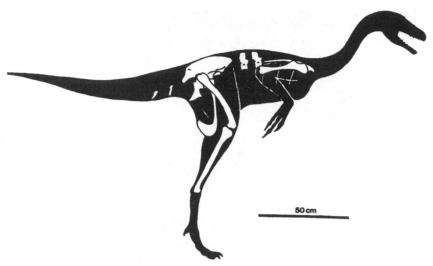

50 cm

Unenlagia comahuensis,
MCF PVPH 78, recon-
structed holotype skeleton.
This taxon was originally
described as a nonavian
theropod dinosaur. Scale =
50 cm. (After Novas and
Puerta 1997).

Archaeopteryx and other birds; pubic distal expansion
or "boot" large as in coelurosaurs, although, as in
birds, primitive forward "toe" of boot is lost.

According to Novas and Puerta, *Unenlagia* provides new information regarding the morphology of
"proavian" dinosaurs that may clarify aspects of forelimb function as related to the emergence of avian
flight. As interpreted by these authors, the glenoid
cavity of the scapula or shoulder joint in this genus is
laterally oriented, a derived feature present in *Archaeopteryx* and other birds, but not as yet reported in
other nonavian dinosaurs. This orientation suggests
that the forelimbs of *Unenlagia* could be raised extensively, producing a full upstroke in the avian manner, anticipating a down and forward flight stroke.
This orientation constitutes a step towards the wing-
folding critical in the protection of long wing feathers. (No evidence of feathers was preserved with the
holotype of *U. comahuensis.*)

Unenlagia was clearly a flightless animal, as evidenced by its relatively large size and short forelimbs,
and one, according to its systematic position, not derived from a flying form. Nevertheless, this genus had
already acquired unusual, almost birdlike forelimb
movements not present in more remote outgroups. As
noted by Novas and Puerta, the upstroke capability
present in *Unenlagia* would have been "a prerequisite
for powered, flapping flight, offering necessary thrust
to lift winged theropods from the ground," nor do the
structure of the forelimbs suggest a gliding stage before the acquisition of avian flight. Novas and Puerta
further postulated that the evidence of this new taxon
"reinforces the hypothesis that a bipedal, cursorial
theropod was ancestral to birds, and used its arms not
only in predation, but probably also in maintenance
of balance and to control its body attitude while running and leaping" (see also Ostrom 1976*c*, 1986).

Because main differences between forelimb bones

of this genus and those of *Archaeopteryx* pertain more
to relative proportions than with acquiring structural
novelties, Novas and Puerta suggested that flight capabilities may have developed "more as changes in
body proportions (that is, enlarged forelimb, reduction in body size and mass) and integument transformations (enlargement of feathers to increase wing surface) than as the acquisition of specific osteological
and muscular features."

Subsequent to the original description of *Unenlagia*, Forster, Sampson, Chiappe and Krause (1998)
challenged its assessment as a nonavian but very birdlike theropod in their paper describing the new Late
Cretaceous bird *Rahonavis* (see below).

Nonosseous Evidence

Accepting that birds are theropod dinosaurs,
Gatesy and Middleton (1997) made a comprehensive
study of bipedalism, flight, and the evolution of locomotor diversity in theropods, the authors' analysis
focusing upon proportions of the main limb bones. As
noted by Gatesy and Middleton, basal theropods are
generally characterized as having but a single "locomotor module" (*i.e.,* "anatomical subregions of the
musculoskeletal system that are highly integrated and
act as functional units during locomotion") comprising the morphologically and functionally coupled
hind limbs and tail (see also Gatesy and Dial 1996).
Birds or "flying theropods" (as Gatesy and Middleton
referred to them), by contrast, have three highly integrated locomotor modules composed of the wings,
hind limbs, and tail. The evolution of flight in
theropods "has been characterized as a shift from one
to three locomotion modules." Gatesy and Middleton
observed that hind limb proportions among nonavian
theropods are relatively homogeneous while those of
birds are quite diverse. This suggested to the authors
that nonavian theropods were primarily terrestrial bipeds possessing a body plan that remained relatively conservative in design throughout the Mesozoic.

Despite sometimes vast differences in body size
among nonavian theropods, Gatesy and Middleton
found no evidence for greatly reduced hind limbs in
these animals, nor specializations "for diving, pad-
dling, wading, trunk climbing, or perching" as in
birds. In coelurosaurs closely related to birds (*e.g.,*
manuraptorans), however, significant transformations
occurred in tail size, the retraction mechanism of the
hind limb, scaling, and the morphology of the pelvis,
these changes resulting in the eventual decoupling of
the hind limb and tail into separate pelvic and tail
modules and the origination of the wing module, a
flight apparatus formed by an allegiance of the pectoral

and caudal modules (see Gatesy and Dial). With this increased modularity, birds may have been allowed more locomotor "options" than nonavian theropods, the ability to fly easing constraints on the hind limbs and permitting specializations for habitats and lifestyles denied to nonavians. Gatesy and Middleton proposed that the ability to fly "increased modular flexibility, resulting in more disparity and locomotor diversity in birds than in nonavian theropods."

Implications of the relationships of dinosaurs to birds may also arise from a recent study published by Larson (1997b). Larson noted that the avian respiratory system is unique (possessing air sacs, its own blood chemistry, and "one-way" lungs), and that this uniqueness is reflected by features of the bones of modern birds, some of them also being known in the bones of dinosaurs and other Mesozoic taxa. Some of these shared features (e.g., similarities in the cervical and dorsal vertebrae — all with diverticula and pneumatic openings — of Archaeopteryx, theropods, sauropods, and pterosaurs) may be interpreted to be the "fingerprints of the avian respiratory system."

If Larson is correct, the following implications (most of them potentially controversial) can be derived from this study: 1. Archaeopteryx, pterosaurs, theropods, and sauropods all possessed the "one-way" avian respiratory system and the ability to breathe with an efficiency similar to that of living birds; 2. if the former groups did possess this respiratory system, they must also have shared other characters (e.g., "a large four chambered heart, a double circulatory system, high arterial blood pressure, nucleated erythrocytes [red blood corpuscles], high blood levels of glucose and globulin protein and the ability to tolerate high levels of blood alkalinity during hyperventilation"); 3. that these groups were endothermic (see previous section); 4. that sauropods could breathe comfortably with their long necks via an avian respiratory system (as do long-necked whooping cranes); 5. it is unlikely that this unique and complex respiratory system evolved more than once; 6. prosauropods and ornithischians apparently did not possess this kind of respiratory system; 7. Archaeopteryx and other birds, theropods, sauropods, and pterosaurs share numerous characters, some regarded as the "fingerprints of the avian respiratory system," these groups, therefore, belonging in a monophyletic group and having the same common ancestor; 8. Ornithischia, Prosauropoda, Herrerasaurus, and Staurikosaurus do not possess characters regarded as the "fingerprints of the avian respiratory system," and must, therefore, not have possessed such a system, these taxa consequently not belonging to the above monophyletic group; 9. consequently, Dinosauria is not a monophyletic group; and 10. theropods and sauropods are more closely related to birds and pterosaurs than to ceratopsians and prosauropods (see "Systematics" chapter).

The Feathers Issue

Of course, among the best evidence supporting a dinosaur-to-bird evolutionary progression would be the discovery of a theropod specimen unquestionably possessing feathers. As pointed out by Padian (1998b), only birds, among all living creatures, have been known to possess feathers. Therefore, the presence of feathers has traditionally been used as a diagnostic feature of birds, and was one of the few major criteria for originally identifying Archaeopteryx as a primitive bird.

Although some paleontologists had long suspected that at least some kinds of theropods may have been feathered, and many modern life restorations have depicted theropods, at least the smaller ones, as feathered (e.g., see the book Predatory Dinosaurs of the World, written and illustrated by Gregory S. Paul 1988b, who has portrayed some theropods as feathered for more than a decade), no dinosaur specimen had ever been found in which signs of features were preserved (see Compsognathus entry, D:TE).

Such evidence seemed to be present in specimens of Sinosauropteryx prima (Ji and Ji 1996), a small theropod recently discovered in China. Debate continued regarding interpretations of the integumentary structures visible in these specimens (see Sinosauropteryx entry) over whether they represent feathers, incipient feathers (also called "protofeathers"), or something else. Yet more recently, the small Chinese theropods Caudipteryx zoui and Protarchaeopteryx robusta (e.g., Currie 1998; Ji, Currie, Norell and Ji 1998; see Caudipteryx and Protarchaeopteryx entries), found with definite feather impressions, have provided unequivocal hard evidence regarding the presence of feathers in some dinosaurs. In examining the systematic positions of both of these new genera, Ji et al. concluded that the presence of feathers could no longer be regarded as a diagnostic feature to identify birds (see "Systematics" chapter); that the presence of feathers on flightless theropods negates the theory that feathers evolved concurrently with flight; and that "the presence of remiges, rectrices and plumulaceous feathers on nonavian theropods provides unambiguous evidence supporting the theory that birds are the direct descendants of theropod dinosaurs."

As earlier pointed out by Quinn (1998), locomotion and thermoregulation — functions that are often suggested as being the primary forces behind the initial evolution of feathers — may not be the only alternatives to explain the origin and function of protofeathers within the ancestors of birds. According to Quinn, protofeathers could originally have had an informational functionality, the earliest of these being "used as sexual signals, warning signs, terrestrial cues, threatening stances, or other information-based behaviors." Well-documented communication via feathers among modern birds is regarded by many scientists as a secondary function of specialized behaviors, exotic feathers, or species-specific adaptations. If originating as devices for information, noted Quinn, "a strong positive-feedback loop" may have been developed resulting in the rapid evolution of this new feature with individuals possessing longer, wider, or novel protofeathers conveying their visual messages more effectively and, consequently, augmenting their overall fitness. Based upon this hypothesis, Quinn suggested that locomotion and thermoregulation are actually secondary functions within an historical context. This hypothesis, Quinn added, is supported by the presence of feather-like structures in both *Sinosauropteryx prima* and the nondinosaurian reptile *Longisquama insignis*.

A Possible Evolutionary Scenario

Assuming that birds did arise from theropod dinosaurs, Long and McNamara (1997) offered ideas on how this evolution may have occurred. The authors noted that heterochrony (*i.e.,* "changes to the timing or rate of developmental events relative to the ancestral condition") is a mechanism which played a driving role in dinosaurian evolution. There are two kinds of heterochrony: 1. "If sexual maturity occurs earlier in the descendant than in the ancestor (progenesis) a juvenile morphology occurs in the descendant adult (paedomorphosis)"; however, "if onset of maturity is delayed (hypermorphosis), extensional of rapid juvenile growth trajectories will result in attainment of a larger body size, and morphologically more 'developed' adults (peramorphosis)."

According to Long and McNamara, the "evolutionary novelties that lead to the success of the birds" include the following paedomorphic characters: Small body size, unfused bones, large orbit, tooth shape, and subsequent tooth loss. *Archaeopteryx*, the authors pointed out, resembles a juvenile theropod in the shape of its skull and orbits. As Elźanowski and Wellnhofer earlier pointed out, in *Archaeopteryx* the expanded rostral blade of the prearticular may incorporate the reduced coronoid, a condition known in the embryonic development of *Taeniopygia*, a modern bird. Long and McNamara also noted that both *Archaeopteryx* and juvenile theropods display such paedomorphic characters as a relatively inflated braincase and tooth reduction; that the skeletal elements in *Archaeopteryx* show less fusion (a juvenile feature) than

do those in living birds; and that adult Mesozoic birds reveal characters that occur early during the ontogeny of living birds.

Long and McNamara further noted that, in contrast to the situation found in theropod dinosaurs, *Archaeopteryx* also shows the peramorphic enlargement of the forelimbs. (Earlier, Thulborn 1985 had argued that a relatively long manus, forelimbs, and pes are juvenile characters in theropod dinosaurs, further suggesting that birds could be, in effect, paedomorphic theropods.) This suggested to the authors that a peramorphic enlargement of the forelimbs occurred by the time *Archaeopteryx* had evolved.

Though Long and McNamara found that paedomorphosis seems to have played a more dominant role in dinosaurian evolution in general, both paedomorphic features (*e.g.,* retention of juvenile features of the skull) and peramorphic features (growth of forearms and digits, leading to wings) were seen as about equally important in the transition from theropods to birds, the latter being particularly important in regards to flying birds.

More Supporting Evidence

Additional evidence that seems to support the theropod-to-bird hypothesis was the discovery of what was originally named *Rahona ostromi* (its generic meaning "menace/threat" or "cloud" in Malagasy), a bird more primitive than *Archaeopteryx* (in fact, one of the most primitive birds known), but one that lived some 80 million years later. The new type species was described by Forster, Sampson, Chiappe and Krause (1998*a*), founded upon a single "raven-sized," adult partial skeleton (UA 8656) collected in 1996 by a joint expedition of the State University of New York at Stony Brook and the Université d'Antananarivo from a small quarry in the Late Cretaceous sandstone of northwestern Madagascar. (The quarry had previously yielded the only known skeleton of another primitive bird, *Varona berivotrensis*.) (Shortly after this new taxon was named and described, Forster *et al.* 1998*b* discovered that the generic name was preoccupied — by the lymantrid lepidopteran *Rahona* Griveaud 1975, a butterfly — and proposed for it the replacement name *Rahonavis*, its translated name adding the suffix "bird").

According to Forster *et al.* (1998*a*), this specimen exhibits both dinosaurian and avian features. Saurischian features include hyposphene-hypantral vertebral articulations on the dorsal vertebrae; theropod features include a pubic foot; and avian features include a reversed hallux (a feature unique to birds), splintlike fibula, and ulnar papillae ("six low, slightly elongate papillae that become less distinct distally," interpreted by the authors as quill knobs for the attachment of secondary flight feathers). The most striking feature of the skeleton is found on the hind foot, which exhibits a robust, hyperextendible pedal digit II terminating in a sickle-like claw like that seen in troodontid and dromaeosaurid manuraptoran theropods. Although Forster *et al.* (1998*a*) did not rule out the possibility that two different animals might be represented by the type specimen, they remained adamant that both the forelimbs and hind limbs are those of primitive birds.

Performing two phylogenetic analyses, one including and the other excluding the forelimb elements of *Rahonavis*, Forster *et al.* (1998*a*) concluded that *Unenlagia* (see above) belongs within Aves and that this genus represents the sister taxon to a *Rahonavis-Archaeopteryx* clade. According to Forster *et al.* (1998*a*), this clade is united by four unambiguous characters of the pelvis (preacetabular process of ilium twice as long as postacetabular process; postacetabular process shallow [less than 50 percent of depth at acetabulum], drawn back into pointed process; pubic foot projecting caudally only) and femur (femoral neck lost). This unification "places them on a side branch of early bird evolution and supports the suggestion that *Archaeopteryx* was not a direct precursor of modern birds." Forster *et al.* (1998*a*) noted, however, that the characters uniting these taxa seem to "represent primitive characters for birds rather than synapomorphies of a separate primitive bird lineage." According to these authors, the combination of morphological characters found in this new genus "strongly supports its membership in Aves, as well as its theropod ancestry, and thus the dinosaurian origins of birds."

Some, though not all, vertebrate paleontologists who have considered this material have accepted the above interpretation (see Gibbons 1998). Among those workers agreeing with Forster *et al.*'s assessment were systematist Paul C. Sereno, who found that the best way to explain the dinosaur-avian appearance of this new genus is that birds evolved from dinosaurs. Fossil bird and pterosaur specialist Peter Wellnhofer found the specimen to constitute strong evidence supporting a theropod ancestry for birds, Wellnhofer further stating that the retention of many primitive dinosaurian features in this genus made "it a living fossil in its own time." According to Peter Dodson, even if all the bones are avian, the specimen's overall impression is dinosaurian, indicating that *Rahonavis* should be regarded as an animal somewhere between dinosaurs and birds.

Those dissenting from the interpretation of Forster *et al.* (1998*a*) include John Ruben, who believed that the holotype of *R. ostromi* is really a chimera comprising a theropod's hindquarter and a bird's forelimbs. Agreeing with Ruben's evaluation of the fossil, Larry D. Martin stated that this genus is really a dinosaur. Provocatively, Martin added that the avian parts of the specimen could belong to *Varona berivotrensis*, whose only known skeleton is missing the wings.

New insights regarding the relationships between dinosaurs and birds also may be gleaned from a research project by Chapman, Weishampel, Hunt and Rasskin-Gutman (1997) on sexual dimorphism — reflected as size or shape differences between the sexes — in dinosaurs. Chapman *et al.* arbitrarily defined sexual dimorphism in its standard form as occurring "when males are larger or exhibit more extreme morphologies" than females, with reversed sexual dimorphism defined as the opposite. The authors noted that most kinds of dinosaurs examined in this study (*e.g.*, lambeosaurine hadrosaurs, pachycephalosaurs, and ceratopsians) show the standard form; the theropods studied, primarily *Syntarsus* and *Tyrannosaurus* (see entries, *D:TE*), display the reverse form. As pointed out by Chapman *et al.*, most archosaurian sexual dimorphism patterns "show the standard form to be predominant but with the potentially significant exception among the predatory birds."

The question of whether or not birds descended from nonavian theropods may have been answered, with the presence of feathers, as well as other so-called "avian" features, no longer an issue. As stated by Padian (1998*b*), "The evolution of carnivorous dinosaurs through basal coelurosaurs into birds shows some unmistakable trends. As their evolutionary history has become better known, we have seen wishbones, breastbones, hollow bones, long arms and hands, sideways-flexing wrists, nesting behaviour and rapid growth rates all disappear from the avian catalogue of exclusive features. Like feathers, as Ji and colleagues' work shows, these features first evolved in coelurosaurs for purposes completely unrelated to flight."

Recently, Zhao and Xu (1998) reported the discovery of a therizinosaur — a kind of theropod now believed by some workers to belong within the Coelurosauria (see systematics chapter) — recovered from the Early Jurassic (Sinemurian) dull, purplish beds of the Lower Lufeng Formation of Eshan County, Yunnan, China, represented by a specimen (IVPP V11579) including most of the left dentary and part of the splenial. As the authors noted, this find extends the age of this group of unusual dinosaurs, previously known only from the Late Cretaceous (Albian–Maastricthian), back by an additional 94 million years. This discovery also constitutes the earliest positive record of the Coelurosauria — a group including birds and all other theropods more closely related to

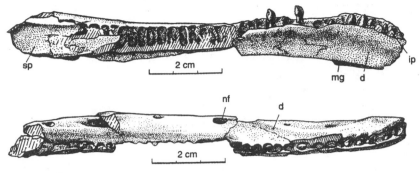

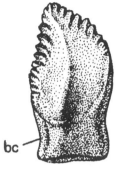

IVPP V11579, Early Jurassic therizinosaur from the Lufeng Formation of Yunnan, China, including *top:* left mandible (medial view), *middle:* dentary (dorsal view), and *bottom:* tooth crown (lateral view). (After Zhao and Xu 1998).

birds than to Carnosauria — therefore lessening the divergence time for members of this clade.

According to Zhao and Xu, the most significant aspect of this discovery is the information it imparts regarding the relationships between dinosaurs and birds. The fossil record of coelurosaurians, until this therizinosaur was found, has been interpreted by some scientists as inconsistent with a close relationship of birds and other members of this group, as most of the diversity of nonavian coelurosaurians can be seen taking place later than *Archaeopteryx* in the Late Jurassic. "The presence of a nonavian coelurosaurian in the Early Jurassic," Zhao and Xu stressed, "indicates that the major clade of this group must have already diverged, well before *Archaeopteryx* appears in the fossil record."

Has this long-running debate finally been settled and the mystery of avian evolution solved?

No doubt, some or perhaps all of the above evidence supporting the dinosaur-to-bird scenario will be disputed and argued over, some to be inevitably disproven and discarded. For the present, however, there seems to be little doubt that the denouement may have been revealed, the book perhaps closed.

As in *D:TE*, then, birds — presently considered here to be very successful feathered theropods, totaling almost 10,000 in their number of species, and reigning among the dominant vertebrate life forms in today's world — constitute a dinosaurian group mostly excluded from the general discussions in this text.

Dinosaur Extinctions

Arguably the question on Morales' list of unresolved controversies most asked by the public concerns not how they lived or why they were so successful, but "How and why did dinosaurs become extinct?"

The extinction of all the remaining dinosaurian groups (excluding birds, if they are regarded as avian theropods), as well as all other terrestrial animals weighing in excess of 25 kilograms, at the end of the Cretaceous period, 65 million years ago, continues to arouse the interest and puzzlement of both scientists and laymen alike. Adding to this mystery of the dinosaurs' extinction is the fact that other groups of Mesozoic life-forms (*e.g.*, pterosaurs, marine reptiles, various families of birds and marsupial mammals, calcareous plankters, ammonites, and numerous plants) also perished at this time, while many (but not all) crocodiles, lizards, snakes, turtles, placental mammals, and neornithine birds survived as groups.

As in the past, the more spectacular and often catastrophic scenarios, generally intended to explain a relatively sudden rather than gradual extinction (the scenario favored by the present writer) of these animals, win the most coverage in the popular press and seem to hold the greatest fascination with nonscientists.

The Impact Theory

Approximately two decades ago, Nobel Prize-winning physicist Luis W. Alvarez and colleagues (see Alvarez, Alvarez, Asaro and Michel 1980) introduced the theory that the extinction of the dinosaurs, as well as numerous other (though not all) species, may have been caused by an asteroid colliding with the Earth. Briefly stated, the idea was that an enormous asteroid struck the Earth at the end of the Cretaceous, releasing huge amounts of energy, darkening the sky and, consequently, interrupting the food chain and changing the biosphere in various other ways so that dinosaurs, as well as other creatures, could not survive.

Over the years, since this spectacular postulation — sometimes referred to as the "asteroid theory" or "bad day hypothesis" — was first proposed, scientists in various fields have voiced and published assenting and dissenting opinions on the subject (see *D:TE*). The majority of paleontologists now, however, apparently agree that an impact of some very large extraterrestrial body with this planet did occur during Late Cretaceous times. However, scientists remain divided in their opinions as to whether or not this apparent impact was, in fact, the major cause of these mass extinctions. Recently, based upon more current studies, a yet larger number of paleontologists seem to be leaning toward accepting this so-called "asteroid theory" to explain the extinctions at the Cretaceous–Tertiary, or K-T (also KT, or K/T, depending on one's preference) boundary.

Indeed, an ever-growing body of evidence now supports the ideas that at least one of the following events occurred at the culmination of the Cretaceous period: 1. increased volcanic activity (evidenced by thick flows of basalt covering much of southwestern India, especially the Deccan Traps in this area; see

Chatterjee and Rudra 1996), producing environmentally detrimental pollutants over an extended length of time; or 2. the impact of some celestial body (what appear to be the craters of huge asteroids or comets having been recently discovered; see below).

Other questions, however, remain: What effect did these events have on the dinosaurs and other selected animals living at that time which became extinct, and would these creatures have suffered extinction regardless of any such event or events?

Favoring the cataclysmic theory of dinosaur extinction, Chatterjee (1992, 1995a, the latter a preliminary report), and Chatterjee and Rudra (1993, 1996), noted that a number of crater sites have been linked to this extinction at the K-T boundary for over a decade. Of these, the Chicxulub Crater in Yucatán, near Mexico, has been regarded as the most likely candidate for hard evidence of a meteorite impact that some scientists (Hildebrand, Penfield, King, Pilkington, Camaro, Jacobson and Boynton 1991) believe resulted in the final extinction of the dinosaurs.

However, the more recently discovered Shiva Crater, identified from subsurface data at the India-Seychelles rift margin in the northwest Indian Ocean, may also be a potential impact structure. According to Chatterjee (1995a; see also Chatterjee and Rudra

1996), the main evidence supporting this site as an impact structure "is the Bombay High Field, a giant offshore oil basin in India, and associated alkaline intrusives, presumably melt ejecta, emplaced radially around the crater."

Chatterjee (1995a) noted that the Shiva Crater is the correct K-T boundary age and reveals "the morphology of a complex impact scar with a distinct central uplift represented by the Bombay High, an annular trough, and a collapsed outer rim."

As described by Chatterjee (1995a) and Chatterjee and Rudra (1996), the crater is oblong in shape, and measures about 600 kilometers in length, 450 kilometers in diameter, and 12 kilometers deep. Chatterjee and Rudra noted that the crater's age "is inferred from its Deccan lava floor, Paleocene age of the overlying sediments, isotope dating (~65Ma) of presumed melt rocks, and the Carlsberg rifting event (chron 29R) within the basin."

Chatterjee (1995a) and Chatterjee and Rudra (1996) speculated that the projectile that created the Shiva Crater was about 40 kilometers in diameter and struck obliquely at the continental shelf of western India in a southwest-northeast trajectory. The authors further theorized that the synchrony and near-antipodal positions of both the Indian and Mexican

One of artist Neave Parker's Mesozoic scenes published during the 1950s in the *Illustrated London News*, this one depicting dinosaurs (in somewhat dated life restorations grouped together from different Late Cretaceous levels) facing extinction amid a time of geologic change. From left to right: the ankylosaur *Euoplocephalus*, ceratopsian *Triceratops*, theropod *Gorgosaurus*, hadrosaur *Edmontosaurus*, theropod *Tyrannosaurus*, and ceratopsians *Torosaurus* and *Styracosaurus*, pterosaurs overhead. In the foreground, tiny mammals seem to be patiently awaiting the world they will soon inherit.

Courtesy *Illustrated London News*.

craters and their same age could suggest two possible alternate yet linking origins: 1. Both craters originated from the splitting of a meteorite having a larger diameter, or 2. a large impact produced a similar impact on the opposite side of the planet "by axial focusing of seismic waves."

According to Chatterjee (1995b) and Chatterjee and Rudra (1996), the central uplift of the Shiva Crater is mostly represented by the Bombay High; annular basin by the Surat Basin, Dahanu Depression, Panna Depression, and Amirante Depression; and the crater rim is formed by the Panvel Flexure, Amirante Arc, and Narmada Fault.

Considering India as "ground zero" for both the Shiva impact and Deccan volcanism, Chatterjee and Rudra (1996) assessed the causal relationships and biotic effects of both scenarios, determining that volcanism began some million years before the impact, its "origin attributed to the Deccan-Réunion hotspot," the enormous area covered by the Deccan Traps explained by "intercanyon flows along the drainage of the Narmada, Godavari, and Cambay rift basins."

As noted by Chatterjee and Rudra (1996), Maastrichtian dinosaur fossils of any kind are extremely rare in India. Theropods, sauropods, and ankylosaurs flourished there during the early stage of Deccan eruptions, but died out suddenly, the last dinosaur bones being found in this area occurring at the boundary of the Cretaceous–Tertiary impact (or exactly at the iridium layer), evidence apparently supporting a sudden extinction event. This also suggested to the authors that, although both impact and volcanism could have been involved in these dinosaurs' extinction, contributing significantly to the breakdown of stable ecological communities and disrupting the biosphere, the impact seems to have played the more salient role as a killing mechanism.

Further support for the impact scenario was offered in a brief report by Pillmore (1998a), who announced that the K-T boundary "is preserved in a sequence of coal-bearing, fluvial rocks in the lower part of the Raton Formation (Late Cretaceous and Paleocene) at more than 20 sites in the southern and east-central parts of the Raton basin in northern New Mexico and southern Colorado." This boundary, found at the top of a 2- to 2.5-centimeter thick kaolinitic claystone bed (termed the "fireball layer") in an interval of coal and carbonaceous shale, is defined by the abrupt disappearance of several fossil pollen taxa, and correlates with quite similar claystone beds found at the palynological boundary at sites in Wyoming and Montana, and north into Alberta and Saskatchewan. According to Pillmore, the claystone layer "contains anomalously high concentrations of iridium and shock quartz grains, signatures of asteroid impact." The fossil plant record, Pillmore pointed out, is indicative of continent-spanning disruption of the terrestrial ecosystem at the Cretaceous–Tertiary boundary.

In a follow up report, Pillmore (1998b) announced that dinosaur tracks found in sandstone beds of the lower part of the Raton Formation in the Raton basin constitute "convincing evidence that dinosaurs were present and probably thriving in this part of the Western Interior, either until or only a very short time before, the asteroid impact at the end of the Cretaceous Period." More dinosaur tracks were also found at several horizons located farther below the boundary. These trace fossils, consisting both of impressions and natural casts, represent a tyrannosaurid theropod, hadrosaurid ornithopods, and ceratopsid ceratopsians. Pillmore (1998b) noted that these tracks are significant as "some occur where the K/T boundary clay layer is present and visible above the track layers and the exact stratigraphic position of the tracks is known."

Also, López-Martinez, Ardévol, Arribas, Civis and Gonzalez-Delgado (1998) showed — in a "poster" presented at the Third European Workshop on Vertebrate Palaeontology in May 1998 at the Natuurhistorisch Museum, Maastricht, Netherlands — that biostratigraphic and paleomagnetic analyses of rocks from the Ager syncline of the Tremp Formation, in the south-central Pyrenees, Spain, have allowed for the location of the K-T boundary. At least four species of dinosaurs, represented by numerous individuals, are known from the Ager area below the boundary, while no dinosaurs are known from even the earliest Palaeocene rocks. Evidence of dinosaurs below the boundary include fossil footprints (including those of a large three-toed ornithopod, and large and relatively small sauropods) representing the youngest dinosaur remains documented in Europe to date. This evidence illustrated that at least four dinosaurian species were living in the Ager area just before the end of the Cretaceous, a record that, according to López-Martinez et al., "supports the catastrophic scenario of dinosaur extinction."

Other Observations

A less spectacular interpretation of what may have occurred at the end of the Cretaceous, though one including an extraterrestrial impact, was proposed by Archibald (1996), who tested various hypotheses of extinction of dinosaurs and other vertebrates at the K-T boundary, based upon the fossil record.

Testing these hypotheses first necessitated determining whether disappearances of species are actually extinctions rather than artifacts of taxonomy, of ecology, or of preservations. According to Archibald, the only well-documented record of vertebrates across the K-T boundary is in the Western Interior of North America. When these three artifacts are considered, the record shows that 52 of 107 species (or 49 percent) survived the boundary, this being only about a 10 percent lower level of survival than for intervals of time just before and after the boundary. Also, if the 20 rare species disappearances at the boundary are survivals, then survival could rise as high as 67 percent (72 of 107 species) at the boundary, true survival levels for vertebrate species, therefore, being between 49 (more likely closer to being correct) and 67 percent at the boundary.

Archibald found that extinction is not uniform for the dozen major taxonomic vertebrate groups (sharks and relatives, bony fishes, amphibians, multituberculates, placentals, marsupials, turtles, lizards, champsosaurs, crocodilians, saurischian dinosaurs, and ornithischian dinosaurs) across the K-T boundary, but rather concentrated into five groups (sharks and relatives, marsupials, lizards, saurischians, and ornithischians), each of these suffering at least 70 percent extinction, and accounting for 41 of 55 (=75 percent) of the species extinctions across the boundary in the Western Interior of North America.

According to Archibald, comet or asteroid impact, or massive volcanism (also worldwide fires, sharp decreases in temperature, and acid rain) correctly predict only five of the 12 turnover patterns (extinctions or survivals) for the dozen major vertebrate groups across the boundary, with marine regression (see below) and habitat fragmentation predicting 11 out of 12. The latter scenarios account for the disappearance from the Western Interior of sharks and their relatives, with the loss of close contacts with oceanic waters; the decline of marsupials with the appearances of new and potentially placental competitors that crossed newly formed land bridges; and the disappearance of both saurischian and ornithischian dinosaurs with the reduction and fragmentation of low coastal habitats. Archibald ruled out extraterrestrial impacts or massive volcanism as the sole cause of the extinctions at the K-T boundary, and concluded that neither of these causes, nor that of marine regression, taken separately (and occurring at other times when mass extinctions did not take place), can sufficiently explain all major extinctions. According to Archibald, these causes, taken together, "explain the patterns of faunal and floral turnover" at the Cretaceous–Tertiary boundary.

In a "short review" discussing the Cretaceous extinction of ammonites, invertebrate paleontologist Peter D. Ward (1997) accepted that the Chicxulub impact event took place 65 million years ago, but addressed a problem regarding the demise of this highly diverse group of mollusks, one of the various nondi-nosaurian groups that also went extinct at that time. Ward pointed out that, during their more than 300 million-year history, ammonites had survived a great deal of environmental change, including the most catastrophic mass extinction of all, the Permian–Triassic event. Therefore, the extinction of the ammonites at Mesozoic's end was indeed curious.

Ward (1997) noted that, from the end of the Campanian through that of the Maastrichtian, ammonites had become less diverse, and their numbers remained equally constant until the very end of the Cretaceous period. Given their very long history, during which they survived numerous catastrophes, Ward (1997) could find no "terrestrial" cause for their extinction, and concluded "that only some extraordinary circumstance could have caused their final demise." Ward postulated it was not the Chicxulub impact event itself that caused the extinction of the ammonites, but rather environmental effects resulting from that event — mainly, the destruction of the plankton upon which so many creatures, including the ammonites, depended for sustenance and reproduction.

While stating that evidence for a giant impact at the end of the Cretaceous period is "overwhelming," Ward (1997) added that debate continues as to the possible environmental effects of the impact, and to whether they resulted in mass extinctions, with dinosaurs and ammonites being the main possible victims. This debate, Ward pointed out, has currently settled upon three questions: 1. Was there one — or more — extinction events; 2. if the latter, was the extinction gradual, suddenly, or a combination of both; and 3. was the mass extinction single or multicausal?

Based on invertebrate-fossil samplings from seven strategic locations in France and Spain, Ward (1997) found that, at least in that region, "two distinct intervals of extinction could be discerned."

The first interval involves inoceramid bivalves, the vast majority of which became extinct about two millions years before the "final crisis" (coinciding with the placement of the iridium layer, roughly corresponding to the base of the Hell Creek Formation). This extinction, as verified by the fossil record, was gradual, the causes for it unknown.

The second interval involved ammonites and a small number of other invertebrate taxa. Ward (1997) first recognized a minor extinction interval involving the extinction of six ammonite species just prior to the K-T boundary. This interval was associated with Late Cretaceous marine regressions. Regression (see below) would have resulted in both dramatically altering habitats, and also in reducing the amount of rock material, thus noticeably altering the fossil samplings. At the K-T boundary, Ward (1997) recognized the extinction of about 16 ammonite species, plus various other invertebrate taxa, "that may well have been caused by the end–Cretaceous impact."

Although accepting that an impact did occur on the Yucatán Peninsula some 65 million years ago, Kellar (1998) noted that very little evidence has been offered to link it to the mass extinctions of dinosaurs or any other groups of organisms. Kellar pointed out that two major sets of data from the fossil record are detrimental to the impact hypothesis: 1. The K-T mass extinction is mostly restricted to the tropics, with no major extinctions known to have occurred in high latitudes (this suggesting that a mass kill resulting from the Yucatán impact was largely restricted to low latitudes, therefore not being global in scope); and 2. biotic diversity steadily decreased during the five million years preceding the impact with no new species evolving.

Furthermore, Kellar noted, the climate significantly cooled during this time until about 300,000 years before the K-T boundary, then warmed and finally cooled again during the last 100,000 years of the Cretaceous. These changes in temperature "caused a progressive mass extinction and predisposed the survivor fauna to eventual extinction." Faunas in high latitudes that were more tolerant to environmental changes survived into the later Tertiary; environmentally sensitive tropical and subtropical faunas in low latitudes progressively succumbed as the climate decreased. Kellar concluded that, though the impact may have contributed to the mass extinctions of the Late Cretaceous fauna, it was not the primary cause.

Gradual Extinction Theories

Not all workers, however, have accepted the "asteroid impact" theory as the final explanation for the extinction of the dinosaurs, instead considering the demise of this great group of animals to have been gradual and requiring a long period of time.

Wroblewski (1996), as had Archibald, addressed the question as to whether dinosaurian extinction was a result of marine regression. Analyzing assemblages of theropod teeth from several terminal Cretaceous formations, Wroblewski found significant similarity in the relative abundance and taxonomic diversity between samples of the teeth from those formations, and suggested that paleoecological controls had more effect than did time factors in determining the composition of local theropod faunas in the Late Cretaceous.

Based "on new paleogeographic data from southern Wyoming," Wroblewski found reason to reject theories that dinosaurs became extinct due to loss of coastal plain habitats in a response to a lowering of sea level, pointing out that the results of this "regression

were buffered locally by rapid subsidence of the Hanna Basin which caused persistence of marine and deltaic deposition until mid–Lancian time." In conclusion, Wroblewski found it an oversimplification to depict both "terminal Cretaceous marine regression and dinosaurian extinction as constant in both duration and local magnitude."

Sloan (1997) suggested that plate tectonics — the movement of large land masses via plates that make up the Earth's core — had two major effects on dinosaurs and their abundance (and eventual final extinction):

1. Because of the breakup of the "super-continent" Pangaea, there was a world-wide dinosaur fauna in the Jurassic; but with numerous isolated land masses developing in the Early–Late Cretaceous, dinosaur faunas became regional, this leading to the greater number of Late Cretaceous dinosaurs.

2. With plate tectonics, oxygen and carbon dioxide in the atmosphere varied. Increased rates of sea floor production led to a rapid increase in carbon dioxide (a greenhouse gas), but also increased photosynthesis leading to increased oxygen, the amount of which was a balance between the rate of carbon dioxide production, rate of carbon burial (as oil or coal), and the atmosphere's rate of oxygen loss resulting from rock weathering.

According to Sloan, the dinosaurs enjoyed two major radiations, each one ending in an extinction. The first radiation led to the Middle Jurassic–Early Cretaceous fauna dominated by sauropods, stegosaurs, and large theropods, gradually leading to the Early Cretaceous with an extinction of 64 percent, including all large dinosaurs. The second, basically Late Cretaceous, radiation included hadrosaurs, ankylosaurs, pachycephalosaurs, ceratopsians, and manuraptoran theropods, terminating in a gradual extinction in the last 10 million years of that period.

Sloan stated that the first of these two extinctions occurred during the Early Cretaceous, with the atmosphere's oxygen content measuring at 22 percent; the second took place in the Late Cretaceous, when the spreading of the sea floor doubled due to Pacific superplumes, with oxygen rising to 35 percent and dropping to 27 percent by the end of the period (today it is 21 percent). Sloan speculated that as dinosaurs do not ventilate their lungs as efficiently as do birds and mammals, the large forms suffered extinction during times when the level of oxygen dropped.

Sereno (1996), however, in a brief preliminary report on an upcoming major study on the phylogenetic structure and evolutionary implications of dinosaur descent (see systematics chapter), suggested that dinosaurian extinction may be less related to the breakup of continents than to other factors. According to Sereno, "Mesozoic biogeographic patterns are dominated by regional extinction and dispersal as opposed to a hierarchic vicariance pattern that mirrors the fragmentation of Pangaea."

A rather traditional hypothesis to explain dinosaur extinction — that herbivorous forms were unable to adapt to eating the angiosperms (flowering plants) that arose in the middle of the Cretaceous and were abundant by the end of that period, replacing gymnosperms (mostly conifers) in biomass production dominance — was examined from a new perspective by Taggart and Cross (1996).

As stated by Taggart and Cross, "high populations of herbivores are sustained by the dominant plants, defined in terms of biomass production, of the communities in which they occur." Hadrosaurs radiated early in the Cretaceous, a time when conifers were the dominant land plants, in terms of biomass, analysis of rare stomach contents from Wyoming and Alberta indicating that these duckbilled dinosaurs continued preferential consumption of conifers even after the major radiation of flowering plants. By the end of the Cretaceous, the major change in biomass production from gynmosperms to angiosperms would have been detrimental to any group of large, plant-eating animals (*e.g.*, hadrosaurs and sauropods) that persisted in preferring to exploit conifers. Thus, the feeding preferences of certain herbivorous dinosaurs may "have contributed to the vulnerability of specific groups when subject to stresses associated with K/T boundary events."

Taggart and Cross noted that the above scenario does not necessarily apply to ceratopsians (and perhaps ankylosaurs), the adaptive radiation of which, coupled with their probable reconstruction as herb- and shrub-level grazers in their communities, may have led toward a utilization of a flowering-plant biomass.

Sereno (1996), contrary to the above study, proposed that "the evolution of feeding adaptations among dinosaurian herbivores argues strongly against any correlation with the rapid mid–Cretaceous rise of angiosperms."

Although much had already been published in the literature attempting to explain dinosaur extinction as gradual, occurring over many millions of years, it was the opinion of Fastovsky and Sheehan (1997) — after evaluating various ideas and theories supporting the gradual-extinction scenario, and utilizing data derived from the fossiliferous Hell Creek Formation in the Western Interior of North America — that two misconceptions are commonly put forth to "falsify the idea that" the dinosaurs' extinction was due to the impact of an asteroid with the Earth. Quoting these authors:

"Myth 1—*If an asteroid really caused the extinc-tions, one should find a death horizon with abundant fossils. A corollary to this myth, common in popular accounts, is that if the asteroid scenario is correct, bones should be found covered by an iridium-bearing 'impact layer.'*"

Commenting on the above, Fastovsky and Sheenan noted the following: So-called "Signor-Lipps Effects" (codified by Signor and Lipps 1982, who proposed that the cumulative probability of finding fossils decreases as one nears an arbitrary boundary) result even in an instantaneous extinction that produces a fossil record indicating an apparent gradual extinction; the fossil record produced by time averaging of the record and by rate of deposition are about the same for sudden or gradual extinctions; and impact clay is not always preserved, a few millimeters of clay preserved on a dinosaur skeleton being very unlikely.

"Myth 2—*Dinosaurs are not present in the 2–3 m below the impact horizon, and the evidence thus strongly suggests that they disappeared before the end of the Cretaceous.*"

Recarding the above, Fastovsky and Sheenan stated that the impact layer is known only at two Hell Creek sites, and there has only local distribution; the exact position of this layer is unknown, therefore the 3-meter interval cannot be identified, nor can this idea be tested (though it may in the future, based on the use of pollens to locate the precise boundary); and no evidence currently suggests that dinosaurs are less common in this interval than in any other Hell Creek 3-meter interval.

Fastovsky and Sheenan considered their admittedly limited database — restricted as it was to but one area of a single continent — to be the "litmus test" for global events (as proposed by Archibald and Bryant 1990). What the authors found significant was not that there are thick sequences of terrestrial outcrops barren of fossils at the Hell Creek K-T boundary, but rather that such outcrops do preserve fossils. The paucity of K-T dinosaur fossils found outside North America was attributed to the lack of fossiliferous sequences as opposed to a diminished role for latest Cretaceous dinosaurs. According to Fastovsky and Sheenan, only the preservation of latest Cretaceous, high-diversity tetrapod ecosystems without dinosaurs can be really used "as evidence that dinosaurs had become a diminished force in terrestrial ecosystems at the end of the Cretaceous," such outcrops not being known, this suggesting to them "that the North American situation epitomizes latest Cretaceous events."

The authors therefore concluded "that the extinction of the dinosaurs and other organisms globally can be most easily — indeed, most parsimoniously — explained by the catastrophic impact of an asteroid with the earth."

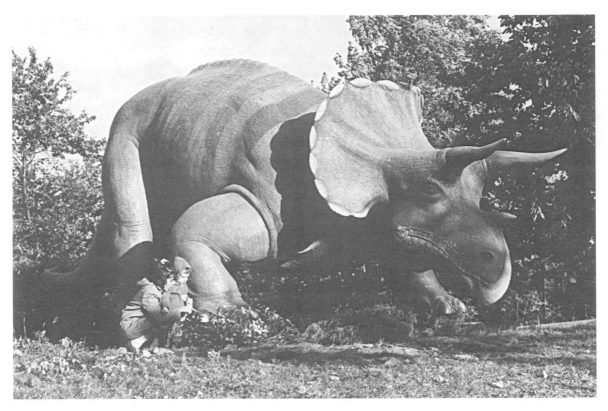

Louis Paul Jonas Studios' life-sized mechanical model (equipped with moving head) of *Triceratops*, possibly the last dinosaurian genus to become extinct, made for the 1964 New York World's Fair. This figure, nicknamed "Uncle Beazley" (and no longer mechanized), now resides outside the National Museum of Natural History, Smithsonian Institution, Washington, D.C.

Zinsmeister (1997) offered a somewhat different interpretation of events, though one including an impact event, at the end of the Cretaceous period. According to this author, new fossil data and the reassessment of old information from the mid and low latitudes show the terminal Cretaceous mass extinctions were not abrupt, but "that the Earth's biosphere was already under severe stress" that had begun during the Campanian, "and experienced a decline in global diversity well before the end of the Cretaceous."

As reported by Zinsmeister (1997), recent discoveries of a fossil-fish bone layer immediately above the K-T iridium anomoly in the James Ross Basin of Seymour Island, on the northeast tip of the Antarctic Peninsula, could represent the first documentation of a mass kill caused by an impact event at the end of the Cretaceous period. Zinsmeister (1997) stated, "The absence of any other extirpation horizons in the Upper Cretaceous and Lower Tertiary sequence strongly suggests that the fish kill is related to the event that produced the iridium anomaly." Also, the disappearance in Antarctica of ammonites and other species before the formation of this anomaly and the fish bone horizon indicates "that the Terminal Extinction Event was not the result of a single factor, but the conjunction of several events with the impact precipitating the final extinction." Data from Seymour Island and nearby Antarctic islands suggested to Zinsmeister (1997) "that the decline in diversity and extinction and of important cosmopolitan marine groups in the

high latitudes began earlier [during the Late Campanian] and was more severe than in the lower latitudes."

Zinsmeister (1997) pointed out that the Earth is "a biotically robust world." The fact that mass extinctions did not follow a number of other catastrophic geologic events (*e.g.*, the Middle Ordovician Millbrig–Big Bentonite volcanic event, the Late Devonian Alamo Impact, also earlier postulated Mesozoic impact events that did not cause mass extinction of dinosaurs) indicated to the author that the planet's biosphere is amazingly "resilient to major geologic catastrophes with mass extinction events occurring only when there is a conjunction of geologic events."

Zinsmester (1997) offered that, if the biosphere had not been under a long-term period of stress beginning as far back as the Campanian, the Maastrichtian impact event may have had little or no effect on the biosphere. In other words, the impact may have been something akin to the proverbial "straw that broke the camel's back" that led to the extinction of dinosaurs and other life-forms that might otherwise have survived.

The K-T Boundary: Precisely What Is It?

Recently coming into question was precisely just *when* the great extinction of the dinosaurs actually

occurred and what it entailed. Ward (1996), in a preliminary report to his 1997 paper, pointed out the present nonexistence of any commonly agreed upon definition of the K-T boundary, and posed the following questions: "What was the duration [of the Late Cretaceous mass extinctions]? Do we include only the extinctions clustered at the boundary, or include precursor events observed from Maastrichtian Stage strata, or even from the Campanian Stage? Do we include early Tertiary events as part of the K/T catastrophe, and if so, which ones? What died out, and when? Was there a latitudinal component?" Ward stated further that all mass extinctions required some finite time period to unfold; therefore, mass extinctions should be viewed as having discrete time intervals (*e.g.*, an onset phase, one or more periods of greatest extinction, and concluding phases).

Furthermore, Sullivan (1996*b*, 1998) stated in brief reports that dinosaur extinction was neither catastrophic nor unique, emphasizing that, throughout the Mesozoic, species-level dinosaur extinction differed in no way from that observed at the K-T boundary, and that nonavian dinosaur species declined significantly from late Campanian to late Maastrichtian time. According to Sullivan, the fossil record does not support the selective extinction of large-bodied dinosaurs due to the impact of an asteroid at or near the Cretaceous–Tertiary boundary; instead, the decline of such animals may be most adequately "explained by dwindling taxonomic diversity during late Mesozoic time and environmental 'deterioration' brought about by global tectonics, coupled with the diversification of the avian lineage of the Dinosauria" (Sullivan 1996*b*).

As with other controversies, then, many questions remain unanswered regarding the final extinction of the dinosaurs.

Incomplete skull referred to *Triceratops* sp., a relic of the final days of the last dinosaurs at the end of the Cretaceous period.

II: Dinosaurian Systematics

D inosaur classifications continue to evolve, with the introduction of new taxa and repositioning or removal of old taxa (see *D:TE*). Our concepts of classifying dinosaurs are influenced by new discoveries; more advanced techniques in the recovery, preparation, and study of fossils; new phylogenetic analyses; and by reassessments of previously known taxa. One worker's cladogram often conflicts with or invalidates another's. A number of new and sometimes contradicting phylogenies for various dinosaurian groups have been proposed by systematists since the publication of *D:TE*. It will remain to be seen which new schemes, or parts thereof, will become adopted by the majority of workers.

Dinosauria

Although virtually all workers now agree to the monophyly of the Dinosauria, not everyone's conception of just what constitutes a dinosaur is necessarily the same.

Fraser and Padian (1995), in a brief report, called attention to the recent tendency to rediagnose and redefine the Dinosauria in order to allow the inclusion of certain key taxa within this monophyletic group, this instability making difficult the establishment of relationships of new material. Therefore, these authors supported "a previously suggested node-based definition of Dinosauria that is restricted to Saurischia plus Ornithischia." Fraser and Padian will later publish "a modified set of diagnostic characters that may allow disassociated elements to be referred to or excluded from the Dinosauria."

A consensus has yet to be reached as to which genera represent the earliest known dinosaurs.

Though most workers seem to regard *Eoraptor* and *Herrerasaurus* either as basal dinosaurs outside of Saurischia or as basal theropods (*e.g.*, Currie 1995; Sereno 1995), others have suggested that they may belong outside of Dinosauria (Holtz 1995*a*, 1995*b*; Holtz and Padian 1995) altogether.

Holtz (1995*b*) regarded *Eoraptor* and the Herrerasauridae as sister taxa to either the theropod-sauropodomorph clade or to Dinosauria *sensu strico* (=Saurischia plus Ornithischia). Holtz and Padian (1995) further suggested that *Eoraptor* and herrerasaurids are not theropods, are probably outside Saurischia plus Ornithischia, probably outside Saurischia, and perhaps nondinosaurian, but nestled within Ornithodira and retaining, as do theropods, various ornithodiran features lost by ornithischians and, to some extent, by basal sauropodomorphs.

Sereno (1996), in preparing a major cladistic reorganization of the Dinosauria, briefly announced some of his findings, analyzing the higher-level relationships of dinosaurs "by establishing basal cladistic structure within the group followed by analyses of the subgroups Ornithischia, Sauropodomorpha and Theropoda."

Sereno's (1996) analyses suggested that key locomotor and trophic adaptations of each subgroup arose before dinosaurs dominated terrestrial faunas near the end of the Triassic period, and that basal lineages within each subgroup arose by the end of the Triassic or beginning of the Jurassic, with notable missing lineages in each subgroup.

The following trends were observed by Sereno (1996): Phylogenetic trends in body size show stepwise increases, stepwise reduction observed only in coelurosaurs; obligate quadrupedality assumed among herbivores; increase in number of cervical and sacral vertebrae; neck elongation; miniaturization of forelimbs; and loss of external manual and pedal digits.

Novas (1996*b*) criticized numerous earlier attempts (his own included) to list characters presumably diagnostic of Dinosauria, stating that "most of the alleged dinosaur synapomorphies have broader distributions among Archosauria, whereas other features are diagnostic to less inclusive groups than Dinosauria." As examples, Novas (1996*b*) pointed out various cranial features ("'S' flexed curved neck, loss of clavicle-interclavicle, digitigrade pes, loss of osteoderms, *etc.*") that are also present in the Pterosauria and basal ornithodiran *Marasuchus* (formerly *Lagosuchus*), and which have been "hypothesized as present in the common ornithodiran ancestor" (see Gauthier and Padian 1985; Gauthier 1986; Sereno 1991).

Novas (1996*b*) cited other features previously regarded as diagnostic of the Dinosauria, but which are shared by *Marasuchus* ("*e.g.*, deltopectoral crest down the humerus shaft; concave glenoid, facing mostly posteroventrally") and the dinosaur-like archosaur *Lagerpeton* ("*e.g.*, pedal digit five very reduced and nondivergent"). Consequently, these represent synapomorphies of the larger clades Dinosauriformes (including *Marasuchus lilloensis*, *Pseudolagosuchus major*, Dinosauria [including Aves], and all descendants of their common ancestor) or the more inclusive Dinosauromorpha.

In this new analysis of Dinosauria, Novas (1996*b*)—considering taxa ranging from Carnian to Recent—defined Dinosauria as including Ornithischia, Saurischia, and all descendants of their common ancestor, regarding the Herrerasauridae (including *Herrerasaurus* and *Staurikosaurus*) and *Eoraptor* as saurischian theropods rather than basal dinosaurs or nondinosaurian archosaurs.

Evaluating data from various earlier studies (Gauthier 1986; Novas 1992*a*, 1992*b*, 1994; Sereno

Partial skull of the large "ceratosaurid" theropod *Ceratosaurus nasicornis* displayed in the Dinosaur Valley museum in Grand Junction, Colorado, in right lateral view. This North American species from the Upper Jurassic Morrison Formation was one of the relatively few known carnivorous dinosaurs bearing prominent cranial horns.

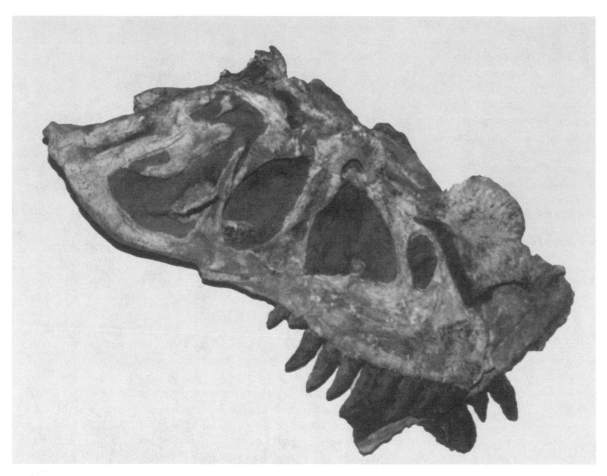

Photograph by the author, courtesy Museum of Western Colorado.

1991; Sereno and Arcucci 1994*a*, 1994*b*; Sereno and Novas 1990, 1992, 1994; Sereno, Forster, Rogers and Monetta 1993), Novas (1996*b*) found the monophyly of Dinosauria to be supported by 17 derived traits, four of which (postfrontal bone absent; post-temporal foramen present; quadrate head laterally exposed; ectopterygoid dorsal to transverse flange of pterygoid) he regarded as equivocal cranial synapomorphies.

Aside from the above features, Novas (1996*b*) diagnosed Dinosauria by the following characters: 1. Temporal musculature extended anteriorly onto skull roof; 2. epipophyses on cervical vertebrae; 3. deltopectoral crest distally projected; 4. manual digit IV with three or fewer phalanges; 5. at least three sacral vertebrae; 6. perforate acetabulum; 7. brevis shelf on lateroventral side of postacetabular blade of ilium; 8. ischium with slender shaft and ventral keel (obturator process) restricted to proximal third of bone; 9. reduction of tuberosity that laterally bounds ligament of femoral head; 10. prominent anterior (lesser) trochanter on femur; 11. tibia overlapping anteroproximally and posteriorly ascending process of astragalus; 12. calcaneum with concave proximal articular surface (for reception of distal fibular end); and 13. distal tarsal 4 proximodistally depressed and triangular-shaped in proximal view.

This analysis suggested to Novas (1996*b*) that "a sustained modification of hind limb morphology occurred in the early evolution of Ornithodira, because most of the diagnostic features of this and less inclusive groups (*e.g.*, Dinosauromorpha, Dinosauriformes, and Dinosauria) pertain to the femur, tibia, tarsus, and pes."

Novas (1996*b*) further suggested that the transformation of the ilium, ischium, and pubis, and presumably the musculature originating from them "was delayed with respect to the hind limbs, since most important pelvic modifications occurred at the Dinosauria node, but not before," with forelimb transformation being less profound.

Saurischia

Theropoda

Of the two major dinosaurian groups, the Saurischia has been most subject to revision in recent years, mainly regarding the groups Theropoda and Sauropoda.

The Theropoda — an assemblage of saurischians accounting for more than one third of the known

dinosaurian genera — is the clade undergoing the most revision, with more proposed revised phylogenies either published or in preparation than any other dinosaurian group.

In a recent new analysis of the Theropoda, Holtz (1995*b*) excluded *Eoraptor* and Herrerasauridae from this group, and perceived a basal split of Theropoda into Ceratosauria and Tetanurae.

Sereno (1995), positing that *Eoraptor* and herrerasaurids are primitive theropods and considering the early evolution and major patterns of diversification of the Theropoda, proposed the following scenario: *Eoraptor* is the earliest recorded possible theropod and more closely approximates "the hypothetical dinosaurian condition than any other dinosaurian subgroup"; more derived than *Eoraptor* are *Herrerasaurus* and its allies, which were widely distributed across Pangaea. All remaining theropods (neotheropods) diverged along the lines Ceratosauria and Tetanurae before the end of the Carnian, the Late Triassic "ceratosaur" radiation giving way to a tetanuran radiation during the Early and Middle Jurassic. Independent spinosaurid, allosauroid, and coelurosaurian lineages were apparently present and globally distributed by the mid–Jurassic, long before the part-

ing of any major land masses, during which time the sequence of structural changes occurred that climaxed in the evolution of avian power flight. During the Cretaceous, three tetanuran lineages on three different land masses independently achieved domination and radiation — coelurosaurs in Laurasia, "ceratosaurs" in South America, and spinosaurids in Africa. Sereno's (1995) analysis kept tyrannosaurids within Coelurosauria.

Currie (1995) regarded Theropoda as a monophyletic taxon including living birds, with *Eoraptor* and *Herrerasaurus* as the earliest known members of this group. According to Currie (1995), most large theropods belong to the group Carnosauria (a taxon abandoned by some workers, *e.g.*, Holtz 1994; see also *D:TE*), a monophyletic taxon united by more than a dozen synapomorphies "including the universal presence of opisthocoelic cervical vertebrae."

Hunt (1996) briefly introduced a new unnamed clade of primitive, herrerasaurid-like theropods including *Chindesaurus bryansmalli* (originally referred to the Herrerasauridae), as well as two as of yet undescribed genera from the Upper Triassic Bull Canyon Formation of Eastern New Mexico. Hunt noted that these taxa share several generally accepted herrerasaurid synapomorphies (*e.g.*, pyramidal ascending process of

Skeletons (casts) of the carnosaur *Allosaurus fragilis* and camarasaurid *Camarasaurus supremus* mounted at Dinofest™ (1998), the former posed as though attacking the latter. These mounts represent two of the main groups of saurischian dinosaurs, respectively, the Theropoda and Sauropodomorpha.

Skeleton (cast reconstructed from holotype UC OBA 1, missing elements cast from *Allosaurus fragilis*) of the "megalosaurid" theropod *Afrovenator abakensis*, mounted and temporarily displayed in 1994 at the Harold Washington Library Center, Chicago. This large carnivorous dinosaur was collected along with other fossil vertebrates, including a new and unnamed sauropod, by Paul C. Sereno and team from Lower Cretaceous rocks of the Sahara Desert.

astragalus; anteroposteriorly-shortened posterior dorsal centra) and several derived characters (*e.g.*, gracile unbooted pubis; proximally flared scapula). According to Hunt, these characters suggest that this new taxon is the sister group to the Herrerasauridae, restricted to the "Revueltian" (early to middle Norian) of western North America.

These characters indicated to Hunt a Late Triassic, pre–Norian faunal exchange between North America and South America. Hunt recognized three faunal exchanges during this time on the basis of theropods: 1. Gondwana — herrerasaurids but no "ceratosaurs"; 2. southern Laurasia — herrerasaur-like clade and "ceratosaurs"; and 3. northern Laurasia — exclusively "ceratosaurs."

Ceratosauria was found by Currie (1995) to be definable only by plesiomorphic characters if the genus *Ceratosaurus* is included. Cervical centra of *Ceratosaurus* approach the opisthocoelic condition found in Carnosauria, one reason, in Currie's (1995) opinion, that *Ceratosaurus* should be removed from Ceratosauria, redefined, and regarded as the sister taxon

of Carnosauria. Currie (1995) also concluded that most remaining well known theropods (including avimimids, caenagnathids, dromaeosaurids, ornithomimids, oviraptorids, troodontids, and birds) belong to the monophyletic group Coelurosauria.

Among the paleontologists most actively attempting to bring stability to the Theropoda and organize this entire group based upon parsimonious cladistic analysis is Thomas R. Holtz, Jr. Holtz (1995*b*) noted that, among "ceratosaurs," *Elaphrosaurus* shares more derived characters with the Coelophysoidea than with the Neoceratosauria (including *Ceratosaurus* [regarded by Holtz as a "ceratosaur," *contra* Currie 1995] plus Abelisaurida).

Holtz and Padian (1995) defined Ceratosauria as all theropods closer to *Ceratosaurus* than to birds, and Tetanurae as all theropods closer to birds than to *Ceratosaurus*. Within Tetanurae, Holtz and Padian included the stem-taxa Carnosauria, defined by them as tetanurans closer to *Allosaurus* than to birds, and Coelurosauria, defined as tetanurans closer to birds than to *Allosaurus*.

Holtz (1995*b*) predicted that the common ancestor of all theropods was a megapredatory form, and suggested that the small size of some members of Ceratosauria and Coelurosauria was secondarily derived (although the paucity of small theropods in the fossil record also could be explained by collecting and taphonomic bias). Though Holtz (1996) accepted Spinosauridae (having largely been regarded in recent years as synonymous with Baryonychidae; see below) as a valid tetanuran (or tetanurine) family, he believed that the phylogenetic position of this taxon may lie elsewhere.

In describing the new theropod, *Angaturama* (see entry), Kellner and Campos (1996) recognized the Spinosauridae (including Baryonychidae) as a clade comprising *Spinosaurus aegyptiacus* and the anterior portions of two premaxillae (MNHN GDF 365 and 366) from the Elrhaz Formation (Aptian) of Gadoufaoua (Niger), referred to the Spinosauridae by Taquet (1984; see *Baryonyx* and *Irritator* entries, *D:TE* and this volume), *Baryonyx walkeri*, and *Angaturama limai*.

Kellner and Campos diagnosed the Spinosauridae by the following synapomorphies: Teeth with subcircular transverse sections; external nares displaced backwards (directly seen only in *Baryonyx*, indicated in *Angaturama* and in specimens referred to Spinosauridae from Gadoufaoua; seven premaxillary teeth (observed in *Baryonyx*, *Angaturama*, and Gadoufaoua specimens); anterior portion of the lower margin of the upper jaw concave (as in *Baryonyx*, *Angaturama*, and Gadoufaoua specimens), conforming to convexity of dentaries (seen in *Baryonyx* and in the lower jaw of *S. aegyptiacus*); anterior portion of upper and lower jaws laterally expanded (as in *Baryonyx*, the lower jaw of *S. aegyptiacus*, and the upper jaw of *Angaturama* and Gadoufaoua specimens).

Milner (1996) recognized the Baryonychidae as a group of unusual, long-snouted theropods known from the early Cretaceous (Wealden) of Europe, Albian–Cenomanian of North Africa, and Albian of northeast Brazil, noting that cranial material from the Upper Cretaceous of Morocco — a partial maxilla described by Buffetaut (1989) as *Spinosaurus* — closely resembles that of the lost *Spinosaurus aegyptiacus* type material and shares derived characters with *Baryonyx*. As *Baryonyx* lacks several important synapomorphies of Tetanurae, Milner suggested that these dinosaurs could represent a surviving lineage of more primitive theropods having a largely Gondwanan distribution.

Skeleton (cast) of the oviraptorid theropod *Ingenia yanshini* (here mislabeled *Oviraptor*), prepared and mounted by paleontologist Kenneth Carpenter in a brooding pose over its nest, displayed at the third Dinofest[TM] event in 1998.

Photograph by the author.

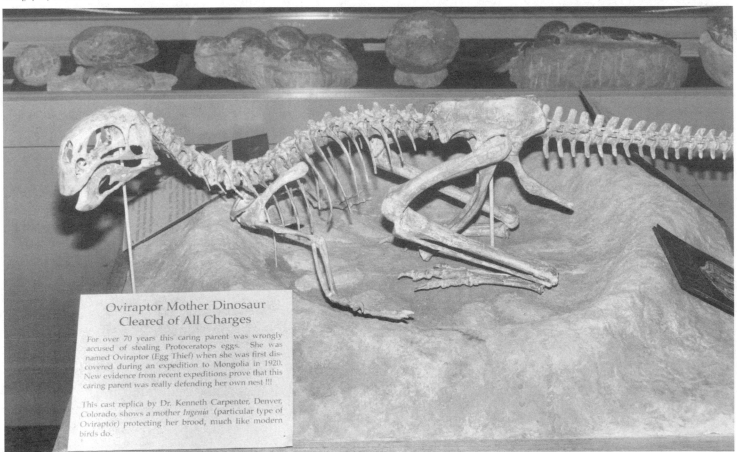

Oviraptor Mother Dinosaur
Cleared of All Charges

For over 70 years this caring parent was wrongly accused of stealing Protoceratops eggs. She was named Oviraptor (Egg Thief) when she was first discovered during an expedition to Mongolia in 1920. New evidence from recent expeditions prove that this caring parent was really defending her own nest !!!

This cast replica by Dr. Kenneth Carpenter, Denver, Colorado, shows a mother *Ingenia* (particular type of Oviraptor) protecting her brood, much like modern birds do.

Milner noted that all "spinosaur" material has been found in "low-lying deltaic coastal flood plain or lagoonal horizons and shows specialized skull and dental characters possibly interpreted as adaptations to a piscivorous diet."

Charig and Milner (1997), in their monograph on *Baryonyx walkeri*, argued for retaining Baryonychidae and Spinosauridae as distinct taxa, but added that these families could be linked based upon characters found in *Angaturama*. As noted by Charig and Milner (1997), *Angaturama* shares certain apomorphous characters with *Spinosaurus*, but also shares others with *Baryonyx* that could not be demonstrated in *Spinosaurus* owing to the incompleteness of its type material. This implied a relationship between the two families that justified their inclusion in a new "superfamily" of basal tetanurans, the Spinosauroidea (see *Baryonyx* entry), defined by Charig and Milner by the following apomorphies: 1. Jaws elongated, particularly in prenarial region; 2. greater or lesser tendency (greater in upper than lower jaw) to develop terminal

rosette; 3. lower jaw turned upwards at extreme anterior end, constricted transversely just behind it; 4. increase from five to seven premaxillary teeth; and 5. teeth showing reduction in a. compression of whole tooth in labio-lingual direction, b. recurvature of crown, and c. size of denticles on anterior and posterior carinae of crown.

Charig and Milner included in the Spinosauroidea the Baryonychidae (*Baryonyx*), Spinosauridae (*Spinosaurus*, *Angaturama*, and the Moroccan specimen), but excluded *Torvosaurus* and *Eustreptospondylus*. These authors further suggested that the Albian *Irritator*, known from a partial skull, might be a spinosaurid, sharing various characters with *Angaturama* (see entry; also *Irritator* entry, *D:TE*).

Regarding the Baryonychidae and Spinosauridae as sister taxa, Charig and Milner noted that the degree of reduction shown in the tooth characters (b. and c., above) is significantly less in Baryonychidae than in the considerably later Spinosauridae, this exhibiting a trend that seemingly increased much during the

Skeleton of the Asian allosaurid *Szechuanosaurus campi* mounted in an active pose at the third Dinofest™ event, held in Philadelphia, Pennsylvania, in 1998. This Late Jurassic species is known from a number of specimens recovered in China. The reconstructed skull on this mount is largely hypothetical.

Photograph by the author.

interval of time between the Barremian and Cenomanian. In their reanalysis of the systematic position of *Baryonyx* and its allies within Theropoda, Charig and Milner introduced the new taxon Neotetanurae, which is essentially the same as Avetheropoda, with *Baryonyx* the sister taxon to this clade. *Megalosaurus* and *Torvosaurus* (genera assigned to the family "Megalosauridae"), respectively, were regarded by these authors as progressively more distant outgroups to a combined clade comprising Spinosauroidea plus Neotetanurae [=Avetheropoda].

Supposedly related to the Spinosauridae is the new monotypic family Sigilmassasauridae, which Russell (1996) established while describing the new Moroccan genus *Sigilmassasaurus*, the latter including material originally described by Stromer (1934) as "*Spinosaurus* B." As interpreted by Russell, this family seems to be made up of atypical theropods with comparatively small heads, relatively long, yet strong and maneuverable necks, and ornithopod-like tails (see *Sigilmassasaurus* entry for diagnosis).

Holtz (1996) offered a new analysis of the non-avian tetanurines, proposing that "Megalosauridae" (*Megalosaurus* plus *Torvosaurus*), Spinosauridae, *Eustreptospondylus*, and *Piatnitzkysaurus* form a basal polytomy with regards to Avetheropoda, an exclusive clade diagnosed by the presence of a furcula. Within Avetheropoda is the monophyletic Carnosauria, with *Monolophosaurus* regarded as the sister group to Allosauroidea (Allosauridae plus Sinraptoridae).

Holtz (1996) regarded *Cryolophosaurus* as a basal carnosaur, and *Giganotosaurus* and Carcharodontosauridae as allosauroids closer to Allosauridae than to Sinraptoridae; *Compsognathus*, *Dryptosaurus*, and Manuraptoriformes forming a basal trichotomy; and the monophyletic Arctometatarsalia (Tyrannosauridae plus Bullatosauridae) and Manuraptora (Oviraptorosauria plus *Microvenator* plus Therizinosauroidea) plus (Dromaeosauridae plus Aves) supported. Holtz (1996) stated that this "new analysis confirms that several characters which previously unambiguously diagnosed Tetanurae or subgroups (*i.e.*, loss of the obturator foramen, loss of metatarsal IV, presence of the arctometatarsalian pes) are found to have evolved two or more times within the clade."

In a preliminary study of theropod vertebrae, Britt (1995) found that phylogenetic hypotheses can be tested by the presence of internal or external pneumatic diverticula in these bones; that the highest-level diagnostic pneumatic characters are based upon internal structure; and that other characters are diagnostic at lower taxonomic levels.

According to Britt, both camerate (simple) and camellate (complex) internal structures are present in theropod vertebrae, with camellate, however, restricted (except for *Ceratosaurus*, which has notably camellate pneumatic vertebrae) almost entirely to the Avetheropoda. The neural arches of camerate vertebrae are made up of simple laminae "which intersect to form deep, external ossae and all but the bases of the apophyses are apneumatic"; those of camellate vertebrae "are pneumantic, swollen ('inflated'), and thin walled" as in living birds.

Britt concluded that the camerate vertebrae of dromaesaurids and camellate vertebrae of troodontids corroborate the hypothesis that Deinonychosauria (a name formerly and incorrectly used to embrace both Dromaeosauridae and Troodontidae; see Currie and Padian 1997*a*; Currie 1997*b*) is a polyphyletic group (see also Holtz and Padian 1995); and that the camerate vertebrae in dromaeosaurids suggest that this condition is a synapomorphy of Dromaeosauridae within Avetheropoda, or that Dromaeosauridae is incorrectly placed within the latter group. Britt further stated that at least some dorsal vertebrae of *Archaeopteryx* are pneumatic, the nature of their internal structure yet to be determined, and that this determination should help clarify this genus' relationship to theropods and extant birds.

A new analysis of the Coelurosauria, based on characters of the vertebrae, was proposed by Makovicky (1995). Makovicky subjected 42 vertebral characters to cladistic analysis, with *Dilophosaurus* and Allosauroidea used as successive outgroups. Results of this analysis support the monophyly of Coelurosauria.

Makovicky found that, within this taxon, the Troodontidae, Ornithomimidae, and Avimimidae form a crown group with an oviraptorosaur-*Microvenator*-*Ornitholestes* clade as the closest sister group; their common sister group consists of an avialan-dromaeosaurid-*Ornitholestes* clade, with dromaeosaurids and *Ornitholestes* forming a monophyletic taxon; Tyrannosauridae and *Coelurus* are the next outgroups within Coelurosauria. Makovicky accepted inclusion of Tyrannosauridae within Coelurosauria and the close relationships between therezinosauroids-oviraptorosaurs and troodontids-orithomimosaurs, respectively, but did not accept the monophyly of Arctometatarsalia.

Chen, Dong and Zhen (1998), in their joint paper describing the Late Jurassic or Early Cretaceous Chinese theropod *Sinosauropteryx prima*, revived the primitive coelurosaurian family Compsognathidae Marsh 1882 to embrace *Sinosauropteryx* and the Late Jurassic European genus *Compsognathus*. Chen *et al.* diagnosed the Compsognathidae by several characters shared by both of these genera, including the following: Premaxillary teeth unserrated, but maxillary teeth serrated; neural spines of dorsal vertebrae fan-shaped;

Holotype skeleton (IVPP 84019) of the medium-sized Middle Jurassic carnosaur *Monolophosaurus jiangi* mounted at Dinofest™, 1998. This species — distinguished by its midline crest, formed by the paired premaxillary, nasal, lacrimal, and frontal bones — is now considered to be a sister taxon to the Allosauroidea.

caudal transverse processes rudimentary or absent; powerful manual phalanx I-1 (diameter of shaft greater than that of radius); pubic boot with limited anterior expansion; and ischium having prominent obturator process.

In a preliminary report, Holtz (1997) proposed a revised phylogenetic analysis of the coelurosaurian family Tyrannosauridae, comprising "the best known and taxonomically most diverse group of large thero-pods of the Late Cretaceous." In this new analysis, Holtz (1997) reached the following conclusions: Monophyly of the Aublysodontinae (including *Alectrosaurus*, *Aublysodon*, and more fragmentary forms) is weakly supported by lack of serrations on premaxillary incisiform teeth, other characters of this subfamily, where they can be evaluated, being plesiomorphic for Tyrannosauridae; remaining tyrannosaurids include the Tyrannosaurinae (*Alioramus*, plus a well

Photograph by the author.

Skeleton of the large Late Jurassic sinraptorid allosauroid *Yangchuanosaurus shangyouensis* at Dinofest™ in 1998. The skeleton has been mounted in an outmoded "tail dragging" rather than a correct horizontal pose.

supported clade consisting of *Albertosaurus, Gorgosaurus, Daspletosaurus,* and *Tyrannosaurus*).

According to Holtz (1997), because of the fragmentary nature of the other tyrannosaurids, "it is only this latter clade which can confidently be diagnosed by the typical 'tyrannosaurid' manual synapomorphies."

Therizinosauroidea and its junior synonyms Enigmosauridae, Segnosauria, and Segnosauridae — an assemblage of unusual, possibly herbivorous taxa known exclusively from the Late Cretaceous of Asia and possibly North America — has been moved about phylogentically over the years, being originally placed within the Theropoda (Perle 1979), somewhere between Prosauropoda and Ornithischia (Paul 1985), and close to "broad-footed sauropodomorphs" (Gauthier 1986), before being referred back again to the Theropoda (Russell and Dong 1993) (see *D:TE* for more details).

Although most authors seem to have accepted the assessment that therizinosaurs are unusual theropods (*e.g.,* Holtz 1996), recently Dong and Yu (1997), in describing the species *Nanshiungosaurus bohlini,* offered a new interpretation of this group that is arguably the most radical one yet proposed. According to Dong and Yu, therizinosaurs [=segnosaurs

of their usage] should be raised to the rank of a new dinosaurian "order," the Segnosaurischia, which can then be subdivided into two distinct families, the Segnosauridae ("segnosaurs" similar to theropods) and the Nanshiungosauridae ("segnosaurs" similar to sauropods). Unfortunately, the authors did not provide details to defend this intriguing assessment. Needless to add, the appearance of a new order, with members resembling both theropods and sauropods as late as the Cretaceous, should present major problems to systematists.

Holtz and Padian (1995) strictly defined Manuraptora*, a taxon within Coelurosauria, as including all descendants of the common ancestor of *Dromaeosaurus* and birds; stem-defined Arctometatarsalia as all coelurosaurs closer to *Ornithomimus* than to

---

Charig and Milner (1997) pointed out that the name Maniraptora (as previously spelled), which was proposed by Gauthier (1986), is etymologically incorrect: "Manus (which is Latin, not Greek as stated by Gauthier), meaning hand, is a fourth-declension feminine noun with the root manu- (see International Code of Zoological Nomenclature, 3rd edition, 1985: 215), not man- as Gauthier obviously supposed. His replacement of the English adjective manual with 'manual,' op. cit., is presumably based on the same incorrect supposition." Charig and Milner proposed that this term be corrected to "Manuraptora."

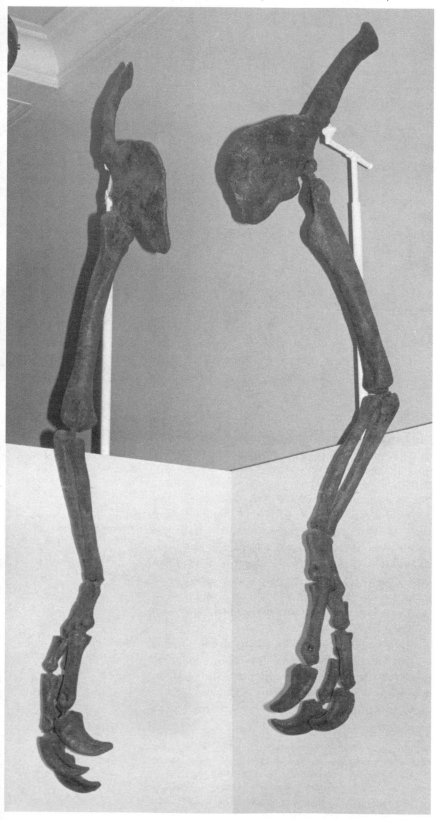

Deinocheirus mirificus, cast of holotype (ZPAL MgD-1/6) shoulder girdles and forelimbs, an apparently giant theropod sometimes regarded as an unusually large member of the Ornithomimidae, or a form possibly related to ornithomimids. However, its true affinities may not be known until more material relating to this enigmatic animal is found and studied.

birds; and identified the node connecting Arctometatarsalia with Manuraptora as the new taxon Manuraptoriformes (Holtz 1995*b*).

More recently, Padian, Hutchinson and Holtz (1997), in pointing out the necessity of maintaining node- or stem-based definitions of taxa for purposes of communication, proposed a nomenclature for the major theropod groups.

According to Padian *et al.*, if *Eoraptor* and Herrerasauridae are regarded as theropods, then the remaining taxa would form the node Neotheropoda.

The assemblage of higher theropods then forms the stems "Ceratosauria" (including Abelisauroidea, all taxa closer to *Carnotaurus* than to "Ceratosauridae") and Tetanurae. Within Tetanurae, the node Avetheropoda consists of the stems Carnosauria (=all taxa closer to *Allosaurus* than to Aves, with the group Allosauroidea, its principal node, comprising the stem-taxa Allosauridae and Sinraptoridae) and Coelurosauria.

According to Padian *et al.* (1997), Coelurosauria includes various basal forms and also Manuraptoriformes, the main stems of which are Arctometatarsalia (=superfamily Tyrannosauroidea plus Bullatosauria [Troodontidae plus Ornithomimosaura], or all taxa closer to *Ornithomimus* than to Aves), Oviraptorosauria (=Therizinosauroidea plus [Oviraptoridae plus Caenagnathidae], or all taxa closer to *Oviraptor* than to Aves), and Manuraptora (all taxa closer to Aves than to *Ornithomimus*). Within Manuraptora, the stem taxa Deinonychosauria (all taxa closer to *Deinonychus* than to Aves) plus Aviale (*Archaeopteryx* and extant birds plus descendants of their most recent common ancestor) are united as a new proposed node which the authors named Eumanuraptora.

Sues (1997), in reassessing the oviraptorosaurian genus *Chirostenotes* (see entry), also reevaluated the families Elmisauridae and Caenagnathidae. Considering the "caenagnathid" genus *Caenagnathus* to be synonymous with the "elmisaurid" *Chirostenotes*, Sues consequently agreed with the earlier suggestion of Currie and Russell (1989) that Elmisauridae should be regarded as a subjective junior synonym of Caenagnathidae. Performing his own cladistic analysis, Sues found that the group Oviraptorosauria includes the families Oviraptoridae and Caenagnathidae; also, preliminary analysis indicated that the taxa Therizinosauroidea and Oviraptorosauria share a sistergroup relationship.

Sues defined Caenagnathidae as including *Chirostenotes pergracilis* (upper Campanian–lower Maastrichtian, Alberta) and *C. elegans* (upper Campanian, Alberta), an as yet unnamed caenagnathid (upper Maastrichtian of North and South Dakota, United States; see Currie, Godfrey and Nessov 1994; Triebold and Russell 1995), *Elmisaurus rarus* (Maastrichtian,

Skeleton (ROM 672) of the giant tyrannosaurid theropod *Gorgosaurus libratus*. Until recently, this Late Cretaceous species was generally regarded as belonging in the genus *Albertosaurus* (see *Albertosaurus* and *Gorgosaurus* entries, *D:TE* and this volume).

Mongolia) [Sues also regarding *Elmisaurus* as possibly synonymous with *Chirostenotes*], *Caenagnathasia martinsoni* (Turonian, Uzbekistan), and their most recent common ancestor.

Sues rediagnosed Caenagnathidae as follows (based on *C. pergracilis*): Antorbital fossa on maxilla with pronounced rim; medial wall of antorbital fossa extensive, without accessory antorbital fenestra; mandible with long, low, undivided external mandibular fenestra; braincase much deeper than long, having distinctly verticalized basicranial region; otic region having deep but anteroposteriorly narrow lateral depression; manual digit III longer than I, with very slender phalanges; synsacrum comprising six coossified vertebrae with pneumatic foramina; proximal end of metatarsal III distinctly constricted, pinched between II and IV.

While redescribing the holotype of *Dryptosaurus aquilunguis* (see *Dryptosaurus* entry), Carpenter, Russell, Baird and Denton (1997) referred the genus *Dryptosaurus* to its own monotypic family, Dryptosauridae Marsh 1890. One of these authors (Denton) believed *Dryptosaurus* to belong within Coelurosauria, while all

four considered this genus to be a probable manuraptoran.

In describing the birdlike theropods *Protarchaeopteryx* and *Caudipteryx*, Ji, Currie, Norell and Ji (1998), through phylogenetic analysis, found both to lie outside Avialae as nonavian coelurosaurs. According to Ji *et al.*, these genera are more primitive than *Archaeopteryx*, the earliest known avialan, representing "stages in the evolution of birds from feathered, ground-living, bipedal dinosaurs." Ji *et al.* joined *Caudipteryx* and *Protarchaeopteryx* to form an unnamed clade within Manuraptura. *Caudipteryx* was found to be the sister taxon to the Avialae; *Protarchaeopteryx* to be unresolved from the Velociraptorinae root. Avialae was found to be monophyletic, this placement "supported by the unequivocal presence of a quadratojugal that is joined to the quadrate by a ligament," "absence of a quadratojugal squamosal contact," "and reduced or absent processes of the ischium." Furthermore, this study indicated to the authors "that feathers are irrelevant in the diagnosis of birds," and that it could "no longer be certain that isolated down and semiplume feathers discovered in

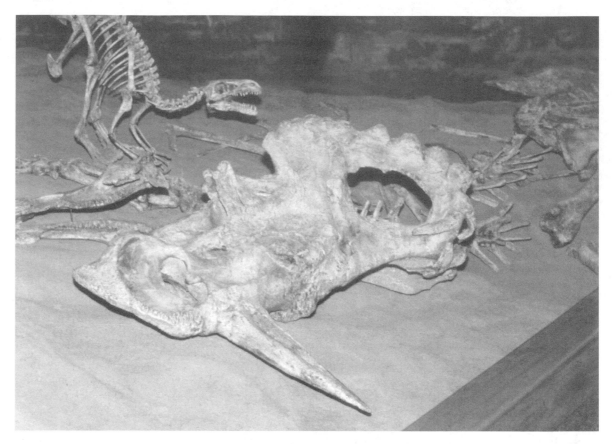

Skeleton of the relatively small dromaeosaurid theropod *Dromaeosaurus albertensis*, mounted over remains of the centrosaurine ceratopsian *Centrosaurus*. Dromaeosaurids are believed to have been active predators that possibly hunted in groups or packs in order to bring down such large prey.

Photograph by the author, courtesy Royal Tyrrell Museum/Alberta Community Development.

Mesozoic rocks belonged to birds rather than to non-avian dinosaurs."

Sauropodomorpha

Gauffre (1995) noted that the very homogeneous postcranial anatomy of members of the Prosauropoda — the more primitive group within the Sauropodomorpha — makes studying the relationships of these dinosaurs no simple task; furthermore, existing cladograms are inaccurate. Gauffre, therefore, proposed a new phylogenetic analysis of the Prosauropoda using lagosuchids, basal sauropods, and *Herrerasaurus* as outgroups.

Gauffre's proposed (but unpublished and not adopted) cladogram for this taxon suggests the following: 1. The Prosauropoda is confirmed to be a monophyletic taxon; 2. the ingroup comprises two monophyletic taxa, the first including two European (*Sellosaurus* and *Plateosaurus*) and two South African genera (*Euskelosaurus* and *Massospondylus*), and one South American genus (*Coloradisaurus*); the second including two Chinese (*Lufengosaurus* and *Yunnanosaurus*) and two North American (*Anchisaurus* and *Ammosaurus*) genera, and one South American genus (*Riojasaurus*); 3. taxa from remote geographical areas (*e.g.*, *Plateosaurus* and *Coloradisaurus*) can be

very close phylogenetically; 4. the temporal extent of close taxa is quite different, indicating that the *Massospondylus*, *Lufengosaurus*, and *Yunnanosaurus* lineages originated in lower Norian times; and 5. prosauropods and sauropods diverged as early as — or earlier than — the first record of either sister group (?early Carnian for prosauropods; see Olsen and Galton 1984; also Gauffre 1993*a*).

Noting the commonly held "assumption that the ancestral saurischian was a relatively small, bipedal, erect, and cursorial animal," Van Heerden (1997) addressed the problem that some light-bodied prosauropods (*e.g.*, *Thecodontosaurus*, *Massospondylus*, and *Anchisaurus*) appear relatively late in the fossil record compared to the heavily built more primitive forms (*e.g.*, *Riojasaurus*, *Euskelosaurus*, and *Melanorosaurus*), all of these forms being known from a somewhat large area in the southern part of Gondwana. Rejecting the notion that this disparity might be the result of preservational or collecting biases, Van Heerden proposed two alternative hypotheses regarding prosauropod systematics:

1. The Prosauropoda is a monophyletic group, stemming from a heavily built, quadrupedal, and possibly herbivorous "thecodontian," which first gave rise to the heavier built prosauropods; and 2. the Prosauropoda is a polyphyletic group, with the more heavily built and more lightly built forms having two

Skeleton (juvenile) of the Early Jurassic melanoro-saurid prosauropod *Lufen-gosaurus hueni* mounted at Dinofest™ in 1998, Phila-delphia. This Chinese species is known from more than 30 specimens, which display an ontogenetic range from juvenile to adult.

Photograph by the author.

separate origins leading from "thecodontians" to dinosaurs. The latter hypothesis would also imply that both the Dinosauria and Saurischia are polyphyletic taxa.

For the present, however, little evidence (P. M. Galton, personal communication 1997) has been offered to support either Gauffre's or Van Heerden's proposals.

Next to the Theropoda, the group undergoing the most extensive revisions is the Sauropoda. This group, while including some of the most well known of all dinosaurian genera, has long been rather poorly understood, especially in regards the relationships between genera and the correct assignment of these genera to higher taxa. In *D:TE*, the systematic breakdown of the Sauropoda was still relatively traditional, including six basic families — Vulcanodontidae, Cetiosauridae (with subfamilies Cetiosaurinae and Shunosaurinae), Brachiosauridae, Camarasauridae (with the subfamilies Camarasaurinae and possibly Opisthocoelicaudinae), Diplodocidae (with the subfamilies Diplodocinae and Dicraeosaurinae), plus the taxon Titanosauria (including the families Andesauridae and Titanosauridae).

Although much work has been done in the past century regarding the classification of these giant dinosaurs and the relationships between the numerous genera and species, none has ever proven to be entirely satisfactory, much of it having been based upon superficial or supposedly diagnostic characters that are not sustained by modern cladistic methods of phylogenetic analysis. Perhaps the Sauropoda has not been as thoroughly studied as much as other groups in the past for sheer practical reasons. For example, skulls of these dinosaurs are rarely preserved, postcranial bones are often extremely heavy and therefore difficult to handle, and much of the type material, some of it restored in plaster, has been mounted for museum display and is virtually inaccessible.

A substantial amount of original work on this group of dinosaurs has been done in just the past few years and continues in an attempt to resolve, at long last, this major problem of sauropod systematics. To date of this writing, a number of new (and sometimes quite radical) phylogenies have been proposed, leaving sauropod classification currently in a rather chaotic state. Sauropod specialist John S. McIntosh (personal communication 1998) disagrees "with many of the recent attempts and to some degree all of them," but has reserved, for the present at least, a detailed critique of any of them. Following, therefore, is a compendium of much of this work, the present writer conservatively noting that at least some of these more recent classifications will probably change yet again in the future.

Based upon earlier work by McIntosh (1990*a*, 1990*b*), Hunt *et al.* (1994) acknowledged eight sauropod families, although at least two of these were regarded as questionable: Barapasauridae (previously considered to be a possible synonym of the Vulcanodontidae) and Cetiosauridae (both of these families regarded by Hunt *et al.* as paraphyletic, based upon plesiomorphic characters), Brachiosauridae, Camarasauridae, Diplodocidae, Euhelopodidae (=Mamenchisauridae; see below), Dicraeosauridae (considered by McIntosh 1990*a*, 1990*b* to be a subfamily of Diplodocidae), and Titanosauridae.

Regarding the Barapasauridae (the name having priority over Vulcanodontidae; see Olshevsky 1991; also Salgado, Coria and Calvo 1997) as a group of primitive sauropods, Hunt *et al.* interpreted the diagnostic characters proposed by McIntosh (1990*b*) for this family as plesiomorphic, observed by him as also occurring in the Prosauropoda, and suggested that all of the perceived sauropod features of this group (*e.g.*, straight rather than sigmoidal femur) may relate to large body size rather than bear any taxonomic significance.

Hunt *et al.* (1994) agreed with Benton (1990) that the relatively primitive family Cetiosauridae is also based upon plesiomorphic characters, and that Shunosaurinae, one of the subfamilies assigned to this taxon, could be the sister group of the Diplodocidae, based on the presence of (possibly synapomorphic) forked chevrons in the midtail caudal vertebrae. Hunt *et al.* considered the Cetiosaurinae and Shunosaurinae, both taxa proposed by McIntosh (1990*b*), to be paraphyletic, with Middle to Upper Jurassic stratigraphic ranges.

Not all workers, however, have agreed that the Cetiosauridae should be abandoned as a valid family. In a preliminary report on the classification of sauropods from Sichuan Basin, China, based on newly obtained data from relatively complete specimens collected during the past 10 years by various Chinese geologists and paleontologists, Zhang and Chen (1996) published the following revised diagnosis of Cetiosauridae: Primitive sauropods of medium to large size; skull relatively low; external nares in dorso-anterior part of skull; orbits broad in midposterior part of skull; lower jaw comparatively slender; teeth of medium size, relatively more teeth in upper and lower jaw; neck not greatly elongate, approximately up to 25 presacral vertebrae; pectoral and pelvic girdles solidly constructed; ilium low; front legs two-thirds to three-fifths length of hind legs; radius three-quarters length of humerus; tibia more than half length of femur.

More than two decades ago, Berman and McIntosh (1978) proposed that the Diplodocidae is a monophyletic taxon; later, McIntosh (1990*b*) divided the Diplodocidae into the subfamilies Diplodocinae, Mamenchisaurinae, and Dicraeosaurinae. This previous interpretation of the Diplodocidae more recently came under the criticism of Hunt *et al.*, who noted that not all of the characters uniting diplodocids are present in every genus referred to this family, and also that these characters essentially only define diplodocines.

Olshevsky (1991) opined that both the Mamenchisaurinae and Dicraeosaurinae should be elevated to family rank, with Mamenchisauridae made a junior synonym of the earlier published taxon Euhelopodidae. Olshevsky's proposal was supported by Russell and Zheng (1993), who described the first cranial material (including a *Euhelopus*-like quadrate) belonging to *Mamenchisaurus*. Russell and Zheng also described *Mamenchisaurus* mandibles that are distinct from those of all diplodocines, having a long tooth row with teeth resembling those of *Brachiosaurus* and *Camarasaurus*.

Citing cranial similarities between *Mamenchisaurus* and *Euhelopus*, Hunt *et al.* proposed that these genera belong in the same family, Euhelopodidae, its members differing from brachiosaurids and camarasaurids in such features as more elongate skulls and a greater number of cervical vertebrae.

In their report, Zhang and Chen accepted the Euhelopodidae [=Mamenchisauridae of their usage] as a valid family, proposing for it the following revised diagnosis: Large to huge sauropods; skull moderately high; teeth spatulate; neck especially elongate, with 19 cervical vertebrae; cervicals long, opisthocoelous; cervical neural spines low, long; hollow structure in side of centra developed; cervical ribs long; 12 dorsal vertebrae, weakly opisthocoelous; dorsal neural spines relatively low, moderately and transversely developed; four sacral vertebrae, the first normal, second to third fused; ilium relatively high, pubic peduncle of ilium situated at middle part of ilium; pubis plate-shaped; ischium slender; forelimbs relatively short; ratio of length of humerus to that of femur about 4.5; ulna equal to three-fifths or four-fifths length of humerus; tibia one-half to two-thirds length of femur. Zhang and Cheng included two genera in this family, *Mamenchisaurus* and *Omeisaurus*.

Hunt *et al.* further suggested that "dicraeosaurs" (including *Nemegtosaurus* and *Quaesitosaurus*, both of which were referred to the new family Nemegtosauridae by Upchurch 1994, and *Antarctosaurus*, usually classified as a titanosaurid) are distinct from all other diplodocids (as defined by McIntosh 1990*b*) "in not increasing the number of cervical vertebrae at the expense of the dorsals." Hunt *et al.* agreed with Olshevsky that the Dicraeosaurinae warrants family status. Furthermore, Hunt *et al.* stated that similar cranial features shared by diplodocids and dicraeosaurids may suggest that these two groups together make up a monophyletic "superfamily" Diplodocoidea, and that the Diplodocidae, Dicraeosauridae, and Euhelopodidae could be united by other synapomorphies (*e.g.*, diplodociform chevrons).

Wilson (1996), in reporting new material pertaining to the sauropod *Amphicoelias* (generally classified as a diplodocine; see entry), conducted a phylogenetic analysis that suggests that the Diplodocoidea is a monophyletic group, with *Amphicoelias* the sister taxon to the Diplodocidae (including *Apatosaurus*, *Barosaurus*, and *Diplodocus*) and Dicraeosauridae (including *Dicraeosaurus* and *Amargasaurus*).

Bonaparte (1996*b*) maintained that the Dicraeosauridae is a valid family of medium-sized sauropods represented by two genera, the Tanzananian *Dicraeosaurus* and Argentinian *Amargasaurus*. As Bonaparte (1996*b*) pointed out, the dorsal vertebrae of these taxa are quite distinct in the following features: Lack of pleurocoels, which seem to be secondarily cancelled; centra proportionally small; the few nonbifurcated dorsal neural spines paddle-shaped; cervical, dorsal, and sacral vertebrae very derived; girdles rather primitive; limb bones blunt.

In describing the new species *Rebbachisaurus tessonei* (see *Rebbachisaurus* entry), Calvo and Salgado (1995) accepted the Diplodocoidea (embracing such taxa as *Apatosaurus* and *Diplodocus*) as a monophyletic clade including *Dicraeosaurus*, but introduced the new taxon Diplodocimorpha to represent a larger clade including *R. tessonei*, Diplodocidae, and all descendants of their common ancestor, this new group considered to be the sister group of the Diplodocoidea.

Calvo and Salgado diagnosed Diplodocimorpha as sauropods sharing the following synapomorphies: 1. Teeth pencil-like; 2. anterior extension of quadratojugal located beyond anterior border of orbit; 3. basipterygoid processes forwardly directed; 4. quadrate inclined posterodorsally; 5. infratemporal fenestra oval or slit-shaped; 6. narial opening located above orbit; 7. "whip-lash" tail; 8. tall neural arch in posterior dorsal vertebrae higher than centra; 8. tall neural arch in caudals, at least 1.5 times higher than centra; 9. tall neural arch in caudal vertebrae, at least 1.5 times higher than centra; 10. wing-like transverse process in caudals; 11. ratio of humerus/femur less than 0.70.

Upchurch (1997) published a preliminary report

of a major new cladistic analysis of sauropod phylogeny utilizing a data-matrix of 205 characters for 26 sauropod taxa. Upchurch's (1997) analysis resulted in two most parsimonious trees, differing only in the relationships between the Chinese genera *Euhelopus*, *Omeisaurus*, and *Mamenchisaurus*.

According to Upchurch's (1997) analysis, the Euhelopodidae constitutes a monophyletic assemblage of Chinese sauropods (including *Shunosaurus*) united by seven synapomorphies (including laterally compressed cranial cervical centra). Euhelopodidae is the sister group to a clade including "cetiosaurids" and the Neosauropoda (see below). The genera *Haplocanthosaurus*, *Cetiosaurus*, and *Patagosaurus* represent successively more distant sister taxa to the Neosauropoda, this again suggesting that the Cetiosauridae is paraphyletic. Neosauropoda subdivides into two clades, the "Brachiosauria" (comprising the broad-nostrilled *Camarasaurus*, brachiosaurids, and titanosaurids) and the Diplodocoidea (including nemegtosaurids, dicraeosaurids, diplodocids, and *Rebbachisaurus*). *Phuwiangosaurus*, from the Lower Cretaceous of Thailand, may be a basal titanosauroid, based on its possession of a robust radius, shortened ischium, as well as other derived features. Titanosauroidea now includes *Opisthocoelicaudia*, at least four apomorphies being present in that genus and *Saltasaurus*, but absent in *Alamosaurus* and other titanosauroids. Upchurch (1997) concluded that some forms, such as *Haplocanthosaurus*, "are influenced by the inclusion or exclusion of certain taxa (*e.g.*, *Rebbachisaurus*) which possess unusual combinations of derived and primitive states," this suggesting that analyses founded upon fewer taxa and characters may reach "spurious results."

Among the sauropods being subjected to the most salient revision since *D:TE* went "to press" are those generally referred to as "titanosaurs," a group that seemed to have originated during the Late Jurassic and persisted into the Late Cretaceous. Previously, the Titanosauria had been subdivided into two families, the more primitive Andesauridae (including the genera *Andesaurus*, *Argentinosaurus*, and *Epachthosaurus*) and the more advanced Titanosauridae (including *Aegyptosaurus*, *Aeolosaurus*, *Alamosaurus*, *Ampelosaurus*, *Argyrosaurus*, *Hypselosaurus*, *Iuticosaurus*, "*Laplatasaurus*" [=*Titanosaurus*], *Loricosaurus*, *Magyarosaurus*, *Neuquensaurus*, *Saltasaurus*, *Titanosaurus*, and possibly *Antarctosaurus* and *Janenschia*).

Recently, Bonaparte (1996*b*) published the following emended diagnosis for the Andesauridae: Titanosaurs with dorsal vertebrae having small pleurocoels located in anterior part of a pleurocoelian, ovoid depression; two or three triangular, deep depressions on lateral side of neural arch; neural arch tall, with elongate neural spine; well-developed hyposphene-hypantrum; amphiplatyan to slight opisthocoelian dorsal vertebrae; central caudal vertebrae (proximal ones unknown) with somewhat short prezygapophysial processes.

Bonaparte (1996*b*) cautioned that while, primarily because of older age, it may be tempting to think of *Andesaurus delgadoi* as ancestral to typical titanosaurids, the presence of procoelian central caudal vertebrae in the Aptian Rayoso Formation "suggests that titanosaur evolution did not follow a linear change in the development of the caudal procoelian and probably of the dorsal opisthocoelian vertebrae, but more probably a mosaic evolution with precocious and delayed lineages." Acknowledging that the Andesauridae could be ancestral to the Titanosauridae, Bonaparte (1996*b*) speculated that titanosaurids differentiated and colonized the Patagonian area and displaced the andesaurids; also, that, historically speaking, the migratory events on the "super-continent" including South America, Africa, and India most likely played an important historical and evolutionary role for which good evidence is scarce.

Earlier, however, Hunt *et al* had noted that the most commonly cited characteristic of the Titanosauridae is the presence of procoelous anterior caudal vertebrae, and pointed out that weakly procoelous anterior caudals are also present in other sauropods (*e.g.*, *Diplodocus*, *Apatosaurus*, and *Bellusaurus*). These authors found more useful synapomorphies of this family to be the transversal expanded ischium (Jacobs, Winkler, Downs and Gomani 1993), as well as the possession of dermal armor.

Among sauropods, the various higher taxa grouping together dinosaurs genera referred to as "titanosaurs" have undergone much recent revision, some of these studies being in conflict with each other:

Two of the most comprehensive examinations of the phylogenetic relationships within the family Titanosauridae were conducted — one by Salgado, Coria and Calvo (1997), a parsimonious cladistic analysis based upon postcranial evidence, the other by Salgado and Calvo (1997), based upon cranial evidence. Although both studies focused upon titanosaurid evolution and the phylogenetic relationships between members of the Titanosauridae, they also brought new and original insights to other groups within

Skeleton of the eusauropod *Bellusaurus sui* exhibited at Dinofest™ in 1998. This species is known from at least 17 rather small specimens, each one that of a juvenile individual (juvenile sauropods being rare in the fossil record).

Photograph by the author.

Sauropoda. Results of these studies yielded a number of "new" sauropod higher-level taxa, including Eusauropoda (see comments below of Wilson and Sereno 1998), Camarasauromorpha, and Titanosauriformes (all proposed by Salgado *et al.*; see below) and some surprising (and also rather controversial) interpretations of former taxa.

In undergoing this analysis, Salgado *et al.* included ten relatively well-known terminal taxa in the ingroup Titanosauria:

Saldago *et al.* newly defined the encompassing taxon Sauropodomorpha as the clade including the most recent common ancestor of Prosauropoda and Sauropoda and all of its descendants. The authors diagnosed this group by the following postcranial synapomorphies: At least 10 moderately elongated cervical vertebrae (Gauthier 1986); metacarpals arched (Sereno 1989); pollex robust, with enlarged ungual (Gauthier 1986); pedal ungual I subequal or longer than all other phalanges (Sereno 1989); ungual of hallux enlarged; hind limbs equal to or shorter than trunk; tibia shorter than femur (all Gauthier 1986); and ascending process of astragalus keyed into descending process of tibia (Benton 1990).

Salgado *et al.* defined the group Sauropoda as the clade including the most recent common ancestor of *Vulcanodon karibaensis* and Eusauropoda and all of its descendants. The authors rediagnosed the Sauropoda by the possession of the following postcranial synapomorphies: Cervical and anterior trunk vertebrae opisthocoelous; at least four sacral vertebrae; ilium with pubic peduncle much longer than ischiatic articulation; femur almost straight in lateral view; and metatarsals shorter than metacarpals. Other probable synapomorphies (12 cervical vertebrae [Gauthier 1986]; carpus and tarsus reduced to one or two elements each [McIntosh 1990*b**] number of manual phalanges greatly reduced [Gauthier 1986]; only manual digit I retaining claw, number of phalanges reduced in pedal digits IV and V [McIntosh 1990*b*]) were not included because of their poorly known distribution among basal sauropods.

Eusauropoda was defined by Salgado *et al.* as the clade including the most recent common ancestor of *Barapasaurus tagorei* and Neosauropoda and all of its descendants. It was diagnosed by at least these two synapomorphies: Femur without anterior trochanter; and anteroposterior diameter of distal end of tibia subequal/greater than distal width.

Neosauropoda, a taxon previously introduced by Bonaparte (1986*a*), was defined by Salgado *et al.* as the clade including the most recent common ancestor of Diplodocidae and Camarasauromorpha and all of its descendants. Neosauropoda was rediagnosed by these authors by two synapomorphies not found in

B. tagorei: Presacral vertebrae with pleurocoels; and at least five sacral vertebrae.[†]

Salgado *et al.* defined Camarasauromorpha as the clade including the most recent common ancestor of Camarasauridae and Titanosauriformes and all of its descendants. The authors diagnosed this group by the following synapomorphies: Posterior trunk and sacral centra opisthocoelous; anterodorsal edge of neural spine placed anteriorly with respect to anterior root of midcaudal postzygapophysis; anterior caudals with open hemal canal; metacarpals relatively long; and ischium with dorsoventrally expanded pubic articulation.

Titanosauriformes was defined by Salgado *et al.* as the clade including the most recent common ancestor of *Brachiosaurus brancai, Chubutisaurus insignis* (see below, also *Brachiosaurus* entry), and Titanosauria and all its descendants. The new taxon was diagnosed by these authors by the following synapomorphies: Presence of medial prespinal lamina in posterior trunk vertebrae; neural arches of mid- and

---

*According to McIntosh (1990*b*), this is the condition for the "typical sauropod carpus," although there are exceptions: Shunosaurus presents three elements, "the larger one covering metacarpals I and II, the smaller, metacarpals II and III"; Lavocat (1955) reported three distal carpals in a large, primitive (Middle Jurassic) sauropod from Madagascar referred by him to "Bothriospondylus"; and the diplodocid Apatosaurus has but one element above metacarpals II and IV, a condition which may or may not be true of other members of its family.*

[†]*J. S. McIntosh (personal communication 1998) cautioned about utilizing the number of sacral vertebrae as a diagnostic character for sauropod classification. According to McIntosh, "The basic sauropodomorph sacrum has two vertebrae, not three (e.g., Riggs 1903*b*, who stated that there are three sacral vertebrae in sauropods). These vertebrae are those numbers '2' and '3' in Diplodocus, Apatosaurus, Camarasaurus, etc. A caudal referred to as a 'caudo-sacral' is early on taken into the sacrum ('no. 4'), followed by a second caudo-sacral ('no. 5'), and finally a 'dorso-sacral' ('no. 1'). In many instances, a second dorso-sacral is added, bringing the total to six. However, when are one of these modified dorsal or caudal vertebrae considered to be a sacral? In juveniles, all sacral centra are free, as are all sacral ribs and the arches except those of the true sacrals, 'nos. 2' and '3.' A suture line is never seen between the postzygapophysis of 'no. 2' and the prezygapophysis of 'no. 3.' The caudo-sacrals become more 'sacrylized' than the dorso-sacral. In most, if not all, Camarasaurus skeletons, the centrum of sacral '1' is not fused to the other four sacrals, even in adults. This vertebra should be considered a sacral because the ribs contribute (weakly) to the sacral yoke. In some old individuals, the still-clearly dorsal-like ribs of dorsal '12' fuse to the ilium. This vertebra should probably not be considered a dorsal, but this is partly a matter of definition. Shunosaurus is said to have four sacrals. The last dorsal might be regarded as a dorsal or may be modified enough to be considered a sacral. It is a matter of degree as to when a vertebra is modified enough to be removed from the dorsals and caudals and put into the sacrum. This modification changes with age in some cases. Assigning a definite 'I' or 'O' to this character is, therefore, very dangerous."*

posterior caudal centra anteriorly positioned; manual digit I with claw reduced or absent; preacetabular lobe of ilium broadly expanded, directed upwardly; pubic peduncle perpendicular to sacral axis; and presence of prominent lateral bulge in femur below greater trochanter.

Included within Titanosauriformes was the newly introduced yet unnamed taxon, designated "Unnamed taxon I" by the authors and including the taxa *Chubutisaurus insignis, Andesaurus delgadoi, Epachthosaurus sciuttoi, Malawisaurus dixeyi, Argentinosaurus huinculensis, Opisthocoelicaudia skarzynskii,* Titanosaurinae indet. (DGM "Serie B," Powell 1986), *Aeolosaurus, Alamosaurus sanjuanensis, Neuquensaurus australis, Saltasaurus loricatus* [*N. australis* plus *S. loricatus* = Saltisaurinae], and all descendants of their most recent common ancestor. This group was diagnosed by Salgado *et al.* by a single synapomorphy: Tibia with distal end broader transversely than anteroposteriorly.

Titanosauria (Bonaparte and Coria 1993), a group originally erected to embrace the families Andesauridae and Titanosauridae (Powell 1986), was redefined by Salgado *et al.* as the clade including the most recent common ancestor of *Andesaurus delgadoi* and the Titanosauridae and all of its descendants. Salgado *et al.* rediagnosed this taxon by the following derived character states: Trunk vertebrae with eye-shaped pleurocoels; posterior trunk vertebrae with ventrally widened, slightly forked infradiapophyseal laminae; presence of centro-parapophyseal lamina in posterior trunk vertebrae; anterior caudal vertebrae procoelous; and pubis considerably longer than ischium.

As the family Andesauridae was found by Salgado *et al.* to be paraphyletic, these authors suggested that it be abandoned.

The monophyletic Titanosauridae was redefined by Salgado *et al,* as including *Epachthosaurus sciuttoi, Malawisaurus dixeyi, Argentinosaurus huinculensis,* Titanosaurinae indet. (DGM "Serie B"), *Opisthocoelicaudia skarzynskii, Aeolosaurus, Alamosaurus sanjuanensis,* and Saltisaurinae and all of its descendants. It was rediagnosed by Salgado *et al.* by these synapomorphies: Absence of hyposphene-hypantrum articulation in posterior trunk vertebrae; six sacral vertebrae; anterior caudals strongly procoelous, with "ball and socket" articular faces*; mid- and posterior caudals strongly procoelous; sternal plates semilunar in shape; absence of claw on manual digit I; manual phalanges absent; and preacetabular lobe of ilium almost horizontal, outwardly projected.[†]

Although cavernous osseous tissue and the possession of dermal armor have been used as criteria to diagnose the Titanosauridae, Salgado *et al.* suggested

that these be abandoned, pointing out that 1. except for the osteoderms assigned to *Saltasaurus loricatus,* this assignment was never unquestionable, and 2. the phylogenetic relevance of the comparative development of cavernous osseous tissue is not clear.

Included within the Titanosauridae were five new taxa, designated by Salgado *et al.* "Unnamed taxon II" through "Unnamed taxon VI." "Unnamed taxon II" was defined by Salgado *et al.* as the clade of derived titanosaurids, including *Argentinosaurus huinculensis, Opisthocoelicaudia skarzynskii,* Titanosaurinae indet. (DGM "Serie B," Powell 1986), ?*Aeolosaurus, Alamosaurus sanjuanensis, Neuquensaurus australis,* and *Saltasaurus loricatus.* The authors diagnosed this group by the following synapomorphies: Medial prespinal lamina formed down to base of neural spine in posterior trunk vertebrae (Bonaparte and Coria 1993) (trunk vertebrae poorly preserved in *Aeolosaurus,* this genus' placement in this group therefore tentative); coracoids quadrangular. "Unnamed taxon III" was defined by the authors as the clade including *Argentinosaurus huinculensis, Opisthocoelicaudia skarzynskii,* Titanosaurinae indet. (DGM "Serie B," Powell 1986). It was diagnosed by the following synapomorphy: Trunk vertebrae with accessory spinodiapophyseal laminae. "Unnamed taxon IV" included *Opisthocoelicaudia skarzynskii* and Titanosaurinae indet. (DGM "Serie B," Powell 1986), and was diagnosed by Salgado *et al.* by the following synapomorphy: Posterior trunk vertebrae without diapo-postzygapophyseal laminae. "Unnamed taxon V" included *Aeolosaurus, Alamosaurus sanjuanensis, Neuquensaurus australis,* and *Saltasaurus loricatus.* Salgado *et al.* diagnosed this group by these synapomorphies: First caudal vertebra biconvex; dorsal prominence present on inner face of scapula.[§] Finally, "Unnamed taxon VI," including *Alamosaurus sanjuanensis, Neuquensaurus australis,* and *Saltasaurus loricatus,* was diagnosed by Salgado *et al.* by the following synapomorphies: Mid- and posterior caudal centra depressed, with dorsoventrally convex lateral faces; pronounced lateral ridge on base of neural arch in midpart of

---

As a consequence of this analysis, Salgado et al. (1997) deduced that the opisthocoelous caudal vertebrae of Opisthocoelicaudia skarzynskii *evolved from a procoelous condition.*

[†]*J. S. McIntosh (personal communication 1998) does not entirely agree with this last criterion, noting that the character is very prominent in taxa from Patagonia and Argentina, but may not be the case for all titanosaurids.*

[§]*According to J. S. McIntosh (personal communication 1998), Powell's 1986 unpublished thesis on the revision of the Titanosauridae of South American figures a very characteristic titanosaurid sacrum from Brazil having a prominent ball on the back of sacral "6." The first caudal vertebra of this dinosaur could not, therefore, have possessed a biconvex centrum.*

tail; and ischium with relatively short posterior process.

Saltisaurinae, a name introduced by Powell (1986), was defined by Salgado *et al.* as the clade including the most recent common ancestor of *Neuquensaurus australis* and *Saltasaurus loricatus*. The authors diagnosed this taxon by the following synapomorphies: Cervical prezygapophyses short, articular facets located near level of diapophyses; anterior caudal centra depressed, with dorsoventrally convex lateral faces; and anterodorsal edge of neural spine located posteriorly relative to anterior root of midcaudal postzygapophyses. The Saltisaurinae seems to be a more restricted group endemic to South America.

From the above study, Salgado *et al.* determined that *Brachiosaurus brancai*, a species traditionally nestled within the long established family named Brachiosauridae (see *Brachiosaurus* entries, *D:TE* and this volume), is the most basal titanosauriform; and that *Chubutisaurus insignis* (previously considered to be a tentative "brachiosaurid") is the sister taxon of the Titanosauria, sharing one apomorphy (distal end of tibia expanded more transversely than anteroposteriorly) with that group. *Opisthocoelicaudia skarzynskii*, which had been tentatively classified as a camarasaurid (see *D:TE*), was reinterpreted by Salgado *et al.* as a titanosaurid, apparently allied to Titanosaurinae indet. (DGM "Serie B") by the absence of diapo-postzygapophyseal laminae.

In the related subsequent study, Salgado and Calvo examined various sauropod skulls — those referred to titanosaurids being mostly fragmentary — in order to determine if that information would corroborate the results that Salgado *et al.* obtained based upon postcranial characters. Specimens examined by Salgado and Calvo included the following: *Diplodocus* sp. (AMNH 696; CM 11161 and 3452), *Camarasaurus lentus* (AMNH 545 and 467; CM 11338), *Apatosaurus* sp. (CM 11162), *Antarctosaurus wichmannianus* (MACN 6904), *Amargasaurus cazaui* (MACN-N 15), *Saltasaurus loricatus* (PVL 4017-161 and 4017-162), and *Pleurocoelus* sp. (UMNH 898).

As Salgado and Calvo related, it had long and traditionally been assumed that titanosaurids possessed what was believed to be a more "advanced" *Diplodocus*-type skull (rather long; external nares located posterodorsally between orbits; peglike teeth restricted to front of mouth; quadrate anteriorly inclined; basioccipital condyle ventrally directed; basipterygoid process slender, anteroventrally oriented) rather than a more "primitive" *Camarasaurus*-type skull (short and high; broad nares separated by premaxilla and nasals; spoon-shaped teeth along entire margins of maxilla and dentary; quadrates almost vertically oriented; basioccipital condyle directed posteroventrally; basipterygoid processes ventrally projecting).

Despite titanosaurid cranial material being extremely rare and fragmentary, Salgado and Calvo reinterpreted the titanosaurid skull as actually being *Camarasaurus*-like, but having peglike teeth restricted to the extremity of the jaws, and exhibiting wear facets that are sharply inclined relative to the labio-lingual axis.[*] As the latter character is shared with *Brachiosaurus altithorax* and *Pleurocoelus* (both classified as brachiosaurids), this character was interpreted by the authors as a probable synapomorphy of Titanosauriformes.

Several characters (including long recurved paroccipital processes becoming slender downwards; reduced, narrow supratemporal fenestra) were regarded by Salgado and Calvo as synapomorphies of Titanosauria or of a less inclusive group, or as synapomorphies (teeth peglike; teeth restricted to anterior region of snout; mandibular symphysis perpendicular to long axis of lower jaw) within Titanosauridae.

In reexamining the skulls of *Nemegtosaurus mongoliensis* (see *Nemegtosaurus* entries, *D:TE* and this volume) and *Quaesitosaurus orientalis*, Salgado and Calvo found them to be more *Camarasaurus*-like than *Diplodocus*-like, as had previously been supposed, possessing various characters (see *Nemegtosaurus* entry) indicating that these taxa are related to the Titanosauridae rather than to the Diplodocidae, or the Dicraeosauridae as had previously been believed.

Salgado *et al.*, and Salgado and Calvo, determined that *Vulcanodon* and *Barapasaurus* do not belong in a single family, and agreed with various other recent workers that the Cetiosauridae is a paraphyletic group that should be abandoned.

In turn, the Brachiosauridae, a family long regarded as valid, was found by these authors to be an unnatural assemblage of basal sauropods, basal titaniforms, and basal titanosaurs, including numerous poorly represented forms, many of them incorrectly linked together based upon characters that are actually synapomorphies of Titanosauriformes. Other characters (*e.g.*, opisthocoelous dorsal centra; probably relatively elongated forelimbs) used to include various taxa (*e.g.*, *Bothriospondylus*, *Lapparentosaurus*, *Volkheimeria*, and *Ischyrosaurus*) in the Brachiosauridae are plesiomorphic for the Titanosauriformes.

---

[*]As observed by J. S. McIntosh (personal communication 1998), the well-preserved "titanosaur skull" found in March 1997 by paleontologist Rubén Darío Martínez in the Upper Cretaceous of Chubut Province, Patagonia, shown in a photograph published in the December 1997 issue of National Geographic, *is, if correctly identified, generally diplodocid with broad teeth (see Clark 1997).*

Concerning various taxa that had generally been regarded as brachiosaurids or possible brachiosaurids (see *D:TE*, respective entries), Salgado and Calvo found the following: *Brachiosaurus* (see entries, *D:TE* and this volume) was regarded as a basal titanosauriform, some of the characters previously used to diagnose this genus found to be synapomorphies of the Titanosauriformes. No evidence supported the inclusion of type species *Bothriospondylus suffosus* and referred species "*B.*" *madagascariensis* in a single genus, nor were synapomorphies found to support either of their inclusion within the Titanosauriformes. *Pelorosaurus conybeari*, *P. mackensoni*, and "*Bothriospondylus*" *nougaredi* were all regarded as titanosauriforms close to titanosaurs and basal titanosaurs. Also considered to be a titanosauriform was *Macrurosaurus*. The five specimens (QM F3390, F6737, F7291, F7292, and F7880) referred by Coombs and Molnar (1981) to *Austrosaurus* sp., exhibit several synapomorphies of the Titanosauriformes (*e.g.*, caudal neural arches forwardly displaced; femur with pronounced lateral bulge); the character of relatively long metacarpals is shared with other camarasauromorphs. *Iuticosaurus valdensis* [="*Titanosaurus*" *valdensis* of their usage], from the Barremian of the Isle of Wight, was regarded as probably the oldest of known titanosaurids, suggesting a probable European origin for the Titanosauridae.

The above phylogeny, however, has proven to be controversial as well as innovative. For example, Wilson and Sereno (1998), in their major, comprehensive monograph on the early evolution and higher-level phylogeny of sauropods, criticized the phylogenetic study of Salgado *et al.* on numerous issues, among these the following: Many of the conclusions reached by Selgado *et al.* were founded upon sparse evidence, some of the clades within Titanosauria being supported by only a single character. Also, Eusauropoda, *contra* Salgado *et al.*, is not a new taxon but a name introduced by Upchurch (1995), for a group in-

Femur (QM F3390), one of five specimens referred to the titanosauriform sauropod *Austrosaurus* sp. (After Coombs and Molnar 1981).

cluding *Shunosaurus* (and other "euhelopodids") plus Neosauropoda. Upchurch's original stem-based definition of Eusauropoda was a monophyletic assemblage including all sauropods except for vulcanodontids (Upchurch's definition being the one followed by Wilson and Sereno in their study). According to Wilson and Sereno, the major contribution of Salgado *et al.* in their analysis was "the proposal of and support for Titanosauriformes," a novel arrangement that includes *Brachiosaurus* and Titanosauria.

Wilson and Sereno defined Sauropoda (known temporal range: earliest Jurassic [Hettangian] to latest Cretaceous [Maastrichtian]) as sauropodomorphs more closely related to the genus *Saltasaurus* than to the prosauropod genus *Plateosaurus*. These authors diagnosed Sauropoda by the following characters: Obligatory quadrupedal posture with columnar orientation of principal limb bones (humerus, radius-ulna, femur, and tibia-fibula); four or more sacral vertebrae (one caudosacral added); humerus with low deltopectoral crest; olecranon absent; proximal end of ulna triradiate; distal end of radius subrectangular, posterior margin for ulna flattened; ilium having low ischial peduncle; ischial blade equal to or longer than pubic blade; ischial shafts having dorsoventrally flattened distal ends; cross section of femur eliptical (with transverse long axis); fourth trochanter of femur reduced to low crest or ridge; astragalus lacking anterior fossa and foramina at base of ascending process; distal tarsals 3 and 4 absent (no ossified distal tarsals); proximal ends of metatarsals I and V subequal in area to that of metatarsals II and IV; metatarsal V 70 percent or more of length of IV; ungual of pedal digit I enlarged, deep, narrow (sickle-shaped).

Wilson and Sereno's cladistic analysis of the Sauropoda, focusing upon the higher-level relationships within this group, was based upon 109 characters (32 cranial, 24 axial, and 53 appendicular) for 10 sauropod taxa, the latter "selected for analysis on the basis of completeness and as a representative sample of sauropod morphology." The most parsimonious arrangement of these taxa resulted as follows: Four genera — *Vulcanodon*, *Shunosaurus*, *Barapasaurus*, and *Omeisaurus*, the latter three included in the group Eusauropoda — were positioned as a sequence of sister taxa to the Neosauropoda, a group of advanced sauropods.

Basically following Upchurch work, Eusauropoda (known temporal range: Early Jurassic [Pliensbachian] to latest Cretaceous [Maastrichtian]) was defined by Wilson and Sereno as sauropods more closely related to *Saltasaurus* than to *Vulcanodon*. Eusauropoda was diagnosed by these authors as follows: External nares retracted posterodorsally; snout having stepped narial margin; absence of antorbital fossa; maxillary border of external naris long; absence of anterior process of prefrontal; absence of squamosal-quadratojugal contact; anterior ramus of quadratojugal elongate, distally expanded; infraorbital region of cranium shortened anteroposteriorly; supratemporal region of cranium shortened anteroposteriorly; supratemporal fossa broadly expanded laterally; quadrate shaft having elongate posterior fossa; lateral ramus of palatine narrow; maximum depth of anterior end of dentary ramus about 150 percent minimum depth of ramus; tooth rows broadly arched anteriorly; tooth crowns spatulate; enamel having wrinkled texture; crown overlap; crown-to-crown occlusion precise; V-shaped wear facets (interdigitating occlusion); at least 13 cervical vertebrae; cervical centra opisthocoelous; midcervical neural arches tall (height greater than posterior face of centrum); dorsal neural spines broader transversely than anteroposteriorly; distal chevrons having anterior and posterior processes; carpals block-shaped; phalanges on manual digits II and III reduced (II-ungual, III-3 and ungual absent; manual phalangeal formula 2-2-2-2-2 or lower); manual phalanges (except for unguals) broader than long; iliac blade having semicircular dorsal margin and expanded preacetabular process; pubic apron canted posteromedially; tibia with laterally projecting cnemial crest; posteroventral process of tibia reduced; fibula having lateral trochanter; length of metatarsal III 25 percent or less that of tibia; minimum shaft width of metatarsal I greater than that of metatarsals II–IV; metatarsals with spreading configuration; nonterminal phalanges of pedal digits short; ungual of pedal digit I longer than metatarsal I; penultimate phalanges of pedal digits II–IV rudimentary or absent; unguals of pedal digits II–III sickle-shaped; ungual of pedal digit IV rudimentary or absent.

Barapasaurus, *Omeisaurus*, and Neosauropoda were grouped together by Wilson and Sereno as an unnamed assemblage (known temporal range: Early Jurassic [Pliensbachian] to latest Cretaceous [Maastrichtian]), diagnosed as follows: Posterior cervical and anterior dorsal neural arches having interprezygapophyseal laminae; anterior dorsal centra opisthocoelous; middle and posterior neural arches having composite lateral laminae (spinodiapophyseal plus supraprezygapophyseal); sacricostal yoke; fibula with triangular articular scar for tibia; astragalar posterior fossa divided by crest; pedal ungual asymmetrical.

Wilson and Sereno united *Omeisaurus* and Neosauropoda as an unnamed assemblage (known temporal range: Late Jurassic [Oxfordian] to latest Cretaceous [Maastrichtian]), diagnosed as follows: Frontal excluded from supratemporal fossa; supratemporal fossa transversely oriented; 17 or fewer dentary teeth; presacral pleurocoels deep, invaginated; cervical pleurocoels divided; 12 or fewer dorsal vertebrae; five or more sacral vertebrae (at least one dorsosacral added); shafts of cervical ribs positioned below centra; acromion more than 150 percent of minimum width of scapular blade; metatarsals III and IV having minimum transverse shaft diameters 65 percent or less than that of metatarsals I and II.

Neosauropoda (known temporal range: Late Jurassic [Oxfordian] to latest Cretaceous [Maastrichtian]) was defined by Wilson and Sereno as *Diplodocus*, *Saltasaurus*, their common ancestor, and all its descendants, including Diplodocoidea and a new taxon, Macronaria. These authors diagnosed Neosauropoda as follows: Preantorbital fenestra developed; ventral process of postorbital broader transversely than anteroposteriorly; lack of jugal-ectopterygoid contact; external mandibular fenestra closed; tooth crowns lacking denticles; two or fewer carpal elements; metacarpals bound, having long intermetacarpal articular surfaces; metacarpus having U-shaped proximal articular surface (270-degree arc); ilia preacetabular process laterally divergent; proximal end of tibia subcircular; astragalus with ascending process extending to posterior margin; astragalus wedge-shaped in anterior view.

Diplodocoidea (including Diplodocimorpha; known temporal range: Late Jurassic [Kimmeridgian] to Early Cretaceous [Hauterivian], possibly Late Cretaceous [Campanian–Maastrichtian]) was defined by Wilson and Sereno as neosauropods more closely related to *Diplodocus* than to *Saltasaurus*, including *Rayososaurus*, *Amphicoelias*, dicraeosaurids, and diplodocids. These authors diagnosed the taxon by the following synapomorphies: Dentary having ventrally projecting "chin" and transversely narrow symphysis; subcylindrical tooth crowns; narrow subcylindrical basipterygoid process (length at least four times basal diameter) that project anteroventrally or anteriorly; atlantal intercentrum having anteroventrally expanded occipital fossa; cervical ribs shorter than their respective centra; arches of dorsal and caudal vertebrae tall (more than two and one-half times length of dorsoventral centrum height); whiplash tail (at least 30 elongate, biconvex posterior caudal vertebrae).

Wilson and Sereno introduced the new taxon Macronaria (know temporal range: Late Jurassic [Kimmeridgian] to latest Cretaceous [Maastrichtian]), defined as a clade including neosauropods more closely related to *Saltasaurus* than to *Diplodocus* (i.e., ?*Haplocanthosaurus*, *Camarasaurus*, and Titanosauriformes. The authors diagnosed Macronaria as follows: Middle and posterior dorsal neural spines having transversely flared distal ends; chevrons with open proximal articulations; distal ischial shafts coplanar.

Camarasaurus and Titanosauriformes (known temporal range: Late Jurassic [Kimmeridgian] to latest

Cretaceus [Maastrichtian]) were combined into an unnamed assemblage, diagnosed by Wilson and Sereno as follows: Maximum diameter of naris greater than maximum diameter or orbit; quadrate fossa deep; depth of surangular more than twice that of angular; opisthocoelous posterior dorsal centra; length of longest metacarpal 45 percent more than that of radius; metacarpal I longer than metacarpal IV; puboischial contact deep dorsoventrally.

Titanosauriformes (known temporal range: Late Jurassic [Kimmeridgian] to latest Cretaceous [Maastrichtian]) was defined by Wilson and Sereno as *Brachiosaurus*, *Saltasaurus*, their common ancestor, and all of its descendants, including Brachiosauridae and the new taxon Somphospondyli. These authors diagnosed Titanosauriformes as follows: Pterygoid lacking dorsomedially oriented basipterygoid hook; dorsal ribs having pneumatic cavities; distal condyle of metacarpal I undivided, with reduced articular surface; iliac preacetabular process semicircular; proximal one-third of femoral shaft deflected medially.

Restoring the family Brachiosauridae (known temporal range: Late Jurassic [Kimmeridgian] to Early Cretaceous [?Albian]), Wilson and Sereno defined this taxon as titanosauriforms more closely related to *Brachiosaurus* than to *Saltasaurus*, including the French "*Bothriospondylus*" *madagascariensis* (but excluding *Bothriospondylus* material from Madagascar), *Brachiosaurus*, "*Eucamerotus*" [=*Chondrosteosaurus*], and *Pleurocoelus*. Wilson and Sereno diagnosed Brachiosauridae by the following synapomorphies: Muzzle subrectangular (twice as long as deep); cervical centra elongate (attaining maximum of seven times as long as deep); centra having deep accessory depressions; humerus elongate (subequal to femur in length); humerus having prominent deltopectoral crest.

Somphospondyli (known temporal range: Late Jurassic [Kimmeridgian] to latest Cretaceous [Maastrichtian]) was defined by Wilson and Sereno as titanosauriforms more closely related to *Saltasaurus* than to *Brachiosaurus*, uniting *Euhelopus* and Titanosauria. This new taxon was diagnosed by the authors as follows: Cervical neural arches having reduced lamination; presacral vertebrae composed of spongy bone; anterior and middorsal neural spines posteroventrally inclined; six sacral vertebrae (one dorsosacral vertebra added); scapular glenoid deflected medially.

Titanosauria (known temporal range: Late Jurassic [Kimmeridgian] to Late Cretaceous [Maastrichtian]) was defined by Wilson and Sereno as titanosauriforms more closely related to *Saltasaurus* than to *Brachiosaurus* or *Euhelopus* (for the present, this definition including *Aeolosaurus*, *Alamosaurus*, *Ampelosaurus*, *Andesaurus*, *Argentinosaurus*, *Epachtho-saurus*, *Magyarosaurus*, *Malawisaurus*, *Nemegtosaurus*, *Neuquensaurus*, *Opisthocoelicaudia*, and *Saltasaurus*). The authors diagnosed Titanosauria as follows: Anterior caudal centra having prominently convex (hemispherical) posterior face; anterior and middle caudal vertebrae with prespinal and postspinal laminae; sternal plates having strongly concave lateral margins; ulna with prominent olecranon process; carpals unossified or absent; ischium longer than pubis.

From the above study, Wilson and Sereno noted that traditional characters previously supporting a diplodocoid-titanosaur sister-group relationship (*e.g.*, cylindrical tooth crowns, procoelous anterior caudal centra, and unossified calcanea) are homoplastic, having appeared independently in these and also other sauropod lineages. Indeed, "the distribution of several classic sauropod features" were shown to be homoplastic, appearing independently in a number of sauropod subgroups, these including narrow tooth crown proportions, bifid neural spines, elongate cervical centra, and increased length and numbers of cervicals.

Also perceived from the above study was "the evolutionary sequence of many functionally significant sauropod adaptations." According to Wilson and Sereno, sauropods were characterized early in their evolution by appendicular adaptations that facilitated the columnar support of great weight. Specializations in the teeth (*e.g.*, interlocking and overlapping crowns; V-shaped wear facets) are present in basal sauropods and modified further (*e.g.*, loss of overlapping crowns, narrow crown proportions, reduction in number of teeth) in some subgroups, the latter occurring before the Late Jurassic well preceding the Cretaceous diversification of angiosperms. Early in their evolution, sauropods increased the lengths of their necks by incorporating two trunk vertebrae into the neck (thereby moving the shoulder girdle posteriorly) and adding one cervical. Specific sauropod subgroups further increased their neck length via at least seven events in their evolution, these also including the lengthening of cervical vertebrae.

As Wilson and Sereno pointed out, the fossil record shows that sauropods originated during the Middle Jurassic period. All major sauropod clades were established before the Late Jurassic, a time when substantial faunal interchange was yet possible among major continental regions. Furthermore, an initially global distribution of neosauropods in the Late Jurassic seems to have continued without the influence of continental fragmentation, their "lineages flourishing and diversifying in some areas and decreasing in diversity or becoming extinct in others."

However, even as Wilson and Sereno's phylogeny was awaiting publication, yet another analysis of the

Titanosauria was being prepared by Elizabeth M. Gomani. In an abstract for an intended paper presenting new information concerning the titanosaurid *Malawisaurus* (see entry, *D:TE* and this volume), and taking the data regarding that genus into consideration, Gomani (1998) diagnosed Titanosauria by the following features: Paroccipital processes short, dorsoventrally curved; osteoderms; six sacral vertebrae; anterior caudal centra strongly procoelous; olecranon process of ulna projecting above proximal articulation; ischial blade expanded; puboischial contact dorsoventrally extended.

Based on her preliminary cladistic analysis of sauropods and incorporating the new information pertaining to *Malawisaurus*, Gomani concluded that *Janenschia* is the most basal titanosaurian; that *Malawisaurus*, *Andesaurus*, and *Epachthosaurus* form a clade with *Malawisaurus*, supported by the possession of shallow dorsal pleurocoels and rudimentary cervical neural arches, occupying the most basal position in that group; and that *Aeolosaurus*, *Opisthocoelicaudia* plus *Titanosaurus*, and a clade including *Alamosaurus* plus *Neuquensaurus* and *Saltasaurus* make up an unresolved trichotomy.

Ornithischia

Thyreophora

For more than two decades, the Ankylosauria, a group of armored dinosaurs belonging to the ornithischian group Thyreophora, has been neatly subdivided into two families (see Coombs 1978) — the more primitive Nodosauridae (characterized by such features as a longer, pear-shaped head surmounted by bony plates, dermal plates arranged in transverse bands along the neck back and tail, and an upright body, some genera possessing outward-projecting lateral spines) and the more advanced Ankylosauridae (distinctive features including a triangular head bearing horns, a robust body, some genera possessing cone-shaped dorsal spines, and a tail terminating in a club).

Based on features seen in more recently collected ankylosaurian specimens, including remains of a new genus that would later be named *Gastonia* (see entry) by Kirkland in 1998, *Polacanthus*, and *Mymoorapelta maysi*, Kirkland (1996), in a preliminary report, proposed that a third family, the resurrected Polacanthidae Wieland 1911, embrace these three taxa, which were considered by him to be most ornate of all known ankylosaurs. Kirkland (1996) described this clade as possessing a "chimera of ankylosaurid and nodosaurid characters," and distinguished by the possession of grooved shoulder spines (a primitive character; K. Carpenter, personal communication 1997), hollow-based triangular caudal plates, a sacral shield of fully fused armor, and also what Kirkland (1996) then identified as a spinelike or "proto tail" club.

From patterns observed earlier by Kirkland and Carpenter (1994) in a specimen of *M. maysi*, Kirkland suggested that advanced members of the Polacanthidae possessed large, erect shoulder spines in addition to the lateral shoulder spines, as well as laterally extending spines and platelike elements common to all of the group's members. Caudal plates are present along the sides of the tail. The tail's perceived "protoclub," Kirkland speculated, was most likely a defensive weapon, as evidenced by adaptations for tail swinging. Kirkland further theorized that some members of this group, those possessing forward directed eyes (unlike the new ankylosaur that would be named *Gargoyleosaurus*, described by Carpenter in 1998; see entry and below), probably used their necks and shoulder spines for both display purposes and in intraspecific shoving matches.

Carpenter, Kirkland, Miles, Cloward and Burge (1996) (also other authors, *e.g.*, Vickaryous and Ryan 1997), in a later preliminary report (that mentioned the still unnamed *Gastonia* and *Gargoyleosaurus*), decided that this group does not warrant family status, but should be regarded as Polacanthinae Wieland 1911, a subfamily of the Nodosauridae. According to Carpenter *et al.* (1996), both new genera, as well as *Mymoorapelta*, share features in common with nodosaurids (*e.g.*, lateral temporal opening visible in lateral aspect; occipital condyle without neck; laterally projecting neck, body, and tail spines; prominent scapular spine or pseudoacromion process) and ankylosaurids (asymmetrical skull armor; caudolateral cranial and jugal horns; no ridge separating cutting edge of beak and maxillary tooth row; broad postocular shelf). Both taxa share "a uniquely derived notch in the anterior part of the premaxillary beak"; *Gargoyleosaurus* possesses premaxillary teeth and an elongated premaxillary scoop (characters considered plesiomorphic for the Ankylosauria); spiny armor found associated with *Gastonia* and fused sacral armor in *Mymoorapelta* indicate close relationships with *Polacanthus*; and *Polacanthus* seemed to possess a small incipient tail club, implying affinities with ankylosaurids rather than nodosaurids. Carpenter *et al.* suggested that both of these new taxa, and perhaps *Mymoorapelta*, are united with *Polacanthus* in the Polacanthinae. This clade represents various highly ornate genera, with ankylosaurid-like heads and nodosaurid-like bodies, known from Europe and North America, spanning the Late Jurassic through Early Cretaceous.

More recently, Kirkland (1998*a*), in formally

Paleontologists Harley G. Armstrong *(left)* and James I. Kirkland *(right)* examine dermal armor (MWC collection) of *Mymoorapelta maysi*, an ankylosaur from the Upper Jurassic Morrison Formation, at the Museum of Western Colorado.

naming and describing *Gastonia*, conducted a preliminary analysis of the Polacanthinae. Although Kirkland (1998a) noted that members of this clade exhibit characters indicative of both the Nodosauridae and Ankylosauridae, as well as others outside of these two families, this analysis supported the idea that the Polacanthinae is a monophyletic group belonging not to the Nodosauridae, as previously surmised, but to the Ankylosauridae, and located at the base of the latter group. Polacanthinae was found at this time to be the most primitive subfamily within the Ankylosauria and the sister group to the more primitive clade Shamosaurinae Tumanova 1983 (including the Early Cretaceous Mongolian genus *Shamosaurus* and various new taxa to be named by Kirkland and Carpenter), although Kirkland subsequently suspected that Polacanthinae may be the more primitive group (J. I. Kirkland, personal communi-

cation 1998). Both of these subfamilies were found to be successive sister groups to other taxa (the genus *Tsagantegia*, the genus *Pinacosaurus*, an unnamed clade including *Saichania* and *Tarchia*, and an unnamed clade including *Euoplocephalus* and *Ankylosaurus*, respectively) belonging to the Ankylosauridae. (According to J. I. Kirkland, personal communication 1998, these remaining ankylosaurid genera — with the probable exception of *Tsagantegia*, which has a simple narial structure and seems to lack a tail club — may, for now at least, be grouped together into their own subfamily, Ankylosaurinae, a taxon proposed by Baron Franz Nopcsa in 1918.)

Kirkland (1998a) diagnosed the Polacanthinae as follows: Ankylosaurid-like skull, almost straight, with parallel tooth rows, long basipterygoid processes; scapula having well-developed acromion flange arising from dorsal margin of scapula, ischia with ventral

Photograph by the author, courtesy
Natural History Museum of Los Angeles County.

Reconstructed partial skeleton (LACM 3719/16440) of
the most derived stego-
saurid thyreophoran genus
Stegosaurus, referred to the
species *S. stenops.*

flexion at midlength as in Nodosauridae; armor including sacral shield of fused (not sutured) elements; elongate, posteriorly grooved shoulder spines; large, elongate, laterally directed, symmetrically-hollow-based, triangular caudal plates extending down the tail.

To this clade, Kirkland (1998a) referred the Early Cretaceous genera *Polacanthus*, *Hoplitosaurus*, and *Gastonia*, the Jurassic *Mymoorapelta*, possibly the Early Cretaceous *Hylaeosaurus*, and also possibly the Late Jurassic *Gargoyleosaurus* (J. I. Kirkland, personal communication, 1998).

Ornithopoda

As previously discussed (see *D:TE*), the Fabrosauridae, once regarded as a group of basal ornithopods including a number of genera, was later considered by various workers to be an unnatural, paraphyletic grouping (see Sereno 1986; Gauthier 1986; Weishampel and Witmer 1990).

More recently, however, following Peng's (1990) description of the Middle Jurassic primitive ornithischian *Agilisaurus louderbacki* (see *D:TE*), founded upon a beautifully-preserved, almost complete skeleton (ZDM6011), Peng (1997) reinstated Fabrosauridae as a valid family representing a group of "small, unarmored, and most primitive-looking ornithischians yet discovered," these dinosaurs occurring in the

Upper Triassic through Early Jurassic of Africa and the Middle to Upper Jurassic of China.

Peng (1997) regarded the Fabrosauridae (embracing *Fabrosaurus*, *Agilisaurus*, and probably *Gongbusaurus*, the latter genus seemingly more closely related to *Agilisaurus* than to the former) as a monophyletic taxon diagnosed by the following unequivocal synapomorphies: 1. Lacrimal inserting into narrow slot in apex of maxilla; 2. mandible with peculiarly salient finger-like retroarticular process; 3. particularly short forelimb, approximately 40 percent length of hind limb; 4. ilium having supra-acetabular flange over anterior half of acetabulum; 5. posterior process of ilium having distinctive brevis shelf that first turns medially, then downwards; 6. ischium with dorsal groove on proximal shaft; and 7. reduced pedal digit I, having splintlike shaft of metatarsal I and ungual extending just beyond end of metatarsal II.

Peng (1997) considered fabrosaurids to be unique in their tooth morphology and structure, differing from prosauropods in having a less symmetrical tooth crown, with fewer erect denticles of unvarying size on both anterior and posterior edges. Fabrosaurid teeth differ from those of other primitive ornithischians (*e.g.*, heterodontosaurids and hypsilophodontids) in being thinly and uniformly enameled on both sides, each having a single round central vertical ridge.

Restored skeleton (cast) of *Xiaosaurus dashanpensis*, an ornithischian of uncertain affinities from China, displayed at Dinofest™ in 1998.

Photograph by the author.

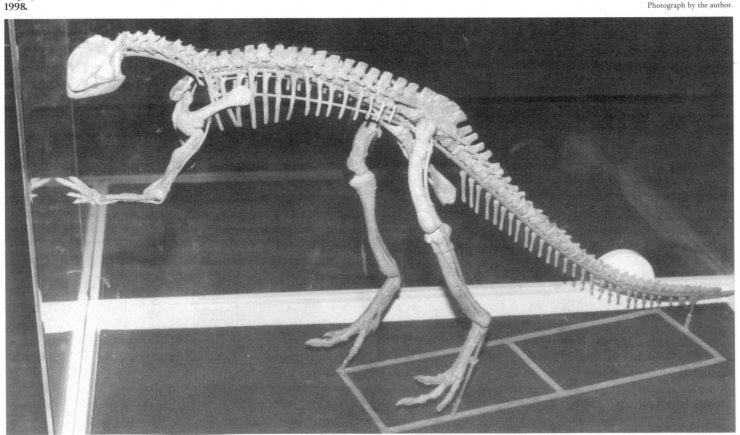

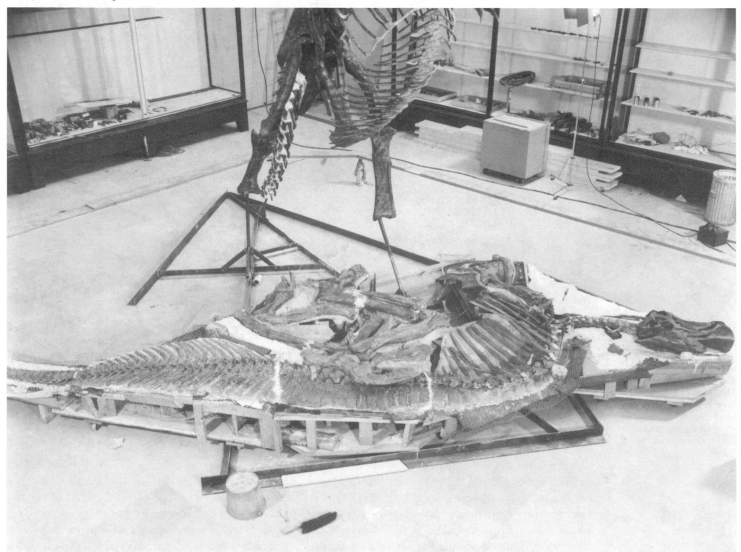

Peng (1997) described fabrosaurids as small (1- or 2-meters in length) dinosaurs having a triangular, largely fenestrated skull with large laterally placed orbits (indicating large eyes). Fabrosaurids may have possessed a horny beak (suggested by the position of the first maxillary tooth, set back slightly from the tip of the premaxilla, and the general structure of this area), the lower beak fitting inside the upper one to form an effective cropping instrument. The form of the teeth and structure of the jaws show only vertical jaw mechanism, the simplest among known ornithischians.

As Peng (1997) observed, fabrosaurids possess a very lightly constructed skeleton, with very short neck and trunk, and a long tail making up almost half of the body length. The limb bones are slender and hollow, possessing thin walls. The forelimbs, terminating in a very small manus, are only about 40 percent the length of the hind limbs. These features indicate bipedality, the tail presumably used as a counterbalance for the body weight during locomotion and to compensate for shifts in the center of gravity. Furthermore, the tibia considerably exceeding the femur in length and metatarsal III being greater in length than half the femur suggest that fabrosaurids were cursorial.

Winkler, Murry and Jacobs (1997), in interpreting their new ornithopod species *Tenontosaurus dossi* (see *Tenontosaurus* entry), proposed that two of the characters—width of frontal and ossified hypaxial tendons—previously used to support a monophyletic Hypsilophodontidae should be removed from the diagnosis of this family, noting that they are also found in the Iguanodontian genus *Tenontosaurus*.

Furthermore, Winkler *et al.* suggested that several key synapomorphies (*e.g.*, loss of premaxillary teeth, single ventral predentary process) used to define the base of Iguanodontia be likewise removed, as these

Almost complete articulated skeleton (FMNH PR380; skull of another individual, FMNH PR1479) of the lambeosaurine hadrosaurid *Lambeosaurus lambei* under preparation for display in 1956 at the (then named) Chicago Natural History Museum. The skeleton, found in a death pose, was collected by Elmer S. Riggs, George F. Sternberg, and J. B. Abbott during the Marshall Field Exhibition to Alberta, Canada, in 1922. It was given to the museum in 1947 by the University of Chicago.

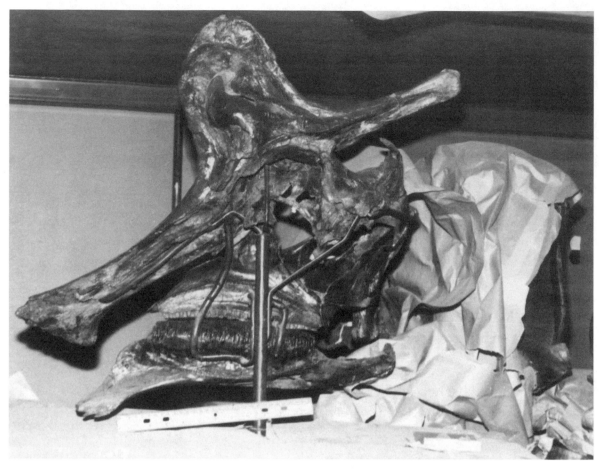

Lambeosaurus lambei, holotype incomplete skull (CMN [formerly NMC] 2869), left lateral view. This Late Cretaceous lambeosaurine hadrosaurid is known from a number of good specimens, representing juveniles to adults.

characters are also found in *Tenontosaurus*, unless the genus is removed from this group (see below).

In naming and describing the new basal iguanodontian *Gasparinisaura cincosaltensis* (see *Gasparinisaura* entry), Coria and Salgado (1996) erected the new taxon, Euiguanodontia, to embrace an assemblage of Late Jurassic–Late Cretaceous ornithopods. Coria and Salgado defined this new taxon as comprising *Gasparinisaura* plus Dryomorpha [=Dryosauridae plus Iguanodontidae plus Hadrosauridae], but excluding *Tenontosaurus* and all other ornithopods.

The Euiguanodontia was diagnosed by Coria and Salgado as including ornithopods sharing these unequivocal synapomorphies: Jugal-postorbital articulation facing laterally; maxillary teeth with prominent lateral primary ridge; brevis shelf well-developed; and metatarsal I reduced or absent.

Coria and Salgado accepted as valid the taxa Euornithopoda Sereno 1986, defined by them as including the Hypsilophodontidae and Iguanodontia, and Ankylopollexia Sereno 1986, the latter including iguanodontians more advanced than dryosaurids.

Forster (1997), in a preliminary report, stated that the Iguanodontia plus Hadrosauridae form a diverse, almost globally distributed clade of Late Jurassic–Late Cretaceous ornithopods. A cladistic analysis by Forster confirmed that the "Iguanodontia forms a paraphyletic assemblage of taxa spread along the branch leading to Hadrosauridae," with no subclades perceived within iguanodontians. Forster's analysis revealed "a sequence of character transformation with a low level of homoplasy appearing up through the iguanodontian clade." These changes, beginning with the most primitive taxon, *Tenontosaurus*, and culminating with the most derived, *Telmatosaurus*, include the following: Co-ossification of carpus and MC I; rhomboidal arrangement of epaxial tendons; hatchet-shaped sternal plates; increase in body size; loss of pedal digit I; loss of antorbital fenestra; loss of angular foramen; and loss of jugular process on maxilla.

This analysis confirmed that the Hadrosauridae is a monophyletic group supported by many synapomorphies, including the following: Number of vertical tooth positions increased to at least 40 in adults; loss of fused carpus and manus digit I; and extreme dorsoventral expansion on anterior jugal.

As the term "Hadrosauridae" has, in the past, been used in different ways by different workers, Forster proposed a node-based definition of this group "restricting this clade to the Lambeosaurinae plus Hadrosaurinae and their most recent common

Photograph by the author.

Skull (cast by Triebold Industries here labeled as a possible *Pachycephalosaurus*) presumably belonging to the spike-headed pachycephalosaur *Stygimoloch spinifer*, displayed at Dinofest™ in 1998. Found in Upper Cretaceous rocks in North America, this species is one of the largest of known pachycephalosaurid taxa.

ancestor," a definition consistent with the original meaning of the family's name. According to Forster's analysis, all taxa lying outside this restricted group, including *Telmatosaurus*, belong within the Iguanodontia.

More recently, Norman (1998) proposed a new phylogeny in which he rediagnosed Euornithopoda as follows: Antorbital fenestra smaller in area than antorbital fossa it overlies; sinuous lower margin to jugal arch; space separating lower edge of quadratojugal from lateral margin of jaw articulation; pleurokinetic hinge (lateral rotation of cheek teeth developed); anterior process of pubis comparable in length to (or exceeding in length) anterior process of ilium; medioventral edge of shaft of ischium with discrete, finger-shaped obturator process; shallow anterior intercondylar groove on distal end of femur; ?angle between anterior and posterior pubic ramus less than 100 degrees.

Norman's phylogeny basically defined Euornithopoda as consisting of the new group Hypsilophodontia (including the genus *Tenontosaurus* and possibly *Muttaburrasaurus*, see entries) plus Dryomorpha.

Hypsilophodontia was diagnosed by Norman as follows: Maxillary teeth with labial surface marked by low vertical striae, dentary teeth with lingual surface characterized by sharp, prominent, approximately centrally positioned primary ridge; quadratojugal large, fenestrate; quadrate lateral wing with large, shallow embayment for attachment of quadratojugal; shaft to ischium laterally compressed, straight, caudally directed (rather than curved ventrally); obturator process positioned near midlength of ischium (between 30 and 50 percent); hypaxial ossified tendons.

Dryomorpha was diagnosed by Norman by the following characters: Paired ventrolateral process on predentary; lateral and medial rostral processes on maxilla separated by oblique channel for caudolateral premaxillary process; teeth also supported by bone of alveolous, molded around each root and crown; development of specialized premaxilla-maxilla hinge as part of functional evolution of pleurokinesis; channel-like anterior intercondylar groove on femur; prominent articular head developed on posterior side of proximal end of humerus; quadratojugal reduced to small element separating jugal and quadrate; quadrate with notchlike embayment in its lateral wing, forming caudal margin of quadrate (paraquadratic) foramen; close-packed teeth in maxillary and dentary dentitions; width across orbital region of skull roof greater than that across occipital region; ischial shaft arched ventrally along its length; development of small distal boot with flat medial surface on ischium; obturator process situated proximally on shaft of ischium (within 25 percent of ischium's total length).

According to Norman's classification, Dryomorpha includes the family Dryosauridae, new taxon Camptosauria, and Iguanodontia.

Camptosauria was diagnosed by Norman by the following: Prominent primary ridge on labial surface of maxillary crowns; inrolling of enamel on lower half of mesial edge of crown (in lingual view), forming oblique cingulum; maxillary crowns narrower and more lanceolate (in labial view) than dentary crowns (in lingual view); heavy ossification of carpus (metacarpal I shortened, incorporated obliquely into carpus; consequent partial fusion of modified carpus into two blocks — metacarpal 1 + radiale + intermedium + adjacent distal carpals, and ulnare + distal carpals 4 and 5 — these articulating via broad concave facets with distal end of radius and ulna); short, divergent digit I of manus and sub-conical manus digit I ungual (Sereno 1986, regarding *Camptosaurus*); digits II and III dominant, ending in dorsoventrally flattened unguals; digits displaying ability to hyperextend and well-defined articular relationships (indicating use in weight support/locomotion; manus digit III having lost one phalanx (unknown in dryosaurids, but recognized in *Tenontosaurus*, this feature either acquired independently in weight-supporting manus, or supports Iguanodontia *sensu* Sereno 1986).

Iguanodontia, which includes Iguanodontidae plus *Probactrosaurus* plus Euhadrosauria (Weishampel, Norman and Grigorescu 1993), was rediagnosed by Norman as follows: Digit I of manus with conical, pointed, strongly divergent ungual; elongate and ligamentously bound ("bundled") metacarpals II–IV; metacarpals IV subequal in length to III, both considerably longer than metacarpal II; metacarpal II and its first phalanx approximately equal in length to III; metacarpal II proximal to III and IV, projecting into recess on distal surface of carpus; digits II and III with flattened, distally rounded ungual phalanges; sternal bone having caudolateral process; dorsoventrally expanded distal end of anterior pubic process; posterior pubic process shorter than ischium; pedal ungual phalanges of digits II–IV flattened, broad; lattice-like ossified tendons flanking dorsal, sacral, and proximal caudal neural spines.

The Iguanodontidae was rediagnosed by Norman by these characters: Dentary teeth broad, asymmetrical, with distally off-set but relatively low primary ridge, separated by shallow trough from parallel secondary ridge which meets apex of crown at a mesial "shoulder" (a variable number of parallel tertiary ridges running down crown surface, usually taking their origin from bases of marginal denticles); dentary and maxillary teeth interlocking through shape of their adjacent crowns (little evidence of cementum locking crowns and roots of teeth into battery); lacrimal locked on to fingerlike process at apex of maxilla, extensively overlain by premaxilla and prefrontal; palpebral 1 (supraorbital) with large baseplate articulating loosely against prefrontal alone; palpebral curving upward and backward, following line of orbital margin (forming equivalent of a prominent brow ridge) terminating near postorbital and sometimes followed by loose (rarely preserved) accessory palpebral; jugo-maxillar suture complex, consists of finger-like caudolateral process of maxilla, which slots into large recess of medioventral surface of jugal (the two meeting in externally sinuous sutural line); ungual phalanx of manus digit I hypertrophied as long, medially directed, robust conical spike, articulating against its metacarpal via flattened, disklike first phalanx

Skeleton of the primitive ceratopsian *Psittacosaurus sinensis* displayed at Dinofest™, Philadelphia, 1998. Known from a wealth of fossil specimens from the Lower Cretaceous of Asia, *Psittacosaurus* seems to have been ancestral to all the later ceratopsian dinosaurs.

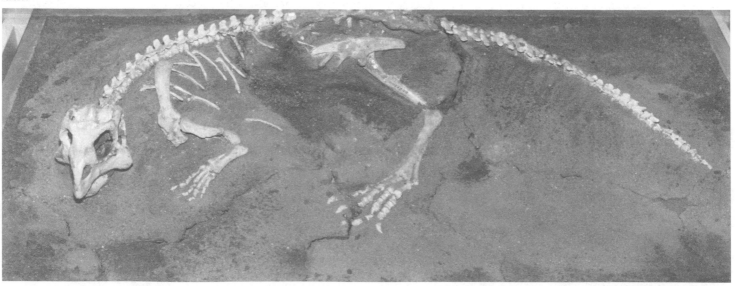

Photograph by the author.

(this ungual may be subequal to, or greater in length to digit II of manus); manus digit V showing evidence of hyperphalangy, diverging strongly from digits II-IV; carpal bones and metacarpal 1 fused indistinguishably into two bone blocks.

Euhadrosauria was rediagnosed by Norman as follows: Maxillary crowns miniaturized; cemented magazines of teeth; dentary alveoli forming parallel-sided vertical furrows; localization of enamel to just labial and lingual surfaces of crowns of maxillary and dentary crowns, respectively; near symmetry of lingual and labial aspects of dentary and maxillary crowns, respectively; closure of mandibular and surangular fenestrae; complete loss of digit I on manus; reduction of carpus into two small elements; straight femoral shaft distal to fourth trochanter; anterior intercondylar groove on femur completely roofed over.

Ceratopsia

The Ceratopsia has remained a fairly stable group over the past few years, in part due to the fact that many well-preserved ceratopsian skulls, crucial in regards identifying and diagnosing members of this clade, in addition to postcranial skeletons, have been collected for study.

In performing a systematic analysis of *Psitta-cosaurus* (see entry), Xu (1997) found that some of the species assigned to this genus can be divided into two distinct (but unnamed) sister groups — the more primitive of which he named "Clade A," the more derived "Clade B." As early as 1986, Paul C. Sereno questioned the monophyly of the taxon Protoceratopsidae, commonly accepted as the more primitive of the two families usually nestled, along with the Ceratopsidae, within the Neoceratopsia. Because of this uncertainty, some workers (*e.g.*, Ryan and Currie 1996; Sampson, Ryan and Tanke 1997) have informally referred the taxa generally designated as "protoceratopsids" simply as "protoceratopsians."

A brief report on a new analysis of basal Neoceratopsia was presented by Chinnery and Weishampel (1996; detailed cladistic analysis in press as of this writing), particularly concerning the position of the primitive ceratopsian *Montanoceratops cerorhynchus*. This analysis showed that Protoceratopsidae, as previously understood, is a paraphyletic group, with *Montanoceratops* (generally classified as a protoceratopsid) the most advanced basal neoceratopsian, thereby representing the sister group to Ceratopsidae; with *Leptoceratops* more advanced than previously believed and the next outgroup to Ceratopsidae; and with *Microceratops* and *Bagaceratops* the most primitive of basal neoceratopsians.

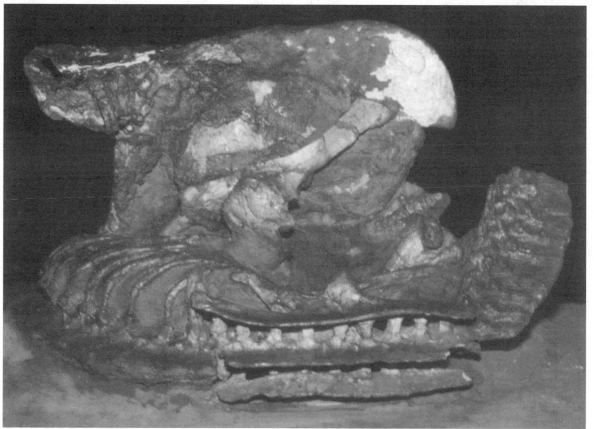

Almost complete skeleton (AMNH 6418) of the "protoceratopsid" ceratopsian *Protoceratops andrewsi*. The matrix covering much of this specimen gives the illusion of integument, although no traces of skin are preserved in that covering. The overall effect does, however, suggest in some ways how the animal may have appeared in life.

Photograph by the author, courtesy American Museum of Natural History.

Reconstructed holotype (AMNH 5464) skeleton of the Late Cretaceous species *Montanoceratops cerorhynchus*, originally described as a new species of *Leptoceratops*. This species, formerly classified as the most derived of known "protoceratopsids," is now interpreted as the most advanced basal neoceratopsian.

More recently, Dong and Azuma (1997), while describing the new genus *Archaeoceratops*, also used it as the basis for a new neoceratopsian family, Archaeoceratopsidae, diagnosed by them as follows: Primitive neoceratopsian; body lightly built; bipedal to quadrupedal; jugal shallow; three to four premaxillary teeth; palpebral; frill short or absent; hind limb relatively long (compared to protoceratopsids); metatarsus long, narrow.

To this new family, Dong and Azuma also referred the genera — both previously classified as protoceratopsids — *Microceratops* and *Kulceratops*. The family was regarded by its authors as closely related to the Protoceratopsidae and as a possible sister group to the Psittacosauridae. However, the Archaeoceratopsidae has not yet achieved much acceptance as a valid family.

Wolfe and Kirkland (1998), in naming and describing *Zuniceratops* (see entry) — a new genus possessing some features showing affinities to both the more derived ceratopsids (*e.g.*, large skull with elongate frill, brow horns) and others to primitive horned dinosaurs (*e.g.*, single-rooted teeth) — noted that this taxon, consequently, falls outside the crown group definition (*i.e.*, the ancestor of the family and all of its descendants) of the Ceratopsidae ("large quadrupeds with large skulls, frills made up of the parietals and squamosals, and nasal and postorbital horns at least

early in ontogeny"). Further pointing out that the fragmentary central Asian genus *Turanoceratops* is known to possess brow horns and apparently both single- and double-rooted teeth, and that this taxon also falls outside the Ceratopsidae, Wolfe and Kirkland referred both genera to a new neoceratopsian clade, Ceratopsomorpha. The Ceratopsomorpha was diagnosed by these authors as ceratopsians with paired orbital brow horns ancestrally. It includes "both *Zuniceratops* and *Turanoceratops* with the Ceratopsidae and additionally would include even less derived taxa as long as they possessed brow horns."

Concerning more advanced ceratopsians, Forster, Sereno, Evans and Wore (1993) had previously published a cladogram showing inferred phylogenetic relationships within the ceratopsid subfamily Chasmosaurinae based upon a phylogenetic analysis of nine cranial characters. Forster *et al.* had concluded that the biogeographic history implied by these relationships suggests that a single southward dispersal event cannot explain the biogeographic exchange between the northern and southern species.

However, in his paper describing the "El Picacho ceratopsian" (see section on new discoveries and ideas), Lehman (1996) found the analysis of Forster *et al.* to be "contrary to traditional views of chasmosaurine evolutionary trends." Consequently, Lehman advocated an alternative and more traditional phylogeny:

Forster *et al.* had considered the possession of long supraorbital horncores and the anterior curvature of horncores as primitive character states for the Chasmosaurinae, *Chasmosaurus belli* therefore regarded as among the most primitive chasmosaurines.

Lehman (1996), however, pointed out that members of the "Protoceratopsidae" and Centrosaurinae have either no, or very small, supraorbital horns, and that centrosaurine brow horns, when present, exhibit posterior curvature; that, as the Chasmosaurinae is universally regarded as more derived than the "Protoceratopsidae" and Centrosaurinae, it is reasonable to assume that small posteriorly curved brow horns represent the basal chasmosaurine condition; and that evidence in adult chasmosaurines indicates that anteriorly curved horncores is a condition that developed ontogenetically from a posteriorly curved (juvenile) condition. Lehman (1996) favored the traditional interpretation of large supraorbital horncores as derived character states in the Chasmosaurinae, exhibited in the latest representatives of this group, and associated with such other features, usually regarded as advanced for the subfamily, as "1) large body size and more massive postcranial skeleton, 2) closure of the postfrontal fontanelle and development of frontal sinuses, 3) development of sinuses in the base of the horncores, and 4) lengthening of the tooth row and number of tooth positions."

Forster *et al.* considered the development of the premaxillary flange (regarded by these authors to be basically an extended ossification of the internarial septum) as a derived condition in chasmosaurines and as further evidence for the status of *Chasmosaurus* as a derived member of the Chasmosaurinae.

According to Lehman (1996), ossification of the internal septum is much more extensive in centrosaurines, which are usually thought to be more primitive than chasmosaurines. Lehman (1996) regarded the presence of this flange in *Chasmosaurus* as a retained primitive condition and its reduction in members of the subfamily as a derived character state.

The presence of a fingerlike premaxillary process, its tip isolated on the nasal bone, was regarded by Forster *et al.* as a derived condition.

According to Lehman (1996), this process is found only in *Chasmosaurus* and *Pentaceratops* among centrosaurines; is variable in its development between different *Chasmosaurus* specimens; is present, though weakly-developed, in some centrosaurines (*e.g.*, *Centrosaurus apertus* specimen CMN 348); and is well-developed in at least one protoceratopsid, *Leptoceratops gracilis* and somewhat developed in *Protoceratops andrewsi*. The premaxillary process in the very primitive protoceratopsid *Bagaceratops rozhdestvenskyi* is separated from the maxilla by a large foramen, a small

foramen having the same position in *Chasmosaurus* and *Pentaceratops*. This process was, consequently, regarded by Lehman (1996) as a retained primitive condition in both of these chasmosaurines.

Forster *et al.* interpreted a wide frill to be a derived character in *Chasmosaurus*.

According to Lehman (1996), other ceratopsians (including the chasmosaurines *Torosaurus latus* and *Triceratops horridus*, as well as some protoceratopsids and psittacosaurs) also have relatively wide frills. Therefore, this character may have little phylogenetic significance and may be a primitive character state for the Ceratopsidae.

Contrary to Forster *et al.*, Lehman (1996) suggested that large parietal fenestrae may have been primitive for the Ceratopsidae, with the contraction or closure of these openings in the frill interpreted to be a derived condition. As observed by Lehman (1996), the parietal openings in adult individuals of *P. andrewsi* (*e.g.*, AMNH 6466 and 6408) are almost as large, relative to the preorbital length of the skull, as those in *Chasmosaurus* and *Pentaceratops*, and the lateral bar of the parietal in some *P. andrewsi* specimens (*e.g.*, AMNH 6466 and 6429) strikingly resembles that in *Chasmosaurus*. Lehman (1996) further noted that all ceratopsids except *Chasmosaurus* and *Pentaceratops* have comparatively smaller parietal openings than *Protoceratops*, and that the lack of such openings in *T. horridus* is usually considered to be a secondarily derived condition.

Forster *et al.* interpreted the jugal-squamosal contact below the infratemporal fenestra as a derived condition in chasmosaurines. However, Lehman (1996) noted that such a contact has been described in centrosaurines (*e.g.*, *Centrosaurus apertus* and *Pachyrhinosaurus canadensis*) and may develop ontogenetically, this condition not being present in juvenile centrosaurines (*e.g.*, *Avaceratops lammersi*). Lehman (1996) added that this contact is not found in protoceratopsids and, therefore, may represent the primitive condition for the Neoceratopsia; also, that its occurrence in both centrosaurines and some species of *Chasmosaurus* suggests that "this feature is primitive for ceratopsids, or less likely, that it was acquired independently by centrosaurines and *Chasmosaurus*."

Finally, Forster *et al.* considered to be a primitive character the absence of a marked embayment along the posteromedial border of the parietal. As Lehman (1996) pointed out, *Chasmosaurus*, which Forster *et al.* regarded as the most derived of chasmosaurines, has no such embayment, although marked embayments are present in the parietal margins of many centrosaurines (including *C. apertus* and *Styracosaurus albertensis*). According to Lehman (1996), this character, which includes much ingroup and

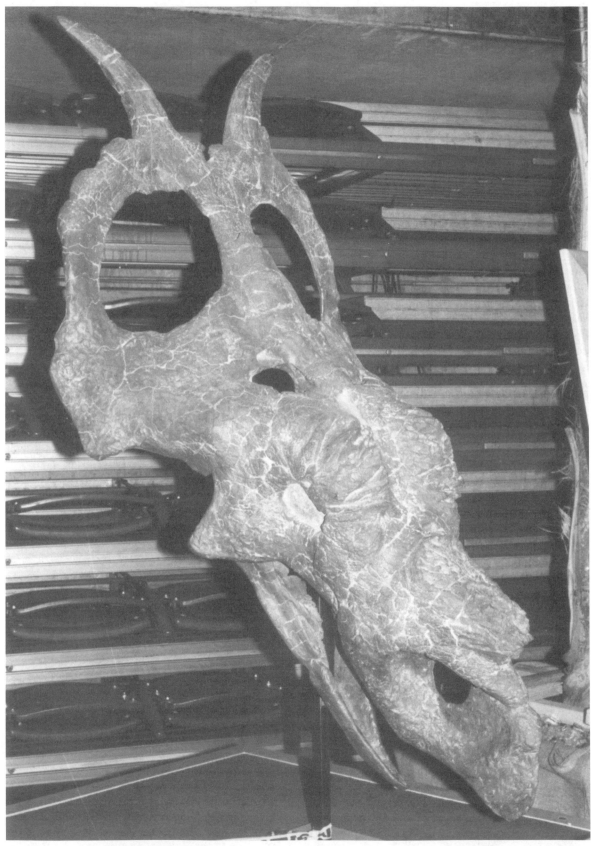

Skull (cast of holotype MOR 485) of the centrosaurine ceratopsian *Achelousaurus horneri*, right three-quarter view, displayed at Dinofest™ International (1996), in Tempe, Arizona. This large species from the Upper Cretaceous of Montana seems to be closely related to *Pachyrinosaurus canadensis* and *Einiosaurus procurvicornis*.

intraspecific variation, probably has little phylogenetic importance.

Lehman (1996) favored the more traditional phylogeny proposed by Dodson and Currie (1990), emphasizing the significance of supraorbital horncores in the evolution of the Chasmosaurinae, with *Triceratops* regarded "as exhibiting the culmination in chasmosaurine phylogenetic trends."

According to Lehman (1996), it is possible "that the ceratopsian dinosaurs of the American Southwest represent the result of a unique dispersal event to the south from more diverse northern ceratopsian faunas," this event resulting "in the introduction of a chasmosaurine population of the *Chasmosaurus* 'grade' into the region, perhaps in middle Campanian time," with protoceratopsids, centrosaurines, and other chasmosaurines unable to immigrate into the region.

Lehman (1996) further speculated that *Chasmosaurus mariscalensis* and *Pentaceratops sternbergi* could have been derived from a more primitive chasmosaurine (*e.g.*, *Chasmosaurus belli*), and that the "El Picacho ceratopsian may represent a taxon further derived from the same lineage."

The presence of *Torosaurus utahensis* in the middle–late Maastrichtian could, according to Lehman (1996), indicate a second dispersal event to the south, succeeded by isolation from *T. latus* populations in the north, the more abundant former species possibly representing the culmination of the southern chasmosaurine lineage.

The following outlining of the Dinosauria — based upon and revised from that which appeared in *D:TE*, and reflecting some of the more recently published ideas offered above and elsewhere in the text — is the present author's conservative (and subjective) attempt to organize the various taxa above the level of genus into a convenient and usable system, based upon currently available published data. In some areas, choices had to be made as to which of the new phylogenies to follow, based upon the writer's opinions, which may and probably will change as future volumes of this series are published.

What should be evident in the following breakdown is how dramatically some parts of the outline have changed since the publication of *D:TE*, especially

Skeleton of a flat-headed hadrosaurid *Edmontosaurus*, among the last dinosaurian genera to become extinct.

in regards the Theropoda and Sauropoda, and how many new higher taxa have been introduced. No doubt, revisions among these groups will continue to change significantly in the years to come, as more phylogenetic analyses are performed on them.

As in *D:TE*, this is not, by any means, the author's attempt to offer an "official" organization of these taxa; nor does it include cladograms, as one worker's cladogram can differ from another's, sometimes in the extreme, depending upon the criteria used. Obviously, this organization does not — and surely cannot — incorporate all of the sometimes conflicting views that have been recently proposed in the literature. As in *D:TE*, then, any attempt at organizing a phylogeny of the Dinosauria can only be regarded as tentative.

The terms "family," "subfamily," and "super-family" have been retained for use in this text, although some authors no longer use them. A family can be identified by the suffix "-idae," a subfamily by "-inae," and a "super-family" by "oidea." (For diagnoses and definitions of most of the following taxa, as well as authors' names, junior synonyms, generalized descriptions, geologic age, geographic distribution, and lists of genera belonging to these groups, see *D:TE*.*)

_____

A number of systematists, each a specialist in one or more dinosaurian groups, are currently joining forces over the Internet, pooling their knowledge, expertise, and opinions in a major combined attempt to produce, in cyberspace, the closest approximation yet of a "definitive" phylogeny of the Dinosauria. When this massive cladistic work — titled the "Tree of Life Project" — is completed and presumably published, more significant changes in dinosaurian classification will undoubtedly be seen.

DINOSAURIA

    I. SAURISCHIA
      THEROPODA
        Eoraptor
        HERRERASAURIDAE
        [unnamed clade including *Chindesaurus*]
        NEOTHEROPODA
          "CERATOSAURIA"
            COELOPHYSOIDEA
            NEOCERATOSAURIA
              ?"CERATOSAURIDAE"
              ABELISAUROIDEA
                NOASAURIDAE
                ABELISAURIDAE
        TETANURAE
          SPINOSAUROIDEA
            "MEGALOSAURIDAE"
            EUSTREPTOSPONDYLIDAE
            BARYONYCHIDAE
            SPINOSAURIDAE
            Piatnitzkysaurus
            ?SIGILMASSASAURIDAE
        AVETHEROPODA
          CARNOSAURIA
            ?*Cryolophosaurus*
            Monolophosaurus
            ALLOSAUROIDEA
              SINRAPTORIDAE
              ALLOSAURIDAE
              CARCHARODONTOSAURIDAE
          COELUROSAURIA
            COMPSOGNATHIDAE
            ?DRYPTOSAURIDAE
            MANURAPTORIFORMES

MANURAPTORIFORMES (cont.)
ARCTOMETATARSALIA
TYRANNOSAURIDAE
AUBLYSODONTINAE
TYRANNOSAURINAE
BULLATOSAURIA
TROODONTIDAE
ORNITHOMIMOSAURIA
HARPYMIMIDAE
GARUDIMIMIDAE
ORNITHOMIMIDAE
?AVIMIMIDAE
?THERIZINOSAUROIDEA
ALXASAURIDAE
THERIZINOSAURIDAE
OVIRAPTOROSAURIA
Microvenator
OVIRAPTORIDAE
OVIRAPTORINAE
INGENIINAE
CAENAGNATHIDAE
MANURAPTORA
?*Ornitholestes*
EUMANURAPTORA
DROMAEOSAURIDAE
DROMAEOSAURINAE
VELOCIRAPTORINAE
?[unnamed] clade including *Protarchaeopteryx* plus *Caudipteryx*]
?AVIALE [=AVES]
SAUROPODOMORPHA
PROSAUROPODA
THECODONTOSAURIDAE
ANCHISAURIDAE
MASSOSPONDYLIDAE
YUNNANOSAURIDAE
PLATEOSAURIDAE
MELANOROSAURIDAE
BLIKANASAURIDAE
SAUROPODA
VULCANODONTIDAE
EUSAUROPODA
Shunosaurus
BARAPASAURIDAE
Omeisaurus
?"CETOSAURIDAE"
NEOSAUROPODA
DIPLODOCOIDEA
Rayososaurus
Amphicoelias
DIPLODOCIDAE
DICRAEOSAURIDAE
MACRONARIA
Haplocanthosaurus
CAMARASAUROMORPHA
CAMARASAURIDAE

TITANOSAURIFORMES
BRACHIOSAURIDAE
SOMPHOSPONDYLI
EUHELOPODIDAE
TITANOSAURIA
Janenschia
ANDESAURIDAE
TITANOSAURIDAE

II. ORNITHISCHIA
Pisanosaurus
Technosaurus
Lesothosaurus
GENASAURIA
THYREOPHORA
Emausaurus
Scutellosaurus
Scelidosaurus
EURYPODA
STEGOSAURIA
HUAYNAGOSAURIDAE
STEGOSAURIDAE
ANKYLOSAURIA
NODOSAURIDAE
ANKYLOSAURIDAE
?*Gargoyleosaurus*
POLACANTHINAE
SHAMOSAURINAE
?*Tsagantegia*
Pinacosaurus
[unnamed clade including *Saichania* plus *Tarchia*]
[unnamed clade including *Euoplocephalus* plus *Ankylosaurus*]
ANKYLOSAURINAE
CERAPODA
ORNITHOPODA
FABROSAURIDAE
HETERODONTOSAURIDAE
EUORNITHOPODA
?"HYPSILOPHODONTIDAE"
IGUANODONTIA
?*Tenontosaurus*
?*Muttaburrasaurus*
Rhabdodon
EUIGUANODONTIA
[unnamed clade including *Gasparinisaura*]
DRYOMORPHA
DRYOSAURIDAE
ANKYLOPOLLEXIA
CAMPTOSAURIA
IGUANODONTIDAE
?*Probactrosaurus*
HADROSAURIDAE
?*Bactrosaurus*
?*Telmatosaurus*
Secernosaurus
EUHADROSAURIA

EUHADROSAURIA (cont.)
LAMBEOSAURINAE
HADROSAURINAE

MARGINOCEPHALIA
Stenopelix
PACHYCEPHALOSAURIA
HOMALOCEPHALIDAE
PACHYCEPHALOSAURIDAE
CERATOPSIA
PSITTACOSAURIDAE
NEOCERATOPSIA
"PROTOCERATOPSIDAE"
Leptoceratops
Montanoceratops
CERATOPSOMORPHA
Zuniceratops
?Turanoceratops
CERATOPSIDAE
CENTROSAURINAE
CHASMOSAURINAE

Somewhat dated models by Century Dioramas Studios of representatives of the two major groups of Dinosauria, Ornithischia (the ceratopsian *Triceratops horridus*) and Saurischia (the theropod *Tyrannosaurus rex*). This tableau, based directly on a mural (see *D:TE*) by Charles R. Knight at The Field Museum, was originally produced for the 1933 Chicago World's Fair. It was later displayed at the end of the popular coal mine exhibit in Chicago's Museum of Science and Industry. The diorama is now in storage.

III. Dinosaurian Genera

This section comprises an alphabetically arranged compilation of dinosaurian genera, many of which are new to this volume, while others are revised from entries published in the original *Dinosaurs: The Encyclopedia*.

Entries marked with a dagger (†)—*e.g.*, *ALLOSAURUS*— identify genera which originally appeared in *D:TE*, but in this volume offer new, revised, or corrected data or new, updated, or otherwise different illustrations. Within these dagger-marked entries, basic introductory information (*e.g.*, relating to classification, age, diagnosis, and so forth) is included only when it is new or has been revised. Information presented in this volume which conflicts with that appearing in *D:TE* supplants that information which was previously published. Most photographs and drawings of type specimens, referred fossil material and life restorations relevant to dagger-marked entries can be found in the original entries.

Revised or new diagnoses, definitions, and generalized descriptions and explanations of higher taxa, with broader applications to each genus or species, can be found in the preceding chapter; unchanged data relevant to those topics will be found in the original book.

The following genera have their own entries which are new to this volume: *Abrosaurus, Altirhinus, Angaturama, Animantarx, Archaeoceratops, Augustia, Bagaraatan, Caudipteryx, Eobrontosaurus, Eolambia, Gasparinisaura, Gastonia, Gojirasaurus, Guaibasaurus, Hudiesaurus, Jainosaurus, Jingshanosaurus, Ligabueino, Megaraptor, Pellegrinisaurus, Protarchaeopteryx, Rayososaurus, Saurophaganax, Scipionyx, Shanxia, Sigilmassasaurus, Siluosaurus, Sinosauropteryx, Sonorasaurus,* and *Zuniceratops.*

The following genera (this list not including taxa now regarded as junior synonyms, *e.g.*, *Laplatasaurus* and *Rioarribasaurus*) had their own entries in *D:TE*, but also have entries in this volume, some of them presenting new species:

Abelisaurus, Acrocanthosaurus, Albertosaurus, Allosaurus, Amargasaurus, Ampelosaurus, Amphicoelias, Antarctosaurus, Apatosaurus, Argentinosaurus, Argyrosaurus, Arstanosaurus, Bactrosaurus, Barapasaurus, Baryonyx, Brachiosaurus, Camarasaurus, Campylodoniscus, Carcharodontosaurus, Carnotaurus, Centrosaurus, Chasmosaurus, Chirostenotes, Chubutisaurus, Coelophysis, Compsognathus, Cryolophosaurus, Dacentrurus, Daspletosaurus, Datousaurus, Deinonychus, Deltadromeus, Dilophosaurus, Diplodocus, Drinker, Dryptosaurus, Dystrophaeus, Edmontosaurus, Epachthosaurus, Euhelopus, Gargoyleosaurus, Genyodectes, Giganotosaurus, Gorgosaurus, Gryposaurus, Hadrosaurus, Haplocanthosaurus, Iguanodon, Indosaurus, Indosuchus, Irritator, Lexovisaurus, Magyarosaurus, Maiasaura, Majungatholus, Malawisaurus, Mamenchisaurus, Marshosaurus, Massospondylus, Melanorosaurus, Microvenator, Minmi, Muttaburrasaurus, Nanshiungosaurus, Nedcolbertia, Nemegtosaurus, Neovenator, Neuquensaurus, Noasaurus, Omeisaurus, Onychosaurus, Ornithomimus, Oviraptor, Pachyrhinosaurus, Pararhabdodon, Parasaurolophus, Pelecanimimus, Pentaceratops, Plateosaurus, Pleurocoelus, Probactrosaurus, Procompsognathus, Protoavis, Protoceratops, Psittacosaurus, Rebbachisaurus, Saltasaurus, Sauropelta, Scelidosaurus, Shunosaurus, Sinornithoides, Spinosaurus, Stokesosaurus, Struthiosaurus, Stygimoloch, Supersaurus, Tarchia, Tenontosaurus, Thescelosaurus, Titanosaurus, Torosaurus, Triceratops, Troodon, Tyrannosaurus, Utahraptor, Velociraptor, Velocisaurus, Vulcanodon, and *Xenotarsosaurus.*

†ABELISAURUS

Saurischia: Theropoda: Neotheropoda: "Ceratosauria": Neoceratosauria: Abelisauroidea: Abelisauridae.

Diagnosis of genus: Skull characterized by three distinctive features: 1. large infratemporal opening bordered posteriorly by almost straight quadratojugal in line with posteroventral process of squamosal; 2. preantorbital fenestra reduced, located very near preorbital fenestra; and, 3. dorsal process of maxilla very reduced anteroposteriorly (Bonaparte 1996*b*).

Comments: *Abelisaurus*, a quite large theropod from Argentina, is still known from only a single specimen. Since the holotype skull (MC 11098) was originally named and described by José F. Bonaparte and Fernando E. Novas in 1985, this specimen has been reexamined by the senior author.

In a later report, Bonaparte (1996*b*) noted the following additional "interesting features" of the skull of the type species *A. comahuensis*: Dorsal roof of the orbit showing "contact between the lacrimal and postorbital, avoiding that the prefrontal and frontal border the orbit"; nasals bearing a rough, rugose external surface (except around nasal opening) suggesting a very coarse dermal covering; quadrate and quadratojugal fused; ventral projection of the lacrimal anteriorly concave, posteriorly convex; and snout very deep.

According to Bonaparte, if high and narrow muzzles are signs of fierce predation, then the very high snout (as well as the high, narrow skull) of *Abelisaurus* suggests that type of behavior in this genus. Other indications that this theropod was a formidable predator are the large infratemporal and preorbital openings (apparently for the housing of large jaw muscles) and sharp, transversely narrow and short-crowned teeth (only a few having been preserved).

Key references: Bonaparte (1996*b*); Bonaparte and Novas (1985).

ABROSAURUS   Zhang and Chen 1996

Saurischia: Sauropodomorpha: Sauropoda: Eusauropoda: Neosauropoda: Macronaria: Camarasauromorpha: Camarasauridae.

Name derivation: ?Latin *abruptus* = "broken off/abrupt" + Greek *sauros* = "lizard."

Type species: *A. gigantorhinus* Zhang and Chen 1996.

Other species: [None.]

Occurrence: Lower Shaximiao Formation, Zigong, China.

Age: Middle Jurassic.

Known material: Incomplete skull with teeth, postcranial remains including cervical and dorsal vertebrae, forelimb and hind limb elements.

Holotype: [At press time, the holotype is unknown to the present writer, though it may be identical to the above material.]

Diagnosis of genus (as for type species): Skull relatively low, lightly constructed, with very large openings separated by particularly narrow portion; external nares and antorbital fenestrae very large, elliptical and triangular in outline, respectively; pair of supratemporal fenestrae in close proximity, separated by narrow parietal; mandible long, thin, mandibular foramen small; five premaxillary, 15 maxillary, and 16–18 dentary teeth; neck not extremely long, with about 13 cervical vertebrae; cervical centra about one and one-third times length of dorsals, cervical neural spines relatively low; 13 dorsal vertebrae; posterior cervical and anterior dorsal neural spines slightly forked, remainder of dorsal spines broadening transversely; dorsal centra platycoelous or weakly amph-

icoelous; forelimbs three-fourths length of hind limbs (Zhang and Chen 1996).

Comments: The type species *Abrosaurus gigantorhinus* is known from cranial and postcranial remains collected from the Lower Shaximiao Formation, Dashapu, Zigong, China (Zhang and Chen 1996). It was first unofficially named in an unpublished master's thesis written by H. Ouyang (1986) of the Zigong Dinosaur Museum.

Key references: Ouyang (1986); Zhang and Chen (1996).

†ACROCANTHOSAURUS

Saurischia: Theropoda: Neotheropoda: Tetanurae: Avetheropoda: Carnosauria: Allosauroidea: Carcharodontosauridae.

Occurrence: Antlers Formation, Twin Mountains Formation, Texas; Antlers Formation, Oklahoma, United States.

Known material: Three incomplete skeletons, two including partial skulls, fairly complete skull, ?isolated teeth.

Holotype: OMNH 8-0-S9, incomplete skull, incomplete postcrania including ninth cervical and sixth dorsal vertebrae, dorsal spine.

Diagnosis of genus (as for type species): Theropod having co-ossified frontals and parietals; jugal process of palatine bifurcated; pronounced, laterally-projecting knob on surangular shelf; large caudal surangular foramen; reduced divisory ridge in mandibular glenoid; teeth with continuous apical denticulation; pronounced pleurocoelous fossae and foramina on all presacral and sacral vertebrae; presacral, sacral, and proximal caudal vertebrae having elongate (some having length of more than 2.5 times centrum length) neural spines possessing inter- and supraspinous ligament insertion sites with numerous associated asymmetrical fossae and foramina; cervical vertebral centra having camellate interiors; cervical neural spines with triangular cranial processes that insert into caudal overhangs; abrupt transition from craniocaudally broad to narrow neural spines at eighth cervical; large, centrally located pleurocoelous fossa with two foramina on axis; axis with reduced distal neural spine; axis with large epipophyses; cranial dorsal vertebrae having multiple fossae and foramina on lateral surfaces of neural spine; transverse processes of medial and caudal dorsal vertebrae having strong dorsocaudal angulation, deep fossae on lateral surfaces separated by very thin laminae, arched pre- and postsygapophyseal facets, prezygapophyseal facets contiguous with hypantral facets; neural spines of caudal dorsal vertebrae strongly angled cranially; rudimentary pleurocoelous fossae on proximal caudal verte-

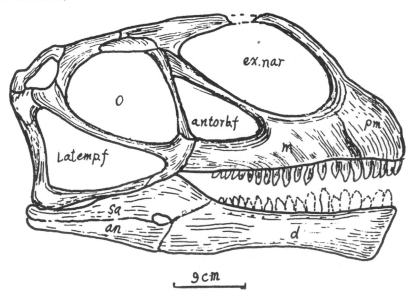

Abrosaurus gigantorhinus, reconstructed skull right lateral view. (After Zhang and Chen 1996.)

brae; multiple foramina located within proximal and distal fossae on neural spines of proximal caudal vertebrae; medial caudal vertebrae with accessory transverse processes; sagittal portion of gastralia consisting of single element; ischium having deep, elongate, ovoid fossa on proximal, dorsocaudal surface (Harris 1998).

Comments: The genus *Acrocanthosaurus* had been founded by Stovall and Langston (1950) upon very incomplete skeletal remains (OMNH 8-0-S9; originally MUO 8-0-59) recovered from the Lower Cretaceous Antlers Formation (Trinity Group) of Texas. Stovall and Langston based their original diagnosis and description of the type species, *A. atokensis*, on both the type specimen and also the paratype (OMNH 8-0-S8; originally MUO 8-0-58), a partial postcranial skeleton collected from the same locality. For decades following the original description by these authors, the two specimens comprised the only good fossil remains attributable to this taxon.

In recent years, however, new material belonging to *A. atokensis* has been recovered. Among these remains is a well-preserved skull and articulated skeleton originally owned by Geological Enterprises and prepared by the Black Hills Institute of Geologic Research, Inc. The skull was exhibited in April 1996 at the second Dinofest™ International, hosted by Arizona State University in Tempe. A cast of this skull subsequently went on exhibit in the newly renovated "Dinosaur Hall" of The Academy of Natural Sciences of Philadelphia.

Russell (1998) briefly reported that the North Carolina State Museum of Natural Sciences acquired this specimen (NCSMNS 14345) in November, 1997. The specimen, Russell noted, had been recovered from the Antlers Formation (late Aptian–early Albian) in McCurtain County, Oklahoma, within a channel associated with abundant woody stems (with diameters measuring from 4 to 5 centimeters) and a chelonian carapace (A. Graffham, personal communication to Russell, 1998).

According to Russell, evidence supports the late Aptian–early Albian, North American coexistence "of a boreal 'Hadrosaur Assemblage,' an interior, low diversity 'Deinonychus-Tenontosaurus Assemblage' and a meridional, coastal 'Acrocanthosaurus-Pleurocoelus Assemblage.'" The subtropical to tropical environments in which *Acrocanthosaurus* lived were also favored by sauropods and archaic angiosperms.

As noted by Russell, no dinosaurian genera in the "*Acrocanthosaurus-Pleurocoelus* Assemblage" are yet known from the then biogeographically joined continents of Africa and South America. Major dinosaurian groups that may so occur (including carcharodontoisaurid theropods, titanosaurid sauropods, and long-spined iguanodonts) could have differentiated in

Photograph by the author.

Acrocanthosaurus atokensis skull (cast of NCSMNS 14345; original specimen owned by Geological Enterprises) from Oklahoma, as displayed at Dinofest™ International (1996) in Tempe, Arizona.

southern North America after immigration from Africa via Europe during Barremian time. The arrival during late Albian time of dinosaurs of Asian-American affinities on the Colorado Plateau coincided with the debut of angiosperm trees and disappearance of dinosaurian genera exemplified by the "*Acrocanthosaurus-Pleurocoelus* Assemblage," although the region inhabited by this assemblage could have been originally shielded from invading biota by north-south floral and faunal gradients. Russell further noted that, based on fossil-trackway evidence from the Gething Formation of British Columbia, the Asian-American dinosaur assemblage may have arrived in higher latitudes earlier, entering "the Colorado Plateau with the Albian midcontinental seaway and associated maritime environments from the north."

More recently, Harris (1998) published a major reanalysis (including a revised diagnosis) of *A. atokensis*, based upon the holotype and paratype specimens, and also a 70 percent complete, partial articulated skeleton (SMU 74646, each element assigned its own catalog number; also catalogued as FWMSH 93-B9). (This study, originally completed in partial fulfillment of Harris' requirements for a Master of Science degree at Southern Methodist University, was apparently written before the preparation of the above recently collected material.)

As recounted by Harris, this new specimen was discovered by Philip R. Hobson at Hobson Ranch, in the Upper Cretaceous (late Aptian) Twin Mountains Formation (defined by Fisher and Rodda 1996), lowest member of the Trinity Group, in Parker County, west of Forth Worth, in north-central Texas. The site, occurring in a cross-bedded and concretionary sandstone facies, was first reported in 1990. The well-preserved specimen includes elements that had previously

Acrocanthosaurus atokensis incomplete referred skeleton (SMU 74646), schematic diagram showing preburial position based upon positions of the bones as found in the field. (After Harris 1998.)

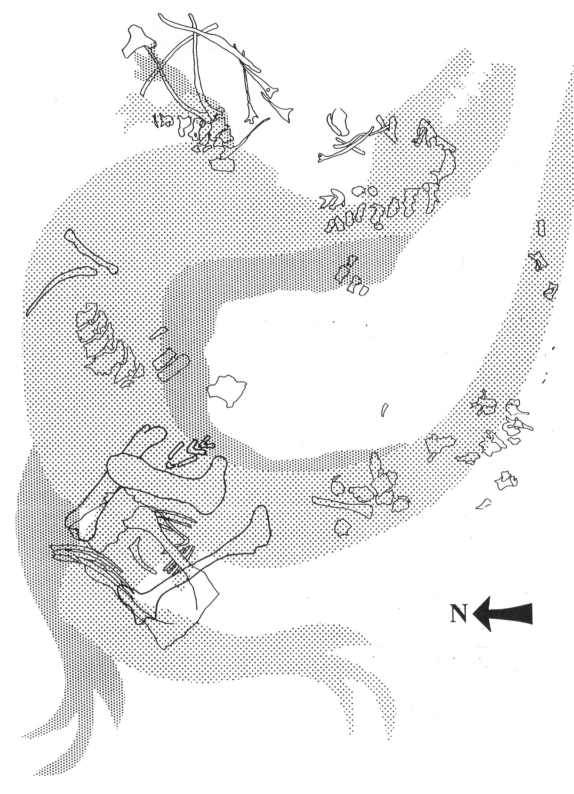

N ←

been insufficiently known (*e.g.*, palatine, surangular, articular, prearticular, teeth, cervical, dorsal, sacral, and caudal vertebrae, scapulae, ischia, and femora). It was found lying on its right side, the head, neck, and tail arched backwards, this position implying exposure before burial. The presence of two crocodilian teeth

and the tooth of a possible fish suggest that some of the missing elements had been scavenged.

After performing cladistic analyses of *Acrocanthosaurus*, Harris cited autapomorphies of the Allosauroidea present in this genus, primarily the following: Jugal process of the palatine distally expanded; basioccipital absent from the basal tubera; and surangular twice as deep as the angular. *Acrocanthosaurus* is most closely allied with the African (Albian or Cenomanian) genus *Carcharodontosaurus*, sharing with it laterally expanded, reniform caudal articular facets on the cervical vertebrae, and rudimentary caudal pleurocoelous fossae. *Acrocanthosaurus* was found by Harris also to be closely related to such allosauroids as the European *Neovenator*, Asian *Chilantaisaurus*, and South American *Giganotosaurus*, and more distantly related to *Allosaurus*.

Harris agreed with Sereno, Dutheil, Iarochene, Larsson, Lyon, Magwene, Sidor, Varrichio, and Wilson (1996) (see *Carcharodontosaurus* entry) "that the closest (well-known) theropod to *Acrocanthosaurus* is *Carcharodontosaurus*, forming the monophyletic clade Carcharodontosauridae," with *Allosaurus* one step removed, one node further out including Sinraptoridae (*Sinraptor* plus *Yangchuanosaurus*).

According to Harris, the "relative closeness of *Acrocanthosaurus* to *Carcharodontosaurus* implies that dispersal of their common ancestor probably occurred through South America and into Africa prior to the separation of North and South America sometime in the Early Cretaceous before the Aptian."

From what was originally revealed by the holotype and paratype specimens, *Acrocanthosaurus* was known to have been a very large theropod possessing rather long neural spines. Although not enough material belonging to this dinosaur had yet been recovered, various attempts were made over the years to depict *Acrocanthosaurus* as it may have appeared in life. Because little was known of the animal's skull, these life restorations — all of them appearing in popular books (*e.g.*, Sattler 1983, illustration by Pamela Carroll) — were largely guesswork. Most of these illustrations were somewhat based on *Allosaurus*, with emphasis on the elongated neural spines.

The first published life restoration of *Acrocanthosaurus* was prepared by Joseph Sibal for John H. Ostrom's (1964) book, *The Strange World of Dinosaurs*, with the tall neural spines creating a small fin from the back of the head to the end of the tail. A new interpretation of *Acrocanthosaurus*, drawn by George Olshevsky and first appearing on the cover of Olshevsky's (1978) publication *Mesozoic Meanderings*, depicted the animal with the spines embedded in a thick fleshy ridge (as in some mammals, such as bison).

In 1995, following the recent collection of the more complete Oklahoma *Acrocanthosaurus* material (and subsequently the new Texas specimen), a number of more accurate portrayals of this dinosaur were attempted by artists including Robert F. Walters. Saurian Studios (see abstract by Alden 1996) produced one of the first of these depictions. The Saurian Studios restoration, a sculpture by Tim Barry based in part on the Geological Enterprises specimen, correctly showed the lacrimal horns as part of a unit comprising the nasals, and with a ridge extending just behind the skull to the middle of the tail.

Notes: A tooth resembling that of *Acrocanthosaurus* was reported by Ratkevich (1997) as matching bite marks on sauropod bones found in the Turney Ranch Formation or southeastern Arizona (see *Sonorasaurus* entry).

New observations concerning Roland T. Bird's Paluxy River dinosaur trackway (one section of which is displayed in the Texas Memorial Museum, Austin, the other at the American Museum of Natural History, New York) were offered by artist David A. Thomas (1996), who stated that Bird (1941) was correct in believing that these tracks recorded a theropod (possibly *Acrocanthosaurus*) attack upon a sauropod (possibly *Pleurocoelus*).

The trackway was interpreted by Thomas as

Life restoration of *Acrocanthosaurus atokensis* painted by Robert F. Walters.

Excavation in 1938 by Roland T. Bird's American Museum of Natural History crew of a Paluxy River dinosaur trackway (AMNH 3065). These tracks seem to record a large theropod (tracks named *Irenesauripus* [formerly *Eubrontes*] *glenrosensis*, possibly made by *Acrocanthosaurus*) stalking a sauropod (tracks named *Brontopodus birdi*, possibly made by *Pleurocoelus*).

revealing the theropod and sauropod trackmakers walking in the same rhythm for 12 consecutive steps. According to Thomas, it is to a predator's benefit to match the rhythm of its prey, for when this occurs, "the prey is standing still relative to the predator, which can then pick its time and point of attack very precisely." Thomas' interpretation was based largely on a study of 38 videotaped chases of African animals, which, though not strictly analogous, showed the predators availing themselves of the advantages of picking up the rhythm of their prey.

In a subsequent article coauthored by Thomas and Farlow (1997), the writers determined that the conspicuous "skip" or drag mark evident in the Austin segment of the trackway, made by the sauropod, seemingly occurred just after being struck by the pursuing theropod.

Stanford and Stanford (1998) reported a trackway of large theropod tracks "speculatively attributed to *Acrocanthosaurus*" from the Lower Cretaceous of Maryland.

Key references: Alden (1996); Bird (1941); Harris (1998); Olshevsky (1987); Ostrom (1964); Ratkevich (1997); Russell (1998); Sereno, Dutheil, Iarochene, Larsson, Lyon, Magwene, Sidor, Varrichio, and Wilson (1996); Stanford and Stanford (1998); Stovall and Langston (1950); Thomas (1996); Thomas and Farlow (1997).

†ALBERTOSAURUS Osborn 1905 — (=?*Deinodon*)

Saurischia: Theropoda: Neotheropoda: Tetanurae: Avetheropoda; Coelurosauria: Manuraptoriformes: Arctometatarsalia: Tyrannosauridae: Tyrannosaurinae.

Name derivation: "Alberta [Canada]" + Greek *sauros* = "lizard."

Type species: *A. sarcophagus* Osborn 1905.

Other species: [None.]

Occurrence: Horseshoe Canyon Formation, Alberta, Canada; Dinosaur Park Formation, Montana; ?Lance Formation, Wyoming, United States.

Age: Late Cretaceous (late Campanian–early Maastrichtian).

Known material: Two fragmentary skulls with associated postcrania, skulls, skeletons, fragmentary postcrania.

Holotype: CMN [formerly NMC] 5600, incomplete skull including braincase, palatal region, and lower jaws.

Diagnosis of genus (as for type species): Premaxilla very short and broad anteroposteriorly, little visible in side view; preantorbital fenestra located well anterior to maxillary opening, visible in lateral aspect; maxillary opening taller than long, separated from antorbital opening by thin bar of maxillary; lacrimal horn moderately developed; surangular foramen comparatively small (for a tyrannosaurid); trunk apparently shorter than that of *Gorgosaurus libratus*; distal end of scapular blade strongly inflected forward; tibia more gracile than in *G. libratus* (Carpenter 1992).

Comments: The genus *Albertosaurus*—in the past couple of decades generally regarded as synonymous with the slightly larger and geologically older *Gorgosaurus* (see †*Gorgosaurus* entry; also *Albertosaurus* entry, *D:TE*)—was founded upon an incomplete, poorly preserved skull (CMN 5600) collected from the Laramie Formation [now Horseshoe Canyon Formation] at Kneehills Creek, Red Deer River, Alberta, Canada.

This specimen, and also a smaller partial skull (CMN 5601) with lower jaws and associated postcranial remains (including fragments of sacral vertebrae and an ilium, the distal end of a tibia with astragalus, metatarsal IV, and three pedal ungual phalanges), collected by the Geological Survey of Canada from Kneehills Creek, were referred to *Laelaps incrassatus* by Cope (1893). With the name *Laelaps* preoccupied and replaced by *Dryptosaurus*, Lambe (1903, 1904) later described this material in greater detail as *D. incrassatus*. Finally, Osborn (1905) referred this material to

a new genus and species, *Albertosaurus sarcophagus*, designating CMN 5600 the holotype and CMN 5601 the paratype.

Osborn originally diagnosed *A. sarcophagus* simply as having 15 mandibular teeth, including one small anterior tooth.

Parks (1928) described a new species, *A. arctunguis*, based on partial postcranial remains (ROM 807) including a sacrum with vertebrae, a left scapulocoracoid, left forelimb, the left half of a pelvis, and associated limb bones, recovered in 1923 by a University of Toronto expedition from the Edmonton [now Horsehoe Canyon] Formation, on the west side of Red Deer River, along Kneehills Creek. This specimen was mounted without head and tail at the Royal Ontario Museum of Palaeontology.

Parks defined this new species mostly by details in which the fourth metatarsal of ROM 807 differed from that of CMN 5601. For example, in ROM 807 this element is relatively longer and heavier. These differences, Parks noted, might be attributable to ontogeny, while others could be due to crushing or to the poor condition of the fossil material.

Russell (1970), in his study of tyrannosaurids of western Canadian, found the identifying features perceived by Parks of ROM 807 to be both pathologic (a condition also noted by Parks) and due to postmortem breakage, stating that "it is not possible to separate the type of *A. arctunguis* from the type and paratype of *A. sarcophagus* on morphological grounds, and the great resemblance of each of these specimens to the corresponding region of the skeleton of *A. libratus* argues convincingly for their inclusion within a single species." Furthermore, Russell observed that the forelimb of ROM 807 is apparently slightly shorter and the pubis slightly larger than in the holotype of *Gorgosaurus libratus*.

Note: In a preliminary report, Gonzales-Leon

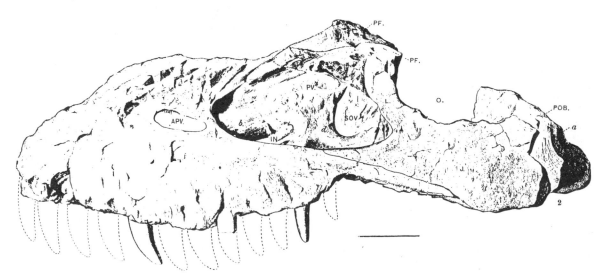

Albertosaurus sarcophagus, CMN 5601, incomplete paratype skull originally referred to *Laelaps incrassatus* in left lateral view. Scale = 6 cm. (After Lambe 1904.)

Albertosaurus

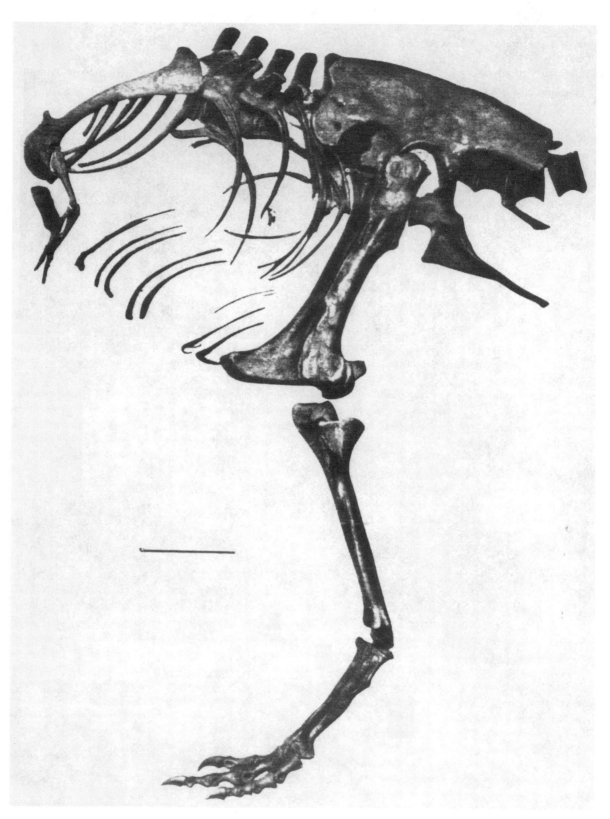

and Lucas (1996) noted that isolated teeth of large theropods, resembling teeth referred to cf. *Albertosaurus*, were collected from the Cabullona Group, Cabullona Basin (Late Cretaceous; late Campanian–Maastrichtian, based on nonmarine mollusc taxa, pollen, charophytes, and various vertebrate remains), northeastern Sonora, Mexico. Among other fossils recovered from this locality are remains of hadrosaurids (the most common Cabullona Group dinosaur, material including very abundant isolated vertebral centra, two left humeri, and a distal phalanx), ceratopsians (represented by posterior cervical or anterior dorsal centra), fishes (lepisosteids [gars], represented by scales, and amiids [bowfins], known from vertebrae), trionychid turtles (known from shell fragments), crocodilians (eusuchians, represented by isolated vertebrae), and a teiid lizard (*Champos segnis*, known from a right dentary).

Key references: Carpenter (1992); Cope (1893); Lambe (1903, 1904); Osborn (1905), Parks (1928); Russell (1970).

†**ALLOSAURUS**—(=*Antrodemus, Apatodon, Creosaurus, Epanterias, Hypsirophus* [in part], *Labrosaurus, Saurophaganax*)

Saurischia: Theropoda: Neotheropoda: Tetanurae: Avetheropoda: Carnosauria: Allosauroidea: Allosauridae.

New species: *A. maximus* (Ray 1941).

Occurrence of *A. maximus*: Morrison Formation, Oklahoma, United States.

Age of *A. maximus*: Late Jurassic (Kimmeridgian–Tithonian).

Known material of *A. maximus*: Fragmentary cranial remains including right postorbital, two partial quadrates, three poorly preserved tooth crowns, vertebral remains including atlas, cervicals, dorsal neural arch, caudal centra, and chevrons, pelvic elements including ilium, ischium, and pubis, forelimb elements including humerus, and manual digits with claws, hind limb including femur, pes, representing at least two individuals of equal size; also, much as yet unidentified or unpublished material.

Holotype of *A. maximus*: OMNH 01123, middorsal neural arch.

Diagnosis of *A. maximus*: Allosaurid reaching extremely large size; differing from other allosaurids in presence of horizontal lamina along base of each side of neural spine; this lamina arising from spine base cranially, free caudally, roofing over craniocaudally elongated space floored by dorsal surface of transverse process; differs from other allosaurids in that atlas lacks prezygapophyses for proatlas, does not roof over neural canal, chevrons craniocaudally expanded distally (Chure 1995).

Comments: The large carnosaur *Allosaurus* remains, to date, the most completely known and best understood of all Late Jurassic theropod genera.

In 1995, Daniel J. Chure, a paleontologist stationed at Dinosaur National Monument in Utah, a site which has yielded significant *Allosaurus* remains, proposed the new generic name *Saurophaganax* for a gigantic theropod that has been known and occasionally alluded to (though has not been sufficiently understood) for more than five decades. Generally, this dinosaur, originally named *Saurophagus maximus*, has been regarded as a probable junior synonym of the better known *Allosaurus*, though a particularly big individual belonging to that genus (*e.g.*, Hunt and Lucas 1987; Paul 1988*b*).

As detailed by Chure, the first known remains of this theropod were collected during the 1930s by the University of Oklahoma. The material, mostly partial postcrania (see *Saurophagus* entry, *D:TE*, for photographs), were recovered from Quarry 1 (for which no maps exist) in the Morrison Formation (equivalent to the upper part of the Brushy Basin Member of this formation on the Colorado Plateau; F. Peterson, personal communication to Chure, 1994), east of Kenton, in Cimarron County, Oklahoma. Much of the preparation of these fossils was done in the 1930s by untrained laborers hired by the WPA (Works Progress Authority), the result being that much of the original material was damaged.

In a popular article, Ray (1941) named these remains *Saurophagus maximus*, but did not provide detailed descriptions or substantial figures illustrating the material. Ray did, however, publish a photograph of an alleged articulated hind limb belonging to this new species. According to Langston (1989; also, W. Langston, Jr., personal communication to Chure 1993), however, this picture was "staged" in Permian redbeds near Norman, Oklahoma; nor is there evidence indicating that these bones were found in association with one another.

Chure, assuming that all large theropod bones from Quarry 1 belong to this taxon, compared this dinosaur to *Allosaurus* and other large theropods. As assessed by Chure, this form is closely allied with *Allosaurus* morphologically and should be classified with the Allosauridae, though being about 25 percent larger than any *Allosaurus* specimen yet described (size alone being of questionable systematic value). However, Chure found *S. maximus* to differ morphologically from that genus in having expanded chevrons that are derived in comparison "to the condition seen in primitive theropods, abelisaurids, and primitive tetanurans (megalosaurids, allosauroids, and torvosauroids [=megalosaurids])" (similar chevron morphology apparently arising independently in Tyrannosauridae); in lamina present along the base of the neural spine (a feature unique among Theropoda); and in the morphology of the atlas, which resembles that in some tyrannosaurids.

Because of the above features and the large size of this theropod, Chure regarded "*Saurophagus*" as generically distinct from *Allosaurus*. Chure added that *Epanterias amplus*, a giant theropod species founded upon a fragmentary holotype and sometimes regarded as synonymous with either "*Saurophagus*" or *Allosaurus* (*e.g.*, Bakker 1986), cannot be distinguished from either of these genera, though it is nearer in size to the former.

Camp, Welles and Green (1953) noted that the name *Saurophagus maximus* is both a *nomen nudum* and preoccupied (Swainson 1831), this assessment followed by subsequent authors (*e.g.*, Chure and McIntosh 1989 in their bibliography of the Dinosauria). Hunt and Lucas arguing that the name, though preoccupied, was correctly established, designated a right tibia (OMNH 4666) as the lectotype.

Not certain as to whether or not Ray's informal description of *S. maximus* met the criteria of the International Code of Zoological Nomenclature, Chure pointed out that OMNH 4666 is not distinctive, and that the taxon it represents is not differentiable; therefore, Chure proposed the new name *Saurophaganax* (suggested to Chure by Ben Creisler) for the Quarry 1 theropod, with a distinctive middorsal neural arch (OMNH 01123) designated the holotype.

As Chure noted, very little data has actually been published concerning the size of this theropod, although Stovall (in Ray 1941), based upon the length of the bones in the composite hind limb, estimated the animal to be about 14 meters (approximately 47 feet) long, comparable to *Tyrannosaurus rex*. According to Chure's calculations based upon the same composite

limb, this estimate seems to be correct, although *S. maximus* appears to have been as massive or "bulky" (*contra* Paul and Ray) as *T. rex*. Following a method proposed by Anderson, Hall-Martin and Russell (1985) for determining weight in dinosaurs based upon long-bone circumference, John S. McIntosh estimated the weight of *S. maximus* to have been about 2720 kilograms (almost 3 tons). (At date of this writing, Chure is preparing a more detailed description of the material referred to *S. maximus*.)

However, subsequent to Chure's renaming of the above material, its status as a valid genus was questioned by David K. Smith after studies by Smith of the wealth of material that has, over the years, been referred to *Allosaurus* (see below).

Much of what is known about *Allosaurus* has resulted from studies of numerous disarticulated specimens belonging to this genus, representing various ontogenetic stages. The majority of these remains have been recovered from the Cleveland-Lloyd Dinosaur Quarry, located in the Brushy Basin Member of the Morrison Formation (Upper Jurassic) of Utah, and, to a lesser extent, from Como Bluff, Wyoming, and the Dry Mesa Dinosaur Quarry, near Dry Mesa, western Colorado. All three of these sites were deposited within approximately three million years of each other (B. J. Kowallis, personal communication to Smith, 1996). As more *Allosaurus* specimens from these quarries are studied and evaluated, new data concerning

Allosaurus maximus, A. OMNH 01338, left ilium, lateral view; B. OMNH 01737, proximal end of right ischium, lateral view; C. OMNH 01425, distal half of right pubis, lateral view; D. OMNH 01708, right femur, E. anterior, F. medial, G. posterior, and H. lateral views; OMNH 01370, right tibia, K. posterior, L. anterior, and M. lateral views; OMNH 01935, left humerus, O. posterior, P. anterior, and Q. medial views, originally referred to *Saurophaganax maximus.* Scale = 10 cm. (A–D, E–H, I, J–M, and N–Q sharing same scale bar). (After Chure 1995.)

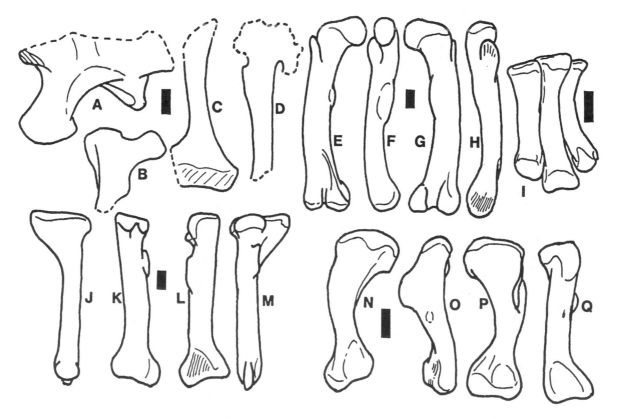

Photograph by the author, courtesy Royal Tyrrell Museum/Alberta Community Development.

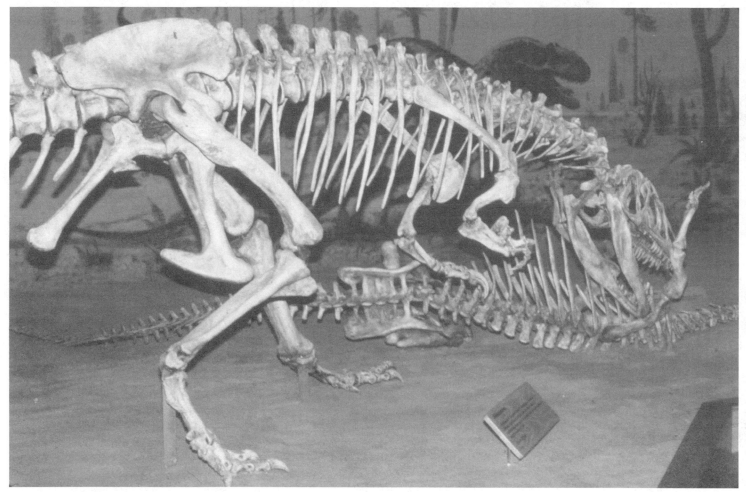

Allosaurus fragilis skeleton mounted in feeding pose.

the various aspects of this dinosaur continue to surface.

In the past, various modern workers (*e.g.*, Paul 1988*b*; Britt 1991) have suggested that more than a single valid species (*i.e., A. fragilis*) could exist at the above three sites. More recently, Smith (1996) tested that idea by performing a discriminant analysis of *Allosaurus* material from the Cleveland-Lloyd Dinosaur Quarry, Como Bluff locality, and Dry Mesa Dinosaur Quarry, using several different strategies to construct the discriminant functions for this genus. Utilizing a discriminant analysis, Smith attempted to allocate various *A. fragilis* specimens to the quarries from which they were extracted. Smith noted that, if correctly identified, the specimens could reveal consistent morphological differences reflecting evolutionary or geographic trends in *Allosaurus* populations from the three quarries, and that, given a set of measurements, an isolated element could therefore be related to its respective quarry.

Smith found that Cleveland-Lloyd *Allosaurus* specimens could be correctly distinguished from those from the other quarries, but only if size was retained as a factor (possibly due to such proposed untestable

hypotheses as "selective preservation of young individuals, sub-optimal environmental conditions, or a gene-flow filter between this population and those to the east and south"); also, that those from Como Bluff and Dry Mesa tended to be confused with one another. Little or no shape difference was observed in *Allosaurus* bones from any of the three sites, this suggesting to Smith that only one valid species, *A. fragilis*, should be retained as valid.

Subsequently, Smith (1998) published a morphometric analysis of population variation in *Allosaurus* based upon specimens found at Como Bluff, Dry Mesa, Dinosaur National Monument (Utah), Garden Park (near Canyon City, Colorado), and the Cleveland-Lloyd Dinosaur Quarry. Smith (1998) patterned his study in part upon a morphometric study by Weishampel and Chapman (1990) of 33 femora of the prosauropod *Plateosaurus* from the Trössingen quarry in Germany, in which two morphs, similar to the pattern observed by Smith in *Allosaurus*, were revealed. These different morphs in *Plateosaurus* were regarded by Weishampel and Chapman as having sexual rather than taxonomic significance.

Allosaurus

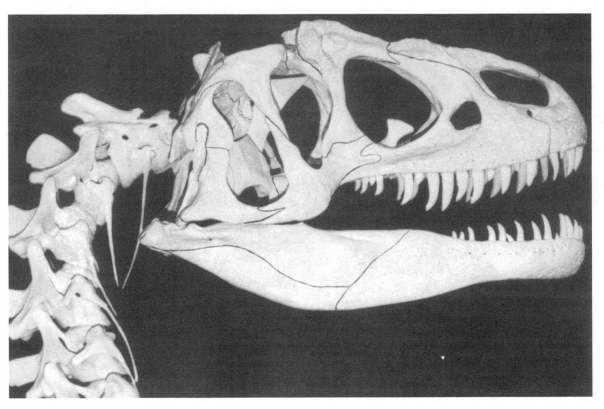

Allosaurus fragilis, reconstruction of skull and anterior presacral vertebrae, based on material recovered from the Cleveland-Lloyd Dinosaur Quarry. *Allosaurus* is the most common representative of the fauna from this site. (After Madsen 1976.)

From his extensive study, Smith (1998) could not find justification, utilizing morphometric methods, for the existence of more than one species of *Allosaurus* within the type species *A. fragilis*. Variation among femora heads constituted the only variable where an anomalous pattern was seen, these differences therefore regarded by Smith (1998) as having no systematic importance. Most morphometric and morphological variation was observed to occur in the skull, these differences appearing to be gradational with no well-defined clustering and, therefore, interpreted as a result of individual variation (Smith, Richmond and Bybee, in preparation).

Regarding *Saurophaganax*, Smith (1998) found the material assigned to this genus to lie on the same growth trajectory in almost every instance, therefore "The presence of unique morphological characters described by Chure (1995), combined with the results presented here, suggest that *Saurophaganax* is a distinct, large species of *Allosaurus* that should be referred to as *Allosaurus maximus*.

Addressing Britt's (1991) suggestion that two *Allosaurus* morphologies (one "low-cheeked," the other "high-cheeked") from the Dry Mesa Quarry may represent distinct species, Smith (1998) noted that these differences fall within the expected range variation for *A. fragilis*. Noting that the second of these morphs was also identified as having a lower crested lacrimal, Smith (1998) pointed out that shape variation in other *Allosaurus* elements is sometimes greater than that seen in that bone.

The first study on variation in aspects of the tympanic pneumatic system in a population of *A. fragilis* was made by Chure and Madsen (1996a) and published in a preliminary report. (As pointed out by Chure and Madsen, this system in theropod dinosaurs has generally been only poorly understood and mostly unrecognized, mostly due to "the historical failure of morphologists to recognize this system in theropods.") Their study was based on a series of 17 basicrania (UUVP 2850, 5849, 0033, 3287, 6912, 5942, 3203, 5943, 5843, 5748, 2067, 5969, 3304, 5583, 5346, 40-540, and 294). The specimens were collected from the Cleveland-Lloyd Dinosaur Quarry. These 17 basicrania comprise a population sample from one locality. (See Miller, Horrocks and Madsen 1996 for the first extensive article concerning this quarry and its fauna [80 percent of which have been identified as *A. fragilis*], including a history of the site and detailed quarry map; also Miller 1996).

From examination of these specimens, Chure and Madsen found depressions on the basicranium and also the presence of pneumatic foramina, evidence indicating to them that, as in many other theropods, a diverticulum of the tympanic pneumatic system was present in *Allosaurus*, bound medially by the lateral surface of the basisphenoid and laterally by the medial surface of the ala basisphenoidalis.

According to Chure and Madsen, the tympanic pneumatic system in *A. fragilis* exhibits both ontogenetic and individual variation:

Anteriorly, diverticula invade the basipterygoid process in the smallest individuals and withdraw with age, sometimes becoming lost with increasing basicranial length. Basipterygoidal recesses are present on both sides and symmetrically distributed, unlike the general pattern observed in theropods (reported by Currie and Zhao 1993), wherein asymmetry in size and number of sinuses is not uncommon.

Posteriorly, the caudoventral extension of the lateral basisphenoidal depression exhibits marked individual variation "as to degree of development and also left/right asymmetry in the presence or absence of the recesses." Chure and Madsen noted that degree of development of this extension is unrelated to the individual's size and variation is typical of that reported in other theropods (see Currie and Zhao).

Chure and Madsen noted that well-developed recesses on basipterygoid processes have been reported in several theropod families, including the Allosauridae (*Piatnitzkysaurus floresi*; Bonaparte 1986*b*), Itemiridae (*Itemirus medullaris*; Kurzanov 1976), and Family indet. (?*Stokesosaurus clevelandi* braincase from the Cleveland-Lloyd Dinosaur Quarry; see *Stokesosaurus* entry), the adult condition in these taxa strongly resembling, or being more pronounced than, the condition observed in juvenile *A. fragilis* individuals. Although no ontogenetic series exists for these taxa, Chure and Madsen speculated that this adult condition is retained from an earlier growth stage. Because the known occurrences of pronounced basipterygoidal recesses in adults is widespread systematically, Chure and Madsen suspected that this condition can probably be attributed to parallelism, with no phylogenetic importance.

Taphonomic evidence suggesting the scavenging of an *Allosaurus* individual was reported by Chure, Fiorillo and Madsen (1997). A partial skeleton of a large (ilium length of 811 millimeters) *Allosaurus* from the Morrison Formation of Wyoming exhibits numerous, subparallel tooth marks on the foot of the pubis, one of the most massive bones of the skeleton. The caudal two-third of the right side of the bone is missing; and the ventral margin of the missing piece is a smooth, gentle curve suggestive of the curve, as seen in ventral view, of the tooth row of a large carnivorous dinosaur.

As interpreted by Chure *et al.* (1997), the tooth marks probably resulted from a single bite of the lateral and anterolateral part of the tooth row of a large theropod, this idea being supported by the curvature of the bite and the fact that the tooth marks do not cross. (Because of the large number of tooth impressions, multiple bites would have been employed only if the snout of the biter were used, which would almost surely have resulted in crosscutting instead of

Photograph by the author, courtesy American Museum of Natural History.

Allosaurus fragilis, (AMNH 5753), detail of skull (cast) showing lacrimals, right three-quarter view. According to a 1998 study by paleontologist David K. Smith, the size and shape of lacrimals in the genus *Allosaurus* seem to be the result of allometry and individual variation.

subparallel marks and a scalloped rather than curved outline.)

Based on the size of the bite, the authors found *Ceratosaurus* or *Torvosaurus* to be the most likely candidates for the makers of the tooth marks. Owing to the size of the *Allosaurus* individual, and to the massiveness of the pubic foot and its position in the skeleton, Chure *et al.* (1997) deemed it more plausible that the bites were made after the animal was dead rather than during an attack.

Laws (1997) published a preliminary report on a study of abnormalities in the bones of a skeleton (MOR 693) of an 87 percent-grown, subadult male *A. fragilis*, nicknamed "Big Al," from the Morrison

Formation of Big Horn County, Wyoming. Pathologic bones include five dorsal ribs, cervical vertebra 6, dorsals 3, 8, and 13, caudal 2, chevron 2, gastralia, a scapula, manual phalanx I-1, pedal phalanges III-1 and II-3 (ungual), metatarsals III and V, and an ilium. The bones were compared by Laws to pathologic theropod specimens from the Cleveland-Lloyd collections housed at Brigham Young University, Provo, Utah, and at the Museum of the Rockies, in Bozeman, Montana.

As interpreted by Laws, these bones were so afflicted as the result of trauma, infection, or aberrancy. The condition of all of these pathologic bones suggested that infection and injury were common to theropod dinosaurs. Laws deduced that the Big Horn County *Allosaurus* "may have incurred some infection while standing on carcasses and some injury during competition with other males and pursuit of prey." Laws further speculated that "allosaurs possessed an immune response which allowed them to live with microbial infection in their bones, probably by keeping it localized."

Breithaupt (1998) reported that the partially articulated "Big Al" skeleton, which had been discovered in 1991 north of Shell, Wyoming, near the American Museum of Natural History's famous Howe Quarry, is one of the most complete (95 percent) individual specimens of this genus ever found in Wyoming.

Note: Williamson and Chure (1996) reported a large allosaurid represented by a partial postcranial skeleton (NMMNH P-26083), including an incomplete pelvic girdle (comprising part of the right ilium, right and left ischia), two sacral vertebrae (?numbers 4 and 5), the anterior part of the tail (first through fourth caudal vertebrae, four chevrons), a partial left hind limb (femur, tibia, fibula, several phalanges), and a right femur, discovered by Ron and Rod Peterson in the Brushy Basin Member of the Morrison Formation, on the east flank of Mesa Gigante, in west-central New Mexico. The bones were found either in articulation or in close association, indicating that they all belonged to a single individual. The specimen, the most complete Jurassic theropod yet found in that

Two *Allosaurus fragilis* individuals confronting a *Ceratosaurus nasicornis*, the latter utilizing its heavy tail to kick out with its feet. Illustration by Gregory S. Paul (from *Predatory Dinosaurs of the World*), a specialist in the restoration of theropods.

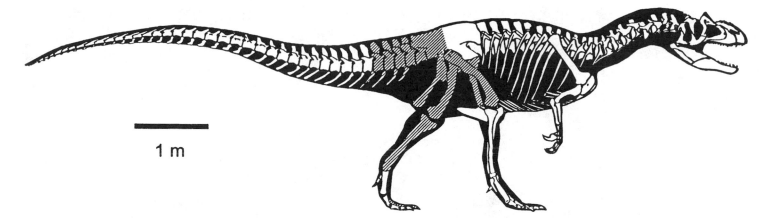

Skeletal reconstruction based on preserved elements (hatched areas) of allosaurid specimen NMMNH P-26083. (After Williamson and Chure 1996.)

state, was salvaged from the base of a coarse-grained, well-cemented sandstone that was in the process of being rapidly removed by headwall erosion during strong but brief summer torrential rains. The locality, one of the richest in the Morrison Formation of New Mexico, also yielded numerous isolated sauropod elements, including ribs, vertebrae, and a partial skull belonging to a diplodocid.

The specimen was of particular interest to Williamson and Chure because of its size (femur having a preserved length of 991 millimeters and estimated complete length of approximately 1100 millimeter, rivalling material which Chure had referred to *Saurophaganax maximus*) and because of its occurrence, being the most southern-known theropod from the Morrison Formation.

As NMMNH P-26083 lacks important diagnostic elements, Williamson and Chure were unable to refer this specimen with certainty to any particular genus, although some comparisons with other large, Morrison Formation theropod taxa were possible. In the hind limb, the elevated femoral head and wing-like lessert trochanter of the femur, and tall ascending process of the astragalus (inferred from a scar on the tibia), are features of Tetanurae, the authors thus excluding close affinity with *Ceratosaurus* (apparently regarded by them as a "ceratosaur"; see "Systematics" chapter). The expanded distal end of the ischium and short postacetabular portion of the ilium separate the specimen from the Coelurosauria. Though the ischium is not complete, its straight ischial shaft and the short, squared-off posterior end of the ilium remove it from referral either to *Marshosaurus* or *Torvosaurus*. The ischia of NMMNH P-26083 resemble those of *Allosaurus* in having a long, straight and slender shaft and characteristic distal expansion, indicating that the specimen belongs in the Allosauridae. Although NMMNH P-26083 could belong to *Allosaurus fragilis* or some other Morrison Formation allosaurid species (*e.g.*, *A. maximus*, for which the ischium is, at best, only poorly known), or may repre-

sent a new taxon, Williamson and Chure could not make such a determination based on the collected material.

Erratum: In *D:TE*, p. 113, the figured holotype neural spine (AMNH 5731) of *Hypsirophus discursus* (a composite species established on elements of both *Allosaurus* and *Stegosaurus*) belongs to *Stegosaurus armatus*. The stegosaur material belonging to this specimen may represent a valid genus (K. Carpenter, personal communication 1998).

Key references: Bakker (1986); Breithaupt (1998); Camp, Welles and Green (1953); Chure (1995); Chure, Fiorillo and Madsen (1997); Chure and Madsen (1996*a*); Chure and McIntosh (1989); Currie and Zhao (1993); Hunt and Lucas (1987); Langston (1989); Laws (1997); Paul (1988*b*); Ray (1941); Smith (1996, 1998); Williamson and Chure (1996).

ALTIRHINUS Norman 1998

Ornithischia: Genasauria: Cerapoda: Ornithopoda: Euornithopoda: Iguanodontia: Euiguanodontia: Dryomorpha: Ankylopollexia: Iguanodontidae.

Name derivation: Latin *altus* = "high" + Greek *rhinus* = "nose."

Type species: *A. kurzanovi* Norman 1998.

Other species: [None.]

Occurrence: Khuren Dukh, Dornogov', Mongolia.

Age: Early Cretaceous (late Aptian–Albian).

Known material: Five specimens, including cranial and postcranial remains, adults and juveniles.

Holotype: PIN 3386/8 (some elements numbered 3388), cranial remains including much of left side of well-preserved skull, right side of skull crushed, damaged, and represented by isolated right nasal, predentary, dentary, pterygoid fragments, quadrate, squamosal, postorbital, jugal, surangular, angular, prearticular, and paroccipital wing), postcrania including left and right atlas neural arches, left scapula, left coracoid, pubes, ischia, manus digit V, ungual of manuses IV and III, three pedal phalanges including one ungual.

Altirhinus

Altirhinus kurzanovi, holotype skull (PIN 3386/8), left lateral view.

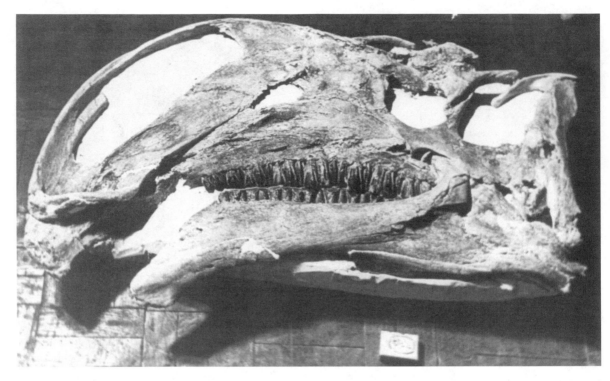

Diagnosis of genus (as for type species): Euornithopod measuring up to 8 meters in length; rostral tip of nasals strongly arched; external surface of nasals smooth, no depression on lateral surface for extension of (presumed) extranarial pouch; midline internasal

Altirhinus kurzanovi, PIN 3389, referred left manus, dorsal view. (After Norman 1998.)

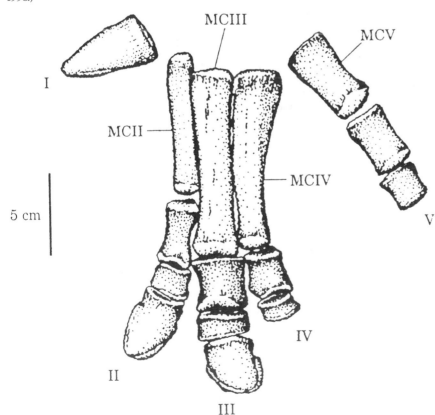

groove; rostral portion of premaxilla decurved; lateral flaring of premaxilla (to widen oral cavity) not bounded by raised rim; no antorbital fenestra; lacrimal articulating with finger-shaped dorsal process of maxilla; large curved (left) palpebral articulating with prefrontal; quadrate (paraquadrate) foramen between quadratojugal and quadrate; rostral end of jugal tapering to a point; jugal articulating with caudolaterally directed finger-like process on maxilla; postpalatine foramen present; surangular with two lateral foramina; dentary with down-curved rostral end; two replacement crowns in deeper (caudal) portions of maxillary and dentary dentitions; manus proportions very similar to those of *Iguanodon* spp.; ungual phalanx of manus digit I large, conical, laterally compressed; carpus well ossified, but not co-ossified into two discrete blocks (as in *Camptosaurus, Iguanodon* spp., and *Ouranosaurus*); digit IV of manus with apparently short hooflike ungual; ilium with sinuous dorsal margin, large anterior process, everted dorsal ridge, no brevis shelf; shaft of ischium straight, parallel-sided, with axial twist; femoral shaft curved rostrally; large, finger-shaped lesser trochanter (not flattened and appressed to anterolateral margin of greater trochanter (Norman 1998).

Comments: The genus *Altirhinus* was founded upon a partial skeleton (PIN 3386/8) collected from the Lower Cretaceous ("Khukhtekian" of Jerzykiewicz and Russell 1991) of Khuren Dukh (Xypeh Dyx), northwestern Dornogoĭ (East Gobi Province, south of the town of Choir [Choyr]), Mongolia. Paratype specimens from the same locality, referred to the type species *A. kurzanovi*, comprise the following: PIN 3386/7 (3387), including dentaries, predentary, surangulars, angular, splenial, prearticular, premaxilla, maxillae, jugal, palpebral, prefrontal, frontals, lacrimals, quadrates, pterygoid, palatine, ?vomers, ten isolated teeth, left atlas neural arch, fragmentary cervical and dorsal vertebrae, many ribs, metacarpals, phalanges, and unguals of manus, sternal bones, coracoids, humerus, radius, and ulna; PIN 3386/9 (3389), including scapulae, left coracoid, sternal plates, humeri, radii, right ulna, right manus, metacarpals II–V, unguals of pollex, all phalanges of digits II–IV, phalanges 1 and 2 of digit IV, 1 and 2 of V, metacarpals II–V of left manus, pollex spine, complete digits II–IV, phalanx of digit V, isolated carpal bones, pubes, left femur, right tibia, fibulae, astragali, two sets of metatarsals, all first phalanges, second phalanges of right and left digits I and II, two lateral unguals, and 34 caudal vertebrae; and PIN 3390, including broken limb and girdle bones, some neural arch and jaw fragments, isolated dentary tooth, and PIN 3391, including partial left pes, tibia, four vertebral centra, small fragments, the latter two specimens representing small individuals (Norman 1998).

The holotype of this new taxon — including a high-snouted skull (apparently formerly listed as PIN 3386/50) resembling skulls of *Iguanodon* (see *D:TE*), collected by Sergei N. Kurzanov of the Palaeontology Institute of the Russian Academy of Sciences — was tentatively referred, in various published studies (*e.g.*, Norman 1986; Norman and Weishampel 1990), to *I. orientalis*, a species founded by Rozhdestvensky (1942), based upon dental similarities. Subsequently,

Norman (1996) found that *I. orientalis* was established on nondiagnostic materials, although the Asian species does seem to be closely similar to the European species *I. bernissartensis*, and also that the referred specimen does not belong to the same taxon.

During the 1980s and 1990s, drawings and photographs of this skull began to appear in various technical and popular publications, the skull itself being displayed at various exhibitions including the "Great Russian Dinosaurs" traveling exhibit, which began in 1996, and also the third Dinofest™ event in 1998.

In a preliminary report, Norman and Kurzanov (1997) stated that the specimen including the skull usually referred to as "*Iguanodon*" *orientalis* represents a new genus and species of iguanodontian ornithopod, this dinosaur being very similar, especially in postcranial anatomy, to *Iguanodon*. Subsequently, Norman (1998) officially referred PIN 3386/8 to its own iguanodontid genus and species, *Altirhinus kurzanovi*.

According to Norman (1998), *Altirhinus* differs only slightly from *Iguanodon*, the major differences and their potential implications being as follows: 1. Enlargement and depression of the premaxillary and dentary beak in *Altirhinus* altering the cropping mode, probably facilitating regular feeding on a diversity of low browse; 2. increase in length of diastema, facilitating a bimodal jaw action, whereby the cropping action can operate without interfering with the normal chewing action (as in extant mammals); and 3. depth of maxillary and dentary dentitions required for a second replacement tooth possibly indicating a more abrasive diet, though there are limitations to this

Altirhinus kurzanovi, ilium of unregistered specimen (juvenile) associated with this species in collections from Khuren Dukh, left lateral view. (After Norman 1998.)

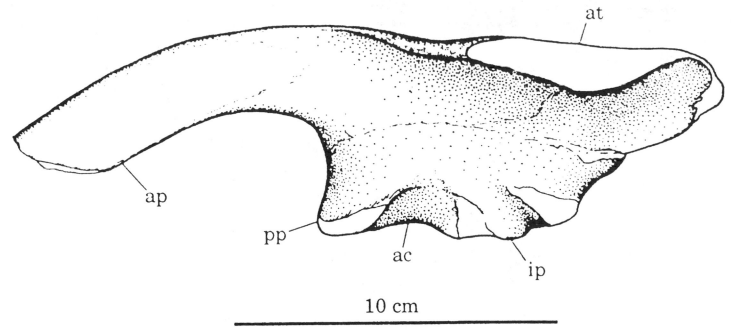

10 cm

strategy, a second replacement crown being present only in the deepest part of the jaw.

Norman (1998) regarded *Altirhinus* as a derived member of the Iguanodontidae, the anatomy of *A. kurzanovi* being comparable to that of *Iguanodon* (Norman 1980, 1986) in both the general framework formed by most of the cranial bones and in numerous aspects of the postcranial skeletons, most notably the form of the manus. This species also bears some superficial resemblances to members of the Hadrosauridae. However, apomorphic traits observed by Norman (1998) in this new genus (*e.g.*, expanded external nares and elevated nasals, diastema, ventral offset of beak, increase in replacement teeth in maxillary and dental batteries) and apparent reduction in the co-ossification of the carpus were perceived as convergent with hadrosaurids rather than as synapomorphies with the Hadrosauridae.

As Norman (1998) speculated, the appearance of very "European" large ornithopods in Asia may be explained by contemporaneous though episodic land links between the Northern Hemisphere land masses during the Barremian–Albian interval. The appearance of derived forms such as *Altirhinus* in Asia could be attributed to the isolation of Asia from the European "domain" during the Late Cretaceous (Albian), this suggesting an Asian origin for the Hadrosauridae in "Middle" Cretaceous times.

Norman (1998) noted various anatomical adaptations in the skull of *A. kurzanovi*: Vertical expansion of dorsal nasal cavity; lateral expansion and lowering of cropping beak relative to jaw line; increase in number of replacement teeth (but no significant miniaturization of crowns) and trend toward formation of more integrated cheek-teeth battery (seen to varying degrees in several mid–Cretaceous ornithopods). These adaptations, Norman (1998) suggested, "can be

interpreted within the context of an evolutionary trend culminating in the cranial complexity seen in the terminal lineage of ornithopods represented by the Late Cretaceous Hadrosauridae." The skull modifications seen in *A. kurzanovi* were interpreted as broadly analogous to those also seen in some iguanodontians (*e.g.*, *Ouranosaurus* and *Muttaburrasaurus*) and some hadrosaurine hadrosaurids (*e.g.*, *Brachylophosaurus* and *Gryposaurus*), this seeming trend in narial expansion among ornithopods apparently having functional and ecological significance.

Functionally, Norman (1998) noted, some of these modifications can be related to what may be regarded as "improvements" to the efficiency of gathering and processing food, which could "represent increased niche partitioning and/or responses to increasingly tough and abrasive (xeric adapted) foliage." Other changes, most significantly modifications in the nasal cavity (possibly associated with providing space for a counter-current turbinal system for conserving moisture; see "Ectothermy Versus Endothermy" section, p. 40), may suggest "a biological response to increasingly seasonal/xeric conditions in the middle of the Cretaceous Period or changes in the floral composition of these times."

Key references: Norman (1980, 1986, 1996, 1998); Norman and Kurzanov (1997); Norman and Weishampel (1990); Rozdestvensky (1952).

†AMARGASAURUS

Saurischia: Sauropodomorpha: Sauropoda: Eusauropoda: Neosauropoda: Diplodocoidea: Dicraeosauridae.

Comments: Among the more atypical sauropods to be named and described in the past decade is *Amargasaurus* (Salgado and Bonaparte 1991), a genus distin-

Amargasaurus cazaui, original reconstruction of holotype skeleton (MACN-N 15). (After Salgado and Bonaparte 1991.)

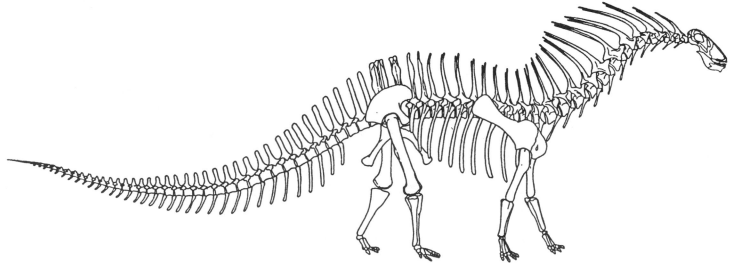

Photograph by Brian Franczak, courtesy José F. Bonaparte and Museo Argentino de Ciencias Naturales.

Amargasaurus cazaui, reconstructed skeleton MACN-N 15 (skull based on *Dicraeosaurus*) mounted at the Museo Argentino de Ciencias Naturales, Buenos Aires.

Postcranial skeleton (LACM 6058 131865, cast of holotype MACN-N 15) of the unusual sauropod *Amargasaurus cazaui*, displayed as found in the field.

Photograph by the author, courtesy Natural History Museum of Los Angeles County.

Above and opposite: Two unusual saurischian dinosaurs from the Late Cretaceous of Argentina: The high-spined sauropod *Amargasaurus cazaui* (above) and horned theropod *Carnotaurus sastrei* (opposite page), as restored by Robert F. Walters.

guished by exceptionally long cervical neural spines, which may have supported a kind of membranous frill along the neck, or simply arose as individual units somewhat resembling a porcupine's quills.

Bonaparte (1996*b*) hypothesized that these exceptionally long spines in *Amargasaurus*, in a proportion presently unknown in any other sauropod, probably imposed a different behavior of the neck and head movements of this genus than in the more conservative neck of *Dicraeosaurus.* The characters of higher degree of bifurcation in the dorsal neural spines and elongate cervical neural spines in the Late Cretaceous *Amargasaurus* compared with *Dicraeosaurus* of the Late Jurassic "suggest an evolutionary trend of these characters within this clade of sauropods."

According to Bonaparte, the presence of the re-

lated *Dicraeosaurus* in Africa and *Amargasaurus* in South America, and their absence in Laurasia, suggest that dicraeosaurids could have differentiated in Gondwana, perhaps not dispersing to Laurasia for paleogeographic reasons. Bonaparte found the inclusion by McIntosh (1990) of the Mongolian genera *Nemegtosaurus* and *Quaesitosaurus* (now possibly a junior synonym of *Nemegtosaurus*; see entry in *D:TE*) in the "Dicraeosaurinae" to be not supported by convincing arguments (see *Nemegtosaurus* entry, this volume).

Erratum: The photo caption on p. 124 of *D:TE* should state that the skull of *Amargasaurus cazuai* was reconstructed after that of *Dicraeosaurus*, not *Diplodocus.* (See also *Apatosaurus* entry, "Erratum," this volume.)

Key references: Bonaparte (1996*b*); Salgado and Bonaparte (1991).

†AMPELOSAURUS

Saurischia: Sauropodomorpha: Sauropoda: Eusauropoda: Neosauropoda: Macronaria: Camarasauromorpha: Titanosauriformes: Somphospondyli: Titanosauria: Titanosauridae.

Comments: Titanosaurid sauropods are rare in the Upper Cretaceous of Europe, having thus far been recorded only from Campanian and early Maastrichtian rocks of the Ibero-Armorican Island, a land mass including the Iberian Peninsula, France, and much of Germany. One of the best known titanosaurids from this area is *Ampelosaurus atacis*, a type species from the late Campanian to early Maastrichtian of France.

To date of this writing, Jean Le Loeuff— who named this taxon and presented a preliminary de-

scription of same in 1995 — has not yet published his announced monograph on this genus and species (see *D:TE*). However, in a more recent abstract (1998), Le Loeuff stated that *A. atacis* is a 15-meter (over 50-foot) long animal known not only from the upper Aude Valley, but also the Petites Pyrénées, and the Chaînon de Saint-Chinian.

Notes: Le Loeuff (1998) briefly mentioned four additional as yet unnamed and not formally described titanosaurid species from the latest Cretaceous of the Ibero-Armorican Island:

1. A smaller new genus and species from the (late Campanian–early Maastrichtian) Spanish Basque Country (Sanz, Powell, Le Loeuff and Martinez, in press);

2. Some poorly preserved midcaudal vertebrae

found by a Mr. Degeix in upper Campanian marine deposits at Vanxains, near Ribérac (Dordogne), original characters being that "their neural arch is placed very anteriorly, and the pedicles cover only the anterior third of the centrum";

3. Caudal vertebrae and a scapula, recently discovered at (early Maastrichtian) Fox Amphoux (Var) by amateur paleontologists Patrick and Annie Méchin, the scapula "characterized by a system of ridges and protuberances at the base of the scapular blade," this feature being unknown in all other titanosaurids; and

4. A late Maastrichtian form from Els Nerets (Catalonia, Spain).

Le Loueff (1998) added that one or even several more titanosaurid species may have evolved during the latest Cretaceous on the Ibero-Armorican Island. According to the author, "This number is much higher than previous figures, and thus raises questions about the ecological or stratigraphical differences between these species."

Key references: Le Loeuff (1995, 1998).

†AMPHICOELIAS

Saurischia: Sauropodomorpha: Sauropoda: Eusauropoda: Neosauropoda: Diplodocoidea.

Diagnosis of genus: Autapomorphies including basal tubera with pendant lateral processes; pleurocoels of cervical vertebrae surrounded by well marked fossa; slender femur with subcircular cross section at midshaft (Wilson and Smith 1996).

Comments: One of the earliest sauropods to be discovered, *Amphicoelias*, named and described by pioneer North American paleontologist Edward Drinker Cope (1877*b*), is a relatively rare genus known from little fossil material, some of which has been misplaced.

Recently, Wilson and Smith (1996) announced new material pertaining to this dinosaur. These remains, representing a single individual, include a partial skull, 12 presacral and seven vertebrae, complete pelvis, and a femur, collected from the Upper Jurassic Morrison Formation of Park County, Montana. Wilson and Smith identified the specimen as referable to *Amphicoelias* because of "the extreme slenderness of the femur, the subcircular femoral cross-section at mid shaft, and reduced pleurocentral opening in the posterior dorsal centra."

Generally, *Amphicoelias* has been regarded as a member of the Diplodocidae. In their brief report on the new material, however, Wilson and Smith removed the genus from that position, noting that it exhibits various synapomorphies of Diplodocoidea (dentary with ventrally projecting "chin," dentary symphysis narrow, cervical ribs short).

According to Wilson and Smith, *Amphicoelias*

lacks most diplodocid plus "dicraeosaurid" synapomorphies, and, despite some homoplasy, remains in a basal position within Diplodocoidea; plesiomorphic features include ventrally directed basipterygoid processes, a rounded dentary ramus, and pubis having a weakly developed ambiens process.

Wilson and Smith pointed out that *Amphicoelias* lacks two of the most characteristic features of Diplodocidae plus "Dicraeosauridae" (the anteriorly directed basipterygoid processes, which position the jaw articulation beneath the anterior margin of the orbit, and the squared muzzle), this suggesting that these features "constitute a correlated feeding innovation of advanced diplodocoids."

Key references: Cope (1877*b*); Wilson and Smith (1996).

ANGATURAMA Kellner and Campos 1996 — (=?*Irritator*)

Saurischia: Theropoda: Neotheropoda: Tetanurae: Spinosauroidea: Spinosauridae.

Name derivation: Aboriginal Brazilian Tupi *angaturama* = "noble."

Type species: *A. limai* Kellner and Campos 1996.

Other species: [None.]

Occurrence: Santana Formation, Southern Ceará, Brazil.

Age: Early Cretaceous (Albian).

Known material/holotype: GP/2T-5, incomplete anterior part of skull.

Diagnosis of genus (as for type species): Anterior part of skull strongly compressed, narrowest near sixth premaxillary tooth; anterior portion of premaxilla less broad ("spoon-shaped") than in *Baryonyx*; well-developed premaxillary sagittal crest (Kellner and Campos 1996).

Comments: The genus *Angaturama* was founded upon part of a skull (GP/2T-5) collected from the Romualdo Member (Albian; see Pons, Bethou and Campos 1990) of the Santana Formation, Araripe Basin, Southern Ceará, Northeastern Brazil. The type specimen, contained in a calcereous nodule brought to the attention of Alexander W. A. Kellner in 1991, is significant as the first dinosaur to be described from Brazil for which skull material, excluding the lower jaws (see *Staurikosaurus* entry, D:TE), is known. No complete teeth were preserved in the specimen (Kellner and Campos 1996).

As described by Kellner and Campos, the premaxilla has a total of seven teeth, which seem to decrease in size from the first to the third, gradually decrease from the third to the sixth, then increase to the third maxillary tooth. The fourth maxillary alveolus is smaller than the previous one, suggesting that the teeth may decrease in size posteriorly. All teeth seem

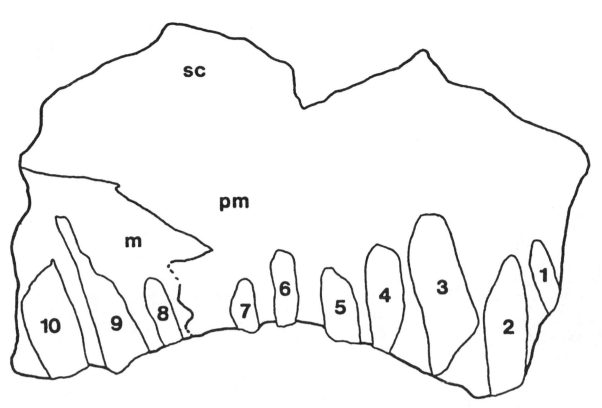

Angaturama limai, GP/ 2T-5), holotype partial anterior part of skull, right lateral view. Scale = 50 mm. (After Kellner and Campos 1996.)

to be long and forwardly directed, with subcircular transverse sections; they have very long roots, and at least the basal portion of the anterior and posterior keels are not serrated, resembling the condition found in *Spinosaurus*.

Because of several synapomorphies shared by *Angaturama* and various other unusual theropods attributed to spinosaurids, the authors referred this genus to the Spinosauridae (see "Systematics" chapter).

Key reference: Kellner and Campos (1996).

ANIMANTARX Carpenter, Kirkland, Burge and Bird 1998

Ornithischia: Genasauria: Thyreophora: Nodosauridae.

Name derivation: Latin *animant* = "living" + Latin *arx* = "fortress or citadel."

Type species: *A. ramaljonesi* Carpenter, Kirkland, Burge and Bird 1998.

Other species: [None.]

Occurrence: Cedar Mountain Formation, Utah, United States.

Age: Early Cretaceous (Albian–Cenomanian).

Known material/holotype: CEUM 6228, partial skull and right mandible, cervical and dorsal vertebrae, ribs, scapulocoracoids, fragment of sternal plate, right humerus, left ilium with ischium, left femur.

Diagnosis of genus (as for type species): Parietal region highly domed (as in *Struthiosaurus*, *Pawpawsaurus*, and *Silvisaurus*, as opposed to moderately

domed as in *Sauropelta* and *Panoplosaurus*, and slightly domed in *Edmontonia*); postorbital "horns" very small (prominent in *Pawpawsaurus*, absent in *Sauropelta*, *Edmontonia*, *Silvisaurus*, *Panoplosaurus*, and *Struthiosaurus*); lateral notch in skull roof for supratemporal fenestra moderately developed in dorsal view (as in *Edmontonia*, well developed in *Pawpawsaurus*, absent in *Silvisaurus*); skull roof having indistinguishable armor pattern (as in *Silvisaurus* and *Gastonia*, well developed pattern in all other known nodosaurids); quadratojugal "horn" small, rounded (as in *Niobrarasaurus*, as opposed to large, pointed in *Sauropelta*, large, rounded in *Pawpawsaurus* and *Silvisaurus*); exoccipitals and supraoccipital forming prominent dorsal and lateral rim to foramen magnum (as in *Struthiosaurus*, rim absent or moderately developed in other nodosaurids); armor on mandible restricted to half mandibular length (as opposed to three-fourths length in *Edmontonia* and *Panoplosaurus*); armor not prominent (as in *Silvisaurus*, very prominent in *Sauropelta*, *Edmontonia*, and *Panoplosaurus*); coracoid elongate, approximately 63 percent length of scapula (similar to 62 percent in *Panoplosaurus*, unlike 27 percent in *Sauropelta*); humerus having very slender shaft (as in other nodosaurids), but deltopectoral crest very high, near level of humeral head (unlike that in other known nodosaurids); oblique ridge on anterolateral surface of femur below lesser trochanter (as in *Texasetes*) (Carpenter, Kirkland, Burge and Bird 1998).

Comments: The genus *Animantarx* was founded

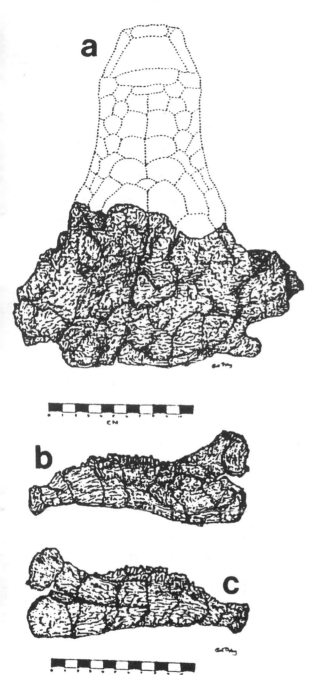

Animantarx ramaljonesi,
CEUM 6228, holotype a.
posterior part of cranium
(dorsal view), and b.–c.
lower jaw (medial and lateral views, respectively),
originally referred to cf.
Pawpawsaurus. (After
Burge 1996.)

upon a partial skele-
ton with partial skull
(CEUM 6228), dis-
covered by Ramal
Jones at the Carol
Site, just above the
base of the Mussen-
tuchit Member of the
Cedar Mountain
Formation, in a band
of the formation ex-
tending east-west,
south of the Books
Cliffs in northern
Grand County and
Emery County, east-
ern Utah. Jones
found the specimen
in an area where no
bones were exposed
on the surface utiliz-
ing a modified scin-
tillometer (see Jones
and Burge 1995), this
being the first time a
dinosaur specimen
has been found via
radiological survey-
ing. The type speci-
men was, at first,
briefly described by
Burge (1996) as a
nodosaurid possibly
referable to *Pawpaw-
saurus* (Carpenter,
Kirkland, Burge and
Bird 1998).

The Mussentu-
chit Member is the
geologically youngest
of four successively
older members, de-
fined by Kirkland, Britt, Burge, Carpenter, Cifelli,
DeCourten, Eaton, Hasiotis and Lawton (1997), of
the Cedar Mountain Formation, and was dated by
these authors as of Albian–Cenomanian age.

As estimated by Carpenter *et al.*, the *Animantarx*
individual represented by the holotype, based on its
postcranial remains, seems to be about comparable in
size to *Texasetes pleurohalio.*

Notes: Carpenter *et al.* also reported unidentifiable nodosaurid isolated teeth collected from the
east side of the San Rafael Swell, in the middle of the
Mussentuchit Member of the Cedar Mountain Formation.

According to Kirkland *et al.*, three successive dinosaur faunas, supported by the stratigraphic distribution of ankylosaurs, can now be recognized in the
Cedar Mountain Formation — subdivided by these
authors into the Yellow Cat Member, Poison Strip
Sandstone, the Ruby Ranch Member, and the
Mussentuchit Member. As noted by Carpenter *et al.*,
ankylosaurs are rare in the latter two members, but are
the most common of dinosaurs found in the upper
part of the Yellow Cat Member and Poison Strip Sandstone, this disparity possibly being a collecting artifact. "Nevertheless," Carpenter *et al.* noted, "ankylosaur dinosaurs indicate a three-fold division of the
Cedar Mountain dinosaur faunas and suggest that the
formation spans at least the last half of the Lower Cretaceous."

Key references: Burge (1996); Carpenter, Kirkland, Burge and Bird (1998); Jones and Burge (1995);
Kirkland, Britt, Burge, Carpenter, Cifelli, DeCourten, Eaton, Hasiotis and Lawton (1997).

†ANTARCTOSAURUS

Saurischia: Sauropodomorpha: Sauropoda: Eusauropoda: Neosauropoda: Macronaria: Titanosauriformes: Somphospondyli: Titanosauria: Titanosauridae.

Age: Late Cretaceous (Coniacian).

Holotype: MACN 6904, partial skull including
 braincase, quadrate, quadratojugal, squamosal, incomplete mandible with teeth, also cervical vertebra, scapula, radius, ulna, incomplete elements of
 pelvis, hind limb elements.

Comments: Among the relatively few titanosaurid taxa for which skull material is known (none
of which is complete, even most partial crania being
poorly preserved) is the very large South American
type species *Antarctosaurus wichmannianus.* The holotype (MACN 6904) of this taxon includes a partial
skull. Huene (1929) originally restored this skull as resembling that of *Diplodocus,* the appearance it has
mostly retained for nearly 70 years. Only recently have
the cranial elements of the type specimen been
significantly reevaluated and the skull reconstruction
been revised to reflect a more up to date understanding of this species.

As recounted by Bonaparte (1996*b*), in a review
of the Cretaceous tetrapods of Argentina, this skull
was collected in 1916 by R. Wichmann from the Río
Colorado Formation (Coniacian) of Río Negro Province. Although the cranial material is very incomplete,
the mandibular symphysis, Bonaparte observed, "is
built by a transversial plane of both dentaries, resulting in a wide anterior part of the snout, perhaps an
[*sic*] special adaptation for some alimentary habits,"

Photograph courtesy James I. Kirkland.

Animantarx ramaljonesi, CEUM 6228, associated holotype postcranial elements including left scapulocoracoid, right humerus, rib, posterior dorsal vertebra, right femur, and left ilium with co-osified ischium (entire ischium not figured in Carpenter, Kirkland, Burge and Bird 1998) originally referred to cf. *Pawpawsaurus.* (After Kirkland, Britt, Burge, Carpenter, Cifelli, DeCourten, Eaton, Hasiotis and Lawton 1997.)

such wide mouths in herbivorous mammals usually indicative of nonselective grazing habits, this suggesting that *A. wichmannianus* was a browser rather than a grazer.

In an extensive study of titanosaurid skulls in which they offered a new reconstruction of the skull of *A. wichmannianus,* Salgado and Calvo (1997) found that this skull shares the following exclusive characters with that of *Saltasaurus loricatus,* a species whose type material includes a skull in which the braincase (PVL 4017-161) and skull roof (PVL 4017-162) are preserved: 1. Parocciptal process long, recurved, becoming slender downwards; and 2. supratemporal fenestra reduced, narrow.

Salgado and Calvo noted that the second of these characters was listed by Powell (1986) as diagnostic for the Titanosauridae, thereby integrating the respective diagnoses of both *A. wichmannianus* and *S. loricatus* and are, consequently, apomorphies of these two species. Also, the skull of *A. wichmannianus* presents a character unknown in *Saltasaurus*— mandibular symphysis perpendicular to long axis of mandible — and is distinguished from other sauropods (except *Nemegtosaurus*) by its almost vertical mandibular symphysis.

After their restudy of the cranial elements of both *Antarctosaurus* and *Saltasaurus,* Salgado and Calvo proposed that the *A. wichmannianus* braincase is oriented like that of *Camarasaurus* rather than of *Diplodocus* (see "Systematics" chapter). If that is correct, then the ventral direction of the basipterygoid

processes in *A. wichmannianus* (also possibly in *Saltasaurus*) suggests that the mandibular articulation was positioned somewhat posteriorly, just below the occipital condyle, the quadrate axis therefore being vertical rather than anteriorly inclined (as in diplodocids).

Another species referred to *Antarctosaurus, A. giganteus* Huene 1929, was founded on two femora, fragments of pubis, the distal end of a tibia, and two incomplete caudal vertebrae (MLP 23-316), recovered by personnel of the La Plata Museum from the Río Neuquén Formation (Aptian; Bonaparte used the former and mostly abandoned stratigraphic designation "early Senonian," basically identifying the lower part of the Lower Cretaceous), Neuquén Province, Argentina. As observed by Bonaparte, the femora of this species are longer and more slender than in the type species, and display little expansion in the areas of proximal and distal articulation.

McIntosh (1990*b*) doubted that Huene's assignment of this species to *Antarctosaurus* was correct. Likewise, Bonaparte found that the affinities of the type material of this species with *A. wichmannianus* do not imply that it belongs to this genus, the gross similarities of the femora in both *A. giganteus* and *A. wichmannianus* possibly due to convergence in giant titanosaurs. Bonaparte cautioned that femora generally are not diagnostic at the genus level and pointed out that the material assigned to *A. giganteus* was collected from an older level than was the type species.

Bonaparte and Bossi (1967) had referred to *Antarctosaurus* sp. (see *D:TE*) a specimen (PVL 3670)

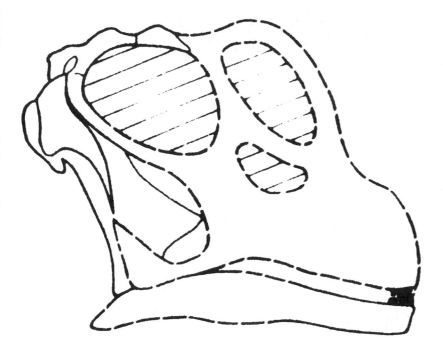

Antarctosaurus wichmannianus, new reconstruction of holotype partial skull (MACN 6904). (After Salgado and Calvo 1979.)

comprising a left premaxilla, one cervical and some caudal vertebrae, an incomplete humerus, ulna, radius, small fragment of ilium, incomplete pubis and ischium, the major portion of a femur, tibia and fibula, collected in 1982 by José F. Bonaparte, Jaime E. Powell, and assistants from the Los Blanquitos Formation (?Campanian), in the Salta Province of Salta, Argentina. This material is significant as "the first evidence of titanosaurid sauropods for the Salta Group of the Andean Basin (Reyes & Salfity 1973), and was an important argument to interpret the geological age of the bearing beds (Bonaparte & Bossi 1967)." For now, it constitutes the "only associated remains that documents the presence of Titanosaurinae in that region of Argentina" 1996b).

Powell (1979), observing that the radius differs significantly from that in *Antarctosaurus*, suggested that the above specimen could represent a new genus belonging to an undetermined higher taxon. Bonaparte observed the following in PVL 3670: Premaxilla high, somewhat short, externally convex, with large axial plane for contact with other premaxilla; premaxilla bearing four alveoli, three having erupting teeth; morphology of premaxilla suggesting anterior part of muzzle to be proportionally narrow (differing much from what is indicated by wide symphysial region of lower jaw of *A. wichmannianus*).

Bonaparte speculated that *Antarctosaurus*, though a gigantic sauropod, was probably among the most slender of titanosaurids.

Key references: Bonaparte (1996b); Bonaparte and Bossi (1967); Huene (1929); McIntosh (1990b); Powell (1979, 1986); Reyes & Salfity (1973); Salgado and Calvo (1997).

†**APATOSAURUS**—(=*Brontosaurus, Elosaurus*; =?*Atlantosaurus*)

Saurischia: Sauropodomorpha: Sauropoda: Eusauropoda: Neosauropoda: Diplodocoidea: Diplodocidae.

Comments: *Apatosaurus*, perhaps the most well known of all dinosaurian genera, continues to interest both scientists and laymen. Recent studies of this gigantic sauropod have involved such topics as the dinosaur's phylogenetic placement, anatomy, and name.

The classification of *Apatosaurus* as a diplodocid was recently questioned by Bonaparte (1996a). From a comparative study of presacral vertebrae of the genera *Apatosaurus, Diplodocus*, and *Camarasaurus*, Bonaparte (1996a), in a preliminary abstract that has not to date been developed into a detailed paper, interpreted the vertebrae of *Apatosaurus* (referred by Berman and McIntosh to the Diplodocidae) as unique, and concluded that they correspond to a distinct non-diplodocid sauropod family, the Apatosauridae.

Bonaparte (1996a) characterized these vertebrae in *Apatosaurus* as follows: (Cervicals) progressive shortening backwards of four last cervicals; hypertrophy of parapophysis; hypertrophy of capitulum and tuburculum of ribs; neural arches proportionally high, representing three-fourths of total height in cervicals 14 and 15; (anterior dorsals) supradiapophysial laminae making anterolateral border of neural spines; absence of infradiapophysial anterior lamina in fourth dorsal; postspinal lamina in fourth dorsal; (central and posterior dorsals) infradiapophysial anterior lamina absent, except in last dorsal; symmetric position of pre and postspinal laminae, also lateral laminae along neural spine; suprapostzygapophysial lamina bifurcated, one branch on lateral lamina, another fused to postspinal lamina. Bonaparte (1996a) observed that the cervical vertebrae in the diplodocid *Diplodocus* show an increasing complexity in their morphology posteriorly, and also in their proportional length, none of these complexities being present in *Apatosaurus*; also, the morphotype of the posterior cervicals of *Diplodocus* continues posteriorly into the two anterior dorsals, while the reverse condition occurs in *Apatosaurus*, as the anterior dorsal morphotype is present in the posterior cervicals. These differences indicated to him "a different type of and evolutionary 'tendency' increasing the posterior cervical morphotype in *Diplodocus*; and increasing the anterior dorsal morphotype in *Apatosaurus*." According to Bonaparte (1996a), these morphotypes may be linked to different muscular arrangements and, probably, to different habits. Bonaparte's (1996a) referral of *Apatosaurus* to its own family has not been adopted (see "Systematics" chapter).

Only slightly disarticulated dorsal and caudal vertebrae (FMNH P25112) of the sauropod *Apatosaurus excelsus* as found in 1901 in the Grand River Valley, Fruita, Colorado, a site now called "Dinosaur Hill." This specimen was described by Elmer S. Riggs two years later at the Field Columbian Museum.

Cranial material relating to sauropods in general has always been rare in the fossil record, including that pertaining to the well known genus *Apatosaurus* (see *D:TE*). In an abstract, Connely (1997) reported the discovery of the first known complete skull and jaw of the species *Apatosaurus excelsus*, recovered in the fall of 1996 by field crews from Casper College, Casper, Wyoming, from Como Bluff, Wyoming.

From preliminary studies of this skull, Connely observed striking differences in the head-neck carriage between *A. excelsus* and the closely related *Diplodocus* spp. According to Connely, *A. excelsus* seems to have had less leverage than all *Diplodocus* species relative to the area of the head-neck joint. This suggested that differences in head-neck posture reflect adaptive divergence of sympatric herbivores not unlike those observed today in modern antelope. Connely suggested that by "reconstructing the joint capsule structures and head-neck musculature, it may be possible to determine the mechanical and behavioral consequences of the variation on osteology and thus generate a model which describes the feeding ecology of these large herbivores." The author further suggested "that closely related sauropod species differ more in the head-neck structure than in dentition or jaw musculature."

Bakker (1998), in a detailed survey report on the Jurassic–Cretaceous transition in Wyoming and Colorado, pointed out salient differences between the above skull (TATE 099) of *A. excelsus* and that (CM 11162) allocated to the type species *A. ajax* by Berman and McIntosh (1987) (see *D:TE*). As stated by Bakker, the braincase of CM 11162 "has the basitubera located just forward of the occipital condyle, far posterior to the position seen in [TATE 099]." These differences in the braincase could indicate that *A. ajax* and *A. excelsus* do not belong to a single genus (Connely and Hawley, in preparation, to date of this writing). If this assessment proves to be correct, then the latter species—originally named *Brontosaurus excelsus* by Marsh (1879)—would be reinstated under that generic name according to the rules of the International Commission on Zoological Nomenclature. In that event, both *Apatosaurus* and the better known

Apatosaurus excelsus, composite skeleton before its unveiling to the public in 1958: Anterior part, FMNH P27021; posterior part, FMNH P25112 including right femur; skull cast of CM 12020 (of *Camarasaurus*); neck, forelimbs, more than last half of tail, and other elements cast from a variety of specimens. In the opinion of Robert T. Bakker, this species should revert to its originally published name of *Brontosaurus excelsus*.

name *Brontosaurus*, regarded as synonyms for almost a century (see Riggs 1903*b*; also *D:TE*), would each be a valid genus.

Erratum: Brian Franczak's sauropod painting reproduced on p. 124 of *D:TE* was mislabeled *Amargasaurus cazaui* and really depicts *Apatosaurus louisae*.

Key references: Bakker (1998); Bonaparte (1996*a*); Connely (1997); Connely and Hawley (in preparation); Marsh (1879); Riggs (1903*b*).

ARCHAEOCERATOPS   Dong and Azuma 1997

Ornithischia: Genasauria: Cerapoda: Marginocephalia: Ceratopsia: Neoceratopsia: "Protoceratopsidae."

Name derivation: Greek *archaio* = "ancient" + Greek *keratos* = "horned" + Greek *ops* = "face."

Type species: *A. oshimai* Dong and Azuma 1997.

Other species: [None.]

Occurrence: Xinminbao Group, Gansu Province, China.

Age: Early Cretaceous.

Known material: Two partial skeletons.

Holotype: IVPP V 11114, incomplete skeleton with nearly complete skull, series of dorsal, six sacral, and three caudal vertebrae.

Diagnosis of genus (as for type species): Primitive, lightly built; three to four premaxillary teeth; skull narrow, long; width across quadrato-jugal reaching 75 percent basal length of skull; snout relatively long; snout hook-shaped in lateral view; pair of small external narial openings; mandible shallow, with straight ventral margin; frill short or absent; large antorbital fossa located at premaxilla-maxilla suture; teeth differing between upper and lower jaws (*Protoceratops*-like in upper jaw, *Psittacosaurus*-shaped in lower); hind limb relatively long compared to "protoceratopsids" (Dong and Azuma 1997).

Comments: The type species *Archaeoceratops oshimai*, most primitive and stratigraphically the oldest of all known neoceratopsians, was founded upon an

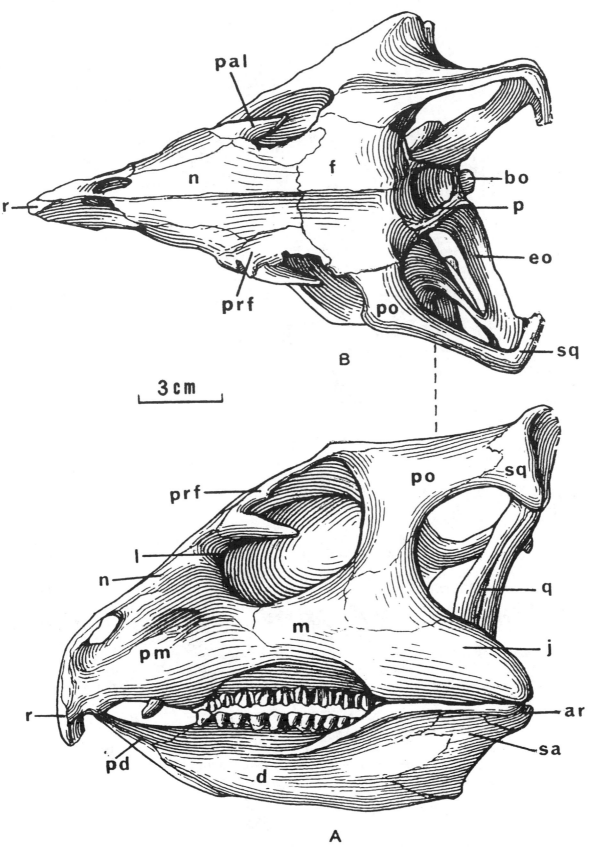

Archaeoceratops oshimai (IVPP V. 11114), holotype skull in A. left lateral and B. dorsal views, as drawn by Chen Wenlong. (After Dong and Azuma 1997.)

3 cm

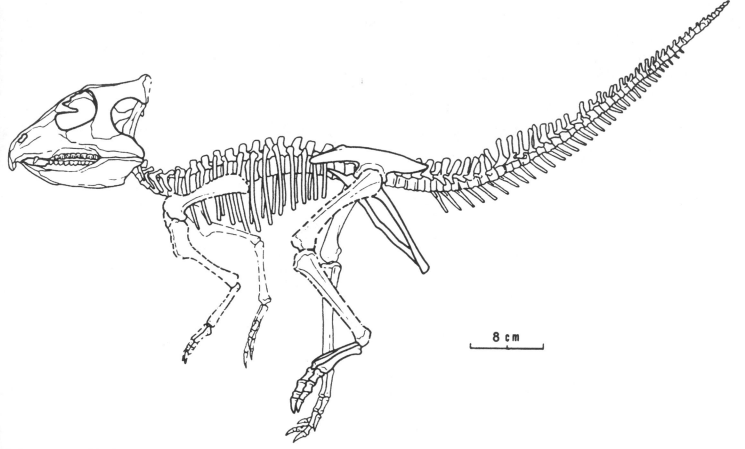

Archaeoceratops oshimai, reconstructed skeleton based on holotype (IVPP V. 11114), two caudal vertebrae and part of pelvis from paratype (IVPP V. 11115), front limbs restored by Chen Wenlong after *Psittacosaurus*. (After Dong and Azuma 1997.)

incomplete skeleton (IVPP V. 11114) including a relatively well-preserved skull, collected during the Sino-Japanese Silk Road Dinosaur Expedition (Dong 1997*b*) from the Xinminbao Group, Gongpoquan Basin of the Mazongshan Area of Gansu Province, China. A paratype specimen (IVPP V. 11115) consists of an incomplete skeleton including a relatively well-preserved tail, partial hind limb, and complete pes (Dong and Azuma 1997).

The forelimbs are unknown in the collected *Archaeoceratops* material. However, the hind limbs are relatively long compared to those of other known "protoceratopsids," and exhibit strong similarities to those of *Psittacosaurus*. Therefore, in reconstructing the skeleton of *A. oshimai*, Dong and Azuma incorporated the forelimbs of that more primitive genus. As surmised by the authors, *Archaeoceratops*, with its lightly built body and relatively long hind legs, was probably a cursorial animal capable of both quadrupedal and bipedal locomotion.

Dong and Azuma referred *Archaeoceratops* to the Neoceratopsia on the basis of two features: 1. The holotype skull seems to be typical for ceratopsians, having a rostral bone on the summit of the snout, and 2. the maxillary teeth are similar to those in "protoceratopsians." As there is no suggestion of nasal or brow horncores, the relationships of this new form could be close to "protoceratopsids."

However, the presence of distinct teeth in the upper and lower jaws (*Protoceratops*-like and *Psittacosaurus*-like, respectively) distinguish this genus from all previously described "protoceratopsians," Maryańska and Osmólska (1975) having previously noted that the teeth of all "protoceratopsids" are quite similar in general structure. Consequently, Dong and Azuma referred this new genus (as well as various others previously classified as "protoceratopsids"; see "Systematics" chapter) to the new family Archaeoceratopsidae, which, the authors suggested, may be sister taxon to the "Psittacosauridae."

Key references: Dong (1997*b*); Dong and Azuma (1997).

†ARGENTINOSAURUS

Saurischia: Sauropodomorpha: Sauropoda: Eusauropoda: Neosauropoda: Macronaria: Titanosauriformes: Somphospondyli: Titanosauria: Titanosauridae.

Comments: Remains of this genus — among the most gigantic of sauropod dinosaurs — were first collected in 1980 by F. Romero and assistants; more

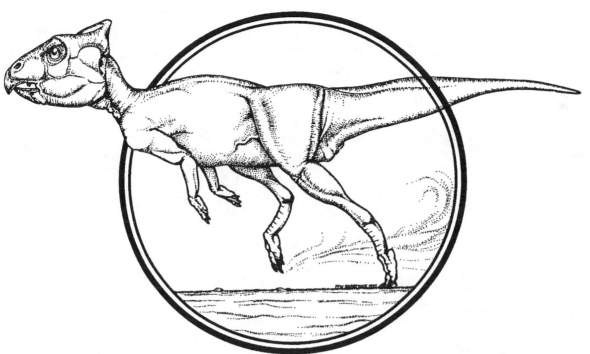

material was recovered in 1989 by José F. Bonaparte, Martin Vince and assistants (Bonaparte 1996*b*).

As Bonaparte pointed out, *Argentinosaurus* is the best known and probably largest of South American titanosaurs, the fibula measuring 1.60 meters in length and suggesting a femur 2.30–2.50 meters long. The genus may also be the largest of all post–"Neocomian" [or Bonaparte's usage] Cretaceous sauropods. From what is known about these animals, gigantic forms seem to have lived from the Aptian (Rayoso Formation) through Coniacian (upper part of the Río Neuquén Formation), with smaller sauropods following.

Key reference: Bonaparte (1996*b*).

†ARGYROSAURUS

Saurischia: Sauropodomorpha: Sauropoda: Eusauropoda: Neosauropoda: Macronaria: Titanosauriformes: Somphospondyli: Titanosauria: Titanosauridae.

Occurrence: ?Bajo Barreal Formation, Chubut Province, Argentina.

Known material: Incomplete postcranial remains.

Holotype: MLP 77-V-29, left humerus, radius, ulna, and manus.

Diagnosis of genus: Humerus heavily constructed (more so than in *Antarctosaurus*); scapula showing "different angle" between longest axis of blade and that of acromial-glenoid expansion; proximal caudal vertebrae having centrum and neural arch very short anteroposteriorly and deep (Bonaparte 1996*b*).

Comments: As recounted by Bonaparte (1996*b*) in a preliminary report, this genus, probably the best documented of all Late Cretaceous Argentinian titanosaurids, was established upon a left forelimb (MLP 77-V-29) missing the phalanges, collected circa 1900 by C. Ameghino, possibly from the Bajo Barreal Formation of Chubut Province, Argentina.

Other material, including three dorsal and three caudal vertebrae, a left scapula, humerus, both radii, and rib fragments (PVL 4628), was recovered in 1982–1983 by José F. Bonaparte, Martin Vince, Jaime E. Powell, and assistants from the Bajo Barreal Formation. These additional remains were referred to *Argyrosaurus* by Powell (1986), who had doubts that they belonged to the type species.

Powell observed in the forelimb of *Argyrosaurus* similarities to that of the forelimb in the North American genus *Alamosaurus*, but found the proportions of their respective metacarpals to be much different.

Key references: Bonaparte (1996*b*); Powell (1986).

†ARSTANOSAURUS

Ornithischia: Genasauria: Cerapoda: Marginocephalia: Ceratopsia: Neoceratopsia *incertae sedis.*

Comments: Although the type species *Arstanosaurus akkurganensis* has generally been regarded as a duckbilled dinosaur because of the various hadrosaurid specimens referred to this taxon, its holotype — an incomplete left maxilla (IZ 1/1) — possesses double-rooted teeth, a feature unique to ceratopsians. (The hadrosaurid remains will eventually be referred

Argyrosaurus superbus, MLP 77-V-29-1, holotype left forelimb. Scale = 500 mm. (After Huene 1929.)

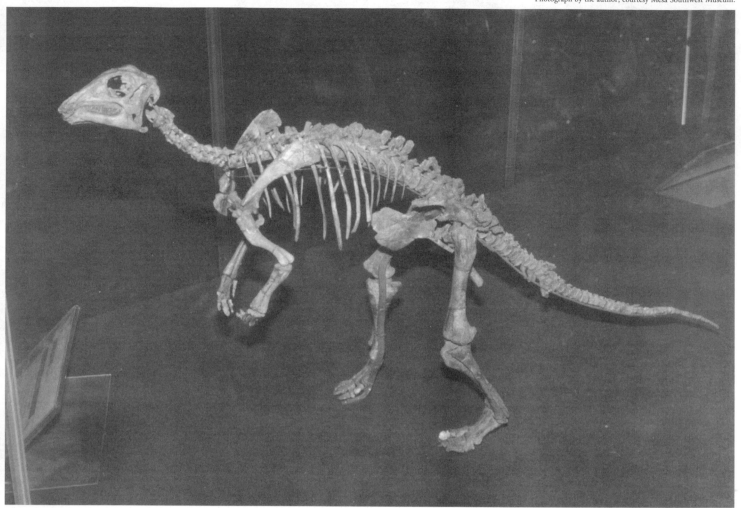

"Arstanosaurus" sp. skeleton (juvenile) displayed in the "Great Russian Dinosaurs Exhibition" (1996), Mesa Southwest Museum, Mesa, Arizona.

to a new genus and species by David B. Norman [M. K. Brett-Surman, personal communication 1997]).

Notes: New hadrosaurid material that has been referred to *"Arstanosaurus"* includes the skeleton of a young individual (pictured in *The ICI Catalogue of The Great Russian Dinosaurs Exhibition 1993–95*; Vickers-Rich and Rich 1993), collected from the Bayn Shireh Formation (Late Cretaceous, Santonian), in the Gobi Desert, People's Republic of China. The skeleton was mounted and displayed as part of the [Qantas] "Great Russian Dinosaurs Exhibition," which toured in various countries beginning in 1992.

As noted by Vickers-Rich and Rich, the exhibited skeleton represents a dinosaur perhaps three to four years old. Juveniles ranged in height from 40 to 50 centimeters (over 15 to about 19 inches). Studies of bone microstructure suggest that the young grew quite rapidly, this size within a year of hatching. Adults apparently grew up to 15 meters (about 50 feet) long and from 6 to 7 meters (over 20 to almost 24 feet) high.

Key reference: Vickers-Rich and Rich (1993).

AUGUSTIA Bonaparte 1998

Saurischia: Sauropodomorpha: Sauropoda: Eusauropoda *incertae sedis.*

Type species: *A. ligabuei* Bonaparte 1998.

Other species: [None.]

Occurrence: Lohan Cura Formation, Neuquén Province, Argentina.

Age: Late Cretaceous (Aptian).

Known material/holotype: Postcranial remains including sequence of 19 incomplete neural arches, nine dermal ossifications located on neural spines, right tibia and fibula with incomplete astragalus, five left metatarsals.

Diagnosis of genus: [None yet published.]

Comments: In recent years, a number of bizarre sauropods have been described from South America, some of them armored or bearing atypical dermal adornments. A new and apparently strikingly armored sauropod, *Augustia ligabuei*, was originally named as such and briefly described by Bonaparte (1998) in an abstract. This taxon was founded upon partial postcranial remains, including "outstanding dermal ossifications," collected in the Aptian continental sediments of the Lohan Cura Formation, in the southern Neuquén Province of Argentina.

Bonaparte described the dermal ossifications of this unique sauropod as follows: Anterior dorsal and possibly cervical vertebrae have an axial, symmetrical ossification measuring 21 centimeters in height. Posteriorly, the form of this ossification alters to become a transversely broadened plate measuring 65 centimeters in width and having pronounced laterodorsal projections. Further posteriorly, the unpaired plate splits into two laminar ossifications measuring 40 centimeters in length, and from which extend somewhat cylindrical spikes measuring 50 centimeters in length, projecting laterodorsally. These spikes become laminar on the sacral vertebrae and measure 75 centimeters long. The more anterior ossifications are joined to the neural spine through a separate ossification; paired osteoderms are connected to the transversely broad summit of the neural spine by a set of two small bones, perhaps of dermal origin.

Bonaparte was unable to assign this new taxon to any sauropod group, given the paucity of material presently available, but noted that "the information from the incomplete neural arches plus the presence of the unique type of dermal ossifications suggest that *Augustia ligabuei* represents a new family of Aptian sauropoda for South America, and possibly for other continents of Gondwana."

To date of this writing, this new type species awaits formal description.

Note: The name *Augustia* is preoccupied, and so the sauropod "*Augustia*" will have to be renamed (G. Olshevsky, personal communication).

Key reference: Bonaparte (1998).

†BACTROSAURUS

Ornithischia: Genasauria: Cerapoda: Ornithopoda: Euornithopoda: Iguanodontia: Euiguanodontia: Dryomorpha: Ankylopollexia: ?Hadrosauridae: Euhadrosauria.

Comments: Relatively little has been published about *Bactrosaurus*, usually regarded as the earliest

B

Bactrosaurus johnsoni, cast of reconstructed skeleton, based on more recently collected material, prepared by the Saurus Corp. and exhibited at the second Dinofest™ International (1966) in Tempe, Arizona.

Photograph by the author.

known lambeosaurine, since the original material was first discovered in Mongolia in 1923 (see Gilmore 1933).

As related by Currie and Eberth (1993), several more recent expeditions have collected fossils (including remains of *Bactrosaurus*) from the low-relief exposures of the Iren Dabasu Formation, at Iren Nor, Inner Mongolia, People's Republic of China, since dinosaur remains were first found at this comparatively small area in 1922.

(According to Currie and Eberth, the generally accepted Cenomanian age ascribed to the Iren Dabasu Formation at Iren Nor may be too old. Based on the occurrence of the turtle *Lindholmemys martinsoni* in both that formation and in the younger parts of the Bayn Shireh Formation, the Iren Dabasu Formation seems to be equivalent to the uppermost levels of the latter. The theropods *Saurornithoides* and *Avimimus* are present in the Iren Dabasu Formation, Djadokhta Formation [Campanian], and also in younger Mongolian sediments, but not in the Bayn Shireh. Therefore, Currie and Eberth concluded that the Iren Dabasu Formation at Iren Nor is younger than Cenomanian, best not considered early "Senonian," although preliminary data suggests that it could actually be as young as Campanian.)

Currie and Eberth noted that among the as yet undescribed Iren Dabasu duckbilled dinosaur material are "immense collections in Hohhot, Erenhot and Beijing of type species *Bactrosaurus johnsoni* and *Gilmoreosaurus mongoliensis*," with "the potential to reveal complete anatomical information for these primitive hadrosaurine and lambeosaurine hadrosaurs, including growth and variation."

As this book goes to press, a paper — not then available to the present writer for examination — was published by Godefroit, Dong, Bultynck, Li and Feng (1998) in which this French-Chinese team stated that *Bactrosaurus* is not a primitive lambeosaurine, as previously believed (see *D:TE*), but rather a basal hadrosaurid. Godefroit *et al.* proposed that *Bactrosaurus* and another primitive genus, *Telmatosaurus*, be placed within a new taxon, Hadrosauroidea, the latter lying outside of Hadrosauridae.

Also, Rasmussen (1998), in a preliminary report on the phylogenetic relationships of hadrosaurs and related ornithopods based upon forelimb morphology, found the "Hadrosauridae to be a well-supported monophyletic group with the exclusion of *Bactrosaurus*."

Key references: Currie and Eberth (1993); Gilmore (1933); Godefroit, Dong, Bultynck, Li and Feng (1998); Rasmussen (1998).

BAGARAATAN Osmólska 1996

Saurischia: Theropoda: Neotheropoda: Tetanurae: ?Avetheropoda *incertae sedis*.

Name derivation: Mongolian *baga* = "small" + Mongolian *araatan* = "predator."

Type species: *B. ostromi* Osmólska 1996.

Other species: [None.]

Occurrence: Nemegt Formation, Omnogov, Mongolia.

Age: Late Cretaceous (?mid–Maastrichtian).

Known material/holotype: ZPAL MgD-I/108, incomplete left mandible, incomplete postcranium.

Diagnosis of genus (as for type species): Mandible with two surangular foramina; articular with oblique posterior surface and short retroarticular process; caudal vertebrae with hollow, very thin-walled centra; hyposphene-hypantrum articulation stout, present in at least 16 proximal caudals; prezygapophyses in proximal caudals with ridges on lateral surfaces; ilium with two deep depressions, crestlike projection on lateral surface of postacetabular process; femur with anterior crest below lesser trochanter; tibia and fibula fused distally with each other and with coalesced astragalocalcaneum (Osmólska 1996).

Comments: The twelfth theropod species known thus far from the Nemegt Formation, *Bagaraatan ostromi* was established on a partial skeleton (ZPAL MgD-I/108), discovered during the Polish-Mongolian Paleontological Expedition of 1970 by Zofia Kielan-Jaworowska, in the sand layer of the lower portion of that formation (?mid–Maastrichtian; Jerzykiewicz and Russell 1991), in the eastern part of the Northern Sayr (Gradziński and Jerzykiewicz 1972), at Nemegt, Mongolia (Osmólska 1996).

As noted by Osmólska, the type specimen (identified by Gradziński and Jerzykiewicz as a "coelurid dinosaur") includes a left mandible missing its midsection and tooth crowns; a sacral spine; 25 caudal vertebrae, 21 constituting a series; several chevrons and fragments of chevrons, a few in articulation with caudals; damaged postacetabular processes of left and right ilium; proximal half of left pubis, articulated with acetabular part of ischium; proximal and distal portions of left femur; complete left tibia; fibula (ascending process fragmentary); and left pedal phalanges II-2 and IV-1. It was found with all bones anterior to the pelvis much weathered and represented only by scraps. Judging from its position and the arrangements of the weathered postcranial fragments, the mandible surely belonged to the same individual as the hindquarters and tail.

According to Osmólska, *B. ostromi* is, "by dinosaur standards," a moderate-sized theropod with a relatively small head, strong, toothed lower jaws somewhat resembling those of some "carnosaurs," probably a somewhat slender neck, strong hips, and slender hind limbs. The mandible, as preserved, measures 63 millimeters, the entire length of the animal

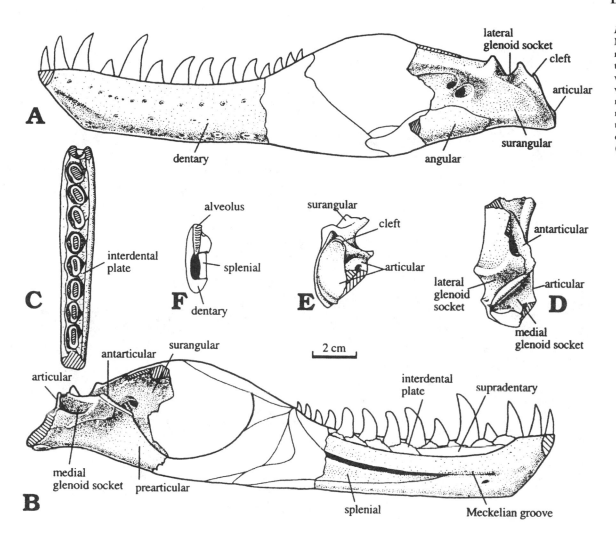

Bagaraatan ostromi, ZPAL MgD-I/108, holotype left mandible, A–B. reconstruction in lateral and medial views, C. dentary in dorsal view, D–E. posterior part of mandible, dorsal and posterior views, and F. cross section through dentary at end of preserved fragment. (After Osmólska 1996.)

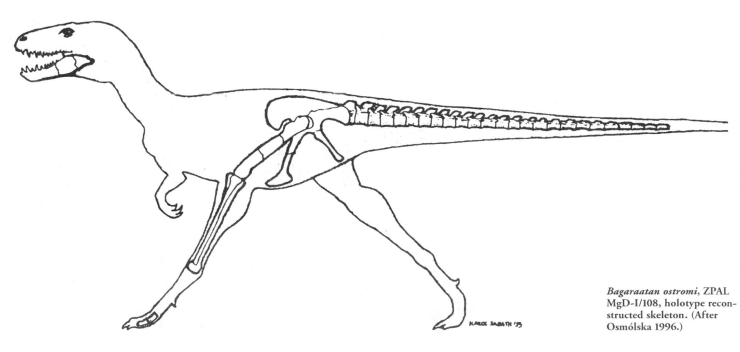

Bagaraatan ostromi, ZPAL MgD-I/108, holotype reconstructed skeleton. (After Osmólska 1996.)

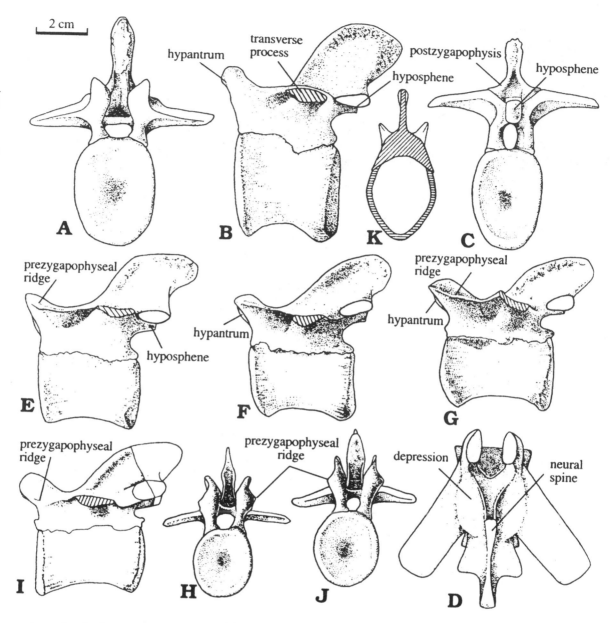

estimated to be from 3.0 to 3.5 meters (about 10.3 to almost 12 feet), the height at the hips less than 1 meter (less than 3 feet). The strong fusion between the sacral ribs and ilium, the co-ossification of the shin bones with the proximal tarsals, and the probable presence of the antarticular in the mandible indicate that the type specimen represents a mature, possibly old, animal.

Osmólska found details of the tail to be peculiar, even extraordinary, forming a suite of features autapomorphic to this taxon, these including the following: Centra with extremely thin walls; hyposphene-hypantrum articulation massive and extensively persistent (resulting in a comparatively rigid tail); prezygapophyses laterally angled; neural spines rough and expanded; dorsal depressions at bases of proximal transverse processes. As nothing in the preserved remains indicates that the presacral part of the animal's body was particularly heavy (the low ilium and slender legs suggesting a relatively gracile thorax), Osmólska surmised that the tail, though probably massive and muscular, did not serve exclusively as a counter-balance; rather, its rigidity was most likely a modification for speed.

Other unusual features of this taxon, discussed by Osmólska, are the evidence (two large depressions) for apparently "overgrown musculature" on the postacetabular portion of the ilium, and the anteroproximal crest on the femur below the lesser trochanter, the latter bearing a distinct scar for muscular or ligamental attachment (not found in other known dinosaurs). Osmólska found it reasonable to associate this scar with the insertion of a muscle (probably the m. pubioschiofemoralis [pars dorsalis]) that abducted and protracted the femur; a roughly similar cranial and

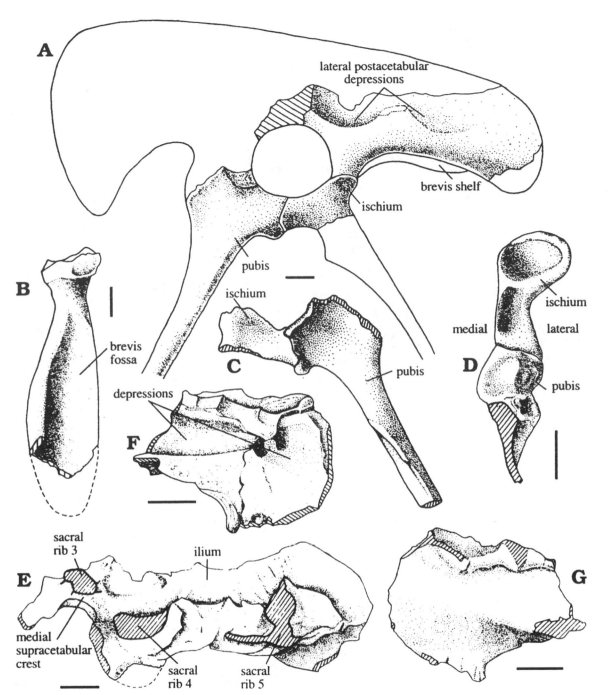

Bagaraatan ostromi, ZPAL MgD-I/108, holotype reconstructed pelvis, A. left lateral view, B. reconstructed right postacetabular process of ilium, ventral view, C–D. fragment of left pubis and ischium, medial and dorsal views, E. right postacetabular process of ilium, medial view, and F–G. fragment of ?right preacetabular process of ilium, ?lateral and ?medial views. Scale = 2 cm. (After Osmólska 1996.)

dorsal location of the insertion area of this muscle is found in crocodilians (Rowe 1989), although neither the femora of crocodilians nor other theropods have a crestlike insertion site.

Comparing the postacetabular portion of the ilium of *Bagaraatan* with other reptiles, Osmólska offered the following: The two depressions most likely served as origin sites of two separate heads of the m. iliofemoralis, or the anterior of the two served as the origin of the m. iliotrochantericus. The dorsomedially inclined femoral head indicates that the femur seemed to have been directed laterodistally. Also (though the

poor state of preservation prevents knowing if the femur was bowed), the medially concave tibiotarsus brought the pes near the sagittal plane beneath the dinosaur's center of gravity, this curvature compensating for the assumed laterodistal deviation of the femur from the sagittal plane.

In comparing ZPAL MgD-I/108 to other theropods, Osmólska noted a number of features in *Bagaraatan* also found in the Ceratosauria, although most of these are theropod plesiomorphies, while others may be homoplasies. The author concluded that this genus is best accommodated in the Tetanurae, displaying synapomorphies (loss of obturator foramen; proximally placed lesser trochanter; position of cnemial crest, similar to that of the two cnemial crests in "*Maleevosaurus novojilovi*" [= *Tyrannosaurus bataar*] and *Allosaurus fragilis*) with Avetheropoda (as defined by Holtz 1994a). Although some features of the mandible and the general shape of the long and slender shin bones resemble those found in the Dromaeosauridae, Osmólska cautioned that others (*e.g.,* propubic pelvis; structure of caudals; lack of ossified caudal tendons) make any close relationship of *Bagaraatan* with dromaeosaurids unlikely. Finally, the incompleteness of the *B. ostromi* holotype preclude any determination of its more exact affiliation.

As pointed out by the author, this species' occurrence in the Nemegt Formations strongly supports her (Osmólska 1980) earlier conclusions regarding "the strong diversity of theropods and the approximately equal proportions of herbivores to carnivores biological productivity during the Nemegt Formation sedimentation times," the latter thereby seemingly invalidating the predator/prey ratio as means to evaluate dinosaurian metabolic rates.

Key references: Gradziński and Jerzykiewicz (1972); Osmólska (1996).

†BARAPASAURUS

Saurischia: Sauropodomorpha: Sauropoda: Eusauropoda.

Diagnosis of genus (as for type species): Posterior dorsal vertebrae having slit-shaped neural canal, margins of which are deeply inset fore and aft, and infradiapophyseal fossa opening into neural canal (Wilson and Sereno 1998, based on Jain, Kutty, Roy-Chowdbury and Chatterjee 1979).

Comments: Wilson and Sereno (1998) rediagnosed the type species, *Barapasaurus tagorei*, based upon published illustrations of the material, and also on their own observations of remains housed in the collections of the Indian Statistical Institute (Wilson, unpublished data).

Key reference: Jain, Kutty, Roy-Chowdbury and Chatterjee (1979); Wilson and Sereno (1998).

†BARYONYX

Saurischia: Theropoda: Neotheropoda: Tetanurae: Spinosauroidea: Baryonychidae.

Occurrence: Wealden, Surrey, Wessex Formation, Isle of Wight, Ashdown Sand, East Sussex, England; Encisco Group, La Rioja, Spain; Elrhaz Formation, Gadoufaoua, Niger.

Age: Early Cretaceous (Hauterivian–Aptian).

Known material: Skeleton, bone fragments, teeth.

Holotype: BMNH R9951, well-preserved incomplete skull and portcranial skeleton, including conjoined premaxillae, conjoined vomers, anterior portion of left maxilla, conjoined nasals, left lacrimal, left prefrontal, left postorbital, anterior end of braincase (right frontal, right parietal, right orbitosphenoid, right laterosphenoid), posterior end of braincase with occiput (both prootics, both opisthotics, basisphenoid, supraoccipital, exoccipitals, basioccipital), left jugal, quadrates, dentaries, splenials, right surangular, angulars, right coronoid, some upper teeth *in situ*, numerous isolated teeth of unknown position in jaws, axis and four further cervical vertebrae, 12 dorsal vertebrae, three or four basal caudal vertebrae, three distal caudals, axial rib, three other cervical ribs, many dorsal ribs, abdominal ribs, five chevrons, sternum, scapulae, coracoids, humeri, left radius, left ulna, left pollex with huge ungual, complete left digit II or digit III, isolated left and right phalanges, right ilium, pubes, left ischium, proximal end of left femur, distal end of right femur, right fibula, right calcaneum, metatarsal fragments, pedal ungual.

Diagnosis of genus (as for type species): Prenarial region of snout extended into extremely narrow rostrum terminating in spatulate, horizontal expansion ("terminal rosette"); snout slightly down-turned in lateral aspect, jaws with sigmoidal margins; external naris long, low, far back on side of snout; complex articulation of premaxilla and maxilla unfused above subrostral notch; small median knob at posterior end of conjoined nasals on dorsal surface, cruciform in dorsal view, anterior limb of cross drawn forwards into low, thin median crest; occiput deep, paroccipital processes directed horizontally outwards; basipterygoid processes descending far below basioccipital, diverging only slightly laterally; anterior end of dentary upturned in lateral aspect; six to seven premaxillary teeth, eight maxillary teeth (preserved; probably about 15 in all), 32 dentary teeth generally smaller than those in upper jaw, more than twice as numerous per unit length of jaw; prominent bony wall on lingual side of all teeth; tooth crowns flattened only slightly labiolingually, lightly fluted on lingual side; anterior and posterior carinae finely serrated (about seven denticles per millimeter); tooth rows exceptionally long and slender; axis small, hyposphene well-developed; cervical vertebrae with flat zygapophyses and well-developed epipophyses; ends of centra not offset, so probably no upward curve to neck; neurocentral sutures unfused; neural spines generally short, those of caudal vertebrae expanded into large, flattened plates; cervical ribs short, crocodiloid, slightly overlapping; humerous relatively well-developed, both ends broadly expanded but flattened, distal rotated 35 degrees

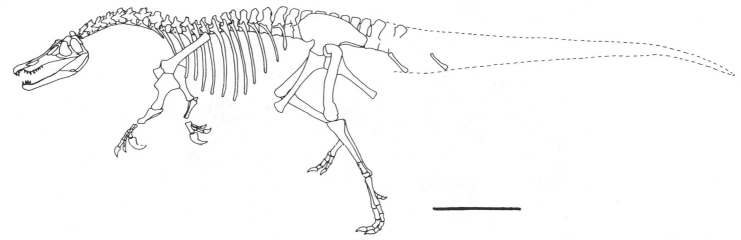

Baryonyx walkeri, reconstruction of holotype skeleton (BMNH R9951). Scale = 1 m. (After Charig and Milner 1997, figure 44).

against each other from plane of proximal, shaft massive and almost straight; radius stout, slightly less than half length of humerus; ulna stout, somewhat longer than radius, olecranon robust; manual ungual phalanx exceptionally large, not laterally compressed, probably from digit I; pubic foot not expanded; ischium with obturator flange proximally continuous with anterior margin (Charig and Milner 1997).

Comments: In 1986, Alan J. Charig and Angela C. Milner of (what is now called) The Natural History Museum, London, named and described *Baryonyx walkeri*, a new and unusual theropod discovered in 1983 in the Barremian of Surrey, England. A second report by these authors followed in 1990, while a major monograph on this type species would appear in 1997.

Following the above rather brief preliminary writings, Viera and Torres (1995) referred to *B. walkeri* a left maxillary fragment (Museo de San Telmo, San Sebastian, GA-2065) about 75 percent the size of that in BMNH R9951, recovered from the Encisco Group, Barremian of Igea, La Rioja, Spain.

Charig and Milner's monograph on *B. walkeri* was not published until 1997, just one month after the death of its senior author. In this new work, the authors noted more precisely that the holotype (BMNH R9951) was found in the Lower Cretaceous, Wealden Series, Upper Weald Clay, *Cypridea clavata* zone, near the base of the Barremian, at the Smokejack's Brickworks locality, Ockley, near Dorking, Surrey, England.

In their monograph, Charig and Milner (1997) referred to *Baryonyx* sp. tooth crowns (IWCMS 3642 and IWCMS 5120 from Hanover Point; IWCMS 1522, IWCMS 1995 207-209, and UOP 97, all unlocalised) from the Wessex Formation (=Wealden Shales, Barremian) of the Isle of Wight, described as possibly "baryonychid" by Martill and Hutt (1996); a crown (MNEMG 1996.133) collected in the mid-

1980s by Dr. E. A. Jarzembowski from the Upper Weald Clay (Barremian), Surrey; a crown (BEXHM: 1993.485) collected by Dr. D. Brockhurst in 1993 from Ashdown Sand (Hauterivian), Bexhill-on-Sea, East Sussex; and fragments (MNHN GDF 365 and 366) from the Elrhaz Formation (Aptian) of Gadoufaoua, Niger, described as mandibular symphyses of a spinosaurid by Taquet (1984; see *D:TE*).

Originally, Charig and Milner (1986) made no claims as to the classification of *Baryonyx* other than that it was a "typical large theropod" resembling such taxa as *Allosaurus*. Phylogenetic assessments began with Buffetaut's (1989) referral of a partial maxilla from the Upper Cretaceous of Morocco to *Spinosaurus*, a very large African genus distinguished by vertebrae possessing very elongated neural spines. The holotype of *Spinosaurus* included a fragmentary maxilla, but the specimen was destroyed during World War II (see *Spinosaurus* entries, *D:TE* and this volume). Buffetaut, consequently, referred the maxilla from Morocco to *Spinosaurus* (using for the latter dentary teeth and alveoli and isolated teeth) based on teeth and their alveoli, the only structures common to both specimens. Comparing the *Spinosaurus* holotype and Moroccan specimen to *Baryonyx*, Buffetaut concluded that both of these genera could belong in the same family; for the present, though, Buffetaut preferred keeping the Spinosauridae and Baryonychidae separate but regarded as closely related.

Subsequently, Charig and Milner (1990) recognized that *Baryonyx* warranted its own family, Baryonychidae, and observed similarities between their genus and *Spinosaurus*, but denied that *Baryonyx* was a member of the Spinosauridae; nor could the authors fit the genus into any other theropod taxon based on Gauthier's (1984, 1986) cladistic breakdown of the Theropoda. Initially, Charig and Milner (1990) interpreted the specimen described by Buffetaut as

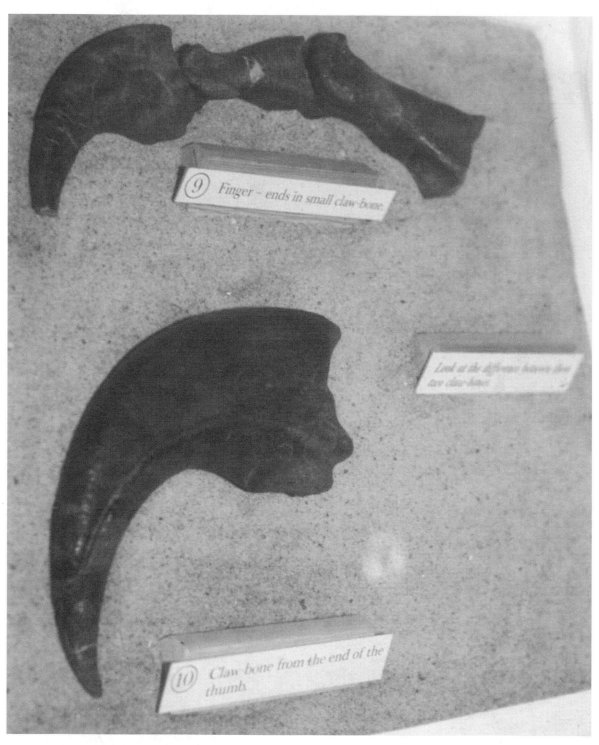

Baryonyx walkeri, holotype (BMNH R9951) manual phalanges and unguals, as exhibited in the mid–1980s at the formerly named British Museum (Natural History).

resembling *Baryonyx* more closely than *Spinosaurus*, and argued that it should be referred instead to the Baryonychidae as an indeterminate member of this clade; later, Charig and Milner (1997) agreed with Buffetaut's assessment of the Moroccan fossil and his proposal that a particular relationship exists between the two families.

Although later authors have generally referred *Baryonyx* to the Spinosauridae (and either explicitly or implicitly regarded Baryonychidae as a junior synonym of that family), Charig and Milner (1997) pointed out that such assessments were founded upon their own earlier and preliminary descriptions which, the authors admitted, contained a number of errors that were discovered following additional preparation and study of the type material (*e.g.*, possession of at least one elongated neural spine). Furthermore, Charig and Milner (1997) argued against synonymizing the two families based upon these considerations: 1. *Baryonyx* is known from more complete type material than *Spinosaurus* and would therefore constitute a much more informative type genus for its family, and the lost type material of the latter genus precludes comparisons; 2. the most distinguishing feature of the Spinosauridae is the elongation of the neural spines not seen in *Baryonyx*; and 3. as currently known, the similarities between these two genera are insufficient to justify their treatment, for cladistic analysis, as a single operational taxonomic unit. In conclusion, Charig and Milner (1997) determined that the Baryonychidae and Spinosauridae, though separate taxa, are close enough to each other for inclusion in a new superfamily, Spinosauroidea (see "Systematics" chapter).

Charig and Milner (1997) noted that (based upon work by Ross and Cook 1995 on the Smokejack's locality) *Baryonyx* lived in a fluvial and mudplain environment with lagoons and marsh. Flora in this environment included ferns and aquatic or marsh-dwelling plants, horsetails, club mosses, and conifers. Invertebrates included insects, thriving in great numbers and varieties, and also ostracods, isopods, conchostracans, and bivalves. Vertebrates included bony fishes, sharks, crocodiles, pterosaurs, and dinosaurs, mostly the ornithopod *Iguanodon*.

In speculating upon the feeding habits of *Baryonyx*, Charig and Milner (1997) noted the following: 1. Scales and teeth of the common Mesozoic fish *Lepidotes*, and also bony remains identified as belonging to *Iguanodon*, were found in the stomach region of *B. walkeri*; and 2. certain characters of the jaws and teeth in this dinosaur are analogous to adaptations in modern crocodilians in catching and swallowing fish. This led Charig and Milner (1997) to envision *Baryonyx* as a fish-eater that caught small to moderate-sized fishes in a crocodilian manner, that is, "it seized them with the end of its pincer-like jaws and gripped them transversely in its subrostral notch and lateral teeth; the shape of the jaws and the nature of the teeth accord well with the suggestion that they somehow helped the grasping and manoeuvering of slippery prey. The animal might then have tilted its head back and manoeuvered the fish around so that the fish slid head-first down the gullet into its stomach, as do modern crocodilians."

Baryonyx may have also, on occasion, actively preyed upon small to medium-sized land-based animals. However, Charig and Milner (1997) noted that this theropod was apparently ill-equipped for capturing and dismembering live prey, pointing out the following: 1. The middle part of each mandibular ramus is wafer thin; 2. teeth are only slightly laterally compressed, unlike those of typical large predacious theropods (*e.g.*, *Allosaurus*); and 3. denticles on the carinae of the teeth are unusually fine.

Expanding upon the issue of feeding, Charig and Milner (1997) noted the following regarding *Baryonyx*: 1. The long, narrow jaws could have been used to dip, either into water to seize fish, or into the body cavity of a large carcass to seize entrails; 2. the lateral, rather posteriorly located external nostrils, would have allowed the animal to breath with its snout deep in water or in the body cavity of a carcass; 3. the large and seemingly heavy head would have restricted neck mobility; 4. the cervical centra are not "offset," indicating that the neck was probably not held in the sigmoid curve typical of most theropods; 5. cervical vertebrae have well-developed epipophyses, but low neural spines lacking spine tables, these features suggesting that strong intervertebral muscles and a highly mobile neck that would have enhanced feeding activities were absent; 6. the humerus is quite robust, with broadly expanded ends, the pectoral girdle is well-developed, and the sternum ossified, all facilitating the powerful adduction, abduction, and possibly rotation of the entire forelimb; 7. radius and ulna are comparatively short, but robust and powerful, the olecranon remarkably long, producing a mechanical advantage (*i.e.*, leverage) during extension of the forearm; and 8. the enormous manual ungual would have been an extremely powerful offensive weapon.

The above features implied to Charig and Milner (1997) that this dinosaur's greatest offensive and defensive weapons were its exceptionally powerful forelimbs and talons, particularly that of the thumb, that "would have enabled the animal not only to catch and kill its prey (if necessary), but also to rip and tear it to pieces," the enlarged claws also possibly used for "gaffing," that is "hooking or flipping fishes out of the water as is done today by grizzly bears." The teeth, with their fine denticles suitable for piercing and smoothly cutting prey, and the jaws were probably primarily used for seizing fish and, during occasional scavenging, entrails.

Charig and Milner (1997) envisioned *Baryonyx* as mainly a fish-eating theropod that "probably crouched on the banks of lakes, creeks and rivers or waded in the shallows," securing prey in its jaws or by "gaffing," with small fishes swallowed whole and larger ones broken up by the forelimbs. On occasion, however, *Baryonyx* may have been an active predator, and also acquired food as an opportunistic scavenger. (It could not be determined if the *Iguanodon* remains found within the ribcage of *Baryonyx* were the result of predation or scavenging.)

Charig and Milner (1997) rescinded their (1986) earlier suggestion that *Baryonyx* could have walked on all fours, noting that the anatomy of this dinosaur, as now interpreted, displays no evidence of a gait differing from that of any other typical theropod. However, the animal would have had to come down to a crouching or (utilizing its massive forearms) quadrupedal position, either on the edge of the water or in it, while capturing its aquatic prey.

As the holotype was found somewhat intact (most of the tail missing, the lower teeth having fallen from their sockets) though its bones were mostly disarticulated and somewhat scattered, Charig and Milner (1997) hypothesized that the animal most likely died where its remains were found, its skeleton resting in sediments that were mostly submerged in shallow water but exposed for brief periods to the air. The bones had been trampled and broken, presumably under the feet of large dinosaurs such as *Iguanodon*, before fossilization occurred, and no evidence was perceived in the specimen indicative of scavenging or of the cause of death.

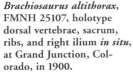

Brachiosaurus altithorax, FMNH 25107, holotype dorsal vertebrae, sacrum, ribs, and right ilium *in situ*, at Grand Junction, Colorado, in 1900.

Key reference: Buffetaut (1989, 1992); Charig and Milner (1986, 1990, 1997); Martill and Hutt (1996); Taquet (1984); Viera and Torres (1995).

†BRACHIOSAURUS

Saurischia: Sauropodomorpha: Sauropoda: Eusauropoda: Neosauropoda: Macronaria: Camarasauromorpha: Titanosauriformes: Brachiosauridae.

Comments: For the more than 90 years since the North American type species *Brachiosaurus altithorax* was named and first described by Field Columbian Museum paleontologist Elmer S. Riggs (1903*a*), the genus *Brachiosaurus* has remained one of the relatively few sauropod genera most familiar to laymen. The depiction of this huge dinosaur, with its raised nostrils, very long neck, long forelimbs and relatively short hind limbs, downward sloping back, and rather short tail, is recognizable in most books written about dinosaurs.

Courtesy The Field Museum (neg. #4027).

Brachiosaurus altithorax, FMNH 25107, holotype right humerus and Field Columbian Museum of Natural History paleontologist Harold W. Menke (assistant to Elmer S. Riggs) in 1900 at Quarry 16, Grand Junction, Colorado.

Courtesy The Field Museum (neg. #3934).

Traditionally, *Brachiosaurus* (and the species referred to it: *B. brancai* from Africa, ?*B. atalaiensis* from Portugal, and *B. nougardei* from Africa) has occupied what has seemed to be a stable position within its own family, the Brachiosauridae, for many years one of the various sauropod taxa accepted as valid by most workers (*e.g.*, McIntosh 1990*b*; see also *D:TE*). Indeed, the occurrence of species of *Brachiosaurus* in both North America and Africa has long been regarded as evidence for a land connection between Laurasia and Gondwana during the Late Jurassic. In the recent past, however, not only has the relationship between the species of *Brachiosaurus* been challenged, but also the validity of the Brachiosauridae itself.

In two subsequent studies on the evolution of titanosaurids, Salgado, Coria and Calvo (1997), and Salgado and Calvo (1997) interpreted the characters largely used to diagnose the Brachiosauridae as plesiomorphic for basal titanosaurs, regarding some of the characters diagnosing *Brachiosaurus* as synapo-

Holotype (FMNH 25107) of *Brachiosaurus altithorax* being jacketed in 1900, at Quarry 13, Grand Junction, Colorado, for shipment to the Field Columbian Museum in Chicago.

morphies for Titanosauriformes, a new taxon introduced by Salgado *et al.* The species *B. altithorax* was, therefore, considered by these authors to be a basal titanosauriform, with the Brachiosauridae regarded by them as an artificial assemblage of primitive titanosauriformes (see "Systematics" chapter).

According to Salgado and Calvo, no unequivocal synapomorphies unite the type species with *B. brancai*, the primary criterion linking these taxa being the high ratio of humerus to femur length (an opinion expressed in noncladistic terminology 80 years earlier by Lull 1919). However, as noted by Paul (1988*a*), the femur of the best preserved specimen of *B. brancai* (HMN S11) is incomplete; therefore, the extremely elongate forearms in *B. altithorax* could be an autapomorphy of that species rather than a synapomorphy of *Brachiosaurus*. Also, a relatively high ratio of humerus to femur is apparently not characteristic

of brachiosaurids, as similar ratios are also known in titanosauriforms, basal titanosaurs, as well as other primitive sauropods.

Because the femur of ?*B. atalaiensis* does not exhibit the pronounced lateral bulge characteristic of the Titanosauriformes, Salgado and Calvo removed the tentative species from this clade.

Performing their own cladistic analysis of various sauropod taxa, Wilson and Sereno (1998) criticized numerous points regarding the conclusions of the Salgado *et al.* and Salgado and Calvo (see "Systematics" chapter), and retained the Brachiosauridae as a stable clade within Titanoformes.

Not until the late 1970s was *Brachiosaurus*, with its approximate 24-meter length and possibly 45-metric ton weight, seriously challenged as a size contendor by other, newly discovered sauropods. During that period, paleontologist James A. Jensen discovered in

Reconstructed skeleton of the gigantic sauropod *Brachiosaurus altithorax* (including cast of holotype specimen FMNH 25107) mounted by the PAST company in The Field Museum's prestigious Stanley Field Hall.

the Dry Mesa Dinosaur Quarry of the Morrison Formation, Colorado, remains of a diplodocid which was publicized as being the largest sauropod known. In 1979, Jensen found at Dry Mesa what seemed to be a brachiosaurid even larger than the diplodocid. Jensen (1985) named these, respectively, *Supersaurus vivianae* and *Ultrasaurus macintoshi.*

More recently, Curtice, Stadtman and Curtice (1996) identified the holotype dorsal vertebra (BYU 9044) of *U. macintoshi* as diplodocid and referred it to *S. vivianae.* However, a huge scapulocoracoid (BYU 9462), which Jensen had referred to *U. macintoshi,* was identified by Curtice *et al.* as belonging to the Brachiosauridae, based on various brachiosaurid characters (*e.g.,* narrow scapular neck, distal blade expansion, irregular shape of coracoid), and was referred by them to *Brachiosaurus* sp. Although this specimen was initially regarded as belonging to an exceptionally large brachiosaurid, Curtice *et al.* noted that almost all earlier estimates of its size and weight were founded on the misconception that dorsal vertebra BYU 9044 is brachiosaurid and that BYU 9462 is larger than any other known *Brachiosaurus* scapulocoracoid. Curtice *et al.* and Curtice (1996) pointed out the following:

BYU 9462 is 250 centimeters long, while the largest known *Brachiosaurus* scapula (HM Sa 9 from Tendaguru), lacking a coracoid, is 193 centimeters. If the Tendaguru specimen had a coracoid 40 centimeters in length, the total length would approximate that of BYU 9462. Also, HM Sa 9 is wider than BYU 9462 at midshaft, proximal and distal ends, and generally thicker.

These measurements and proportions indicated to Curtice *et al.* that the Dry Mesa *Brachiosaurus* is no larger than the mounted composite skeleton (holotype HM SI and SII) of *B. branchai* displayed in the Humboldt Museum für Naturkunde (see *D:TE* for photograph).

Key references: Curtice, Stadtman and Curtice (1996); Jensen (1985); Lull (1919); McIntosh (1990*b*); Paul (1988*a*); Riggs (1903*a*); Salgado and Calvo (1997); Salgado, Coria and Calvo (1997); Wilson and Sereno (1998).

†**CAENAGNATHUS**—(See *Chirostenotes.*)

†**CAMARASAURUS**—(=*Cathetosaurus, Caulodon, Morosaurus, Uintasaurus.*)
Saurischia: Sauropodomorpha: Sauropoda: Eusauropoda: Neosauropoda: Macronaria: Camarasauromorpha: Caramasauridae.

Camarasaurus

Camarasaurus supremus
mounted skeleton.

Holotype of *C. lewisi*: BYU 9047, tooth, cervical vertebrae (numbers 1–8 complete, with ribs; 9–12 fragmental), dorsal vertebrae (1–7 fragmental to incomplete, 8–12 complete), dorsal ribs (12 almost complete, well represented on left side, 10 mostly incomplete on right side), sacral vertebrae (1–5 complete except for right ribs), caudal vertebrae (1–26 mostly complete, 17 middle ones and posterior ones not in articulation, of which only 11 are now available), 18 mostly complete chevrons (?2-6, 12-3, 15-9, 21-2, ?24-7), right humerus, radius, ulna, distal carpal, metacarpals (1–5), phalanges (I-2 [claw] and II-1), incomplete left ilium, left pubis, right and left ischia.

Diagnosis of genus: Lacrimal having long axis directed anterodorsally; quadratojugal with short anterior ramus that does not extend anterior to laterotemporal fenestra; quadratojugal-squamosal contact; conspicuous groove passing anteroventrally from surangular foramen to ventral margin of dentary; ischial blade directed posteriorly so that long axis of its shaft passes through pubic peduncle; fibula having dorsoventrally deep tibial scar (Wilson and Sereno 1998).

Diagnosis of *C. lewisi*: Very deep, narrow bifurcation of neural spines of presacral vertebrae persist-

ing back from thirteenth cervical through eleventh dorsal vertebra, with a trace showing in twelfth dorsal; increased angle (about 20 degrees) between axes of sacrum and ilium, with much more strongly developed ossified ligaments in posterior dorsal and particularly sacral regions linking spine of one vertebra with diapophyses of succeeding vertebra; articular surfaces of pre- and postzygapophyses large, rectangular; heads of chevrons strongly bridged over with bone, each with two distinct articular surfaces of equal dimension, anterior one articulated with preceding vertebra being horizontal, posterior one articulating with succeeding vertebra oriented downward at 60-degree angle (McIntosh, Miller, Stadtman and Gillette 1996).

Comments: *Camarasaurus* ranks among the best known of Late Jurassic, North American sauropods, numerous specimens referred to this genus having been recovered for more than a century. Indeed, this genus, with its box-like head and approximately equal-length legs, constitutes one of the relatively few sauropod images known to the public.

In a recent cladistic analysis of higher-level sauropod phylogeny, Wilson and Sereno (1998) defined *Camarasaurus* as a genus comprising the species *C. grandis*, *C. lentus*, *C. lewisi*, *C. supremus*, probably *C. alenquerensis*, their ancestor, and all its descendants.

Camarasaurus lentus skull (cast of CM 12020) without lower jaws, left lateral view.

Photograph by the author, courtesy The Field Museum.

The authors commented, however, that these four species are in need of revision.

Of the above-mentioned species, *C. lewisis* was originally described as the type species of a new genus, *Cathetosaurus*, which Jensen (1988) had founded upon a two-thirds complete, well-preserved postcranial skeleton (BYU 9047 [misprinted as 9740 in Jensen's paper]), recovered in 1967 by him from the Brushy Basin Member (Late Jurassic [Tithonian] or Early Cretaceous [Hauterivian or "Neocomian"]) of the Morrison Formation, in Mesa County, Colorado. As later noted by McIntosh, Miller, Stadtman and Gillette (1996), the site is on Star Mesa, on the eastern part of the Colorado Plateau, above the confluence of Big and Little Dominguez Creeks, several kilometers from where these combined creeks meet the Gunnison River; also, nonrecovered material belonging to this species, described by Jensen in his field notes as "atlas and axis very punky bone like dirt," probably represented the posterior part of the skull, most likely the occipital region.

This taxon was accepted by Miller, McIntosh, Stadtman and Gillette (1992) as a valid species, but one rather belonging to *Camarasaurus*. According to McIntosh *et al.*, Jensen's *Cathetosaurus* so closely resembles *Camarasaurus* (and differs in various features from *Brachiosaurus* and *Haplocanthosaurus*) that it can only be regarded as a junior synonym of the latter, its referral to *Camarasaurus* based on the following: Possession of the same presacral and sacral vertebral formula (12 cervicals, 12 dorsals, 5 sacrals); presacrals with same very large pleurocoels (for which Cope 1877*a* named *Camarasaurus*); cervical arches placed forward on centra, spines bifid; cervical ribs very long and slender, extending as far posteriorly as the two succeeding vertebrae; morphology of twelfth cervical rib transitional between typical cervical and dorsal ribs; presacrals (including posterior dorsals) strongly opisthocoelous; posterior dorsal spines tending to be relatively short, massive, set on high arch; sacrum with same general construction as in other *Camarasaurus* species; caudal vertebrae and forelimb virtually indistinguishable from *C. grandis* (YPM 1901); especially manus agrees very closely in having long, slender metacarpals; pelvic bones closely resembling those of *C. supremus*, except for relationship of ilium to sacrum. Regarding the above latter feature in BYU 9047, Jensen had emphasized the large degree of forward rotation of the axis of the ilium relative to that of the sacrum, the first record of this feature in any known sauropod.

C. lewisi was considered to be a species distinct from the other three valid species of *Camarasaurus* (*C. supremus*, *C. grandis*, and *C. lentus*) based on several characters illustrating "a greater stage of development of morphological change within the genus": 1. deep narrow cleft in cervical spines; 2. deep V-shaped (instead of U-shaped) cleft in dorsal spines, extending farther posteriorly in column to dorsal 11 (as opposed to 5 or 6); 3. dorsal-sacral vertebra (or sacral 1) more "sacralized" and second caudo-sacral vertebra (or sacral 5) less so than in *C. supremus* and *C. lentus*; 4. much greater development of sacrocostal plate than in other *Camarasaurus* species; 5. divided articular facets of anterior and middle chevrons occupying different transverse planes, anterior facet horizontal, posterior facet sloping more posteroventrally (about 60 degrees); and 6. forelimb (very similar to that of *C. grandis*) distinctly more slender than in *C. lentus*.

Following completion of the preparation of BYU 9047, McIntosh *et al.* published the definitive osteology of *C. lewisi*. The holotype of this species includes numerous ligaments and tendons in the pelvic region, the first "evidence of the intricate nature of these typically unrecorded connective tissues in sauropods," and evidence that, as McIntosh *et al.* pointed out, that BYU 9047 clearly represents a quite old individual.

Further work was conducted by Fiorillo (1996) on the patterns of microwear and resource partitioning in teeth of *Camarasaurus* and *Diplodocus*, the two most common Morrison Formation sauropods. From the patterns of occurrence of pits, coarse scratches, and fine scratches on the surface of these teeth, Fiorillo deduced that adult *Camarasaurus* individuals ate coarser food than did those of *Diplodocus*. Enamel in these teeth, as evidenced by their similar microstructure, did not play a role in the observed wear patterns.

According to Fiorillo, most teeth belonging to *Camarasaurus* adults exhibit signs of ingestion of coarser food, while those of juveniles show a wear pattern similar to that seen in *Diplodocus*, this suggesting that *Camarasaurus* young and *Diplodocus* adults ate the same kinds of vegetation, dietary divergence in *Camarasaurus* occurring when individuals reached adult size. Also, Fiorillo noted that the profound longitudinal, climatic gradient in the Morrison Formation, expressed by the occurrence of a large alkaline playa lake in the upper part of the formation, apparently had no effect upon the patterns of resource partitioning in adult forms of either *Camarasaurus* or *Diplodocus* (see also Fiorillo 1998).

Tidwell and Carpenter (1997) reported that the Denver Museum of Natural History had recently rediscovered one of the original sauropod quarries in Garden Park, Colorado, worked by pioneer paleontologist Edward Drinker Cope during the nineteenth century. From this site museum workers collected 33 bones — including a well-preserved axis, a pubis, ischium, and anterior caudal vertebra — offering excellent material for comparison with Cope's *C. supremus* specimens. Much of the rest of the specimen had been severely damaged due to weathering and was of lesser value for comparison.

According to Tidwell and Carpenter, the specimen constitutes the only well-preserved remains of this *Camarasaurus* species to be collected since Cope's time at the site, offers an excellent historical connection to the man's Garden City quarries, and also gives new information as to the layout of the local quarries popularly referred to as "saurian hill."

Key references: Fiorillo (1996, 1998); Jensen (1988); McIntosh, Miller, Stadtman and Gillette (1996); Miller, McIntosh, Stadtman and Gillette (1992); Tidwell and Carpenter (1997); Wilson and Sereno (1998).

†CAMPYLODONISCUS

Saurischia: Sauropodomorpha: Sauropoda: Eusauropoda: Neosauropoda: Macronaria: Camarasauromorpha: ?Titanosauriformes: ?Somphospondyli: ?Titanosauria *incertae sedis*.

Occurrence: ?Chubut Group, Chubut Province, Argentina.

Holotype: MACN A-10863, incomplete left maxilla with seven alveoli, one complete tooth, one replacement tooth, isolated fragmentary tooth.

Comments: *Campylodoniscus* is another sauropod known only from very incomplete material.

In a preliminary report on Argentinian tetrapods, Bonaparte (1996*b*) found *Campylodoniscus*, based on a maxilla (MACN A-10863) collected possibly from the upper Chubut Group of Chubut Province, Argentina, to be "one of the most interesting genera among the Cretaceous sauropods of Argentina" because of the information it yields regarding the possible origin and differentiation of the cylindrical teeth in titanosaurids and diplodocids. The preserved maxillary tooth possesses a crown that appears intermediate between the spatulate "cetiosaurid" type and the cylindrical, pencil-like type seen in titanosaurs, diplodocids, and dicraeosaurids. According to Bonaparte, MACN A-10863 constitutes "good evidence that different groups of sauropods lived in the Late Cretaceous of Patagonia."

Key reference: Bonaparte (1996*b*).

†CARCHARODONTOSAURUS

Saurischia: Theropoda: Neotheropoda: Tetanurae: Avetheropoda: Carnosauria: Allosauroidea: Carcharodontosauridae.

Diagnosis of genus (as for type species): (Dental characters) posterior crown margin only slightly convex at midlength, convex distally; enamel ornamentation including transverse bands and arcuate wrinkles near crown margins; (cranial) antorbital fenestra length 30 percent and height 25 percent of those of cranium; ventral margin of antorbital fossa everted; prefrontal absent or co-ossified; postorbital ventral ramus having robust lateral process with groove and pit; postorbital-squamosal articulation helical; paroccipital process and basal tubera situated far ventral to occipital condyle; (postcranial) postaxial cervical vertebrae having kidney-shaped posterior articular faces, short neural spines, robust transverse processes, strong ventral keels; anterior caudal vertebrae pleurocoelous; distal caudals having narrow anteroposteriorly

Life restoration of *Carcharodontosaurus saharicus* painted by Robert F. Walters.

©1996 Walters

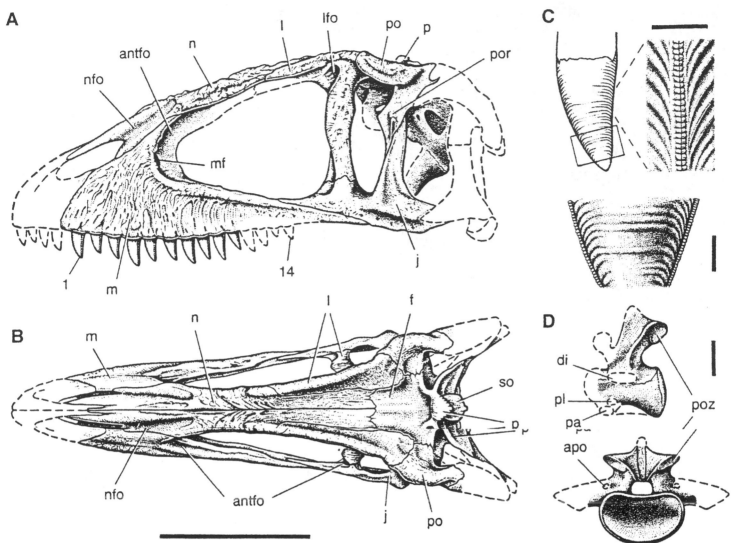

A

nfo
antfo
n
l
lfo
po
p
por
mf
j
1
m
14

B

m
n
l
f
so
p
nfo
antfo
j
po

C

D

di
pl
pa
apo
poz

Carcharodontosaurus saharicus, reconstructed skull (SGM-Din 1) from Kem Kem, A. left lateral and B. dorsal views (scale = 50 cm), C. maxillary tooth, with (right) magnified views of posterior margin and (left) lateral surface (scale = 5 mm [above], 1 cm [below]), D. midcervical vertebra, (top) left lateral and (bottom) posterior views (scale = 5 cm). (After Sereno, Dutheil, Iarochene, Larsson, Lyon, Magwene, Sidor, Varricchio and Wilson 1996).

compressed neural spines (Sereno, Dutheil, Iarochene, Larsson, Lyon, Magwene, Sidor, Varricchio and Wilson 1996).

Comments: A very large North African theropod discovered during the early 1930s, the genus *Carcharodontosaurus*, until the recent discovery and collection of new material, has remained a relatively obscure and elusive genus known from just a few fossils, its type specimen having been destroyed during World War II (see *D:TE*).

The best *Carcharodontosaurus* material yet recovered is an incomplete skull (missing the snout, posteriormost parts, and lower jaws) and associated cervical vertebrae, discovered in summer, 1995, during a joint U.S.-Moroccan expedition, led by Paul C. Sereno of the University of Chicago (Lemonick 1996).

This skull (SGM-Din 1), found in Late Cretaceous (Cenomanian) beds in the Kem Kem region (informally called the "Kem Kem beds") of southeastern Morocco, would measure, if complete, some

1.6 meters (about 5.4 feet) in length, that length equal to or greater than that of the largest known *Tyrannosaurus rex*, a longer-limbed, taller, and less heavy species. Various diagnostic dental features identified this material as belonging to *C. saharicus* (Sereno *et al.* 1996).

Cast reconstructions of this skull have been placed on exhibit at Explorers Hall, The National Geographic Society Museum in Washington, D.C., and at the University of Chicago.

Opinions have varied regarding the phylogenetic position of *Carcharodontosaurus*. Based on studies of the Kem Kem remains and after cladistic analysis of basal tetanurans, Sereno *et al.* concurred with Rauhut (1995) that *Carcharodontosaurus* belongs within the allosauroid clade. Sereno *et al.* further suggested that this genus is closely allied with *Acrocanthosaurus* and *Giganotosaurus*, and that these three taxa should be united as carcharodontosaurids by the following characters: Broad orbital shelf (formed by lacrimal and postorbital bones) and squared anterior end of lower

Photograph by the author, courtesy University of Chicago.

Carcharodontosaurus saharicus, reconstructed skull (including cast of SGM-Din 1) prepared under the direction of Paul C. Sereno and displayed at the Crerar Library, University of Chicago.

jaw. Sereno *et al.* pointed out that particularly broad cervical centra and anterior caudal vertebrae with small pleurocoels are present in both *Carcharodontosaurus* and *Acrocanthosaurus*.

African dinosaurs have been more poorly known than those of any other continent, save for Antarctica and Australia, the best specimens including the more recently collected *C. saharicus* material from Morocco and the holotype skeleton of *Deltadromeus agilis*, the latter also recovered by Sereno's team. Similarities between the Kem Kem *Carcharodontosaurus* remains and fossils belonging to non–African allosauroid taxa have led to a new possible scenario for Late Cretaceous (Cenomanian) faunal differentiation. According to Sereno *et al.*, large "carcharodontosaurid predators" underwent a global radiation during the Early Cretaceous. The close relationships between the African *Carcharodontosaurus*, North American *Acrocanthosaurus*, and South American *Giganotosaurus* reveal a "carcharodontosaurid radiation that had achieved a transcontinental distribution before the end of the Early Cretaceous (ca. 100 Ma)." Possibly, the African genus may have been isolated on its continent during the Cenomanian (ca. 90 Ma), although its "carcharodontosaurid progenitors were able to colonize north-

ern and southern landmasses during the Early Cretaceous" (see *Deltadromeus* entry, *D:TE*).

Additional remains referred to *C. saharicus* were reported by Russell (1996), this material including a maxillary fragment (CMN [formerly NMC] 4189), various isolated teeth (CMN 41908, 41910, 41817, 41818, and 41819), and a cervical vertebra (CMN 50792). It was collected from the "Middle" Cretaceous of the Tafilalt, Morocco (see *Spinosaurus* entry).

Key references: Lemonick (1996); Rauhut (1995); Russell (1996); Sereno, Dutheil, Iarochene, Larsson, Lyon, Magwene, Sidor, Varricchio and Wilson (1996).

†CARNOTAURUS

Saurischia: Theropoda: Neotheropoda: "Ceratosauria": Neoceratosauria: Abelisauroidea: Abelisauridae.

Occurrence: La Colonia Formation, Chubut Province, Argentina.

Age: Early–Late Cretaceous.

Comments: This large, rather short-faced, horned abelisaurid (and presently the best known Gondwanan theropod) was collected by José F. Bonaparte and assistants in 1984 and first briefly described by Bonaparte the following year; more recently, the genus was reviewed by Bonaparte (1996*b*).

Carnotaurus

Photograph by the author, courtesy Natural History Museum of Los Angeles County.

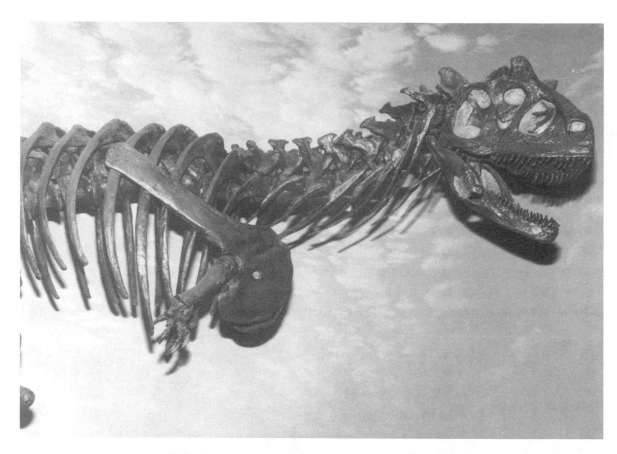

Skeleton (LACM 5509/ 23504, cast of holotype MACN-CH 894) of *Carnotaurus sastrei* showing the very small yet massive bones of the forearm that had functionally become part of the hand.

Photograph by the author, courtesy Natural History Museum of Los Angeles County.

Life-sized sculpture of *Carnotaurus sastrei* by Stephen A. and Sylvia J. Czerkas, both of whom assisted Professor José F. Bonaparte in the recovery of the holotype skeleton. In the background is a cast (LACM 5509/23504) of that specimen (MACN-CH 894), which, along with preserved skin impressions belonging to this species, served as the model for the sculpture.

Bonaparte (1996*b*) noted that the holotype (MACN-CH 894) of the type species *C. sastrei*, consisting of a nearly complete skeleton with skin impressions, was not recovered from the Gorro Frigio Formation as indicated by Bonaparte, Novas and Coria (1990), but rather from the lower section of the La Colonia Formation (early Late Cretaceous), based on studies by Ardolino and Delpino (1987). Also, Bonaparte (1996*b*) stated that the extreme shortness and massiveness of the radius and ulna in this genus indicate that these bones had become functionally part of the hand.

Bonaparte (1996*b*) speculated that this genus was most likely "a very agile and slim hunter, with a skin externally decorated with modest knobs distributed every 10 cm or so on most of the body, except on the snout where the knobs probably changed to spiny protuberances, according with osseous rugosities on the nasals."

The first accurate life restorations of *Carnotaurus*— indeed, probably the first of any kind of theropod in which the integument was correctly shown — was made by husband and wife sculptors Stephen A. and Sylvia J. Czerkas, the most significant (and spectacular) of these being a life-sized, three-dimensional model commissioned during the mid–1980s by the

Natural History Museum of Los Angeles County for exhibition accompanying a cast of the holotype skeleton.

Later, Czerkas and Czerkas (1997) chronicled in detail the development and construction of the figure: The figure was sculpted in clay over a steel armature incorporating fiberglass casts of numerous skeletal elements, including the scapula, bones of the pelvis, hind limbs, scapula, forelimbs, and the entire skull with jaws. Molds were made of skin impressions preserved with the original skeleton, these allowing the artists to show how the integument of this dinosaur probably appeared in life. "The fossilized skin impressions of the theropod, *Carnotaurus*," the authors stated, "reveals that large carnivorous dinosaurs were covered in nonimbricating scales similar to those which are known from herbivorous dinosaurs. Additionally, the skin of *Carnotaurus* may be distinguished by the presence of conical studs arranged in irregular rows on the sides of the neck, back and tail."

Key references: Bonaparte (1985, 1996*b*); Bonaparte, Novas and Coria (1990); Czerkas and Czerkas (1997).

CAUDIPTERYX   Ji, Currie, Norell and Ji 1998
Saurischia: Theropoda: Neotheropoda: Tetanurae:

Caudipteryx zoui, holotype NGMC 97-4-A, part of National Geographic Society's "China's Feathered Dinosaurs" exhibit at The Field Museum in 1998–99.

Photograph by the author, courtesy The Field Museum.

Caudipteryx

Caudipteryx zoui, paratype NGMC 97-9-A, displayed at National Geographic Society's "China's Feathered Dinosaurs" exhibit.

Avetheropoda: Coelurosauria: Manuraptoriformes: Manuraptora: Eumanuraptora: Dromaeosauridae.

Name derivation: Latin *cauda* = "tail" + Greek *pteryx* = "feather."

Type species: *C. zoui* Ji, Currie, Norell and Ji 1998.

Other species: [None.]

Occurrence: Chaomidianzi Formation, Liaoning Province, People's Republic of China.

Age: ?Early Cretaceous.

Known material: Two skeletons including skulls, feather impressions.

Holotype: NGMC 97-4-A, complete skeleton with feather impressions.

Diagnosis of genus (as for type species): Derived features of short tail (less than 23 caudal vertebrae) and arms having remiges attached to digit II (Ji, Currie, Norell and Ji 1998).

Comments: Among the most important (and surprising) of recent dinosaur fossil discoveries has been *Caudipteryx*.

The new genus was founded upon an almost complete skeleton (NGMC 97-4-A) collected from the Jiulongsong Member of the Chaomidianzi Formation (underlying the Yixian Formation, of apparent Late Jurassic–Early Cretaceous age), in the Sihetun area of Liaoning Province, China. A paratype specimen (NGMC 97-9-A), another almost complete skeleton, was recovered from the same locality. Both specimens include concentrations of small, polished,

**Life-sized model of
Caudipteryx zoui, a nona-
vian theropod with
plumage, made by sculptor
Brian Cooley for National
Geographic Society's
"China's Feathered Dino-
saurs" exhibit.**

rounded pebbles in the stomach region — gastroliths
measuring up to 4.5 millimeters in diameter, though
most measure considerably less than 4 millimeters.
However, the most interesting and sensational feature
of these specimens is that both include feather impressions (Ji, Currie, Norell and Ji 1998).

Before the type species, *C. zoui*, was formally

named and described, a preliminary report written by
theropod authority Philip J. Currie was published in
National Geographic (Currie 1998*b*) magazine, along
with photographs of the fossil material and a sculp-
tured life restoration by artist Brian Cooley. The new
taxon is significant in being based upon the first dinosaur specimens found including unquestionable

feather impressions, thereby offering the strongest evidence relating birds directly to nonavian theropods.

According to Currie's initial notice, the first specimen—which would later be named *Caudipteryx*—was presented to him by Ji Qiang, the director of the National Geological Museum of China. The specimen had been found in the Sihetun locality (radiometric dates and other evidence tentatively pointing to an Early Cretaceous age; see Smith, You and Dodson 1998; Padian 1998*b*), which had already yielded three other recently discovered feathered animals—the nonavian theropods *Sinosauropteryx* and *Protarchaeopteryx* (then still regarded as a bird; see entry), and the primitive bird *Confuciusornis*. At the time, Ji believed the specimen to be the best one yet of *Protarchaeopteryx*. Indeed, the specimen closely resembled remains of the latter genus, and also clearly showed distinctive feather impressions in the regions of the arms and tail.

Three months later, while comparing this specimen to two other skeletons referred to *Protarchaeopteryx*, Currie and Ji noticed various inconsistencies. Although all three skeletons were approximately the same size and showed feather impressions, two of them—including the one presented earlier to Currie—had much shorter, theropod-like arms. Following preparation by Kevin Aulenback of the Royal Tyrrell Museum of Palaeontology, the latter two specimens were closely examined by Currie, Ji, and Aulenback, who found in them other theropod features, including long, sharp, and serrated conical teeth. As Currie noted, these teeth were confined to the front of the upper jaw, pointing more forward than downward, and had possibly "been incorporated into a birdlike beak with only the tips protruding." Currie speculated that the tail feathers in *Caudipteryx* probably fanned out for display.

In describing the holotype of *C. zoui*, Ji *et al.* noted that at least 14 remiges are attached to the second metacarpal, phalanx II-1, and the base of phalanx II-2. Each remex possesses a well-preserved rachis (also spelled "rhachis") and vane. The most distal remex measures less than 30 millimeters in length; the second most distal remex measures 63.5 millimeters, is symmetrical, and has barbs of 6.5 millimeters in length on either side of the rachis; the fourth most distal is 95 millimeters in length, longer than the humerus. The distal ends of the remaining remiges are not preserved.

According to Ji *et al.*, ten complete and two partial rectrices are preserved in the holotype, 11 attached to the left side of the tail (probably paired with another 11, not preserved, on the right side). Two rectrices are attached to each side of the last five or six caudals, but not to the anterior ones. The paratype preserves most of nine rectrices. Each rachis has a basal diameter of 0.74 millimeters and tapers distally. Each feather appears to be symmetrical, although in most of them the tips of the barbs of adjacent feathers overlap.

In the holotype, the body is covered by small, plumulaceous feathers, especially in the hip area and at the base of the tail.

As pointed out by Ji *et al.*, the remiges of *Caudipteryx* have symmetrical veins, and birds possessing asymmetrical feathers (including *Archaeopteryx*) are generally regarded as those capable of flight. In *Caudipteryx*, the arms are shorter than those of most nonavian coelurosaurs; the remiges are just slightly longer that the humerus; and the distal remiges are shorter than the proximal remiges. These features indicated to the authors that *Caudipteryx* was not a flier. Furthermore, the relatively long legs and the high-positioned, anteromedially-oriented hallux, indicate that this genus was a cursorial ground dweller.

Ji *et al.* grouped *Caudipteryx* and *Protarchaeopteryx* into an unnamed clade of manuraptoran theropods which they regarded as the sister group of the Velociraptorinae (see "Systematics" chapter). As stated by Currie in his original report, "*Caudipteryx* and *Protarchaeopteryx* make the dividing line between dinosaurs and birds even less distinct and strengthen the theory that birds evolved from small carnivorous ground-dwelling dinosaurs" (see introductory chapter, section on "Dinosaurs and Birds"; see also "Systematics" chapter.)

Key references: Currie (1998*b*); Ji, Currie, Norell and Ji (1998).

†CENTROSAURUS—(=?*Monoclonius*)
Ornithischia: Genasauria: Cerapoda: Marginocephalia: Ceratopsia: Neoceratopsia: Ceratopsomorpha: Ceratopsidae: Centrosaurinae.

Comments: *Centrosaurus*, a centrosaurine ceratopsian distinguished by such features as a long nasal horn, is one of the most common and best known horned dinosaurs. Much information about this genus has surfaced from the study of numerous specimens recovered from bonebeds, with more of these mass burial sites continuing to be found and explored, containing concentrations of *Centrosaurus* skeletal remains.

In a brief preliminary report, Eberth (1996) counted a total of nine monogeneric ceratopsian bonebeds (preserving disarticulated centrosaurine remains, eight dominated by *Centrosaurus*, one by *Styracosaurus*), each representing a minimum of 300 to 400 individuals, found in exposures of the Judith River Group, Dinosaur Park Formation, Dinosaur Provincial Park, Alberta, Canada. All nine bonebeds occur in the lower half of the formation; the *Centrosaurus*

Photograph by the author, courtesy Royal Tyrrell Museum/Alberta Community Development.

Centrosaurus apertus referred skull, right lateral view.

bonebeds were found in the lowest part of the formation, the *Styracosaurus* bonebed at a higher level. Four of the *Centrosaurus* bonebeds are associated with thin mudstone facies of overbank origin. Analyses of two of these four bonebeds yielded data suggesting that the preserved fossil *Centrosaurus* assemblages represent two mass kills, each possibly pertaining to a large population of animals that fell victim to a major flooding event. Eberth estimated that the entire *Centrosaurus* population, if all four mudstone bonebeds are related to each other, totaled more than 10,000 individuals.

Getty, Eberth, Brinkman, Tanke, Ryan and Vickaryous (1997) reported on the taphonomy of two overbank bonebeds in the lower half of the Dinosaur Park Formation of Alberta, more than 90 percent of the identifiable remains at these sights belonging to the type species *Centrosaurus apertus*, the remaining material to hadrosaurs and theropods (represented by shed rootless teeth).

According to Getty *et al.*, the large number of theropod teeth to other vertebrate microfossils and the presence of theropod tooth marks on 3 percent of the *Centrosaurus* (mostly axial) elements suggest that the teeth were lost during scavenging.

Getty *et al.* proposed that the combination of stratigraphic, sedimentologic, and taphonomic data intimates that these bonebeds were subjected to numerous events of flooding, scavenging, and reworking, similar to histories that have been proposed for

in-channel bonebeds. Evidence of chemical etching of the bones and lack of evidence for weathering further suggested to the authors "an acidic chemical environment and possibly a short residency time on the floodplain prior to final burial," the taphonomic signature in these bonebeds apparently "typical of a humid, subtropical, coastal plain setting."

Koppelhus (1997) reported on a sampling of four *Centrosaurus* bonebeds for palynological analysis in connection with sedimentological logging, these monogeneric fossil sites covering the lowermost 20 meters of the Dinosaur Park Formation in Alberta.

Yielded by these samples were diverse and well-preserved palynological assemblages, those from below indicating "environments dominated by low but probably dense ground cover consisting of ferns along with angiosperms of unknown affinity," the background vegetation consisting of tall trees. According to Koppelhus, all samples studied thus far have yielded several megaspore species suggesting that "waterferns were either floating on the surface of water or were growing in shallow water." Over 100 palynomorph species were identified in these samplings, representing bryophytes, pteridophytes, gymnosperms, and angiosperms; freshwater algae were not found to be common in any sampling, nor have any marine influences yet been found.

Koppelhus noted that further research in this area may someday "make it possible to understand the

Photograph by the author, courtesy Royal Tyrrell Museum/Alberta Community Development.

Recreation of a small area of a *Centrosaurus* bonebed.

vegetative cover when thousands of *Centrosaurus apertus* perished on this floodplain paleoenvironment."

Notes: Williamson (1996) reported the first centrosaurine to be documented from the southern Rocky Mountain region of North America and possibly the oldest known ceratopsid from that continent. The specimen (NMMNH P-25052) is a partial skeleton comprising disarticulated skull elements (including an almost complete left squamosal, left jugal, left dentary, and predentary) and associated postcrania (including a partial cervical bar, numerous dorsal vertebrae, a partial sacrum, many ribs, a partial left ilium, and left femur. The material was recovered from the Upper Cretaceous (lower Campanian) Allison Member of the Menefee Formation, a widespread alluvial floodplain deposit of the San Juan Basin, New Mexico. The skeleton was found closely associated with a small vertebrate fauna including the dromaeosaurid cf. *Saurornitholestes*, a new species of the alligatoroid *?Brachychampsa*, and trionychid and baenid turtles.

According to Williamson, though the squamosal of NMMNH P-25052 is clearly that of a centrosaurine comparable in size to *Centrosaurus*, this spec-

imen cannot be referred to this or any other genus, lacking key cranial elements (*e.g.*, nasal and brow horns, parietals) required for generic identification.

In a study of a pathologic skull of the centrosaurine genus *Pachyrhinosaurus* (see entry), Rothschild and Tanke (1997) noted that two specimens assigned to "*Monoclonius*," the horncore of AMNH 3944 and reconstructed horncore of NMNH 8897, have a morphology different from that of other horncores of *Centrosaurus*. Therefore, their referral to *Centrosaurus* requires additional assessment.

Although, for many decades, some authors (*e.g.*, Brown 1914) have regarded *Monoclonius* as a junior synonym of *Centrosaurus*, others (*e.g.*, Sternberg 1938) believed that each is generically distinct. Sampson, Ryan and Tanke (1997), in a study of craniofacial ontogeny in centrosaurines, argued that *Monoclonius* is not, in fact, a valid taxon, but a subadult form of *Centrosaurus*, *Pachyrhinosaurus*, *Styracosaurus*, *Einiosaurus*, or *Achelousaurus*, lacking distinctive skull ornamentation, but possessing features similar to those seen in juveniles and subadults of these genera. Sampson *et al.* further pointed out that a number of specimens, including postorbitals with well-developed horncores and parietal fragments having well-developed processes, found among *Monoclonius*-like frill fragments in an unexcavated bonebed in Dinosaur Provincial Park, Alberta, make *Centrosaurus* the most likely of the above candidates.

Sampson *et al.* also stated that perhaps the most convincing evidence against the validity of *Monoclonius* are the parietals found in low diversity bonebeds. As the authors noted, a number of parietals found in *Centrosaurus*, *Pachyrhinosaurus*, and *Einiosaurus* bonebeds in Montana and Alberta are of the typical *Monoclonius* type — adult-sized, comparatively thin, having simple margins lacking hooks, spikes, or horns. Had they been found isolated, these elements might have been referred to *Monoclonius*, thus suggesting that this taxon was preserved alongside other centrosaurine genera.

Contrary to Sampson *et al.*, Dodson and Tumarkin (1998), in a brief preliminary report citing Long and McNamara's (1997) application of the principles of heterochrony to the ontogeny of ceratopsians (see introductory chapter), posited that the very large species *Monoclonius crassus* (see *D:TE*) is a neotenic form, that is, one having retained juvenile morphology to large adult size. (Using the same criteria, Dodson and Tumarkin interpreted *Avaceratops*, regarded as a juvenile by Sampson *et al.*, as a progenic form, that

is, one that reached sexual maturity at a smaller size than in other centrosaurines; see *D:TE*).

Key references: Brown (1914); Dodson and Tumarkin (1998); Eberth (1996); Getty, Eberth, Brinkman, Tanke, Ryan and Vickaryous (1997); Koppelhus (1997); Sampson, Ryan and Tanke (1997); Sternberg (1938); Williamson (1996).

†CHASMOSAURUS

Ornithischia: Genasauria: Cerapoda: Marginocephalia: Ceratopsia: Neoceratopsia: Ceratopsomorpha: Ceratopsidae: Chasmosaurinae.

Diagnosis of *C. mariscalensis*: Moderate-sized chasmosaurine having long, broad, dorsally curved squamosals with convex lateral margins bearing six to ten pronounced marginal undulations, with or without attached epoccipitals; slender medially indented parietal bar with narrow posterolateral rami enclosing very large, triangular parietal fenestrae; anteromedian process of nasals separating premaxillae; large posteriorly curved supraorbital horncores arising directly over orbits; distinguished from *Pentaceratops sternbergii* by posterior curvature of supraorbital horncores, dorsal curvature of squamosals, and slender construction of parietal (Lehman 1996).

Comments: In 1989, Thomas M. Lehman described a new species of the genus *Chasmosaurus*, which he named *C. mariscalensis*, based upon a bonebed

Mounted skeleton of *Chasmosaurus belli*, left lateral view.

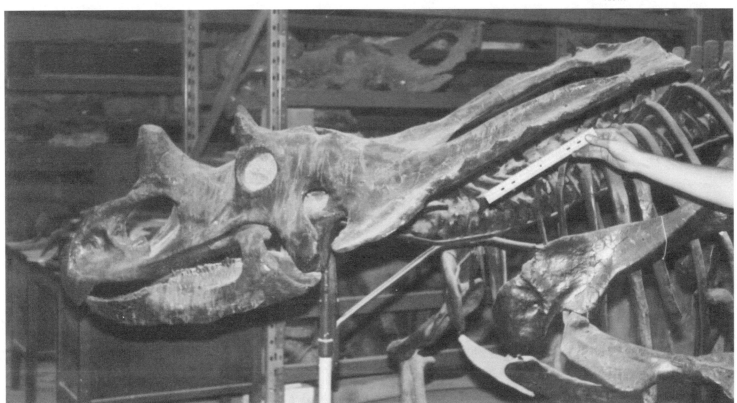

Chasmosaurus

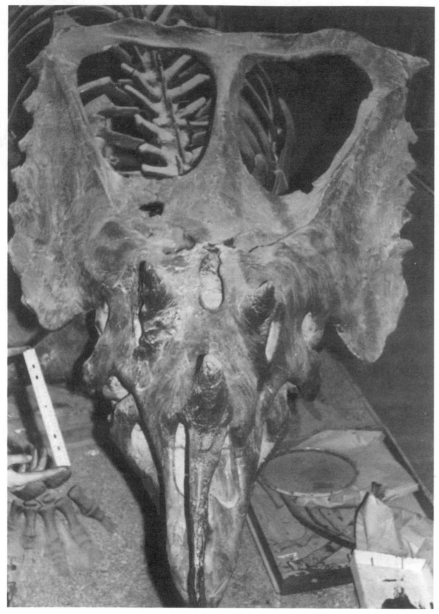

Chasmosaurus belli skeleton, front view.

accumulation of numerous disarticulated skulls and postcranial skeletons. Later, Forster, Sereno, Evans and Rowe described and figured a well-preserved skull (TMM 43098-1) belonging to this species (see *D:TE*).

Lehman (1996) has more recently criticized various points made by Forster *et al.* in their description of TMM 43098-1, including the following: Forster *et al.* stated that the ten squamosal epoccipitals present in this species are the most recorded for any ceratopsian. As noted by Lehman, some specimens of *Pentaceratops sternbergii* have at least that many, the total number varying ontogenetically. Also, Forster *et al.* had described and figured epoccipitals along the lateral edge of the squamosal in TMM 43098-1. According to Lehman, only the first six of the ten mar-

ginal undulations of the squamosal have such processes preserved; the lost epoccipitals would most likely have been large and triangular in shape, as are those in other specimens (*e.g.*, UTEP P.37.7.054 and 046) of *C. mariscalensis*, and not low and elliptical as shown by Forster *et al.* Furthermore, the shape of the epoccipitals varies among *C. mariscalensis* and *S. sternbergii* individuals.

Although Forster *et al.* regarded the convex lateral frill in *C. mariscalensis* as especially diagnostic, Lehman (1996) pointed out that the same condition is also true for other chasmosaurines, including *Triceratops*.

According to Lehman (1996), Forster *et al.* were incorrect in stating that the supraorbital horncores in *C. mariscalensis* straighten and become more erect during ontogeny, and that all referred horncores in adults show almost vertical orientation. As shown previously by Lehman (1989, 1990), some small and presumably juvenile horncores are vertically directed, while some larger and presumably adult horncores are curved posteriorly.

Later, Lehman (1998) briefly reported on a partial skeleton of *C. mariscalensis* that had been collected in 1938 by Wann Langston, Jr., for the University of Oklahoma. This specimen, though fragmentary, allowed for the first accurate reconstruction of this dinosaur's body proportions and also for a detailed assessment of the population structure in the "herd" represented at the type locality. According to Lehman (1998), this species is presently known from eight localities, each one found within a stratigraphic interval in the lower part of the upper shale member of the Aguja Formation, all but one in coastal plain deposits that accumulated near the paleo-shoreline. The distinctive pollen and wood assemblage in these deposits suggest "that the preferred habitat of *C. mariscalensis* was open low lying brackish marsh between areas of dense cypress and palm swamp."

According to Lehman (1998), the maximum adult size of this species, as revealed by isolated specimens of adult or near-adult individuals collected from five of these localities, is about 2500 kilograms (about 1.9 tons), about the same as *C. belli*. At least 20 individuals (representing a "herd" that perished as the result of a mass mortality event) have been recovered from the holotype bonebed, although only the holotype specimen was a full adult, the remaining individuals being subadults and juveniles. Fragments representing very small individuals have been found at two other localities. Lehman (1998) interpreted this disparity between specimens found at the different localities to suggest that the youngest animals (*i.e.*, hatchlings) lived apart from the older individuals, joining the "herds" later during their ontogeny.

The species *C. russelli* was considered by Lehman (1996) to be a junior synonym of *C. belli*, but he did not demonstrate their alleged synonymy.

Key references: Forster, Sereno, Evans and Rowe (1993); Lehman (1989, 1990, 1996, 1998).

†**CHIROSTENOTES**—(=*Caenagnathus, Macrophalangia,* ?*Ricardoestia*; =?*Dromaeosaurus,* ?*Elmisaurus*)
Saurischia: Theropoda: Neotheropoda: Tetanurae: Avetheropoda: Coelurosauria: Manuraptoriformes: Oviraptorosauria: Caenagnathidae.
Type species: *C. pergracilis* Gilmore 1924.
Other species: ?*C. elegans* (Currie, Godfrey and Nessov 1994).
Occurrence: Dinosaur Park Formation, Horseshoe Canyon Formation, Alberta, Canada.
Age: Late Cretaceous (Turonian–Maastrichtian).
New material: Partial mostly disarticulated but associated skeleton including left maxilla, probable left palatine, partial braincase, vertebrae (three cervical, two dorsal, and five caudal), synsacrum composed of six co-ossified vertebrae, anterior and posterior cervical rib, middorsal rib, fragments of ilia,

right ischium, pubes, partial distal end of right tibia, several badly crushed unidentifiable bones, adult.

Diagnosis of genus (as for type species): Aside from larger size, mandible distinguished from that of *C. elegans* by possession of more elaborate and shallower dentary, proportionately longer mandibular symphysis, and presence of median ridge on dorsal (lingual) aspect of mandibular symphysis (Sues 1997).

Comments: The taxonomic history of the rare, medium-sized and lightly built, birdlike dinosaur *Chirostenotes pergracilis* has been long and fairly complicated (see entry, *D:TE*); and a better understanding of this species surfaced with the identification by Hans Dieter-Sues of a specimen of *C. pergracilis* that had been collected almost 75 years earlier.

As recounted by Sues (1997), this specimen—a partial skeleton (ROM 43250)—was recovered on June 12, 1923, by G. E. Linbald, while leading a field party from the Royal Ontario Museum of Palaeontology, from the Horseshoe Canyon Formation (Late Campanian–Early Maastrichtian), along the Red Deer River, in southern Alberta. Linbald identified the specimen in his field diary as a possible

Chirostenotes pergracilis, ROM 43250, partial braincase in A. occipital, B. lateral, and C. anterior views. Scale = 2 cm. (After Sues 1997.)

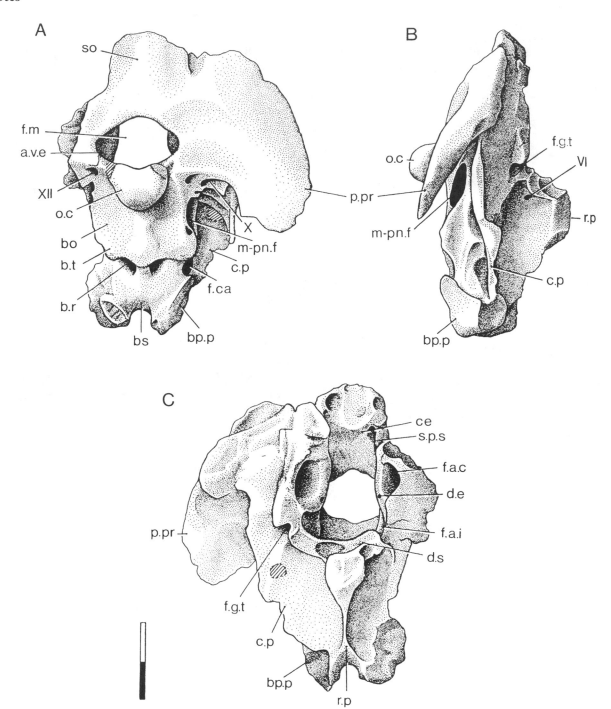

ornithomimid; decades later, Russell (1972), in his review of Late Cretaceous ostrich dinosaurs of western Canada, referred to the specimen — collected in two blocks and still unprepared — as unidentified ornithomimid. The larger block was taken out of storage in 1988 and its plaster jacket briefly opened for inspection, during which time various postcranial bones including a few vertebrae were removed. After this removal, both blocks were rejacketed and put back into storage.

Sues' examination of these vertebrae in 1988 re-

vealed that the specimen did not belong to an ornithomimid. Further preparation of these fossils revealed a close similarity between certain elements of ROM 43250 to corresponding bones of a partial postcranial skeleton RTMP 79.20.1 of *C. pergracilis* described by Currie and Russell (1988) (see also *D:TE*), particularly in the distinctive structure of the synsacrum in both specimens. Each synsacrum comprises six co-ossified vertebrae that decrease in length and dorsoventral height toward the anterior end of the series. The centra of the sacral vertebrae possess distinct pneumatic openings. Also, both specimens possess a similarly shaped ischium. Because of these shared features, Sues referred ROM 43250 to *C. pergracilis*.

Though Currie and Russell were the first authors to speculate that *Caenagnathus* could be a junior synonym of *Chirostenotes* (see entry, *D:TE*), no homologous elements were available at the time to confirm their suspicion, the holotype of *Caenagnathus collinsi* being an almost complete mandible (CMN 8776; R. M. Sternberg 1940). Based upon the close structural correspondence between the maxilla of ROM 43250 and CMN 8776, Sues regarded *C. collinsi* as a junior synonym of *C. pergracilis*.

ROM 43250, therefore, represented the second record of *C. pergracilis* from the Horseshoe Canyon Formation, the first being a left metatarsal II (CMN 9570) (see Russell 1984). This more complete specimen was especially useful in that it preserved certain elements — including skull parts, presacral and caudal vertebrae, cervical ribs, and both pubes — that had previously been unknown in this taxon.

With ROM 43250 substantially augmenting what had been known of the skeletal structure of *Chirostenotes*, Sues published a detailed description of this specimen. Also, Sues proposed a new diagnosis of the type species, based upon ROM 43250 and also the following specimens: CMN 2367 (holotype of *C. pergracilis*), incomplete articulated left and right manus (Gilmore 1924); CMN 8538 (holotype of *Macrophalangia canadensis*), distal portion of right tibia with part of astragalus, two distal tarsals, and right pes (C. M. Sternberg 1932); CMN 8776 (holotype of *C. collinsi*); and CMN 9570, left metatarsal II (Russell 1984).

Currie and Russell had previously identified two "morphs" among the various postcranial specimens referred to *C. pergracilis* — one being larger and more robust, the other smaller and more gracile — which these authors interpreted as indicative of sexual dimorphism (see *Chirostenotes* entry, *D:TE*). Subsequently, Currie (1989) referred three *Chirostenotes*-like tarsometatarsi (including ROM 781, the holotype of *Ornithomimus elegans* Parks 1933, comprising complete metatarsals II and IV, incomplete distal tarsal IV, and metatarsal III), to *Elmisaurus* as a second species of that genus, *E. elegans* (see *Elmisaurus* entry, *D:TE*).

Sues regarded the differences between the larger and smaller morphs as having taxonomic rather than sexually dimorphic significance, the larger morph (including ROM 43250) being representative of *C. pergracilis*. Also, Sues found unconvincing the criteria used by Currie to refer ROM 781 to *Elmisaurus*, and also questioned those differentiating *Chirostenotes* from *Elmisaurus* at the generic level (*e.g.*, absence of fusion in tarsometatarsus and also overall larger body size in *Chirostenotes*; see Currie 1989, 1990; also, presence of proximolateral process on distal fourth tarsal

Chirostenotes pergracilis, ROM 43250, synsacrum, lateral view. Scale = 2 cm. (After Sues 1997.)

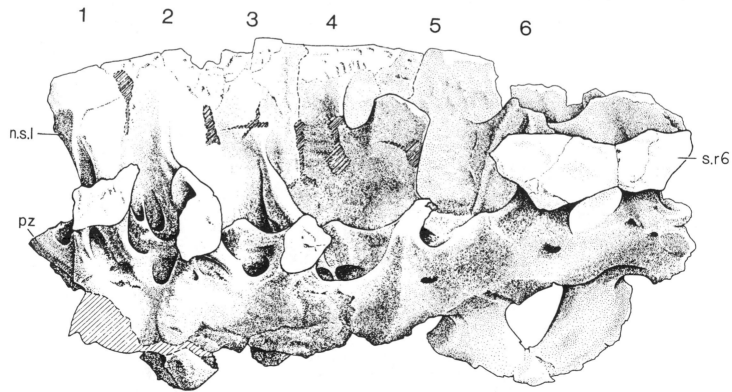

in *Elmisaurus* specimens from Alberta and Mongolia; Currie 1990). According to Sues, then, the smaller of the two above mentioned "morphs," documented by RTMP 79.20.1 and ROM 781, represents a possible second species of *Chirostenotes* (as first suggested by C. M. Sternberg 1934), the available binomen for this taxon being *C. elegans*, while the genus *Elmisaurus* seems to be referable to *Chirostenotes*.

Earlier, Cracraft (1971) had erected the new and smaller species *Caenagnathus sternbergi* upon a right mandibular fragment (CMN 2690); more than two decades later, Currie *et al.* tentatively referred to this species several partial dentaries, all of these specimens of *C. sternbergi* having been recovered from Alberta (see *Caenagnathus* entry, *D:TE*).

Acknowledging that Currie and Russell had already suggested that the two "morphs" represented by postcranial remains might correspond to the two types of mandibular remains, and based upon appropriate size, Sues tentatively associated the mandibular material of *C. sternbergi* with the postcrania of ?*C. elegans*.

Osmólska (1981) had referred *Chirostenotes* to her newly erected family Elmisauridae, which Sues (following an earlier suggestion by Currie and Russell) regarded as a subjective junior synonym of Caenagnathidae (a taxon, along with the taxa Oviraptoridae and Therizinosauroidea, nestled within Oviraptorosauria; see "Systematics" chapter).

Sues listed the following craniomandibular apomorphies shared by *Chirostenotes* with the Oviraptoridae (see Barsbold 1983; Barsbold, Maryańska and Osmólska 1990; Currie *et al.* 1994): 1. Upper and lower jaws edentulous; 2. maxillae having broad palatal shelf bearing two longitudinal ridges and with posteromedial toothlike processes; 3. mandible with large external mandibular fenestra; 4. rami bowed laterally at about midlength; 5. dentary with medial (lingual) ridge; 6. dorsal margin of dentary deeply concave; 7. dentary having two long posterior processes separated by mandibular fenestra; 8. co-ossification of articular, surangular, and (possibly) coronoid into single element; 9. coronoid process inflected dorsomedially; articular facet convex (in lateral aspect), distinctly expanded laterally and medially, raised above dorsal margin of mandibular ramus. According to Sues, *Chirostenotes* and the Oviraptoridae also share the presence of six or seven sacral vertebrae with pneumatic openings, and (at least) the proximal caudals are extensively pneumatic. Also, Sues noted that, based on ROM 43250, *Chirostenotes* shares two derived conditions with the therizinosaurid *Erlikosaurus*: 1. Presence of accessory antorbital fenestra, and 2. reduced rim around antorbital fossa. These characters shared by *Chirostenotes* with the Oviraptoridae and Ther-

izinosauridae support the position of the Caenagnathidae within the Oviraptorosauria.

Key references: Barsbold (1983); Barsbold, Maryańska and Osmólska (1990); Cracraft (1971); Currie (1989, 1990); Currie, Godfrey and Nessov (1994); Currie and Russell (1998); Gilmore (1924); Osmólska (1981); Parks (1933); Russell (1972, 1984); C. M. Sternberg (1932, 1934); R. M. Sternberg (1940); Sues (1997).

†CHUBUTISAURUS

Saurischia: Sauropodomorpha: Sauropoda: Eusauropoda: Neosauropoda: Macronaria: Titanosauriformes: Somphospondyli: Titanosauria: Titanosauridae.

Occurrence: Cerro Barcino Formation, Chubut Province, Argentina.

Age: Early Cretaceous (?Aptian).

Holotype: MACN 18222, posterior dorsal centrum, dorsal neural arch, dorsal neural spine, 10 incomplete caudal vertebrae, complete left femur, tibia, humerus, radius, and ulna, four metacarpals, some fragmentary remains.

Comments: The holotype (MACN 18222, consisting of partial postcrania) of this large, heavily built sauropod was collected by Guillermo del Corro and O. A. Gutiérrez in 1965 from the Cerro Barcino Formation of Chubut Province (Bonaparte 1996*b*).

McIntosh (1996*b*), in a review of the Sauropoda, placed *Chubutisaurus* in the Brachiosauridae (see "Systematics" chapter), but Bonaparte (1996*b*) disagreed with that assessment. According to Bonaparte, the humerus/femur ratio used by McIntosh to assign this genus to the Brachiosauridae is not different from that of primitive titanosaurs from Patagonia; also, Salgado (in preparation) observed several characters of the prespinal lamina of this genus which are different from those of *Brachiosaurus*, with "not one unequivocal derived character shared by *Chubutisaurus* and the brachiosaurids" (see also Salgado, Coria and Calvo 1997). Bonaparte speculated that *Chubutisaurus* differs from titanosaurs and represents a distinct family which, based on the available material, cannot yet be well defined.

Key references: Bonaparte (1996*b*); McIntosh (1996*b*).

†COELOPHYSIS—(=*Longosaurus, Rioarribasaurus*; =?*Podokesaurus*, ?*Syntarsus*)

Saurischia: Theropoda: Neotheropoda: "Ceratosauria": Coelophysoidea.

Type species: *C. bauri* (Cope 1887).

Other species: *C. longicollis* (Cope 1887) [*nomen dubium*], *C. willistoni* (Cope 1889) [*nomen dubium*].

Vertebrate paleontologist Edwin H. Colbert at the Royal Tyrrell Museum of Palaeontology, while attending the Dinosaur Systematics Symposium in 1986, studies *Coelophysis bauri* fossils collected from the Ghost Ranch quarry prior to completion of his 1989 monograph on this dinosaur.

Comments: The small, Late Triassic "ceratosaur" *Coelophysis* is one of the best known dinosaurs of any kind. The genus is represented by hundreds of skeletons recovered from various sites. Most of these specimens, some complete and articulated and preserved in various stages of ontogeny, have been collected from a single site, the Whitaker quarry, at Ghost Ranch, New Mexico.

Although this dinosaur has long been well known both to scientists and the general public, there has recently been considerable controversy regarding its name. Questions arose: Should this dinosaur be called *Coelophysis*, the name given by Cope (1887*b*) to various fragmentary specimens found at a different locality, or *Rioarribasaurus*, the new name given by Hunt and Lucas (1991) to the Ghost Ranch skeletons (see *Coelophysis* and *Rioarribasaurus* entries, *D:TE*, for details)?

As editorial work was completed on the original *Coelophysis* and *Rioarribasaurus* entries for *D:TE*, the International Commission on Zoological Nomenclature (ICZN) had not yet published its ruling as to which of these names would be the official one for the small theropod represented by numerous specimens collected from the Whitaker Quarry, Ghost Ranch, New Mexico.

Very briefly summarizing:

David Baldwin, working for early paleontologist Edward Drinker Cope in 1881, collected the fragmentary remains of a small dinosaur in the Petrified Forest Member of the Chinle Formation, Rio Arriba County, in northwestern New Mexico. Cope (1887*a*) referred this material to two new species of the genus *Coelurus*, which he named *C. longicollis* and *C. bauri*. Subsequently, Cope (1887*b*) removed these species from *Coelurus*, referring them to a new genus, *Coelophysis*, with *C. bauri* the type species.

More than half a century later (in 1947), George Whitaker, assistant to then American Museum of Natural History paleontologist Edwin H. Colbert (1947, 1961, 1989, 1990, 1995), discovered a bonebed of skeletons, some of them articulated, representing hundreds of individuals belonging to a single genus of small theropod at Ghost Ranch, in Rio Arriba County, New Mexico. Colbert assigned these remains to *Coelophysis*, which, due to the abundance and

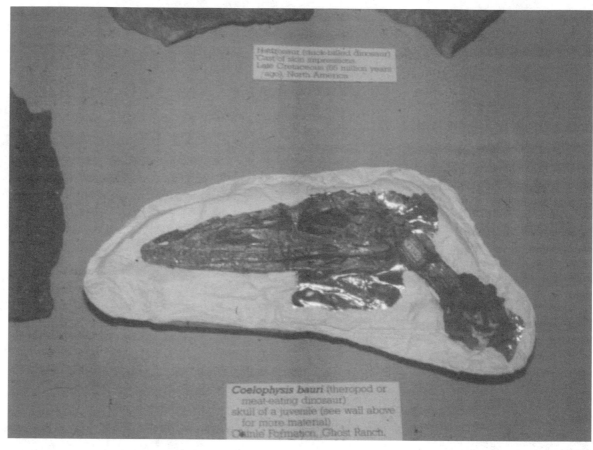

Skull of the small theropod dinosaur *Coelophysis bauri* from Ghost Ranch, New Mexico.

excellent preservation of the specimens and the ontogenetic range exhibited by them, has become one of the best known of all dinosaurian genera.

Indeed, *Coelophysis* became a familiar theropod, both in technical articles and in the popular press, and was even designated the official state fossil of New Mexico. In recent years, however, the generic name for this dinosaur was questioned, particularly as related to the Ghost Ranch specimens. Padian (1986), in reviewing the taxonomic status of Cope's *Coelophysis* material, inquired whether or not the Whitaker quarry specimens could be referred to this genus. Hunt and Lucas (1991) later regarded *Coelophysis* as a *nomen dubium*, founded on material exhibiting no diagnostic features. Furthermore, Hunt and Lucas removed the Ghost Ranch specimens from the genus *Coelophysis* and erected for them a new genus and species, *Rioarribasaurus colberti*, selecting specimen AMNH 7224, the best skeleton recovered from the Whitaker quarry, as the holotype.

In December 1992, paleontologists Dr. Colbert (Museum of Northern Arizona, Flagstaff), Dr. Alan J. Charig (The Natural History Museum, London), Prof. Peter Dodson (School of Veterinary Medicine, University of Pennsylvania, Philadelphia), Dr. David D. Gillette (Division of State History — Antiquities, Salt Lake City, Utah), Dr. John H. Ostrom (Yale Peabody Museum of Natural History, New Haven, Connecticut), and Dr. David B. Weishampel (School of Medicine, Johns Hopkins University, Baltimore, Maryland) applied to the Commission (Case 2840) requesting that AMNH 7224 be designated the neotype of Cope's fragmentary species *Coelurus bauri*, thus rendering *C. bauri* a senior objective synonym of *R. colberti*; that *Coelophysis* again be the regarded as the correct name for the Ghost Ranch theropod specimens; and that the genus *Rioarribasaurus* and binomen *R. colberti* be rejected and considered invalid by the ICZN.

The above application elicited strong sentiments, both pro and con, and submitted to the ICZN, from various members of the vertebrate paleontology community.

Comments supporting the application and published in the *Bulletin of Zoological Nomenclature* were offered by Dr. Hans-Dieter Sues (Royal Ontario Museum, Toronto), Dr. Hilde L. Schwartz (Los Alamos National Laboratory, Los Alamos, New Mexico), Dr. Ralph E. Molnar (Queensland Museum, South Brisbane), Prof. Zdenek V. Spinar (Prysk, Czech Republic), Dr. Thomas R. Holtz, Jr. (Geological Survey, U.S. Department of the Interior, National Center, Reston, Virginia), Prof. Farish A. Jenkins, Jr. (Museum of Comparative Zoology, Harvard University,

Cambridge, Massachusetts), Dr. Benjamin S. Creisler, Dr. Nicholas Hotton III (National Museum of Natural History, Smithsonian Institution, Washington, D.C.), Dr. Dale A. Russell (Canadian Museum of Nature, Ottawa, Ontario), Dr. Elizabeth L. Nicholls (Royal Tyrrell Museum of Palaeontology, Drumheller, Alberta), Prof. Louis L. Jacobs (Southern Methodist University, Dallas, Texas), Donald F. Glut, and Prof. Armand de Ricqlés (Université de Paris).

Opposing comments, published in the *BZN*, were submitted by Dr. Adrian P. Hunt (University of Colorado at Denver), Dr. Spencer G. Lucas (New Mexico Museum of Natural History and Science, Albuquerque), Dr. Robert M. Sullivan (The State Museum of Pennsylvania, Harrisburg; see also Sullivan 1996*a* [Sullivan believes that *Coelophysis* displays diagnostic characters and that *Rioarribasaurus* is gener-

ically distinct from that taxon), Dr. Samuel P. Welles (Museum of Paleontology, University of California, Berkeley), George Olshevsky, and Dr. Philip Huber (Ohio University, Athens).

Considering that Cope's (1887*a*, 1887*b*) original *C. bauri* material is fragmentary, but also noting that the name *Coelophysis* has been used since 1947 to designate the better preserved Ghost Ranch specimens and that the applicants "sought to secure this meaning in the interest of stability," members of the Commission were invited to vote on the issue on December 1, 1995. Voting ended on March 1, 1996, with the results published as "Opinion 1842" in the *Bulletin of Zoological Nomenclature* 53 (2), June 1996. There were 18 affirmative and eight negative votes.

As stated by one of the Commission's affirmative voters (Hahn) in the *Bulletin*: "The problem in this

Coelophysis bauri as restored by Gregory S. Paul. The small-headed robust morph is on the left. The larger-headed gracile morph is left of center. From *Predatory Dinosaurs of the World* (1988).

case is ... the type material is insufficient to be useful in identifying the taxon concerned. Of the nominal genera involved, *Coelophysis* is the most important in phylogenetic discussions and the name is well used in the literature. Therefore, to conserve 'common usage' it is necessary to approve the proposals of Colbert *et al.*"

Another voter (Heppell) favoring the application stated: "It is clear that the lectotype of *Coelurus bauri* is manifestly not able to fulfill the essential function of a type specimen [providing] 'the objective standard of reference by which the application of the name it bears is determined' (Article 61a of the Code). If the type specimen is inadequate to support this function the name it bears is inevitably a nomen dubium. If, as here, varying interpretations of its identity are current, the pragmatic solution is to set aside its type status in favor of a neotype ... I [believe] it is better to clear the ground of dubious or ambiguous impedimenta and leave the way open for future taxonomic and stratigraphic assessment of this important theropod material."

Therefore, *Coelophysis* now remains the official name for the small "ceratosaur" represented in such great numbers at the Ghost Ranch quarry.

Note: Sullivan (in press) will name and describe a second small theropod genus found in the Ghost Ranch quarry (R. M. Sullivan, personal communication 1998).

Key references: Colbert (1947, 1961, 1989, 1990, 1995); Cope (1887*a*, 1887*b*); Hunt and Lucas (1991); Padian (1986).

†COMPSOGNATHUS

Saurischia: Theropoda: Neotheropoda: Tetanurae: Avetheropoda: Coelurosauria: Compsognathidae.

Comments: One of the tiniest known dinosaurs, the Late Jurassic theropod *Compsognathus longipes* is represented by only two specimens, the holotype (BSP 1563) and best specimen being an almost complete articulated skeleton excellently preserved in its original "death pose" in lithographic limestone.

In their paper describing the new theropod *Sinosauropteryx* (see entry), Chen, Dong and Zhen (1998) referred both that genus and *Compsognathus* to the reinstated family Compsognathidae Marsh 1882, based upon various characters shared by both genera (see "Systematics" chapter). At the same time, Chen *et al.* cautioned about using some characters to diagnose *Compsognathus*, particularly "the presence of a relatively large skull and short forelimbs" (see Norman 1990; *D:TE*), pointing out that relative skull length in theropods can be highly variable. Ratios involving skull and length of elements of the forelimb and hind limb depend upon the absolute size of the individual animal, "mostly because of negative allometry experienced by the tibia during growth or interspecific size increase." Chen *et al.* found more useful results for diagnostic purposes in comparing the lengths of the humerus plus radius with femur length.

Griffiths (1993) had identified as eggs various polygonal irregularities, found inside and outside the body cavity of the holotype of *C. longipes* and originally thought to be armor (Huene 1901; see *D:TE*). Chen *et al.* doubted Griffiths' interpretation of these structures as eggs, noting that they were much greater

First three-dimensional skeleton of *Compsognathus longipes*, this cast made by Bruce J. Mohn. Once believed to possess a manus with two digits, *Compsognathus* was probably three-fingered, such as the compsognathid *Sinosauropteryx*.

in number and also much smaller (about 10 millimeters in diameter) than two definite eggs found within the body cavity of *Sinosauropteryx* (see entry).

Bruce J. Mohn attempted the first three-dimensional mount of *C. longipes*. As Mohn (1996) pointed out, in an abstract, mounting skeletons of small vertebrates for museum display creates special problems. Mounting an original specimen can result in damage to the fossil bones through the processes of preparation. Furthermore, mounting a specimen limits its accessibility for study purposes. It is, therefore, more practical and reasonable to mount casts or sculpted reproductions of the original bones for exhibit.

As the bones in the almost complete type specimen of *C. longipes* are laterally compressed, it was impractical for Mohn to make casts of the original remains for the mount. Instead, Mohn studied several small theropods to suggest the form and number of the bones missing from the holotype, and to sculpt areas of the specimen that were obscured by matrix and overlying bones.

Mohn sculpted the bones in clay and formed delicate features (*e.g.*, cervical thoracic ribs, gastralia) from copper or steel wire. Molds were prepared, after which casts were made in polyester resin over steel armatures. The cast bones were then assembled in an "active" pose (see also Mohn 1998*a*).

Key references: Chen, Dong and Zhen (1998); Griffiths (1993); Huene (1901); Mohn (1996, 1998*a*).

†CRYOLOPHOSAURUS

Saurischia: Theropoda: Neotheropoda: Tetanurae:
    Avetheropoda: Carnosauria: Allosauroidea.

Age: Early Jurassic.

Comments: A relatively recently named theropod distinguished by an unusual, furrowed cranial crest, *Cryolophosaurus* was first announced in a preliminary report by Hammer and Hickerson in 1993, then described by these authors the following year.

Subsequent to those original articles, Hammer (1997) more precisely dated the remains of this theropod as of Early Jurassic age (based on the presence of a large tritylodont and a large plateosaurid prosauropod similar to *Plateosaurus* and *Lufengosaurus*).

Hammer noted that *Cryolophosaurus* is a relatively large animal (approximately 8 meters, or 27 feet in length), displaying all of the general features of other theropods. The author then referred *Cryolophosaurus* to the Allosauroidea as the most primitive known member of that family (approximately 50 million years older than any other known member of this group), considering the genus to be an early relative of *Allosaurus* and *Monolophosaurus*. Because of its age, Hammer was not surprised that *Cryolophosaurus* retains some primitive features—especially in the femur and foot (Hammer and Hickerson 1994)—compared to other allosauroids.

Holtz (1996), in a major new phylogenetic analysis of the Theropoda, regarded *Cryolophosaurus* as a basal member of Carnosauria (see "Systematics" chapter).

Archaeopteryx lithographica being chased by a predaceous *Compsognathus longipes*, as restored by Gregory S. Paul, this scenario suggesting one of the possible origins of flight. From *Predatory Dinosaurs of the World* (1988).

Cryolophosaurus

Cryolophosaurus elliotti, life restoration by William Stout, an artist who specializes in reconstructing the environments and inhabitants of prehistoric Antarctica. This painting of the crested theropod was made with the consultation of paleontologist William R. Hammer using, as a model, a cast of the reconstructed holotype skull.

In a more recent abstract, Hammer and Hickerson (1998) stated that features of the high, narrow skull of *Cryolophosaurus* suggest that this genus is a tetanuran related to Late Jurassic to Early Cretaceous forms found mainly on northern continents, although the highly bowed femur retains plesiomorphic features (*e.g.,* a shallow extensor groove and declined head of the greater trochanter) typical of some "ceratosaurs," while primitive characters can also be seen in other postcranial elements. If indeed a tetanuran,

according to the authors, *Cryolophosaurus* "precedes all other members of that clade by tens of millions of years, therefore the retention of primitive features is not unexpected."

Pointing out that a partially articulated foot and portion of a femur, belonging to the prosauropod, were found among the scattered bones of *Cryolophosaurus*, and that several long cervical ribs, possibly belonging to this prosauropod, were found in the mouth of *Cryolophosaurus*, Hammer surmised that this theropod had been feeding when it died. Hammer further speculated that, since the ribs extend all the way back to the theropod's neck region, this *Cryolophosaurus* individual may have choked to death on its prosauropod prey.

Hammer also guessed that a single, postcanine tooth, found with the *Cryolophosaurus* remains, may have been among the theropod's stomach contents. The tooth is that of a tritylodont, an early relative to mammals the size of a beaver.

Antarctic dinosaurs are rare, Hammer (1998) pointed out, for a number of reasons, these including the following: 1. Access to Antarctica is difficult, with very few paleontologists ever having visited the continent; 2. more than 98 percent of the continent is covered with glacial ice averaging more than two kilometers (one mile) in thickness, with very little rock exposed; and 3. the geology and age of the exposed rocks limit the probability of dinosaur finds.

Regarding the latter reason, Hammer (1998) explained that the majority of the continent's exposed sediments, which are of early Middle Jurassic age, occur in the Transantarctic Mountains atop the highest peaks intruding the underlying sediments. The Early Jurassic Falla Formation, containing the youngest sediments in this range, are only found in quite limited and relatively inaccessible areas near the southern end of the range. *Cryolophosaurus* was found in Antarctica's only Cretaceous sediments on the peninsular islands, these limited exposures comprising marine sediments that rarely produce dinosaurs. Hammer (1998) speculated that "the most promising region for discovering additional Antarctic dinosaurs is in the older sediments of the southern Transantarctic Mountains," although Late Triassic forms might be found in the upper part of the Fremouw Formation underlying the Falla Formation.

Key references: Hammer (1997, 1998); Hammer and Hickerson (1993, 1994, 1998); Holtz (1996).

†DACENTRURUS

Diagnosis of genus (as for type species): Twelve cervical vertebrae, vertebral centra of posterior third of neck and of dorsal series massive, so maximum transverse width is greater than maximum length; solid, pedicel-like region in dorsal vertebrae from posterior two-thirds of series short, minimum angle between each transverse process and neural spine 55 degrees; sacrum having seven co-ossfied centra with two dorsosacral vertebrae anteriorly; centra of anterior caudal vertebrae massive, short neural spines having massive, rounded tops; anterior process of ilium short, broadening anteriorly; distal part of ischium tapering, straight in lateral aspect; ratio of maximum lengths of humerus to radius 1:0.69, of humerus to ulna 1:0.79, of femur to humerus is 1:0.68, of femur to ilium 1:0.85; dermal armor including at least small plates with thick base, two pairs of stocky caudal spines with expanded base, and four pairs of long caudal spines with small base (Galton 1991, modified from Galton 1985*b*).

Comments: Following various previously published writings by Peter M. Galton (*e.g.,* 1981, 1985*b*, 1990*c*), in which he discussed *Dacentrurus*— the first stegosaurid ever to be described, founded upon an articulated, fairly complete postcranial skeleton (BMNH 46013), originally the holotype of the species *Omosaurus armatus* Owen 1875 (see *D:TE*)— Galton (1991) offered a detailed description of remains referred to this genus collected from Upper Jurassic beds in France and Portugal, as well as an emended diagnosis of the genus and type species.

The material from France consists of the holotype (MHNH A; destroyed, no casts) of *Omosaurus* (=*Dacentrurus*) *lennieri* (Nopcsa 1911*a*), a partial skeleton excavated by Emile Savalle and Gustav Lennier (1899), and also a second specimen (Boine A), the distal half of a left femur (Galton and Boine 1980), found at the base of the cliff at La Brière; both specimens were found in the Argiles d'Octeville (lower Kimmeridgian), at the base of the cliffs at Octeville, Cap de la Hève, Normandy.

Specimens (not yet catalogued; designated with letters by Galton 1991 on an interim basis) from Portugal, all originally described by Lapparent and Zbyszewski (1957) and mostly referred by them to *Dacentrurus armatus* and *D. lennieri*, included a partial skeleton (MSGP A) from beds (?middle upper Kimmeridgian) at the top of the sea cliff of Pedras Muitas, east of Baleal; partial skeleton (MSGP B) from beds (?middle upper Kimmeridgian) of the Murteiras ravine, near Bouro; partial skeleton (MSGP C) from beds (?middle to lower upper Kimmeridgian) southeast of Alfeizerão; partial skeleton (MSGP D) from beds (?upper lower Tithonian) on the edges of a ravine near Lourinhã; two damaged anterior caudal vertebrae, and centra of three middle and four posterior caudals (MSGP E), from beds (?upper lower Tithonian) of the sea cliff next to the beach of

Areia Branca; partial skeleton (MSGP E; holotype of *Astrodon pusillus*, referred by Galton 1981 to *D. armatus*) from beds (?upper upper Kimmeridgian–lower lower Tithonian) of the Casal de Pedreira, near Lourinhã; slightly eroded caudal centrum (MSGP G; referred by Lapparent and Zbyszewski to *A. pusillus*, by Galton 1981 to *D. armatus*) of a juvenile individual from beds (?upper lower Tithonian) of Areia Branca; right femur with eroded ends of a juvenile from beds (?upper upper Kimmeridgian–lower lower Tithonian) of Lourinhã; ?lateral end of a sacral rib (MSGP I; referred as proximal end of metacarpal by Lapparent and Zbyszewski to *A. pusillus*) from beds (?upper upper Kimmeridgian–lower lower Tithonian) of Porto do Mos; base of right stocky dermal tail spine (MSGP J) from beds (?upper upper Kimmeridgian–lower lower Tithonian); base of left long tail spine (MSGP K) from beds (?upper upper Kimmeridgian–lower lower Tithonian) at Porto Nova (Maceira); and a bone (MSGP L) from beds (?upper upper Kimmeridgian–lower lower Tithonian) northeast of Pombal, this badly damaged specimen identified by Lapparent and Zbyszewski as the base of a tail spine, but, because of its size, is possibly sauropod (Galton 1991); right femur (IST A) from beds (?middle or lower upper Kimmeridgian) in cliffs of the beach of San Bernardino.

In addition to the foregoing material, Galton described the following specimens from Portugal—a well-preserved right stocky dermal tail spine (FUB A), and the proximal part of a right dorsal rib (FUB B), both found in beds (?upper Tithonian) between Porto de Barcas and Porto Pinheiro, near Lourinhã (B. Krebs, personal communication to Galton).

Although the holotype of *D. armatus* includes a single dermal nuchal plate, no armor was found among the specimens from France, and only dermal spines are included among the Portuguese material (the "nuchal plate" of Lapparent and Zbyszewski identified by Galton 1991 as an incomplete neural arch of a dorsal vertebra).

Galton (1991) noted that three of the spines from Portugal belonging to *Dacentrurus* are massive, possessing a stocky shaft steeply set in a large, oval-shaped base with thick edges notched by numerous grooves, these resembling spines in the holotype (BMNH 46320) of *O. hastiger* (=*D. armatus*). In one (not the second, the third being too poorly preserved for verification) of these spines, the ventral surface of the base is transversed by two longitudinal ridges (also present in BMNH 46320). Galton (1991) pointed out that these spines also resemble the pair of holotype spines (USNM 4937) of *Stegosaurus sulcatus* (=*Stegosaurus armatus*), which display such a ridge, and also the stocky shoulder spines of *Kentrosaurus*, which lack this

ridge. Bakker (1988) had postulated that the spines of "*S. sulcatus*," the bases of which are too large to fit at the end of the tail, should be placed in the shoulder region or at the base of the neck (see *Stegosaurus* entry, *D:TE*). However, Gilmore (1914) had observed that the spines of "*S. sulcatus*" touched one another, joined by cartilage along a rugose surface on the medial edge of their respective bases, and could, consequently, not have occurred above the shoulders. For the above reasons, Galton (1991) suggested that the stocky spines of *Dacentrurus* probably occurred in the sacral region or, more likely, at the base of the tail.

The three remaining dermal spines, Galton (1991) observed, have a slender shaft set at a more shallow angle to a smaller, subcircular base, comparable to two pairs of long spines seen in *Kentrosaurus*. They differ from one another, and also from the long tail spine of BMNH 46013, in their cross section and in the form of their ventral surfaces. As four somewhat different kinds of long dermal spines have presently been identified in *Dacentrurus*, Galton (1991) concluded that this dinosaur possessed at least four pairs of long spines.

Galton (1990*c*), in a review of the Stegosauria, had listed the referred species *D. lennieri*—originally considered to be distinct from *D. armatus* on the basis of having proportionally shorter cervical vertebrae and a greater degree of ossification of the bones—as a junior synonym of *D. armatus*, but did not demonstrate their synonymy. Later, Galton (1991) detailed his reasons for that assessment, pointing out that 1. the cervical vertebrae in MHNH A are not proportionally shorter than those of BMNH 46013; 2. differences in the proportions of the sacral centra of these two specimens are matched within the preserved sacra of a specimen of the stegosaurid *Kentrosaurus aethiopicus*, this difference, therefore, probably explained by individual variation; and, 3. vertebrae originally referred to *D. armatus* have fused ribs, so different degrees of ossification may be due to individual variation, pathology, or have specific significance. Galton (1991) concluded that, because "the differences are so few, [because of] the destruction of the holotype in 1944, and the lack of any casts or alternative specimens showing the same characters as MHNH A," *D. lennieri* is best regarded as a junior synonym of *D. armatus*.

Note: In 1983, Galton referred an isolated left dermal plate (FUB C), found between Porto Pinheiro and Porto de Barcas (Early Cretaceous: possibly lower Berriasian; B. Krebs, personal communication to Galton, rather than Late Jurassic: upper Kimmeridgian, as previously believed), Portugal, to the nodosaurid ankylosaur *Dracopelta*. More recently, Galton (1994) reinterpreted this specimen as probably a left dorsal plate of a stegosaur, noting that *Dacentrurus* is already known from this locality (FUB A, B). If the site is correctly dated, Galton (1994) pointed out, then FUB A and B, and probably C, represent the second record of stegosaurs from the Cretaceous of Europe.

Key references: Bakker (1988); Galton (1981, 1983, 1985*b*, 1990*c*, 1991, 1994); Galton and Boine (1980); Gilmore (1914); Lapparent and Zbyszewski (1957); Nopcsa (1911*a*); Owen (1875); Savalle and Lennieri (1899).

†**DASPLETOSAURUS**—(=?*Deinodon*, ?*Gorgosaurus*)
Saurischia: Theropoda: Neotheropoda: Tetanurae:
   Avetheropoda; Coelurosauria: Manuraptoriformes:
   Arctometatarsalia: Tyrannosauridae: Tyrannosaurinae.

Comments: Among the largest and rarest of North American tyrannosaurids, *Daspletosaurus*, a genus thus far known only from Alberta, Canada, is usually regarded as a valid genus, although some workers have questioned that status. In his book *Predatory Dinosaurs of the World*, Paul (1988*b*) considered *Daspletosaurus* to be a subgenus of *Tyrannosaurus*—which he named *Tyrannosaurus (Daspletosaurus) torosus*—an assessment that has not been adopted.

More recently, in a brief preliminary report for a proposed systematic revision of Albertan, Judith River Group tyrannosaurids, Carr (1995) stated that tyrannosaurids are now among the best represented nonavian theropods, and that "the taxonomy of tyrannosaurids is dominated by a typological approach that misconstrues the significance of ontogenetic and sexual variation." Study of the type specimens and additional skull material from the Dinosaur Park Formation suggested to Carr that both *Gorgosaurus libratus* and *Daspletosaurus torosus* were founded upon ontogenetic differences and sexual dimorphism, and that "size increase and related changes in craniofacial pneumaticity produced distinct morphotypes that have historically been considered diagnostic." According to Carr, only *G. libratus* is a valid taxon, this assessment implying that *D. torosus* might be referable to *Gorgosaurus*.

Most workers, however, accept the generic validity of *Daspletosaurus*, a name which may also apply to one of the better known tyrannosaurid exhibit specimens:

In 1956, the Chicago Natural History Museum (now The Field Museum) displayed in its spacious

Courtesy The Field Museum (neg. #GEO81592).

Skull (FMNH PR308) originally referred to *Gorgosaurus libratus*, but probably belonging to the similar and somewhat larger tyrannosaurid *Daspletosaurus*.

Daspletosaurus

Skeleton (FMNH PR308) of the tyrannosaurid theropod (originally referred to *Gorgosaurus libratus*, but probably *Daspletosaurus*) standing in an outmoded upright pose over the skeleton (FMNH PR380; skull FMNH UC1479) of the hadrosaur *Lambeosaurus lambei*, as originally mounted in 1956 by Orville L. Gilpin for the Chicago Natural History Museum's magnificent Stanley Field Hall. Much of the missing posterior part of the skeleton was reconstructed based on *G. libratus* skeleton AMNH 5458, most of the gastralia after holotype CMN 2120. The skull, too heavy for mounting, has been replaced here by a cast (FMNH PR87469) (see Zangerl 1956).

Stanley Field Hall a fine and well-preserved, almost complete tyrannosaurid skeleton (FMNH [then CNHM] PR308), including the skull, collected in 1914 by Barnum Brown from the Little Sandhill basin, along the Red Deer River in Alberta. The specimen was purchased as a gift to the museum by members of its board of trustees from the American Museum of Natural History. The skeleton was mounted standing tall, tail on the ground, above a downed skeleton of the duckbilled dinosaur *Lambeosaurus lambei* (FMNH [then CNHM] PR380 and UC1479) by Chief Preparator of Fossils Orville L. Gilpin, aided by Assistant Curator of Fossil Mammals William D. Turnbull, and Preparator Cameron E. Gifford. The skull on the mount was a cast (the original remaining in the collections, where it was accessible for study), and the missing elements were restored in plaster (see *D:TE* for additional photographs).

The exhibit was, for many years, one of the most popular displays at the Chicago museum, the speci-

men distinguished as the first such fossil ever mounted using no external supports (Zangerl 1956). The skeleton was originally identified as and labeled *Gorgosaurus libratus*, a name it retained until decades later when it was changed to *Albertosaurus*, reflecting Russell's (1970) formal referral of the genus *Gorgosaurus* to *Albertosaurus*. The skull of this specimen was figured by Russell as exemplary of the genus *Albertosaurus* and the species *A. libratus*, becoming the one upon which a number of subsequent studies of that species would be based and with which other skulls were compared.

Over the years, however, various workers began to notice unusual features in the skull of FMNH PR308. Bakker, Williams and Currie (1988) pointed out that FMNH 308 represents a Judith River gorgosaur "with relatively small teeth and a high tooth count (15 in the maxilla)." In contrast, another Judith River gorgosaur, represented by USNM 12814 and AMNH 5336, exhibits "relatively large teeth and a

low tooth count (13 in the maxilla)." Consequently, Bakker *et al.* referred to The Field Museum specimen as *Gorgosaurus* sp.

About the same time, Paul observed that "It is interesting and important that two types of *A. 'libratus'* heads have been found." In the first kind, represented by the most skulls assigned to *G. libratus*, the preorbital bone points upward, forward, and forms a shorter triangle; in the kind represented by FMNH PR308, the horn is longer, more horizontal, and rectangular. Paul also noted differences in the suture patterns of the skull roof bones of both kinds of skulls, and that the first has larger and possibly fewer teeth. Only tentatively accepting FMNH PR308 as belonging to this species, Paul suggested that the two kinds of skulls represented a "gracile" and "robust" morph, possibly having sexual or some other significance (see *Gorgosaurus* entry, comments on AMNH 5664).

FMNH PR308 was still labeled *Albertosaurus li-bratus* in the early 1990s when the skeleton was dismantled, moved, and remounted in a more dynamic and "modern" pose for The Field Museum's new Mesozoic hall (see introductory chapter). By now, other paleontologists had begun to scrutinize this specimen more critically and question its referral to *Gorgosaurus* or *Albertosaurus* (see [Anonymous] 1994). Among them, both Robert T. Bakker and Currie independently concluded that the skull seems to resemble that of *Daspletosaurus* more than it does any other collected *Gorgosaurus* skulls (P. J. Currie, personal communication). Eventually, this skeleton will probably be formally referred to *Daspletosaurus* and described in a paper possibly to be co-authored by Bakker and Currie.

Key references: [Anonymous] (1994); Bakker, Williams and Currie (1988); Carr (1995); Paul (1988*b*); Russell (1970); Zangerl (1956).

Reconstructed skeleton (FMNH PR308), now labeled *Albertosaurus libratus* but probably *Daspletosaurus*, remounted with the real skull in 1993 and in a more dynamic pose, over the skeleton of *Lambeosaurus lambei*, for The Field Museum's new "DNA to Dinosaurs" (now called "Life Over Time") exhibit.

Life restoration of *Daspletosaurus torosus* running through a cattail marsh in the Judith River, painted by Gregory S. Paul.

†DATOUSAURUS

Saurischia: Sauropodomorpha: Sauropoda: Eusauropoda *incertae sedis*.

Diagnosis of genus: Huge, comparatively primitive, more than 14 meters in length; skull large, heavy, short, with pair of external nares at front; antorbital fenestra small; quadrate forwardly inclined; mandibular bone relatively high, heavily built; teeth large, strong, spatulate; four premaxillary, 10–12 maxillary teeth, 12–14 dentary teeth; presacral vertebrae solidly constructed; 13 cervical vertebrae, centra opisthocoelous, opisthocoels rather large; cervical neural spines low; lamellar structure reduced; 12 dorsal vertebrae, with platycoelous centra; four sacral vertebrae, anterior neural spines fused; cervical centrum length 2.5 times that of dorsals; chevrons fork in midposterior caudals; girdles heavy, with well-developed sacriostal yoke; limbs robust; five digits in manus and pes (Zhang and Chen 1996).

Comments: Zhang and Chen (1996) revised the diagnosis for *Datousaurus bashanensis*—a very large, though not one of the most gigantic of sauropods—based, in part, on more recently collected specimens recovered by Chinese scientists.

From various features (*e.g.*, big and heavy skull, relatively high and thickly built mandible, anteriorly steep dentary, large and strong spatulate-shaped teeth, and tooth formula of Pm4/M10-12/D12-14) the authors suggested that this species, previously classified as a "cetiosaurid" (see "Systematics" chapter), be referred to the Camarasauridae (an assessment to which McIntosh does not agree; J. S. McIntosh, personal communication 1998).

Key reference: Zhang and Chen (1996).

†DEINONYCHUS

Saurischia: Theropoda: Neotheropoda: Tetanurae: Avetheropoda: Coelurosauria: Manuraptoriformes: Manuraptora: Eumanuraptora: Dromaeosauridae: Velociraptorinae.

Comments: Among the better known theropod genera of the past three decades has been *Deinonychus*, famous for the large "sickle claw" of each foot, the stiff tail, and the very active lifestyle this dinosaur seems to have lived. However, the history of *Deinonychus* began almost four decades before this genus was formally named and described.

Partial skeletal remains of this theropod were first collected (along with remains of other then-unnamed dinosaurian taxa) between 1932–1933, from the Cloverly Formation of Montana, by American Museum of Natural History expeditions directed by staff paleontologist Barnum Brown. These remains consisted of an incomplete postcranial skeleton (AMNH 3015) and fragmentary bones of the manus and pes (AMNH 3037).

As recounted by Chure and McIntosh (1989) in their benchmark bibliography of the Dinosauria, Brown had planned to name and describe all of this

Reconstructed skeleton of *Deinonychus antirrhopus* including AMNH 3015 (collected during the 1930s by the American Museum of Natural History at Buster Creek, near Billings, Montana) and also elements cast from other specimens. This is the only mounted skeleton currently on display to incorporate real fossil material.

material, the theropod originally to be called "Daptosaurus agilis." Although Brown never formally published this or the other intended names, he did use them in public lectures, preliminary skeletal reconstructions drawn under his supervision, photographs of the material, and, temporarily, on specimens displayed at the American Museum.

This theropod remained virtually unknown and unstudied for almost four decades. During the late 1960s, more material belonging to this dinosaur was collected by a Yale Peabody Museum of Natural History crew led by Professor John H. Ostrom, from a single quarry in the Cloverly Formation, east of the town of Bridger, in Carbon County, south-central Montana. The dinosaur was finally named *Deinonychus antirrhopus* and described by Ostrom (1969*a*, 1969*b*, 1970).

(Chure and McIntosh noted that the name "D. agilis" was never officially published; nor were Brown's other unofficial names for Cloverly Formation dinosaurs, including the ankylosaur "Peltosaurus" sp. [named *Sauropelta edwardsi* by Ostrom], ornithopod "Tenantosaurus kaiseni" [Ostrom's *Tenontosaurus tilleti*], and small theropod "Megadontosaurus ferox" (Ostrom's [*Microvenator celer*]. Therefore, Ostrom's names are well established taxa having priority.)

Importantly, Ostrom's work on *Deinonychus*, published at a time when dinosaurs were still regarded by most vertebrate paleontologists as little more than curious and interesting evolutionary "dead ends," led the way to new insights and theories about dinosaurian biology and behavior, particularly suggestions that dinosaurs may have been warm-blooded and that theropods were the direct ancestors of modern birds. Indeed, Ostrom's work on this taxon and the attention it attracted, both in the scientific community and with the public, directly inspired the so-called "Dinosaur Renaissance" of the early 1970s, largely fueled by subsequent work by paleontologist Robert T. Bakker. Repercussions of this new era of interest and research healthily continue to this day.

All known skull material of *D. antirrhopus* had been collected from that one quarry back in the 1960s.

Deinonychus

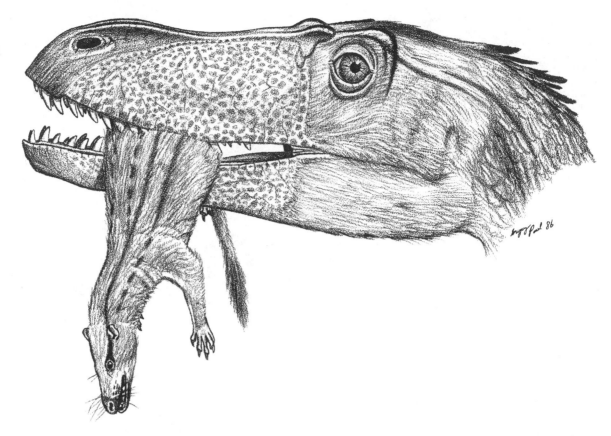

In 1993, the quarry was reopened by a Museum of the Rockies crew which collected new material. These newly recovered remains include a cervical vertebra, several caudal vertebrae, a radius and ulna, two manuses, and portions of the skull (including prefrontal, frontal, parietal, quadrate, laterosphenoid, and braincase portions, all elements previously unknown, and the best examples of nasal, lacrimal, and ectopterygoid yet collected) (Maxwell and Witmer 1996).

In briefly describing the skull, Witmer and Maxwell (1996) noted the presence of details not observed in earlier collected specimens: Pneumatic accessory cavities in all bones (*e.g.*, maxilla, nasal, lacrimal, jugal, and palatine) surrounding the antorbital cavity, this condition usually only found in large-bodied theropods (*e.g.*, allosauroids); messethmoid ossification similar to that in *Hesperornis* and neornithine birds; and prefrontal bone (not present in *Velociraptor*).

According to Witmer and Maxwell, this new material confirms that, as in other derived coelurosaurs, the braincase of *Deinonychus* possessed dorsal and caudal tympanic recesses, a fenestra cochlea, metotic strut, and caudally directed vagal canal. As the skull lacks depressed nasals and enlarged premaxillary teeth, and exhibits more of a robust, *Dromaeosaurus*-like roof, *Deinonychus* is not as similar to *Velociraptor* as generally believed.

As noted by Tyson and Gatesy (1997), the morphology of the tail in theropods was significantly modified during their evolution. In *Deinonychus* and other dromaeosaurs, the tail is distally stiffened and rodlike, such a tail supposedly having functioned as a dynamic stabilizer for providing balance and stability while the dinosaur jumped or reared up one limb. In this preliminary report on the evolution of tail flexibility in theropods, Tyson and Gatesy pointed out that, if the above idea is correct, then "the proximal caudal vertebrae should have been modified from the general theropod condition to provide increased dorsoventral flexibility and thus tail maneuverability."

Synthesizing beam theory and data from living animals, Tyson and Gatesy were able "to predict features of vertebral morphology favoring flexibility at intervertebral joints," these including low, long centra; low, narrow; neural spines and transverse processes; and short chevrons. Testing scaled measurements of dorsal and caudal vertebrae from *Deinonychus* and five other dromaeosaur genera against the model to assess relative flexibility, the authors observed the following: The "proximal caudals of *Deinonychus* match predicted morphological criteria for hypothetical flexible vertebrae"; and "the dorsals of *Deinonychus* and the dorsals and proximal caudals of other theropods, particularly large forms, match a hypothetical stiff morphology."

Similarities in tail morphology between dromaeosaurs

and *Archaeopteryx* suggested to Tyson and Gatesy that their manuraptoran common ancestor also had such a narrow and mobile tail, a dynamically stabilizing tail possibly representing "a functional intermediate between the counterbalancing tails of basal theropods and the aerodynamically stabilizing tails of birds."

Key references: Chure and McIntosh (1989); Maxwell and Witmer (1996); Maxwell and Witmer (1996); Ostrom (1969a, 1969b, 1970); Tyson and Gatesy (1997).

†DELTADROMEUS

Saurischia: Theropoda: Neotheropoda: Tetanurae: Avetheropoda: Coelurosauria *incertae sedis*.

Comments: Although the text entry for this Late Cretaceous, large but rather slender-limbed cursorial coelurosaurian genus was included in *D:TE*, the illustration (Sereno, Dutheil, Iarochene, Larsson, Lyon, Magwene, Sidor, Varricchio and Wilson 1996) of its remains was not available in time for inclusion in that volume; therefore, the illustration is reproduced herein.

Key reference: Sereno, Dutheil, Iarochene, Larsson, Lyon, Magwene, Sidor, Varricchio and Wilson (1996).

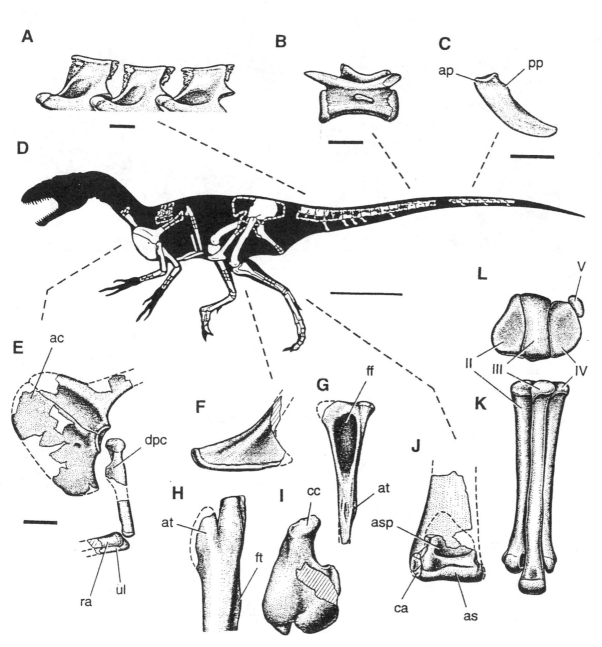

Deltadromeus agilis, SGM-Din 2, holotype A. neural spines of anterior caudal vertebrae, left lateral view, B. midcaudal vertebra, left lateral view, C. midcaudal chevron, left lateral view, D. skeletal reconstruction, E. scapulocoracoid and forelimb (composite left and right), left lateral view, F. pubic foot, left lateral view, G. proximal left fibula, medial view, H. proximal left femur (reversed from right), left lateral view, I. tibia (reversed from right), proximal view, J. distal tibia, astragalus, and calcaneum (reversed from right), anterior view, K. left metatarsals II–V, anterior view, L. left metatarsals II–V, proximal view. Scale (D) = 1 cm; (E) = 10 cm; (others) = 5 cm. (After Sereno, Dutheil, Iarochene, Larsson, Lyon, Magwene, Sidor, Varricchio and Wilson 1996.)

Deltadromeus agilis, skeletal reconstruction (including cast of holotype SGM-Din 2) prepared and mounted under the direction of paleontologist Paul C. Sereno for display at the Crerar Library, University of Chicago.

†DILOPHOSAURUS

Saurischia: Theropoda: Neotheropoda: "Ceratosauria": Coelophysoidea.

Type species: *D. wetherilli* (Welles 1954).

Other species: ?*D. sinensus* Hu 1993.

Comments: *Dilophosaurus*, a medium-sized Early Jurassic "ceratosaur" bearing a double cranial crest, may provide some key information regarding dinosaurian metabolism, and also (see "Notes" below) the possible relationships of nonavian theropods to birds.

Tkach (1996) performed a multi-element osteohistological study of the type species, *D. wetherilli*, using as materials thin sections made from long bones (femur, metatarsal, tibia, and phalanges) and ribs of referred specimen UCMP 37303. As had Curry (1996) with her materials (see introductory chapter, section on "Ectothermy Versus Endothermy"), Tkach found that all of these bones possess "a matrix of well vascularized, woven fibro-lamellar bone" resembling that in the "ceratosaur" *Syntarsus*, the sauropodomorph *Massospondylus*, and the manuraptoran theropod *Troodon*.

Tkach also observed the following: Smaller bones, like ribs, exhibit predominance of longitudinal vascularization, larger bones both longitudinal and plexiform vascularization; all bones show two to three lines of arrested growth (LAGs), characterized by avascular annuli; and scattered Haversian canals formed near perimeter of marrow cavity.

Tkach deduced that *D. wetherilli* could have attained growth rates of from 30 to 35 kilograms in its early life. Histological comparisons of this species to the ceratosaurs *Coelophysis bauri* and *Syntarsus rhodesiensis* and to the prosauropod *Massospondylus carinatus* suggested to Tkach "that the plexiform bone of *D. wetherilli* largely reflects rapid growth rate and has little phylogenetic value other than its consistency with the pattern already shown to be characteristic of other dinosaurs and pterosaurs."

Although the putative Asian species ?*Dilophosaurus sinensis* Hu 1993 was discussed in *D:TE*, an illustration of the type material (KMV 8701) was not available for inclusion in that volume. Since publication of that book, the mounted holotype skeleton of ?*D. sinensis* was exhibited in 1998 at Dinofest™ in Philadelphia. A photograph of that skeleton is herein included.

Photograph by the author, courtesy Natural History Museum of Los Angeles County.

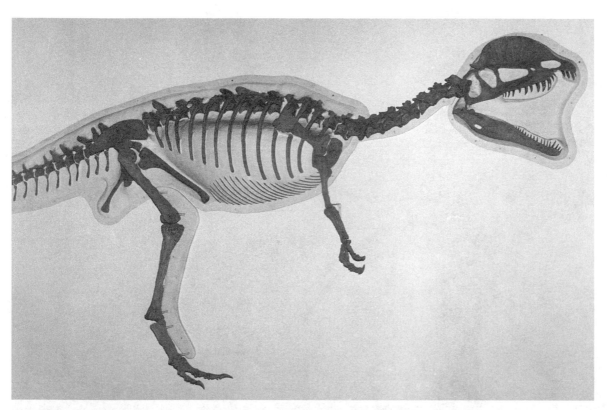

Dilophosaurus wetherilli skeleton (LACM 4462/ 118118, cast of holotype UCMP 37302). Bone histologies suggest rapid growth in this species.

?*Dilophosaurus sinensis*, KMV 8701, holotype skeleton mounted at Dinofest™, held in Philadelphia in 1998. This species may be referable to another genus. Photograph by the author.

Dilophosaurus wetherilli depicted in a swimming mode, with only (as evidenced by some fossil trackways) the tips of its pedal claws digging into the mud below. Illustration by Gregory S. Paul (from *Predatory Dinosaurs of the World*).

Notes: *Dilophosaurus* is a suspected trackmaker of tridactyl footprints called *Kayentapus hopii* and *Dilophosauripus williamsi*. These ichnotaxa, named and described by Welles (1971), were found in the Kayenta Formation (Lower Jurassic) in northern Arizona, this being the same formation that yielded the original specimens of *D. wetherilli*.

In 1993, Gerard Gierlinski, a specialist in ichnotaxa, visited the Pratt Museum in Amherst, Massachusetts, where he had access to the vast treasury of fossil footprints collected during the mid-nineteenth century by Edward Hitchcock, most of them from the Early Jurassic of New England. Gierlinski's original interest was to compare the tracks in this collection with similar material found in his native Poland.

Previously, Gierlinski (1991) had described such comparable Early Jurassic dinosaur tracks from the Holy Cross Mountains, in Poland, as *Kayentapus soltykovensis*—which he originally named *Grallator* (*Eubrontes*) *soltykovensis*—finding the "dilophosaur" form to be the most appropriate candidate for making these tracks. Later, Gierlinski and Ahlberg (1994)

would assign to the same species Early Jurassic tracks found in the Hoganas Formation of southern Sweden.

According to Gierlinski (1996, 1997), one famous Early Jurassic ichnite specimen in the Hitchcock Collection, AC 1/7, could alter what is known of dinosaurs like *Dilophosaurus*.

AC 1/7 is preserved in the fine-grain shale of the Portland Formation, Lily Pond Quarry, near Amherst. The specimen is of comparatively rare form in that it constitutes a trace preserving a medium-sized "dinosaur sitting" imprint, made while the animal was resting. Although this trace has been attributed to an ornithischian dinosaur by some workers, others, including Gierlinski, have interpreted it as having been made by a "ceratosaurian" theropod.

The specimen preserves a pair of tridactyl footprints, between which is the very rare impression of the trackmaker's belly, below which is the more frequently preserved heart-shaped imprint of a cushiony pad called the ischiadic callosity. Curiously, the belly imprint includes traces which, as observed by Gierlinski, resemble the furry-like plumage on the bellies of juvenile birds, especially ducklings. After devoting four years of study to AC 1/7, Gierlinski concluded that the feather-like imprints were not really scale drag marks or the traces of plants or invertebrates. In 1997 (as related in *Dinosaur World*, number 4, 1998), Gierlinski announced that a full-scale model of a feathered *Dilophosaurus*, possibly resembling the dinosaur responsible for AC 1/7, had been made by artist Arta Szubert for exhibit at the Geological Museum of the Polish Institute, in Warsaw, Poland. The figure (nicknamed "Dyzio") measures 5 meters in length and 2.5 meters in height. According to Gierlinski (1998), the figure—which resembles more a stuffed animal than a sculpture—"was restored from the osteological and ichnological data, employing quite sophisticated technology, and highly unusual components."

Erratum: References to Welles (1964) in *D:TE* should be corrected to Welles (1954).

Key reference: Gierlinski (1991, 1996, 1997);

Gierlinski and Ahlberg (1994); Hu (1993); Tkach (1996); Welles (1954, 1971).

†DIPLODOCUS

Saurischia: Sauropodomorpha: Sauropoda: Eusauropoda: Neosauropoda: Diplodocoidea: Diplodocidae.

Comments: For the past several decades, diplodocid sauropods, primarily the very long but relatively slender genus *Diplodocus*, have been portrayed in life restorations as utilizing their large and long "whiplash" tails, employing rapid, forceful whiplike movements, as defensive weapons against attacking theropods.

More recently, Christiansen (1996) reconsidered this popular theory, noting that it has become widespread and "fits well with the new concepts that started gaining acceptance in the 1970s, of dinosaurs as lively, energetic and probably endothermic" animals. What inspired this idea is the caudal morphology (not yet found in other dinosaurs) of *Diplodocus*

Skeleton of *Diplodocus hayi* (subadult) including holotype CM 662, referred CM 94, and skull cast of *D. carnegii* (CM 11161). The use of the whiplash tail in *Diplodocus* as a weapon has recently been questioned.

Photograph by the author, courtesy Houston Museum of Natural Science.

Diplodocus

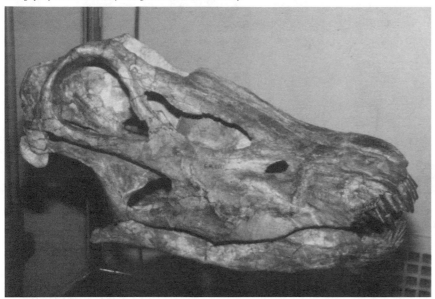

Complete and uncrushed skull (CM 11161) referred to *Diplodocus* sp. This excellent specimen, described by Carnegie Museum of Natural History director William J. Holland in 1924, was collected from the Carnegie quarry at what is now Dinosaur National Monument, near Jensen, Utah.

and *Apatosaurus*, diplodocids for which almost complete caudal vertebral columns are known. Both genera possess a large number of caudal vertebrae and also a long distal "whiplike" part of the tail comprising 30 to 40 rod-like, axially greatly elongated vertebrae. Christiansen, however, offered that this theory was apparently based on hardly more than the possession of a long, tapering tail and is not necessarily supported by anatomical characters.

According to Christiansen, the idea seems to have begun with Holland (1915) who, upon observing that the long, thin tails of certain monitor lizards were sometimes used as weapons against aggressors, speculated that sauropod tails could have worked in a similar though more forceful way. However, as Christiansen pointed out, little evidence other than tail length has subsequently been offered to support Holland's theory, based as it had been upon animals whose tails are "10 times shorter and three orders of magnitude lighter" than those of these giant dinosaurs.

Christiansen pointed out that a whiplike movement of the tails of diplodocid sauropods "could not have been similar to a true whip, in which a standing wave travels from the centre of force application, the handle, along the longitudinal axis of the whip, due to the unreasonably high degree of flexibility this requires. Rather, the tail would probably have to be swung rapidly laterally until reaching the point where the vertebrae would be in their outer positions of mobility and the tendons stretched, whereupon the motion was instantly reversed in order to set up a whiplike wave along the longitudinal axis of the long thin distal section." Such action on the part of a diplodocid would require a substantial lateral mobility, with the centers of force application probably being the prox-

imal and median parts of the tail, equivalent to a whip handle, and the thin part of the tail comparable to the whip itself. The tail strike would have to be powerful to be effective against a large theropod such as an adult allosaurid, "and slow lateral sinusoid movements of the proximal and median part of the tail would not be able to generate the force required to strike in a whiplike fashion."

In considering the tails of diplodocids, Christiansen made such observations as the following: Diplodocids did not possess greater tail flexibility than did the shorter-tailed camarasaurids and brachiosaurids, nor do the centra of diplodocid caudal vertebrae show adaptations for mobility most likely required to swing such an enormous tail rapidly enough to be effective. The circumcentral fusion of adjacent caudal vertebrae in sauropods like *Diplodocus* (see *D:TE*), due to ossification of strong ligaments bridging adjacent centra (this condition found in 50 percent of the specimens with this part of the tail preserved), would have compromised the flexibility of the tail. No real difference concerning power and size can be seen between the hypaxial muscular system of long-tailed and short-tailed sauropods, with diplodocids apparently lacking the muscle power and size required for rapid swinging of their enormous tails.

Also, Christiansen questioned whether the many small and thin distal caudal vertebrae in the diplodocid tail could survive impacts of the magnitude to ward off a theropod weighing several tons. As the long, thin "whip" of the tail seems to have been covered only by skin and light subcutaneous muscle, its small, thin vertebrae do not appear capable of withstanding the enormous stress imposed by a forceful strike. Christiansen speculated that a better strategy would be for the diplodocid to use the middle part of the tail, with its substantially greater mass, as a weapon to knock their carnivorous aggressors off their feet.

Christiansen noted that some sauropods apparently did possess tails suggesting antagonistic behavior. The Chinese sauropods *Omeisaurus* and *Shunosaurus* both possessed tail clubs, which apparently had an intraspecific function or, more likely, were used as weapons against theropod aggressors. Though the central morphology of the proximal caudals in these forms resembles closely that of diplodocids, the tails in these genera are shorter and stockier, therefore being more effective as weapons; also, "striking with a tail club probably requires less rapid lateral movements than would be required to set up a whiplike action in the tail, and the club also seems built to withstand a hard impact with another large object."

Christiansen did not deny the possibility that *Diplodocus* and its kin used their tails like weapons as in the scenarios so often portrayed, especially given the similarities in caudal morphology between diplodocids and the club-tailed Chinese sauropods. However, it seemed more likely that the giant diplodocids were safe from predators simply by nature of their size and probable herding behavior. Adult diplodocids, Christiansen surmised, would more likely have "used their bulk to crush theropods underfoot." (For other hypotheses regarding the use of the whiplash tail, see also introductory chapter, section on "Sauropods.")

Note: The external look of sauropods has been reinterpreted during the past decade. In 1992, Stephen A. Czerkas, one of the foremost modern sculptors of paleontologically accurate dinosaur models and a specialist in fossilized dinosaur skin impressions, published a brief report on "conical or spine-like elements" recovered from the Howe Quarry—a site on the Barker Howe ranch, below the Big Horn Mountains, near Shell, Wyoming—which he interpreted as dermal spines belonging to diplodocid sauropods resembling *Diplodocus* (see entry, *D:TE*) and *Barosaurus*. Based on this evidence, Czerkas proposed that diplodocids, and possibly all, sauropods were much more reptilian in appearance than usually portrayed, possessing a median row of such spines on the tail—not unlike those seen on the tails of modern iguanas and crocodiles—and possibly also on the neck and body (see also Czerkas 1997). The discovery of these structures indicated to Czerkas that previously published life restorations of sauropods may not have been entirely accurate, and that some aspects of their external appearance are not necessarily indicated by what has usually been preserved in the fossil record.

Indeed, in recent years, various sauropod taxa have been found possessing diverse external adornments not previously suspected for these kinds of dinosaurs—*e.g.*, armor scutes (*Saltasaurus*), clubbed tails (*Shunosaurus*), much elongated spines (*Amargasaurus*), and even plates and spikes (the genus originally named *Augustia*; see entry). Therefore, discovering unusual external structures in other kinds of sauropods should not be as surprising as they would have been a decade or more ago.

With the publication of that original report, some paleontologists, most of whom had not examined the structures firsthand, rejected Czerkas' findings or regarded them with skepticism (the present author also having treated them with doubt in the *Diplodocus* entry in *D:TE*), while others accepted them. In fact, various "paleo-artists" (including Gregory S. Paul, Mark Hallett, and Michael W. Skrepnick) promptly began to incorporate Czerkas' interpretation into many of their life restorations of sauropods.

Czerkas (1994) subsequently published another,

more detailed study of these elements, including in that follow-up paper a history of the discovery of sauropod skin impressions and the workings at Howe Quarry.

According to Czerkas (1994, 1997), based on his own personal observations of the original fossil materials, sauropod skin is not smooth, leathery or elephant-like, as has usually been depicted in life restorations, but scaly like that of a reptile. One skin specimen (no collection number given) from Dinosaur National Monument, Czerkas (1994) noted, presumably associated with cervical vertebrae assigned to *Barosaurus*, possesses quite large scales (25 by 12 centimeters), with the smallest scales surrounding the progressively larger scales in the center of what seems to be an ornamental cluster pattern (similar to that observed on some hadrosaurs). Another specimen (no collection number given), in the Carnegie Museum of Natural History collections, is different in having scales of just moderate size (about 1 centimeter in diameter), and shows a more uniform pattern. Czerkas (1994) further pointed out that the possible skin represented by a carbonaceous layer, observed by Gilmore (1925) between the ribs of a fine juvenile specimen (CM 11338; see *D:TE*) of *Camarasaurus* from Dinosaur National Monument, has no discernible scale pattern. Considerable variation, then, does exist in the scalation of sauropod skin.

As recounted in detail by Czerkas (1992, 1994), the Howe Quarry had yielded, during the collecting years of Barnum Brown, numerous sauropod skeletons and also a relatively large amount of sauropod skin, the latter only briefly described by Brown in various semipopular articles (*e.g.*, Brown 1935).

Czerkas (1994) related that the Howe Quarry was reopened during 1990–1991 by Siber and Siber Enterprises, as part of a project of the Aathal Dinosaur Museum in Switzerland. Following the work abandoned more than half a century before by Brown, collectors recovered more sauropod bones and additional samplings of sauropod integument. Only a few sections of skin, however, could be reliably associated with bones so as to represent their natural positions, although it seemed "that portions of the lower sides and belly region are preserved with ribs and gastralia." As described by Czerkas (1994), the scales seen on these sections are of moderate sizes (mostly from 2 to 3 centimeters), arranged in nonoverlapping, rosette patterns in "typical dinosaurian fashion."

Unexpected discoveries during the first field season included "large scales and ornamental structures like spikes or frills." More of these nonossified structures were found during the second season. Czerkas (1992, 1994) interpreted these elements as dermal spines which, because of their nonossified nature, are rarely preserved.

As further noted by Czerkas (1994), much of the skin impressions found during the Siber excavation was not directly associated with skeletal remains. The separation of soft body parts from skeletal remains was attributed to unique preservational conditions that had resulted from considerable predation, evidence for this including numerous shed theropod teeth and also footprints.

The spines as preserved, Czerkas (1994) observed, include at least three different morphological groupings, though all are "variations on the same pattern, representing progressive differences according to size and probable positioning on the body." The first grouping consists of small, conical spines that are tall, sharply pointed, and laterally compressed; spines of the second grouping are considerably smaller, but compressed laterally to a greater extent and relatively longer; those of the third, which may not have belonged to the row including the first and second types but were placed elsewhere on the body, consist of both large and small spines that are relatively much shorter and blunt.

According to Czerkas (1992, 1994), the only direct physical evidence regarding how these dermal spines were arranged in life are in two small patches of skin (noted as "#F-27-29" and "#K-27-8") that surround a few distal caudal vertebrae, these spines clearly, the author noted, following one another on the dorsal median line that forms a single row of spines. Regarding how these structures may have appeared elsewhere on the body, Czerkas (1992, 1994) determined that "the most conservative interpretation to account for the larger isolated dermal spines should have them continue anteriorly along the summit of the tail. This would create an ornamental crest of spines along the entire length of the tail with the largest spines near the proximal end." Although no other dermal spines were directly associated with bones, Czerkas (1992, 1994) speculated that, as in various other dinosaurs and extant reptiles, this "crest" might continue along the neck and rest of the body.

Czerkas (1994, 1997) also suggested that such spines may have served as defense structures that strengthened the hide of the tail, ornamentation that played a role in visual recognition, or created a "vertical fin" which enhanced the animal's ability to swim.

Extrapolating from this interpretation that these structures indeed represent dermal spines, Czerkas (1994) further stated, "The inference that dermal spines can be attributed to all the varied types of sauropods, may or may not, eventually prove to be warranted. Certainly there must have been variations between different taxa, with more or less spines, or possibly, none at all. But to portray any sauropods without dermal spines, at least on the tail, falsely implies that evidence exists to the contrary of what has been revealed by the current discovery of dermal spines. Indeed, if may be appropriate to incorporate dermal spines not only on all sauropods but also on their distantly related ancestors, the prosauropods."

A series of conical structures, probably nonosseous dermal spines, is present above at least part of the tail of the sauropod represented by fossil bones found at the Howe quarry (J. S. McIntosh, personal communication 1998). Future additional studies of these structures, perhaps including cross-sectional analysis, may forever resolve any remaining controversy over them, determining precisely what they are, if they were present in places other than the tail, and if they occurred in taxa other than the Howe Quarry sauropod. Indeed, their discovery offers some interesting and exciting new possibilities in reinterpreting the external appearance of these giant dinosaurs.

Key reference: Brown (1935); Christiansen (1996); Czerkas (1992, 1994, 1997); Gilmore (1925); Holland (1915).

†DRINKER

Comments: In a report on the dinosaurian habitats at Como Bluff, Wyoming, Bakker (1996b) noted that the only common dinosaur found in the Ward's Ranch Facies, Indian Fort Member (vertical divisions of the Morrison by Bakker and Allen 1996) of the Como Morrison Formation, is the tiny primitive ornithopod *Drinker nisti*. More recently collected remains indicate that this dinosaur had an approximate snout to tail-tip length of 300 millimeters (about 11.5 inches) and "a weight not much larger than a big chicken, making this the smallest adult ornithischian."

As noted by Bakker, 30 skeletons of this genus, some of them articulated, were recovered from this site at the Becky Quarry. The specimens were dug out of a single oval mass of mudstone measuring about one meter across. As the remains show no signs of scavenging, nor are fossils of any other kind found here, Bakker suggested that this site could represent a communal burrow. Other *Drinker* remains, numbering several dozen specimens, were collected throughout the outcrop area. No *Drinker* material was found outside the Ward's Ranch Facies.

According to Bakker, the Ward's Ranch Facies and entire Indian Fort Member at Como is made up "of swamp beds, lake-swamp beds, and swamp-river channels and floodplains." Consequently, *Drinker* was interpreted as a dinosaur that favored very swampy terrain, Bakker pointing out that its foot structure matches its chosen habitat. According to Bakker (1996a 1996b), *Drinker*'s very long, spreading hind toes and its ankle joints "allowed the animal to grasp

uneven terrain or branches for climbing." Bakker (1996*b*) also suggested that the long claws on its outer toes were suitable for digging, these supposed abilities to dig and climb affording *Drinker* a tall vertical foraging range.

Key references: Bakker (1996*a*, 1996*b*).

†DRYPTOSAURUS

Saurischia: Theropoda: Neotheropoda: Tetanurae: Avetheropoda: ?Coelurosauria: Dryptosauridae.

Holotype: ANSP 9995, fragment of right maxilla, fragment of right dentary, prearticular, nine caudal vertebrae, right humerus, manual phalanges I-1, I-2, and II-2, left and right pubes, fragment of right ischium, left humerus, left femur, left tibia, left fibula, astragalus, numerous fragments.

Diagnosis of genus (as for type species): Maxillary teeth with gaps between serrations equal to half width of a serration; blood grooves ["perpendicular to the longitudinal axis of the tooth"] of maxillary teeth

not extending onto crown (as with most theropods, *e.g.*, allosaurids, carcharodontosaurids, tyrannosaurids, dromaeosaurids); dentary slender (not deep, as in mature tyrannosaurids); humerus with well-developed deltopectoral crest occupying proximal one-third of shaft (unlike small, proximally located deltopectoral crest of tyrannosaurids); manus ugual I-2 very large relative to phalanx I-1, exceeding *Baryonyx* in ungual/humeral ratio; phalanx I-1 straight (lacking twist in shaft seen in allosaurids and tyrannosaurids); other manual phalanges relatively straight-sized (as in tyrannosaurids, not hourglass-shaped in dorsal view, as in most theropods); hind limb gracile; lesser trochanter lower than femoral head, spike-like (as in tyrannosaurids); femur lacking deep intercondylar groove anteriorly; no deep groove separating cnemial crest and fibular condyle (as in *Allosaurus* and tyrannosaurids); astragalus with bulbous medial condyle; ascending process of astragalus probably tall, centrally located (as in *Deinonychus*, not anterolateral as in tyrannosaurids and other theropods); metatarsal not

Dryptosaurus aquilunguis, ANSP 9995, holotype A. maxillary fragment; detail of maxillary tooth serrations in B. medial and C. posterior views; right dentary fragment in D. medial (arrow indicating replacement tooth) and E. lateral views; detail of second dentary tooth serrations in F. medial and G. posterior views. Scale = 5 cm. (After Carpenter, Russell, Baird and Denton 1997.)

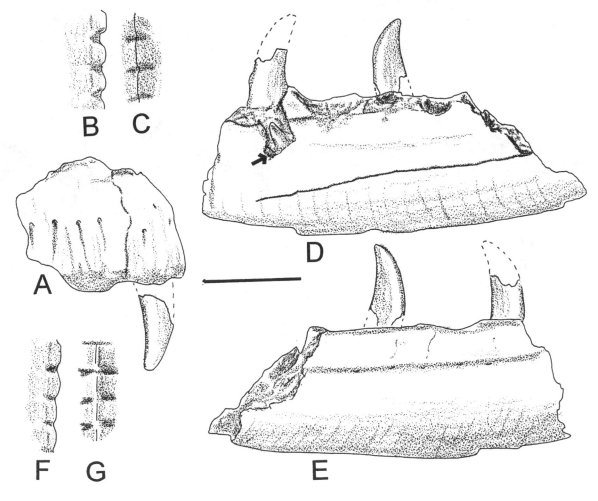

of arctometatarsal type (Carpenter, Russell, Baird and Denton 1997).

Comments: Historically significant as the first North American theropod to be named and described (as *Laelaps aquilunguis* Cope 1866), remains of this dinosaur — distinguished by its large manual claw — were found in early 1866 in a West Jersey Marl Company by workmen under the supervision of J. C. Voorhees, south of Barnsboro, in Mantua Township, Gloucester County, New Jersey.

For more than a century, *Dryptosaurus* has remained a poorly understood taxon. During most of those years, the genus has been classified either with the "Megalosauridae" or Tyrannosauridae (the latter then still regarded as a "carnosaurian" family), mostly based upon gross and superficial similarities between *Dryptosaurus* and members of those groups of generally large theropods (for details, see *D:TE*; and Carpenter, Russell, Baird and Denton 1997).

More recently, Denton (1990), in a preliminary report, challenged the earlier long-standing notions as to the phylogenetic standing of *Dryptosaurus*, suggesting that the closest relationships of this genus might be found somewhere within the Coelurosauria.

Denton pointed out various coelurosaurian features observed in *D. aquilunguis* (*e.g.*, generally gracile skeleton; laterally compressed teeth with strong posterior serrations; metatarsal IV similar to that in dromaeosaurs; manual claw huge and recurved; femur with fourth trochanter poorly developed; forelimbs relatively large; ornithomimid-like phalanges and tarsus).

Later, Carpenter *et al.* reassessed the holotype skeleton of *D. aquilunguis* and its phylogenetic relationships, at the same time determining just what elements belong in ANSP 9995.

Also, Carpenter *et al.* discussed AMNH 2438, a left metatarsal which they surmised "might have been collected by a worker at the time of the original find or uncovered subsequently as the quarry was extended," and which Edward Drinker Cope, who first described this theropod, had kept in his personal collection that was eventually sold in 1902 to the American Museum of Natural History. Later, Huene (1932) described and figured this specimen for the first time from a cast in the British Museum (Natural History). According to Carpenter *et al.*, the surface of the original bone "is badly corroded and is unlike the other

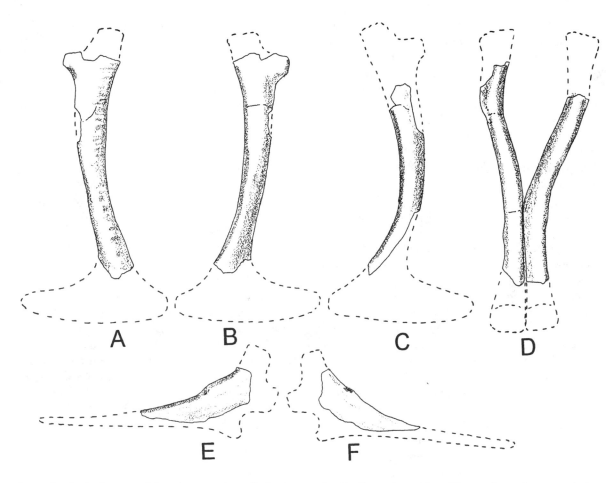

Dryptosaurus aquilunguis, ANSP 9995, holotype pelvic elements: Right pubis in A. lateral and B. medial views; C. left pubis in lateral view; D. view of right and left pubis in articulation; ?right ischium fragment in E. lateral and F. medial views. (After Carpenter, Russell, Baird and Denton 1997.)

bones in the holotype raising the question of whether the bone actually belongs to the holotype," a question that, for the present at least, probably cannot be answered.

Carpenter *et al.* were in agreement with Marsh (1890*b*) that *Dryptosaurus* warrants its own monotypic family Dryptosauridae. The authors also agreed that *Dryptosaurus* possesses some features (*e.g.*, "feebly developed fourth trochanter and expanded ascending process of the astragalus") that qualify its inclusion in the Coelurosauria, although other features (*e.g.*, "relatively well-developed forelimbs; simple, laterally

Dryptosaurus aquilunguis, schematic drawing of ANSP 9995 skeletal elements. Scale = 50 cm. (After Carpenter, Russell, Baird and Denton 1997.)

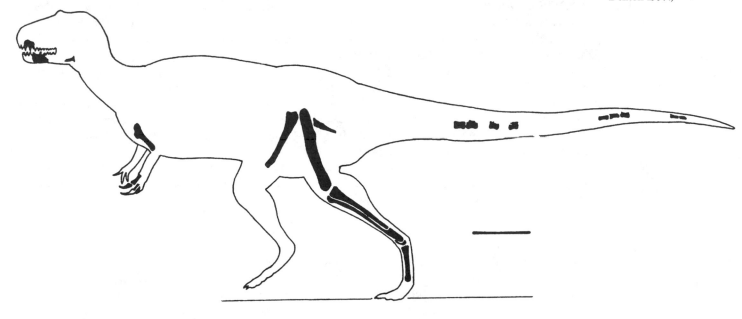

compressed teeth; straight-sided, nonhypertrophied pedal phalanges; poorly developed femoral anterior intercondylar groove") are plesiomorphic and functionally similar to those of all generalized theropods.

One of the authors (Denton) maintained his earlier position that *Dryptosaurus* is a coelurosaur, although his co-authors found the presently available material to be too fragmentary and, therefore, insufficient for cladistic analysis and subsequent assignment to some higher taxon. Although Carpenter *et al.* found *Dryptosaurus* to be most likely a manuraptoran, they could not unequivocally state this due to the lack of diagnostic elements in the holotype.

Gallagher (1995, 1997) reported that numerous theropod teeth have been collected over the past decade by New Jersey State Museum field crews at Phoebus Landing and vicinity along the Cape Fear River in North Carolina, and also from other localities in that state and New Jersey. After making a statistical analysis of these teeth, Gallagher (1995) determined that these specimens, exhibiting a wide range in sizes, suggest a population of different ages and growth stages of the same kind of dinosaur, probably *Dryptosaurus*.

Also, Gallagher (1997) stated that, because of the large manual claw, *Dryptosaurus* was interpreted by him as a manuraptoran, and that this theropod was consequently reconstructed "as a modified and scaled-up version of John Ostrom's *Deinonychus*, only with a large claw on the hand."

Key references: Carpenter, Russell, Baird and Denton (1997); Cope (1866); Denton (1990); Gallagher (1995, 1997); Huene (1932); Marsh (1890*b*).

†DYSTROPHAEUS

Saurischia: Sauropodomorpha: Sauropoda: Eusauropoda: Neosauropoda *incertae sedis*.

Known material: Partial postcrania representing one or two individuals, more material apparently *in situ*.

Holotype: USNM 2364, partial postcrania including half a right scapula, almost complete right ulna, upper part of right radius, left metacarpals 1, 2, and 3 (identification of holotype elements by McIntosh 1997).

Comments: *Dystrophaeus* remains an enigmatic and problematic sauropod. Based on very incomplete material, the genus was named by Cope (1877*c*), who incorrectly believed it to be of Late Triassic age. Only recently has this dinosaur been seriously reevaluated. Though little is still known about the skeleton of *Dystrophaeus* and the affinities of this genus within Sauropoda, new studies by Gillette (1996*a*) and McIntosh (1997), after rediscovery of the type locality

and the collection of more material, has revealed additional information regarding this dinosaur's stratigraphic position and its evolutionary implications.

In 1859, when Professor John S. Newberry, a geologist, discovered the holotype (USNM 2364) and only known specimen belonging to this dinosaur (a partial postcranial skeleton) in the Morrison Formation in southeastern Utah, he declared that much of the specimen had been left *in situ* (see *D:TE* and McIntosh 1997 for details). Until recently, however, the precise location of the site that yielded the original material (and presumably still preserves the rest of the specimen) has remained a mystery.

As recounted by sauropod specialist John S. McIntosh (1997), that author's interest in *Dystrophaeus* originated during the middle 1960s while attempting to understand the relationship of this genus to other Morrison forms. McIntosh's study of USNM 2364 "revealed interesting and unusual features, and it became evident that the discovery of more material would be of great importance." Attempting to locate the actual site of this, the first sauropod discovery in the New World and the second dinosaur found in the western United States, McIntosh found Newberry's report — which provided clues as to where Newberry's so-called "*Saurian Bones*" had been discovered — among the rare books at the Yale Sterling Library. McIntosh then contacted James A. Jensen, a paleontologist with a knack for finding important dinosaur specimens. Jensen, in turn, contacted Fran Barnes, a writer and historian of Western lore, who subsequently became almost obsessed with finding the discovery site. Checking the necessary records, Barnes uncovered information that led to the rediscovery (first announced by Gillette, Barnes, Gillette and McIntosh 1989; see also Gillette 1993; McIntosh 1996) of the site in 1987 in East Canyon, San Juan County, Utah (see Barnes 1988 for the full account of this discovery).

In 1989, a partial phalanx or metacarpal (UMNH collection), belonging to the holotype, was recovered during a preliminary excavation of the rediscovered type locality under the supervision of David D. Gillette, then the State Paleontologist of Utah. Assisting in this digging were Peggy Bechtel, Wilson Bechtel, Lynette Gillette, and members of the Utah Friends of Paleontology. More of the specimen yet remains to be removed (Gillette *et al.* 1989; Gillette 1996*b*). Through this excavation it was determined that the specimen lay at the bottom of the Tidwell Member of the Morrison Formation (Upper Jurassic), or alternatively (according to more recent revisionary stratigraphy) in the Tidwell Member of the Summerville Formation (Middle Jurassic San Rafael Group).

Dystrophaeus viaemalae, USNM 2364, holotype metacarpals in storage in the National Museum of Natural History collections.

(See Gillette 1996*a* for a detailed report concerning the determination of the stratigraphic position of the type locality, established by Fred Peterson and Christine Turner, and on the major issue of the currently disputed position of the J-5 unconformity of Pipiringos and O'Sullivan 1978, a member usually mapped as the Morrison's lower boundary, atop which the formation's sediments were deposited).

Despite the recovery of the above new material, Gillette (1996*a*) noted (see also McIntosh 1990*b*, 1997) that the type material is insufficient for a diagnosis of the genus.

Mostly based on the osteology of the front limb bones, Huene (1904) referred the type species *D. viaemalae* to the "Cetiosauridae" (not presently regarded by all workers as a valid taxon; see "Systematics" chapter).

In his review of the Sauropoda, McIntosh (1990*b*) stated that *Dystrophaeus* probably belongs to the Diplodocidae, the relatively short metacarpals precluding referral to the Camarasauridae or Brachiosauridae and suggesting a relationship to the Diplodocidae. Later, McIntosh (1997) noted similarities between the partial scapula of *Dystrophaeus* and those of the diplodocids *Diplodocus* and *Supersaurus*

(the contour of the posteroventral margin of the shaft exhibiting a distinct cusp). Therefore, according to McIntosh (1997), based upon this and other admittedly "flimsy evidence," the preserved remains "suggest that *Dystrophaeus* belongs to the Diplodocidae or Cetiosauridae with a slight preference for the former view."

Gillette (1996*a*), pointing out that Upchurch (1995) had considered *Haplocanthosaurus* to be a sister taxon to *Camarasaurus*, proposed that the affinities of *D. viaemalae* are most likely to be found within the "Cetiosauridae," Titanosauridae, Camarasauridae, or Diplodocidae, a more precise assignment pending the hoped for recovery of more material once excavation of the type locality later resumes.

Though imperfectly known, *Dystrophaeus* is an important taxon considering its possibly critical role in the evolution of North American sauropods. As related by Gillette (1996*a*): A lengthy period of relatively low diversity and abundance spanned the Late Triassic origin of dinosaurs to the Late Jurassic explosion of new and abundant forms in North America, the latter represented by the diverse dinosaurian fauna of the Morrison Formation of the Colorado

E

Plateau and surrounding areas of the western United States. The origin of the Morrison dinosaurs included introducing sauropods to North America, where these animals did not appear until the end of the Middle Jurassic. North American prosauropods are known (through fossil bones and tracks; see Lockley and Hunt 1995) from the Late Triassic through Middle Jurassic. As sauropods originated in the Early Jurassic, achieving almost worldwide distribution by the Middle Jurassic (McIntosh 1990*b*; Upchurch 1995), their North American ancestry cannot be among the prosauropods of that continent, but originated by emigrating from other continents during Callovian or Oxfordian times.

Dystrophaeus, Gillette (1996*a*) noted, is one of four known sauropods recognized from the bottom of the Morrison Formation (or, alternatively, from the Summerville Formation), the others being *Camarasaurus* (Summerville Formation, New Mexico), an unidentified form (Tidwell Member of the Morrison Formation, Colorado National Monument, Colorado), and *Apatosaurus* sp. (Morrison Formation, Colorado). As indicated by the stratigraphic position of *Dystrophaeus*, this genus appears to be the oldest of these four, or at least ranks among the oldest of all North American forms (see also McIntosh 1997), and must be, consequently, ancestral to other Morrison sauropods (*e.g.*, *Apatosaurus*, *Barosaurus*, *Brachiosaurus*, *Camarasaurus*, *Diplodocus*, *Haplocanthosaurus*, *Seismosaurus*, *Supersaurus*). North American sauropods may have originated from Europe (indigenous genera including *Cetiosaurus*, *Cetiosauriscus*, *Bothriospondylus*, *Camarasaurus*), South America (*Amygdalodon*, *Patagosaurus*, *Volkheimeria*), Africa (*Cetiosaurus*), Asia (*Shunosaurus*, *Datousaurus*, *Tienshanosaurus*), or, less likely, from Australia (*Rhoetosaurus*) or Madagascar (*Bothriospondylus*, *Lapparentosaurus*), the ancestry of the North American forms probably lying within the families represented by those genera. Gillette (1996*a*) suggested that *Dystrophaeus* could be one of those genera or a descendent of one.

In conclusion, Gillette (1996*a*) emphasized that, whatever the affinities of *D. viaemalae*, this species' stratigraphic position critically relates to the timing of the origin and evolution of all Morrison Formation dinosaurs. If *D. viaemalae* emigrated to North America during the earlier determined time (before the J-5 unconformity), it could represent a species, genus, or family thus far unknown from the Middle Jurassic of North America, and it or its descendants might be ancestral to some of the Morrison sauropods (*Apatosaurus*, etc.); if, however, this species or its ancestors emigrated to North America later (after the termination of the J-5 unconformity), the time span separating the four Tidwell Member sauropods (*Dy-*

strophaeus, etc.) from later Jurassic sauropods is not as great, with *Dystrophaeus* included among the Morrison genera yet still possibly old enough to be related to sauropods of other continents.

As stated by McIntosh (1997), the intended future return to the type locality to collect more material "could result in very significant progress in understanding the evolution of the sauropods and aid the cladistic analysis of this group."

Key References: Barnes (1988); Cope (1877*c*); Gillette (1993, 1996*a*, 1996*b*); Gillette, Barnes, Gillette and McIntosh (1989); Huene (1904); McIntosh (1990*b*, 1997).

†EDMONTOSAURUS

Ornithischia: Genasauria: Cerapoda: Ornithopoda: Euornithopoda: Iguanodontia: Euiguanodontia: Dryomorpha: Ankylopollexia: Hadrosauridae: Euhadrosauria: Hadrosaurinae.

Comments: The best known of all hadrosaurid genera, this classic "duckbilled dinosaur" is documented by numerous specimens collected over a period of more than a century.

More recently, Tedesco, Halvorsen and Cooper (1998) briefly reported on a hadrosaurid mass mortality site, or bonebed, found in the Lance Creek Formation (Late Cretaceous, Maastrichtian) in east central Wyoming, and dominated by the genus *Edmontosaurus*.

As described by Tedesco *et al.*, the bonebed measures about one meter in thickness, the primary bed occurring in the upper meter of an organic-rich siltstone unit. White, cross-bedded sandstone capped by rippled sandstone forming the resistant cap rock — interpreted by the authors as representing fluvial channel deposits — overlies the siltstone. Lenses of fine-grained, dark gray, extremely organic-rich mudstone are interspersed with the channel sandstones. Organic debris found in this mudstone — interpreted by Tedesco *et al.* as representing oxbow lake or stagnant water ponds within the floodplain complex — include numerous cones, seeds, and entire leaves.

The fossil bed is composed of the disarticulated bones of hundreds of individuals, most of these remains belonging to *Edmontosaurus*. However, the site also contains a rich fauna of ceratopsian dinosaurs, plus nondinosaurian aquatic animals including turtles, crocodiles, and gar. Organic debris includes mostly leaf litter, but also seeds and amber. Tedesco *et al.* interpreted the rocks at this site as representing "a fluvial/deltaic complex draining a region of temperate climate. Fox Hills sediments are coeval with Lance Creek Formation sediments and are coastal, lagoonal, and deltaic sandstones that mark the approximate location of the shoreline."

Photograph by the author, courtesy Natural History Museum of Los Angeles County.

From the evidence preserved at this site, Tedesco *et al.* speculated that a herd of hadrosaurs, mostly consisting of *Edmontosaurus* individuals, crossed the river during a flood. Many of these dinosaurs did not make it across, their bodies washing downstream, later to become scavenged and disarticulated. Later flooding buried some of these remains and washed others further downstream, the result of this event being "an accumulation of many different bones randomly scattered throughout the layer, as well as in pockets of channel floor sediments."

As pointed out by the authors, this bonebed "is significant in that it extends the known migration range of *Edmontosaurus* further south and east than previously reported."

Key reference: Tedesco, Halvorsen and Cooper (1998).

EOBRONTOSAURUS Bakker 1998

Saurischia: Sauropodomorpha: Sauropoda: Eusauropoda: Neosauropoda: Diplodocoidea: Diplodocidae.

Name derivation: Greek *eos* = "dawn" + *Brontosaurus*.

Type species: *E. yahnahpin* (Filla and Redman 1994).

Other species: [None.]

Occurrence: Morrison Formation, Wyoming, Colorado, United States.

Age: Late Jurassic.

Known material: Two partially articulated incomplete postcranial skeletons, various postcranial elements.

Holotype: TATE 001, partially articulated incomplete skeleton, including both sternal plates, sternal ribs.

Diagnosis of genus (as for type species): Differs from all other "apatosaurine" species in retaining long cervical ribs and very primitive scapulocoracoid; upper scapular blade expanded, scapulocoracoid suture at right angle to long axis of scapular blade, coracoid shallow dorsoventrally and rounded (not angular anteriorly and posteriorly) (Bakker 1998).

Comments: The new genus *Eobrontosaurus* was established on an incomplete skeleton (TATE 001)—originally named *Apatosaurus yahnahpin* by Filla and Redman (1994)—collected from the "Bertha" Quarry, located in the lower half of the Morrison Formation in southeastern Wyoming. Specimens referred to the type species, *E. yahnahpin*, include TATE 066 (formerly CM 563), a partially articulated incomplete skeleton, TATE 067, vertebrae from Wyoming, and also cervical, dorsal, and sacral vertebrae, and a hind foot, from Felch Quarry 1, just below the Brushy Basin Member of the Morrison Formation, in Cañon City, Colorado, figured by Marsh (1896) as belonging to *Diplodocus longus* (Bakker 1998).

This species was first diagnosed by Filla and Redman as follows: Closest to *Apatosaurus excelsus*, but differs in retention of these primitive characters: upper scapula blade greatly expanded; scapula spine (deltoid ridge) perpendicular to long axis of scapula blade; coracoid shallow, not enlarged ventrally, humerus with very narrow shaft; additional primitive character possibly the retention of very long cervical ribs.

Originally, Filla and Redman described what they interpreted to be gastralia, or "belly ribs," in the

Edmontosaurus annectens, articulated skeleton (LACM 7233/23504), juvenile specimen collected by Harley J. Garbani.

Eobrontosaurus

Photograph by the author, courtesy Pink Palace Museum, Memphis, Tennessee.

Skull of duckbilled dino-
saur *Edmontosaurus an-
nectens*.

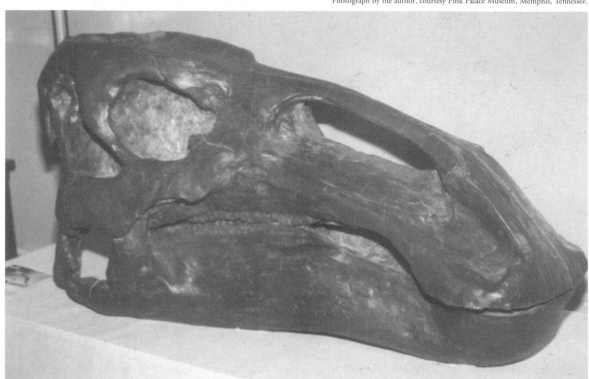

Eobrontosaurus yahnahpin,
holotype sternal ribs (originally identified as gastralia)
of *Apatosaurus yahnahpin*,
internal (A, B, and C) and
posterior-edge (J, K, and L)
views, arrows indicating
front of torso. Scale = 10
cm. (After Filla and Red-
man 1994).

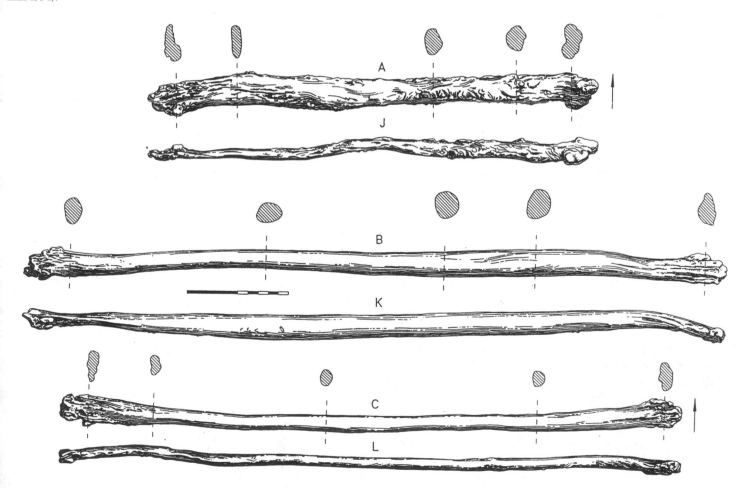

holotype, hailed as the first definite gastralia found in any sauropod specimen; more recently, however, Leon Claessens, in his master's thesis centering upon gastralia in dinosaurs (Utrecht University), identified these bones as sternal ribs (L. Claessens, personal communication to J. I. Kirkland, 1996). Filla and Redman envisioned this species as a stoutly built sauropod having very powerful and flexible forearms, able to run and rear up on its hind legs to feed or engage in intraspecific neck "butting" (see Bakker 1986), its [sternal ribs] serving both as a protective basket and to contribute to the functioning of the respiratory system. (See *Apatosaurus* entry, *D:TE*, for additional details on this species.)

Bakker, in renaming and rediagnosing this species, informally used the term "apatosaurine" to indicate all diplodocids possessing massive limbs, and wide necks and tails (*e.g.*, *Eobrontosaurus*, *Apatosaurus*, and "*Brontosaurus*"), and "diplodocine" for those with slender limbs, and slender necks and tails (*e.g.*, *Diplodocus*, *Barosaurus*, and *Amphicoelias*).

As pointed out by Bakker, the two scapulocoracoids of the holotype, when first excavated, were incorrectly thought to be those of a "haplocanthosaur" or "camarasaur," Bakker further noting that, if found isolated, these elements would not have been referred to a diplodocid. However, two "eobrontosaur" skeleton have been recovered possessing "a typical apatosaur forelimb firmly articulated into the glenoid, and both specimens are accompanied by typical apatosaurine caudal vertebrae." As Bakker observed, the forelimb of *E. yahnahpin* differs from that of all other known "nonapatosaurs" in having a short humeral shaft, humeral head that is in line with the shaft (not displaced inward), and a much more massive forearm and manus than in any other known Morrison sauropod (see McIntosh 1990*b*; Filla and Redman 1994).

Key references: Bakker (1998); Filla and Redman (1994); Marsh (1896).

EOLAMBIA Kirkland 1998

Ornithischia: Genasauria: Cerapoda: Ornithopoda: Euornithopoda: Iguanodontia: Euiguanodontia: Dryomorpha: Ankylopollexia: Hadrosauridae: Euhadrosauria: ?Lambeosaurinae.

Name derivation: Greek *eos* = "dawn" + "lambeosaurine."

Type species: *E. caroljonesa* Kirkland 1998.

Other species: [None.]

Occurrence: Cedar Mountain Formation, Utah, United States.

Age: Early–Late Cretaceous (Albian–Cenomanian).

Known material: Five partial skeletons, two with skulls, adult and juvenile.

Holotype: CEUM 5258, partial skeleton with skull, crania including paired frontals, partial parietals, (poorly preserved) braincase, both maxillae, both jugals, right postorbital, lower portion of right quadrate, left dentary, postcrania including atlas, cervical vertebrae, anterior dorsal vertebrae, proximal ischium, fragment of tibia, right fibula, adult.

Diagnosis of genus (as for type species): Large hadrosaurid unique in possessing a combination of the following: skull having nondenticulate premaxilla enrolling around narial opening, lacking ventral foramen (as in lambeosaurines), no evidence of telescoping of premaxilla and nasals over frontals to form crest; sagital crest extending above back of skull; squamosals meeting at midline in juveniles, with short paroccipital processes; jugals long, low; maxilla lacking narial process (as in lambeosaurines), with 32 tooth positions in adults; lower jaw deepening rostrally with almost no diastema; 30 tooth files, with at least three teeth per file; teeth having single central carina; at least seven sacral vertebrae with ventral groove (as in hadrosaurines); proximal caudal vertebrae highspines; scapula expanding slightly; forelimb massive, long; ilium having slender preacetabular process, poorly developed supra-acetabular crest [formerly "antitrochanter"], well-developed brevis shelf; ischium long, stout, with large and flaring, blade-like distal end (Kirkland 1998*b*).

Comments: To date the oldest hadrosaurid known from significant skeletal evidence, the new genus and species *Eolambia caroljonesa* (informally referred to as "Eohadrosaurus caroljonesi" by Kirkland 1997) was established upon a disarticulated partial skeleton with incomplete skull (CEUM 9758), found in 1993 by Carol and Ramal Jones at what would be referred to as the "Carol Site," in the basal Mussentuchit

Eolambia caroljonesa, CEUM 9758, holotype partial skull including left maxilla (lateral view) and right dentary (medial view).

Courtesy James I. Kirkland.

Eolambia

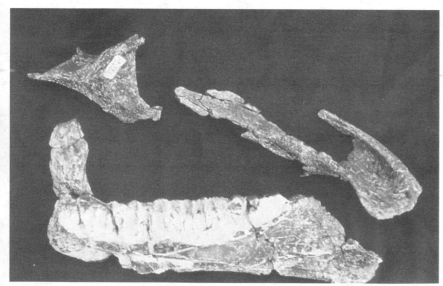

Top: Eolambia caroljonesa, CEUM 9758, holotype dentary teeth, medial view. **Left: Eolambia caroljonesa,** juvenile skull material including OMNH 28916, left squamosal (dorsal view), OMNH 28919, right premaxilla (lateral view), and OMNH 28511, left dentary (medial view).

imen was somewhat damaged by roots. Paratype specimens include CEUM 5212, a partial skull and forelimb representing a large adult, with more of the specimen yet to be recovered, from the "Carol Site," and also the following specimens collected in the region of the southwestern San Rafael Swell by the Oklahoma Museum of Natural History: a partial juvenile skeleton including many vertebral centra and neural spines, scapulae, right ulna, right ilium, partial ischium, fragmentary distal femora, right and partial left tibia, distal two-thirds of right and fragment of left tibia, metatarsals, and phalanges; partial juvenile skeleton with parts of the skull, including right premaxilla, left squamosal, left exocciptal, left prefrontal, left dentary, a dorsal vertebra, isolated neural arch, left and proximal right humeri, right ulna, metacarpals, and partial right tibia; partial skeleton (OMNH 27749) with sacrum and ischium (more elements to be excavated); an isolated left ischium (OMNH 24389); a mostly unexcavated partial skeleton (OMNH 32812) including two caudal vertebrae and a partial scapula. Indeed, *E. caroljonesa* is currently the most common dinosaur known from these strata (Kirkland 1998*b*).

Member (dated to be of Albian–Cenomanian age by Kirkland, Britt, Burge, Carpenter, Cifelli, DeCourten, Eaton, Hasiotis and Lawton 1997) of the Cedar Mountain Formation, along the west side of the San Rafael Well, in Emory County, east of Castle Dale, Utah. The Joneses brought their find to the attention of Donald L. Burge, director of the College of Eastern Utah, Prehistoric Museum, in Price, who, with museum staff members and volunteers, excavated the skeleton. Buried just beneath the surface, the spec-

(According to M. K. Brett-Surman [personal communication, 1998], Kirkland's statements regarding 32 tooth positions, number of tooth files, slenderness of the preacetabular process, the massiveness of the forelimb, and the poor development of the supra-acetabular crest "are all subjective, and relative, statements that cannot be used in a diagnosis.")

In a preliminary cladistic analysis attempting to place *Eolambia* within the Hadrosauridae, Kirkland found this genus to exhibit but one of six character states used to define the Hadrosaurinae — groove on ventral surface of sacrum (independently acquired in the iguanodontid *Ouranosaurus*), this state, also found in the Ankylosauria and Ceratopsia. On the contrary, *Eolambia* possesses four of the seven characters uniting all previously known lambeosaurines — absence of premaxillary foramen; external nares surrounded by premaxilla (partly so in *Eolambia*); development of maxillary shelf; and caudal vertebrae having very tall neural spines. Two other lambeosaurine characters — circumnarial depression extending up onto nasal, and shortened parietal (independently acquired in *Ouranosaurus*) — are not present in *Eolambia*. However, these character states relate to the development of a nasal crest.

As *Eolambia* has no such crest but does possess the above other cited features usually regarded as indicative of the Lambeosaurinae, Kirkland concluded that *Eolambia* seems to be a basal, crestless lambeosaurine. If this assessment is correct, then Kirkland proposed that this group of duckbilled dinosaurs be redefined as "all taxa that have lost the premaxillary foramen, have partial enrollment of external nares by premaxilla, have developed the maxillary shelf, have developed tall proximal caudal spines, and have developed a robust forelimb."

However, Kirkland noted that *Eolambia* might also be interpreted to be the sister taxon of the Lambeosaurinae. Whichever assessment may be correct, Kirkland concluded that the possession of both hadrosaurine and lambeosaurine synapomorphies in this genus "suggests that *Eolambia* may represent the hadrosaurid morphological stage near the divergence of hadrosaurines and lambeosaurines."

Considering that the occurrence of the primitive hadrosaurid *Eolambia* might suggest a North American origin for the Hadrosauridae, Kirkland noted that the presence of the closest known relatives of this group — *Ouranosaurus* in Africa and *Probactrosaurus* in Asia — suggests an origin outside of North America. *Eolambia* establishes that both the Hadrosaurinae and the Lambeosaurinae originated early in the history of the Hadrosauridae. With the occurrence of another possible hadrosaurid — "*Trachodon*" [=? *Telmatosaurus*] *canta*possible *bridgiensis* [see *Telmatosaurus*]

Courtesy James I. Kirkland.

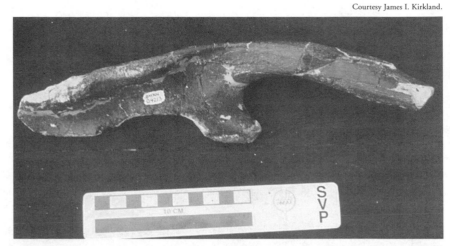

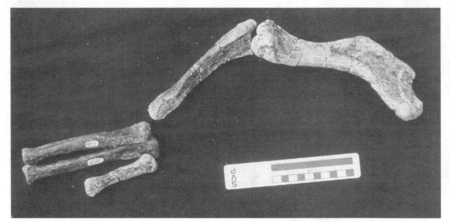

Courtesy James I. Kirkland.

entry, *D:TE*, based on a tooth from the base of the Cenomanian Cambridge Greensand, described by Lydekker (1888) — Kirkland found it obvious that the Hadrosauridae were widely distributed across the Northern Hemisphere by the end of the Early Cretaceous period.

Notes: Trace fossils found in the Mussentuchit Member of the Cedar Mountain Formation may pertain to *Eolambia*. In Kirkland *et al.*, DeCourten reported large ornithopod tracks, possibly representing this genus, found near the Long Walk Quarry east of Castle Dale, Utah.

Abundant transported eggshell having a reticulate surface pattern and thickness of about 2 millimeters — found in the Cedar Mountain Formation associated with isolated hadrosaurid teeth, may be referable to *Eolambia*. From the same stratigraphic level of this area and possibly pertaining to this genus are Cedar Mountain eggshell specimens described by Jensen (1970) (K. Hirsch, personal communication to Kirkland; also Bray 1998).

Also possibly belonging to *Eolambia* is part of an embryonic maxilla which, along with the above skeletal and trace specimens, could, according to Kirkland,

Top: Eolambia caroljonesa, OMNH 04213, juvenile right ilium (lateral view). *Bottom: Eolambia caroljonesa*, forelimb elements including right humerus (OMNH 28915), right ulna (OMNH 28917), and second, third, and fifth metacarpals (OMNH 30999, 31004, and 30998, respectively).

Epachthosaurus

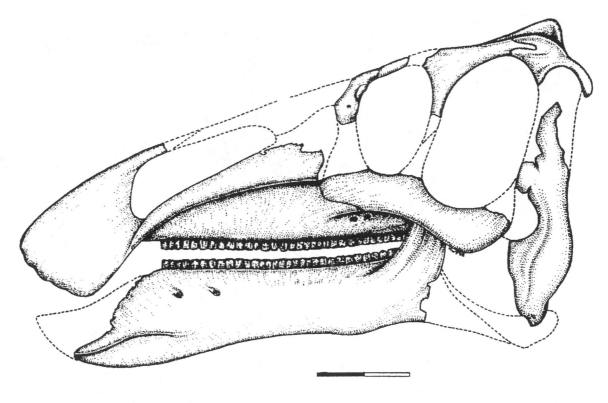

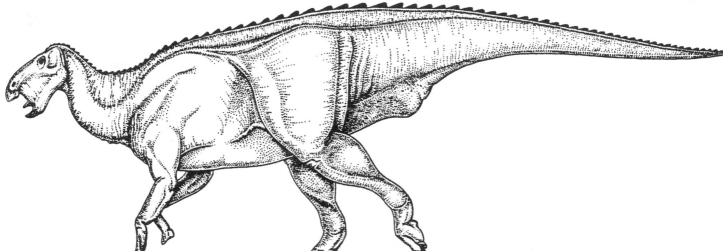

eventually lead to the documentation of the entire growth history of this common dinosaur.

Key references: Bray (1998); Jensen (1970); Kirkland (1998*b*); Kirkland, Britt, Burge, Carpenter, Cifelli, DeCourten, Eaton, Hasiotis and Lawton (1997).

†EPACHTHOSAURUS

Saurischia: Sauropodomorpha: Sauropoda: Neosauropoda: Macronaria: Titanosauriformes: Somphospondyli: Titanosauria *incertae sedis*.

Comments: This South American titanosaur, remains of which were first collected by José F. Bona-

parte and assistants in 1981, is presently under reevaluation by various workers. Recently, both the diagnosis of this genus as well as the correct referral of all fossil remains referred to it have come under question.

In commenting upon *Epacthosaurus*, Bonaparte (1996*b*) observed that the paraplastotype specimen — MACN-CH 13689, a cast of an incomplete sequence of dorsosacral vertebrae — affords more interesting information than does holotype vertebra MACN-CH 1317: Centra of dorsal vertebrae wider than high, with somewhat flat and extended central surface; pleurocoels rather large (more so than in any other known

titanosaur); neural arch typically titanosaurian, with single neural spine possessing modest prespinal lamina which bifurcates (as in holotype MACN-CH 1767), lateral side of neural arch showing typical angled depressions, generally two for each side; vertebrae with very derived hyposphene-hypantrum structure (similar to that in *Argentinosaurus*).

Bonaparte noted that, during excavation of this material, an osseous bar was seen above the sacral neural spines extending above the last two dorsal vertebrae, this feature possibly representing "an ossified supraspinal cartilage for a stronger dorso-sacral connection." However, identification of MACN-CH 13689 with *Epachthosaurus* may not be correct (see below).

In a paper in which he names and describes the new genus and species *Pelligrinisaurus powelli* (this book), Salgado (1996) suggested that the type species *Epachthosaurus sciutto* requires a new diagnosis based upon proven derived characters, as some of the characters originally used by Powell (1986) to diagnose this taxon are probably plesiomorphic features. As noted earlier by Salgado and Martínez 1993), though Powell (1986, 1990) interpreted the presence of a ventrally forked prespinal lamina on the posterior dorsal vertebrae as an apomorphy of *Epachthosaurus*, this character is probably plesiomorphic for all titanosaurids, being also present in *Andesaurus delgadoi* and most likely in the brachiosaurid *Brachiosaurus brancai*. Salgado noted that the anteroposteriorly compressed neural spine in the posterior dorsals is not unique to the holotype of *E. sciuttoi*, as it is also found in other titanosaurids including *Saltasaurus* (Powell 1986).

Contra Bonaparte, Salgado rejected referral of MACN-CH 13689 to *Epachthosaurus*. The accessory intervertebral articulation of the dorsal vertebrae mentioned by Powell (1986) in this specimen are not present in MACN-CH 1317, although similar articulations are known in *Argentinosaurus huinculensis*, reasons for which Bonaparte and Coria (1993) had previously (and correctly, Salgado noted) related MACH-CH 13689 to that species.

In diagnosing *E. sciuttoi*, Powell (1990) proposed that the dorsal centrum width to height ratio being equal or more than 1.5 is an apomorphy of the holotype. Salgado, pointing out that other sauropods — including *Brachiosaurus*, *Austrosaurus*, and *Opisthocoelicaudia* — display basically the same ratio, proposed that this feature be considered invalid in the diagnosis until the condition can be established through cladistic analysis in the common titanosaurid ancestor.

The only autapomorphy recognized as valid by Salgado in the holotype of *E. sciuttoi* is the interprezygapophyseal shelf — an unusual feature unknown

in titanosaurids — which Powell (1990) described in some detail but did not include in his diagnosis of the species. This apomorphy was also observed in UNPSJB 920 (R. D. Martínez, personal communication to Salgado), an almost complete and articulated specimen from the Bajo Barreal Formation of Chubut, Argentina, the same locality and stratigraphic unit that yielded the holotype, referred to *Epacthosaurus* and described by Martínez, O. Giménez, J. Rodriguez and M. Luna (1990).

Key reference: Bonaparte (1996*b*); Martínez, Giménez, Rodriguez and Luna (1990); Powell (1986, 1990); Salgado (1996); Salgado and Martínez (1993).

†EPANTERIAS — (See †*Allosaurus*.)

†EUHELOPUS

Saurischia: Sauropodomorpha: Sauropoda: Eusauropoda: Neosauropoda: Macronaria: Titanosauriformes: Somphospondyli: Euhelopodidae.

Diagnosis of genus (as for type species, *E. zdanskyi*): Produmbent teeth with asymmetrical enamel (*i.e.*, anterior crown-root margin being closer to apex of crown), well-developed crown buttresses on lingual crown surface; acute anteroventral margin of naris; presacral neural spines having divided coel above prezygapophyseal-postzygapophyseal lamina; increase in number of cervical vertebrae (three or four added for total of 16 or 17 cervicals) Wilson and Sereno (1998).

Key reference: Wilson and Sereno (1998).

†GARGOYLEOSAURUS Carpenter, Miles and Cloward 1998

Ornithischia: Genasauria: Thyreophora: Ankylosauria: Ankylosauridae: ?Polacanthinae.

Name derivation: "Gargoyle" [roof spout carved to represent a grotesque animal or human figure] + Greek *sauros* = "lizard."

Type species: *G. parkpini* Carpenter, Miles and Cloward 1998.

Other species: [None.]

Occurrence: Morrison Formation, Wyoming, United States.

Age: Late Jurassic (Tithonian).

Known material/holotype: DMNH 27726, partial skeleton with skull articulated with first three cervical vertebrae and first two cervical rings.

Diagnosis of genus (as for type species): Differs from all other known ankylosaurids in presence of seven premaxillary teeth; crown base of cheek teeth not swollen into typical ankylosaur cingulum;

Gargoyleosaurus

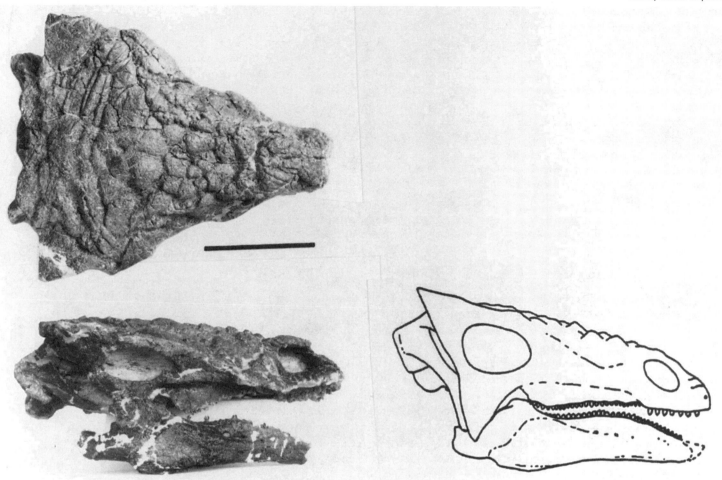

Gargoyleosaurus parkpini, DMNH 27726, holotype skull in (top) dorsal, (lower left) right lateral (as preserved), and (lower right) same (reconstructed by Carpenter) views. Scale = 10 cm. (After Carpenter, Miles and Cloward 1998.)

premaxilla having notch at front in inverted "U" shape; no secondary palate in roof of mouth; nostril openings facing laterally (as in *Ankylosaurus, Shamosaurus,* and most nodosaurids); vomer not expanded upwardly to bisect nasal cavity; air passage straight, not convoluted (as in later ankylosaurids); all vertebral centra elongated (unlike short, wide centra of *Mymoorapelta*); tips of caudal neural spines not expanded (as in *Mymoorapelta*); first armor ring of neck consisting of five partly fused plates; at least two elongated spines extending from each shoulder; body armor consisting of thin-walled cones (unlike solid conical armor of *Mymoorapelta*) (Carpenter, Miles and Cloward 1998).

Comments: The genus *Gargoyleosaurus* was founded upon a partial skeleton (DMNH 27726) with skull (the first known for any Jurassic ankylosaur) discovered by J. Parker and T. Pinegar in the upper part of the Morrison Formation, Bone Cabin Quarry, Albany County, Wyoming. Although small (about 3 meters, or approximately 10 feet in length), the specimen represents an adult individual, as evidenced by the closure of the sutures in the vertebral column (Carpenter, Miles and Cloward 1998).

As observed by Carpenter *et al.*, the type species *G. parkpini* presents a combination of characters later seen in both Cretaceous families of ankylosaurs, the Nodosauridae and Ankylosauridae.

Ankylosaurid features seen in *G. parkpini* include the following: In dorsal view, the skull is triangular in shape, and possesses large, triangular armor scutes at the rear corners; the cheek tooth row is inset very deeply. (However, the cheek teeth are reminiscent of those found in primitive ornithischians [*e.g.,* the Upper Triassic African genus *Lesothosaurus*] in being simple, leaf-shaped, and with slightly expanded bases. Also, the conical, slightly compressed premaxillary teeth have denticles along their margins similar to those observed in the primitive stegosaur *Huayangosaurus* [and also in the rear-most teeth of *Lesothosaurus*], this similarity offering support to the proposal [*e.g.,* Coombs 1978*a*] that the Stegosauria and Ankylosauria are related groups.)

Nodosaurid features noted by Carpenter *et al.* include these: The scooped beak, formed by the premaxillary bones, is long and narrow; not present within the snout are the complex, looped air passages formed by the secondary palate found in some (but not all) Cretaceous ankylosaurids (as revealed by computerized axial tomography (CAT) scan, the secondary palate did not develop, the air passage being simple and direct); the vomer plate, formed by a vertical sheet of bone in the palate, does not extend to the underside of the skull (this condition known only in one nodosaurid, *Pawpawsaurus*, and in no ankylosaurids), forming instead a simple "T" with the palatines as in less specialized ornithischians (*e.g.*, *Hypsilophodon*). Additional CAT scans revealed to the authors that the brain of *Gargoyleosaurus* "had a sharp bend or flexure similar to that seen in *Hypsilophodon* and the nodosaurids *Struthiosaurus* and *Polacanthus*, rather than the moderate flexure seen in the ankylosaurid *Euoplocephalus*.

According to Carpenter *et al.*, the possession of the various nodosaurid-like features in *Gargoyleosaurus* seem to be primitive for the Ankylosauria, being also present in other ornithischians. Ankylosaurid features of the skull indicate a close relationship between this new taxon and the ankylosaurids of the Late Cretaceous. Therefore, *Gargoyleosaurus* was regarded by Carpenter *et al.* as the most primitive, or basal, member of the Ankylosauridae. This assessment supports the proposal that the Ankylosauria originated from a single ancestor (*e.g.*, Coombs 1978*a*; Sereno 1986; Coombs and Maryańska, 1990), the following step in ankylosaurian evolution being the radiation in the Cretaceous of the Nodosauridae and Ankylosauridae.

Key references: Carpenter, Miles and Cloward (1998); Coombs (1978*a*); Coombs and Maryańska (1990); Sereno (1986).

GASPARINISAURA   Coria and Salgado 1996

Ornithischia: Genasauria: Cerapoda: Ornithopoda: Euornithopoda: Iguanodontia; Euiguanodontia: Dryomorpha

Name derivation: "[Dr. Zulma B. de] Gasparini" + Greek *saura* [feminine] = "lizard."

Type species: *G. cincosaltensis* Coria and Salgado 1996.

Other species: [None.]

Occurrence: Río Colorado Formation, Río Negro Province, Argentina.

Age: Late Cretaceous (Coniacian–Santonian).

Known material: Skull, partial crania and postcrania representing approximately 15 individuals, juvenile to adult.

Holotype: MUCPv-208, almost complete skull with atlas and axis in articulation, sacrum, pectoral and pelvic girdles, humeri (missing distal ends), almost complete hind limbs, juvenile.

Diagnosis of genus (as for type species): Anterior process of jugal wedged between maxilla and lacrimal;

ascending process of jugal anteroposteriorly wide, contacts ventral process of postorbital; infratemporal fenestra narrowing ventrally into ventroposteriorly directed slot bordered by quadratojugal; apex of arched dorsal margin of infratemporal fenestra located posterior to mandibular articulation; sacrum with four true sacrals; first and second sacral ribs not fused; chevrons in midcaudal region subtriangular, anteroposteriorly expanded; ilium with long pubic peduncle; femur with fully fused greater and lesser trochanter; femur without intercondylar groove; condylid of femur laterally placed; inner and outer maleoli approximately level ventrally; astragalus with low ascending process; metatarsal II transversely compressed in anterior aspect (less than 15 percent of transverse width of three metatarsals), anteroposteriorly developed (Salgado, Coria and Heredia 1997.)

Comments: The first basal iguanodontian known from the Late Cretaceous of South America, *Gasparinisaura* was founded upon a well-preserved skull and partial postcranial skeleton collected from the Anacleto Member of the Río Colorado Formation, Upper Cretaceous (Coniacian–Santonian; Cruz, Condat, Kozlowski and Manceda 1989; Legareta and Gulisano 1989; Bonaparte 1991), southeast of Cinco Saltos City, northwestern Río Negro Province, Patagonia, Argentina (a locality where remains of sauropods, theropods, turtles, crocodilians, and fishes have also been collected; see Powell 1986). Referred to the type species, *G. cincosaltensis*, was another specimen (MUCPv-212), consisting of a nearly complete, articulated tail, the distal end of both tibiae, and the proximal ends of both metatarsals (Coria and Salgado 1996). As pointed out by Coria (1998) in a later abstract, this taxon constitutes "the first record of ornithopods other than hadrosaurs for the South American continent."

Originally, Coria and Salgado diagnosed the genus (and type species *G. cincosaltensis* as follows: Anterior process of jugal wedged between maxilla and lacrimal, ascending process anteroposteriorly wide and contacting posteriorly with ventral process of postorbital; ventral part of infratemporal fenestra narrowed, ventroposteriorly directed, completely surrounded by quadratojugal; anterior part of postorbital process of squamosal located posteriorly relative to position of mandibular articulation; midcaudal vertebrae with subtriangular, anteroposteriorly expanded chevrons; greater and lesser trochanters of femur fully fused together; condylid of femur laterally positioned.

Coria and Salgado referred *G. cincosaltensis* to the new taxon Euiguanodontia, comprising this species plus Dryomorpha (see "Systematics" chapter).

In analyzing *G. cincosaltensis*, Coria and Salgado noted that this taxon shares the following characters

Gasparinisaura

Gasparinisaura cincos-altensis, MUCPv-208, holotype skull (A. and B.) left lateral view. (After Coria and Salgado 1996.)

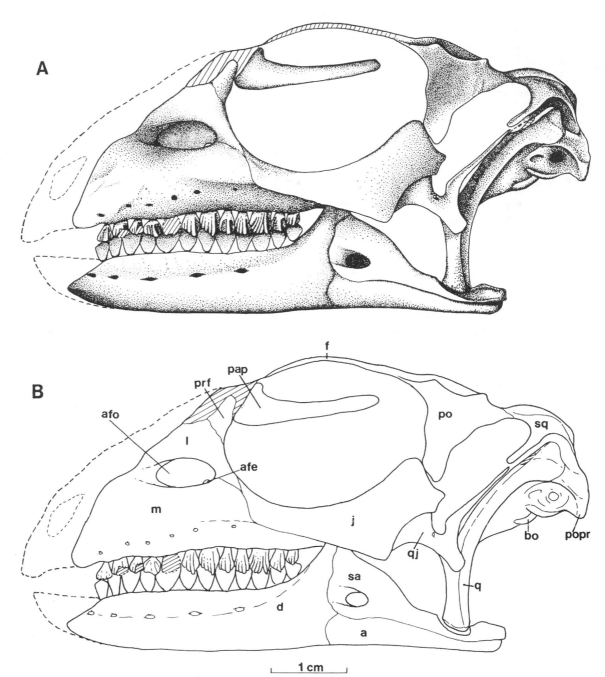

A

B

1 cm

with Dryomorpha: Laterally-facing jugal-postorbital articulation; presence of prominent lateral primary ridge in maxillary teeth; well-developed brevis shelf; and metatarsal I reduced or absent. However, the species is excluded from this group as it retains such plesiomorphic features as a well-developed quadratojugal (contact between quadratojugal and prequadratic process of squamosal absent in Dryomorpha), low maxillary tooth crowns (crowns high in Dryomorpha), and a laterally compressed ischial shaft (cross section rounded in Dryomorpha).

Subsequent to the introduction of *G. cincosaltensis*, Salgado, Coria and Heredia (1997) described

new specimens from the same locality belonging to this type species, this new material — ranging from juvenile to adult — including the following: (MUCPv-212) almost complete, articulated caudal vertebrae, distal ends of tibiae, proximal ends of both metatarsals; (MUCPv-213) dentary, posterior dorsal, articulated last dorsal, dorso-sacral, and first dorsal vertebrae, isolated sacral vertebra, incomplete humeri articulated with radii and ulnae, incomplete right ilium, incomplete left pubis, incomplete right femur, distal portion of tibia and fibula in articulation with astragalus and calcaneum, proximal ends of right metatarsals articulated with distal tarsals, several

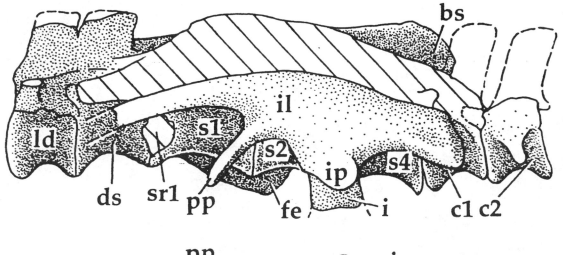

Gasparinisaura cincosaltensis, referred sacrum, partial pelvic girdle, and right femur (MCS-3) in (top) lateral and (bottom) ventral views. (After Salgado, Coria and Heredia 1997.)

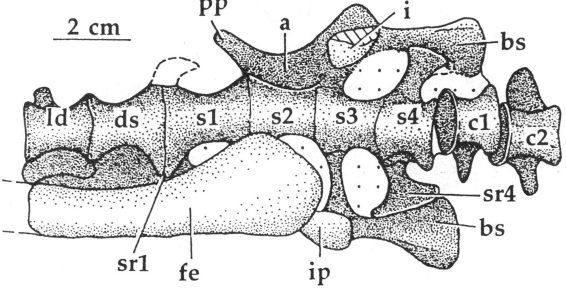

unidentified fragments; (MUCPv-214) five incomplete dorsal vertebrae, three caudal centra, proximal end of left femur, distal end of right femur, proximal portion of right tibia, distal end of left tibia, distal end of right tibia articulated to distal end of fibula; right astragalus and calcaneum; proximal end of right metatarsals articulated with distal tarsals I and II, unidentified appendicular fragments; (MUCPv-215) two dorsal vertebrae, fragmentary sacral vertebrae, four caudal centra, distal end of radius, distal end of right femur, distal end of phalanx, appendiculary fragments; (MUCPv-216) proximal portion of right tibia; (MUCPv-217) proximal portion of left tibia; (MUCPv-218) fragmentary vertebral centra, unidentified fragments, proximal portion of metatarsal, distal end of tibia, phalanges; (MUCPv-225) distal end of left femur; (MUCPv-226) distal portion of right femur, proximal ends of both tibiae; (MUCPv-227) two caudal vertebrae sheathed within ossified tendons; (MCS-1) almost complete tail, part of pelvis; (MCS-2)

right tibia and fibula with complete pes and part of left pes; (MCS-3) complete sacrum (including last dorsal, a dorsosacral, and four true sacral vertebrae), two caudals, ilia, partial femora, right tibia, right astragalus and fibula, partial right ischium, partial left pubis, proximal portion of left metatarsals.

Based upon the above new material, Salgado *et al.* recognized seven new postcranial characters which the authors recognized as autapomorphies of the species and published a revised diagnosis. A new analysis of the phylogenetic relationships of the species, incorporating data from the new specimens, resulted in an additional iguanodontian synapomorphy — condylid of femur slightly overlapping posterior intercondylar (flexor) groove.

Salgado *et al.* noted that most of these specimens were found distributed over a distance of 200 meters (about 680 feet) and concentrated in an interval of red mudstone 2 meters (about 6.8 feet) thick, with no particular orientation of the bones. Unweathered to

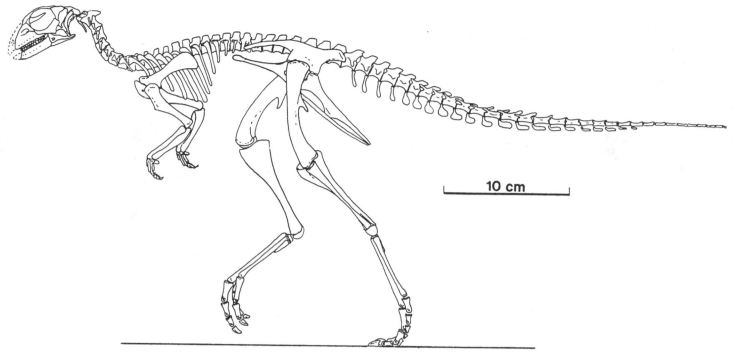

Gasparinisaura cincos-altensis, reconstructed skeleton based on holotype MUCPv-208 and referred specimen MUCPv-212. (After Coria and Salgado 1996.)

10 cm

cracked surface textures of the bones suggested surface exposure prior to burial for most specimens. A relatively large hole in the latero-proximal area of the femur of MUCPv-213 indicates probable predation or scavenging, the action of carnivorous animals possibly having contributed to the dismembering and scattering of the carcasses before burial. Absence of hatchlings implied that Cinco Saltos was not a nest site; rather, the authors speculated, it was "a special area for the exploitation of some necessary resource."

As several partially articulated specimens (mostly juveniles) were found well preserved, while others are badly preserved, Salgado *et al.* proposed that the death of these animals was not the result of a single, catastrophic event. The authors further speculated that all of the specimens found at this locality represent a single population ranging from juveniles to adults, and that populations of this genus were most likely characterized by a high density level.

Notes: Coria (1998) briefly reported that in 1993 Roberto Saldiva, a local farmer from Plaza Huincul, brought to the Museum "Carmen Funes" several ornithopod bone fragments collected from the Huincul Member of the Río Limay Formation (Cenomanian), south of Plaza Huincul. Subsequently recovered from this locality were four almost complete, partially articulated skeletons representing a new iguanodontian that is larger and more derived than *Gasparinisaura*, and also more derived than *Tenontosaurus*.

With this new material, Coria hypothesized that the South American forms constitute a sister group of Dryomorpha, and that they form a monophyletic group with *Gasparinisaura*. The presence of this new form, along with *Gasparinisaura* and also *Loncosaurus* (formerly classified as a theropod; see *D:TE*), reveals an unexpected diversity of early Late Cretaceous, South American basal iguanodontians prior to the land connection with North America, this apparently supporting the idea that a lineage of Jurassic iguanodontians, such as *Dryosaurus*, survived into the Late Cretaceous of South America.

Key references: Coria (1998); Coria and Salgado (1996); Salgado, Coria and Heredia (1997).

GASTONIA Kirkland 1998

Ornithischia: Genasauria: Thyreophora: Ankylosauria: Polacanthinae.

Name derivation: "[Robert] Gaston [discoverer of type locality]."

Type species: *G. burgei* Kirkland 1998.

Other species: [None.]

Occurrence: Cedar Mountain Formation, Utah, United States.

Age: Early Cretaceous (Barremian).

Known material: Skull, more than a thousand mostly disarticulated bones, armor, representing at least five individuals.

Holotype: CEUM 1307, skull, adult.

Diagnosis of genus (as for type species): Medium-to-large (6 meters in length) ankylosaur closest to *Polacanthus* and *Hoplitosaurus*, differing in having three sacral vertebrae, as opposed to four in *Polacanthus*; ilia with slender, diverging preacetabular processes, which are short, almost parallel in *Polacanthus*; femoral head and greater trochanter not as well offset from shaft as in *Hoplitosaurus* and *Polacanthus*; anterior trochanter fused, forming ridge, unlike free trochanter in *Hoplitosaurus*; tibia considerably shorter than in *Polacanthus* and *Hoplitosaurus*; acromium flange-like, but more erect than in *Polacanthus* and *Hylaeosaurus*; no plates with tall slender spines as in *Hoplitosaurus* and *Polacanthus*; unique among polacanthines in possessing dorsal armor characterized by scutes bordered by radially directed ridges; skull unique among all known ankylosaurs in its broad premaxillary notch, posteriorly placed narial openings, and basisphenoid with elongate basipterygoid processes (Kirkland 1998*a*).

Comments: One of the most completely known Early Cretaceous ankylosaurs, the genus *Gastonia* was founded upon an almost perfect skull (CEUM 1307) discovered in the Yellow Cat Member of the Cedar Mountain Formation, Grand County, in eastern Utah. Numerous additional and mostly scattered specimens (CEUM and BYU collections) from the original site, some possibly belonging with the holotype, and including remains of four individuals smaller than the holotype, have since been referred to the type species, *G. burgei* (Kirkland 1998*a*).

The Yellow Cat Member is the earliest of four members of the Cedar Mountain Formation. Defined by Kirkland, Britt, Burge, Carpenter, Cifelli, De-Courten, Eaton, Hasiotis and Lawton (1997), this member is apparently restricted to the Paradox Basin. It was dated as of Barremian age based on the presence of certain ankylosaurs (*i.e.*, a polacanthine, *Gastonia*), iguanodonts, and sauropods that indicate close temporal and geographic ties to the Barremian of Europe (*Polacanthus foxi* occurring in England).

James I. Kirkland announced the discovery of this dinosaur and briefly described its remains as early as 1996, but did not yet assign it a name; subsequently, the informal name appeared in various publications (*e.g.*, Kirkland's entry on the Cedar Mountain Formation in *The Encyclopedia of Dinosaurs*; see Currie and Padian 1997). As Kirkland (1996) observed, distinctive gross features of this new form, relative to other ankylosaurs, include a triangular head, large curved beak, and proportionally short front legs.

As observed by Kirkland (1998*a*), *Gastonia* exhibits a mosaic of characters previously referred either to the Nodosauridae (*e.g.*, simple nasal passage; paroccipital process and temporal fenestra visible in lateral view; scapula with strong, blade-like scapular spine; blade-like ischium ventrally flexed near midlength) or Ankylosauridae (*e.g.*, triangular skull slightly longer than wide, somewhat domed above the eyes; premaxillary scoop wider than long ventrally;

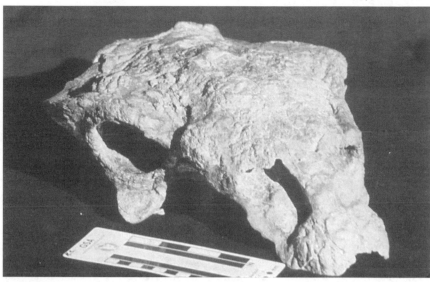

Gastonia burgei, CEUM 1307, holotype skull, right three quarter view.

kidney bean–shaped occiput inclined ventrally without neck, made up by basioccipital centrally and exoccipitals laterally; scapular spine extending upward from dorsal scapular margin; coracoid subequal in length and height; large deltopectoral crest extending to midpoint of humerus). The new genus also displays various primitive (*e.g.*, no armor fused to the skull) and derived (*e.g.*, femur with fusion of the anterior trochanter to greater trochanter) characters unknown in either of these well established ankylosaurian families.

Kirkland (1998*a*) acknowledged that the mixture of features exhibited by *Gastonia* seems to suggest a chimera, possessing an ankylosaurid type head joined to a nodosaurid type body. However, following a preliminary cladistic analysis, Kirkland (1998*a*) determined

Gastonia burgei, CEUM 1236, fusion of sacral shield.

Gastonia

Gastonia burgei, miscellaneous armor including shoulder spines and tail plates.

that *Gastonia*— along with the Early Cretaceous genera *Hoplitosaurus*, *Hylaeosaurus*, and *Polacanthus*, and the Jurassic genus *Mymoorapelta*— should be grouped together within the resurrected taxon Polacanthinae Wieland 1911. In early reports, the author (*e.g.*, Kirk-

land 1996) tended to regard the Polacanthinae as a subfamily of the Nodosauridae. However, although Kirkland (1998*a*) subsequently admitted that it was difficult to deduce whether this clade is more closely related to the Nodosauridae or Ankylosauridae, the preliminary analysis resulted in finding Polacanthinae to be a monophyletic group nested within Ankylosauridae (see "Systematics" chapter). This conclusion, Kirkland (1998*a*) pointed out, suggests that the Ankylosauria had a more complicated early radiation than previously believed, and necessitates a reevaluation of all the better known ankylosaurian genera in order to clarify the higher level systematics of this group.

Kirkland (1998*a*) produced what he considered to be a reasonably accurate reconstruction of the skeleton and armor of *Gastonia*, the latter based upon the kinds of armor preserved and by comparisons with that of other known related ankylosaurs including its closest relative, the European *Polacanthus*, and the North American *Mymoorapelta*: Two rings of cervical armor are present (as in all known ankylosaurs except *Sauropelta*). Numerous laterally compressed hollow-based plates, rather asymmetrical from side to side and most of them triangular in shape, seem to project

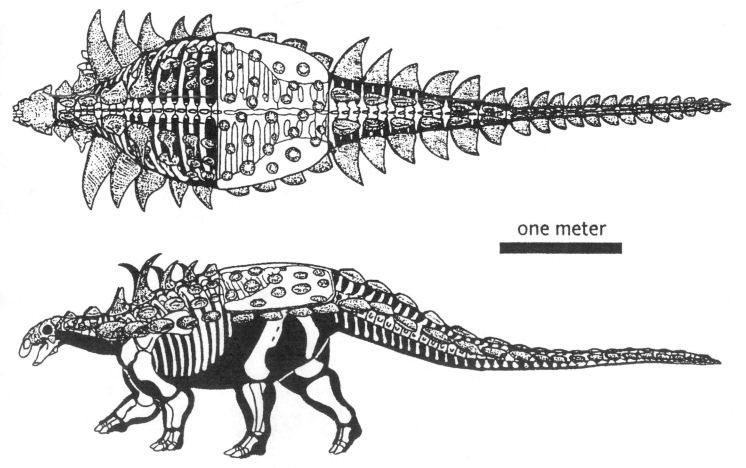

one meter

Gastonia burgei, reconstruction of skeleton in dorsal and left lateral views drawn by Tracy L. Ford, modified by James I. Kirkland. (After Kirkland 1998.)

Life restoration of heavily armored *Gastonia burgei* sculpted by Robert Gaston and Jennifer Schoenbach.

laterally along the tail. Much less abundant tall, asymmetrical spines with hollow bases were most likely located in the shoulder region. Elongate plates of intermediate abundance, having flaring, longer-than-tall hollow bases seem to have been located along the sides of the hips. The sacral shield of fused armor (similar to that in *Polacanthus*) possesses scutes, most of which are ornamented by a margin of radial ridges. Abundant tear-drop-shaped scutes may have formed bands across the back, as in *Gargoyleosaurus* (K. Carpenter, personal communication to Kirkland). In all, Kirkland (1998*a*) concluded that the above array of armor distinguishes *Gastonia* as one of the most ornate ankylosaurs ever described.

Based upon the anatomy and ornamentation of *Gastonia*, Kirkland (1998*a*) offered some speculations as to the possible range of behaviors of this dinosaur.

Regarding intraspecific competition, Kirkland (1998*a*) noted that this dinosaur would have presented an intimidating vision when seen from the front, with its large dorsal and lateral spines. Nevertheless, it seems to have been equipped for head-butting: The eyes were directed forward, an unusual condition in herbivorous animals; the skull is domed and thickened, its occipital condyle ventrally directed so that the snout was held downward; and the articulation between basisphenoid and pterygoids is well developed, allowing for some relative motion between the braincase and the rest of the solidly fused skull, this movement perhaps serving as a shock absorber.

The powerful tail, fortified with large triangular

plates, could effectively slash back and forth as a defensive weapon. As *Gastonia* seems to be the most common dinosaur preserved in the Yellow Cat Member of the Cedar Mountain Formation, Kirkland (1998*a*) further speculated that this heavily armored animal may have been virtually immune to predation by the largest predator known from that locality, the giant dromaeosaur *Utahraptor*.

Key references: Kirkland (1996, 1998*a*).

†GENYODECTES

Saurischia: Theropoda: Neotheropoda *incertae sedis*.

Holotype: MLP 26-39, incomplete premaxillae united to anteroventral sections of maxillae, anterior half of both dentaries with upper and lower teeth.

Comments: As noted by Bonaparte (1996*b*), the holotype (MLP 26-39) of the type species *Genyodectes serus*—a theropod of undetermined relationships with other theropods, from the ?Late Cretaceous of Argentina—was collected ca. 1895 by S. Roth.

Bonaparte observed in the specimen that the "distance between the alveolar border and the lower rim of the narial opening is rather large and resembles the abelisaurid snout condition"; also, both maxillary and dentary teeth are laterally compressed. However, Bonaparte found that MLP 26-39 offers "limited information to attempt a serious interpretation on the systematics of *Genyodectes*.

Erratum: The figure on p. 436 of *D:TE* depicting

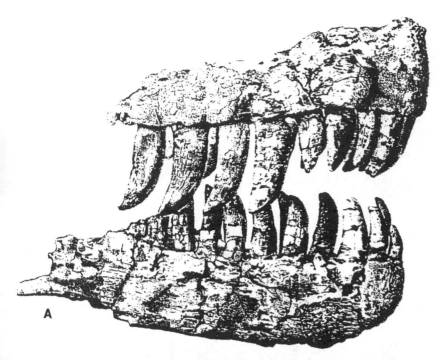

A

Genyodectes serus, MLP 26-39, holotype incomplete premaxillae and partial maxillae, right lateral view. (After Woodward 1901.)

the skull of *Genyodectes serus* should have been credited to Bonaparte (1978), not Woodward (1901).

Key references: Bonaparte (1978); Woodward (1901).

†GIGANOTOSAURUS

Saurischia: Theropoda: Neotheropoda: Tetanurae: Avetheropoda: Carnosauria: Allosauroidea.

Comments: Among the largest known theropods, *Giganotosaurus carolinii* is now known from additional but as yet undescribed material from the Lower Cretaceous of Argentina. These new remains indicate that this dinosaur may have been even larger than previously suspected (R. A. Coria, personal communication; see also *D:TE*).

Giganotosaurus carolinii, cast of partial holotype skeleton (MUCPvCH-1) reconstructed by Valley Anatomical Preparations, on display at The Academy of Natural Sciences of Philadelphia.

Photograph by Tosh Odano, courtesy Valley Anatomical Preparations, Mary J. Odano, and Don Lessem.

The first accurate life restoration of *Giganotosaurus* was prepared by artist Robert F. Walters. According to Walters (1996), as recounted in an abstract, the artist worked in close consultation with Rodolfo A. Coria, the paleontologist who, with Leonardo Salgado, first described this dinosaur (see Coria and Salgado 1995), and also with paleontologist Peter Dodson. Walters began his restoration by studying the original fossil material and also any other available images, these used as a basis to generate a reasonably accurate complete skeletal reconstruction. Musculature was then added with modern archosaurs — ratite birds and crocodilians — used as reference models, supplemented by earlier restorations of other theropods. Skin was based upon samples of fossilized skin impressions of *Carnotaurus*, another Argentinian theropod, supplied by José F. Bonaparte and Stephen A. Czerkas. Coloration, always hypothetical in reconstructing dinosaurs, was based on that of somewhat analogous modern animals and upon the advice of paleontologists.

A mounted cast reproduction of the reconstructed skeleton, made by Valley Anatomical Preparations under the supervision of Rodolfo A. Coria and Philip J. Currie, was exhibited in 1997 at The Academy of Natural Sciences of Philadelphia.

Key reference: Coria and Salgado (1995); Walters (1996).

GOJIRASAURUS   Carpenter 1997

Saurischia: Theropoda: Neotheropoda: "Cerato-sauria": ?Coelophysoidea.

Name derivation: "Gojira" [Japanese name for prehistoric monster of Japanese motion-picture *Gojira*, known in the United States as "Godzilla"] + Greek *sauros* = "lizard."

Type species: *G. quayi* Carpenter 1997.

Other species: [None.]

Occurrence: Cooper Canyon Formation of the Dockum Group (see Carpenter 1997 for explanation), New Mexico, United States.

Age: Late Triassic (early Norian).

Known material/holotype: UCM 47221, lateral tooth, cervical rib, two anterior dorsal ribs, posterior dorsal rib, four middorsal ribs, middorsal neural arch, anterior chevron, two ?gastralia, right scapula, right pubis, left tibia, metatarsal.

Diagnosis of genus (as for type species): Tooth serrations closely spaced, restricted to carina, cutting

Giganotosaurus carolinii, as painted by Robert F. Walters. The first accurate life restorations of this giant theropod dinosaur were done by Walters working under the supervision of vertebrate paleontologist Rodolfo A. Coria.

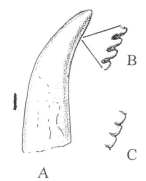

A

Gojirasaurus quayi, UCM 47221, holotype tooth (A), detail of serrations (B) compared with those (C) of *Coelophysis* (DMNH 32156). Scale = 5mm. (After Carpenter 1997.)

edges of serrations curving upwards as in *Saurornitholestes*; neural spines very tall relative to height of centrum as in *Ceratosaurus* (in contrast to *Coelophysis*, *Liliensternus*, *Syntarsus*, and *Herrerasaurus*); scapula expanded distally, with straight ventral margin as in *Coelophysis* and *Liliensternus* (not straplike as in *Her-* *rerasaurus*, or bowed as in *Ceratosaurus*); pubis with single large, oval obturator fenestra (not double as in *Syntarsus*, or notched as in *Liliensternus*); pubic apron narrow as in *Liliensternus* (unlike moderately wide as in *Coelophysis*, or wide as in *Staurikosaurus* and *Herrerasaurus*); distal end of pubis without "foot," slightly

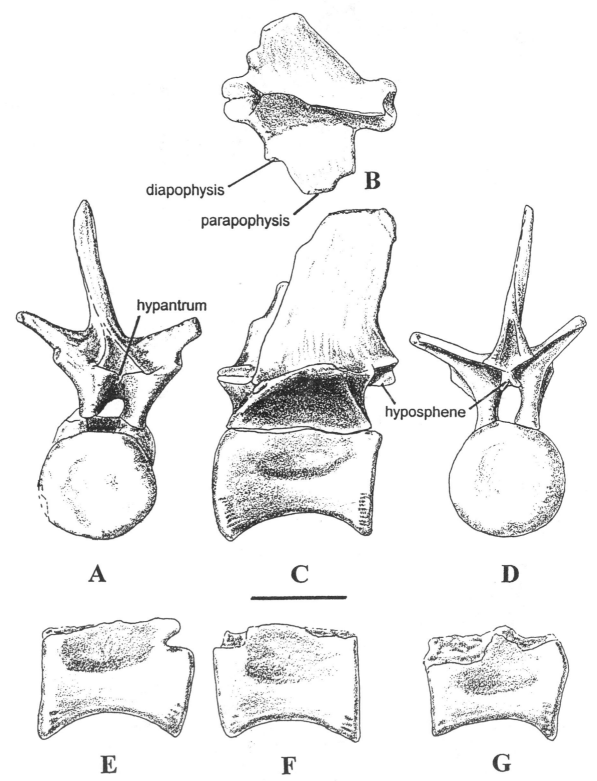

Gojirasaurus quayi, UCM 47221, holotype mid- or posterior dorsal vertebrae in A. anterior, B. dorsal, C. left lateral, and D. posterior views; E. centrum B, F. centrum C, and G. centrum D in lateral views. Scale = 5 cm. (After Carpenter 1997.)

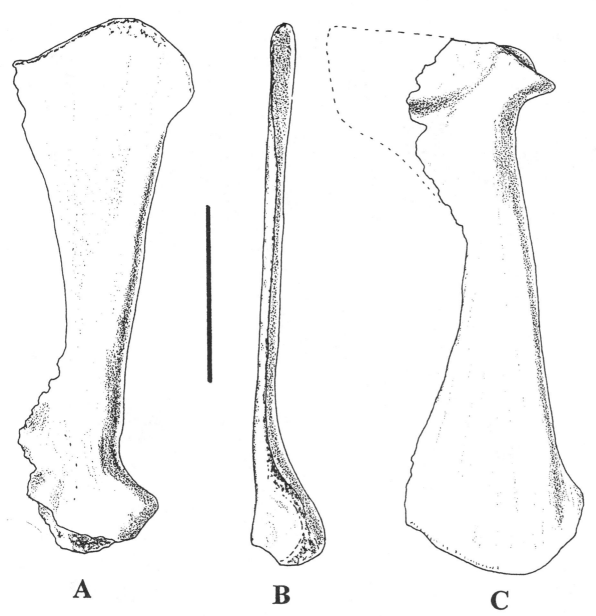

Gojirasaurus quayi, UCM 47221, holotype scapula in A. medial, B. dorsal, and C. lateral views. Scale = 10 cm. (After Carpenter 1997.)

A   **B**   **C**

expanded as in *Coelophysis*, more expanded than in *Liliensternus*; less so than in *Dilophosaurus*; medial tibial condyle larger than lateral condyle as in *Liliensternus*, condyles equal in size to those in *Dilophosaurus*, *Staurikosaurus*, and *Syntarsus* (lateral condyle larger in *Herrerasaurus* and *Chindesaurus*); astragalar facet well developed (unlike condition in *Staurikosaurus* and *Herrerasaurus*) (Carpenter 1997*a*).

Comments: One of the largest known Triassic theropods, *Gojirasaurus quayi* was founded upon a tooth and partial postcranial remains (UCM 47221; first mentioned by Carpenter and Parrish 1985, then Parrish and Carpenter 1986, and various subsequent authors including Hunt and Lucas 1989, Lucas and Hunt 1989, Parrish 1989, and Long and Murry 1995) recovered from the Canyon County Formation, Dockum Group (early Norian, based on magne-

tostratigraphy; see Molina-Garza, Geissman and Lucas 1993), "from a purple weathering mudstone along the upper rim of the badlands along the eastern side of the Revuelto Creek drainage in Quay County," eastern New Mexico (Carpenter 1997*a*).

As observed by Carpenter, the neural arches of the specimen are not fused to the centra, the pelvic bones are not fused together, and the astragalus is not fused to the tibia — signs, according to the author, that UCM 47221 represents an immature individual. The estimated 5.5-meter (nearly 19 feet) length of the specimen, based on the body proportions of *Coelophysis*, is, therefore, below that of an adult; it is substantially greater than the estimated lengths of *Eoraptor* and *Procompsognathus* (1 meter each), *Staurikosaurus* (2.1 meters), *Coelophysis* (2.8 meters), *Herrerasaurus* and *Liliensternus* (3.8 meters each), and *Chindesaurus*

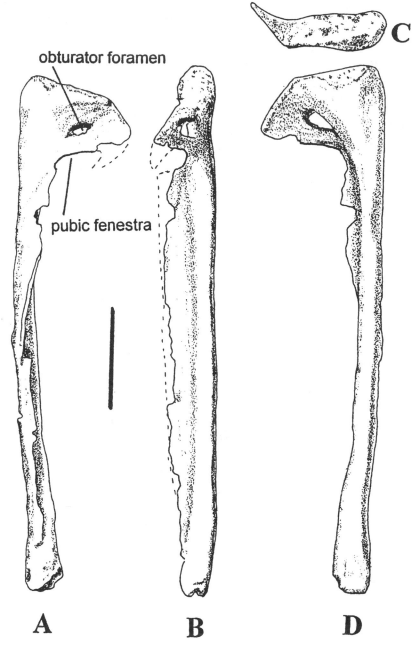

obturator foramen

pubic fenestra

A   **B**   **C**   **D**

Gojirasaurus quayi, UCM 47221, holotype right pubis in A. medial, B. posterior, C. proximal, and D. lateral views. Scale = 10 cm. (After Carpenter 1997.)

(4 meters), and approximately the same as that of *Halticosaurus longotarsus.*

Carpenter pointed out that the recognition of *G. quayi* increases the diversity of North American theropod dinosaurs of the Late Triassic, and supports the observations of previous authors (Hunt 1991; Heckert and Lucas 1995; Hunt, Sullivan, Lucas and Heckert 1995) that the early evolution of theropods was rapid.

According to Carpenter, UCM 47221 shares several apomorphies (*e.g.,* transverse process on neural arch extending length of centrum; parapophysis and diapophysis located on transverse process; "web" of bone connecting tuberculum and capitulum of ribs;

and long, narrow pubis) with other "ceratosauromorphs." The genus most closely resembles *Liliensternus* (see Parrish and Carpenter), *Coelophysis,* and *Syntarsus.*

Key references: Carpenter (1997*a*); Carpenter and Parrish (1985); Hunt and Lucas (1989); Long and Murry (1995); Lucas and Hunt (1989); Parrish (1989); Parrish and Carpenter (1986).

†**GORGOSAURUS** Lambe 1914 — (=?*Daspletosaurus,* ?*Deinodon*)
Saurischia: Theropoda: Neotheropoda: Tetanurae: Avetheropoda; Coelurosauria: Manuraptoriformes: Arctometatarsalia: Tyrannosauridae: Tyrannosaurinae.
Name derivation: Greek *gorgos* = "terrible" + Greek *sauros* = "lizard."
Type species: *G. libratus* Lambe 1914.
Other species: ?*G. sternbergi* Matthew and Brown 1923.
Occurrence: Dinosaur Park Formation, Alberta, Canada; Dinosaur Park Formation, Montana, Fruitland Formation, Kirtland Shale, New Mexico, United States.
Age: Late Cretaceous (middle–late Campanian).
Known material: At least nine partial skulls, three incomplete skeletons, three fragmentary skulls with associated partial postcrania, six relatively complete skulls, teeth, postcrania.
Holotype: CMN [formerly NMC] 2120, skull with associated postcrania, including most of vertebral column, pectoral, and pelvic arches, at least one forearm, hind limbs, ?entire series of gastralia.

Diagnosis of genus (as for type species): Premaxillary openings close to maxillary fenestra; maxillary opening oval, separated by wide bar of maxillary from antorbital fenestra; lacrimal horn very well developed; surangular very large; distal end of scapula broadening gradually; acromion of scapula very deep; tibia more robust than in *Albertosaurus sarcophagus* (Carpenter 1992).

Diagnosis of ?*G. sternbergi:* [No modern diagnosis published.]

Comments: *Gorgosaurus,* the tyrannosaurid genus known from the most collected specimens, was established on a well-preserved, almost complete skeleton (the first Cretaceous theropod specimen found with manus or complete set of abdominal ribs) and skull (CMN 2120), discovered in the summer of 1913 by Charles M. Sternberg in the former Judith River Formation (now recognized as a separate unit, the Dinosaur Park Formation), near Berry Creek, at Red Deer River, Alberta, Canada. The type specimen of what would be named *G. libratus* was recovered later that season by the Geological Survey of Canada,

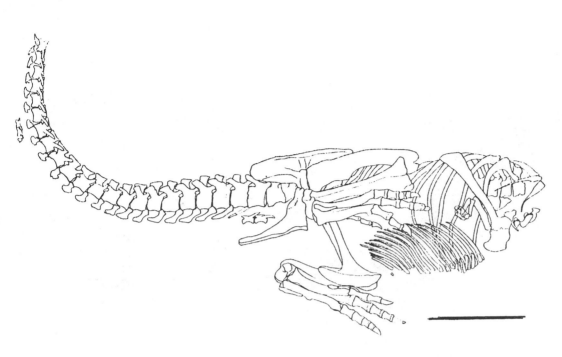

Gorgosaurus libratus, holotype skeleton CMN 2120 as found, drawn by Rudolph Weber and Arthur Miles under the direction of Lawrence M. Lambe. Scale = 90 cm. (After Lambe 1914.)

partly under the direction of chief preparator and collector C. M. Sternberg's father, Charles H. Sternberg.

Lambe (1914a) briefly described the forearm of the specimen, pointing out that the manus has only two digits (with the tiny remnant of digit III appressing II), but did not yet name the material. Subsequently, Lambe (1914b) designated CMN 2120 to be the holotype of the new genus and species *Gorgosaurus libratus.*

G. libratus was originally diagnosed by Lambe (1914b) as follows: Large carnivorous dinosaur reaching length of approximately 29 feet [8.25 meters]; head narrow, moderately elongate; trunk compact; forelimbs very small; hind limbs long, robust; tail almost half total length of animal, tapering, and with only slight lateral compression; skull with large antorbital opening, preceded by very small opening in center of a depressed area; no triangular alveolar plates on inner sides of jaws; foramen in surangular, far back and near its upper border; no presphenial; teeth trenchant, powerful, four premaxillary, 13 maxillary, and 14 dentary; first maxillary tooth similar in shape and size to those of premaxilla; vertebrae slightly amphicoelous, concave on sides and beneath; two cervicodorsal, five sacral, and about 34 caudal vertebrae; neural spines short throughout vertebral column; chevrons short, beginning with first caudal; transverse processes of caudal vertebrae decreasing in size to and ending with fourteenth vertebra; anterior zygapophyses of posterior caudals greatly lengthened; scapula longer than forelimb; humerus twice length of ulna;

two digits (II and III) to manus, with phalangeal formula of 2 II, 3 III, terminal phalanges being clawbones; metacarpal IV represented by proximal vestigial bone; ilium elongate, platelike, with flat upper outline and rounded ends; preacetabular part shorter than hinder portion, of which both are strengthened on outer surface by a prominent, overhanging flange running horizontally at midheight; ischium terminating narrowly below; pubis ending in horizontally expanded "foot," posterior extension of which is greater; femur about same length as tibia; metatarsal I represented distally by short vestigial bone, metatarsal V in similar manner proximally; pes with four clawed digits, viz. Numbers I, II, III and IV, with phalangeal formula of 2 I, 3 II, 4 III, and 5 IV; ventral ribs composite, 16 in number, overlapping at longitudinal midline of body, and bearing distally slender, closely applied supplementaries.

Until the 1970s, the name *Gorgosaurus* was a familiar one in the paleontological literature as well as in popular books. Although initially regarded as a valid genus, its generic status was questioned by Russell (1970) in his study of tyrannosaurs from the Late Cretaceous of western Canada. Russell interpreted *Gorgosaurus* as a junior synonym of the slightly smaller and geologically younger *Albertosaurus* (see *Albertosaurus* entries, *D:TE* and this volume). Russell then stated the following: "The generotypic species of *Albertosaurus* is based on two crania found at different stratigraphic levels within the Edmonton Formation. These specimens so closely resemble skulls referable to

Gorgosaurus

Gorgosaurus libratus, 26-foot long referred skeleton (AMNH 5458) collected by Barnum Brown on the Red Deer River, Alberta, Canada, mounted by Brown (*see in* Matthew and Brown 1923) as if running in pursuit of hadrosaurs. This exhibit is significant as one of the earliest mountings of a dinosaur skeleton in a dynamic and active pose.

Gorgosaurus libratus, from the Oldman Formation, that there can be little question of their generic identity. *Gorgosaurus* is therefore considered as a junior synonym of *Albertosaurus*, and *A. libratus* is in all probability the immediate ancestor of the Edmonton form." More recently, however, Russell's referral of *Gorgosaurus* to *Albertosaurus* has been challenged.

Bakker, Williams and Currie 1988, in their paper naming and describing the so-called "pygmy tyrannosaur" *Nanotyrannus* (see entry, *D:TE*; also *Tyrannosaurus* entry, this volume) considered *Gorgosaurus* to be a genus distinct from *Albertosaurus*. As the authors (Bakker, Currie and Williams) were to demonstrate in an intended subsequent (cited as "in press," but not yet published) paper, "the genus *Albertosaurus* is distinct from the genus *Gorgosaurus*, and these two genera, plus *Tarbosaurus* and *Tyrannosaurus*, make a clade distinct from *Daspletosaurus*. Later, Currie (1992) listed *Gorgosaurus* as a distinct genus, adding that further description and revision of this taxon was required.

Carpenter (1992), pointing out that the holotype and paratype skulls of *A. sarcophagus* are incomplete and crushed, questioned their comparison with *A. libratus* skulls; and, noting various differences (see *Albertosaurus* entry, *D:TE*) between the skulls of these

two species, concluded that *A. sarcophagus* and *A. libratus* may represent different genera, though a final decision on their separation issue should await a complete review of *A. sarcophagus* by Currie based on new skeletons. Also, Olshevsky (1992) listed *Gorgosaurus* as a genus distinct from *Albertosaurus*.

Holtz (1994a) later stated that further work in preparation by Bakker, Currie and Carpenter could justify the reinstatement of *Gorgosaurus*. Later, in a brief preliminary report on a new analysis of the Tyrannosauridae, Holtz (1997) found no support that *A. sarcophagus* and *G. libratus* "were phylogenetically closer to each other than to other advanced tyrannosaurids, so the original generic name of the Judith River form is restored."

Other workers (see references in Currie and Padian 1997; Makovicky and Currie 1998; others) largely have come to regard *Gorgosaurus* as its own valid genus. Consequently, all references to *Albertosaurus libratus* (and all pictures labeled as such, with the probable exception of the skeleton mounted at The Field Museum; see *Daspletosaurus* entry) in *D:TE* should now be considered *Gorgosaurus*.

Taxa that have been referred to *G. libratus* include: *Laelaps incrassatus* [*nomen dubium*] Cope 1876, based on teeth collected from supposed Fort Union beds [=Dinosaur Park Formation], Montana, *L. falculus* [*nomen dubium*] Cope 1876, based on several teeth (not figured), *L. hazenianus* Cope 1876 [*nomen dubium*], *Ornithomimus grandis* Marsh 1890 [*nomen dubium*], and *Dryptosaurus kenabekides* Hay 1899 [*nomen dubium*].

?*Gorgosaurus sternbergi*, a species named and described by Matthew and Brown (1923) and often considered to be a junior synonym of *G. libratus* (see below), is somewhat problematic. ?*G. sternbergi* was based on an almost complete skeleton (AMNH 5664)—missing only the tail, this being the most complete type specimen for any North American tyrannosaurid—discovered by Charles H. Sternberg in the "Judith River" [=Dinosaur Park] Formation at Red Deer River.

Matthew and Brown originally characterized this species as follows: Smaller than and having more slender proportions than *G. libratus*; jaws much less massive, muzzle more slender, maxilla more elongate and shallow, orbital fenestra more circular; tibia considerably longer than femur. However, Matthew and Brown noted that these characters might have ontogenetic significance, as AMNH 5664 represents a juvenile individual in which various elements (*e.g.*, the bones of the pelvis) are not co-ossified.

Over the years, opinions have differed regarding the validity of ?*G. sternbergi* and the interpretation of its elements. Gilmore (1946*a*) interpreted the slenderness of the muzzle in AMNH 5664 as a consequence of crushing. Russell observed that the sutures between the skull roof elements are "widely open, and there is nothing in the morphology of the specimen to suggest that it is not an *A. libratus* approximately two-thirds grown." Russell further noted of the skull of AMNH 5664 that "the supraoccipital alae of the parietals are only about one-fourth as large as in adults, indicating that these crests become more powerfully developed with maturity."

In the years following Russell's referral of ?*G. sternbergi* to *G. libratus* [=*Albertosaurus libratus* of his usage], that synonymy has been questioned. Paul (1988*b*), in his book on predatory dinosaurs, interpreted the holotype skull of *G. sternbergi* as probably that of a juvenile individual. More significantly, Paul noted that the orbital horns of AMNH 5664 are more similar (*i.e.*, "more horizontal,

rectangular, and longer") to those of the skull of **Gorgosaurus** FMNH PR308 (see *Daspletosaurus* entry; also, photographs in *D:TE*) than to most of the skulls assigned to *G. libratus*, including the holotype of that species (this observation perhaps inadvertently implying that ?*G. sternbergi* might actually have affinities with *Daspletosaurus* rather than *Gorgosaurus*). Paul (but not Russell) further observed that the teeth in AMNH 5664 "are literally larger than those of the big specimen" (*i.e.*, FMNH PR308), this suggesting that ?*G. sternbergi* might be a valid species, or, as shown by some skulls apparently representing a growth series, that replacement teeth in such dinosaurs got smaller during ontogeny as an individual approached adult size. In a later personal communication to Olshevsky (1991), Paul expressed his opinion that ?*G. sternbergi* may be a juvenile *G. libratus* or possibly "represent a different tyrannosaurid genus altogether." Consequently, Olshevsky, in his listing of archosaurian taxa, treated *G. sternbergi* as a valid genus and species.

Subsequent workers have been fairly noncommittal regarding *G. sternbergi*. Molnar, Kurzanov and Dong (1990), in their review of "carnosaurs," considered ?*G. sternbergi* to be a possible junior synonym of *G. libratus* [=*A. libratus* of their usage]. In a guidebook to the revamped dinosaur halls at the American Museum of Natural History,

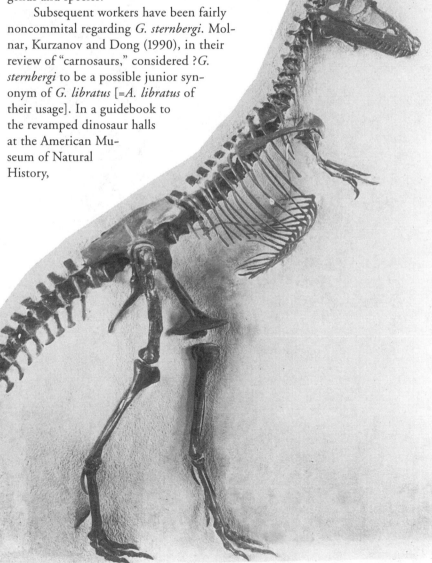

?*Gorgosaurus sternbergi*, AMNH 5664, holotype skeleton (juvenile). This specimen may belong to *G. libratus* or to some other tyrannosaurid taxon (possibly *Daspletosaurus*). The species was named for its collector, Charles H. Sternberg.

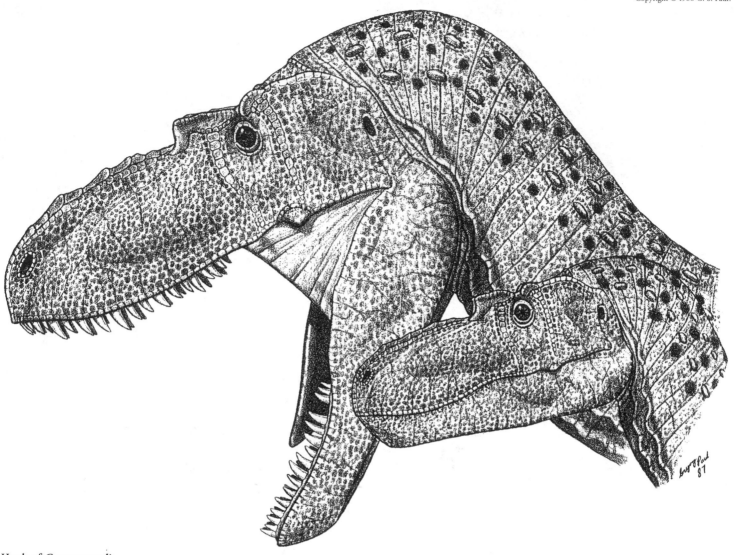

Heads of *Gorgosaurus libratus* and the smaller ?*G. sternbergi*. Illustration by Gregory S. Paul (from *Predatory Dinosaurs of the World*).

Dingus, Gaffney, Norell and Sampson (1995) identified a photograph of the holotype as *G. libratus* [=*A. libratus* of their usage], but noted that the referral of the smaller skeleton to that species "has not been demonstrated conclusively."

For the present, then, ?*G. sternbergi* is included herein as a tentatively valid species of *Gorgosaurus*, although it might also be referable to another genus.

Cooley (1997) reported in *Paleo Horizons*, a publication of Dinamation International Society, that DIS had located — based upon research by Philip J. Currie of the Royal Tyrrell Museum of Palaeontology — in August 1997 a lost and important dinosaur quarry discovered in 1910 by Barnum Brown for the American Museum of Natural History, from which Brown had recovered nine *Gorgosaurus* specimens. Although the material collected by Brown was never formally described and published, Currie regarded it as very important, as some of the remains were articulated

leg bones, this condition suggesting that the animals may have died together and, if so, lived together in a social group. Currie estimated that Brown only collected about 25 percent of this tyrannosaurid material; further excavations will resume at a later date.

Note: The species *Gorgosaurus lancinator* Maleev 1955 was referred by Carpenter (1992) to the new genus *Maleevosaurus*; and *G. lancensis* Gilmore 1946 was referred to the new genus *Nanotyrannus* by Bakker *et al.* (1988). Both of these taxa were later regarded in a preliminary report by Carr (1996) as juveniles of *Tyrannosaurus* (see *Tyrannosaurus* entry).

Erratum: The figure on p. 99 of *D:TE* should have had this caption: "*Gorgosaurus libratus*, holotype skeleton CMN [formerly NMC] 2120, drawn by Rudolph Weber and Arthur Miles under the direction of Lawrence M. Lambe. (After Lambe 1914.)"

Key references: Bakker, Williams and Currie (1988); Carpenter (1992); Carr (1996); Cope (1876);

Photograph by Fernando E. Novas, courtesy Museo Argentino de Ciencias Naturales.

An "unnamed gryposaur," the holotype skeleton of *"Kritosaurus" australis* mounted at the Museo Argentino de Ciencias Naturales.

Currie (1992); Dingus, Gaffney, Norell and Sampson (1995); Holtz (1994*a*, 1997); Lambe (1914*a*, 1914*b*); Makovicky and Currie (1998); Matthew and Brown (1923); Molnar, Kurzanov and Dong (1990); Olshevsky (1991, 1992); Paul (1988*b*); Russell (1970).

†GRYPOSAURUS

Ornithischia: Genasauria: Cerapoda: Ornithopoda: Euornithopoda: Iguanodontia: Euiguanodontia: Dryomorpha: Ankylopollexia: Hadrosauridae: Euhadrosauria: Hadrosaurinae.

Comments: In 1990, Weishampel and Horner regarded as an "unnamed gryposaur" the species *"Kritosaurus" australis*, which Bonaparte, Franchi, Powell and Sepúlveda (1984) had founded upon an incomplete skeleton (MACN-RN 2) collected by José F. Bonaparte and assistants in 1984–1986 from the Los Alamos Formation (Campanian), Río Negro Province, Argentina.

The type specimen of this species includes the posterior part of the skull, a postorbital, some isolated teeth, cervical, dorsal, sacral, and caudal vertebrae, a few ribs, incomplete sternum, both ilia, pubes and ischia, and an incomplete femur. Referred specimens include most of a braincase, several vertebrae, and ribs (MACN-RN 143); an incomplete skull (MACN-RN 144), including the frontal region with its ventral projection fairly well preserved, and incomplete temporal and occipital areas; 11 dorsal and 6 caudal vertebrae, a radius, ulna, the distal portion of a femur, 2 metatarsi, ribs, and a predentary fragment (MACN-RN 145); several vertebrae, an ilium, fragment of ischium, a scapula, and ribs (MACN-RN 146); also, fragmentary remains representing several more individuals. The cast skeleton (see *D:TE* for photographs) mounted at the Museo Argentino de Ciencias Naturales in Buenos Aires is a composite (Bonaparte 1996*b*).

In his preliminary report, Bonaparte found the morphological similarities of this species to be quite similar to the North American species *Gryposaurus* [=*Kritosaurus* of his usage] *notabilis*, "not only in every detail of the pelvic bones and sacrum, but also in the morphology of the frontal and occipital regions of the skull, the scapula, sternum, most of the femur, etc."

However, Bonaparte also noted differences in the distal portion of the femur, the supracondylar canal being roofed in *"K." australis*, but open in the American species. Other differences were perceived "in the shape of the coracoid, the glenoid cavity of the scapula, etc."

Key references: Bonaparte (1996*b*); Bonaparte, Franchi, Powell and Sepúlveda (1984); Weishampel and Horner (1990).

GUAIBASAURUS Bonaparte and Ferigolo 1998
Saurischia: ?Theropoda.
Type species: *G. dandelariai*

Other species: [None.]

Occurrence: Caturrita Formation, Río Grande do Sul, Brazil.

Age: Late Triassic (?late Carnian).

Known material: Two incomplete skeletons.

Holotype: Incomplete skeleton.

Diagnosis of genus: [None yet published.]

Comments: The new primitive saurischian *Guaibasaurus dandelariai*—named and informally described in an abstract—was founded upon two incomplete skeletons collected from a fine-grained fluvial sandstone in the Caturrita Formation (dated as of probable Late Carnian age, based on the occurrence of the dicynodont *Jachaleria*, archosauromorph *Proterochampsa*, cynodont *Exaeretodon*, and rhynchosaur *Scaphonyx*, suggesting "the late Ischigualastian reptilian-age"), near the city of Candelaria, in the state of Río Grande do Sul, in southern Brazil (Bonaparte and Ferigolo 1998).

Although Bonaparte and Ferigolo did not diagnose this taxon, the authors noted that derived characters are present in the distal portion of the tibia. As in *Herrerasaurus*, this section of the bone "is almost square, with a well-defined, ventrally projecting posterior process." Size disparity between the astragalus and calcaneum is great, the ventral side of the calcaneum having a medially directed process. The fifth metatarsal is much reduced and lacks phalanges; metatarsal I is strong and well developed; metatarsal III is almost half as long as the tibia. The tibia and femur have approximately the same length. The pubis is long, laminar, and anterodorsally exposed. The ischium is long and possesses a reduced proximoventral lamina. The ilium and femur are somewhat primitive, the ilium lacking a preacetabular blade, the acetabular portion having a small reduction of the internal wall and pronounced *crista superacetabularis*.

As observed by the authors, this new type species differs from the primitive theropods *Staurikosaurus* and *Herrerasaurus* in the shape of its ilium, which has a prosauropod-like posterior projection, and also in that of the pubis, which lacks an incipient or defined twisting, and also lacks a pubic "foot." The coracoid is low and anteroposteriorly elongated. As in *Eoraptor*, the distal portion of the scapula is expanded.

According to Bonaparte and Ferigolo, this new dinosaur, in addition to other early dinosaurs already described from Argentina, "suggest that a significant radiation of primitive saurischians developed, prior to the dominance of the prosauropods," in the western part of Gondwana.

To date of this writing, *G. dandelariai* awaits formal description.

Key reference: Bonaparte and Ferigolo (1998).

†HADROSAURUS

Ornithischia: Genasauria: Cerapoda: Ornithopoda: Euornithopoda: Iguanodontia: Euiguanodontia:

Cast of incomplete holotype skeleton (ANSP 10005) of *Hadrosaurus foulkii,* body outline indicating the possible life appearance of the entire animal. This type species was the first dinosaur of any kind known in North America from good fossil material.

Photograph by the author, courtesy The Academy of Natural Sciences of Philadelphia.

Hadrosaurus foulkii (right), cast of restored skeleton (including holotype ANSP 10005, originally displayed at The Smithsonian Institution; see *D:TE* for photograph) made by Benjamin Waterhouse Hawkins in 1874, as exhibited in 1894 at the Columbian Museum with skeletal casts of the mammals *Uintatherium* (left) and *Megaloceras* (middle).

Dryomorpha: Ankylopollexia: Hadrosauridae: Euhadrosauria: Hadrosaurinae.

Age: Late Cretaceous (early middle Campanian).

Comments: *Hadrosaurus foulkii*, a species of duckbilled dinosaur for which the skull is not known, is historically important as the first North American dinosaur based upon adequate skeletal material.

Recently, Gallagher (1997) redated the dinosaur-bearing beds in Haddonfield, New Jersey, that yielded the type material of *H. foulkii*. Sampling the shellbed in the Woodbury Formation that yielded the original specimens, and subjecting the shell material to strontium analysis at Rutgers University's Department of Geological Sciences, where a mass spectrograph was utilized, Gallagher found these beds to have an estimate age of 79.5 million years ± one million years, based on ratios given by Peter Sugarman (see preliminary report of Gallagher, Sugarman and Feigenson 1996), the Woodbury Formation thereby being correlative with the Claggett Transgression of the Western Interior Seaway (preliminary report of Gallagher and Paris 1996).

Note: Gallagher reported that various hadrosaur specimens, representing growth stages, have been found in the Atlantic Coastal Plain Upper Cretaceous deposits. Juvenile and adult specimens have been found at the same site in Monmouth County, New Jersey, and isolated remains have been recovered from localities in both southern New Jersey and southeastern North Carolina. Based on this evidence, Gallagher speculated "that hadrosaurs came down to coastal ecosystems to take advantage of the high biomass productivity. They may have brought juveniles with them down from nesting areas which at maximum transgressive phases were probably located to the northwest in the Piedmont uplands.

Key references: Gallagher (1997); Gallagher and Parris (1996); Gallagher, Sugarman and Feigenson (1996).

†HAPLOCANTHOSAURUS

Saurischia: Sauropodomorpha: Sauropoda: Eusauropoda: Neosauropoda: Macronaria.

Diagnosis of genus: Dorsal vertebrae having neural arches lacking anterior central diapophyseal lamina, with elongate infrapostzygapophyseal laminae; dorsal diapophyses projecting dorsolaterally at 45 degrees, approaching height of neural spines; scapular blade with dorsally and ventrally expanded distal end (Wilson and Sereno 1998).

Comments: One of the rarest of Morrison Formation sauropod genera, *Haplocanthosaurus* has generally been regarded as a member of the "Cetiosauridae," a paraphyletic taxon once regarded as a valid family embracing a group of somewhat primitive and related sauropods (see "Systematics" chapter).

In assessing the phylogenetic relationships of the new species *Rebbachisaurus tessonei* (referred by Wilson and Sereno 1998 to *Rayososaurus*; see entry), Calvo and Salgado (1995) also interpreted *Haplocanthosaurus* as being paraphyletic. According to these authors, the referred species *H. delfsi* shares with the type species, *H. priscus*, plus "Diplodocimorpha" (see "Systematics" chapter; also Wilson and Sereno) the following characters: 1. Height of neural arch in anterior dorsal vertebrae at least three times longer than length of centra; 2. dorsal centra in posterior dorsal vertebrae amphyplatyan or amphicoelous; and 3. midprespinal lamina in posterior dorsals occupying entire length of spine.

H. priscus was regarded by Calvo and Salgado as the sister group of the Diplodocimorpha, possessing a widely expanded distal scapular blade (ratio of maximum width/minimum width being greater than 3). As no skull material is known from either of the above species, Calvo and Salgado suggested that several cranial characters considered by them to be diagnostic for Diplodocimorpha may be synapomorphies of a larger group.

In a later preliminary report on a new phylogenetic analysis of the Sauropoda (see "Systematics" chapter), Upchurch (1997) regarded *Haplocanthosaurus* as the sister taxon to the Neosauropoda.

More recently, Wilson and Sereno (1998), while reassessing a number of sauropod taxa, criticized Calvo and Salgado's opinion that *Haplocanthosaurus* is a paraphyletic taxon. According to these authors, the criteria used by Calvo and Salgado, based on the relative width of the scapular blade, were insufficient to warrant such an assessment. Also, the proximal end of the scapular blade in *H. delfsi* was restored (McIntosh and Williams 1988), the ratio in this specimen, consequently, being unknown, while the preserved portion of the distal blade resembles that in *H. priscus*.

Therefore, Wilson and Sereno defined *Haplocanthosaurus* as both species *H. priscus* and *H. delfsi*, their common ancestor, and all of its descendants.

Key reference: Calvo and Salgado (1995); McIntosh and Williams (1988); Upchurch (1977); Wilson and Sereno (1998).

HUDIESAURUS   Dong 1997

Saurischia: Sauropodomorpha: Sauropoda: Eusauropoda: Neosauropoda: Macronaria: Titanosauriformes: Somphospondyli: Euhelopodidae.

Name derivation: Chinese Pingying *Hudie* = "butterfly" + Greek *sauros* = "lizard."

Type species: *H. sinojapanorum* Dong 1997.

Other species: [None.]

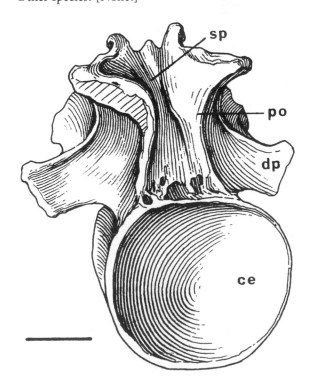

Hudiesaurus sinojapanorum, IVPP V. 11120, holotype dorsal vertebra, posterior view. Scale = 15 cm. (After Dong 1997.)

Occurrence: Kalazha Formation, Xinjiang Uygur Autonomous Region, China.

Age: Late Jurassic.

Known material: Various postcrania, including limb and feet elements.

Holotype: IVPP V. 11120, nearly complete anterior dorsal vertebra.

Diagnosis of genus (as for type species): Gigantic sauropod; top of neural spine of anterior dorsals forming U-shaped shallow cleft; winglike process arising between bases of postzygapophyses and lateral margins of neural spine; neural spine bearing short, anteriorly directed swordlike process on anterior face; lateral faces of centrum with deep pleurocoel; centrum

Photograph by the author.

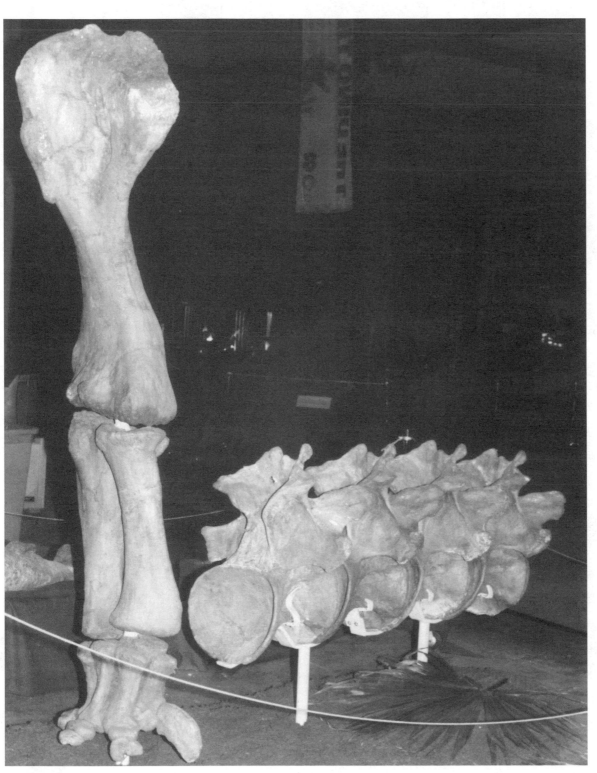

Hudiesaurus sinojapano-rum, IVPP V. 11121, referred right forelimb and foot (left) and articulated dorsal vertebrae (right), displayed at the third Dinofest™ event, held in Philadelphia in 1998.

I

having keel developed along midline on ventral surface (Dong 1997g).

Comments: The new type species *Hudiesaurus sinojapanorum* was established upon a dorsal vertebra (IVPP V. 11120) collected in 1993 during the Sino-Japanese Silk Road Dinosaur Expedition to the Kalazha Formation (Upper Jurassic), Langgou, Qiketia area, Shanshan County of the Turpan Basin (Dong 1997f), Xinjiang Uygur Autonomous Region, China. Referred remains from the same locality include a complete right forelimb comprising humerus, radius,

Photograph by the author, courtesy University Museum, Oxford.

Casts of the holotype skeleton (IRSNB 1534) of *Iguanodon bernissartensis* were made for exhibition at a number of museums, including the Natural History Museum, London, and the Manchester Museum, Manchester, England. This one is on display at the University Museum, Oxford University, Oxford, England.

ulna, and manus elements (metacarpals I-V, phalanges I-2, II-2, III-2, IV-2, and V-1) (IVPP V. 11121-1), and four teeth (IVPP V. 11121-2) (Dong 1997g).

As measured by Dong (1997g), the holotype dorsal centrum of *H. sinojapanorum* has a length of 42 centimeters, 1.5 times longer than the comparable element in the 22-meter (about 75-feet) long mounted holotype skeleton of *Mamenchisaurus hochuanensis*, which was the largest sauropod known from China when it was first described. From these dimensions, Dong (1997g) estimated the total length of *H. sinojapanorum* to be about 30 meters (more than 100 feet) in length.

Key references: Dong (1997f, 1997g).

†IGUANODON

Ornithischia: Genasauria: Cerapoda: Ornithopoda: Euornithopoda: Iguanodontia: Euiguanodontia: Dryomorpha: Ankylopollexia: Iguanodontidae.

Comments: Among the best known of all ornithopod dinosaurs is the spiked-thumbed *Iguanodon*, the second dinosaurian genus to be discovered and named (by Gideon Algernon Mantell in 1825).

As has been documented in numerous accounts, the type species, *I. anglicus* (originally spelled *I. anglicum*) was founded upon some large nonassociated teeth found in the Wealden (Lower Cretaceous) of Sussex (not Kent, as incorrectly stated in *D:TE*), England, during the early 1820s. The teeth resembled those of the modern iguana lizard, hence the name *Iguanodon* (meaning "iguana tooth"). Since that original discovery was made, a number of species have been referred to this genus, some of them based upon equally inadequate fossil materials. The best and most complete of the collected *Iguanodon* specimens are those belonging to the two species *I. bernissartensis* and *I. atherfieldensis* (see *D:TE* for details on all of the above).

Recently a joint formal application, cowritten by (now deceased) Alan J. Charig and Sandra D. Chapman, was submitted to the International Commission on Zoological Nomenclature (published as Case 3037 in the *Bulletin of Zoological Nomenclature*, 55 [2]. June, 1998, pp. 99–104). In their appeal, the authors related in great detail the confused taxonomic history of the genus *Iguanodon* and the various species that have been assigned to it.

Among the many salient and relevant facts pointed out by these authors are the following:

When Mantell (1825) first proposed his new genus *Iguanodon*, he failed to assign it a specific name, nor did he designate a type specimen for the genus. Mantell figured and described seven worn teeth recovered from the sandstone of the Tilgate Forest Beds at Cuckfield, West Sussex, and also mentioned some gigantic bones and vertebrae that he assumed to be those of *Iguanodon*, this latter material not identifiable in the Mantell Collection housed at the Natural History Museum, London.

Holl (1829) later proposed the nominal species *Iguanodon anglicum*, said to have been based upon teeth, several limb bones, and vertebrae collected from the Tilgate Forest in Sussex, this taxon thereby becoming the type species of *Iguanodon*. However, Holl did not describe or illustrate the specimens (though he referred to Mantell's figures of the seven teeth), specify them by catalog number, or select any of them as the holotype.

More recently, David B. Norman (1986), an authority on *Iguanodon* and its species, designated the dentary tooth of the seven syntype teeth originally figured by Mantell as the lectotype of the type species of the genus. At the same time, Norman corrected the species name to the masculine *I. anglicus*. Norman tentatively identified this tooth (plus six others of Mantell's original seven, regarded as paralectotypes, all seven teeth having been long misplaced) in the Palaeontology Department of the Natural History Museum, London. The dentary tooth was listed as BMNH 2392 in both Mantell's catalog and in the registry of the Natural History Museum (inaccurately cited by Norman as BMNH R 2392), London, formerly the British Museum (Natural History), which subsequently purchased Mantell's material.

According to Charig and Chapman, however, BMNH 2392 cannot with certainty be identified with the figures in Mantell's 1825 publication. There is no positive evidence regarding their provenance, and it is not possible, therefore, to know if they all originate from the same locality. Because all of these teeth are isolated, it is impossible to determine whether or not they belong to the same individual or even to the same species. There are differences between these figured teeth and also in teeth illustrated by Mantell in various subsequent publications, and none of them exhibits diagnostic features. In fact, an "examination of all these figures," Charig and Chapman observed, "and of tooth no. BMNH 2392 leads to the conclusion that the figures might be of several different teeth, possibly none of them being 2392. They all represent complete, fully grown dentary (lower) teeth of *Iguanodon*, somewhat worn down at their occlusal surface, but apparently differing in detail. Some are partly encased in rock, others are not; some of the drawings may have been reversed. Much depends upon the accuracy of the artist(s) who drew them."

The species *I. mantelli* was not, the authors further emphasized, founded upon the so-called Maidstone specimen (still bearing Mantell's original cata-

log number 179, but even now not appearing in the Natural History Museum register), an incomplete skeleton from Kent, England, still displayed at the Natural History Museum, London, as has generally been surmised (see *D:TE*). Rather, this species, proposed by Meyer (1832), was again based upon Mantell's original seven teeth.

According to Charig and Chapman, *I. bernissartensis* and *I. atherfieldensis* constitute the first species founded upon substantial type materials, with the former, more robust species—known from a wealth of specimens, some nearly complete and articulated—being the senior of these two taxa. The species *I. anglicus* and *I. mantelli*, to which no additional material has been referred and based upon indeterminate teeth, should be, therefore, regarded as *nomina nuda*.

Charig and Chapman requested the following:

1. That the ICZN utilize its plenary powers to a. "set aside all previous fixations of type species for the nominal genus *Iguanodon*" and designate *I. bernissartensis* (Boulenger, *see in* Beneden 1881) as the type species, and b. "to set aside all previous fixations of type specimens for the nominal species *Iguanodon bernissartensis*" and to designate IRSNB 1534, an almost complete articulated skeleton mounted at the Institut Royal des Sciences Naturelles de Belgique, Brussels—the holotype of *I. bernissartensis*—as the lectotype of the new type species;

2. to place the name *Iguanodon* on the Official List of Generic Names in Zoology; and

3. to place the name *bernissartensis* on the Official List of Specific Names in Zoology, as published in the binomen *Iguanodon bernissartensis* and as defined by the above-designated lectotype.

To date of this writing, the ICZN has not ruled upon the above application.

Key references: Boulenger *see in* Beneden (1881); Holl (1829); Mantell (1825); Meyer (1832); Norman (1986).

†INDOSAURUS

Saurischia: Theropoda: Neotheropoda: "Ceratosauria": Neoceratosauria: Abelisauroidea: Abelisauridae.

Comments: When Friedrich von Huene and Charles Alfred Matley first described the very large Indian theropod they named *Indosaurus*, they considered it to be allied with the Allosauridae (see also Chatterjee 1978).

Later, Molnar (1990), in noting similarities between this genus and the abelisaurid *Carnotaurus*, referred the Indian genus to the Abelisauridae. More

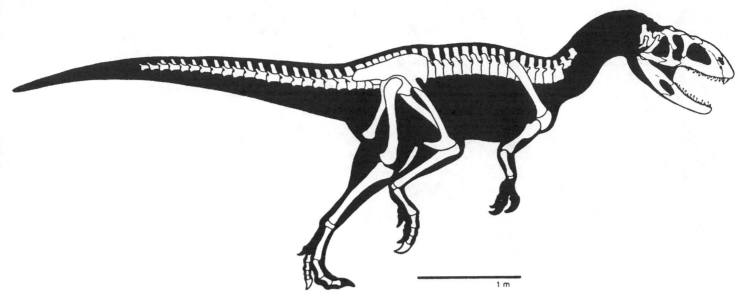

recently, Chatterjee and Rudra (1996) briefly reported the collection of "a *Carnotaurus*-like atlas-axis complex from the Lameta Group of Raiholi area" of India, evidence that supports Molnar's assessment of this genus.

Key references: Chatterjee (1978); Chatterjee and Rudra (1996); Huene and Matley (1933); Molnar (1990).

†INDOSUCHUS

Saurischia: Theropoda: Neotheropoda: "Ceratosauria": Neoceratosauria: Abelisauroidea: ?Abelisauridae.

Comments: Chatterjee and Rudra (1996) reported recently collected remains belonging to the Indian genus *Indosuchus* (and possibly to its type species, *I. raptorius*) from the Bara Simla Hill of

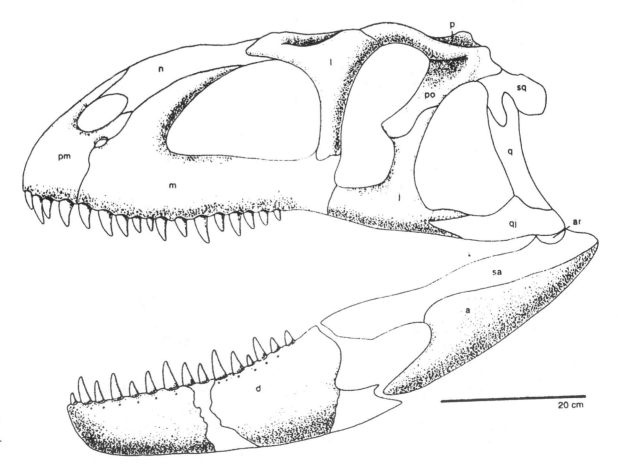

Jabalpur. This material includes a lacrimal, jugal, and the posterior part of the jaw (ISI R 163) and an almost complete skeleton (ISI R 401-454) from the Raiholi site at Gujrat, this specimen comprising disarticulated elements and missing much of the neck, the manuses, and end of the tail.

The authors described the composite skeleton (based on the above material, also on cranial specimens AMNH 1753, 1955, and 1960) thusly: Teeth laterally compressed and serrated, tooth crown extremely low, ratio of crown height to rostro-caudal width 1.5; vertebrae amphicoelous, lacking pleurocoels; scapulocoracoid narrow, with prominent acromial process; iliac blade with deep preacetabular and long postacetabular processes; pubis expanded distally to form "foot"; hind limb bones hollow, thin-walled, stout (resembling those bones in *Carnotaurus*); forelimb short relative to hind limb, ratio of femoral to humeral length about 2, forelimbs (unlike those of *Carnotaurus* and *Tyrannosaurus*) comparable in length to those in allosaurs; femur with spherical, inturned head with distinct neck, lesser trochanter fairly well developed but lower than greater trochanter; tibia robust, with distinct cnemial crest, the latter remaining unfused distally with astragalus; astragalus hemicylindrical in form, with relatively short ascending process.

According to Chatterjee and Rudra, *Indosuchus* seems to be closely related to the South American abelisaurid *Abelisaurus* and may also belong to the family Abelisauridae.

Key reference: Chatterjee and Rudra (1996).

†IRRITATOR—(=?*Angaturama*)

Saurischia: Theropoda: Neotheropoda: Tetanurae: Spinosauroidea: ?Spinosauridae.

Comments: The genus named *Irritator* remains a puzzling (and irritating) genus. In a review of Brazilian dinosaurs, Kellner (1996) criticized the original description of the type species *Irritator challengeri* by Martill, Cruickshank, Frey, Small and Clarke (1996). These authors had placed this taxon in its own manuraptoran family, the Irritatoridae, regarded by them as closely related to Spinosauridae.

From the illustration published by Martill *et al.*, Kellner judged that the type specimen might not yet have been fully prepared when the authors made their study; nor was it clear to Kellner if the matrix from several openings of the skull had been entirely removed before the illustration was made, or if the authors had merely indicated those openings on the picture without removing the matrix.

Kellner stated the following objections:

1. Martill *et al.* did not clarify why they regarded *I. challengeri* as belonging to the Manuraptora. The single character by which Gauthier (1986) diagnosed this group is the absence or reduction of the prefrontal, neither of which can be verified in *I. challengeri*, as the authors only listed this bone and did not illustrate it. Furthermore, Holtz (1994*a*) listed as a manuraptoran synapomorphy the "jugal expressed on the rim of the antorbital fenestra," that of *I. challengeri* apparently not participating in this fenestra.

2. The authors did not compare *I. challengeri* with *Angaturama limai*, a spinosaurid from the same deposit (see *Angaturama* entry) or *Baryonyx*, although they noted similarities between the teeth of *I. challengeri* and those of *Spinosaurus*. Also, Martill *et al.* noted that the mandible of *Spinosaurus* would "not fit with the dental margin of the maxilla and premaxilla" of *I. challengeri*, although in the latter the rostral part of the skull is not preserved.

3. As preliminary comparisons show that *I. challengeri* shares at least two synapomorphies (transverse section of teeth subcircular; external nares displaced backwards) with other spinosaurid taxa, this feature suggests that this species belongs to the Spinosauridae, with the Irritatoridae regarded as a junior synonym of this taxon.

According to Kellner, it is difficult to compare *I. challengeri* with *A. limai*, as both are based upon different parts of the skull. Both species, however, possess unserrated teeth and come from the same deposit, although the preserved posterior part of the skull of the latter seems to be higher and more laterally compressed than the preserved anterior part of the skull of *I. challengeri*. Both specimens may belong to the same taxon, although a positive synonymy cannot be made lacking additional material.

As subsequently noted by Charig and Milner (1997), *Irritator* shares with *Angaturama* elongated jaws, external nares that are set far back, and all tooth characters unique to Spinosauridae (*i.e*, teeth showing reduction in 1. compression of whole tooth in labio-lingual direction, 2. recurvature of crown, and 3. size of denticles on anterior and posterior carinae). Consequently, Charig and Milner concurred with Kellner that this genus is likely a spinosaurid and possibly a senior synonym of *Angaturama*.

Key references: Charig and Milner (1997); Kellner (1996); Martill, Cruickshank, Frey, Small and Clarke (1996).

JAINOSAURUS Hunt, Lockley, Lucas and Meyer 1994

Saurischia: Sauropodomorpha: Sauropoda: Eusauro-

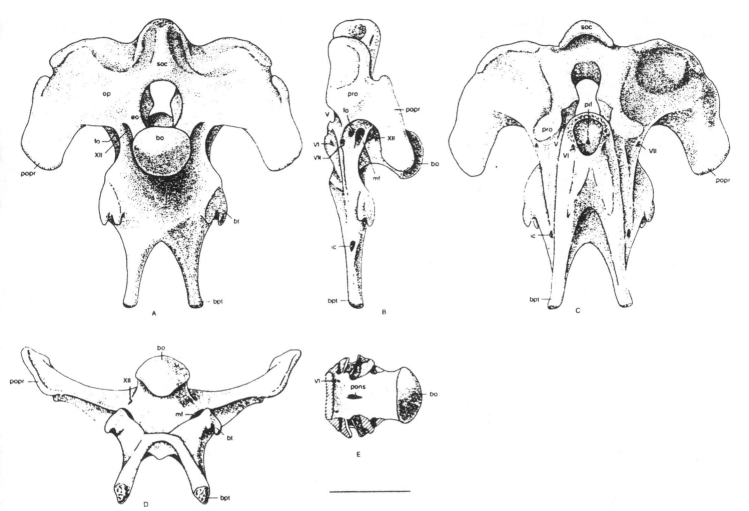

Jainosaurus septentrionalis, ISI R 162, referred braincase, A. caudal, B. lateral, C. rostral, and D. ventral views, E. dorsal view of basioccipital showing pons varioli. Scale = 5 cm. (After Chatterjee and Rudra 1996.)

poda: Neosauropoda: Macronaria: Titanosauriformes: Somphospondyli: Titanosauria: Titanosauridae.

Name derivation: "[Sohan L.] Jain" + Greek *sauros* = "lizard."

Type species: *J. septentrionalis* Hunt, Lockley, Lucas and Meyer (1994).

Other species: [None.]

Occurrence: Lameta Formation, Madhya Pradesh, Bara Simla, India.

Age: Late Cretaceous (Maastrichtian).

Known material: Partial skull with fragmentary braincase, braincase, scapulae, forelimb, ?sternal bone.

Lectotype specimen: GSI K27/497, posterior part of skull, including braincase.

Diagnosis of genus (as for type species): Differs from all other known titanosaurs (except *Titanosaurus*) by possession of flat-sided caudal centra (McIntosh 1990*b*), and from *Titanosaurus* by possession of larger, more gracile limb bones and probably in details of braincase and skull (documented by Berman and Jain 1982; *e.g.,* longer parietals) (Hunt, Lockley, Lucas and Meyer 1994).

Comments: The genus *Jainosaurus* was erected by Hunt, Lockley, Lucas and Meyer (1994) upon large sauropod specimens from the Lameta Formation of India which were originally described by Huene (*in* Huene and Matley 1933) as a new species of *Antarctosaurus* (see entry, *D:TE*), named *A. septentrionalis.* Hunt *et al.* regarded the basicranium (GSI K27/497) figured by Huene as the lectotype and other specimens as paralectotypes, the exact association of the latter with the lectotype unable to be determined. In the event that the lectotype cannot be located (see Berman and Jain), Hunt *et al.* proposed that the left scapula figured by Huene be designated a neotype.

A. septentrionalis was at first diagnosed by Huene (*in* Huene and Matley 1933) as follows: Large but slender; skull with very short base, especially the basisphenoid, the latter characterized by a large, broadly oval median channel; supraoccipital and frontal crest flatter than in *Antarctosaurus wichmannianus*; eighth caudal vertebra intermediate in shape between that in *Titanosaurus* and *Argyrosaurus*; anterior hemapophyses deeply bifurcated, very long, with broader blade than in *Argyrosaurus*; only anterior hemapophysial facets visible in centrum; ribs very broad; scapula very long (relatively much longer and with very different shape than in *A. wichmannianus*), slender, with blade forming slight angle at middle of its upper border; humerus very long and slender; lower forelimb and femur similar to those in *A. wichmannianus*.

McIntosh (1990*b*), in his review of the Sauropoda, suggested that a large associated caudal vertebra referred to "*A.*" *septentrionalis*, with a flat-sided centrum similar to that in *Titanosaurus*, might represent a large species of that genus. Hunt *et al.* regarded the postcrania of *J. septentrionalis* as belonging to a titanosaurid, but interpreted the Argentinian type species *Antarctosaurus wichmannianus* (usually classified as a titanosaurid) as a dicraeosaurid. The authors further noted that, even if *A. wichmannianius* proves not to be a dicraeosaurid, differences in its braincase show that it represents a genus distinct from *Jainosaurus*, the braincase of the latter being similar to that in a specimen found with remains of *Titanosaurus indicus*.

Hunt *et al.* accepted three valid sauropod species from the Lameta Formation: *J. septentrionalis*, *T. indicus*, and *T. blandfordi*. The authors found it possible yet unlikely that future, more complete finds from the Lameta Formation might show that postcrania referred to *Jainosaurus* represents a sexual dimorph or ontogenetic variant of *T. indicus*.

Information possibly regarding the skull of *J. septentrionalis* was provided by a newly collected, finely preserved braincase (ISI R 162) recovered from the Bara Simla site, Lameta Group, of Jabalpur, India. The specimen, representing a young individual, closely resembles the fragmentary braincase described by Huene and Matley (Chatterjee and Rudra 1996) (although to which titanosaurid this new specimen belongs is uncertain; J. S. McIntosh, personal communication 1998). According to Chatterjee and Rudra, the specimen's "most outstanding feature is the highly enlarged basipterygoid processes, which are slender and directed downward" as in *Amargasaurus*, *Nemegtosaurus* and *Saltasaurus*.

Key references: Berman and Jain (1982); Chatterjee and Rudra (1996); Huene and Matley (1933); Hunt, Lockley, Lucas and Meyer (1994); McIntosh (1990*b*).

JINGSHANOSAURUS   Zhang and Yang 1995 —
  (=? *Yunnanosaurus*)
Saurischia: Sauropodomorpha: Prosauropoda: Plateosauridae.
Name derivation: Chinese "Jingshan" [name, meaning "golden hills," of town having jurisdiction over locality] + Greek *sauros* = "lizard."
Type species: *J. xinwaensis* Zhang and Yang 1995.
Other species: [None.]
Occurrence: Lower Lufeng Formation, Yunnan, China.

Jingshanosaurus xinwaensis, Museum of Lufeng Dinosaurs LV003, holotype skull, right lateral view. Scale = 4 cm. (After Zhang and Yang 1994–96.)

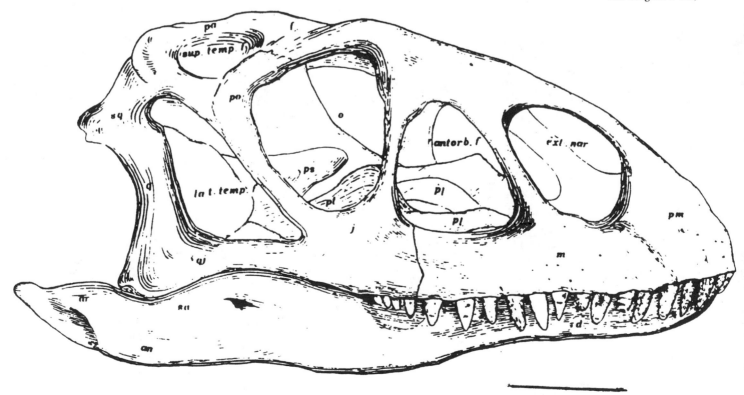

Jingshanosaurus

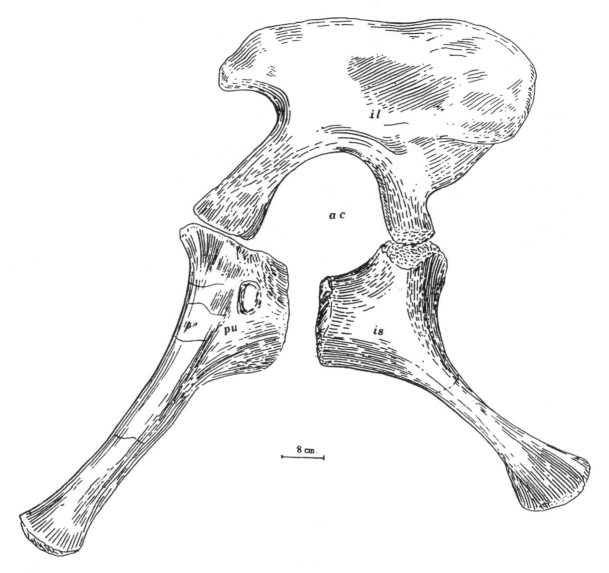

8 cm.

Age: ?Late Triassic.

Known material/holotype: Museum of Lufeng Dinosaurs LV003, almost complete skeleton.

Diagnosis of genus (as for type species): Gigantic prosauropod; heavily built; limb bones hollow but with thick walls; skull relatively small, about 2.4 times length of axis, three times that of first caudal vertebra; anterior region of skull comparatively long, cranium high, with ratio of length to height of skull (including lower jaw) about 1.7; external openings of skull large, bony bars separating openings relatively narrow; external nares subcircular in shape; antorbital fenestra triangular in shape, relatively large; orbits round, of moderate size; quadrate slightly forwardly inclined; lateral temporal fenestra narrow, long, somewhat "ladder" shaped; supratemporal fenestra small, subcircular; parietal comparatively flat; occiput narrow, with precipitous surface; basioccipital short; parasphenoid processes of basioccipital and parasphenoid process of basioccipital and basisphenoid

fairly thick and sturdy; maxilla relatively slight; mandibular ramus comparatively slender; symphysis of dentary weakly developed; posterior jaw articulation located below level of tooth row and is well developed; tooth rows of upper and lower jaws relatively long, with a relatively large number of closely packed teeth; four premaxillary, 16–17 maxillary, and 20–21 dentary teeth; premaxillary teeth long, thick, with sharply tapering crown, somewhat inwardly curving, longitudinal ridge and subtle denticles; middle maxillary teeth similar to premaxillary teeth, with sharp crown, external part of crown gently convex, internal side almost flat, midposterior region of tooth relatively laterally flat (similar to teeth in other prosauropods), anterior and posterior denticles subtle; middle maxillary teeth straight, relatively thick, saw-like anterior and posterior ridges of crest weakly developed; middle region of maxilla with fewer and laterally flattened teeth, anterior and posterior denticles relatively well developed; neck relatively elongate, about one-

third length of body; intercentrum of atlas larger than proatlas, atlas with weakly developed odontoid; neural arch of proatlas thick, short; axis and third cervical vertebra proportionally similar to those in *Plateosaurus* and *Lufengosauruas*, cervical ribs weakly developed; 14 platycoelous dorsal vertebrae, with strongly constructed centra, anterior dorsals with obvious keel and short, narrow neural spines; middle dorsals somewhat contracted, spines platelike, tops not expanded, rectangular in lateral view; three fused sacral vertebrae; articular processes of sacrum fairly well developed; sacral spines low, separate from one another; 38 caudal vertebrae, anterior caudal centra short and stout, articular faces of centra large and round; caudals with strongly developed parapophyses, caudal spines relatively low; chevrons well developed, interior part of anterior chevrons straight, rod-like, middle part "puttyknife" shaped; posterior chevrons short, triangleshaped in anterior view; pectoral girdles solidly constructed; scapula almost straight, relatively constricted in middle portion, comparatively expanded at both ends; coracoid thick, narrow, lateral side slightly convex, with a well-developed ridge for a ligament; fore-limbs proportionately short, humerus short, thick, only about half length of femur; radius and ulna very short, just two-fifths length of tibia; carpals I, II, and III large and fused, carpal IV small and round; metacarpals with phalanges and claw stouter and more robust than in known primitive sauropods; pelvic girdles massive; ilium plate higher than in other prosauropods; pubis and ischium weakly developed compared to *Plateosaurus* and *Lufengosaurus*; femur solidly constructed, with typical S-curvature, fourth trochanter high and fairly well developed, lesser trochanter weakly developed; tibia straight, strong, about four-fifths length of femur; fibula somewhat shorter than tibia, with slender and outward-curving diaphysis; astragalus and calcaneum wedge-shaped, thick, of usual construction; metatarsus with digits and claws relatively shorter than in *Plateosaurus* and *Lufengosaurus* (Zhang and Yang 1995).

Comments: The genus *Jingshanosaurus* was founded upon an almost complete skeleton including a well-preserved skull, lower jaw, atlas, axis, vertebral column, girdles, and limbs, the fourth to tenth cervical centra being heavily damaged due to long exposure

L

in the field. The specimen was collected from the lower part of a dark purple mudstone (the first dinosaur layer, of ?Late Triassic age), in the Lower Lufeng Formation, at Xingwa Village, near Jingshan Town, northeast of Lufeng County, Lufeng Basin, Yunnan Province, China. To date, the skeleton represents the largest (maximum length of up to 8.6 meters or more than 30 feet) and most completely known prosauropod from this formation (Zhang and Yang 1995).

After comparing *Jingshanosaurus* with other prosauropods, Zhang and Yang observed various features (*e.g.*, large body, relatively small head with low skull roof and numerous long, closely arranged teeth, front-hind limb ratio, broad feet) similar to those in plateosaurids, reasons, at least for the present, to refer this genus to the Plateosauridae. The authors regarded this genus as distinct because of such features as the low skull with a well-developed snout, the slender lower jaw with numerous inseparably arranged teeth, premaxillary and anterior maxillary teeth with non-serrated crests on their anterior and posterior edges, the relatively long cervical vertebrae and the remarkably low vertebral neural spines, the extremely short yet strong forelimbs, and the very short but strong first manual claw.

From the nature of other kinds of fossils (*e.g.*, invertebrates and plants) found in the Lufeng Basin, Zhang and Yang surmised that *Jingshanosaurus* lived in an environment with a warm and damp climate, relatively clear lake water, and rather flat land abundant with plants. Based on the dinosaur's body structure, particularly the morphology of its teeth — those of the anterior end of the upper and lower jaws being strong and sharp — the authors suggested that *Jingshanosaurus* was an omnivore, adapted to eating fishes at the river's edge, or snapping the shells off mollusks. The authors further imagined *Jingshanosaurus* utilizing its strong hind legs to stand erect while feeding off the branches and leaves of trees, or using its robust claws to dig up the roots of plants.

In 1951, Yang [Young] had described postcranial remains (IVP AS V100, V91, V98, and V21) which he referred to his dubious theropod genus *Sinosaurus*, although this additional material was not discovered associated with the type specimen (fragmentary jaws with teeth) of *S. triassicus*. These remains included numerous articulated cervical, dorsal, sacral, and caudal vertebrae, and front and hind limbs. Walker (1964) observed that these postcranial remains belonged to a prosauropod.

With the naming of the type species *Jingshanosaurus xinwaensis*, Zhang and Yang compared its holotype with the postcranial material that Yang [Young] (1951) had referred to *S. trassicus*, observing

that the two species compared quite closely. Therefore, Zhang and Yang removed this material from *S. trassicus* and referred it to their new genus and species. The authors further speculated that *Jingshanosaurus* sometimes fell prey to the carnivorous *Sinosaurus*.

Key references: Walker (1964); Yang (1951); Zhang and Yang (1995).

†LAPLATASAURUS—(See † *Titanosaurus*.)

†LEXOVISAURUS

Comments: A new look at *Lexovisaurus*, the first stegosaur known from the Middle Jurassic, was made possible following Peter M. Galton's (1990*a*) restudy of a partial postcranial skeleton (MHBR 0001)—"the earliest associated partial skeleton of a stegosaurid dinosaur from anywhere in the world"—recovered from the Callovian Marls (uppermost Lower Callovian) in the new quarry of the tileworks (Tuileries d'Argences) at Le Fresne d'Argences (Calvados), Normandy, France. The specimen had been found associated with an entirely marine fauna including fishes, reptiles (elasmosaurs, pliosaurs, mesosuchian crocodiles, and an ichthyosaur), and invertebrates (see Bigot 1938; Hofstetter and Brun 1958; Galton 1985*b*, 1990*a*).

The specimen from Normandy (see Galton, Brun and Rioult, 1980; Galton 1990*a*) includes cervical, dorsal, and caudal vertebrae, a left humerus, right femur, right tibia, fibula, astragalus, and calcaneum, and a huge shoulder spine. It was briefly described, but not figured, by Hoffstetter and Brun (1956, 1958), and by Hoffstetter (1957), who referred it (with *Omosaurus durobrivensis* from the Middle Callovian of England) to the new stegosaurid type species *Lexovisaurus durobrivensis* (see also *D:TE*). Later, Galton *et al.* published a preliminary description of the skeleton based on Galton's study of plaster casts of many of the bones (not including most of the neck and tail) and after a brief examination of the actual fossil material. Following the death of Roger Brun in April 1980, much of Brun's collection—which included MHBR 0001—was displayed as La Salle de Normandie au Muséum d'Historie du Havre, France. Among the exhibits was the Normandy skeleton of *L. durobrivensis*, the bones strengthened and mounted so that the individual elements can be removed for study, a situation that was not previously possible.

Galton (1990*a*) published a detailed, illustrated description of this skeleton. Given the incompleteness of this and the other specimens involved, the lack of other diagnostic differences, and the closeness in the geological horizons which yielded the specimens,

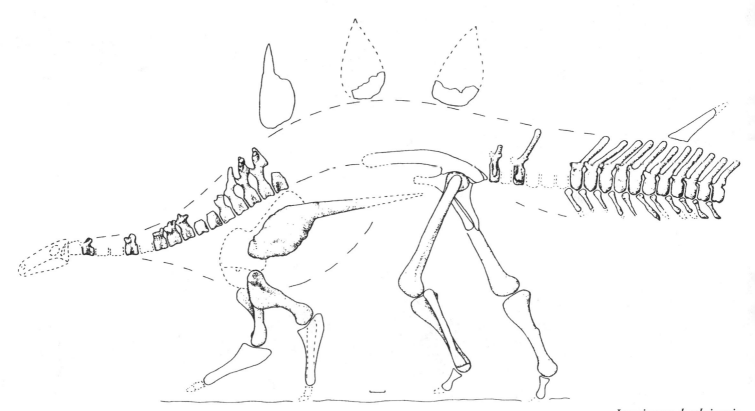

Lexovisaurus durobrivensis, updated skeletal reconstruction based in part on MHBR 0001, elements in dashed lines based upon specimens from the Callovian of England (see Galton 1985*b*). Scale = 50 cm. (After Galton 1990).

Galton tentatively accepted the referral of MHBR 0001 to *L. durobrivensis*. His referral was primarily based upon the close similarity in the form of the caudal vertebrae of the proximal one-fourth of the tail to that of specimens from England belonging to this species: The tops of the neural spines are only slightly expanded transversely in the French and English forms; and the derived form of the transverse processes is also very similar in both (the lateral profile of the ventral surface of the caudal centra is V-shaped in caudals 9 to 12 in the French specimen, 8 to 11 in the English specimen).

The shoulder spine in the French specimen is about twice the size (relative to humeral length) of that of a specimen referred to *L. durobrivensis* (Hulke 1887), and the basal plate is proportionally much larger (Nopcsa 1911*b*). Galton interpreted this disparity in size as possibly representing a sexual dimorphism, the specimen from France being the male morph.

Key references: Galton (1985*b*, 1990*a*); Galton, Brun and Rioult (1980); Hoffstetter (1957); Hoffstetter and Brun (1956, 1958); Hulke (1887); Nopcsa (1911*b*).

LIGABUEINO Bonaparte 1996

Saurischia: Theropoda: Neotheropoda: "Ceratosauria": Neoceratosauria: Abelisauroidea: ?Noasauridae.

Name derivation: "[Dr. Giancarlo] Ligabue" [author of a book about Patagonia; also, supporter of vertebrate paleontology research with extensive grants].

Type species: *L. andesi* Bonaparte 1996.

Other species: [None.]

Occurrence: La Amarga Formation, Neuquén Province, Argentina.

Age: Early Cretaceous ["late Neocomian" of Bonaparte's usage].

Known material/holotype: MACN-N 42, most of cervical neural arch, a dorsal centrum, two posterior dorsal neural arches, complete caudal vertebra, greater portion of right ilium, incomplete pubes, complete left femur, two phalanges, indeterminate bone fragments.

Diagnosis of genus (as for type species): Small abelisaur; cervical and posterodorsal vertebrae with very reduced neural spines; anterior cervical vertebrae with rather flat dorsal surface and triangular, well-marked axial depression in front of base of neural spine; cervicals having long prezygapophyseal process with ridge defining lateral and dorsal planes; posterior dorsal vertebrae elongated, bearing winglike transverse processes and reduced neural spines; femur with trochanteric shelf and modest but well-defined lesser trochanter on anterior dorsal half of trochanteric shelf; fourth trochanter very low and thin; distal section of femur with modest but defined anteriomedial crest; ilium low, elongate, postacetabular blade larger than preacetabular portion (Bonaparte 1996*b*).

Comments: The genus *Ligabueino* was founded

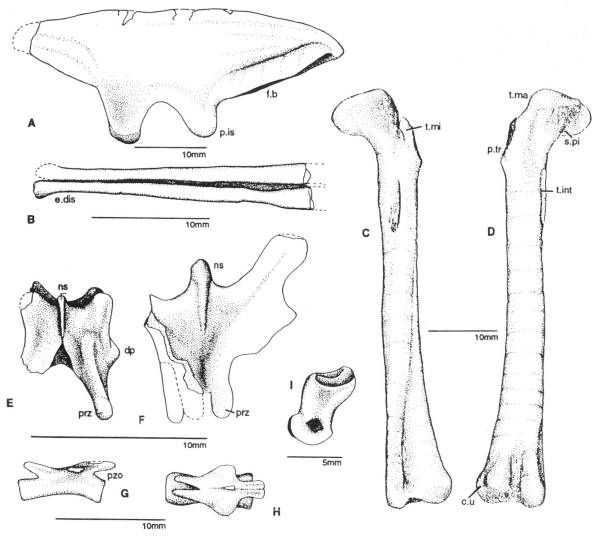

Ligabueino andesi, MACN-N 42, holotype A. left ilium, lateral view, B. middle and distal portions of both pubes, C.–D. left femur, anterior and posterior views, E.–F. incomplete cervical and dorsal neural arches, anterior view, G.–H. caudal vertebra, lateral and dorsal views, I. pedal phalange, lateral view. (After Bonaparte 1996*b*.)

upon partial, rather well-preserved but somewhat distorted (in a few areas) postcranial remains (MACN-N 42) collected by Luis M. Chiappe, José F. Bonaparte, and assistants from the lower section of the La Amarga Formation, Neuquén Basin, Province of Neuquén, Patagonia, Argentina (Bonaparte 1996).

Bonaparte described *Ligabueino* as a small theropod having a femur measuring 62 millimeters in length, a cervical neural arch 6 millimeters wide, and posterior dorsal vertebra measuring 12 millimeters in width.

According to Bonaparte, various morphological features of *Ligabueino* suggest affinities with the Abelisauroidea (*e.g.*, cervical vertebrae with dorsal, somewhat flat surface and very reduced neural spine, a derived character shared only with *Carnotaurus* and *Noasaurus*; similar affinities exhibited in morphology of neural arches of posterior dorsal vertebrae, shafts of pubes, and proximal portion of femur). The morphology of the pubis (with small distal expansion, iliac blade proportionally higher than in *Carnotaurus*,

and presence of section of trochanteric shelf followed by modest lesser trochanter) suggest a less derived form then *Carnotaurus* and *Noasaurus*. Although it was not possible to assign the new genus with certainty to either of the two abelisauroid families on the basis of the paucity of material available, Bonaparte hypothesized that *Ligabueino* was (based upon the cervical neural arch and morphology of the pedal phalanges) probably more closely related to the Noasauridae.

Bonaparte noted that *Ligabueino* represents the oldest record of the Abelisauroidea, indicating that the splitting of this group occurred earlier, probably during the end of the Jurassic to beginning of the Cretaceous.

Key reference: Bonaparte (1996*b*).

†MAGYAROSAURUS

Saurischia: Sauropodomorpha: Sauropoda: Eusauropoda: Neosauropoda: Macronaria: Camarasauromorpha: Titanosauriformes: Somphospondyli: Titanosauria: Titanosauridae.

Comments: *Magyarosaurus dacus*, a very small sauropod from the Late Cretaceous of Transylvania, is undergoing restudy by Coralia-Maria Jianu and David B. Weishampel. In a preliminary report on this "smallest of the largest," Jianu and Weishampel (1998) offered a reevaluation of the theory of Baron Franz Nopcsa (1934) that the relatively small size of this species — as well as other "dwarf" dinosaurs (*e.g.*, the iguanodontian *Telmatosaurus*) — was a consequence of the effects of body size via island habitation.

This reevaluation of Jainu and Weishampel, based upon 20 species distributed among 14 neosauropod genera, takes the following approaches: "1—regression analysis of humeral data as a means of establishing patterns in body size among titanosaurids, and 2—optimization of humeral data onto titanosaurid cladograms to evaluate evolutionary trends within the clade."

Early results of this study — to date of the authors' abstract, based on length and midshaft mediolateral width of the humerus of presumably adult forms, and of three ontogenetic samples spanning postnatal to adult individuals — suggests the following: 1. *M. dacus*, among all other known adult neosauropods, seems to be represented by the smallest individuals; 2. humeri of this species seem to be more similar to those belonging to subadults than to adults of other taxa; and 3. this "juvenile" morphology may indicate dwarfing by heterochronic paedomorphosis in this species.

Key references: Jianu and Weishampel (1998); Nopcsa (1934).

†MAIASAURA

Ornithischia: Genasauria: Cerapoda: Ornithopoda: Euornithopoda: Iguanodontia: Euiguanodontia: Dryomorpha: Ankylopollexia: Hadrosauridae: Euhadrosauria: Hadrosaurinae.

Comments: One of the better known hadrosaurs of recent years has been the type species *Maiasaura peeblesorum*, based upon a wealth of skeletal specimens representing embryonic to adult, as well as

Maiasaura peeblesorum, adult skeleton (cast) displayed at Dinofest™ in Philadelphia, 1998. The exhibit depicts parental care in *Maiasaura*, with this hadrosaur posed tending to a nest of its eggs and hatchlings.

Photograph by the author.

Maiasaura peeblesorum, casts of eggs and skeletons of babies, exhibited at Dinofest™, 1998.

eggs and nests, recovered from the upper part of the Two Medicine Formation in Montana. Most of the published writings about this duckbilled dinosaur have focused upon its possible behavior, particularly in regards to family life.

When *M. peeblesorum* was first named and described by John R. Horner and Robert Makela (1979), the authors believed that the collected material (including fossil bones representing growth stages from apparent hatchling to adult, as well as eggs and nests) constituted evidence suggesting parental care in this genus, with the adults caring for their young at the nest (hence the name, meaning "good mother lizard") for an extended period of time. This interpretation has been largely embraced for more than a decade (*e.g.,* Horner 1982; Horner and Gorman 1988; Horner and Weishampel 1988). Indeed, illustrations depicting the female *Maiasaura* bringing food to her young at the nest have become familiar subjects among artists and ubiquitous ones for modern books about dinosaurs.

More recently, however, this scenario of the "good mother lizard" has come under question and

criticism. Deeming and Unwin (1995) suggested that the size of *Maiasaura* hatchlings may have been greatly underestimated. Apparently indirectly supporting this appraisal was an earlier description by Horner and Currie (1994) of fossils referred to a new hadrosaur species, *Hypacrosaurus stebingeri,* including eggs, embryos, and babies. *H. stebingeri* was presumed to have hatched at about 1 meter in length (*Maiasaura* hatchlings determined to be about 30 centimeters); and its authors did not claim or imply that the young received parental care. Following Deeming and Unwin's idea, Dodson (1995) stated that worn teeth in *Hypacrosaurus* embryos negated the idea that wear facets offer evidence that *Maiasaura* teeth were used in chewing food. Dodson questioned how *Hypacrosaurus* laid soccer ball–sized eggs hatching 1-meter long babies, while the closely related *Maiasaura* laid much more slender eggs hatching babies supposedly less than one-third as large. Dodson postulated that *Maiasaura* hatchlings were larger than reported (possibly as large as those of *Hypacrosaurus*); that *Maiasaura* individuals previously identified as hatchlings may have been embryos; and that undeveloped limb ends, reported in the smallest *Maiasaura* individual as evidence for altriciality, is a feature expected "in an embryo far from hatching" (see *D:TE*).

One year after these opinions were published, Horner (1996) defended his original idea, based on new collections and analyses of hadrosaurine and lambeosaurine nesting horizons that yielded data indicating bimodal life history strategies. According to Horner, eggs referable to *M. peeblesorum* have volumes of about 1,600 milliliters, confirming the idea that the original group of 15 juveniles found in a nest-like structure, represent post-hatchlings, while the larger eggs referred to *H. stebingeri* have a reconstructed volume of 3,900 milliliters. These assessments were supported by taphonomic analyses of the respective nesting horizons, with *Maiasaura* horizons yielding fossil remains of individuals no more than 1.0 meters in length, and *Lambeosaurus* horizons yielding remains of individuals up to 2.0 meters in length.

Horner speculated that, as both *Maiasaura* and *Hypacrosaurus* juveniles seemingly remained in the nesting area after hatching, the evidence continues to indicate at least some degree of parental attention. Also, osteohistological data indicates that post-hatchling juvenile maiasaurs (50 to 75 cm in length) "were incapable of the active mobility in precocial young." As noted by Horner, these *Maiasaura* juveniles possess limb elements in which almost the entire epiphyseal and metaphyseal regions are made up of calcified cartilage; ossified bone is very scarce in these areas, this condition (based on studies of birds) arguing in favor of altricial behavior in this genus.

Morphometric growth analysis was performed on individual forelimb (humerus and ulna) and hind limb (femur, tibia, and metatarsal III) bones of *M. peeblesorum* by Dilkes (1996), who based his research on an ontogenetic sequence of specimens belonging to this species recovered from the Upper Cretaceous of Montana. The sequence, represented by juveniles on a nesting horizon and the disarticulated remains of thousands of adult and subadult individuals from a nearby bonebed (probably victims of some catastrophic event), ranged from nestling (approximately 1 meter in length) to fully mature (up to 7 meters).

Dilkes found that a distinct dichotomy exists between morphometric growth patterns of forelimb and hind limb; positive allometry is present in many internal and external dimensions of the forelimb; and the hind limb exhibits mostly isometry or sometimes negative allometry.

These results supported the hypothesis that the gait selection for *Maiasaura* was dependent on age: "Juveniles walked predominantly as bipeds. As an individual matured and mechanical loads increased on limb bones, its preferred gait shifted to quadrupedality." Dilkes postulated that this transition in posture most likely took place within the first year after hatching.

Evidence relating to the possible diet of *Maiasaura* resulted from a study by Karen Chin (1996a), a leading authority on coprolites, of "large blocky" coprolites recovered from the Upper Cretaceous of Montana. Although it is usually not possible to assign coprolites to any particular dinosaurian species, these specimens were most likely produced by hadrosaurs, as they were found closely associated with bones and nesting areas belonging to *Maiasaura*.

Within different coprolites, Chin recognized a number of refractory organs and tissues of gymnosperms and ferns; also included are wood fragments

Maiasaura peeblesorum, life restoration by Gregory S. Paul, depicting the dinosaur as caring for its young in the nest, an idea originally proposed by paleontologist John R. Horner.

and leaf cuticles (these two groups being most common), and also seeds, petioles, sporangia, and leaf laminae. The contents of the blocky masses consist mostly of conifer stems.

Barreto (1997), utilizing both the light and scanning electron microscopy, made a comparative study of the growth plates (a growth plate being a special disk of cartilage situated near the ends of growing bones, these plates providing a template and the machinery enabling bones to grow in length) in juvenile *Maiasaura* specimens from the Two Medicine Formation, and also in various living animals (a mammal, lizard, and bird).

Barreto found that the growth plate in these dinosaurs most closely resembles that of birds. The basic shape, and also the size, shape, and arrangement of the chondrocytes (special cells which produce and maintain the plate, and which produce a mineralized matrix around themselves), in the growth plates of *Maiasaura* and birds, are remarkably alike. According to Barreto, this identification of homologous characters in both dinosaurs and birds allows the assumption that these characters had the same function in both the extinct and living animals. As birds grow to adult size in a very brief period of development, and because the special structure of the growth plate in birds enables the bone to elongate rapidly, it was logical to conclude that dinosaurs, with such similar plates, were also capable of such rapid growth.

Note: Trexler (1997) reported the recent discovery of fragments of unidentified hadrosaurid eggshell eroding from a hillside in the upper part of the Two Medicine Formation in Pondera County, Montana. This find, the author noted, led to the subsequent discovery of a large concentration of eggshell fragments. The discovery was unusual in that neither bones nor larger portions of eggs were found with the shell fragments. Unfortunately, this dinosaurian nest could not be collected, and so photographs had to suffice in documenting the material.

During excavation of the site, a uniform mudstone layer — forming two-thirds of a circular concavity about 2.50 meters in diameter and 0.60 meters in depth — was uncovered, extending outward and upward from the eggshell, this stratum not present beyond the outer rim. Beneath this layer Trexler found a series of sub-spherical mudstone nodules averaging about 0.50 meters in diameter and forming the rim. Trexler interpreted these layers to be the original nest structure, where the hadrosaurids "formed a ring of mud balls, then overlaid the structure with a smooth mud layer to form a nest," this find constituting the first documentation of this kind of dinosaurian nest-building strategy.

Key references: Barreto (1997); Chin (1996*a*); Deeming and Unwin (1995); Dilkes (1996); Dodson (1995); Horner (1982, 1996); Horner and Currie (1994); Horner and Gorman (1988); Horner and Makela (1979); Horner and Weishampel (1988); Trexler (1997).

†MAJUNGASAURUS [nomen dubium] — (See Majungatholus.)

†MAJUNGATHOLUS — (=*Majungasaurus*)
Saurischia: Theropoda: Neotheropoda: "Ceratosauria": Neoceratosauria: Abelisauroidea: Abelisauridae.
Name derivation: "Majunga [Mahajanga, city in Madagascar]" + Latin *tholus* = "dome."
Known material: Postcranial remains including two partial skeletons (one with nearly complete skull), two partial skulls, partial crania, teeth, partial postcrania, adult and juveniles.
Holotype: MNHN.MAJ 4, partial skull roof with frontal "dome."

Diagnosis of genus (as for type species): Nasals thickened, fused, highly pneumatic, with large bilateral foramina; frontals with median hornlike projection; cervical ribs bifurcate distally; cervical ribs having multiple enlarged pneumatic foraminae proximally (diameter more than 10 millimeters) (Sampson, Witmer, Forster, Krause, O'Connor, Dodson and Ravoavy 1998).

Comments: Until recently, after the collection of some excellently preserved specimens, *Majungatholus* has been a poorly known and rather misunderstood genus. Today it is known to be a rather short-faced carnivorous dinosaur, distinguished as one of the few theropods for which every bone of the skull is known. The history of this genus, however, begins more than a century ago, with material originally referred to the similarly named genus *Majungasaurus*.

As chronicled by Sampson, Krause, Dodson and Forster (1996) in a brief report, Depéret (1896) had established a new species of the "catch all" genus *Megalosaurus*, which he named *M. crenatissimus*. This species was based upon six specimens (comprising two teeth, a terminal phalanx, two sacral vertebrae, and one caudal vertebra) selected from a shipment of vertebrate fossils recovered from an Upper Cretaceous site in the Mahajanga Basin near the town of Mahajanga (formerly spelled Majunga), Madagascar. Depéret named the species without designating any of the above specimens to be the holotype, nor did he speculate as to whether or not any of these specimens belonged to the same individual. Later, Lavocat (1955) referred an incomplete dentary (designated the neotype) from the Mahajanga Basin to this species for which he erected the new genus *Majungasaurus*.

Photograph by John Weinstein, courtesy The Field Museum (slide #GN88283.09c).

Excellently preserved skull (FMNH PR 2100) of the theropod *Majungatholus atopus* in left lateral view.

Sampson *et al.* noted that the precise locality information is not known for the specimens of *M. crenatissimus* described by Depéret and Lavocat, although all of them were discovered in the Mahajanga Basin, southeast of Mahajanga, in northwestern Madagascar.

Additional remains apparently belonging to *Majungasaurus crenatissimus* were reported over the years, including the following: A partial skeleton from the Mahajanga Basin, in the collection of the Service de Paléontologie, Université d'Antananarivo, as yet neither prepared nor studied, reported by Russell, Taquet and Thomas (1976); also, supposedly belonging to this species, isolated teeth and terminal phalanges recovered in Egypt (Gemellaro 1921; Stromer and Weiler 1930), isolated teeth collected in Argentina (Bonaparte and Powell 1980), and a single incomplete tooth from India (Mathur and Srivastava 1987).

Molnar (1990), in a review of problematic "carnosaurs," pointed out that both *M. crenatissimus* and the "Middle" Cretaceous Argentinian abelisaurid

Carnotaurus sastrei have a similarly curved mandible, and that it "is possible that *M. crenatissimus* is an abelisaurid."

Later, Russell (1996) referred to cf. *Majungasaurus* sp. the median portion of the ramus of a right dentary (CMN [formerly NMC] 41861), collected from the Tafilalt, "Grès rouges infracénomaniens" (first of three lithologic entities of the "Trilogie mésocrétacée"; see Choubert 1952), in southern Morocco (see *Spinosaurus* entry.)

In 1979, Sues and Taquet erected the new genus and species *Majungatholus atopus* upon a single and very incomplete cranial specimen (MNHN.MAJ 4). This specimen, collected from the Upper Cretaceous (?Campanian) of Madagascar, was believed by these authors as representing the only pachycepalosaur known from the southern hemisphere (see *D:TE*).

Almost two decades later, in a preliminary report, Sampson, Krause, Forster and Dodson (1996) announced that remains of at least two different theropods had recently been found in the Upper

Majungatholus

Cretaceous (Campanian) Maevarano Formation of the Mahajanga Basin — a large-bodied form represented by several specimens, and a new small-bodied "ceratosaur" represented by isolated elements. Materials belonging to the former included a very well-preserved, undistorted, and almost complete right premaxilla and partial postcrania. This specimen was recovered in the austral winter of 1993 during a joint SUNY-Stony Brook/Université d'Antananarivo expedition to the Mahajanga Basin, from the uppermost white sandstone of the continental Maevarano Formation. Because of the preservational quality and color of this specimen, it was assumed by Sampson *et al.* to have been recovered from the same horizon that yielded the specimens of *M. crenatissimus* described by Depéret and Lavocat. As observed by these authors, the premaxilla is relatively short and deep, having a length (72 millimeters) to height (78 millimeters) index (L/H × 100) of 92.

Sampson *et al.* tentatively assigned this new specimen to *M. crenatissimus* because 1. the serration morphology of the premaxillary teeth is the same as that seen on the teeth described by Depéret, and also on the hundreds of isolated teeth recovered from the Mahajanga Basin in 1993 and 1995, and 2. there is no evidence for more than one large theropod taxon from this area. In the same report, Sampson *et al.* stated that reassessment of the holotype of *M. atopus* "suggests that this specimen may in fact be that of a theropod, perhaps *Majungasaurus*," which, if confirmed, "would remove the only occurrence of pachycephalosaurs in the southern hemisphere, and bring into question the suggestion of prolonged biogeographic links between Laurasia and Gondwana."

In comparing this specimen to skulls of other theropods, Sampson, Krause, Dodson and Forster (1996) noted that the former possesses one unambiguous neoceratosaurian synapomorphy ("short, deep premaxillary body with vertical rostral and caudal margins"), at least one abelisaurid synapomorphy ("reduced to absent palatal process"), and shares several synapomorphies with the holotype (AMNH 1733) of *Indosuchus* ("numerous small foramina on external surfaces, well-developed vertical ridges on fused interdental plates, and [possibly] enlarged dental foramina"), the latter Indian genus purported to be an abelisaurid based on characters of the premaxilla and maxilla (see Buffetaut, Mechin and Mechin-Salessy 1988; Bonaparte 1991).

As the Madagascar specimen differs from the premaxilla of *Indosuchus* in no significant ways other than overall size (AMNH 1733 being about one third larger than FMNH PR 2008), Sampson, Krause, Dodson and Forster concluded that 1. *Majungasaurus* and *Indosuchus*, though geographically disparate, are sister taxa within Abelisauridae, and that 2. Madagascar and the Indian "super-continent" remained part of the same biogeographic province well into the Late Cretaceous. The authors further noted that, even if their assessment of *Majungasaurus* as an abelisaurid proved to be incorrect, or if the Abelisauridae ever proves to be a paraphyletic group, the close relationship between this genus and *Indosuchus* remains.

In a later preliminary report, Sampson, Witmer, Forster, Krause and O'Connor (1997) announced the discovery in July 1996 of a beautifully preserved, almost complete but disarticulated skull and partial skeleton (FMNH PR 2100) in the Maevarano Formation, Majunga Basin, in northwestern Madagascar. An only slightly restored cast of this skull went on display at The Field Museum in 1997.

As subsequently noted by Sampson *et al.* (1998), FMNH PR 2100 is distinguished as "among the best preserved and most complete dinosaur skulls known," its individual elements virtually undistorted, allowing for a comprehensive, detailed study of all its bones. Postcranial remains consist of most of the tail. Sampson *et al.* (1998) observed that, in FMNH PR 2100, a rugose sculpturing covers much of the external surface of many elements. Three median ornamentations—1. thickened, fused nasals, 2. a low frontal horn, and 3. a parietal eminence—adorn the skull roof. The skull measures 57 centimeters (approximately 22 inches) in length; compared to remains of the closely related *C. sastrei*, the total body length would probably have been from about 7 to 9 meters (about 23.5 to 30.5 feet).

According to Sampson *et al.* (1998), two other theropod specimens referable to this taxon were recovered at the same locality as FMNH PR 2100. One of these, UA 8678, comprises an incomplete, disarticulated skull, most of the precaudal axial column (several vertebrae and ribs, especially those in the cervical region, found in articulation), and the left ilium. This specimen seems to represent an immature individual, as evidenced by the small size of the skull (compared to that of FMNH PR 2100) and the lack of fusion between some of the vertebral centra and their corresponding neural arches. Yet a third and smaller specimen, FMNH PR 2099, apparently representing an even more immature individual, possesses a low, divided, and relatively smooth swelling atop its partially fused frontals.

At the same time, Sampson *et al.* (1998) noted that the neotype of *M. crenatissimus*, when compared to remains of other abelisaurids, does not reveal any diagnostic characters, the jaw not differing significantly from that in abelisaurid materials recovered from India. Therefore, owing to the inadequacy of the specimens formerly assigned to *M. crenatissimus*, Sampson *et al.* (1998) regarded this taxon as a *nomen dubium*, having been founded upon undiagnostic fossil materials.

In comparing the recently collected more complete and better preserved specimens with the fragmentary type specimen of the "putative Malagasy pachycephalosaur" *Majungatholus atopus*, Sampson *et al.* (1998) noted the following: Several characteristics seen in this specimen are not present in any known pachycephalosaurs (*e.g.*, lack of radiating arrangement of bony trabeculae in dome, dome occurring entirely within frontals rather than incorporating parietals, ruguse ornamentation), while others are theropod features (*e.g.*, long, divided olfactory tracts), and also derived features seen in FMNH PR 2100 (most significantly, frontal "dome" of MNHN.MAJ 4 being equivalent to frontal "horn" in FMNH PR 2100). The authors, therefore, concluded that the more recently collected specimens are referable to *M. atopus*, which is not a pachycephalosaur but a "domed" theropod.

Subsequently, in another preliminary report, Dodson, Forster, Sampson, Ravoavy and Krause (1998) stated that "*Majungatholus atopus* and *Majungasaurus crenatissimus* represent a single taxon of abelisaurid theropod, sharing a number of characters with abelisaurids from India and Argentina."

Sampson *et al.* (1998) observed the following abelisaurid synapomorphies in *M. atopus*: (Cranial) craniofacial elements with external sculpturing; premaxilla with reduced or absent palatal process; elongate maxilla-jugal contact; rostral process of lacrimal strongly reduced or absent; lacrimal having pronounced suborbital process; lacrimal-postorbital contact broad; long axis of postorbital oriented rostroventral-caudodorsal; postorbital having pronounced suborbital process; high, transversely broad nuchal crest with large squamosal contributions; medial alveolar border of premaxilla, maxilla, and dentary bearing fused interdental plates with series of vertical ridges and grooves; hypertrophied external mandibular fenestra and associated weak contacts between dentary and postdentary elements; (postcranial) elongate postaxial epipophyses.

Sampson *et al.* (1998) noted the following synapomorphies shared by *Majungatholus* and *Carnotaurus*: (Cranial) postorbital rostrocaudally elongate; postorbital having stepped-down ventrolateral fossa; dorsally located median fossa in saddle-shaped depression overlapping contact of frontals and parietals; enlarged, caudodorsally projecting parietal eminence supported ventrally by stout supraoccipital; laterally directed paroccipital process having upturned distal ends; splenial stout, triangular, with straight caudal margin.

Although abelisaurids have been reported from Europe (*e.g.*, Buffetaut *et al.* 1988) and northern Africa (Russell 1996), all based on scanty fossil remains; therefore, Sampson *et al.* (1998) restricted the Abelisauridae, with certainty, to three Gondwanan land masses — South America, Madagascar, and India.

As noted by Sampson *et al.* (1998), most paleogeographic scenarios have depicted the Cretaceous period as the most active interval of Gondwanan fragmentation, with Indo-Madagascar splitting off from Antarctica about 125 million years ago, South America separating from Africa about 100 million years ago, and finally Madagascar separating from the Indian subcontinent from 85 to 90 million years ago (*e.g.*, Ziegler, Scotese and Barrett 1982). Other reconstructions have instead postulated that Indo-Madagascar and Antarctica were joined by a land link across the Kerguelen Plateau — theoretically emplaced after the separation of Indo-Madagascar and Antarctica — that persisted until much later (perhaps until 80 million years ago) than the separation between Africa and South America. This latter reconstruction, Sampson *et al.* (1998) noted, "would predict a greater similarity of the Late Cretaceous terrestrial biota between South America and Indo-Madagascar (via Antarctica) than between South America and Africa," with the faunas of Africa, from the time of that continent's physical isolation from South America, exhibiting increasing endemism (*e.g.*, Storey 1995).

According to Sampson *et al.* (1998), the confirmed occurrence of abelisaurids in Late Cretaceous horizons of Argentina, the Indian subcontinent, and Madagascar is consistent with the second of the above two scenarios, and also with at least two major biogeographic hypotheses: 1. Abelisaurids originated before the major break-up of continents during the Early Cretaceous, spreading throughout most of Gondwana and possibly into Laurasia (the current absence of documented abelisaurids from Africa being due "to poor sampling, differential extinction, or both"); and, 2. abelisaurids originated during the Early Cretaceous following the plate-tectonic isolation of Africa (abelisaurids, consequently, never existing in Africa, dispersing between South America and Indo-Madagascar by way of Antarctica, utilizing the postulated land bridge across the Kerguelen Plateau.

Key references: Bonaparte and Powell (1980); Depéret (1896); Dodson, Forster, Sampson, Ravoavy and Krause (1998); Gemellaro (1921); Lavocat (1955); Mathur and Srivastava (1987); Molnar (1990); Russell (1996); Russell, Taquet and Thomas (1976); Sampson, Krause, Forster and Dodson (1996); Sampson, Krause, Dodson and Forster (1996); Sampson, Witmer, Forster, Krause and O'Connor (1997); Sampson, Witmer, Forster, Krause, O'Connor, Dodson and Ravoavy (1998); Stromer and Weiler (1930); Sues and Taquet (1979).

†MALAWISAURUS

Saurischia: Sauropodomorpha: Sauropoda: Eusauropoda: Neosauropoda: Macronaria: Camarasauromorpha: Titanosauriformes: Somphospondyli: Titanosauria: ?Titanosauridae.

Comments: Gomani (1996) reported additional material belonging to the medium-sized titanosaur *Malawisaurus*, collected from the Early Cretaceous of Malawi, in southeastern Africa. In a follow-up report, Gomani (1998) noted that these remains comprise 50 percent of the cranium (including the premaxilla, jugal, quadrate, basicranium, pterygoid, ectopterygoid, dentary, and a splenial) and 75 percent of the postcranium (including 14 cervical vertebrae, nine dorsals, sacrum, 48 caudals, 19 chevrons, sternal plates, coracoid, two humeri, radius, two ulnae, four metacarpals, two manual digits, ilium, three ischia, femur, tibia, fibula, a metatarsal, and dermal armor). According to Gomani (1996), a large dermal ossicle, similar to that of *Saltasaurus*, measures 19 centimeters (about 7.4 inches) long and 9.5 centimeters (about 3.6 inches) wide. As observed by Gomani (1998*a*), all of these elements, found either in articulation or associated with each other, represent three *Malawisaurus* individuals.

Gomani (1996) noted that, though among the most primitive of sauropods, *Malawisaurus* may also be among the best known in terms of collected specimens, now represented by, according to Gomani (1998*b*), 50 percent of the cranium and 70 percent of the postcranial elements, with a vertebral column complete save for the atlas and axis.

Gomani (1998*b*) cited three different morphs of posterior caudal vertebrae in this genus (the shape of caudal centra and inclination of caudal neural arches sometimes used as taxonomic characters in titanosaurians): In the first, the centra are rectangular in lateral view; in the second and third morphs, the centra are concave ventrally, one having low and pointed rudiments of the posterior neural spines, the other having taller and flat-ended posterior neural spines.

Note: Gomani (1996, 1998*a*) also reported an as yet unnamed sauropod found at this same Malawi locality.

Key references: Gomani (1996, 1998*a*, 1998*b*).

†**MALEEVOSAURUS**—(See † *Tyrannosaurus*.)

†**MAMENCHISAURUS**—(=*Zigongosaurus*)
Saurischia: Sauropodomorpha: Sauropoda: Eusauropoda: Neosauropoda: Macronaria: Camarasauromorpha: Titanosauriformes: Somphospondyli: Euhelopodidae.

Type species: *M. constructus* Yang [Young] 1954.

Other species: *M. hochuanensis* Yang [Young] and Chao 1972, *M. fuxiensis* (Hou, Chao and Chu 1976), *M. sinocanadorum* Russell and Zhen 1993, *M. jingyanensis* Zhang, Li and He 1996, *M. youngsi* Zhang and Chen 1996, *M. anyuensis* Yang, Li and He 1996.

Age: Early–middle Late Jurassic.

Mamenchisaurus hochuanensis mounted skeleton (LACM 5166/125973, cast of holotype and other remains, skull cast from *Diplodocus carnegii*) temporarily displayed in 1992 at the Media Center shopping mall, Burbank, California.

Photograph by the author, courtesy Natural History Museum of Los Angeles County.

Mamenchisaurus

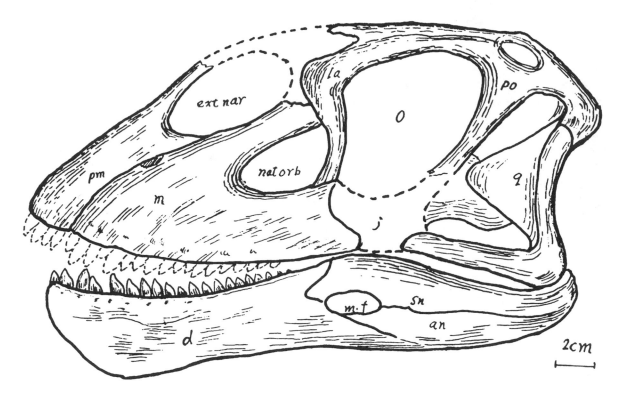

Diagnosis of genus (as for type species): Medium-sized sauropod; hollow degree of presacral vertebrae especially developed, vertebral centra typically opisthocoelous; cervical vertebrae similar to those of *Omeisaurus*; cervical neural spines low, flat; anterior process of cervical ribs well developed, with groove shape; dorsal vertebrae with apparently well-developed pleurocoels; dorsal neural spines low; anterior caudal vertebrae notably precoelous; chevrons in medial part of tail forked; distal end of tibia relatively extended (Zhang and Chen 1996).

Diagnosis of *M. hochuanensis*: Length of neck almost half length of entire body; 19 cervical vertebrae with slightly opisthocoelous centra; 12 dorsal vertebrae, with faintly opisthocoelous centra; first to fourth dorsal neural spines bifurcated; posterior dorsals with typically opisthocoelous centra; four fused sacral vertebrae, neural spines from first to third fused; more than 36 caudal vertebrae, anterior 16 caudals procoelous with transition from platycoelous to amphicoelous centra; fourth sacral neural spine and anterior caudal neural spines convex anteriorly and concave posteriorly; chevrons forked beginning with ninth caudal; ilium high, pubic peduncle located at middle portion; ischium comparatively elongate; tibia and fibula of almost equal length; metarsals short, "claw" of pedal digit I particularly developed (Zhang and Chen 1996).

Diagnosis of *M. fuxiensis*: Medium- to large-sized sauropod; skull relatively high; snout moderately developed; external nares paired, located at anterior part of skull; occipital portion broad; supratemporal fenestra relatively large; teeth medium-sized, spatulate; four premaxillary, 12–14 maxillary, and 15–17 dentary teeth; ?17 cervicals, having opisthocoelous centra with rather large pleurocoels, lamellar structure of neural spines developed; 12 or 13 dorsal vertebrae, anterior neural spines weakly bifurcated; four sacral vertebrae, with three fused anterior neural spines; first and second caudal vertebrae with fanlike flat caudal ribs; chevrons unforked; scapula long, thin, extended at proximal end; coracoid comparatively round; sternum oval in shape; ilium high, with pubic peduncle at middle part of ilium; limb bones relatively flat (Zhang and Chen 1996).

Diagnosis of *M. jingyanensis*: Gigantic, about 20–26 meters in length; skull moderately high and light; naris small, located in anterior part of skull; mandible slender; teeth typically spatulate; four premaxillary, 14–16 maxillary, and 17–19 dentary teeth; cervical vertebrae extremely long, pleurocoels of dorsal vertebrae poorly developed; spines of anterior dorsal vertebrate bifurcated; anterior dorsal vertebrae remarkably procoelous; humerus robust, straight (Zhang, Li and Zeng 1998).

Diagnosis of *M. anyuensis*: [Not currently available.]

Diagnosis of *M. youngsi*: [Not yet published.]

Comments: For the present, the genus *Mamenchisaurus*, a Chinese sauropod with an extremely long neck, is represented by a total of seven species, although

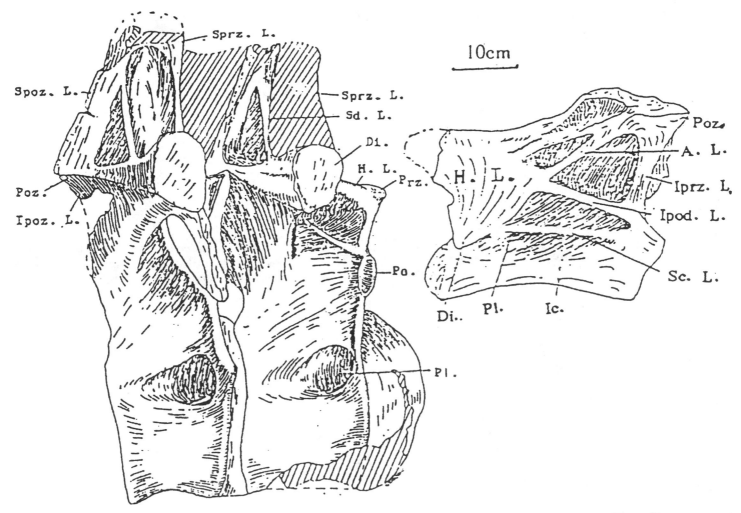

10cm

Mamenchisaurus anyuensis,
AL001, holotype fused dorsal vertebrae and cervical
vertebra, lateral views.
(After Yang, Li and He
1996.)

some of these taxa may eventually prove to be conspecific.

One of these species, *M. jingyanensis*, was originally described by Zhang, Li and He in 1996 (see also
Zhang, Li and Zeng 1998), based on a partial skull
and lower jaw and radius (CV00734), and a referred
ulna (CV00219), from the middle Late Jurassic Shangshaximiao Formation of Jingyan County, Junghsien
County, Sichuan County, Zigong. The species *M.
anyuensis* was described that same year by Yang, Li
and He, founded upon vertebrae (AL001–AL003,
AL101–AL106).

Zhang and Chen (1996) revised the diagnoses
for the genus and most of the species of *Mamenchisaurus*—the type species *M. constructus* from the
early Late Jurassic, Yibin County, Mamenchi; *M.
hochuanensis* from the early Late Jurassic, Hochuan
County, Sichuan; *M. jingyanensis*; and *M. fuxiensis*
from the early Late Jurassic, Wujiabai, Zigong—
based, in part, on more recently collected specimens
recovered by Chinese scientists.

The species *M. fuxiensis* was originally described
by Hou, Chao and Chu (1976) as the new type species

Zigongosaurus fuxienses, then later referred by Dong,
Zhou and Zhang (1983) to the genus *Omeisaurus* (see
D:TE) as new species *O. fuxiensis*. However, Zhang
and Chen found that the stratigraphic position of *Z.
fuxiensis* is higher than that of *Omeisaurus tianfuensis*
or *O. junghsiensis* and lower than that of *M. hochuanensis* or *M. jingyanensis*, the age of *Z. fuxiensis* therefore being between Middle and early Late Jurassic age;
also, the posterior cervical and anterior dorsal neural
spines of *Z. fuxiensis* are weakly bifurcated, representing an intermediateness that is more advanced
than *Omeisaurus* and more primitive than *Mamenchisaurus*. As *Z. fuxiensis* is quite similar to *Mamenchisaurus*, Zhang and Chen suggested that this species
be removed from *Omeisaurus* and referred to the former genus as the new species *M. fuxiensis*.

As reported by Zhang and Chen, the new large
species *M. youngsi*, presumably named in a thesis by
H. Ouyang, was based on an almost complete skeleton (including a well-preserved skull, articular, vertebral column, and limbs) collected by Ouyang and
colleagues from the Zigong Dinosaur Museum. The
skull and teeth of this species are quite similar to those

of *M. jingyanensis*, and its neck comprises 19 cervical vertebrae; its cervicals, dorsals, caudals, and chevrons are exactly like those of *M. hochuanensis*.

Note: Dong (1997*d*) reported the recovery of a possible "mamenchisaurid" [=euhelopodid] tooth (IVPP V. 11124) perhaps representing a new genus and species, collected during the Sino-Japanese Silk Road Dinosaur Expedition from the lower part of the Xinminbao Group (Lower Cretaceous), Mazongshan Area, Gansu Province, China (Dong 1997*b*). The preserved part of the tooth measures 42 millimeters in length. The tooth differs somewhat from teeth of *Mamenchisaurus*, *Euhelopus*, and *Omeisaurus*, having finely rather than more prominently serrated carinae. It resembles the tooth of *Chiayüsaurus* in that the concavity on the lingual surface occupies only the distal half of the crown, the crown is narrow, and the tip of the crown bends inward and backward.

Key references: Dong, Zhou and Zhang (1983); Hou, Chao and Chu (1976); Yang [Young] (1954); Yang [Young] and Chao (1972); Yang, Li and He (1996); Zhang, Li and He (1996); Zhang, Li and Zeng (1998).

†MARSHOSAURUS

Saurischia: Theropoda: Neotheropoda: Tetanurae: Avetheropoda: Carnosauria.

Comments: A newly identified specimen referred to the type species *Marshosaurus bicentesimus*, one of the rarer Morrison Formation theropods, was briefly described in a preliminary report by Chure and Britt (1997).

According to Chure and Britt, the specimen — the most complete one yet belonging to this species — consists of a partial skeleton collected in 1912 from the Late Jurassic Morrison Formation of Dinosaur National Monument. It includes the posterior half of the skull and right mandible, cervical and anterior dorsal vertebrae (dorsals with neural spines having notched craniodorsal margins matching those referred to *M. bicentesimus* from the type locality), a scapula, humerus, and one pathological rib.

Regarding *Marshosaurus* as a primitive carnosaur, Chure and Britt noted the following primitive features: Braincase long; rectangular lateral temporal fenestra; centra having thick walls and camerate pneumatic structure; pubic shaft bowed; pubic foot small with no cranial component; ilium long and low.

Derived features observed in the specimen by Chure and Britt include these: Axial intercentrum inclined (as in *Sinraptor*); cervical epipophyses almost as tall as neural spine; cervical vertebrae opisthocoelous; scapular blade moderately expanded; obturator notch open.

As the humerus in this specimen is "surprisingly short and massive," the authors speculated that the forelimbs of *Marshosaurus* were proportionately small, as in "megalosaurids." Although the materials available made it difficult to assess the exact phylogenetic placement of this genus, Chure and Britt interpreted *Marshosaurus* as "a relatively primitive carnosaurian tetanuran, probably closer to *Megalosaurus* and *Eustreptospondylus* than more advanced carnosaurs."

Key reference: Chure and Britt (1997).

†MASSOSPONDYLUS

Saurischia: Sauropodomorpha: Prosauropoda: Massospondylidae.

Comments: *Massospondylus* is a lightly-built, bipedal, medium-sized (approximately 4 to 6 meters, or 12 to 20 feet) prosauropod of the Early Jurassic period, known mainly from a wealth of specimens (ranging from juvenile to adult) found in South Africa, but also from material collected in the United States (see *D:TE*).

In a study of the skull of the type species, *Massospondylus carinatus*, Gow, Kitching and Raath (1990) interpreted various cranial features as indicating sexual dimorphism. Skulls interpreted as representing males were characterized by a thickening of the dorsal orbital rim and a deepening of the posterior end of the maxilla. Galton (1997*b*), however, based upon his own independent studies, interpreted these "male" features as probably indicative of individual variation.

Erratum: On p. 437 of *D:TE*, in the *Geranosaurus* entry, only the illustrated lower jaws belong in the holotype of the ornithopod *Geranosaurus harriesi*. The other figured parts (*i.e.* the scapulocoracoid, pes, humerus, manus, radius, and ulna, some of which were repeated in that book's *Massospondylus* entry) are actually remains now referred to *M. carinatus*. The pictured foot and forelimb elements are part of the type material (SAM 2769 and 2770) of *Aetonyx palustris*, which is regarded as a junior synonym of *M. carinatus*.

Key references: Galton (1997*b*); Gow, Kitching and Raath (1990).

MEGARAPTOR Novas 1998

Saurischia: Theropoda: Neotheropoda: Tetanurae: Avetheropoda; ?Coelurosauria *incertae sedis*.

Name derivation: Greek *mega* = "large" + Latin *raptor* = "thief."

Type species: *M. namunhuaquii*

Other species: [None.]

Occurrence: Río Neuquén Formation, Neuquén Province, Argentina.

Age: Late Cretaceous (Turonian–Coniacian).

Known material/holotype: MCF-PVPH 79, right ulna, left manual phalanx 1.I (phalanx 1 of left manual digit I), distal half of right metatarsal III, ungual phalanx of digit II of right pes.

Diagnosis of genus (as for type species): Large, gracile theropod with enlarged pedal ungual on digit II, genus and species exhibiting the following autapomorphies: bladelike olecranal process on proximal ulna; distal end of ulna stout, triangular in distal aspect; manual phalanx 1.I subquadrangular in proximal view, with dorsal portion transversely wider than ventral portion; metatarsal III with deep, wide extensor ligament pit (Novas 1998).

Comments: The new taxon *Megaraptor namunhuaiquii* was founded upon a very incomplete postcranial specimen (MCF-PVPH 79), its most impressive element being an enlarged second toe. The holotype was collected from fluvial deposits of the Upper Cretaceous (Turonian–Coniacian; see Leg-

erreta and Gulisano 1989; Cruz, Condat, Kozlowski and Manceda 1989) Río Neuquén Formation, exposed at Sierra del Portezuelo, Neuquén Province, Argentina (Novas 1998).

This discovery was first mentioned in an abstract by Novas, Cladera and Puerta (1996). In this initial report, the authors also reported from this locality four other theropod specimens: 1. The foot of the first troodontid found outside of North America and Asia, 2. a skeleton that would be referred to the new genus *Unenlagia* (see introductory chapter, section on birds), 3. an ornithomimid isolated proximal humerus having a ball-shaped articular head and shallow deltopectoral crest, and 4. four proximal caudal vertebrae of a large indeterminate theropod. Collectively, these finds suggested occasional Late Cretaceous interfaunal exchanges between the partially isolated South America and Laurasia.

Novas described the large pedal claw as measuring

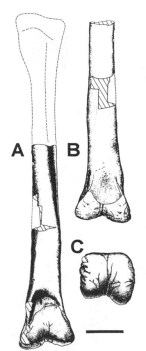

Megaraptor namunhuaiquii, MCF-PVPH 79, holotype distal half of right metatarsal III, in A. dorsal, B. ventral, and C. distal views. Scale = 5 cm. (After Novas 1998.)

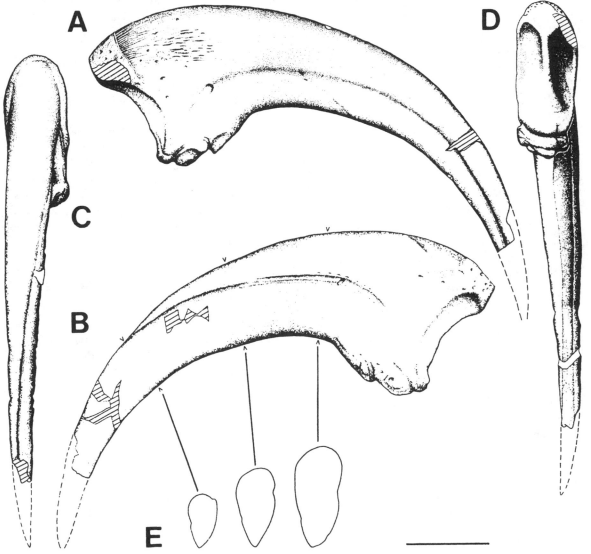

Megaraptor namunhuaiquii, MCF-PVPH 79, holotype ungual phalanx of right pedal digit II, in A. lateral, B. medial, C. cranial, and D. caudal views; E. cross sections. Scale = 5 cm. (After Novas 1998.)

33.9 centimeters along its dorsal edge (about 54 percent larger than that of the giant dromaeosaurid *Utahraptor*). This claw, Novas noted, would have been about 37 centimeters if complete and, when covered with its bony sheath, more than 40 centimeters.

As pointed out by Novas, South American Cretaceous theropods were—until the discovery of *Megaraptor*—mainly represented by abelisaurids. *M. namunhuaiquii*, however, "represents a startling example of a large, although apparently gracile, predatory dinosaur, with a specialized foot bearing a very large raptorial ungual on its second pedal digit." Its large body size (probably totalling 8 meters in length) and the raptorial pedal claw make the new genus an interesting case among dinosaurs from phylogenetic, biomechanical, and behavioral perspectives.

According to Novas, the slender proportions of manual phalanx 1.I and the strong transverse compression inferred for its corresponding ungual (not preserved), suggest that the manus of *Megaraptor* was more slender and proportionally longer than that of *Allosaurus*; except for a few atypical cases (*e.g.*, *Deinocheirus*), the manus of this new genus may be the largest of all known theropods. The transversely compressed pedal claw is dorsoventrally more shallow but more recurved than that of *Utahraptor*. Metatarsal III closely resembles in curvature and cross section that of a large, Aptian dromaeosaurid from Japan (RTMP 95.38.1, cast; see Azuma and Currie 1995 and *D:TE*).

The sickle-like claw present on pedal digit II suggested to Novas some phylogenetic relationship with other theropods possessing such a talon, like troodontids and dromaeosaurids (*e.g.*, Colbert and Russell 1969; Ostrom 1969*b*; Gauthier 1986; others). The enlarged, trenchant ungual indicates specialized articulations in phalanges 1 and 2 of the second digit which allowed hyperextension and flexion (see Ostrom; also Osmólska and Barsbold 1990). However, the morphology of the available forelimb and pedal material of the new genus counters the interpretation that *Megaraptor* is closely related either to troodontids or dromaeosaurids, despite resemblances in the claw. The ulna, for example, is more similar to that of such diverse theropods as *Syntarsus*, *Torvosaurus*, *Allosaurus*, and *Piatnitzkysaurus* (MACN-CH 895) in its retention of an enlarged olecranon, the almost straight caudal margin of the shaft, and proximal processes for articulation with the radius that form an "L"-shaped notch in proximal view (these features possibly functionally related, and therefore, simply homoplasius rather than indicating any relationship; R. E. Molnar, personal communication 1998). In troodontids (*e.g.*, *Troodon* [CMN 12344, cast], *Sinornithoides* [IVPP V9612]) and dromaeosaurids (*Saurornitholestes* [MOR 660, cast], *Deinonychus* [AMNH 3015]), the ulna is

distinguished from that of less derived theropods (including *Megaraptor*) by the presence of these characters: Olecranon process feebly developed, and less prominent proximal processes to receive radius, defining an almost caudally oriented "U"-shaped notch. Furthermore, the ulnar shaft in *Megaraptor* is straight and there is no scar for the M. brachialis; in troodontids and dromaeosaurids, by contrast, the ulnar shaft is caudally bowed (see Gauthier) and there is a well-marked scar for the M. brachialis on the cranial surface of the proximal ulna (see Ostrom).

According to Novas, metatarsal III in *Megaraptor* resembles that of coelurosaurs, rather than that in basal tetanurine theropods (including *Allosaurus* [AMNH 6125], *Eustreptospondylus* [OUM J13558], and *Piatniztkysaurus* [MACN-CH 895]), in being proportionally long and slender, the cranial surface of the distal portion of this element being almost flat. In *Megaraptor,* this element narrows proximally to a degree that resembles the central metatarsal of coelurosaurians *Ornitholestes* (AMNH 619), *Deinonychus* (YPM 5205), and the large dromaeosaurid from Japan, but is not pinched as in arctometatarsalians (including caenagnathids [=elmisaurids of Novas' usage], ornithomimids, and tyrannosaurids; see Holtz 1994*a*). Also in *Megaraptor*, the distal half of this element lacks the lateral and medial projections that overlap metatarsals II and IV, respectively, in troodontids, caenagnathids, and other arctometatarsalians.

Therefore, Novas offered the preliminary conclusion that *Megaraptor* is a more derived theropod than basal tetanurines like *Allosaurus*, *Eustreptospondylus*, and *Piatnitzkysaurus*. Based on the gracile proportions of the metatarsals (see Holtz), Novas tentatively referred *Megaraptor* to the Coelurosauria, noting that, although the large claw of digit II suggests relationships with dromaeosaurids and troodontids, forelimb anatomy indicates that *Megaraptor* could be placed outside of the remaining Coelurosauria (*e.g.*, Tyrannosauridae, Ornithomimosauria, Oviraptorosauria, Troodontidae, and Manuraptora). *Megaraptor* may represent another example of Gondwanan dinosaurs evolving in isolation from those of Laurasia. This genus seemingly corresponding to an evolutionary stage of South American dinosaurs during which some members achieved gigantic size.

Key references: Novas (1998); Novas, Cladera and Puerta (1996).

†**MELANOROSAURUS**—(=*Roccosaurus*)
Age: Late Triassic (Carnian).
Comments: *Melanorosaurus*, which appeared in the early Late Triassic, is among the earliest of known prosauropods (Gauffre 1993*a*). Two species have been

assigned to this large South African genus, the type species, *M. readi* Haughton 1924, represented by two partial postcranial skeletons (SAM 3449 and 3450), and the geologically younger *M. thabanensis* Gauffre 1993*a*, represented by a femur (MNHN LE5-16).

New information regarding the genus and its species has been gleaned after the recovery of two rather well-preserved, nonmineralized, incomplete postcranial skeletons (NM R1551, originally announced in a faunal list by Van Heerden *see in* Anderson and Cruickshank 1978 as *Roccosaurus* [*nomen nudum*]; see *D:TE*) of *M. readi* from the base of the Elliot Formation (Carnian; see Olsen and Galton 1984; also Gauffre 1993*b*) on the Milner farm, Wodehouse (Dordrecht) district, Eastern Cape Province, South Africa. These remains, which represent two individuals of approximately the same size, include vertebrae (one cervical, several dorsals, four associated sacrals, and a number of caudals), and also various girdle and limb bones (Van Heerden and Galton 1997).

Comparing this new material to the type specimens, Van Heerden and Galton observed that the femora and tibiae of SAM 349 are from 2–3 percent smaller than those of the structurally similar NM R1551; also, in SAM 349, the tibia is 72 percent as long as the femur, while in NM R1551 the tibia is between 76 and 80 percent the femoral length (this discrepancy in ratios possibly due to abrasion of the distal end of the tibia of SAM 349).

Although questioning the recognition of *M. thabanensis* as a species distinct from *M. readi*, Van Heerden and Galton noted various differences between the former and the new material: The femur in *M. thabanensis* is shorter and more robust than in *M. readi*, suggesting that the type species was more lightly built; in *M. readi*, the lesser trochanter is positioned on the lateral edge of the femur and visible in posterior view, while in *T. thabanensis*, it is well removed from the lateral edge; and, in *M. thabanesis*, the lower end of the fourth trochanter extends further onto the distal half of the femur and is more distant from the medial margin.

The sixth cervical vertebra of *M. readi* has an inclined anterior articular surface, a feature suggesting to Van Heerden and Galton that this species probably had a neck possessing a natural curvature. As the neck in the prosauropod *Plateosaurus* is somewhat shorter than that of *Riojasaurus*, Van Heerden and Galton therefore surmised that *Melanorosaurus* also had a proportionately shorter neck than *Plateosaurus*.

Comparing the new material to the more stockily built South American genus *Riojasaurus* (and to a recent illustration of the skull and neck of this genus figured by Bonaparte and Pumares, in press), Van Heerden and Galton noted that the sixth cervical in that genus closely resembles its counterpart in *M. readi*, possessing a centrum that is only slightly longer than high, and an axially short neural spine, these similarities indicating that *M. readi* and *Riojasaurus*

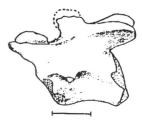

Melanorosaurus readi, sixth or seventh cervical vertebra (MN R1551), left lateral view. Scale = approximately 50 mm. (After Van Heerden and Galton 1997.)

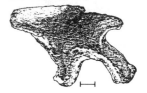

Melanorosaurus readi, right ilium (MN R1551) in lateral view. Scale = approximately 50 mm. (After Van Heerden and Galton 1997.)

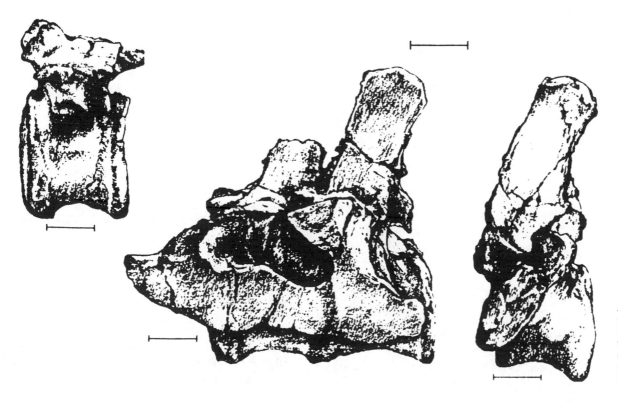

Melanorosaurus readi, first to fourth sacral vertebrae (MN R1551), left lateral view, the second and third ankylosed. Scale = approximately 50 mm. (After Van Heerden and Galton 1997.)

probably had necks of about equal length. *M. readi* has four functional sacral vertebrae, the first coming from the dorsal rather than caudal series (a condition similar to that in theropods), while *Riojasaurus* (as well as all other known prosauropods) possesses but three.

In *M. readi*, the sacral neural spines are comparatively longer than those in *Riojasaurus*; the scapula in the former has parallel long sides, as opposed to the "hourglass" shape seen in *Riojasaurus*; the pubes are relatively long and slender, slightly longer than the ilium, which is a broader and stockier bone in *Riojasaurus*; and the forelimb elements in *Melanorosaurus* are relatively shorter and the limb bones less stockily built than in the South American prosauropod. These features suggested to Van Heerden and Galton that *Melanorosaurus*, or at least the type species, was most likely a facultatively bipedal animal (as opposed to the obligatorily quadrupedal *Riojasaurus*), the longer pubes serving to support the belly when the dinosaur was supported by its hind limbs.

Key references: Anderson and Cruickshank (1978); Gauffre (1993*a*); Haughton (1924); Van Heerden and Galton (1997).

†MICROCOELUS—(See *Neuquensaurus*.)

†MICROVENATOR

Saurischia: Theropoda: Neotheropoda: Tetanurae: Avetheropoda: Coelurosauria: Manuraptoriformes: Oviraptorosauria.

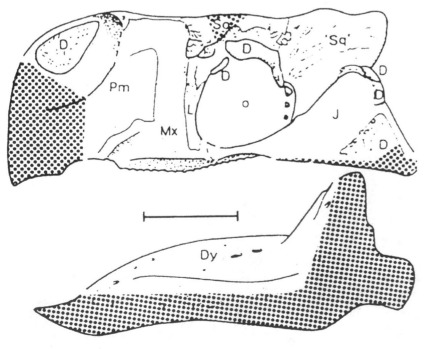

Minmi sp., reconstruction of skull and mandible (QM F18101), left lateral view. Scale = 50 mm. (After Molnar 1996.)

Comments: The small theropod *Microvenator* had been founded upon a partial postcranial skeleton (AMNH 3041) discovered in 1932 during an American Museum of Natural History expedition to the Cloverly Formation (Lower Cretaceous) of Montana. At the time, the type species *M. celer* was neither named nor described (except for a preliminary description), nor was it assigned a type specimen. Almost 40 years later, John H. Ostrom finally performed those duties, although little has been published concerning this dinosaur in the ensuing years.

More recently, Makovicky and Sues (1997) (see also Sues 1998), in a brief preliminary report, reevaluated the genus and species in terms of their phylogenetic affinities. According to Makovicky and Sues, the holotype of *M. celer* exhibits features that are generally interpreted as indicating immaturity in archosaurs (*e.g.*, lack of fusion between centra and neural arches of vertebral column, and between scapula and coracoid). (In his original description of *M. celer*, Ostrom proposed that the type specimen could represent a juvenile.)

Based on their reexamination of AMNH 3041, Makovicky and Sues observed that *Microvenator* can be distinguished from other coelurosaurs by "an enlarged accessory trochanter on the femur and dorsoventrally flattened caudal centra."

From a cladistic analysis utilizing 89 characters, Makovicky and Sues concluded that *Microvenator* is "the sister group of Late Cretaceous Asian oviraptorids, within a monophyletic Oviraptorosauria," this genus representing "the stratigraphically oldest known record of the Oviraptorosauria."

Key references: Makovicky and Sues (1997); Ostrom (1970); Sues (1998).

†MINMI

Comments: In November, 1989, Ian Ievers found a second specimen of the small, Australian ankylosaur *Minmi*. The specimen was discovered on an outcrop of limestone concretions on a low ridge in the Toolebus Formation, Early Cretaceous (Albian), in open country south of the Flinders River on Marathon Station, east of Richmond, in north-central Queensland.

The following January, the specimen (QM F18101) was collected by the Queensland Museum. The nearly complete skeleton (in fact, the most complete dinosaur specimen yet found in Australia) includes most of the skull and body armor and was articulated, except, perhaps, for the feet, distal end of the tail, and axis. The remains were found upside down in marine deposits, associated with numerous shell plates of the mussel *Inoceramus*, a few teeth belonging to the small fossil shark *Echinorhinus*, and an

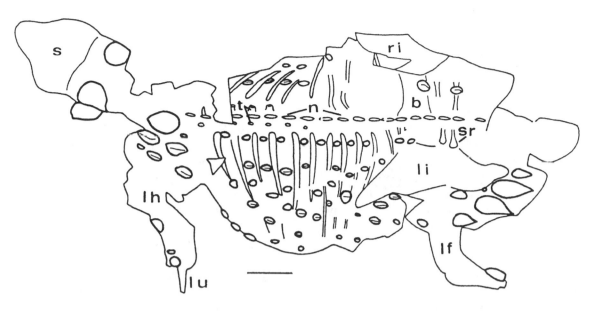

indeterminate ammonite, the body presumably having been washed out to sea (Molnar 1996).

Molnar stated that a detailed description of this specimen (and also a recently discovered, possibly conspecific thyreophoran skeleton), as well as an analysis of its phylogenetic relationships, must await the completion of its preparation and subsequent study. However, discussions of the specimen have appeared in various popular publications (*e.g.*, the Japanese magazine *Kyoryugaku Saizensen [Dino Front-line]*; Molnar 1994) and photographs of the specimen have been printed in a number of books (*e.g.*, *The Ultimate Dinosaur Book*, by Lambert 1993; see also *D:TE*).

According to Molnar, QM F18101, as partially prepared, reveals most of the contacts between cranial bones and preserves most dorsal armor in place. Among the unusual features of the specimen are a seemingly very large inferior process of the premaxilla, thin ventral sheets of the nasals, an apparently

Minmi paravertebra, life restoration painted by William Stout, based upon the collected specimens.

rod-like, vertical lacrimal, and pronounced coronoid process on the mandible. A broad "bridge" of bone joins the ilium to the sacrum, the former structure joining the medial margin of the ilium to the dorsal portions of the neural spines of at least three, perhaps five, sacral vertebrae.

Although small (apparently from 2.5 to 3.5 meters, or 8.5 to nearly 12 feet, in length when complete) when compared with skeletons of other ankylosaurs, QM F18101 was regarded by Molnar, for various reasons, as either "an almost mature, or newly mature, individual": Some early ankylosaurs are small, and *Minmi* is a relatively early member of this group. The holotype of *Minmi paravertebrata* was recovered from marine sediments near an island (see Molnar 1980) from which it possibly derived; if the lineage evolved in an insular environment, a small adult body size is feasible (see *Struthiosaurus* entry, *D:TE*). Most (QM F33565 and F33566 [possibly belonging to the same individual], AM F35259, QM F33286 and the holotype) of the collected specimens referred to *Minmi* measure within 10 percent of the linear dimensions of QM F18101; it seems unlikely (though is not impossible) that six specimens from different populations and geographical locations all represent juveniles. Even though the junctions between the cranial bones are mostly not fused (suggesting immaturity, but also the plesiomorphic state), the contacts in the braincase are fused, while both frontals and parietals are fused along the midline (suggesting adulthood in ankylosaurs; see Coombs and Maryańska 1990). The coracoids are not fused to the scapulae in QM F18101; but Coombs and Maryańska do not consider that to be a juvenile character, while the scapulocoracoids in some adult ankylosaurs are not fused (see Carpenter 1990; Pereda-Suberbiola 1994).

The fact that QM F18101 was found with the small dermal ossicles of the back mostly in place suggested to Molnar (1996) that the skin was present and intact on the animal's back at the time of burial. Molnar (1996) speculated that either the carcass was largely intact when it washed out to sea, floating for a considerable distance (gas bubbles forming during decomposition to facilitate floating) before sinking; or that it had dried out and mummified, floating until it became waterlogged. Of the two possible scenarios, Molnar (1996) favored the latter, the evidence supporting this interpretation including the dorsal sheet of ossiciles in QM F18101 having "sunk" in between the ribs, a condition "consistent with mummification" and difficult to explain otherwise (except that without air or gas bouyancy, such a carcass would sink; K. Carpenter, personal communication 1997).

Key references: Molnar (1980, 1996).

†MUTTABURRASAURUS

Ornithischia: Genasauria: Cerapoda: Ornithopoda: Euornithopoda: ?"Hypsilophodontidae."

Comments: Molnar (1996*a*) published new data relating to the evolution and systematic position of the bulbous-snouted Australian ornithischian *Muttaburrasaurus*, following further preparation of the holotype skeleton (QM F6140) and also the discovery of a new skull (QM F14921).

As related by Molnar, the second and probably more complete skull was collected in 1987 by paleontologist Mary Wade of the Queensland Museum from the Upper Cretaceous (Albian) Allaru Mudstone ("a gray calcareous marine argillite" underlaying the younger Mackunda Formation, from which QM F6140 was recovered) on Dunluce station, between Hughenden and Richmond, in north-central Queensland. The specimen "has been laterally sheared and

A. *Muttaburrasaurus langdoni*, reconstructed holotype skull (QM F6140), and B. *Muttaburrasaurus* sp., skull (QM F14921). (After Molnar 1996.)

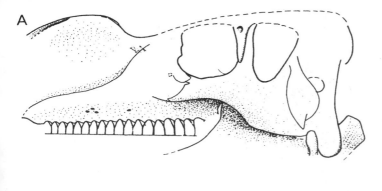

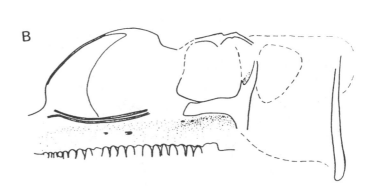

crushed," the nasal bulla (a large and prominent structure) being flattened, the skull roof lying almost coplanar with the right side. The left postorbital region is badly damaged with the postorbital entirely missing.

Because of the general form of this skull, as well as the apomorphic nasal bulla and form of the teeth, Molnar referred QM F14921 to the genus *Muttaburrasaurus*. Due to damage and the as yet unfinished preparation, and also the possession of partly erupted maxillary crowns anteriorly in the tooth row (those of the type species being entirely erupted along the entire visible maxillary tooth row), and differences in form, Molnar found it premature to assign this second skull to *M. langdoni*, referring it instead to *Muttaburrasaurus* sp.

Based on both specimens, Molnar redescribed the skull of this genus with particular attention focused on the structure of the palate and braincase, also the maxilla, postorbital bar, and other relevant cranial features. Further cleaning of the type specimen before preparing a reconstruction of the skeleton revealed the metatarsus to be shorter than initially believed, thereby reducing what had been thought to be a disparity in length between the third and other metatarsals.

Muttaburrasaurus was originally described by Bartholomai and Molnar (1981) as an iguanodontian closely related to *Camptosaurus*, this phylogenetic assessment largely based upon the earlier comparative study, primarily of the ornithopods *Camptosaurus* and *Tenontosaurus*, by Dodson (1980). As pointed out by Molnar, that assessment was somewhat based on the identification of "an incomplete, flattened, tapering element" as possibly representing a thumb-spike, a plausible interpretation if *Muttaburrsaurus* is, in fact, an ankylopollexian. However, as this piece of bone is "poorly preserved, abraded and broken" it cannot be identified as a thumb-spike with certainty and constitute evidence that this genus belongs in the Ankylopollexia.

With access to better material than when the genus was first described, and in lieu of the original and newly revealed character states, Molnar reviewed the systematic position of *Muttaburrasaurus*. This reassessment of the genus was mostly based upon the more recent reinterpretation of ornithischian phylogeny published by Sereno (1986), although, as Molnar pointed out, the incompleteness of the material

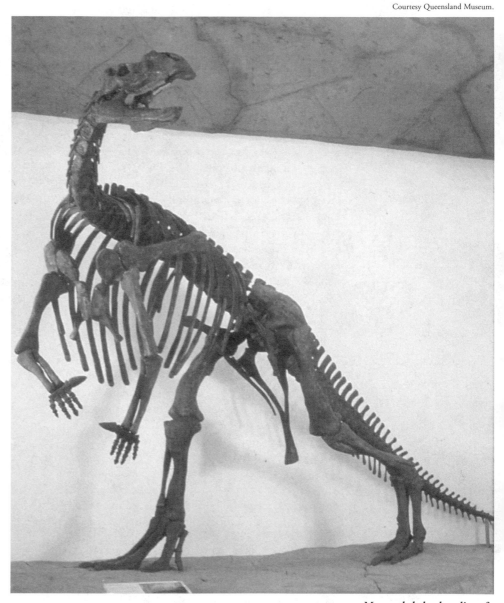

Mounted skeletal replica of *Muttaburrasaurus langdoni*, based upon the incomplete holotype specimen (QM F6140).

precluded many of the character states utilized by Sereno.

From Molnar's new analysis, three of the seven characters used by Sereno to diagnose the Genasauria ("mandibular dentition offset medially; moderate coronoid process; pubic peduncle of ilium less robust than ischial peduncle") were found to be present in *Muttaburrasaurus*, making it reasonable to include this genus in that group; one character ("external opening of the antorbital fossa of moderate size or smaller") out of four used by Sereno to diagnose the Ornithopoda were found in the Australian genus, thereby giving reason to regard *Muttaburrasaurus* as an ornithopod. However, on the basis of what is presently known of it, this genus could not be assigned by Molnar to any group below that of Ornithopoda. According to that author, *Muttaburrasaurus* "may represent

a lineage that diverged from the iguanodont-hadrosaur line prior to the divergence of taxa such as *Dryosaurus* and *Tenontosaurus*."

In comparing the geologically younger holotype skull with QM F14921, Molnar found the former to differ in various unexpected ways, some of them suggesting "a trend toward the evolution of a continuous more-or-less planar sheet of enamel along the labial face of the maxillary dentition." Apparently, the nasal bulla in the type specimen differs somewhat in shape (shorter and slightly deeper in QM F14921) and structure (*e.g.*, in QM F14921, crescentic element makes up anterior part of lateral wall of bulla, possibly being or being part of premaxilla; in holotype, lateral wall seems to consist of single element) from that of the "Dunluce" skull. There may also be other differences between the two morphs (*e.g.*, "form of the jugal-maxillary contact"; "absence of replacement crowns in the maxillary series"), though these could not be determined due to the states of preparation and preservation.

Of five potential explanations for these differences (including pathology and ontogenetic development), Molnar found only three (individual variation, sexual dimorphism, and phylogenetic trends) to be reasonably viable. Of these three, the latter explanation, with *Muttaburrasaurus* sp. considered to be slightly more primitive than the holotype of *M. langdoni*, was deemed the most plausible. If that explanation is correct, then smaller teeth recovered from the Griman Creek Formation at Lightning Ridge may pertain to a more plesiomorphic species of this genus. This would suggest "that the teeth in this lineage evolved to progressively reduce the size of the primary ridge on the maxillary teeth, progressively displace it towards the posterior (distal) edge of the lateral face and increase the number of secondary ridges," thereby providing "a continuous, lightly corrugated strip of enamel along the lateral side of the upper dentition." Molnar noted that this condition is consistent with Barthomolai and Molnar's earlier suggestion of a shearing dentition in this genus, and that the maxillary teeth of the older *Atlascoposaurus* (NMV P157390) are near "to the expected ancestral state of those of *Muttaburrasaurus*.

More recently, Norman observed that the anatomy of *M. landoni* is not consistent with that of a typical iguanodontid; rather, the maxillary dentition of this species resembles that of more derived hypsilophodontids like *Rhabdodon* (see Weishampel, Grigorescu and Norman 1991) and the hypsilophodontian *Tenontosaurus*; and the postcranial skeleton, though imperfect, mostly resembles that of hypsilophodontids.

During the late 1990s, a "skeleton replica" of *M.*

landoni, "based (loosely) on QM F6140" (R. E. Molnar, personal communication 1998), was mounted at the Queensland Museum.

Key references: Bartholomai and Molnar (1981); Dodson (1980); Molnar (1996*a*); Norman (1998); Sereno (1986).

†NANOTYRANNUS—(See *Tyrannosaurus*.)

†NANSHIUNGOSAURUS

Saurischia: Theropoda: Neotheropoda: Tetanurae: Avetheropoda: Coelurosauria: ?Manuraptoriformes: ?Therizinosauroidea: Therizinosauridae.

New species: *N. bohlini* Dong and Yu 1997.

Occurrence of *N. bohlini*: Xinminbao Group, Gansu Province, China.

Age: Late Early Cretaceous or Early Late Cretaceous.

Known material/holotype of *N. bohlini*: IVPP V. 11116, series of vertebrae comprising 11 cervicals (including atlas) and five dorsals, fragmentary ribs.

Diagnosis of *N. bohlini*: Larger than other known therizinosaurs [=segnosaurs of their usage]; centra of

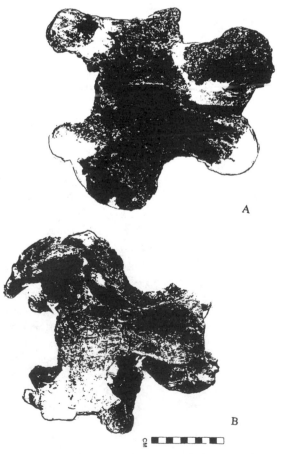

Nanshiungosaurus bohlini, IVPP V. 11116, holotype tenth cervical vertebra, in A. dorsal and B. ventral views. (After Dong and Yu 1997.)

cervical and dorsal vertebrae platycoelous; cervical neural spines low, long; zygapophyses long, wide, located well above neural canals; dorsal neural spines low, narrow; dorsal vertebrae with keels (Dong and Yu 1997).

Comments: This second species of *Nanshiungosaurus*—an Asian genus originally believed to be a rather small and unusual sauropod, but later was considered to be an equally unusual theropod—was founded upon partial postcranial remains (IVPP V. 11116) found in 1992 during the Sino-Japanese Silk Road Dinosaur Expedition (Dong 1997*b*) to the uppermost Xinminbao Group, Gongpoquan Basin of the Mazongshan Area of Gansu Province, China (Dong and Yu 1997). Dong and Yu primarily distinguished *N. bohlini* from the type species, *N. brevispinus*, by features of the neural spines. In the latter, the anterior cervical vertebrae are amphicoelous and the posterior ones are opisthocoelous; the dorsal vertebrae are amphiplatyan and possess broad neural spines.

Although therizinosauroids have generally come to be regarded as a grouping of atypical theropods (see *D:TE*), Dong and Yu interpreted them as establishing the new "order" Segnosaurischia, with the genus *Nanshiungosaurus* belonging in its own "segnosaurischian" family, the Nanshiungosauridae, whose members somewhat resemble sauropods (see "Systematics" chapter).

Key reference: Dong (1997*b*); Dong and Yu (1997).

NEDCOLBERTIA Kirkland, Britt, Whittle, Madsen and Burge 1998

Saurischia: Theropoda: Neotheropoda: Tetanurae: Avetheropoda: Coelurosauria: Manuraptoriformes.

Name derivation: "Ned [Edwin H.] Colbert."

Type species: *N. justinhofmanni* Kirkland, Britt, Whittle, Madsen and Burge 1998.

Other species: [None.]

Occurrence: Cedar Mountain Formation, Utah, United States.

Age: Early Cretaceous (Barremian).

Known material: Three partial associated skeletons (one juvenile, two subadults).

Holotype: CEUM 5071, partial associated skeleton including several fragments of caudal vertebrae, proximal femora, distal right tibia, distal right fibula, both calcanea, lateral halves of main bodies of both astragali, distal and proximal ends of right metatarsals, several partial phalanges, three proximal unguals, portion of distal humerus, numerous unidentified fragments (collected as float, *i.e.* on the surface), excavated quarry material including numerous caudal centra, fragments of pelvis, distal left femur, left tibia, proximal right tibia, left fibula lacking middle of shaft, almost complete set of left metatarsals, 14 phalanges, three pedal unguals, partial pubis, parts of ischium, juvenile.

Diagnosis of genus (as for type species): Small, lightly built, cursorial theropod, having simple pneumatic dorsal vertebrae unlike ornithomimids, tyrannosaurids, and troodontids; manus having long, slender phalanges, deep raptorial first manual ungual with large flexor tubercle, slender second manual ungual indicating differentiated unguals (unlike ornithomimids and *Ornitholestes*); hind leg slender; femur bowed medially, femoral head inclined below greater trochanter, anterior trochanter shorter than greater trochanter (unlike condition in Manuraptoriformes), fourth trochanter well developed on proximal half of femur (unlike *Microvenator*); tibia and fibula longer than femur (as in most small theropods); astragalus extending up almost 25 percent length of tibia (as in Coelurosauria); pes as long as tibia, first digit present (unlike condition in most ornithomimids), metatarsals closely appressed along all but most distal portions, with third metatarsal narrowed proximally, but not excluded from ankle (in a manner similar to that in *Ornitholestes*); pedal unguals long, asymmetrical, triangular in cross section, no raptorial second ungual (as in dromaeosaurids and troodontids) (Kirkland, Britt, Whittle, Madsen and Burge 1998).

Comments: The genus *Nedcolbertia* was founded upon an incomplete skeleton (CEUM 5071) of a

Nedcolbertia justinhofmanni, CEUM 5071, holotype incomplete pelvic elements, including (clockwise) proximal end of left ischium (lateral view), right pubic boot (right side), also pubic boot (right side) of paratype CEUM 5072, and distal end of ischium of CEUM 5071 (lateral view).

Courtesy James I. Kirkland.

Nedcolbertia

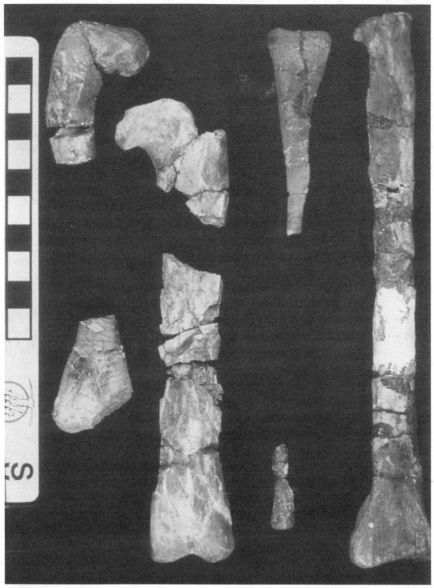

Nedcolbertia justinhof-manni, CEUM 5071, holotype proximal limb elements (left to right) right femur (cranial view), left femur (cranial view), left tibia (lateral view), and right tibia (cranial view).

juvenile individual discovered in 1993 by Christopher Whittle of the University of New Mexico in a drab, green-mauve claystone resting on a thick nodular calcrete at the base of the Yellow Cat Member of the Cedar Mountain Formation (Lower Cretaceous, Barremian), northeast of Gaston Quarry, northeast of Arches National Park and southeast of Cisco (Barremian; see Kirkland, Britt, Burge, Carpenter, Cifelli, DeCourten, Eaton, Hasiotis and Lawton 1997), in eastern Utah. Whittle found the specimen while assisting Donald Burge of the College of Eastern University at excavations at the Gaston Quarry, site of the original *Utahraptor ostrommaysorum* find. Two (subadult) paratype specimens from the same locality include the following: CEUM 5072, a partial associated skeleton comprising a few fragments of dorsal vertebrae, several fragments of caudal vertebrae, fragments

of ilia, fragments of pubis, fused distal pubis, weathered fragments of proximal left and right femora, fragments of proximal and distal tibia, two proximal fibulae, fragments of astragali, proximal and distal ends of metatarsals, numerous partial and complete pedal phalanges, five partial pedal unguals, four ?manus phalanges, two partial first unguals, and one partial second ungual; and CEUM 5073, a partial associated skeleton including numerous fragments and a few complete caudal centra, several fragments of caudal neural arches, several proximal chevrons, large fragments of both coracoids, fragment of proximal humerus, and numerous unidentified fragments. The three specimens, discovered within 50 meters of one another, were mostly found as float, having apparently undergone little transport on exposure to the surface. The presence of associated fossils, including crocodilian teeth and a lungfish tooth plate, suggest that these skeletons were preserved in an aquatic environment. Other material assigned to the type species *Nedcolbertia justinhofmanni* includes material recovered from the Dalton Well Quarry (see Britt and Stadtman 1996), higher in the Yellow Cat Member on the west side of Arches National Park (Kirkland, Britt, Whittle, Madsen and Burge 1998).

Its type material largely excavated by Scott K. Madsen of Dinosaur National Monument, this small theropod was informally mentioned in several preliminary announcements (*e.g.,* Anonymous 1998). The specific name is in honor of New Jersey youth Justin Hoffman, grand-prize winner of the Search for America's Junior Paleontologist co-sponsored by Dinamation International Society and Discover Card.

According to Kirkland *et al.* (1998), the holotype specimen indicates an individual having an estimated total length of about 1.5 meters, with the subadults approximately 3 meters long.

In attempting to classify *Nedcolbertia*, Kirkland *et al.* (1998) found the genus to be "within the Tetanurae because of the expanded pubic foot, reduced fibula, and horizontal groove on the astragalus" (*e.g.,* Gauthier 1986; Holtz 1994a; Sereno 1997). Placing the new genus in the Coelurosauria was problematic, as the ischium in the type material is incomplete, and therefore cannot be shown to be reduced in length relative to the pubis. However, the "expansive ascending process of the astragalus is strongly supportive of *Nedcolbertia*'s inclusion within the Coelurosauria" (*e.g.,* Gauthier 1986; Holtz 1994b). Determining whether or not *Nedcolbertia* belongs in the Manuraptoriformes was difficult due to the poor state of preservation of the forelimb (*e.g.,* Holtz 1994a, 1994b, 1996), although the anterior trochanter does not reach the top of the femur in this genus.

As the structure of the foot excludes *Nedcolbertia*

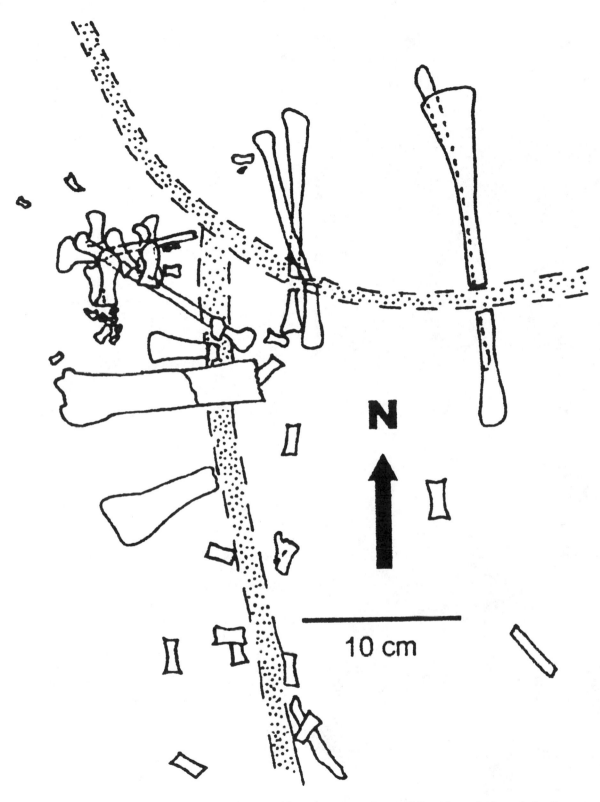

N

10 cm

from the Arctometatarsalia (Holtz 1994a, 1994b, 1996), the well-differentiated manual ungual separates it from the Oviraptorosauria, and the absence of a raptorial second pedal ungual bars it from the Dromaeosauridae. Kirkland *et al.* (1998) found it most parsimonious to regard this genus as a basal coeluro-saur near the small Late Jurassic theropods *Compsognathus* and, especially, *Ornitholestes*, sharing with the latter a similar ankle and foot. Based on what can be determined in the preserved materials of *Nedcolbertia* and in the flattened holotype skeleton of *Compsognathus*, these two genera could share the same kind of

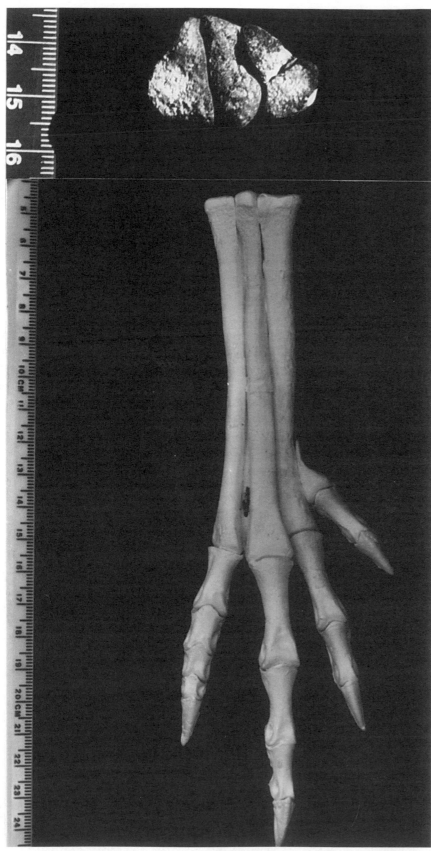

Nedcolbertia justinhofmani (bottom) referred foot of juvenile specimen, (top) proximal view of metatarsals. (After Kirkland, Britt, Burge, Carpenter, Cifelli, DeCourten, Eaton, Hasiotis and Lawton 1997.)

derived ischium. The humerus in *Nedcolbertia* seems to resemble most closely that of *Coelurus fragilis* and *Ornitholestes hermanni*. However, the pubis of *Coelurus* possesses a deeper boot, and the pubes are fused for a greater percentage of their length. *Nedcolbertia* also differs from *Ornitholestes* in various ways: The pubis has a much larger obturator notch; the first manual ungual in *Nedcolbertia* is more robust and has a more prominent flexor tubercle than the other manual ungual; the distal end of the femur is more quadrate; the metatarsals are more closely appressed; and, in cross-section, the pedal unguals are more angulate, with pits instead of a flexor tubercle.

Note: Kirkland *et al.* (1998) noted that a geologically younger, gracile yet larger North American coelurosaurian theropod — known from diverse specimens, all possibly representing a single taxon and collected from strata of Aptian–Albian age — may be related to *Nedcolbertia*. These materials include remains (USNM 6107, including caudal vertebrae, pedal claws, distal metatarsals, and an astragalus) recovered from the Arundel Formation of Maryland, and originally described by Gilmore (1920) as *Ornithomimus affinis* (see *Archaeornithomimus* and *Ornithomimus* entries, *D:TE*); additional material recovered in recent years that could be referable to this taxon (T. Lipka, personal communication to Kirkland *et al.* 1998); incomplete left metatarsals II (YPM 5174) and IV (YPM 5284), and a pedal ungual (YPM 5286) from the Cloverly Formation of southern Montana, described by Ostrom (1970) as *Ornithomimus* sp.; and a large gracile theropod foot (AU 74-16) from the Trinity Group of southwestern Arkansas (Quinn 1973), informally referred to as "Arkansaurus fridayi" (see *D:TE*, "Notes" to *Archaeornithomimus* entry). According to Kirkland *et al.* (1998), the "presence of this taxon together with *Nedcolbertia* suggests an underappreciated radiation of primitive coelurosaurians during the Early Cretaceous."

Key references: Anonymous (1998); Britt and Stadtman (1997); Kirkland, Britt, Burge, Carpenter, Cifelli, DeCourten, Eaton, Hasiotis and Lawton (1997); Kirkland, Britt, Whittle, Madsen and Burge (1998).

†NEMEGTOSAURUS—(=?*Quaesitosaurus*)

Saurischia: Sauropodomorpha: Sauropoda: Eusauropoda: Neosauropoda: Macronaria: Camarasauromorpha: Titanosauriformes: Somphospondyli: Titanosauria: ?Titanosauridae.

Age: Late Cretaceous (Campanian–Maastrichtian).

Comments: Preserved and collected skulls of any kinds of sauropod dinosaurs have always been rare. Delicate in construction, they are usually not preserved with the rest (and more durable) parts of the skeleton, either due to weathering or being separated from the neck. The most complete sauropod cranial material known from the Late Cretaceous are isolated skulls of *Nemegtosaurus mongoliensis* and *Quaesitosaurus orientalis*, both of these species having been found in the Nemegt Formation of Mongolia.

The holotype skull (ZPAL MgD-I/9; see *D:TE* for photograph of nonrestored specimen) of *N. mongoliensis* lacks only its dorsal portion and includes the lower jaws. Nowiński (1979), in originally describing *Nemegtosaurus*, noted that the skull resembles that of *Dicraeosaurus*, an observation also shared by McIntosh (1990*b*) in the latter's review of the Sauropda. Consequently, *Nemegtosaurus*, for almost two decades, has been generally regarded as a dicraeosaurine diplodocid or a dicraeosaurid.

More recent studies by Salgado and Calvo (1992, 1997), Yu (1993), and Salgado, Coria and Calvo (1997), however, have resulted in different interpretations. Salgado and Coria (1992), discerning no synapomorphies linking *Nemegtosaurus* and *Quaesitosaurus* with either the dicraeosaurids *Dicraeosaurus* or *Amargasaurus*, removed the former two genera from the Dicraeosaurinae. Subsequently, Yu (1993), in a cladistic study of the Diplodocidae, agreed with that assessment, erecting for *Nemegtosaurus* and *Quaesitosaurus* the new diplodocid subfamily Nemegtosaurinae.

As pointed out by Salgado and Calvo (1997), Nowiński's assignment of *Nemegtosaurus* to the Dicraeosaurinae was mostly based upon these features: 1. Possession of cylindrical, peg-like teeth restricted to anterior region of jaws; 2. anteroventrally projecting basipterygoid processes; and 3. anterior inclination of quadrate. However, as these characters are uncertain in *Quaesitosaurus*, inclusion of this genus in the Dicraeosaurinae cannot be verified.

In reassessing the type skulls of *Nemegtosaurus* and *Quaesitosaurus*, Salgado and Calvo (1997) interpreted the earlier published reconstructions to be in error, pointing out that the *Nemegtosaurus* skull seems to have been somewhat distorted do to preservational deformation.

New reconstructions of both type skulls by Salgado and Calvo (1997) portray *Nemegtosaurus* and *Quaesitosaurus* as having rather primitive *Camarasaurus*-type skulls rather than more advanced *Diplodocus*-type skulls as was previously believed. Indeed, if this interpretation is correct, the primitive structure of their skulls ("occipital condyle and paroccipital processes posteroventrally oriented, basipterygoid processes ventrally directed and 'camarasauroid' conformation, and disposition of the nares in the skull") suggest that these two genera are closely related to the Titanosauridae (first suggested by Calvo, 1994*a*, 1994*b*) and are not diplodocids.

Salgado and Calvo (1997) also noted that *Nemegtosaurus* and *Quaesitosaurus* probably share the fol-

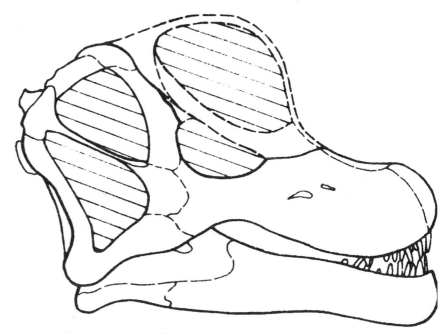

Nemegtosaurus mongoliensis, new reconstruction of holotype skull (ZPAL MgD-I/9). (After Salgado and Calvo 1997.)

lowing plesiomorphic characters with other nondiplodocid sauropods: 1. Lacrimal vertically oriented; 2. jugal not participating in margin of antorbital fenestra; anterior section of suture between premaxilla and maxilla almost vertical; 4. absence of maxillary process clasping anterior end of vomer; and 5. coronoid process of surangular elevated. In their new reconstructions of these skulls, Salgado and Calvo (1997) speculated that the nares were probably double and located anteriorly.

Salgado and Calvo (1997) regarded *Nemegtosaurus* and *Quaesitosaurus* as basically similar genera, but different in various ways. As noted by these authors, the paraoccipital processes in *Quaesitosaurus* project laterally and short basipterygoid processes project ventrally (see Kurzanov and Banikov 1983), while in *Nemegtosaurus* the basipterygoid processes are directed anteroventrally (Nowiński); *Quaesitosaurus* seems to have the unique feature of a deep depression on the lateral face of the quadrate and a prominent channel opening beneath the condyle, the inclination of the quadrate apparently arbitrary (Kurzanov and Banikov), while in *Nemegtosaurus* the condyle slants sharply forward as in diplodocids (Nowiński).

Despite the similarities of these two skulls, the generic validity of *Quaesitosaurus* has recently come into question. Wilson (1997), in a preliminary reevaluation of Mongolian sauropods, observed that both *Nemegtosaurus* and *Quaesitosaurus* are characterized by a unique basipterygoid articulation and other [as yet unlisted] features suggesting that these taxa could be conspecific, with previously noted differences seemingly due to post-mortem deformation.

Wilson basically agreed with Salgado and Calvo (1997), and Salgado, Coria and Calvo (1997) regarding

New reconstruction of holotype skull of *Quaesi-
tosaurus orientalis,* a possible junior synonym of
*Nemegtosaurus mongolien-
sis.* (After Salgado and
Calvo 1997.)

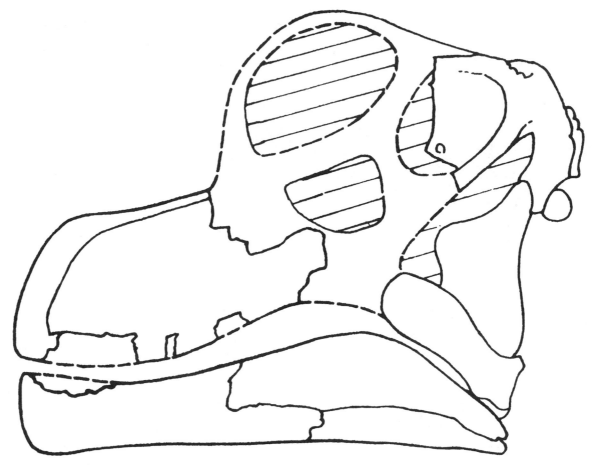

the affinities of *Nemegtosaurus* and *Quaesitosaurus,* noting that the presence of a broad quadrate fossa and enlarged coronoid region on the lower jaw in these genera suggest that they belong in the Neosauropoda (see also Upchurch 1997); furthermore, additional [but not yet mentioned] features of the braincase suggest a close alliance with a group of derived titanosaurs. According to Wilson, given the Campanian–Maastrichtian age and Asian origin of these two taxa, their phylogenetic affinities are particularly relevant to an understanding of Late Cretaceous sauropod lineages when Mesozoic continental isolation was at its peak.

Wilson concluded that, although all major neosauropod lineages ("broad-nostrilled forms and diplodocids") are known from the Late Jurassic to Early Cretaceous, titanosaurs make up almost all of sauropod diversity in the Late Cretaceous. Most of these dinosaurs flourished in South America, although South American titanosaurs do not seem to form a natural group, this, according to Wilson, "suggesting that titanosaurs experienced a complex biogeographic history that can be better understood only with knowledge of their lower-level relationships."

However, although Wilson considered *Quaesitosaurus* to be a junior synonym of *Nemegtosaurus,* some workers are skeptical of that assessment. According to

sauropod specialist John S. McIntosh (personal communication 1998), the more recent reconstructions of the skull of *Nemegtosaurus* may be somewhat inaccurate, with the relationships of the Cretaceous sauropods yet to be understood pending the collection and study of new material.

Note: Dong (1997*d*) reported three teeth and a caudal vertebra (IVPP V. 11123) recovered during the Sino-Japanese Silk Road Dinosaur Expedition from the upper part of the Xinminbao Group (Lower Cretaceous) of the Mazongshan Area, Gansu Province, China (Dong 1997*b*), and referred to the "Nemegtosauridae." The peg-like teeth (IVPP V. 11123-2-3) are similar to those of both *N. mongoliensis* and referred species *N. pachi.* The caudal (IVPP V. 11123-4) is platycoelous and resembles one collected from the Cap de la Heve, Bleville (Upper Albian), Normandy, described by Buffetaut (1984).

Key references: Kurzanov and Banikov (1983); McIntosh (1990*b*); Nowiński (1979); Salgado and Calvo (1992, 1997); Salgado and Coria (1992); Salgado, Coria and Calvo (1997); Wilson (1997); Yu (1993).

NEOVENATOR Hutt, Martill and Barker 1996
Saurischia: Theropoda: Neotheropoda: Tetanurae: Avetheropoda: Carnosauria: Allosauroidea: ?Allosauridae.

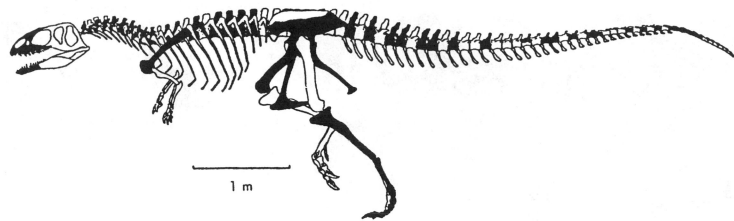

Name derivation: Greek *neo* = "new" + Greek *venator* = "hunter."
Type species: *N. salerii* Hutt, Martill and Barker 1996.
Other species: [None.]
Occurrence: Wessex Formation, Isle of Wight, England.
Age: Early Cretaceous (Barremian).
Known material/holotype: MIWG 6348 and BMNH R10001, most of skeleton including partial skull.

Diagnosis of genus (as for type species): Allosauroid with five premaxillary teeth (shared with *Allosaurus*); external narcs twice as long as high, twice as long as dental margin of premaxilla; maxillary fenestra large, located posteriorly with narrow posterior margin; teeth with crowns one quarter total length of tooth; all dorsal vertebrae pleurocoelous (shared with *Torvosaurus*; see Britt 1991); pedal unguals with distinct dorsal groove (Hutt, Martill and Barker 1996).

Comments: Theropod specimens from the Cretaceous of Europe are rare, especially those from the Wealden Group of England. Many generic and specific names have been given to numerous theropod specimens found in England, most of these names now regarded as *nomina dubia*.

The first reported allosauroid and one of the best represented of the valid theropod taxa from England is *Neovenator salerii*, a type species founded upon a partially articulated skeleton (MIWG 6348 and BMNH R10001) approximately 70-percent complete, excavated in 1978 from a cliff face at Grange Chine, Brighstone Bay, on the west coast of the Isle of Wight, United Kingdom. This specimen, the most complete theropod known from the Isle of Wight, was recovered from a plant debris bed below the Grange Chine Sandstone of the Wessex Formation (Lower Cretaceous), Wealden Group (see Stewart 1981) (Hutt, Martill and Barker 1996).

As cited by Hutt *et al.*, the cranial material of the holotype includes both premaxillae with replacement teeth, a left maxilla, right nasal, the anterior portion of the left dentary with replacement teeth, and a few large isolated teeth; the postcranial skeleton includes at least six cervical vertebrae, 22 caudal vertebrae, three hemal processes together with fragments of cervical and dorsal ribs, several gastralia, shoulder girdle including a fused left scapulocoracoid, pelvic girdle comprising acetabular borders of both ilia and a head and partial shafts of the pubes, a right femur, left tibia and fibula, metatarsals II and IV, and several phalanges including unguals. These bones, preserved in siltstone with some pyrite overgrowths, are mostly three-dimensional, with just slight damage from compaction. The bones, though spread over an approximate 24 square-meter area, are of the same preservational mode, not duplicated, and proportionally correct for a single animal. Taken together, this specimen represents a large but gracile theropod measuring approximately 7.5 meters (about 26 feet) in length.

Hutt *et al.* identified *Neovenator* as a member of the Avetheropoda (see Holtz 1994*a*) based on its possession of a large pubic boot; and of the Allosauroidea, as the nasal participates in the antorbital fenestra (Sereno, Wilson, Larsson, Dutheil and Sues 1994). The authors tentatively assigned *Neovenator* to the Allosauridae based upon characters regarded by Holtz as autapomorphic of that family, these including the possession of a pubic boot that is longer anteriorly than posteriorly and triangular in ventral view, adding that they did not know if those features were present or absent in the Sinraptoridae.

Comparing *Neovenator* to the allosaurid *Allosaurus* and sinraptorid *Sinraptor*, Hutt *et al.* pointed out that all three possess pleurocoelous cervical and dorsal vertebrae, though in the latter two genera the pleurocoels do not continue after the fourth dorsal. *Neovenator* differs from *Allosaurus* in the following features: Snout in the former genus more elongate, with narrow bite of no more than 80 millimeters wide; more strongly procoelous cervical and dorsal vertebrae; relatively shorter and thicker dorsal neural spines; pronounced ischial boot (only a terminal

Neovenator salerii, reconstructed skeleton based on holotype (MIWG 6348 and BMNH R1000), outline based on *Allosaurus* as modified by Madsen (1976). Scale = 1 m. (After Hutt, Martill and Barker 1996.)

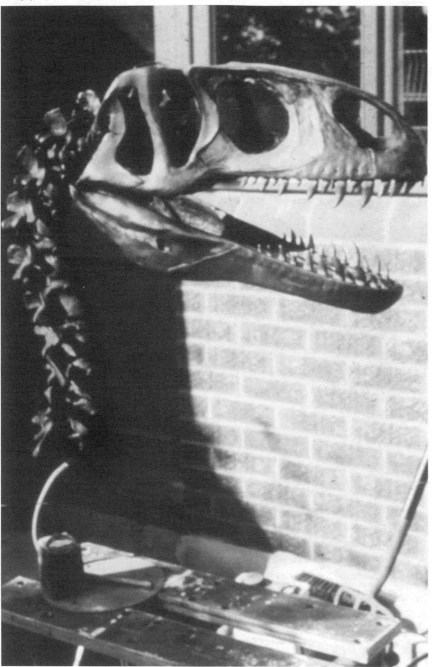

Photograph by the author, courtesy Museum of the Isle of Wight Geology.

Neovenator salerii, skull with cervical vertebrae as reconstructed by paleontologist Steve Hutt during the mid–1980s (then regarded as a possible new species of *Megalosaurus*).

swelling in *Allosaurus*); accessory trochanter on femoral shaft; proximal bulge behind crista fibularis of tibia; dorsal groove on pedal ungual phalanges. It differs from *Sinraptor* in having five rather than four (the usual theropod condition) teeth in the premaxilla.

According to Hutt *et al.*, the discovery of this allosaurid in the Lower Cretaceous of Europe could constitute additional evidence supporting the idea of a Cretaceous Pan-Laurasian dinosaur fauna, although its being distinct from both the North American *Allosaurus* and Asian *Sinraptor* could "indicate postseparation from an earlier pandemic allosaurid stock."

In 1985, more than a decade before this new taxon was formally named and described, a mounted skeleton, including casts of the holotype reconstructed somewhat based on *Allosaurus* and labeled as *Megalosaurus*, was displayed at the Dinosaur Museum in Dorchester (see *D:TE*, *Megalosaurus* entry, for photograph of this exhibit).

Key reference: Hutt, Martill and Barker (1996).

†**NEUQUENSAURUS** Powell *see in* Bonaparte 1987 —(=*Microcoelus*; =?*Loricosaurus*)
Saurischia: Sauropodomorpha: Sauropoda: Eusauropoda: Neosauropoda: Macronaria: Camarasauromorpha: Titanosauriformes: Somphospondyli: Titanosauria: Titanosauridae.
Name derivation: "Neuquén [province of Argentina]" + Greek *sauros* = "lizard."
Type species: *N. australis* (Lydekker 1893).
Other species: *N. robustus* (Huene 1929).
Occurrence: ?Río Colorado Formation, ?Allen Formation, Allen and Río Negro Formations, Neuquén and Río Negro Provinces, Argentina.
Age: Late Cretaceous (Coniacian–Campanian).
Known material: Various postcranial remains.
Holotype: MLP. Ly. 1/2/3/4/5/6, caudal vertebrae.

Comments: The genus *Neuquensaurus* (a *nomen nudum* in *D:TE*) was founded upon varied material first described by Lydekker (1893) as a new species of *Titanosaurus*, *T. australis*.

As detailed by Bonaparte (1996*b*), this species was based upon varied remains including caudal vertebrae (the holotype, MLP. Ly. 1/2/3/4/5/6), as well as several groups of vertebrae, scapulae, coracoids, humeri, ulnae, most postcranial elements, this material collected circa 1891 by S. Roth, then in 1910–1920 by personnel of the La Plata Museum, possibly from the Río Colorado Formation (Coniacian) and Allen Formation (Campanian), Neuquén and Río Negro Provinces, Argentina. As adequate data on the provenance and correct association of the recovered pieces were not available, Lydekker, and then Huene (1929), had to utilize mixed specimens in their respective studies of *T. australis*.

Later, Powell (1986), in his as yet unpublished doctoral thesis, interpreted the remains studied by Lydekker and Huene as representing a genus distinct from *Titanosaurus*, describing the material and renaming it *Neuquensaurus*. The new generic name was first published by Bonaparte (1987), the type species, *N. australis*, subsequently published by Powell (1987).

McIntosh (1990*b*), in a review of the Sauropoda, tentatively referred this taxon to *Saltasaurus* as a second species of that genus, ?*S. australis*.

According to Bonaparte (1996*b*), *Neuquensaurus*

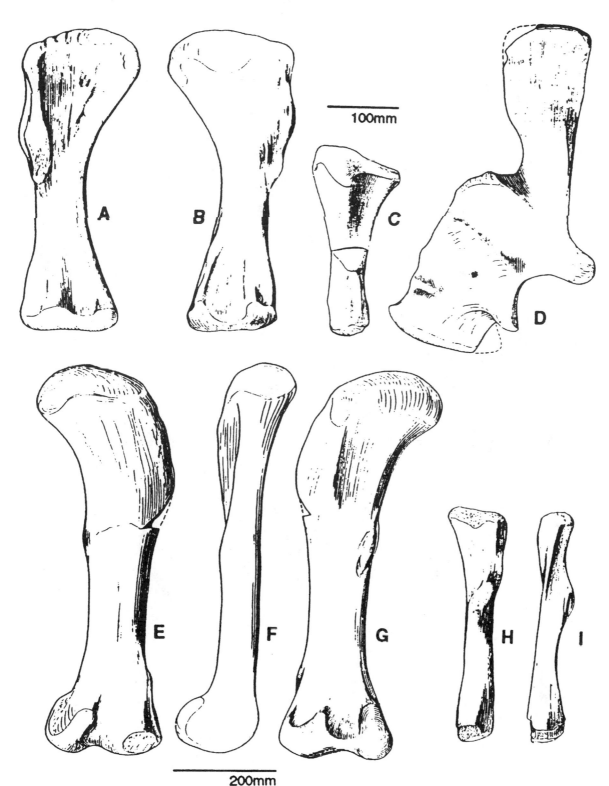

100mm

200mm

mainly differs from *Titanosaurus* in the morphology of the caudal vertebrae and of the forelimb bones. Although *Neuquensaurus* is similar to *Saltasaurus*, the former differs in details of the caudals and sacrum, which are opistholocleian rather than biconvex as in the latter; the limb bones are more slender than in *Saltasaurus*; and the scapula, though having a different outline, has a medial projection on its anterior border similar to that in *Saltasaurus*.

Bonaparte (1996*b*) speculated that both *Neuquensaurus* and *Saltasaurus* had similar ecological roles and belonged to a widely distributed subfamily, and

Neuquensaurus

Neuquensaurus robustus, A.–B.–C. right femur, posterior, medial, and anterior views, D. right fibula, lateral view, E. right tibia, anterior view, F.–G.–H. left ulna, lateral, medial, and posterior views. Scale = 200 mm. (After Huene 1929.)

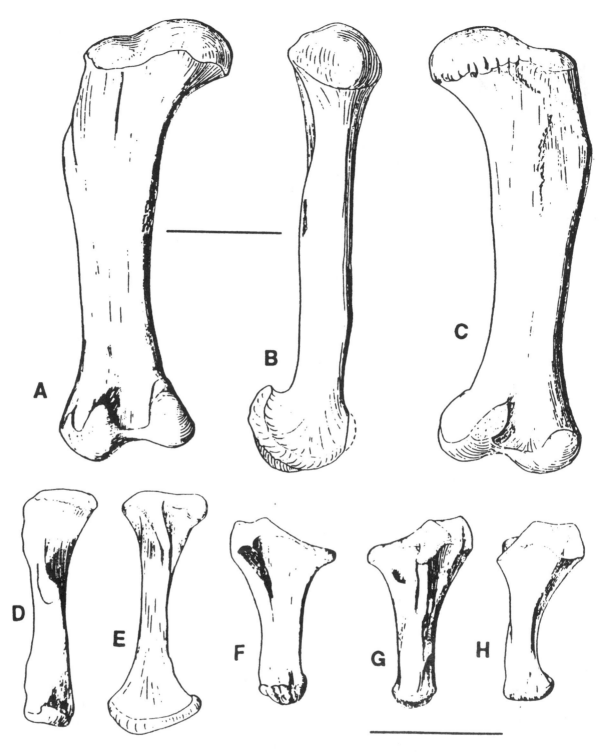

that quite possibly *Neuquensaurus*, like *Saltasaurus*, was armored (though it has never been unequivocally shown that the scutes described by Huene as *Loricosaurus* belong to *Neuquensaurus*; see "Note" below).

As Bonaparte (1996*b*) noted, Huene had proposed the species *Titanosaurus robustus* based upon its more robust limb bones, this taxon having been founded on lectotpe specimens (MLP.CS. 1094, 1095, 1171, and 1480) comprising both ulnae, a left radius,

and left femur, collected from around 1895 to 1910 by S. Roth and personnel of the La Plata Museum, from the Allen Formation and Río Colorado Formation (Coniacian), Río Negro Province. Powell (1986) regarded the heavier condition of the limb bones as insufficient grounds to support specific differentiation and, finding no anatomical differences, considered this species to be a *nomen dubium*. Bonaparte (1996*b*), while regarding this species as belonging to the genus

Nequensaurus, did not discount the possibility that the heavier condition of the bones represents sexual dimorphism or individual variation.

McIntosh referred to ? "*Saltasaurus*" *australis* the type species *Microcoelus patagonicus* Lydekker 1893, based upon an incomplete dorsal vertebra (MLP. Ly. 23) collected from the Río Colorado Formation in Neuquén Province. Earlier, Huene had referred this species to "*Titanosaurus*" *australis*, after which Powell (1986), interpreting the holotype as undiagnostic, regarded this taxon as a *nomen dubium*.

Note: J. S. McIntosh (personal communication 1998) pointed out that an ankylosaur has recently been found in South America, thereby raising the question of whether *Loricosaurus* was an ankylosaur after all; according to McIntosh, however, the armor scutes probably do belong to a sauropod, most likely *Neuquensaurus*.

Key references: Bonaparte (1987, 1996*b*); Huene (1929); Lydekker (1893); McIntosh (1990*b*); Powell (1987, 1980).

†NOASAURUS

Saurischia: Theropoda: Neotheropoda: "Ceratosauria": Neoceratosauria: Abelisauroidea: Noasauridae.

Comments: As noted by Bonaparte (1996*b*) in a brief report on the Cretaceous tetrapods of Argentina, *Noasaurus* is a significant genus, though it was not realized as such when first described by Bonaparte and Powell (1980), as "the first recorded taxon of an endemic, large clade of theropods, the Abelisauria," which in later years would yield important new taxa.

According to Bonaparte, *Noasaurus* was a small theropod with a total length of no more than 1.50 meters (slightly more than 5 feet). Bonaparte further stated that, although there are basic similarities between this genus and both *Abelisaurus* and *Carnotaurus*, there are also differences (*e.g.*, in the maxilla, unfused quadrate and quadratojugal, and different type of cervical ribs), the latter suggesting that *Noasaurus* belongs in its own abelisauroid family, Noasauridae (Bonaparte and Powell 1980).

Key references: Bonaparte (1996*b*); Bonaparte and Powell (1980).

†OMEISAURUS

Saurischia: Sauropodomorpha: Sauropoda: Eusaurapoda.

Type species: *O. junghsiensis* Yang [Young] 1939.

Other species: *O. tianfuensis* He, Li, Cai and Gao 1984, ?*O. changshouensis* Yang [Young] 1958, ?*O. luoquanensis* He, Li and Cai 1998.

Occurrence: Lower Shaximao Formation, Sichuan, China.

Age: Middle Jurassic.

Diagnosis of genus: Ascending ramus of maxilla having dorsoventrally expanded distal end; increase

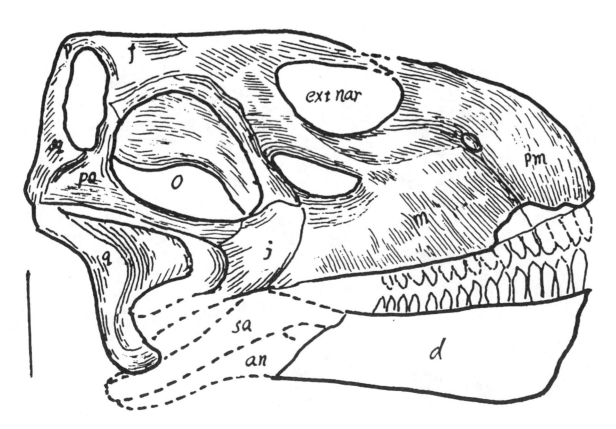

Omeisaurus tianfuensis reconstructed skull in right lateral view. Scale = 12 cm. (After Zhang and Chen 1996.)

Omeisaurus

Photograph by the author.

Omeisaurus tianfuensis, mounted skeleton, its incredibly long neck almost reaching the auditorium ceiling, displayed at Dinofest™, held in Philadelphia in 1998.

in number of cervical vertebrae (probably three added to make total of 16 cervicals); increase in cervical length (midcervical centra almost five times longer than deep), with reduction in height of cervical neural spines (Wilson and Sereno 1998).

Diagnosis of *O. junghsiensis*: ?17 long and opisthocoelous cervical vertebrae, with pleurocoels developed in centra, cervical neural spines low; three platycoelous sacrals, centra and neural spines coalesced; first caudal rib present, fan-shaped (Zhang and Chen 1996).

Diagnosis of: *O. tianfuensis*: Huge; skull heavy, wedge-shaped; ratio of height to length of skull at least about 1.2; maxillary with large ascending process; antorbital fenestra small; external nares in anteromiddle and upper part of skull; mandible high, mandibular foramen small; dentary two-thirds length of mandible; anterior end of dentary relatively high; teeth robust, spatulate; well-developed denticles on anterior edge of teeth, poorly developed on posterior edge; four premaxillary, 11 maxillary, and 13–15 dentary teeth; ?17 cervical, 12 dorsal, four sacral, and more than 36 caudal vertebrae; cervicals long, opisthocoelous, with well-developed ventral keel; dorsal vertebrae opisthocoelous, with developed pleurocoels, neural spines not bifurcated; anterior caudals slightly amphicoelous, first one having fan-shaped rib; chevrons in middle to posterior caudals forked; forelimbs at least four-fifths length of hind limbs; ulna at least two-thirds length of humerus; tibia to femur ratio about 2.3; five digits in both manus and pes; phalangeal formula of manus 2.2.2(?).1, of pes 2.3.3.3.2; manual digit I and pedal digits I–III bearing claws (Zhang and Chen 1996).

Comments: As recounted by Zhang and Chen (1996), the very long-necked sauropod *Omeisaurus* was formerly believed to be of Late Jurassic age, because the horizon from which it came was regarded as the Shangshaximiao Formation in the Upper Jurassic Series. At that time, spatulate sauropod teeth found in this formation at Guangyuan, Changshou were assigned to *Omeisaurus*. In 1977, however, geologists from Sichuan discovered that the rock layer containing *O. junghsiensis* teeth at Hsikuashan Junghsien County, Sichuan, was actually the Lower Shaximiao Formation, slightly higher than the stratigraphic position of *O. tianfuensis* from Middle Jurassic rocks at Dashanpu Zigong, both species being quite similar in features of the cervical and dorsal vertebrae, girdles, and limbs. Thus, both species were considered by Zhang and Chen to be of Middle Jurassic age.

Zhang and Chen revised the original diagnosis for *Omeisaurus* and two of its species, *O. junghsiensis* from Hsikwashan Junghsien County and *O. tianfuensis* from Dashanpu Zigong, based, in part, on

more recently collected specimens recovered by Chinese scientists.

More recently, in a cladistic reassessment of the genus, Wilson and Sereno (1998) defined *Omeisaurus* as the species *O. jungsiensis* and *O. tianfuensis*, their common ancestor, plus all of its descendants. At the same time, these authors rediagnosed the genus *Omeisaurus* based solely on autapomorphies. Of the various other species referred to this genus, Wilson and Sereno pointed out that three (*O. changshouensis*, *O. fuxiensis*, and *O. louquanensis*) were established upon fragmentary material that is difficult to compare with *O. jungsiensis* and are most likely invalid.

Wilson and Sereno commented that, as no tail clubs have yet been found associated with skeletons of *Omeisaurus*, the basis for referral of such clubs to this genus has not been demonstrated (although the most distal caudal vertebrae were not preserved in these specimens). Therefore, this feature cannot, for the present at least, be used a criterion to link *Omeisaurus* with the tail-clubbed sauropod *Shunosaurus*.

Note: Zhang and Chen removed the species *O. fuxiensis*, which was originally described as the type species *Zigongosaurus fuxiensis*, and referred it to the genus *Mamenchisaurus* (see *Mamenchisaurus* entry).

Key references: He, Li and Cai (1988); He, Li, Cai and Gao (1984); Wilson and Sereno (1998); Yang [Young] (1939, 1958); Zhang and Chen (1996).

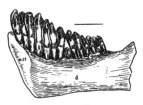

Omeisaurus tianfuensis, right mandible with teeth, lingual view. Scale = 6 cm. (After Zhang and Chen 1996.)

†**ONYCHOSAURUS** Nopcsa 1902 [*nomen dubium*]—(=?*Rhabdodon*, ?*Struthiosaurus*)

Ornithischia: Genasauria *incertae sedis*.

Name derivation: Greek *onyx* = "nail" + Greek *sauros* = "lizard."

Type species: *O. hungaricus* Nopcsa 1902 [*nomen dubium*].

Other species: [None.]

Occurrence: Gosau Formation, Transylvania, Romania.

Age: Late Cretaceous (Turonian).

Known material: Miscellaneous postcranial remains.

Holotype: [Missing] caudal dermal plates, two individuals.

Diagnosis of genus (as for type species): [None published.]

Comments: The type species *Onychosaurus hungaricus* was founded by Nopcsa (1902*b*) upon a number of dermal plates belonging to two individuals collected from an unknown locality in Transylvania, then a part of Hungary.

According to Nopcsa, who did not figure the specimens, the armor plates in the caudal region are of a characteristic type; "the semicylindrical ventral plates possess complex articulation resembling those found in *Polacanthus*, while the dorsal elements are arranged in two longitudinal series." Additional remains of *O. hungaricus* were found in the Szentpéterfalva area of Transylvania (see Nopcsa 1914).

Romer (1956), Kuhn (1964), and Steel (1969) considered *Onychosaurus* to be a member of the Ankylosauria. Subsequently, Carroll (1988) made the genus a junior synonym of *Struthiosaurus*. Later, Norman and Weishampel (1990) referred *O. hungaricus* to the iguanodontian species *Rhabdodon priscus* (see *D:TE*), though without offering evidence supporting this synonymy.

More recently, Pereda-Suberbiola and Galton (1997), in a review of the armored dinosaurs from the Late Cretaceous of Transylvania, found Nopcsa's (1902*b*) original description of *O. hungaricus* to be more indicative of an ankylosaur than an ornithopod. However, as the original type material is currently missing, these authors could not accurately assign this species to any higher taxon, preferring to regard it as a *nomen dubium*.

Key references: Carroll (1988); Kuhn (1964); Nopcsa (1902*b*); Norman and Weishampel (1990); Pereda-Suberbiola and Galton (1997); Romer (1964); Steel (1969).

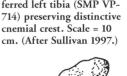

Ornithomimus antiquus, referred left tibia (SMP VP-714) preserving distinctive cnemial crest. Scale = 10 cm. (After Sullivan 1997.)

†ORNITHOMIMUS—(=*Coelosaurus*.)

Saurischia: Theropoda: Neotheropoda: Tetanurae: Avetheropoda: Coelurosauria: Manuraptoriformes: Arctometatarsalia: Bullatosauria: Ornithomimosauria: Ornithomimidae.

Type species: *O. antiquus* (Leidy 1865).

Other species: [None.]

New material: Nearly complete left tibia, juvenile.

Diagnosis of genus: At present, tentatively the same as the diagnosis proposed by Russell (1972; see *D:TE*, also "Comments" below), but expanded to include the character of a generically distinctive cnemial crest (described as forming a prominent anterior ridge that descends along the shaft for almost one-fourth its length; anteriorly-directed upper cnemial crest almost parallel to shaft of tibia for 2.3 centimeters, descending sharply toward shaft, forming distinctive, somewhat angular ridge in medial view) (Sullivan 1997).

Comments: The genus *Ornithomimus*—one of the so-called "ostrich dinosaurs," because of their superficial resemblance to those large flightless birds — was recently reviewed by Robert M. Sullivan, subsequent to his collection on August 16, 1995 of an almost complete left tibia (SMP VP-714) belonging to a small juvenile individual (referred by Sullivan to the species *O. antiquus*) from the De-na-zin member of the Kirtland Formation (Late Cretaceous: late Cam-

panian–?early Maastrichtian) at Willow Wash, in San Juan County, New Mexico. This specimen documents the first definite occurrence of the genus from the De-na-zin Member of that formation (Sullivan 1997).

Comparing SMP VP-714 with the tibiae of the holotypes of *O. antiquus* (ANSP 9222), *O. edmontonicus* (ROM 851), and *Struthiomimus* (=*Dromiceiomimus*) *brevitertius* (ROM 797) (see *D:TE* for illustrations), Sullivan observed that the Kirtland specimen, because of its possession of the distinctive cnemial crest, can only be referred to *Ornithomimus*. As this feature is not present in other known ornithomimid genera but is observed in all three "species" of *Ornithomimus* (*O. velox*, *O. antiquus*, and *O. edmontonicus*), Sullivan interpreted this unique cnemial crest to be a generic character.

The absence of a fused astragalus and calcaneum in SMP VP-714, and also its comparatively small size (25 centimeters in length, slightly more than half that of the tibia of the type specimen of *O. edmontonicus*), indicated to Sullivan that the tibia from New Mexico represents a juvenile animal. (As pointed out by R. E. Molnar, personal communication 1998, fusion is also absent in the holotype of *O. antiquus*, possibly suggesting another juvenile individual or that fusion may be a variable character.)

Regarding the three generally accepted "species" of *Ornithomimus* (*O. velox*, *O. antiquus*, and *O. edmontonicus*; see *D:TE*), Sullivan pointed out that the only criterion formerly used to separate these taxa has been their stratigraphic occurrence, *O. velox* being known from the late Campanian of Colorado, *O. edmontonicus* from the late Campanian–early Maastrichtian of Alberta, and *O. antiquus* from the Maastrichtian of New Jersey. Also, Russell (1972), who did not consider the status of *O. antiquus*, had commented that the species *O. velox* and *O. edmontonicus* cannot be distinguished morphologically based upon the collected material, and were otherwise accepted by that author as valid based solely on their stratigraphic position. Noting that morphology alone and not stratigraphic and geographic position is the only criterion for distinguishing species, Sullivan recognized *O. antiquus* as the single valid species of *Ornithomimus*, with *O. velox* and *O. edmontonicus* considered by him to be junior synonyms.

Sullivan argued that Russell's diagnosis for *Ornithomimus* was mostly based upon relative proportions and is, therefore, subjective, lacking "critical characters necessary to differentiate putative ornithomimid species from one another, making it largely inadequate for diagnostic purposes" (see also Baird 1986). A new diagnosis, Sullivan suggested, utilizing phylogenetic systematic analysis, is now needed for this genus.

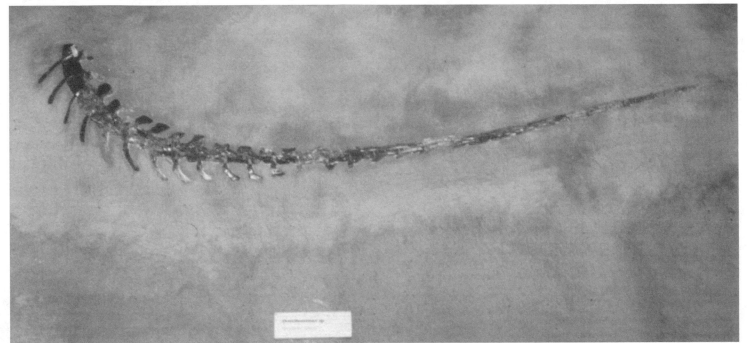

Articulated series of caudal vertebrae referred to *Ornithomimus* sp.

Key references: Baird (1986); Leidy (1865); Russell (1972); Sullivan (1997).

†OVIRAPTOR

Saurischia: Theropoda: Neotheropoda: Tetanurae: Avetheropoda: Coelurosauria: Manuraptoriformes: Oviraptorisauria: Oviraptoridae: Oviraptorinae.

Comments: The type species *Oviraptor philoceratops* is a relatively rare theropod taxon. It was named and first described in 1923 by Henry Fairfield Osborn of the American Museum of Natural History, the genus and species founded a partial skeleton with skull (AMNH 6517) discovered that same year in what is now called Bayn Dzak, in the southern Gobi Desert of Mongolia. Associated with this skeleton was a nest of fossil eggs (AMNH 6508) [belonging to the parafamily Elongatoolithidae Zhao 1975]. Osborn coined the above binomal (meaning "egg thief with a fondness for ceratopsian eggs") believing that the theropod had perished while robbing eggs then presumed to belong to the primitive ceratopsian *Protoceratops*.

In more recent years, however, the interpretation of Osborn's generally accepted scenario represented by this original find has dramatically altered, based upon new discoveries and studies. Various workers (*e.g.*, Mikhailov 1991; Sabath 1991) have, in fact, proposed that the eggs associated with AMNH 6517, as well as others assumed to pertain to *Protoceratops*, are really those of a theropod.

In 1994, Norell, Clark, Dashzeveg, Barsbold, Chiappe, Davidson, McKenna, Perle and Novacek identified an oviraptorid embryo inside an egg similar to those found with the holotype of *O. philoceratops*. The following year, reports of two spectacular discoveries were published: Dong and Currie (1995), in a preliminary report, briefly described a fragmentary skeleton of *Oviraptor*, which had been found atop a nest of eggs at Bayn Mandahu, Inner Mongolia, People's Republic of China; and Norell, Clark, Chiappe and Dashzeveg (1995) described an *Oviraptor* skeleton found on top of another nest of elongatoolithid eggs (see *D:TE*).

As later detailed by Dong and Currie (1996), the specimen (IVPP V9608) was collected by the Sino-Canadian Dinosaur Project expedition in 1990 in the North Canyon, from Upper Cretaceous redbeds (Campanian) near Urad Houqui. When discovered, it was still assumed that the eggs had been laid by a herbivorous dinosaur and that the theropod died in the act of plundering those eggs for food.

IVPP V9608 consists of a partial articulated skeleton (including vertebrae, pectoral girdle, the right front limb, and right hind limb) and also a partial nest of six eggs and fragments of others. According to Dong and Currie (1996), the skeleton and nest would probably have been complete if not lost to wind, water, and root erosion.

According to Dong and Currie (1996), IVPP V9608 can be distinguished as belonging to an oviraptorid by the structure of the manus (Barsbold and Osmólska 1990). At present, only three oviraptorids — *Conhoraptor*, *Ingenia*, and *Oviraptor* — are known from the Upper Cretaceous of central Asia. Metacarpal I

Oviraptor

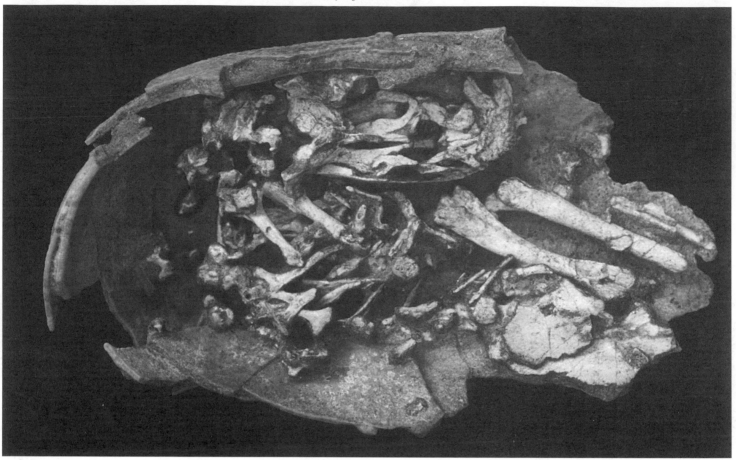

Egg with embryo (cast of AMNH 28507) of an oviraptorid, possibly *Oviraptor philoceratops*, collected during an American Museum of Natural History expedition to Mongolia in 1993.

(32 millimeters long) is less than half the length of II (82 millimeters, though incomplete) as in *Oviraptor* and *Conchoraptor*, in contrast to that in *Ingenia*. The preserved portions of metacarpals II and III are long, the complete bones apparently of nearly equal length, the incomplete bones almost half the length of the humerus, therefore precluding the skeleton's identification with *Ingenia* (in which the metacarpus is only one-third the length of the humerus; see Barsbold, Maryańska and Osmólska 1990). As in *Oviraptor* and *Conchoraptor*, the penultimate phalanges of the manual digits are longer than the more proximal phalanges. All unguals are recurved and possess, as in *Oviraptor* but not in *Conchoraptor*, a dorsoposterior "lip."

As noted by Dong and Currie (1996), the eggs are 15 centimeters long, with short diameters of about 5.5 centimeters. The eggs had been laid in pairs and arranged in a circle. Their longitudinal axes are inclined at low angles to the ground, sloping away from the middle of the nest. In describing these eggs, Dong and Currie (1996) observed that each one has an equatorial region with linearituberculate ornamentation (Mikhailov's variant 1); polar regions are small; and thickness of eggshell is less than 1 millimeter. Further examination of the eggshell via transmitted light mi-

croscopy and scanning electron microscopy revealed the theropod origins of these eggs. Also, they are very similar to the oviraptorid eggs containing embryonic remains described by Norell *et al.* (1994).

Although much of IVPP V9608 had been lost to erosion, it was clear to Dong and Currie (1996) that the theropod was lying a atop the nest, the hind legs folded underneath the body. The pose indicates that the animal had been "trapped in a life pose, sitting on its haunches." As the body had no chance to roll over and was not disarticulated or scavenged, burial must have been rapid. Sediments surrounding IVPP V9608 are fine-grained, reddish and structureless sandstones, which Eberth (1993) interpreted as evidence of very high-energy windstorms. Consequently, Dong and Currie (1996) interpreted the specimen as representing an *Oviraptor* that was lying on its nest when buried during a sandstorm, the authors adding that there "were similar circumstances surrounding the death and burial of the type specimen of *O. philoceratops*.

Dong and Currie (1996) observed the following in IVPP V9608: The right foot is posed in the center of the nest, where there are no eggs, the preserved semicircle of eggs lying anterior, posterior, and to the right of the foot. The right arm is folded back, the

Photography by D. Finnin, courtesy Department Library Services, American Museum of Natural History (neg. #2A23012).

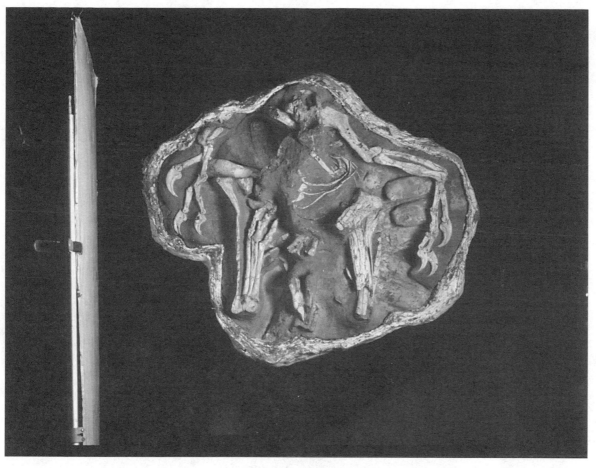

Skeleton of *Oviraptor* positioned over a nest of its eggs (AMNH 5789), collected by the American Museum of Natural History in Bayan Mandahu, Inner Mongolia, People's Republic of China. This specimen was described in 1995 by Mark A. Norell, James M. Clark, Luis M. Chiappe, and Demberelyin Dashzeveg.

hand lying outside the semicircle of eggs at the same level as the eggs. The belly would have been over the middle of the nest, the position of the vertebrae suggesting that the body was stretched out beyond the nest. The skeleton's symmetry suggests the dinosaur was squatting, its feet within the circle of eggs. The back of the right foot is slightly higher in elevation than the eggs, the unguals at the same level, suggesting that the middle of the nest had been filled with sand. The right hand is outside the nest and at the same level as the eggs, this showing that the eggs were probably not buried when the *Oviraptor* sat on the nest.

Evaluating various other interpretations of this specimen, Dong and Currie (1996) discounted the possibility that the association of skeleton and eggs were coincidental, pointing out that "specimens found in this type of bedding at Bayan Mandahu usually occur as untransported, isolated skeletons" (see Jerzykiewicz, Currie, Eberth, Johnston, Koster and Zheng 1993).

Dong and Currie (1996) found Osborn's first interpretation to be unlikely, also, having found no evidence of destruction of any of the eggs before burial, and speculating that "a predatory oviraptorid would probably have either consumed or abandoned its food

long before it was buried by sand and dust carried by a sandstorm."

The most probable interpretation of IVPP V9608, according to Dong and Currie (1996), is that the *Oviraptor* "may have been lying on the nest, incubating and (or) protecting the eggs," this hypothesis supported by the skeleton's position (squatting over the center of the nest), "and the fact that the eggs appear to have been laid by a mature theropod of about the size of IVPP V9608. As the eggs in this specimen are the same size and shape and have the same shell morphology as those found with the holotype of *O. philceratops*, that individual also may have died while caring for its young.

Dong and Currie (1996) concluded that, if their interpretation of IVPP V9608 is indeed correct, it suggests that theropods, "like their descendants, the birds," incubated and protected their eggs, these instincts apparently strong enough for the dinosaur not to have abandoned the nest as it was buried in sand.

Taking their interpretation a step further, Dong and Currie (1996) speculated that the theropod may have been killed while in the act of laying the eggs, this idea supported by the fact that there is no evidence of more than a single layer of eggs. Unfortunately, the

P

theory cannot be tested due to the incompleteness of the specimen.

According to Dong and Currie (1996), the position of the hind foot in this specimen and the open centers of this and all other known elongatoolithid nests seem to indicate that "oviraptorids laid eggs by standing in one spot and turning in a circle." From complete nests containing 30 or more eggs arranged in a spiral around an open area (see Sabath 1991; Mikhailov, Sabath and Kurzanov 1994), it is apparent that the female turned in a single direction laying two eggs at a time. (One nest from Bayan Mandahu exhibited at the Inner Mongolia Museum [Hohot] indicates that "the dinosaur turned clockwise as she laid the eggs.") The first (lowest) layer of IVPP V9608 is in a circle with a relatively wide radius, the spiral tightening as additional layers of eggs were laid; eggs of the lowest layer slope at a low angle away from the nest's center, the angle increasing at higher levels, the decrease in radius and change in angle apparently reflecting "changes in orientation of the cloaca as the animal rose higher on her hind legs." Possibly the dinosaur's hands were used "to scoop sand onto the eggs as they were laid." As the nest's base appears to have

been at ground level, the nest may have formed a mound (Sabath 1991; Thulborn 1992; Mikhailov *et al.* 1994).

As Dong and Currie (1996) pointed out, the importance of IVPP V9608 is the suggestion "that at least some theropod dinosaurs may have practiced birdlike brooding behavior."

Key references: Dong and Currie (1995, 1996); Norell, Clark, Dashzeveg, Barsbold, Chiappe, Davidson, McKenna, Perle and Novacek (1994); Norell, Clark, Chiappe and Dashzeveg (1995); Osborn (1924).

†**PACHYRHINOSAURUS**—(=?*Monoclonius*)
Ornithischia: Genasauria: Cerapoda: Marginocephalia: Ceratopsia: Neoceratopsia: Ceratopsomorpha: Ceratopsidae: Centrosaurinae.

Comments: Once known from only two skulls, the unusual ceratopsian genus *Pachyrhinosaurus*—the geologically youngest of all known centrosaurines, having frill horns and a massive nasal "boss"—is now known from numerous specimens, some of which have yielded fascinating and even surprising evidence concerning this dinosaur.

Artist D. L. Sloan's interpretation of the relationship of *Oviraptor* and its nest of eggs (IVPP V9608), an example of avian brooding behavior in nonavian theropods. (After Doug and Currie 1996.)

D.L.SLOAN '95 ©

Sampson, Ryan and Tanke (1997), in a study of craniofacial ontogeny in centrosaurine taxa based upon specimens recovered from low diversity bonebeds, noted that the juvenile and subadult *Pachyrhinosaurus*, unlike the adult, indeed possessed a long-based nasal horncore. As in all juvenile centrosaurines, this horncore was a direct outgrowth of the two nasal bones overlying most of the narial opening; as in others, it was basically triangular in side view, laterally compressed, and divided longitudinally by a median suture. Late during ontogeny, this horncore fused from the tip down, the two halves becoming entirely co-ossified prior to the development of the adult condition, after which the nasal boss fully and quite rapidly developed. The authors noted that an "ontogenetic series for an undescribed pachyrhinosaur from Alberta shows progressive development from a small, sagittally divided horncore in juveniles to a full-fledged pachyostotic boss in adults," the highly rugose and convoluted texture of the boss suggesting rapid bone deposition "in conjunction with the attainment of adult body size."

Although some workers have suggested that *Pachyrhinosaurus* indeed possessed a nonosseous nasal horn (see Currie 1989), Sampson *et al.* found it unlikely that two independent solutions to the same problem would have evolved (unlike centrosaurine genera that do not have such a boss), and that subadults would lose a nasal horn only to develop a boss during adult life. The authors further speculated that the occurrence of a boss in lieu of a nasal horn in this genus "suggests that the dramatic exostosis in *Pachyrhinosaurus* was a means of creating an osseous platform on the anterior skull roof, perhaps employed in intraspecific competition as a head-butting platform (Farlow and Dodson 1975)."

In the fossil record, evidence of dinosaurian inter-species conflict is rare. Such evidence, involving *Pachyrhinosaurus* with another ceratopsian taxon, has apparently been discovered recently by Bruce M. Rothschild and Darren H. Tanke (1997) through serendipitous observation of a pathologic skull (RTMP 89.55.1234) of this genus collected from the Wapiti Formation of Alberta, Canada.

Rothschild and Tanke pointed out that stress fractures in the feet of humans typically relate to marching or prolonged standing, and that the nonuniform presence of such fractures in ceratopsians implies that prolonged standing was not a factor among these dinosaurs.

Examining RTMP 89.55.1234, Rothschild and Tanke noticed an orbital defect "that extends inferior and anterior to the eye. The defect extends through the right side of the face, almost through to the other side." As described by Rothschild and Tanke, the de-

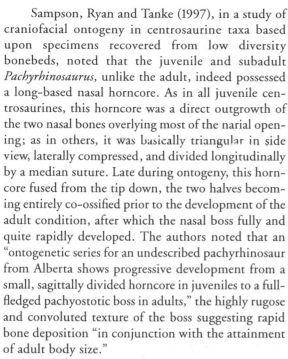

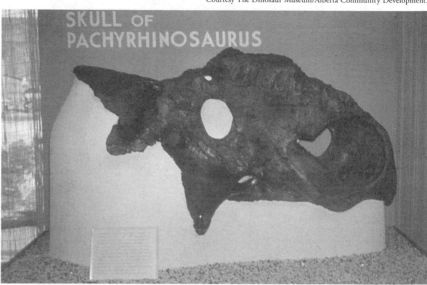

Courtesy The Dinosaur Museum/Alberta Community Development.

fect is rather oval in shape, measures 17 by 15 centimeters at its external surface, and punctures the skull with central tapering. A portion of the subjacent right maxilla had been broken off and a "greenstick" type lesion was observed in the right jugal.

Rothschild and Tanke considered various diagnostic considerations — *e.g.*, cancer, infection (including granulomatous such as tuberculosis and fungus), and trauma — to explain the pathologic condition of this skull. The "greenstick" lesion and absence of resorption centers were difficult for the authors to reconcile with cancer. Infection was deemed unlikely as the main problem, because the specimen exhibited only minimal reactive new bone and no "fronts" of bone resorption. Trauma was also ruled out, as the nature of the injury was not compatible with such potential causes as falls, or wounds inflicted by the claws or teeth of large theropods.

As noted by the authors, the nature of the defect indicates a penetrating or "punched out" injury, its central tapering suggesting that the object that had caused it possessed "a significant tapering morphology." A tree stump was ruled out as the cause of the injury, as the tapering was too marked to match the gradual tapering of a tree stump.

Interaction with another *Pachyrhinosaurus* was also considered. However, possible injury induced by frill horns was discounted because the tapering of frill horns is much greater than the tapering of the noted injury, with all known *Pachyrhinosaurus* frill horns incapable of penetrating to that depth without a considerably wider base. Although a large nasal horn might have caused the injury, no such "appendage" has yet been found in specimens of this genus. (Paleontologists Philip J. Currie, Wann Langston, Jr., and Tanke have speculated that this genus may have

Skull of the centrosaurine *Pachyrhinosaurus canadensis*. Defects found in another skull belonging to this species were apparently made by another centrosaurine, *Centrosaurus nasicornis*.

Pachyrhinosaurus canadensis, life restoration painted by Brian Franczak.

possessed a massive nasal horn, though one lacking a horncore, analogous to the nose horn of a rhinoceros, this idea "predicated upon similarities of the *Pachyrhinosaurus* nasal boss to the bumpy nasal pad on Pleistocene *Elasmotherium* [wooly rhino]," and on the presence of "a long-based and prominent nasal horncore in baby and subadult *Pachyrhinosaurus*.") As a social, herding animal, *Pachyrhinosaurus* would most likely have received injuries from other dinosaurs of its kind, though in the case of RTMP 89.55.1234, a "weapon" relating to this genus could not be identified.

A possible alternative explanation, suggested by Rothschild and Tanke, is interspecific conflict, the injury perhaps having been inflicted by another ceratopsian taxon equipped with the appropriate horn. To determine the identity of this alleged perpetrator of the injury, the authors made a cast of the defect, from which was generated a reverse cast. The reverse cast was then applied to various appropriate ceratopsian horncores, the intent of this comparison being to find a "fit." After comparing the defect with 96 other ceratopsians, Rothschild and Tanke found a "fit" in two specimens labeled "*Monoclonius*" (see *Centrosaurus* entry, "Notes")—the horncore of AMNH 3944 and the reconstructed horncore of NMNH 8897.

Snugly fitting these specimens into the defect, Rothschild and Tanke noticed another, small, and co-

alesced defect in the *Pachyrhinosaurus* skull. The authors then imagined the attacker goring the *Pachyrhinosaurus* almost through its face, the lesser injury possibly occurring as a "skip" lesion, whereby the "*Monoclonius*" horncore tip made a second, though less intense contact with the face.

However, a problem with the above idea, Rothshild and Tanke noted, proved to be the marked geographic separation (sometimes spanning about a thousand miles) of *Pachyrhinosaurus* bonebeds from specimens of other ceratopsian dinosaurs. When also considering the stress fracture data and its relationship to locomotion, the only reasonable explanation for the two taxa meeting is migration. If this interpretation is correct, the injured skull constitutes the first evidence of cohabitation of two ceratopsian species, and, consequently, for migration of at least one species into a shared range. Furthermore, the authors noted, RTMP 89.55.1234 constitutes the first known example of potential horn thrust injury in a centrosaurine.

Erratum: In *D:TE*, the photograph on p. 669 of the holotype skull of *Pachyrhinosaurus canadensis* was inadvertently printed upside down.

Key references: Currie (1989); Farlow and Dodson (1975); Rothschild and Tanke (1997); Sampson, Ryan and Tanke (1997).

†PARARHABDODON

Ornithischia: Genasauria: Cerapoda: Ornithopoda:

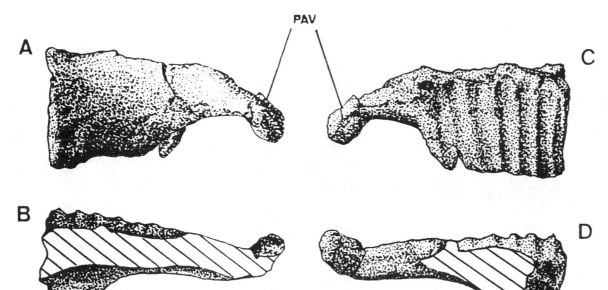

Right maxilla (MDE-Fo1-11) referred to *Pararhabdodon* sp. in A. lateral, B. dorsal, C. medial, and D. ventral views. Scale = 4 cm. (After Laurent, Le Loeuff and Buffetaut 1997.)

Euornithopoda: Iguanodontia: Euiguanodontia: Dryomorpha: Ankylopollexia; Hadrosauridae: Euhadrosauria: Lambeosaurinae.

Type species; *P. isonensis* Casanovas-Cladellas, Santafé-Llopis and Isidoro-Llorens 1993.

New material: Partial skull and postcranial remains, adult and juvenile.

Comments: *Pararhabdodon*, a genus founded upon postcranial material discovered in uppermost Cretaceous rocks (Late Maastricthian; see Ardévol, Casanovas and Santafé 1995) of the Sant Roma a'Abella locality, Catalonia, near Isona, on the Iberian peninsula, was originally described by Casanovas-Cladellas, Santafé-Llopis and Isidoro-Llorens (1993)

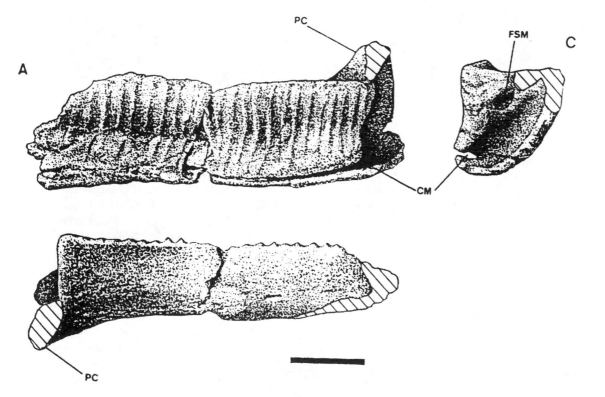

Right dentary (MDE-Fo1-10) referred to *Pararhabdodon* sp. in A. medial, B. dorsal, and C. posterior views. Scale = 4 cm. (After Laurent, Le Loeuff and Buffetaut 1997.)

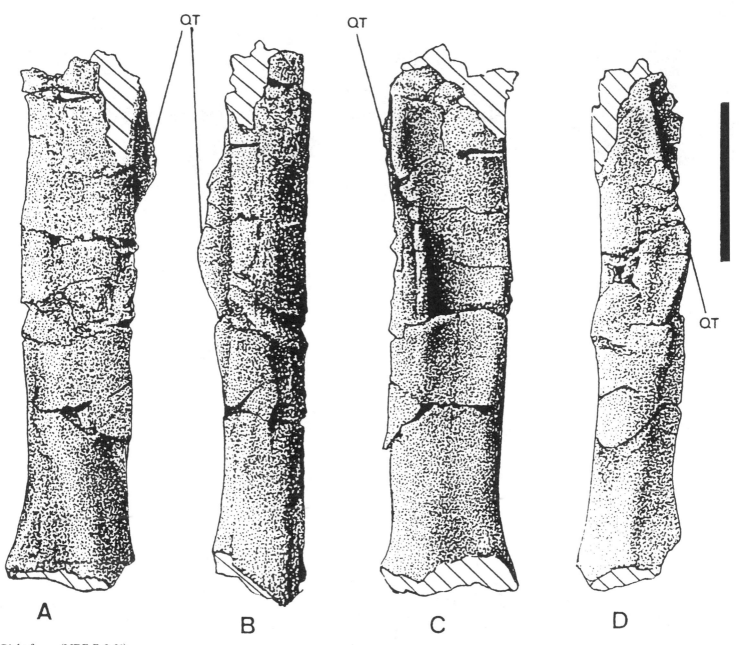

Right femur (MDE-Fo2-01) referred to *Pararhabdodon* sp. in A. anterior, B. lateral, C. posterior, and D. medial views. Scale = 4 cm. (After Laurent, Le Loeuff and Buffetaut 1997.)

as a basal iguanodontian close to *Rhabdodon* (see *D:TE*). Recently, however, this taxon has was referred to the hadrosaurid subfamily Lambeosaurinae by Laurent, Le Loeuff and Buffetaut (1997), based upon new materials which these authors referred to *Pararhabdodon* sp.

As listed by Laurent, Le Loeuff and Buffetaut, these new fossils — recovered from uppermost Cretaceous) rocks of the Corbières orientales, Bexen locality, at Aude, in southwestern France — include the following: A right maxilla (MDE-Fo1-11), a right dentary (MDE-Fo1-10), a fragment of a right dentary (MDE-Fo1-01), teeth (MDE-Fo1-12, 14, and 16), cervical vertebrae (MDE-Fo1-4, 5, 17, 22, 23, and 114), two partial sacral vertebrae (MDE-Fo1-21, 53), ante-

rior caudal vertebrae (MDE-Fo1-61, 97, and 136), a posterior caudal vertebra (MDE-Fo1-30), a right humerus (MDE-Fo1-18), left radius (MDE-Fo1-45), right femora (MDE-Fo2-01 [juvenile], Fo1-19), a partial right femur (MDE-Fo2-148), left tibia (MDE-Fo1-139), a right tibia (MDE-Fo1-143), and the distal end of a right tibia (MDE-Fo1-115).

Laurent *et al.* referred this material to the Hadrosauridae primarily based upon various morphological similarities in the above specimens to corresponding elements in the iguanodontians *Telmatosaurus transsylvanicus* (*Telmatosaurus* presently regarded as a taxon outside of Hadrosauridae; see "Systematics" chapter) and the possibly conspecific *Orthomerus dolloi* (see *Telmatosaurus* and *Orthomerus* entries, *D:TE*), particularly in the maxillae, dentaries, and femora. The authors also noted a number of differences in the elements of these taxa.

According to Laurent *et al.*, *P. isonensis* represents the first record of the Lambeosaurinae in Europe (see also the abstract of Casanovas-Cladellas, Pereda-Suberbiola and Santafé-Llopis 1998).

Pointing out that the name *Rhabdodon*—upon which *Pararhabdodon* was based—is of masculine gender, Laurent *et al.* emended the specific name of the type species *P. isonense* to *P. isonensis*.

Note: Casanovas-Cladellas, Pereda-Suberbiola and Santafé-Llopis also reported a lower jaw with teeth collected in the Ager Syncline (Upper Cretaceous, Maastricthian), near Fontilonga, on the Iberian Peninsula. Based on tooth form, the authors assigned this specimen to the Euhadrosauria (a clade introduced by Weishampel, Norman and Grigorescu 1993), adding that a preliminary study of this material points to its belonging to the Hadrosaurinae.

Key references: Casanovas-Cladellas, Pereda-Suberbiola and Santafé-Llopis (1998); Casanovas-Cladellas, Santafé-Llopis and Isidoro-Llorens (1993); Laurent, Le Loeuff and Buffetaut (1997).

†PARASAUROLOPHUS

Ornithischia: Genasauria: Cerapoda: Ornithopoda: Euornithopoda: Iguanodontia: Euiguanodontia: Dryomorpha: Ankylopollexia: Hadrosauridae: Euhadrosauria: Lambeosaurinae.

New material: Partial skull with jaws.

Comments: Among the rarities of dinosaur fossils are skulls belonging to the lambeosaurine hadrosaurid *Parasaurolophus*, a genus best known for its long, tube-like crest. Until recently, only three skulls of this genus were known since the type species, *P. walkeri* was first named and described in 1922, and only the original find was reasonably complete. (Two referred species *P. crytocristatus* and *P. tubicen*, were based on very incomplete specimens.) In the past, it was believed that the cranial crest housed but two parallel folded tubes for the passage of air, one running the length of the crest, the other corresponding to each nostril.

Our understanding of this dinosaur is changing dramatically in the past few years, however, thanks to studies by paleontologists Robert M. Sullivan and Thomas E. Williamson. Sullivan and Williamson (1996) briefly reported on a recently collected, well-preserved partial skull and jaw (NMMNH P-25100) of the "long-crested species" from the De-na-zin Member of the Kirtland Formation (Upper Cretaceous), San Juan Basin, New Mexico. Preserved in this specimen are an almost complete crest, skull roof, left cheek region, and left mandible.

From this skull, Sullivan and Williamson ob-

served the following details of the crest, previously unknown in this genus: (Externally) ventrally, paired frontals constitute basal part of crest, nasals anterior to frontals above orbit; dorsally, surface is marked by prominent, dorso-posteriorly directed connecting furrows; (internally, as revealed by CT scans) crest is highly complex, comprising a number of paired tubes; crest is divided for entire length by sagittal septum, with no evidence for common medial chamber; up to six chambers near base of crest; "dorsal ascending tract" consists of at least six separate (three pairs) tubes; dorsal pair terminates in large (paired) chamber near crest's tip; "lateral diverticula" are looped, each with dorsal and ventral tract.

According to Sullivan and Williamson, the large internal surface area and prominent vascularization support a thermoregulatory function for this crest.

More recently, Williamson and Sullivan (1997) reassessed a fragmented partial skull (BYU 2467; see *D:TE*) consisting of the distal end of a cranial crest preserved with the internal molds of the narial cavities,

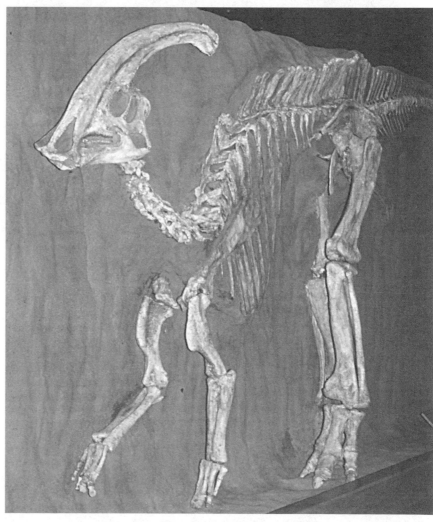

Parasaurolophus walkeri skeleton (cast of holotype ROM 764).

Photograph by the author, courtesy Royal Tyrrell Museum/Alberta Community Development.

Parasaurolophus

Courtesy The Field Museum (neg. #GEO84896D).

Parasaurolophus crytocrys-tatus, reconstruction (cast) of holotype incomplete skull (FM P27393).

recovered from the lower third of the Kaiparowits Formation (Upper Cretaceous), Garfield County, Utah. The specimen had been referred to *Parasaurolophus* sp. by Weishampel and Jensen (1979), who concluded that within larger fragments of its crest only dorsal ascending tracts and ventral ascending tracks are present, while lateral diverticula are absent.

According to Williamson and Sullivan's study of BYU 2465, "several cylindrical segments represent internal molds of portions of the narial chambers," to which adhere "fragments of the crest wall and septa that articulate with the larger fragments of the crest," these segments representing the tubes of the dorsal ascending tracts. Tubes previously identified as dorsal ascending tracts were reinterpreted to be lateral diverticula. According to Williamson and Sullivan, most of the crest of this specimen, posterior to the skull roof, is complete, missing only some 50 millimeters at the point of breakage of the two main pieces.

As Williamson and Sullivan observed, the crest of BYU 2467 resembles in size and shape the holotype skull (FMNH P27393) of *P. crytocristatus*, enough for them to refer with confidence the former specimen to this species. The authors noted that CT scans of BYU 2467 reveal that the lateral diverticula "are not a single pair of tubes for their entire length, as had earlier been reported for *P. crytocristatus*, but are posteriorly each divided by dorso-ventrally oriented septa as in the long-crested *Parasaurolophus* specimen NMMNH P-25100." Williamson and Sullivan further suggested that *P. crytocristatus* could be a primitive species of this genus or represents immature individuals of *P. walkeri*.

Key references: Sullivan and Williamson (1996); Weishampel and Jensen (1979); Williamson and Sullivan (1997).

†PELECANIMIMUS

Saurischia: Theropoda: Neotheropoda: Tetanurae: Avetheropoda: Coelurosauria: Manuraptoriformes: Arctometatarsalia: Bullatosauria: Ornithomimosauria: Ornithomimidae.

Comments: The genus *Pelecanimimus* is a rare and unique member of the Ornithomimosauria and the only member of the group known from Europe. The type species *P. polyodon* is represented by a single specimen—a partial skeleton with skull (LH 7777), from the lacustrine lithographic limestone of the Calizas de La Huerguina Formation (Lower Cretaceous; upper Hauterivian–lower Barremian) of Las Hoyas, Cuenca Province, Spain. Thus far, *Pelecanimimus* is the only known ornithomimosaur possessing teeth, having the highest tooth count of all known theropods (Pérez-Moreno, Sanz, Buscalioni, Moratalla, Ortega and Rasskin-Gutman 1994).

Since *Pelecanimimus* was first described by Pérez-Moreno *et al.*, preserved details that were originally interpreted as "integumentary impressions" (see *D:TE*) have been reidentified through scanning electron microscopy and electron microprobe analyses by Briggs, Wilby, Pérez-Moreno, Sanz and Fregenal-Martínez (1997) as mineralized traces of soft tissue. These impressions occur in the region of the throat, flanking the more proximal vertebrae of the neck, in the vicinity of the ribs, and behind the elbow. According to Briggs *et al.*, they "are preserved both as replicas of the

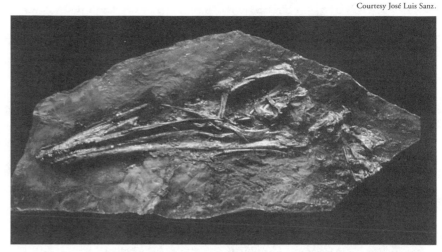

Pelecanimimus polyodon, LH 7777, holotype skull, left lateral view.

original skin and muscle tissue, and as impressions on microbial mats or veils that grew over them." In addition to these impressions, a small triangular area at the back of the skull was interpreted by Pérez-Moreno *et al.* as a possible soft occipital crest.

Briggs *et al.* noted that the Las Hoyas limestones have preserved a diverse biota of plants, insects, crustaceans, fishes, tetrapods, and three birds, some of the latter including feather details (Sanz, Bonaparte and Lacasa 1988; Sanz and Buscalioni 1992); however, no feather impressions were found belonging to the holotype of *P. polyodon*.

As observed by Briggs *et al.*, the soft parts of

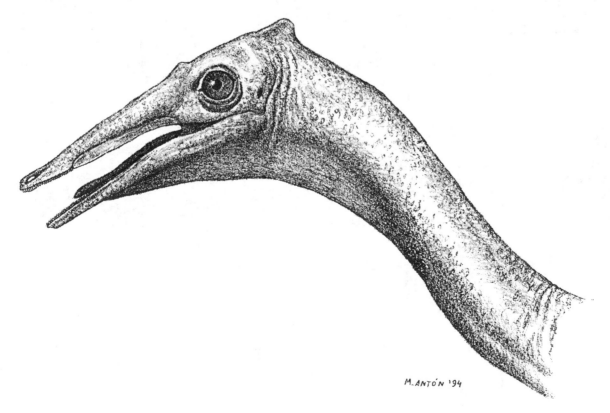

M. ANTÓN '94

Pelecanimimus polyodon, hypothetical life restoration by M. Antón based on holotype remains. (After Pérez-Moreno, Sanz, Buscalioni, Moratalla, Ortega and Rasskin-Gutman 1994.)

Pelecanimimus have been preserved in unusual ways. In the region under the throat, for example, the muscle tissues (replaced in an iron carbonate) have retained some three-dimensional detail, a distinct cross-hatched patterning on the surface of this material representing wrinkling of the dinosaur's hide.

The body outline of *Pelecanimimus* has been preserved by a phosphatized microbial mat — consisting mainly of thin layers of coccoids or circular structures embedded in a film, possibly representing "mucopolysaccharide sheaths surrounding the cells" — that overgrew the carcass, this outline confirming the existence of a dewlap or throat pouch and soft occipital crest.

As noted by Briggs *et al.*, microbial mats have been shown to promote the fossilization of soft tissues in marine Jurassic lithographic limestones of Cerin, France, by concentrating dissolved ions in the vicinity of carcasses (see Wilby, Briggs, Bernier and Gaillard 1996). Mineralization of the mats enveloping the *P. polyodon* specimen was probably facilitated in a similar fashion, with phosphorus released by the decomposing dinosaur to become "trapped and precipitated in the mat where it was directly in contact with the carcass," the mats extending beyond the carcass not becoming mineralized.

Briggs *et al.* pointed out that their study "demonstrates the importance of microbial mats in preserving such details." Furthermore, these authors stressed the importance of "careful monitoring of vertebrate remains for mineralized soft tissues before consigning them to the acid bath in order to release the skeleton from the matrix."

Key references: Briggs, Wilby, Pérez-Moreno, Sanz and Fregenal-Martínez (1997); Pérez-Moreno, Sanz, Buscalioni, Moratalla, Ortega and Rasskin-Gutman (1994).

PELLEGRINISAURUS   Salgado 1996

Saurischia: Sauropodomorpha: Sauropoda: Eusauropoda: Neosauropoda: Macronaria: Camarasauromorpha: Titanosauriformes: Somphospondyli: Titanosauria: Titanosauridae.

Name derivation: "[Lago, or Lake] Pellegrini" + Greek *sauros* = "lizard."

Type species: *P. powelli* Salgado 1996.

Other species: [None.]

Occurrence: Allen Formation, Patagonia, Argentina.

Age: Late Cretaceous (Campanian–lower Maastrichtian).

Known material/holotype: MPCA 1500, four dorsal vertebral centra, 26 incomplete caudal vertebrae, incomplete right femur.

Diagnosis of genus (as for type species): Large titanosaurid (20–25 meters in length), distinguished from other titanosaurid genera by the following autapomorphic characters: midposterior and posterior caudal vertebrae having anteroposteriorly elongated and dorsoventrally depressed neural spines, anterior ends of which are at higher position than posterior ones; dorsal centra strongly depressed; transverse width of centrum of posterior dorsal vertebrae approximately twice maximum dorsoventral depth (Salgado 1996).

Comments: The genus *Pellegrinisaurus* was founded upon parts of vertebrae and a partial right femur (MPCA 1500) found and collected in 1975 by

Pellegrinisaurus powelli, **MPCA 1500, holotype posterior dorsal centrum, A. lateral and B. anterior views. (After Salgado 1996.)**

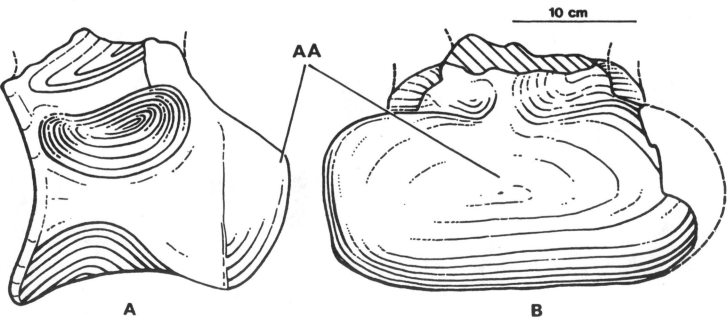

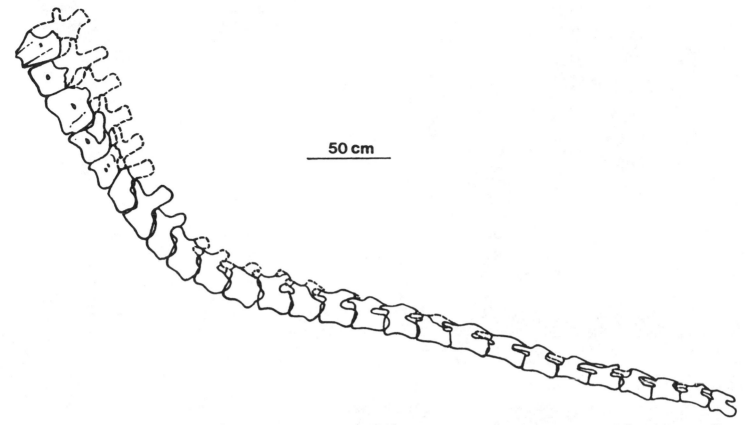

50 cm

Pellegrinisaurus powelli,
MPCA 1500, reconstructed
holotype caudal sequence.
(After Salgado 1996.)

Roberto Abel of the Museo Provincial de "Carlos Ameghino," Cipolletti, and assistants (see Powell 1986), in the Lower Member of the Allen Formation, Malargú Group, Iago Pellegrini, northwestern part of Río Negro Province, Argentina. As caudal vertebrae are of particular importance in titanosaurid systematics, the preservation of a partial caudal series in MPCA 1500 is of particular importance (Salgado 1996).

Powell, in his unpublished revision of the Titanosauridae, had referred MPCA 1500 to cf. *Epachthosaurus* sp., based on similarities (wide dorsal centra, low dorsal neural arches, and development of laminae for reinforcement of apophyses and pleurocoels) with the holotype (MACN-CH 1317) and paraplastotype (MACN-CH 13689) of *E. sciuttoi*. According to Salgado, however, the characters mentioned by Powell, though present in MPCA 1500, do not justify referral of this specimen to *Epacthosaurus*. The dorsal centrum of MPCA is substantially wider than in MACN-CH 1317. Also, osseous reinforcement laminae are also developed in other sauropod families, including Cetiosauridae, Diplodocidae, and Brachiosauridae (see Bonaparte 1986*a*), and may be plesiomorphic for all titanosaurids.

Recognizing Saltasaurinae as a subfamily of Titanosauridae (see Bonaparte and Powell 1980), Salgado interpreted *Pelligrinisaurus* as the probable sister taxon of the "Saltasaurinae," these taxa sharing the presence of low mid- and posterior caudal centra with dorsoventrally convex lateral surfaces.

Salgado pointed out that the titanosaur community at the Iago Pellegrini locality is quite different from those of other Cretaceous localities south of the Río Negro, characterized by *P. powelli* and *Titanosaurus araukanikus*, but devoid of the genus *Aeolosaurus* which is known in other localities, these differences possibly reflecting different environmental conditions of deposition.

Key reference: Powell (1986); Salgado (1996).

†PENTACERATOPS

Ornithischia: Genasauria: Cerapoda: Marginocephalia: Ceratopsia: Neoceratopsia: Ceratopsomorpha: Ceratopsidae: Chasmosaurinae.

Diagnosis of genus (as for type species): Large chasmosaurine with long, straight, narrow squamosals having numerous (generally 8–10) pronounced marginal undulations with or without attached epoccipitals; parietal slender, straplike, with indented medial posterior margin and elongate fenestrae of moderate size; several very large triangular posterior parietal epoccipitals; pair of upturned epoccipitals on midline dorsal surface of posterior part of parietal; epijugals large; large anteriorly curved supraorbital

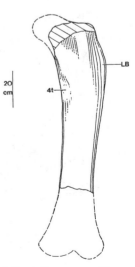

Pellegrinisaurus powelli,
MPCA 1500, holotype right
femur, posterior view.
(After Salgado 1996.)

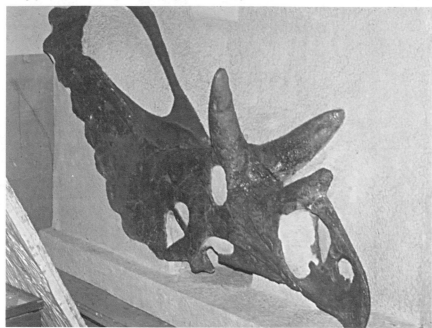

Top: Pentaceratops sternbergii, AMNH 1624, referred skull collected in 1923 by Charles H. Sternberg, the missing parts hypothetically restored in plaster based on other ceratopsian taxa. *Bottom: Pentaceratops sternbergii*, bronze-cast life-sized sculpture by David A. Thomas, made for the New Mexico Museum of Natural History, Albuquerque.

horncores arising directly over orbits; face deep with posteriorly directed jugals; distinguished from *Chasmosaurus mariscalensis* by anterior curvature of supraorbital horncores, straight tapering squamosal, and configuration of posterior parietal margin (Lehman 1996).

Comments: In 1993, Thomas M. Lehman published a composite restoration of the skull of *Pentaceratops sternbergii*, a very large chasmosaurine species distinguished by a particularly long frill. The illustration was based upon several almost complete skulls and a number of fragmentary specimens, as well as other material.

Subsequent to Lehman's publication, Forster, Sereno, Evans and Rowe (1993) figured a skull (MNA 1747) belonging to this species (see *D:TE*).

More recently, Lehman (1996) commented on the illustration of MNA 1747 by Forster *et al.*, pointing out that this specimen is flattened dorsoventrally so that its proportions are distorted in top view; that epoccipital processes shown on the posterolateral corners of the parietal have been lost from this specimen; and that these epoccipitals are shown as overlapped by the squamosals, a condition not known in any ceratopsian.

Lehman, a paleontologist stationed at Texas Tech University specializing in ceratopsians, will describe a gigantic new *Pentaceratops* skull measuring approximately 2.65 meters (about 9 feet) in length (P. Dodson, personal communication 1998).

Key reference: Forster, Sereno, Evans and Rowe (1993); Lehman (1993, 1996).

†PLATEOSAURUS

Comments: *Plateosaurus* remains one of the most common of European dinosaurs. New studies have been made regarding sexual dimorphism and individual variation in *Plateosaurus engelhardti*, the earliest known large dinosaur, and one of the larger prosauropods.

In 1990, Weishampel and Chapman had published their morphometric analysis of the femur of *Plateosaurus*, this study mainly based upon 33 complete femora recovered from the bonebed in the Knollenmergel at the Upper Mill, Trössingen, Würtemberg, Germany (see *D:TE* for more information on this quarry. As stated by Galton (1997*b*) in a later study, Weishampel and Chapman found these elements to be "fairly homogeneous as regards gross dimensions," but also observed two morphs in these bones, differing "in the relative dimensions of the proximal and distal femoral articulations, and in the size and shape of the fourth trochanter." Weishampel and Chapman attributed these differences to intraspecific variation.

Skeleton assigned to *Plateosaurus engelhardti* (originally referred to *P. quenstedti*), collected circa 1911–12 from the bonebed at Trössingen, Germany, exhibited since 1932. The status of *P. engelhardti* has come into question, the Trössingen material possibly referrable to ?*P. plieningeri*.

Photograph by the author, courtesy Museum of Comparative Zoology, Harvard University.

Galton, however, based upon the Trössingen specimens and also material referred to various other prosauropod genera and species, concluded that these proportional differences probably represent a sexual dimorphism — the robust (and less abundant) morph representing the male, the gracile (and more common) morph representing the female.

Regarding the skull, Gow, Kitching and Raath (1990) had interpreted various cranial features observed by them in *P. engelhardti* and also the South African prosauropod *Massospondylus carinatus*, as indicative of sexual dimorphism, with male skulls characterized by thickening of the dorsal orbital rim and deepening of the posterior end of the maxilla. From

Plateosaurus

Skull (YPM cast of AMNH 6810 skull) of *Plateosaurus engelhardti* (originally referred to *P. trössingensis*), left lateral view.

his own studies of material relating to the two species, Galton concluded that these presumed male characters probably represent individual variations.

Galton (1998), in one of a series of papers on the various species that have been referred to the genus *Plateosaurus*, provided notes on the material originally named *Dimodosaurus poligniensis*, which Galton (1985c) had earlier referred to *P. engelhardti*. As de-

tailed by Galton (1998), this taxon had been founded upon "many bones of a gigantic saurian" (first reported by railway engineer Seraphin Chopard in the October 4, 1861, edition of the *Sentinelle du Jura*) uncovered in 1861 during excavation of a cutting of the Bourg-Besançon railway line. These remains represented five individuals; additional specimens referable to this species were found at Vilette near Arbois,

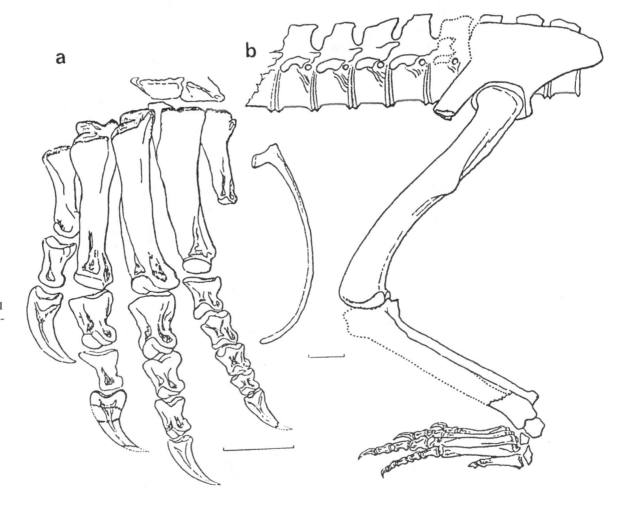

Tentative species ?*Plateosaurus plieningeri* (material originally referred to *Dimodosaurus plieningeri*): a. POL 70, left pes, anterior view (after Pidancet 1863); and b. reconstruction of syntypes (POL 1–4, regarded as the lectotype by Pidancet and Chopard 1862, and POL 7–53, the latter elements probably representing a single individual (after Chopard 1883). Scales = 10 cm. (Reproduced from Galton 1998.)

Domblans, and Beurre near Besançon. The material, housed in the Musée de Poligny, was subsequently described by Pidancet and Chopard two years later. The original material (POL collection, this taxon represented by 107 specimens) remained in the collections of the Musée de Poligny until that institution closed in 1960. (Other prosauropod specimens possibly referable to this species have been recovered from a number of French localities, including a site near Le Chappou [Ain], and others at Violet [Haute-Marne], Le Fechaux in Lons-le-Saunier [Jura], Alzon, and La Chassagne; see Galton 1998 for details.)

As further chronicled by Galton (1998), these specimens were then moved to the Town Hall, and in 1990 to the Université de Paris VI to be restored and described by Gilles Cuny in an as yet unpublished monograph. In 1993, Cuny recatalogued these remains, giving many of the specimens new numbers.

Regarding the taxonomic identity of the material from France, Galton (1997b, 1998) pointed out the following:

The type species, *Plateosaurus engelhardti*, is known from remains representing a large, massively built animal from the Frankonian Feuerletten (including the holotype, also new, mostly as yet undescribed referred material found at Ellingen, near Nürnberg), Bavaria, Germany, and also from the Knollenmergel of Stuttgart-Degerloch (about the same age as the Feuerletten). Unfortunately, the femur of the type specimen of this species is incomplete and cannot be substantially compared with femora of the Trössingen specimens that have been assigned to *Plateosaurus*; however, the femur of the Ellingen specimen is known to have a straight distal end. "*Gresslyosaurus*" cf. *plieningeri*, another prosauropod from Poligny (referred by Huene 1905 to *Plateosaurus plieningeri*, then by Galton 1986 to *P. engelhardti*), also possesses a femur with a straight distal end. However, the femur of "*Dimodosaurus*" *poligniensis* is S-shaped (the more typical condition for prosauropods), and the bones are very similar to those that have been assigned to the Trössingen specimens.

Significantly, the latter specimens were found in rocks that are stratigraphically older than those which have yielded specimens of *P. engelhardti*. Furthermore, the specimens from Trössingen (and possibly others from France and Switzerland) are more gracile than those of *P. engelhardti*, with even the larger individuals being more lightly built and possessing more slender femora and comparatively longer metatarsals. For these reasons, Wellnhofer (1993b) suggested that the name *P. engelhardti* be restricted to the more massively built, geologically younger form.

According to Galton (1998), if *P. engelhardti* is grouped with the specimens from Trössingen, then *P.*

poligniensis should be regarded as a junior synonym of the type species, with the form having a straight femur probably referred to the prosauropod taxon from Ellingen. However, if Wellnhofer is correct in referring the Ellingen material to *P. engelhardti*, then this species is probably also represented at Poligny by remains of "*Gresslyosaurus*" cf. *plieningeri*. Consequently, the material including S-shaped femora would then represent a separate species. Taking a conservative approach, and pending the sorting out of the above systematic alternatives, Galton (1998) tentatively accepted *P.* ("*Dimodosaurus*") *poligniensis* as a species of *Plateosaurus* having an S-shaped femur (though this taxon may be a junior synonym of *P. engelhardti*), and "*Gresslyosaurus*" cf. *plieningeri* for the form with the straighter femur.

Errata: In *D:TE*, p. 710, the mounted skeleton of *Plateosaurus engelhardti* exhibited at the American Museum of Natural History was incorrectly identified in both the text and photograph caption. AMNH 6810 comprises an almost complete skeleton including a complete skull. A cast (YPM 9881) of the disarticulated skull elements of this specimen was placed in the collections of the Yale Peabody Museum of Natural History.

On the same page, the reference to Colbert (1969) should be corrected to Colbert (1968).

Key references: Chopard (1883); Cuny (1993); Galton (1985c, 1986, 1997b, 1998); Gow, Kitching and Raath (1990); Huene (1905); Pidancet (1863); Pidancet and Chopard (1862); Weishampel and Chapman (1990); Wellnhofer (1993b).

†PLEUROCOELUS

Saurischia: Sauropodomorpha: Sauropoda: Eusauropoda: Neosauropoda: Macronaria: Camarasauromorpha: Titanosauriformes: Brachiosauridae.

Comments: *Pleurocoelus* is the most common Early Cretaceous North American sauropod and the first sauropod to be known from that continent. As related by Peter M. Krantz (1998), the original discovery, a tooth (YPM 798) upon which the new type species *Astrodon johnstoni* was erected by Joseph Leidy (1865) (see *D:TE*), was made in late November, 1858 by State Geologist Philip T. Tyson on the property of J. D. Latchford in the Arundel Formation of Muirkirk, Maryland.

As recounted by Krantz, the location of this discovery was substantiated in late 1996 after Latchford's property was inadvertently acquired in December of the previous year by the Maryland–National Capitol Park and Planning Commissions. The latter had sought this property for the development of a dinosaur park as it was adjacent to an active dinosaur

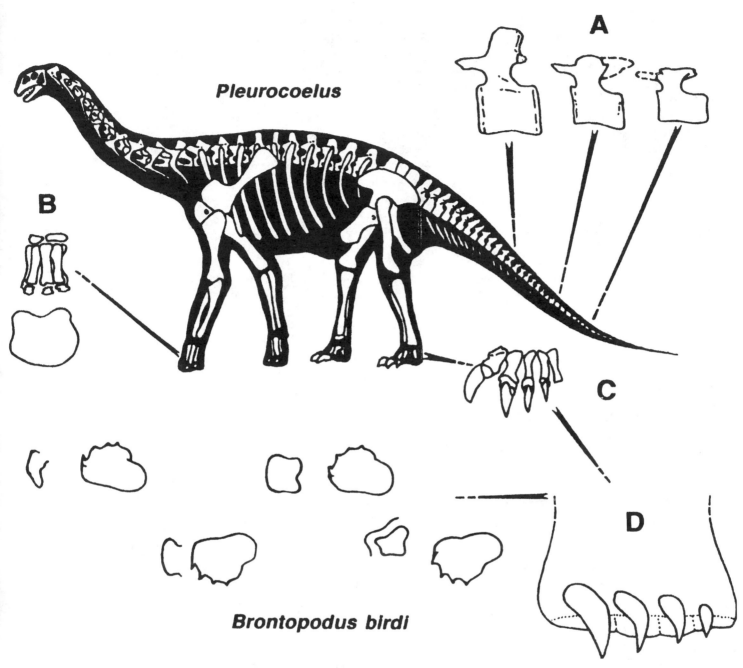

Pleurocoelus

A

B

C

D

Brontopodus birdi

A. *Pleurocoelus* caudal vertebrae (SMU 617.32), B. Roland T. Bird's reconstruction of manus bones of *Brontopodus* trackmaker, C. *Pleurocoelus* left pes (FMNH PR 977), D. *Pleurocoelus* restored left pes (anterior view), and *Brontopodus birdi* tracks, modified from Langston (1974), Farlow, Pittman and Hawthorn (1989), and Gallup 1989. (After Salgado and Calvo 1997.)

fossil site. Discovery of remains at Latchford's house substantiated the property as the actual type locality for the original specimen.

Pleurocoelus (which includes the genus *Astrodon*) has generally been regarded as a relatively small sauropod. More recently, however, remains of this dinosaur have been found that reveal otherwise. As reported by Krantz (1996), Arnold Norden, on May 19, 1991, found some fossil bone fragments in the brick clay pit of Cherokee Sandford Company, at Muirkirk, at a site adjoining and contiguous with the Latchford property. The next day, excavation by a Smithsonian Institution crew yielded "the largest dinosaur bone ever found on the East Coast" (Eugene L. Meyer in a May

25, 1991, article published in the *Washington Post*), an incomplete femur (proximal end missing) belonging to *Pleurocoelus*. According to Krantz, the femur, if complete, may have measured more than 2 meters in length, indicating that the adult animal was a very large sauropod measuring at least 25 meters (about 85 feet) long (see also Krantz 1998).

Pleurocoelus has mostly been regarded as a member of the Brachiosauridae. However, Salgado, Calvo and Coria (1995), in a recent cladistic study, interpreted this genus as the sister taxon of the Titanosauria, and "*Pleurocoelus*" sp. (Langston 1974; Gallup 1989) as a basal titanosaur.

Salgado and Calvo (1997) observed that the distal

end of the tibia in the type species, *P. nanus*, resembles that of *Chubutisaurus insignis* and titanosaurids instead of that of *Brachiosaurus brancai*; as in titanosaurs, the ends of the metacarpals do not show clear articular facets for manual phalanges; opposite to the condition in titanosaurs, the anterior caudals are amphiplatyan, a plesiomorphic condition.

According to Salgado and Calvo, some teeth referred to *Pleurocoelus* possess worn facets that are sharply inclined relative to the labio-lingual axis, probably a synapomorphic condition of the Titanosauriformes, and show "an intermediate morphology between the typical, relatively broad 'brachiosaur'-teeth and the 'peg-like' teeth, typical of titanosaurids" (see Calvo 1994*a*, 1994*b*). The authors speculated that the titanosaur common ancestor probably had teeth like *Pleurocoelus*, and that, consequently, the teeth of *Camarasaurus*, *Brachiosaurus*, *Pleurocoelus*, and the Titanosauridae possess crowns that are comparatively more slender.

Salgado and Calvo pointed out that the most anterior vertebrae of *Pleurocoelus* sp. are mildly procoelous (see Langston), as in the titanosaur *Andesaurus* and in the common ancestor of the Titanosauria (Salgado, Coria and Calvo 1997). Also, an incomplete dorsal vertebra belonging to the specimen Langston described has "the infradiapophyseal lamina slightly forked at its base, and the centro-paraphyseal lamina, both synapomorphies of the Titanosauria" (see Salgado, Coria and Calvo).

More recently, however, Wilson and Sereno (1998), in performing their own cladistic study of numerous sauropod taxa, criticized the above analyses on a number of points (see "Systematics" chapter), concluding that the Brachiosauridae is a valid group within Titanosauriformes, and that *Pleurocoelus* is, in fact, a brachiosaurid.

Gomani, Jacobs and Winkler (1998), although not taking a firm stand on the true affinities of *Pleurocoelus*, while comparing recently excavated remains from Texas referred to this genus with the titanosaur *Malawisaurus*, pointed out the following: Based upon currently available fossil evidence, *Malawisaurus* seems to be more derived than *Pleurocoelus* in possessing the following significant titanosaurian synapomorphies (none of which are present in *Pleurocoelus*): Strongly procoelous anterior caudal vertebrae, presacral vertebrae made up of spongy bone, rudimentary cervical arch laminae, shallow pleurocoels of presacral vertebrae lacking in a sharp lip, and in lacking hyposphene-hypantra articulations. However, *Pleurocoelus* shares with *Malawisaurus* the following potentially useful characters: Tooth morphology, centro-parapophyseal laminae on dorsal vertebrae, and dorsal ribs having proximal pneumatic cavities. On the other hand, both *Pleurocoelus* and *Malawisaurus* share with the brachiosaurid *Brachiosaurus* the following features: Medial caudal vertebrae having anteriorly restricted neural arches, femur with pronounced lateral bulge, and tibia having transversely expanded distal end.

Notes: Salgado and Calvo accepted the interpretation that fossil footprints known as *Brontopodus birdi*, discovered by Roland T. Bird in the Paluxy River Formation of Texas (see *Pleurocoelus* entry, *D:TE*) correspond with the feet of *Pleurocoelus* sp. and that these tracks are consistent with their interpretation of *Pleurocoelus* sp. as a titanosaur. The tracks reveal no traces of a claw of manual digit I (see Farlow, Pittman and Hawthorne 1989; also Gallup), implying that the manus of at least one sauropod trackmaker at this site either possessed no such claw, or that, if present, the claw was imbedded in the foot pad (though McIntosh, Coombs and Russell 1992 noted that these tracks could have been made by a diplodocid with a pes similar to *Dyslocosaurus*.) As this condition is a derived feature not found in *Brachiosaurus* (in which the claw of manual digit I is present though reduced), Salgado and Calvo suggested that its occurrence in *Pleurocoelus* sp. contributes data regarding the evolution of the feet in titanosaurs.

Fossil bones belonging to Early Cretaceous, North American sauropods are comparatively rare, and most of them have, over the years, been attributed to *Pleurocoelus*. In a preliminary report, Winkler, Jacobs and Murry (1997) briefly described an Early Cretaceous sauropod bonebed at the Jones Ranch locality, in the Twin Mountains Formation of Hood County, Texas. The site — discovered by crews from the University of Texas, Austin, and worked by Jeffrey G. Pittman — is particularly significant given its proximity to well-known fossil footprint sites at Glen Rose, Texas (see *D:TE*). Skeletal remains, including articulated segments and isolated bones of at least three sauropod individuals, are known here.

Winkler *et al.* noted that sections of fossil logs, some of which are nearly 4 meters in length, were also found at this site; and that the sauropod bones (also various other vertebrate fragments) were mixed with thick layers of charcoal fragments, conifer cones, and powdered plant debris.

As interpreted by Winkler *et al.*, this site "represents a high-energy and rapid, episodic channel fill event, with subsequent scour and exhumation of parts of the bonebed." According to the authors, the sauropod carcasses had partly decayed before transport and burial, after which "the bones together with the logs jammed and choked the channel of a stream ultimately feeding the tidal flats preserving the contemporaneous sauropod (*Brontopodus*) tracks."

Stanford (1998) reported two very small, associated left and right pes prints and one associated manus print of a hatchling sauropod from the Lower Cretaceous of Travis County, Texas. The pes length is 5.8 centimeters, manus width 3.0 centimeters. The find is significant as the first hatchling sauropod tracks to be documented.

Erratum: In *D:TE*, in the original entry for this genus, the name *Pleurocoelus* was sometimes misspelled as "*Pleurocoelous.*"

Key references: Farlow, Pittman and Hawthorne (1989); Gallup (1989); Gomani, Jacobs and Winkler (1998); Krantz (1996, 1998); Leidy (1865); Salgado and Calvo (1997); Salgado, Calvo and Coria (1995); Salgado, Coria and Calvo (1997); Wilson and Sereno (1998); Winkler, Jacobs and Murry (1997).

†PROBACTROSAURUS

Ornithischia: Genasauria: Cerapoda: Ornithopoda: Euornithopoda: Iguanodontia: Euiguanodontia: Dryomorpha: Ankylopollexia *incertae sedis.*

New species: *P. mazongshanensis* Lu 1997.

Occurrence of *P. mazongshanensis*: Xinminbao Group, Gansu Province, China.

Age: Early Cretaceous.

Known material of *P. mazongshanensis*: Various incomplete cranial and postcranial specimens.

Holotype of *P. mazongshanensis*: IVPP V. 11333, posterior part of incomplete skull.

Diagnosis of *P. mazongshanensis*: Basioccipital with short neck, forming part of border of foramen magnum; ends of paroccipital processes unexpanded; paroccipital processes extending lateroventrally from foramen magnum; frontals distended; maxillary teeth with one highly developed median ridge, other surface smooth; dentary tooth with well-developed main ridge and two lateral less-developed ridges; maxillary and dentary teeth possessing marginal serrations; cervical centra typically opisthocoelous, with one to three small nutritional foramina on lateral sides, well-developed ventral keel retaining same width along its length; ventral keel of dorsal vertebrae undeveloped; height of dorsal centra greater than length; six true sacral vertebrae, lacking ventral groove; anterior caudal vertebrae heart-shaped, several (three–five) mid-caudal vertebrae hexagonal in shape; posterior caudal vertebrae quadrilateral in anteroposterior view; ventral surfaces of anterior caudal centra slightly concave, those of middle centra very concave, those of posterior centra convex; both ends of scapula expanded; shaft of scapula near glenoid cavity strongly contracted; femur with very well-developed, plate-shaped fourth trochanter, anterior intercondylar groove open at distal end of bone, femoral shaft slightly curved; pubis with enclosed obturator foramen, laterally flattened blade of prepubis uneven; pubic shaft rodlike; free ends of posterior hemal arches symmetrically elongated anteroposteriorly (Lu 1997).

Comment: A third species of the iguanodontian *Probactrosaurus*— a genus generally thought of as phylogenetically somewhere between iguanodontid and hadrosaurid — named *P. mazongshanensis*, was founded upon an incomplete skull (IVPP V. 11333) collected in 1992 during the Sino-Japanese Silk Road Dinosaur Expedition (Dong 1997b) from the Early Cretaceous sandstone of the Mazongshan Area, Xinminbao Group, Gansu Province, China. Referred material from the same locality includes four cervical vertebrae, the 10th almost complete (IVPP V. 11334-1); a second

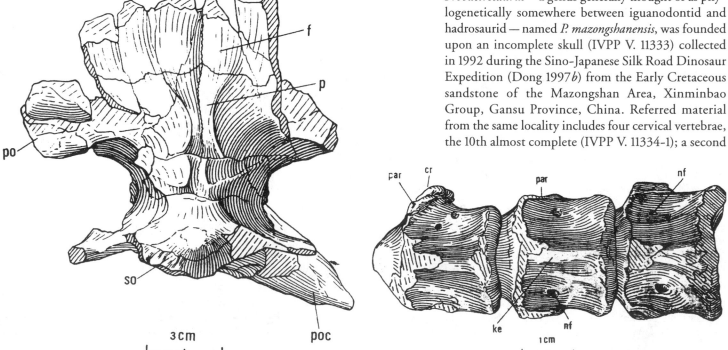

Left: Probactrosaurus mazongshanensis, IVPP V. 11333, holotype posterior part of skull, dorsal view. (After Lu 1997.) *Right: Probactrosaurus mazongshanensis*, IVPP V. 11334-1, referred articulated cervical vertebrae, ventral view. (After Lu 1997.)

dorsal vertebra (IVPP V. 11334-2); an almost complete sacrum (IVPP V. 11334-3); two series of caudal vertebrae, some with spines and hemal arches (IVPP V. 11334-4); a right femur missing proximal portion (IVPP V. 11334-5); portions of both pubes (IVPP V. 11334-6 and 7); part of the anterior process of a left ilium (IVPP V. 11334-8); the posterior portion of a right ilium (IVPP V. 11334-9); two nearly complete maxillary teeth (IVPP V. 11334-10 and 11); four dentary teeth (IVPP V. 11334-12, 13, 14, and 15); part of a left quadrate (IVPP V. 11334-16); a complete left scapula (IVPP V. 11334-17); and a partial left humerus (IVPP V. 11334-18) (Lu 1997).

Lu regarded *P. mazongshanensis* as "a relatively large iguanodontid, with a high skull and a particularly wide occipital region." The species is apparently a "bulky" iguanodontian.

Remains of *P. mazongshanensis* and other new dinosaurs were displayed in the "Dinosaurs of the Silk Road" exhibition by Chinese and Japanese scientists

Key references: Dong (1997*b*); Lu (1997).

†PROCOMPSOGNATHUS

Saurischia: Theropoda: Neotheropoda: "Ceratosauria": ?Coelophysoidea.

Comments: In 1992, Paul C. Sereno and Rupert Wild, upon performing a cladistic analysis of the small theropod *Procompsognathus triassicus*, concluded that the type specimen (SMNS 12591) was, in fact, a chimera, comprising the postcrania of a *Segisaurus*-like theropod and the skull of a sphenosuchian crocodylomorph, *Saltoposuchus connectens*. This assessment was subsequently challenged by Chatterjee (1993) in a brief preliminary report in which he argued that the skull of *P. triassicus* is indeed that of a theropod, with a resemblance to that of *Syntarsus* (see *D:TE*).

More recently, Chatterjee (1998), following detailed preparation of the skull of SMNS 12591, published another brief report maintaining the skull's theropod nature. According to Chatterjee (1998), this skull lacks a number of hallmarks of sphenosuchians: Basal constricted teeth; large tympanic cavity; strong overhang of squamosal at side of quadrate; atrophied descending process of squamosal; tall ascending process of quadratojugal; quadrate/prootic articulation; rostral, dorsal, caudal, articular, and quadrate tympanic recesses; ventral foramina for eustachian tube; large and pneumatic basipterygoid processes; and sagittal crest on parietal.

On the other hand, the skull displays a suite of theropod synapomorphies: Presence of accessory maxillary fenestra; vomers fused rostrally, extended considerably forward to choana; single quadrate head received completely by squamosal without paroccipital contact; laterosphenoid with transverse postorbital process; and fused orbitosphenoids.

Furthermore, Chatterjee (1998) found the braincase of *Procompsognathus* to be quite similar to that of the "ceratosaur" *Syntarsus*.

Key references: Chatterjee (1993, 1998); Sereno and Wild (1992).

PROTARCHAEOPTERYX   Ji and Ji 1997

Saurischia: Theropoda: Neotheropoda: Tetanurae: Avetheropoda: Coelurosauria: Manuraptoriformes: Manuraptora: Eumanuraptora: Dromaeosauridae.

Name derivation: Greek *protos* = "first" + *Archaeopteryx* [generally considered to be the earliest known true bird].

Type species: *P. robusta* Ji and Ji 1997.

Other species: [None.]

Occurrence: Chaomidianzi Formation, Liaoning Province, People's Republic of China.

Age: ?Early Cretaceous.

Known material/holotype: NGMC 2125, almost complete skeleton with preserved feather impressions.

Diagnosis of genus (as for type species): Premaxillary teeth large, straight, maxillary and dentary teeth short, bulbous, all of these teeth primitively serrated; rectrices forming fan at end of tail (Ji, Currie, Norell and Ji (1998).

Comments: One of the first nonavian dinosaurs known positively to have been feathered, the genus *Protarchaeopteryx* was founded upon an almost complete skeleton (NGMC 2125) from the Jiulongsong Member of the Chaomidianzi Formation (underlying the Yixian Formation, tentatively of Late Jurassic–Early Cretaceous age, as determined by radiometric dating and other evidence; see You and Dodson 1998; also Padian 1998*b*), in the Sihetun area near Beipiao City, in Liaoning Province, China (Ji and Ji 1996*b*; 1997; Ji, Currie, Norell and Ji 1998).

The type specimen was first briefly described by Ji and Ji (1996*b*) as belonging to the avian family Archaeopterygidae, this genus and species being more primitive than *Archaeopyteryx*, and possessing feathers described as structurally intermediate between the integumentary structures of *Sinosauropteryx* (interpreted by some scientists as "protofeathers") and the true feathers of *Archaeopteryx*.)

Subsequently, Ji and Ji (1997) formally described *P. robusta* as a primitive bird belonging to a newly proposed family, the Protarchaeopterygidae. This identification was understandable, as the presence of feathers has traditionally been considered to be a diagnostic feature of birds (see "Introduction" section on "Dinosaurs and Birds"; also, "Systematics" chapter), and

Probactrosaurus mazongshanensis, IVPP V. 11334-5, referred incomplete right femur, lateral view. (After Lu 1997.)

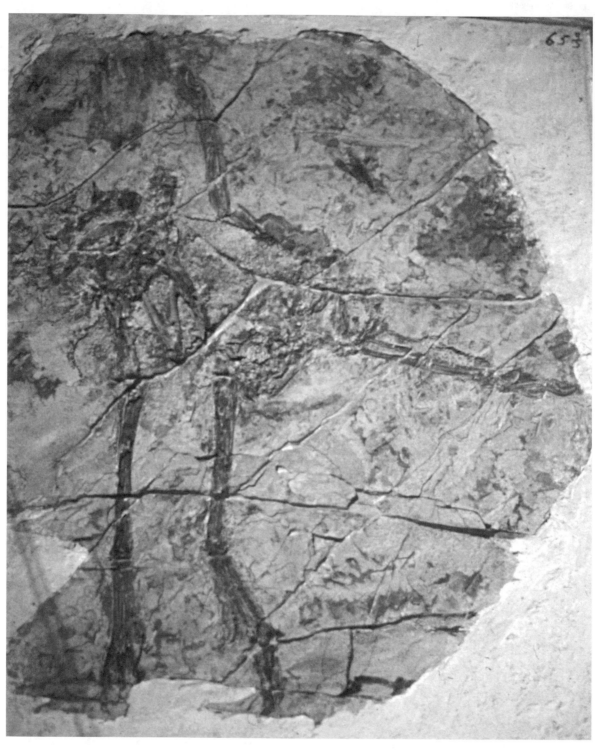

Protarchaeopteryx robusta,
NGMC 2125, holotype
skeleton displayed at Na-
tional Geographic Society's
exhibition of "China's
Feathered Dinosaurs."

the feather impressions preserved in NGMC 2125
leave no doubt as to their identity. Not until the discovery of the related genus *Caudipteryx* (see entry),
also found with feather impressions, was the type specimen of *Protarchaeopteryx robusta* identified (by Ji, Currie, Norell and Ji 1998) as that of a nonavian theropod.

As described by Ji *et al.*, NGMC 2125 preserves
a "clump of at least six plumulaceous feathers" anterior to the chest, some exhibiting well-developed

vanes. Associated with ten proximal caudal vertebrae
are evenly distributed plumulaceous feathers measuring up to 27 millimeters in length. Preserved along the
lateral side of the right femur and proximal end of the
left are plumulaceous feathers measuring 20 millimeters long. Also preserved with the holotype are parts
of more than a dozen symmetrical tail feathers, one of
these extending 132 millimeters from the closest caudal vertebra, with a tapering rachis having a basal

diameter of 1.5 millimeters. The well-formed feather vanes indicate that barbules were present, the vane measuring 5.3 millimeters in width on either side of the rachis. Five barbs come off the rachis at midshaft every 5 millimeters (in contrast with six in *Archaeopteryx*), individual barbs measuring 15 millimeters in length. Barbs at the base of the feather are plumulaceous, as in modern birds.

According to Ji *et al.*, the veins of the rectrices of *Protarchaeopteryx* are symmetrical, a feature generally associated with birds incapable of flight (although "it is possible that an animal with symmetrical feathers could also fly"). The authors pointed out that the relative arm length of *Protarchaeopteryx* is longer than in nonavian coelurosaurs, but shorter than that of *Archaeopteryx* (which possesses asymmetrical veins). However, the high-positioned and anteromedially oriented hallux of *Protarchaeopteryx*, in addition to the long legs, indicate that this genus was a ground-dwelling runner.

Ji *et al.* joined *Protarchaeopteryx* and *Caudipteryx* into an unnamed clade of manuraptorans regarded by these authors as the sister taxon of the Velociraptorinae (see "Systematics" chapter).

Key references: Ji, Currie, Norell and Ji (1998); Ji and Ji (1996*b*, 1997).

†PROTOAVIS

Saurischia: ?Theropoda *incertae sedis*.

Comments: In 1991, Sankar Chatterjee named and described *Protoavis*, a new Late Triassic genus based upon two specimens—the holotype (TTU P 9200), consisting of a partial skull, and a paratype (TTU P 9201), a partial skull and partial postcranial skeleton belonging to a smaller individual—recovered from the Dockum Formation in Garza County, Texas. Chatterjee interpreted these remains as representing the earliest known "protobird."

Chatterjee (1995*c*) subsequently published a new report on *Protoavis* while still maintaining its avian status.

More recently, Chatterjee (1997) unequivocally stated that "*Protoavis* is the basal member of [the Mesozoic avian clade] Ornithothoraces," displaying a number of "improvements for powered flight over the condition in *Archaeopteryx*," these comprising the following: 1. Flight apparatus becoming more robust and pneumatic; 2. coracoid strutlike, elongated ventrally, with expanded sternal end; 3. development of acrocoracoid process to form triosseal canal for supracoracoideus pully that would allow upstroke motion; 4. glenoid facing outward and upward to allow wide excursion of humerus; 5. coracoid with distinct procoracoid process; 6. furcula becoming springlike, with

large interclavicle to withstand compressive force of downstroke; 7. sternum longitudinally directed, with distinct ventral keel for attachment of flight muscles; 8. humerus showing bicipital crest and strongly defined head; 9. radial and ulnar condyles asymmetric and well-developed distally, allowing sliding movement of radius on ulna; 10. in wrist, radiale fairly large, ulnare developing an interlocking articulation with ventral ridge of metacarpal III; 11. second distal carpal showing trochlear surface proximally for sliding of radiale and ulnare, but single facet for reception of metacarpal II; 12. (as in modern birds) acquisition of elbow-wrist linkage system permitting automatic folding and unfolding of wing without muscular effort (see Chatterjee 1995*c*); 13. metacarpals II and III showing quill knobs for attachment of primary feathers; and 14. ilium fused to ischium to withstand thrust from landing gear.

However, a number of workers seem not to have accepted Chatterjee's (1991, 1995*c*, 1997) interpretation. Perhaps the most vocal critic has been John H. Ostrom, an authority on the Late Jurassic bird *Archaeopteryx*. Ostrom (1991) found little support for Chatterjee's claim that *Protoavis* is a bird predating *Archaeopteryx*, criticizing Chatterjee's original 1991 paper as only dealing with the cranial material, which "is fragmentary, disarticulated and severely crushed, and therefore subject to different interpretations—and even different identifications." Ostrom pointed out that every piece of this material has been extracted from the matrix, making spacial associations between the fragments impossible, and found Chatterjee's (1991) analysis of the material to be incomplete, and his sense of the poor quality of preservation inadequate.

Ostrom saw Chatterjee's (1991) photographs of the material as "of miniscule size and marginal quality, arranged in a confusing format (on occasion with 20 or more objects to a page) with brief and sometimes cryptic captions that are discouraging to even the most dedicated readers." Also, Ostrom found Chatterjee's (1991) report to be "padded with accounts of features [*e.g.*, 'Neurosensory organs'] that are not without interest but are irrelevant to the main point," rather than addressing such central questions about the possession of feathers, an avian coracoid, keeled sternum, wishbone, or carpometacarpus. Finally, Ostrom criticized Chatterjee's (1991) description of the cranial material as being from an avian perspective only, not considering "that they might be squamatan, or crocodilian, or pterosaurian, or rhynchocephalian."

Based upon Chatterjee's 1995 report, fossil bird specialist Luis M. Chiappe (1995*c*) found that Chatterjee's (1991, 1995*c*) "interpretation of certain bones (such as furcula, sternum) are questionable, and even the association of elements into specimens and then into a single taxon seems difficult to support." Chiappe further stated that, despite cranial reconstructions, "only portions of the braincase, quadrate and orbital roof are reasonably preserved," concluding that "until better specimens are recovered and support for association of these into a single taxon provided, *Protoavis* should not be considered relevant to avian evolution."

Concurring with Chiappe, Ostrom (1996) published the following contrast between what is known of *Archaeopteryx* and what is not known about *Protoavis*:

1. *Archaeopteryx* (as of 1995) is known from seven complete or almost complete articulated skeletons collected from close localities; *Protoavis* is claimed to be represented by what is thought to be parts of two or three individuals, questionably of the same kind, from two separate sites.

2. *Archaeopteryx* occurs in a well-documented marine sequence that has been precisely dated; *Protoavis* is claimed to have been collected from approximately dated nonmarine deposits.

3. Skeletal specimens of *Archaeopteryx* are available in their natural articulation as when collected; the skull of *Protoavis*, as shown by Chatterjee (1991, 1995c), has been interpreted from fragments to suggest similarities with the Eichstätt *Archaeopteryx* specimen.

Key references: Chatterjee (1991, 1995c, 1997); Chiappe (1995); Ostrom (1991, 1996).

†PROTOCERATOPS

Comments: Among all dinosaurs, one of the best known is the primitive ceratopsian *Protoceratops*, rep-

Skeleton of a hatchling *Protoceratops andrewsi* individual from the Late Cretaceous (Campanian) Djadokhta Formation, Gobi Desert, southern People's Republic of Mongolia, exhibited in the "Great Russian Dinosaur Exhibit" (1996), Mesa Southwest Museum, Mesa, Arizona.

Photograph by the author, courtesy Mesa Southwest Museum.

resented by numerous specimens collected or left *in situ*, representing allometric stages from egg to adult.

In a brief preliminary report, Watabe, Suzuki, Tsogtbaatar, Barsbold and Weishampel (1996) announced the 1994 discovery by the Japan-Mongolia Joint Paleontological Expedition Team of 15 small, well-preserved *Protoceratops* hatchling skeletons, found grouped together in a small area of yellowish-white sandstones (correlated with the Campanian Djadokhta Formation), at the Tugrikin Shire locality, west of Bayn Dzak, Gobi Desert, Mongolia. Fossil eggshell fragments have not yet been identified at this particular site, although eggs have been found elsewhere at Tugrikin Shire.

According to Watabe *et al.*, the skeletons, discovered in different states of preservation, ranged in total (tip of rostral to end of tail) length from 142–186 millimeters (about 5.5–7.2 inches). The skulls possessed weakly developed frills and characteristically large orbits, with one preserving the sclerotic ring bones in its orbit. All individuals were found with their skulls facing one another in a sedimentary environment interpreted as an eolian (created by wind-blown sand) dune. Watabe *et al.* speculated that some catastrophic event (*e.g.*, sand storms or corruption of the nesting hole) could have been the cause for burial of such well-preserved *Protoceratops* remains.

Kirkland (1997b), in the magazine *Paleo Horizons*, a publication of Dinamation International Society, reported what "may be the first record of fossil pupae being found with [a dinosaur] skeleton." The evidence consisted of insect boring and associated pupae found in a well-preserved *Protoceratops* skull discovered in 1997 by Ed Fox during the DIS expedition to Bayan Zag (the so-called "Flaming Cliffs"), Mongolia.

Key reference: Kirkland (1997b); Watabe, Suzuki, Tsogtbaatar, Barsbold and Weishampel (1996).

†PSITTACOSAURUS

New species: *P. mazongshanensis* Xu 1997.

Occurrence of *P. mazongshanensis*: Xinminbao Group, Gansu Province, China.

Age: Early Cretaceous.

Known material/holotype of *P. mazongshanensis*: IVPP V. 12165, almost complete skull, associated cervical, dorsal, and sacral vertebrae, forelimb.

Diagnosis of *P. mazongshanensis*: Snout rather long, especially rostral part of lower jaw; lateral surface of maxilla divided into three planes; maxillary protuberance strongly developed laterally and ventrally; right angle between two planes of lateral surface of jugal, and between planes of ventral surface and medial surface; dorsal part of predentary with lateral protuberance; ventral process along rim of dentary

just posterior to predentary-dentary suture; numerous denticles along edge of tooth crown; secondary ridges on tooth crowns long, slim; pronounced middle lobe consisting of four secondary ridges on lateral surface of maxillary crown; concavity from anteroventral part to posterodorsal part of ventral surface of exoccipital (Xu 1997).

Comments: Of all dinosaurian genera, the parrot-

Protoceratops andrewsi, skeleton (FMNH P12991) and eggs (possibly belonging to this species) collected in 1926 during the Third Asiatic Expedition of the American Museum of Natural History (co-sponsored by the formerly named Field Museum of Natural History) to Mongolia.

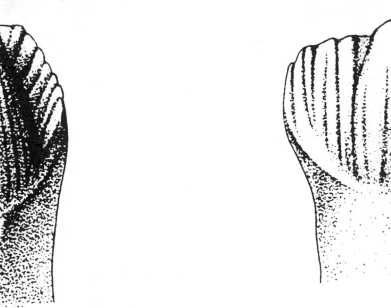

Psittacosaurus mazongshanensis, IVPP V. 12165, holotype A. maxillary and B. dentary teeth. (After Xu 1997.)

Psittacosaurus

Psittacosaurus mazongsha-nensis, IVPP V. 12165, holo-type A. left maxilla, b. atlas neural arch, C. cervical ver-tebrae, D. scapulocoracoid. (After Xu 997.)

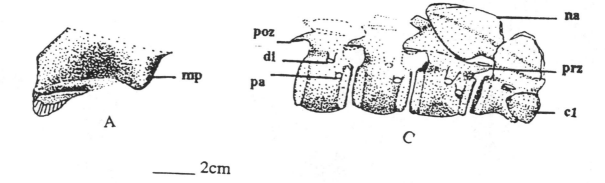

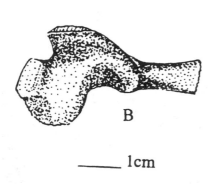

___ 2cm

___ 1cm

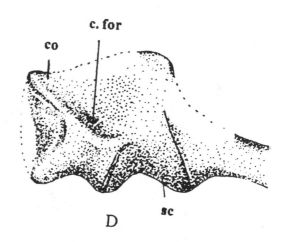

Psittacosaurus mazongsha-nensis, IVPP V. 12165, holo-type basioccipital. (After Xu 1997.)

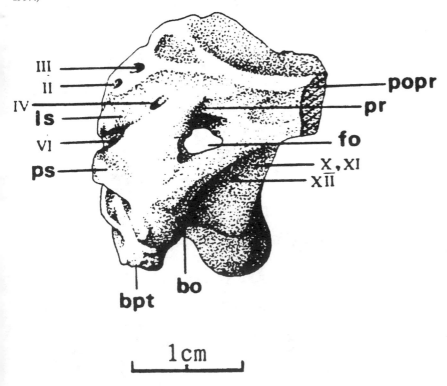

1cm

beaked, primitive ceratopsian *Psittacosaurus* embraces the greatest number of currently accepted species — ten since the genus was first named and described by Henry Fairfield Osborn in 1923 (though not all of these species are necessarily valid [P. Dodson, personal communication 1998]). Now, yet an eleventh species, *P. mazongshanensis*, has been assigned to this genus.

P. mazongshanensis was based upon a nearly com-plete skull and some postcranial remains (IVPP V. 12165), recovered in 1922 from the Xinminbao Group (Lower Cretaceous) during the Silk Road Dinosaur Expedition (Dong 1997*b*) to the Mazongshan Area of Gansu Province, China (Xu 1997).

Xu reported that a group of rounded gas-troliths — pebbles most likely having originated in rivers — were found in the gut area of the holotype, suggesting that this species may have dwelt in the vicinity of rivers. The hypothesis that these stones were probably used in aiding digestion was supported by the following evidence:

1. The 50–60 percent roundness of the pebbles found with the type specimen falls within the range more efficient for grinding food; other gastroliths uti-lized by swimming animals for balance tend to have 80 or more percent roundness.

2. The tooth morphology and jaws of the new species is very different from other psittacosaur species. In *P. mazongshanensis*, the teeth possess more denticles than do those of any other *Psittacosaurus* species, and the articular surface on the lower jaw is

R

cupped rather than perfectly flat as in other species, these features resulting in a relatively poor chewing system.

The structures of the teeth and lower jaws, as well as the association of gastroliths with the holotype, indicated to Xu that *P. mazongshensis* generally ate tough plant material and used the stones to aid in digestion.

Comparing via cladistic analysis the new species with others referred to *Psittacosaurus*, Xu determined that two distinct clades exist within this genus. The more primitive "Clade A" (including the type species, *P. mongoliensis*, also *P. xinjiangensis* and *P. mazongshanensis*) and the more derived "Clade B" (including *P. sinensis* and *P. meileyingensis*). Xu diagnosed "Clade A" by a single synapomorphy (tooth row straight). *P. xinjiangensis* and *P. mazongshanensis* were found to be related to one another by two dental features (*i.e.,* more denticles on tooth crowns; slender secondary ridges on crown surface). "Clade B" was diagnosed by Xu by a number of synapomorphies (skull profile intermediate between rectangular and rounded, with relatively short preorbital region; strongly developed horizontal ridge on postorbital; posterior margin of quadrate deeply sulcate; postorbital region broad; lower jaw V-shaped in ventral aspect; dentary and splenial almost equally contributing to ventral surface of mandible).

Contra Sereno and Chao (1988), Xu found that the presence of a well-developed, pyramid-shaped jugal horn in *P. xinjiangensis* and *P. sinensis* does not indicate a close relationship between these two species, but rather seems to be a character obtained independently by both. According to Xu, this character evolving twice "may reflect a correlation between the morphology of the jugal and the masticatory function of the jaw."

The holotype skull of this species was displayed along with other new dinosaurian specimens in the "Dinosaurs of the Silk Road" exhibition, arranged by Chinese and Japanese scientists.

Key references: Dong (1997*b*); Xu (1997).

RAYOSOSAURUS   Bonaparte 1995

Saurischia: Sauropodomorpha: Sauropoda: Eusauropoda: Neosauropoda: Diplodocoidea.

Name derivation: "Rayoso [Formation] + Greek *sauros* = "lizard."

Psittacosaurus mongoliensis, AMNH 6253, holotype skeleton of *Protiguanodon mongoliensis*, dorsal view.

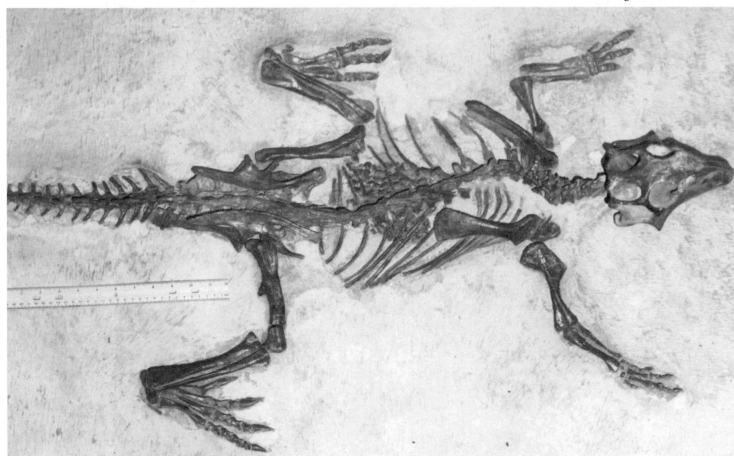

Photograph by Robert A. Long and Samuel P. Welles (neg. #73-345-28). Courtesy American Museum of Natural History.

Rayososaurus tessonei, MUCPv-205, holotype partial skull of *Rebbachisaurus tessonei*, lateral view. (After Calvo and Salgado 1995.)

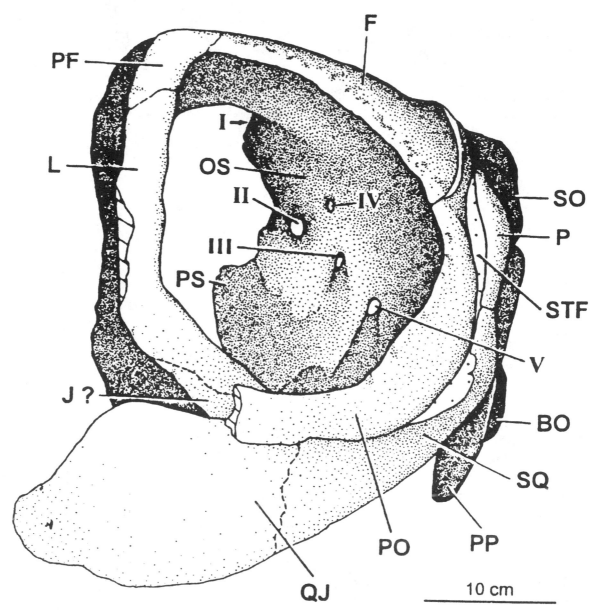

Type species: *R. tessonei* (Calvo and Salgado 1995).

Other species: [None.]

Occurrence: Rayoso Formation, Río Limay Formation, Neuquén Province, Argentina.

Age: "Middle" Cretaceous (Albian–Cenomanian).

Known material: At least three adult incomplete skeletons, partial postcrania, gastroliths.

Holotype: (MACN-N 41), partial postcranial remains including left scapula, incomplete right scapular blade, incomplete left fibula, left femur, fragments.

Diagnosis of genus (as for type species): Scapular blade paddle-like; V-shape angle between acromion and scapular blade; dorsals with absence of hyposphene-hypantrum; neural arch tall; primitive character of single neural spine; parapophysis directed upward at approximately 45-degree angle (Calvo and Salgado 1995).

Diagnosis of *R. tessonei*: "Diplodocimorph" sauropod with these unique derived characters: basipterygoid very thin and short; absence of posterior process of postorbital; articular condyle of quadrate elongated anteroposteriorly; tuberas quite reduced; paroccipital processes not distally expanded; neural spine in posterior cervical and dorsal vertebrae with accessory lamina connecting diapopostzygapophyseal laminae and supraprezygapophyseal laminae; anterior dorsal vertebrae with both supraprezygapophyseal laminae contacting on top of spine; transverse process in anterior caudal vertebrae formed by dorsal and ventral bar directed upward (different than in type species, *Rebbachisaurus garasbae*, which has a true winglike transverse process); shaft of pubis oval in crosssection (Calvo and Salgado 1995).

Comments: The new genus *Rayososaurus* was

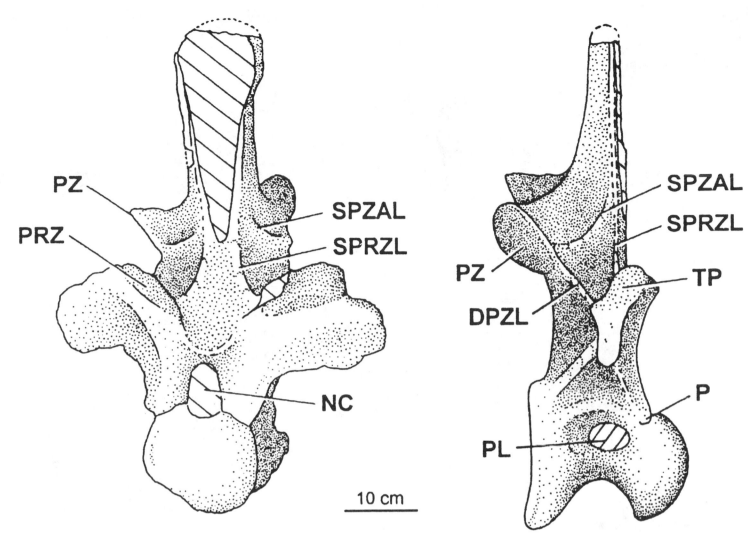

erected by Bonaparte (1995), based upon a left scapula, the distal half of the right scapular blade, proximal half of the left fibula, incomplete left femur, and indeterminate fragments (MACN-N 41), collected by José F. Bonaparte, Martin Vince, and assistants from medium-grained red sandstone of the upper section of the Rayoso Formation (Aptian), south of Agrio del Medio, Departmento Picunches, Province of Neuquén, Patagonia (Bonaparte 1995, 1996*b*).

Bonaparte (1996*b*) originally diagnosed the "type species" [see below], *R. agrioensis*, as follows: Sauropod with prominent spinous acromial process in scapula, internally flat, but externally with rounded edge running obliquely to longer axis of scapula, along middle of acromial process; deep, semicircular separation between acromial process and anterior (dorsal) border of scapular blade, the latter distally much expanded; acromial depression elongated dorsoventrally.

Subsequent to Bonaparte's introduction of *R. agrioensis*, Calvo and Salgado (1995) named and described a second species referred to *Rebbachisaurus*,

R. tessonei, then believed to be the most completely known species assigned to that genus. *R. tessonei* was founded upon a well-preserved, incomplete articulated skeleton (MUCPv-205), including basicranium, disarticulated cervical vertebrae, articulated vertebral column comprising posterior dorsals and all caudals, complete pectoral and pelvic girdles, almost complete hind- and forelimbs (lacking manus), and gastroliths. The specimen was recovered in the continental deposits (Albian–Cenomanian for this area of the basin; see Calvo 1991) at the top of the Candeleros Member and base of the Huincul Member of the Río Limay Formation, Neuquén Group, at the Ezequiel Ramos Mexia lake, southwest of El Chocón locality, Neuquén Province, in northwestern Patagonia, Argentina.

Material referred to this species, from the same locality, includes a disarticulated postcranial skeleton (MUCPv-206, the largest specimen) consisting of two posterior and two anterior cervical vertebrae, one posterior dorsal vertebra, a sternal plate, four metacarpals, ribs, and gastroliths; a partial articulated skeleton

Rayososaurus tessonei,
MUCPv-205, holotype of
Rebbachisaurus tessonei, A.
left scapulocoracoid, lateral
view, B. left humerus, anterior view, C. left ulna, lateral view, and D. left radius, anterior view. (After
Calvo and Salgado.)

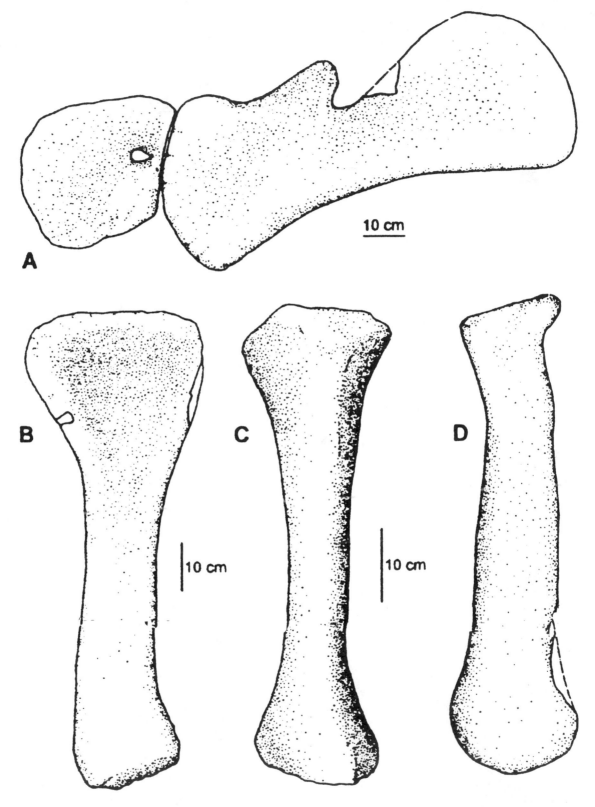

(MUCPv-153, the smallest specimen), comprising two sacral vertebrae, the first six caudals, the pubis, and ischium. Also referred to this species is an un-numbered dorsal vertebra from the Neuquén Province, originally described and figured by Nopcsa (1902), which was referred by him to *Bothriospondy-lus.*

As related by Calvo and Salgado, the holotype was discovered by Leito Tessone in 1988, during a field trip of the Museo de Ciencias Naturales de la

Universidad Nacional del Comahue and (with a team led by Professor José F. Bonaparte) the Museo de Ciencias Naturales "Bernardino Rivadavia" of Buenos Aires. The specimen was briefly reported, though with no detailed information given, by Calvo and Bonaparte (1988) and Calvo and Salgado (1991). The deposits that produced the remains of this species also yielded a dinosaur-dominated vertebrate fauna including the titanosaur *Andesaurus delgado*, the theropod *Giganotosaurus carolinii*, dinosaur trace fossils, and also frogs and undescribed crocodiles. As determined by Calvo and Gazzera (1989), the paleoenvironment of the Candeleros Member of the Río Limay Formation "was represented by a temperate climate with alternate rainy and dry seasons."

According to Calvo and Salgado (1995), *R. tessonei* is characterized by the very broad, racket-shaped blade of the scapula (a character unique to the Sauropoda; see McIntosh 1990*b*), and the quite tall neural spine relative to the height of its centra.

Through phylogenetic analysis, Calvo and Salgado (1995) found the following synapomorphies uniting this species with the Diplodocidae: 1. Teeth pencil-like; 2. anterior extension of quadratojugal situated beyond anterior border of orbit; 3. basipterygoid processes anteriorly directed; 4. quadrate inclined posterodorsally; 5. infratemporal fenestra oval or slit-shaped; 6. narial opening located above orbit; 7. "whip-lash" tail; 8. tall neural arch in posterior dorsal vertebrae three times higher than that of centra; 9. tall neural arch in caudals, at least 1.5 times higher than that of centra; 10. transverse process wing-like; and 11. humerous/femur ratio less than 0.70.

Other synapomorphies that characterize the Diplodocidae were found by Calvo and Salgado (1995) not to be present in *R. tessonei*: 12. cervical neural spine bifurcated; 13. anterior dorsal neural spine bifurcated; 14. hyposphene-hypantrum present in anterior dorsals; 15. anterior caudal vertebrae slightly procoelous; 16. midcaudal chevrons with fore- and aft-directed processes; 17. hemal canal in anterior caudals closed; 18. ratio of maximum width of distal scapular blade/minimum width of scapula blade = 2; 19. prominent ambiens process in anterior part of pubis; 20. distal end of ischia expanded; and 21. dorsoventral contact of both distal ends of ischia wide.

Because of the lack of these latter characters in *R. tessonei*, Calvo and Salgado (1995) erected the new taxon Diplodocimorpha (see "Systematics" chapter; also, Wilson and Sereno 1998) to include this species and all other diplodocids displaying the first 11 of the above characters, and considered this taxon to be the sister group of *R. tessonei* presenting characters 12 through 21.

According to Calvo and Salgado (1995), the pres-

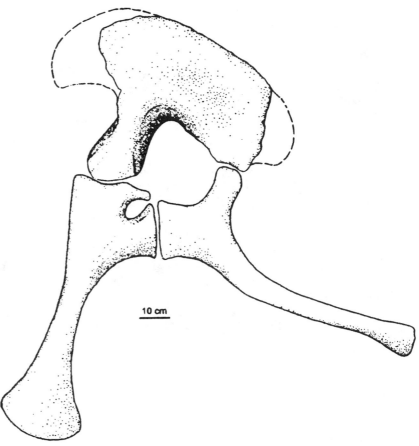

Rayososaurus tessonei, MUCPv-205, holotype reconstructed pelvic girdle of *Rebbachisaurus tessonei*, left lateral view. (After Calvo and Salgado 1995.)

ence of *R. garasbae* in the Aptian–Albian of Morocco and *R. tessonei* in the Albian–Cenomanian of Argentina permits the establishment of a land-bridge connection between Africa and South America up to Albian times. Additional evidence supporting the existence of this land bridge includes remains of other fossil vertebrates including the giant crocodilian *Sarcosuchus* (from the Aptian of Brazil and Niger; see Buffetaut and Taquet 1977), the mesosuchian crocodile *Araripesuchus* (Aptian of Northeastern Brazil and Niger; Buffetaut and Taquet 1979), the turtle *Araripemydiae* (Aptian of Brazil and Niger; De Broin 1980), and coelacanth *Mawsonia* (Aptian–Albian of Brazil and Africa; Wenz 1980). In a later informal article, Calvo and Salgado (1996) observed that the broad distal scapular blade and direction of the acromion process (a supposed autapomorphy of *Rebbachisaurus*) in *R. agrioensis* strongly resemble *R. tessonei*, and found the characters used by Bonaparte to diagnose his new taxon to be apomorphies of *Rebbachisaurus*. Therefore, Calvo and Salgado (1996) regarded Bonaparte's taxon as a *nomen dubium*, referring it to *Rebbachisaurus* sp.

Wilson and Sereno (1998), in a reassessment of various sauropod taxa, noted similarities between *R. tessonei* and the type species of *Rebbachisaurus*,

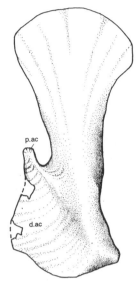

S

Rayosaurus agrioensis, MACN-N 41, holotype left scapula (lateral view) originally referred to *Lapparentosaurus* sp. Total length = 87 centimeters. (After Bonaparte 1996b).

Rayososaurus tessonei, MUCPv-205, holotype reconstructed skeleton of *Rebbachisaurus tessonei*. (After Calvo and Salgado 1995.)

R. garasbae—e.g., broadly expanded scapular blade; broad dorsal neural spines comprising four prominent, perpendicularly oriented laminae—these features apparently synapomorphic at some level. At the same time, however, they also perceived enough differences—e.g., neural arches of *R. garasbae* exhibiting complex lamination pattern ventral to diapophyses and zygapophyses (Wilson, personal observation); dorsal neural spines broadening to nearly twice their minimum width through proximal two-thirds of their height, then tapering sharply towards their summit in *R. garasbae*, but broadening gently towards their distal end in *R. tessonei*—to suggest that both of these species represent distinct genera, *Rayososaurus* and *Rebbachisaurus*. Agreeing that the scapula of *R. tessonei* closely resembles the type scapula of "*R. agrioensis*," Wilson and Sereno recommended that *R. tessonei* be referred to the genus *Rayososaurus*.

Note: The tentative species *?Rebbachisaurus tamesnensis* from Algeria was regarded by Calvo and Salgado (1995) as a camarasaurid.

Key references: Bonaparte (1995, 1996b); Calvo and Bonaparte (1988); Calvo and Salgado (1991, 1995, 1996); McIntosh (1990b); Nopcsa (1902); Wilson and Sereno (1998).

†REBBACHISAURUS

Saurischia: Sauropodomorpha: Sauropoda: Eusauropoda: Neosauropoda: Diplodocoidea: ?Dicraeosauridae.

Comment: A new species, *R. tessonei*, introduced by Calvo and Salgado (1995), was referred by Wilson and Sereno (1998) to the genus *Rayososaurus* (see entry).

Note: *?Rebbachisaurus tamesnensis*, a tentative species from Algeria, was regarded by Calvo and Salgado (1995) as a camarasaurid.

Key references: Calvo and Salgado (1995); Wilson and Sereno (1998).

†RIOARRIBASAURUS—(See *Coelophysis*.)

†SALTASAURUS—(=?*Loricosaurus*)

Saurischia: Sauropodomorpha: Sauropoda: Eusauropoda: Neosauropoda: Macronaria: Camarasauromorpha: Titanosauriformes: Somphospondyli: Titanosauria: Titanosauridae.

Comments: In a brief review of Argentinian tetrapods of the Cretaceous period, Bonaparte (1996b) commented that the armored titanosaur *Saltasaurus*, though of medium size (about 2 meters or less than 7 feet to the dorsal part of the sacral spines, less than 3 meters or about 10 feet to the top of the skull), was quite heavily built, as evidenced by the thickness of the ribs. The short and wide humeri suggest "different habits than in Titanosaurinae and Antarctosaurinae" [these subfamilies not generally adopted; see "Systematics" chapter], which have slender humeri.

Bonaparte speculated that the discovery of five individuals, including juveniles and adults, could be regarded as evidence of gregarious habits in this genus.

Key reference: Bonaparte (1996b).

†SAUROPELTA

Comments: New specimens have been referred to the large North American nodosaurid *Sauropelta*, one of them, for almost three decades, having been referred to other genera of armored dinosaurs.

In 1969, Bodily reported a nodosaurid (BYU 245) specimen found in what is now called the Poison Strip Sandstone, Cedar Mountain Formation, in Grand County, Utah. (The Poison Strip Sandstone is the second oldest of four members of the Cedar Mountain Formation, recently divided and defined by Kirkland, Britt, Burge, Carpenter, Cifelli, DeCourten, Eaton, Hasiotis and Lawton 1997; as *Sauropelta* is also found in the Cloverly Formation [Lower Cretaceous: Aptian–Albian] of Montana, the authors suggested that the Poison Strip Sandstone is also of Aptian–Albian age.)

Bodily's specimen included caudal vertebrae and associated armor. Based upon similarities between the armor in this specimen and armor belonging to

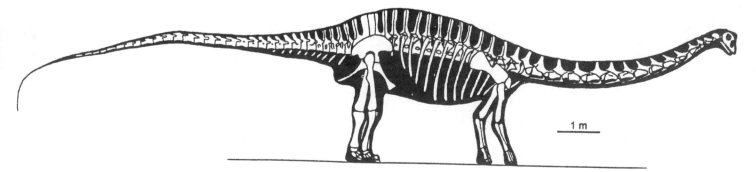

Hoplitosaurus marshi, Bodily referred this specimen to *Hoplitosaurus* sp. Later, Pereda-Suberbiola (1994), who regarded the North American genus *Hoplitosaurus* and English *Polacanthus* as congeneric, tentatively referred BYU 245 to *Polacanthus*.

More recently, Carpenter, Kirkland, Burge and Bird (1998), after a restudy of BYU 245, concluded that this specimen should be referred to *Sauropelta* sp. According to Carpenter *et al.*, the large triangular plates of BYU 245 resemble those of both *Sauropelta* and polacanthines. The large size of the individual and also the structure of the caudal vertebrae, however, are most similar to *Sauropelta*. The caudal neural spines of BYU 245, unlike those of *Sauropelta edwardsi*, are not expanded along their posterior length, this difference indicating to Carpenter *et al.* a possible new species of *Sauropelta*. Perhaps also taxonomically significant, the caudal ribs are more horizontal in *Sauropelta* sp. than in *S. edwardsi*.

Carpenter *et al.* tentatively referred other ankylosaurian fragments from eastern Utah to *Sauropelta* sp. Among this additional material, BYU 9430 (including dorsal vertebrae, ribs, and armor) was collected from the base of the Ruby Ranch Member of the Cedar Mountain Formation (this geologically slightly younger member thus far having yielded the least amount of dinosaurian fossils, also correlating with the Aptian–Albian age of the Clovery Formation, according to Kirkland *et al*). Kirkland *et al.* also reported some very large teeth referable to *Sauropelta* recovered near the Cleveland-Lloyd Dinosaur Quarry in Emery County.

Key references: Bodily (1969); Carpenter, Kirkland, Burge and Bird (1998); Kirkland, Britt, Burge, Carpenter, Cifelli, DeCourten, Eaton, Hasiotis and Lawton (1997); Pereda-Suberbiola (1994).

SAUROPHAGANAX Chure 1995 — (See *Allosaurus*.)
Name derivation: Greek *saurophagos* = "reptile eater" + Greek *anax* = "master, ruler, king."
Type species: *S. maximus* (Ray 1941).

†SAUROPHAGUS — (Preoccupied, Swaison 1831; see *Allosaurus*.)

†SCELIDOSAURUS — (= *Tatisaurus*)
Ornithischia: Genasauria: Thyreophora.
New species: *S. oehleri* (Simmons 1965).
Occurrence of *S. oehleri*: Dark Red Beds, Lower Lufeng Series, Yunnan, People's Republic of China.

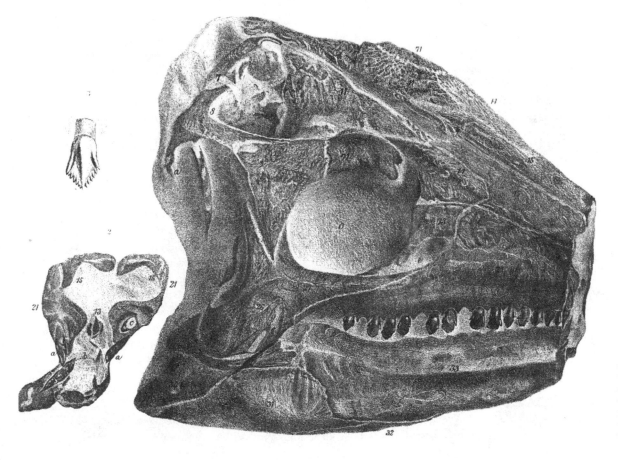

Scelidosaurus harrisonii, upper tooth and skull, this specimen (BMNH R. 1111) currently undergoing new preparation and awaiting a complete description. (After Owen 1861.)

Age: Early Jurassic (?Sinemurian).

Comments: *Scelidosaurus*, as Norman and Charig (1996) pointed out, is particularly significant for several reasons: The genus is one of the most primitive of all known armored ornithischian dinosaurs; one of the earliest of any kind of dinosaur to be described in detail; and known from one of the best-preserved specimens.

Indeed, the finest example of this genus is an excellently preserved, almost complete articulated skeleton (BMNH R. 1111) of the type species, *S. harrisonii*. The skeleton is preserved in a diagenetically carbonate-rich limestone, found in 1858 and originally described by Owen (1861). Norman and Charig found it paradoxical that the anatomy of this dinosaur is still only poorly understood, and that the systematic position of this genus has been enigmatic.

To date of this writing, a new, detailed anatomical study is being conducted on all known material referred to this genus. Norman and Charig noted that acid preparation techniques have been applied to BMNH R. 1111. The extremely fragile skull (previously damaged as a result of handling since its initial preparation by Ron Croucher in the late 1970s) has already been fully etched out, allowing its anatomy to be described for the first time.

Remains of ornithischians are rare in the prosauropod-dominated Lufeng Formation of Yunnan Province, southwestern China, the earliest known ornithischian from this region being the species originally described as *Tatisaurus oehleri* by Simmons (1965), based on an isolated, almost complete left dentary with teeth (FMNH CUP 2088). Although Simmons originally referred *T. oehleri* to the "Hypsilophodontidae," various subsequent workers (*D:TE*) came to regard it as a basal thyreophoran.

More recently, Lucas (1996), in redescribing the holotype of *T. oehleri*, confirmed the thyreophoran affinities of the specimen, and noted its striking resemblance in the dentary structure and lower dentition to *Scelidosaurus*, which was previously known from the Blue Lias (early Sinemurian) of Charmouth (Benton and Spencer 1995) and nearby localities (Newman 1968; Ensom 1987), in southwestern England, and from the Kayenta Formation (possibly early Sinemurian) of Arizona, United States and Asia.

Lucas noted that, although the lower dentition of *Scelidosaurus* has not yet been well described, its dentary is known and its upper dentition permits inferences as to the structure of its lower dentition. *Scelidosaurus* possesses at least 16 upper teeth (true of many ornithischians, including stegosaurs) displaying the same "anticlinal" size gradient as in *Tatisaurus*, particularly significant in *Scelidosaurus* being the "dramatic size increase to the three largest teeth, followed by five teeth that decrease in size posteriorly." Lucas observed that the tooth morphology and thick, robust dentaries of both genera is essentially identical, though that of *Scelidosaurus* is about twice the size of that of *Tatisaurus*.

Based on the close similarities of both genera, and finding it very difficult to recognize *Tatisaurus* as a genus distinct from *Scelidosaurus*, Lucas referred *Tatisaurus* to that genus as the new species, *S. oehleri*. As the British specimens of *Scelidosaurus* are all of early Sinemurian age, Lucas suggested that those from the Kayenta Formation and Lufeng Formation may also be of that age. Lucas further suggested that this genus had a broad Early Jurassic distribution that can be utilized in defining a *Scelidosaurus* biochron — a taxon used as a reference for dating — of Sinemurian age.

Note: New information regarding the external appearance of dinosaurs like *Scelidosaurus* recently surfaced with the examination, by Martill, Loydell and Batten (1997), of a specimen ("obtained from an old collection") belonging to a primitive thyreophoran. The specimen, contained within a cut slab of carbonate mudstone, comprises eight articulated caudal vertebrae that resemble quite closely the comparable elements in *Scelidosasurus*. Unfortunately, the poorly catalogued specimen lacks provenance data, exact horizon and locality being uncertain, although palynomorph analysis by the authors suggested an uppermost Triassic ("Rhaetian") or lowermost Jurassic (Hettangian–Sinemurian) age. Cut longitudinally, the slab revealed *in situ* several hemal arches, unfused (suggesting immaturity) neural arches, and dermal bones.

According to Martill *et al.*, an "envelope of dark brown to amber-coloured preserved soft tissue encloses the vertebral series," which — when subjected to scanning electron microscope analysis, thin-section petrography, and dilute acid preparation — was revealed to be "structured organic material with three distinct zones." In their preliminary description of this specimen, the authors noted that a presumed outer zone of dense organic material overlies two "spongy" layers, within which were perceived a number of places where pigment cells may have been preserved. Within this "multilayered organic sheet" are embedded several dermal ossifications; under the flatter basal surface of the ossifications passes a thin layer or organic material, a somewhat thicker layer passing over the upper surface. According to Martill *et al.*, this arrangement plainly demonstrates that the dermal ossifications in this dinosaur "were not exposed during life, but were covered with a probably toughened keratinous layer of the epidermis much like the covering over the body carapaces of present day Chelonia."

Key references: Benton and Spencer (1995); Ensom (1987); Lucas (1996); Martill, Loydell and Batten (1997); Newman (1968); Norman and Charig (1996); Owen (1861); Simmons (1965).

SCIPIONYX Dal Sasso and Signore 1998

Saurischia: Theropoda: Neotheropoda: Tetanurae: Avetheropoda; Coelurosauria: Manuraptoriformes: *incertae sedis.*

Name derivation: Latin *Scipio* = "[male names for two people: Scipione Bresiak, who first described the Pietraroia Plattenkalk, and Publius Cornelius Scipio, a Roman soldier who fought in the Mediterranean area]" + Greek *onyx* = "claw."

Type species: *S. samniticus* Del Sasso and Signore 1998.

Other species: [None.]

Occurrence: Pietraroia Plattenkalk, Italy, Europe.

Age: Early Cretaceous (Albian).

Known material/holotype: Soprintendenza Archeologica collection, Salerno, nearly complete articu-lated skeleton, missing most of the tail, most of the second right manual claw, and hind limbs distal to the proximal epipodials, includes preserved soft tissues, juvenile.

Diagnosis of genus (as for type species): Differs from all other manuraptoriformes in unique possession of accessory transverse postorbital ridge at fronto-parietal contact; by compressed nature of radiale and semilunate carpal; and in primitive retention of large prefrontal, pronounced scapular acromion, and rounded caudal end of the coracoid (Dal Sasso and Signore 1998).

Comments: The first dinosaur to be found in Italy, the new genus and species *Scipionyx samniticus* is also one of the most extraordinary. The holotype, an almost complete skeleton including exceptionally well-preserved soft tissues, was found in Lower Cretaceous rocks of Pietraroia Plattenkalk (an area known since the eighteenth century for its fossil fishes) of Benevento Province, southern Italy. Preservation of the soft tissues is attributed to "deposition of fine

Scipionyx samniticus, holotype skeleton with internal soft tissues preserved (collection of Soprintendenza Archeologica, Salerno). Scale = 2 cm. (After Dal Sasso and Signore 1998.)

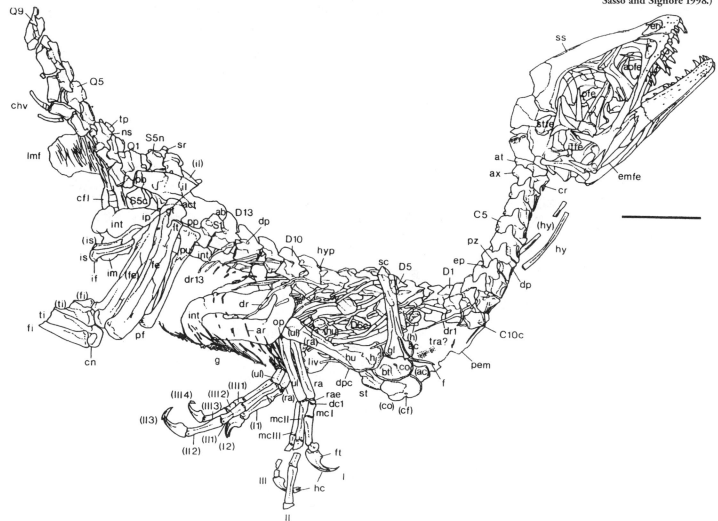

marly limestone in a shallow lagoonal environment, affected by cyclic periods of low oxygen levels." Although the specimen was preserved with the head upturned as in life, the neck is not curved back as with most other articulated theropod skeletons (Dal Sasso and Signore 1998).

Dal Sasso and Signore referred this specimen to the Theropoda because of the synapomorphic presence of denticulate teeth, intramandibular joint, straplike scapular blade, first distal carpal clasping metacarpals I and II, manus lacking digits IV and V, and elongate penultimate phalanges; to the Coelurosauria because of the derived presence of jugal participation in the antorbital fenestra, and metacarpal I being one-third length of metacarpal II; and to the Manuraptoriformes based on the derived presence of a third antorbital fenestra, elongate cervical prezygapophyses, forelimb/presacral ratio of 0.75, ulna bowed posteriorly, semilunate carpal, and slender metacarpal III. The authors noted that this taxon is more primitive than other coelurosaurs as it retains a stout lacrimal and ischial foot (see "Note" below).

As measured by Dal Sasso and Signore, the specimen is 237 millimeters (about 9 inches) in length from the tip of the premaxilla to the ninth (the last preserved) caudal vertebra. Body proportions (*e.g.,* short skull, large orbit, many cranial and postcranial elements unfused, etc.) of the specimen indicated to the authors that the animal was barely more than a hatchling when it died. Furthermore, the symmetry of tooth development in the maxillary rami suggests that the first tooth replacement had not yet taken place, while the low denticle count may also relate to early ontogeny.

Because the specimen displays a mosaic of characters, Dal Sasso and Signore could not refer it to any known theropod family. As noted by the authors, the forelimb ratios and most elements of the skull resemble features seen in the Dromaeosauridae, among these being the following derived characters: Postorbital region sloping; quadrate with single head articulating exclusively with squamosal; paroccipital processes distally slightly twisted posterodorsally; maxillary fenestra dorsally displaced; pneumatization of palatine (however, also known in *Tyrannosaurus rex* and other taxa; R. E. Molnar, personal communication 1998); alignment of dentary foramina into two rows (not in grooves); and splenial emerging externally on lateral surface of mandible. Characters apparently synapomorphic with the Troodontidae include: Small, L-shaped quadratojugal with equal rami; cervical vertebrae with low neural spines; and barely propubic pelvis. Plesiomorphic ornithomimid-like pelvic features include: Ilium posteriorly truncated; and ischium three-fourths length of pubis, with forward-directed "foot." Characters suggesting a more generalized coelurosaurian bauplan include these: L-shaped lacrimal; fan-like coracoid; feeble development of fourth trochanter; and slender, slightly curved chevrons.

Of course, a striking feature of this specimen is the preserved soft tissues, these including muscles, sharp-pointed fibers, most of the intestines, some apparent tracheal rings, and a "large, reddish, well-delimited haematitic halo" tentatively interpreted as traces of the liver. The placement of the intestines — positioned further forward than previously believed, with the colon passing through the pelvic canal, near the vertebral column, ending just above the ischadic foot — results in a gut that was interpreted by the authors as "surprisingly short and deep in section, suggesting a high absorption rate" (although a relatively short gut would be expected in a carnivorous dinosaur, as meat is easier and more efficient to digest than plant material; R. E. Molnar, personal communication 1998; see also, for example, Brett-Surman and Farlow 1997). Depth of the abdomen can be estimated by the position of the gastralia, preserved as in life, which gave support to the posterior intestinal tract.

Very significantly, "the presence of a furcula in this articulated specimen eliminates every doubt about the interpretation of similar structures in other theropods" (see section on "Dinosaurs and Birds," "Introduction").

Note: As pointed out by Molnar (personal communication 1998), many — not all, but enough to be potentially confusing — juvenile character states in theropods are also plesiomorphic character states, this being one reason that adult specimens are the best for use in a cladistic analysis. Possibly, then, *Scipionyx* might be more advanced that the authors have thought.

Key reference: Dal Sasso and Signore (1998).

SHANXIA Barrett, You, Upchurch and Burton 1998

Ornithischia: Genasauria: Thyreophora: Ankylosauria: ?Ankylosauridae.

Name derivation: "Shanxi [Province, People's Republic of China]."

Type species: *S. tianzhenensis* Barrett, You, Upchurch and Burton 1998.

Other species: [None.]

Occurrence: Huiquanpu Formation, Shanxi Province, People's Republic of China.

Age: Late Cretaceous.

Known material/holotype: IVPP V11276, incomplete skeleton including fragmentary skull (braincase, occiput, skull roof, ?quadratojugal), vertebrae (axis,

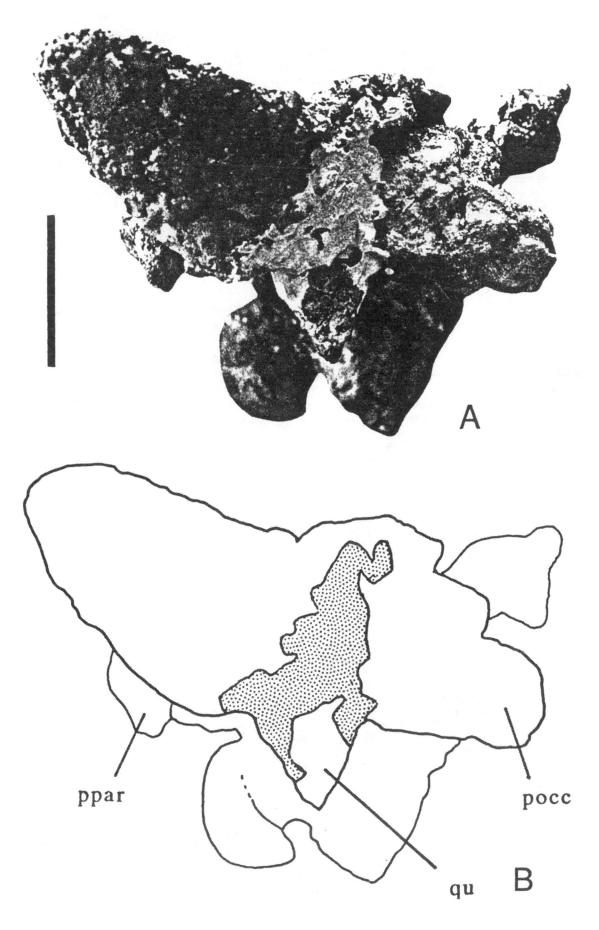

Shanxia

Shanxia tianzhenensis, IVPP V11276, holotype partial skull, lateral view. Scale = 5 cm. (After Barrett, You, Upchurch and Burton 1998.)

ppar

pocc

qu   B

five cervicals, three dorsals, and four caudals), right humerus, fragment of ?ilium, complete right femur, distal portion of left femur, dermal scute.

Diagnosis of genus (as for type species): Ankylosaurid that differs from all other known ankylosaurids in shape of squamosal horns; squamosal horns slender, elongate, posterolaterally inclined at angle of approximately 145 degrees to transverse axis of skull, having narrow junction with skull roof in occipital view, shaped like isosceles triangles in dorsal view (Barrett, You, Upchurch and Burton 1998).

Comments: *Shanxia*—an ankylosaurid genus distinguished by the morphology of its squamosal horn—was founded upon a partial skeleton including a fragmentary skull (IVPP V11276), discovered in 1993 by Messrs. Lu and Li of the Hebei Geological Survey, in the Upper Cretaceous Huiquanpu Formation, Wu Valley, Tian Zhen County, Shanxi Province, west of Beijing, People's Republic of China (Barrett, You, Upchurch and Burton 1998).

Only one dermal scute was preserved in the type specimen. It was described by Barrett *et al.* as oval in outline, sub-triangular in cross section, excavated ventrally, and having a prominent dorsal keel, the maximum height of this keel not exceeding the basal diameter of the scute.

Barrett *et al.* referred *Shanxia* to the Ankylosauridae based on its possession of the following ankylosaurid characters: Skull roof overhanging occiput, obscuring paroccipital process in dorsal view; medial extension of postoccular shelf; large dermal plates fused to squamosals, forming hornlike processes; quadratojugal dermal ossification prominent, wedge-shaped, projecting ventrolaterally; large deltopectoral crest terminating distal to midlength of humerus; deltopectoral crest and transverse axis through distal condyles of humerus occupying same plane; flat radial condyle having oval outline; little distinction between femoral head and proximal femoral trochanters; oval keeled plates deeply excavated; and height of keeled plates not exceeding basal diameter.

Barrett *et al.* noted that IVPP V11276 also exhibits a single "nodosaurid" character—hemispherical occipital condyle oval to subcircular (not crescent shaped) in posterior view, offset from braincase by distinct "neck." However, the authors noted that some caution is required in interpreting this character, as the shape of the occipital condyle in IVPP V11276 is not entirely clear, that the condyle lacks "finished bone edges and may have been prepared into this shape." Also, "new evidence suggests that this character may be primitive for Ankylosauria (W. P. Coombs, pers. comm.) as the occipital condyles of *Talarurus* also appear to be offset from the braincase by a 'neck' (Tumanova, 1987)." The latter, if correct, would preclude the use of this character as a synapomorphy of the Nodosauridae, although the apparent possession of this character may eventually prove to be of some phylogenetic significance.

As pointed out by the authors, the discovery of the new type species *Shanxia tianzhenensis* is significant in apparently being one of only two known valid ankylosaurid genera from China (the other being *Pinacosaurus*). It is also important in being the first dinosaur to be collected from the Huiquanpu Formation, and the most complete dinosaur yet recovered from Shanxia Province. As most ankylosaurids are known to be of Late Cretaceous age, the discovery of *Shanxia* supports an Upper Cretaceous age for the Huiquanpu Formation.

Key reference: Barrett, You, Upchurch and Burton (1998).

†SHUNOSAURUS

Saurischia: Sauropodomorpha: Sauropoda: Eusauropoda.

End of tail of *Shunosaurus lii* with tail club, part of a mounted skeleton displayed at Dinofest™, 1998, Philadelphia.

Photograph by the author.

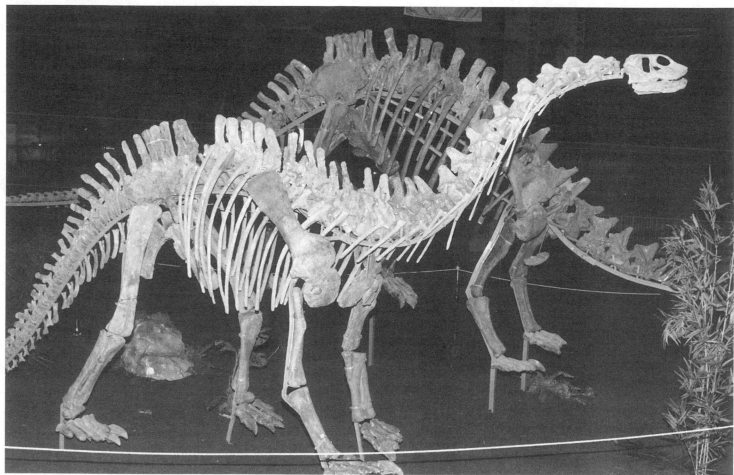

Shunosaurus lii skeleton exhibited at Dinofest™, held in 1998 in Philadelphia.

Diagnosis of genus (as for type species): Prominent anterior portion of axial neural spine; "post-parapophyses" on posterior dorsal vertebrae; terminal tail club composed of at least three enlarged, co-ossified caudal vertebrae with two dermal spines (Wilson and Sereno 1998).

Comments: Zhang and Chen (1996) revised the diagnosis for the type species *Shunosaurus lii*, a club-tailed sauropod, based in part on more recently collected specimens recovered by Chinese scientists. The new diagnosis included numerous characters which were not autapomorphies of the genus and species. More recently, in a study of sauropods in which this taxon was reassessed, Wilson and Sereno (1998) published a diagnosis based solely upon autapomorphies.

Although Zhang and Chen (1996) regarded *Shunosaurus* as a "cetiosaurid," they were not yet certain whether or not this genus should be placed into its own subfamily Shunosaurinae, as referred there by McIntosh (1990*b*). Upchurch, in a new phylogenetic analysis of the Sauropoda, regarded *Shunosaurus* as member of the Euhelopodidae. More recently, Wilson and Sereno found *Shunosaurus* to be a more primitive eusauropod (see "Systematics" chapter).

Key reference: McIntosh (1990*b*); Wilson and Sereno (1998); Zhang and Chen (1996).

SIGILMASSASAURUS Russell 1996

Saurischia: Theropoda: Neotheropoda: ?Tetanurae: ?Spinosauroidea: Sigilmassasauridae.

Name derivation: "Sigilmassa [ancient city, former capital of Tafilalt]" + Greek *sauros* = "lizard."

Type species: *S. brevicollis* Russell 1996.

Other species: [None.]

Occurrence: "Grès rouges infracénomaniens" (first of three lithologic entities of the "Trilogie mésocrétacée"; see Choubert 1952), Morocco, Baharija Formation, Marsa Matruh, Egypt.

Age: Middle–Late Cretaceous (?Albian–?early Cenomanian).

Known material: Numerous isolated vertebrae, also partial postcrania (destroyed).

Holotype: CMN [formerly NMC] 41857, cervical vertebra.

Diagnosis of genus (as for type species and for Sigilmassasauridae): Apomorphies in cervical vertebrae including: spines short, wide transversely (not

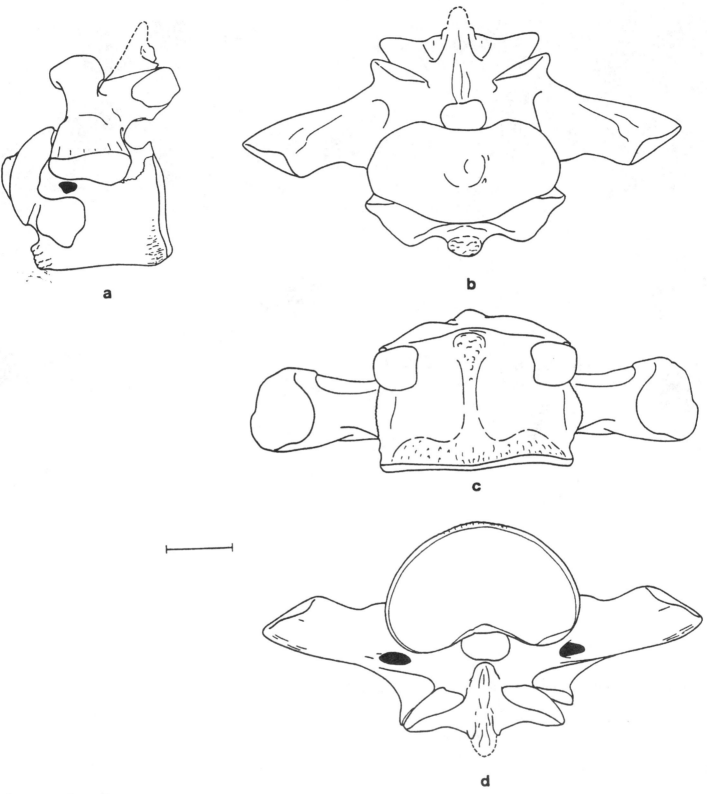

a

b

c

d

Sigilmassasaurus brevicollis, CMN 41857, holotype cervical vertebra in a. left lateral, b. anterior, c. ventral, and d. posterior (inverted) views. Scale = 5 cm. (After Russell 1996.)

long, as in *Spinosaurus*); intercentral articulations wider than high, exceeding length of centrum in width; "transverse" planes through anterior and posterior intercentral articulations converge dorsally, indicating cervical series "U"-shaped in lateral aspect;

parapophyses projecting ventrolaterally beyond rim of intercentral articulations; hypapophyses more powerfully developed in middle of cervical series than in region of cervico-dorsal transition (Russell 1996).

Comments: The genus now called *Sigilmassasaurus*

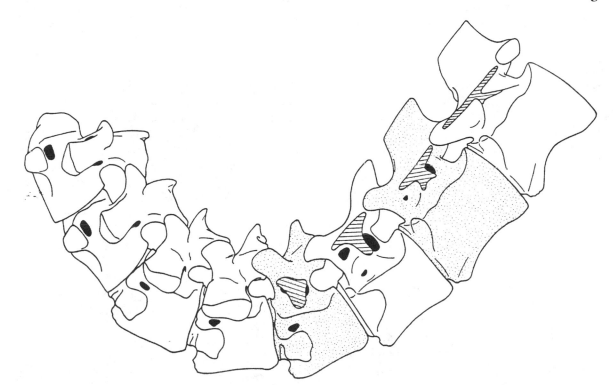

Sigilmassaurus brevicollis, reconstructed anterior presacral vertebral column (left lateral view), reconstrcuted and scaled after CMN 41790, 41774, 41856, 41857 dotted, interpolated), 41858 (dotted, interpolated), and 41850. (After Russell 1996.)

was founded upon an isolated cervical vertebra (CMN 41857), collected by inhabitants of the Tafilalt (see *Spinosaurus* entry) in the Presahara, in southern Morocco. Nonassociated referred remains (listed in a morphologically anteroposterior sequence) includes cervical (CMN 41790, 41774, 41856, [41857; holotype]), dorsal (CMN 41858, 41850, 50428, 50402, 41776, 50407, 50800, 41772, and 41851), and caudal vertebrae (CMN 41854, 41775, 41853, and 41855) (Russell 1996).

According to Russell, *Sigilmassasaurus* represents, in part, the taxon called by Stromer (1934) "*Spinosaurus* B," which he had based on vertebrae, limb bones, and other fragmentary remains (destroyed by American bombers during World War II) recovered from the Baharija Formation, Marsa Matruh, Egypt. Stromer believed that these remains belonged to a species of *Spinosaurus* distinct from the type species, *S. aegyptiacus.* Also, Stromer observed that the limb elements seemingly pertained to a considerably smaller animal than did the vertebrae, and that these vertebrae, although having much shorter spines, appeared to him to resemble those of the holotype of *S. aegyptiacus.*

Russell referred these vertebrae to the type species *Sigilmassasaurus brevicollis*, noting that the cervical vertebrae in this taxon differ greatly from those of *S. aegyptiacus* in the comparative length and breadth of the centra, the angle between the plane of the intercentral articulations and longitudinal axis of the centrum, and the height of the spines, enough to warrant referral to a new family, Sigilmassasauridae.

Also, Russell observed that these vertebrae differ from other Baharija theropods as follows: In a mid-cervical vertebra referred by Stromer (1931) to *Carcharodontosaurus*, the width of the anterior central facet is less than the length of the centrum, and the median keel thickens posteriorly (the reverse condition seen in "*Spinosaurus* B"); proximal caudals referred by Stromer (1931, 1934) to *Carcharodontosaurus* and *Bahariasaurus* have pleurocoels (not present in "*Spinosaurus* B"); and chevrons are bridged in *Carcharodontosaurus* (not bridged in "*Spinosaurus* B").

In describing the Moroccan material, Russell concluded that *Sigilmassasaurus* could represent a highly unusual theropod group. The neck may have comprised a comparatively large number of vertebral segments, as in hadrosaurs (Weishampel and Horner 1990), suggesting more flexibility and a capability of much greater variety of movement than the back. Unlike the condition in theropods with relatively large skulls, the cervical segments do not become more robust posteriorly, suggesting a small head, perhaps comparable in size to that of most hadrosaurs with cervicals of about the same size and similar morphology. The enormous size of the hypapophyses in the posterior cervical region imply that the muscles attached to them would have projected the neck powerfully and swiftly downward. Russell speculated that *Sigilmassasaurus* may have weighed well over a ton (almost 1.2 tons), possessing "rudimentary forelimbs, a neck adapted for pecking and a skull of avian proportions" in comparison to body size, and a tail resembling that of an ornithopod more than that of a theropod.

Russell referred to *Sigilmassasaurus* sp. a posterior cervical centrum (CMN 41629), belonging to a large vertebra, and a distal caudal vertebra (CMN 41862), collected from "Grès rouges." The color of preservation of CMN 41629 is a deep, reddish brown (unlike the white to orange of other specimens in the Canadian Museum of Nature collection), consistent with the darker sediments at the base of the "Grès rouges," suggesting to Russell that this bone was derived from the base of the sequence, and could be tens of millions of years older than the other remains.

Key references: Russell (1996); Stromer (1915, 1931, 1934).

SILUOSAURUS   Dong 1997

Ornithischia: Genasauria: Cerapoda: ?Ornithopoda: ?Euornithopoda: ?"Hypsilophodontidae."

Name derivation: Chinese Pinyon *Silu* (= "Silk Road") + Greek *sauros* = "lizard."

Type species: *S. zhangqiani* Dong 1997.

Other species: [None.]

Occurrence: Xinminbao Group, Gansu Province, China.

Age: Early Cretaceous.

Known material/holotype: IVPP V. 11117 (1-2), complete premaxillary tooth, almost complete cheek tooth.

Diagnosis of genus (as for type species): Smallest known ?"hypsilophodontid," differing from known "hypsilophodontids" by following characters: premaxillary teeth with crown possessing spear-shaped symmetrical on lingual and labial surfaces (width/height = 1/1); relatively long root lacking cingulum; crowns of premaxillary teeth lacking recurved tip, but bearing fine denticles; crowns of cheek teeth asymmetrical, cingulum separated from root; lingual surface of cheek teeth apparently flat, with five fine denticles which are straight and reach base of crown, no center denticle; labial surface of cheek teeth slightly convex, having inclined longitudinal denticles that do not reach base of crown and pronounced triangular-shaped (in outline) central denticle (Dong 1997*e*).

Comments: The small, possible ornithopod genus *Siluosaurus* was founded on a premaxillary tooth (IVPP V. 11117-1) and a cheek tooth (IVPP V. 11117-2), perhaps belonging to the same individual, recovered in 1992 during the Sino-Japanese Silk Road Dinosaur Expedition (Dong 1997*b*), lower portion of the Xinminbao Group (Lower Cretaceous), Mazongshan Area, Gansu, China (Dong 1997*e*).

Dong (1997*e*) tentatively referred the type species *S. zhangqiani* to the Ornithopoda, noting that it seems to be the smallest tooth yet found possibly belonging to that group.

Key references: Dong (1997*b*, 1997*e*).

†SINORNITHOIDES

New material: IVPP V. 11119, two teeth, two caudal vertebrae, partial tibia, distal tarsal, incomplete right metatarsus with metatarsals II, III, and IV, phalanges 1–3 of digit II, phalanges III-1 and IV-1.

Comments: Dong (1997*c*) reported new material (IVPP V. 11119) which he referred to the troodontid theropod *Sinornithoides* sp., collected in the summer of 1992 during the Sino-Japanese Silk Road Dinosaur Expedition (Dong 1997*b*), from the Mazongshan Area of Gansu Province, China, in the same Early Cretaceous horizon as the Xinminbao Group.

As observed by Dong (1997*c*), the specimen is very similar in morphology and size to the type species, *S. youngi*, although it could not be identified below the level of genus.

Note: From the same beds of the Xinminbao Group and recovered during the same expedition, Dong (1997*c*) identified a dozen theropod teeth, one caudal vertebra, and two phalanges (IVPP V. 11122). The teeth (IVPP V. 11122-1, 11122-2, and 11122-3) are all laterally compressed. The longest (possibly maxillary) tooth (IVPP V. 11122-3) measures 24 millimeters in length and may belong to an allosaurid; a medium-sized tooth (IVPP V. 11122-2) is similar to

Siluosaurus zhangqiani, IVPP V. 11117-2, holotype A. labial surface of premaxillary tooth, and B. lingual surface of maxillary tooth. (After Dong 1997.)

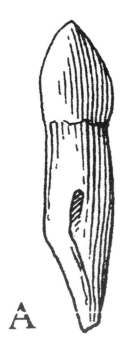

teeth in dromaeosaurids; and a small tooth (IVPP V. 11122-2) is referable to the Troodontosauridae.

Key references: Dong (1997*b*, 1997*c*).

SINOSAUROPTERYX   Ji and Ji 1996

Saurischia: Theropoda: Neotheropoda: Tetanurae: Avetheropoda: Coelurosauria: Compsognathidae.

Name derivation: Greek *Sinai* = "China" + Greek *sauros* = "lizard" + Greek *pteryx* = "wing."

Type species: *S. prima* Ji and Ji 1996.

Other species: [None.]

Occurrence: Yixian Formation, Liaoning Province, People's Republic of China.

Age: Early Cretaceous.

Known material: Three skeletons, at least two possessing fossilized integument, organ pigmentation, two with stomach contents, one with apparent eggs.

Holotype: GMV 2123, complete skeleton preserved in two counterpart slabs, integument, organ pigmentation.

Diagnosis of genus (as for type species): Compsognathid possessing longest tail of all known theropods (64 caudal vertebrae); skull 15 percent longer than femur, forelimb (humerus plus radius) only 30 percent length of leg (femur plus tibia) (in contrast with *Compsognathus*, where skull is same length as femur), forelimb length 40 percent that of leg; within Compsognathidae, forelimb (compared to femur) length shorter in this genus (61 to 65 percent) than in *Compsognathus* (90 to 99 percent); ungual phalanx II-2 shorter than radius (in contrast with all other known theropods); hemal spines simple, spatulate (distally tapering in *Compsognathus*) (Chen, Dong and Zhen 1998).

Comments: Among the more spectacular, provocative and also controversial dinosaur discoveries of recent years is the Chinese theropod *Sinosauropteryx prima*—a small form resembling *Compsognathus*, having a narrow and deep body, rather short and stout forelimbs, and a very long tail (the tails of all collected *Compsognathus* specimens being incomplete; R. E. Molnar, personal communication 1998). The species is controversial in that it may constitute the first real evidence that at least some dinosaurs possessed feather-like structures.

Initial reports in the United States of what seemed to be the first theropod specimen found with unquestionable feather-like fibers—preserved as a dark halo-like marking along the top of the head and down the vertebral column—surfaced at the (early November) 1976 annual meeting of the Society of Vertebrate Paleontology in New York. Chen Pei-ji of the Nanjing Institute of Geology and Paleontology, Academia Sinica, People's Republic of China, showed a photograph of the specimen which had recently been found in China. Naturally, the picture elicited much excitement and also some skepticism among the SVP attendants because of the salient implications of the data the photograph seemed to reveal. If the fiber-like impressions were correctly interpreted, the specimen provided strong and direct evidence linking birds to a dinosaurian ancestry. Moreover, two skeletons had reportedly been collected, both of them displaying the same kinds of markings, making it unlikely that these "feather-like" impressions were an artifact of preservation.

Prior to any formal publications about this creature, the specimen in the photograph promptly became the subject of a drawing by Canadian artist Michael W. Skrepnick (see Skrepnick 1998) of the animal in life as a feathered theropod. Skrepnick's life restoration was subsequently published in various newspapers and magazines along with articles announcing the find.

This new genus and species was founded upon two exceptionally well-preserved skeletons collected from the basal part of the Yixian Formation (Early Cretaceous, as dated by Smith, You and Dodson 1998, primarily based on radiometric dates from basalts within the Yixian and Jiufotang formations), part of a deep sequence of lake sediments interposed with volcanic deposits, in the Jehol Group, Jianshangou-Sihetun area of Beipiao, northeastern People's Republic of China. A third specimen has also been found (Currie 1997*a*, 1998) containing the remains of a small mammal in its abdominal cavity (Currie 1998). The specimens were all found in beds containing a rich biota with freshwater and terrestrial fossils including plants (one possibly representing the oldest known flower), invertebrates, fishes, chelonians, lizards, crocodiles, pterosaurs, dinosaurs, numerous primitive birds (often preserved with feather impressions), and mammals. The slightly smaller

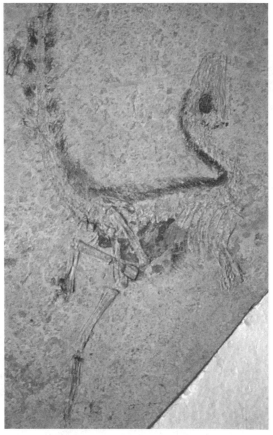

Sinosauropteryx prima, NIGP 127586, counterpart of holotype skeleton GMV 2123, showing integumentary structures and dark indications of possible viscera.

Courtesy Philip J. Currie.

• 323 •

Sinosauropteryx

Sinosauropteryx prima, NIGP 127587, referred specimen including preserved stomach contents (a lizard) and apparent eggs.

skeleton (arguably the best preserved dinosaur skeleton yet found) is contained in two counterslabs, representing a complete skeleton, collected in August of 1996 by local farmers in the same horizon that yielded specimens of the fossil birds *Confuciusornis* and *Liaoningornis.* The main slab of this specimen, designated the holotype (GMV 2123), has been housed in the National Geological Museum of China, in Beijing, and its counterpart (NIGP 127586) at the Nanjing Institute of Geology and Paleontology. The second or referred specimen (NIGP 127587) is nearly complete, missing only the distal half of the tail. This specimen includes stomach contents consisting of a partially articulated skeleton with skull of an undescribed lizard. Also preserved with this (apparently female) specimen, low in the abdomen, anterior to and slightly above the pubic boot, are a pair of what have been identified as small eggs (Ji and Ji 1996; Chen, Dong and Zhen 1998).

Ji and Ji (1996) published the first description of the Beijing slab, naming the animal *Sinosauropteryx prima.* The authors rather briefly described the new genus and species as a bird—in fact, the earliest avian genus yet found in China, and one playing a significant role in the origin of birds. Ji and Ji referred *Sinosauropteryx* to its own avian family, Sinosauropterygidae.

In early March of 1997, Donald L. Wolberg of The Academy of Natural Sciences of Philadelphia dispatched a team of specialists (the first Western scientists permitted to study the specimens in detail) to visit China, where they were to verify the existence of the "feather-like" fibers, and also possibly inspect the field site where the specimens were collected (see Ostrom and Wolberg 1998). The trip would also lay "the groundwork for a new collaboration with the Chinese and for a long-term investigation of the fossils which will most likely continue to raise as many questions as are answered." John H. Ostrom (who wrote of this trip and its results in the Society of Vertebrate Paleontology *News Bulletin,* number 171, October 1997, pp. 39–40) of the Yale Peabody Museum of Natural History served as leader of a team also including the following: Alan Brush, University of Connecticut; Peter Wellnhofer, Munich; Larry D. Martin, University of Kansas; and David Bubier, Academy of Natural Sciences. Wolberg secured funding for the event from the Dinosaur Society, The Academy of Natural Sciences of Philadelphia, and a private sponsor.

As related by Ostrom, the team first examined the slab at Beijing, and later the one at Nanjing, after which the group was taken to the field site. The results of this journey were announced on April 24, 1997, by the researchers at a press conference held at The Academy of Natural Sciences. According to Ostrom's report, the team found the specimen to be similar to though slightly smaller than *Compsognathus longipes,* a theropod from the Upper Jurassic of Europe, but cautioned that both slabs require further preparation and study. The team agreed, however, "that the fibers preserved in both slabs are not like feathers as we know them and probably will require chemical analysis to identify the protein composition to possibly resolve the fiber nature."

Geist, Jones and Ruben (1997), in a preliminary report delivered at the 1997 SVP meeting held in Chicago and a follow up (1998) given at the third Dinofest™ event in Philadelphia, were of the opinion that, upon close examination, the excellently preserved soft tissues seen in specimens of *S. prima* are entirely devoid of feather microstructure and seem "to be limited to the dorsal midline of the body." Geist *et al.* (1997) stated that "the organization of tissues in living animals demonstrates that the tissue preserved on the dorsal midline of the fossil probably consisted of internal collagenous tissue fibers that supported a laterally compressed midline structure"; in other words, in these authors' opinion the fiberlike structures could be remnants of the decomposing dermis that somehow moved to outside the skeleton (although, as pointed out by R. E. Molnar, personal communication 1998, there is no evidence that the fibers were, in fact, structures within the dermis as opposed to structures on the surface, possibly suggesting at least some nonsuperficial similarity to feathers). Furthermore, Geist *et al.* speculated that the very long tail, in conjunction with the above mentioned features (as interpreted by them), suggest *Sinosauropteryx* may be the first theropod known to have been semiaquatic.

Later questioning whether or not *Sinosauropteryx*

Sinosauropteryx prima restored with "protofeathers" by artist Michael W. Skrepnick for the dust jacket of the book *Encyclopedia of Dinosaurs* (1997), edited by Philip J. Currie and Kevin Padian. The illustration was prepared under the supervision of Currie, a specialist in theropod dinosaurs.

might be semiaquatic, as Geist *et al.* had suggested, Mohn (1998*b*), in a brief report, compared the caudal structure of this dinosaur to that of the related theropods *Compsognathus longipes* and *C. corallestris.* Mohn concluded that the tails of these three species could have been used as propulsive organs for swimming, but further pointed out that other characters — most notably the relative proportions and position of the bones of the hind limb — must also be considered. According to Mohn's observations, comparisons of these three dinosaurs with the morphology of modern birds and semiaquatic reptiles "suggest that compsognathids are not typical of such animals," the proportions of the hind limb elements suggesting "possible lifestyle similarities with modern shorebirds and habitually cursorial fowl."

A more heated topic for discussion and argument, of course, are the fiberlike structures preserved in the specimens of *Sinosauropteryx*. Martin (1998) agreed that "it is likely that the structures originally described as feathers in *Sinosauropteryx* are internal rather than external features." Not all workers, however, are convinced that the dark markings preserved on the specimens do not represent feathers (or protofeathers):

In 1997, a new painting by Skrepnick of *S. prima* appeared as the dust-jacket illustration for *Encyclopedia of Dinosaurs*, edited by Philip J. Currie and Kevin Padian. In an entry in that book entitled "'Feathered' Dinosaurs," Currie (1997*a*), who had been among the first Western paleontologists to examine personally the original fossil materials of *S. prima*, stated that the collected skeletons of this approximately 1-meter-long dinosaur "show feather-like structures covering the head, trunk, tail, arms, and legs." According to Currie (1997*a*), these structures — the longest measuring 3 centimeters in length — are more simple than true feathers, each apparently "composed of a central rachis [shaft] and branching barbs" but lacking "the aerodynamic quality of avian feathers." Currie (1997*a*) further noted that the presence of these structures offer additional support to the theories that birds descended directly from theropod dinosaurs and that at least some theropods were warmblooded.

Not until the next year was a formal paper on

S. prima published in English in the journal *Nature*, wherein authors Chen, Dong and Zhen (1998) formally described this species in detail. As described by Chen *et al.*, the genus is comparable in size and morphology, and closely related, to *Compsognathus*, but possesses a three-digit manus (*Compsognathus* was believed to be two-fingered) dominated by digit I, which is longer and thicker than either forearm bone.

Chen *et al.* noted several shared characteristics that indicate a close relationship between *Sinosauropteryx* and *Compsognathus*, these including the following: Possession of unserrated premaxillary but serrated maxillary teeth; manus with powerful phalanx I-1 (shaft diameter greater than that of radius); dorsal vertebrae with fan-shaped neural spines; caudal vertebrae with rudimentary (in *Sinosauropteryx*) or absent (in *Compsognathus*) neural processes; pubic booth having limited expansion; ischium with prominent obturator process. Therefore, these authors referred both *Sinosauropteryx* and *Compsognathus* to the family Compsognathidae Marsh 1882 (see "Systematics" chapter).

Regarding referred specimen NIGP 127587, Chen *et al.* pointed out that the exposed surfaces of the two fossil eggs (measuring 37 by 26 millimeters) are overlain by gastralia, while the left femur protrudes underneath the eggs; therefore, the eggs were certainly preserved within the body cavity. Addressing the possibility that the dinosaur had eaten the eggs, the authors noted that—given the position of the eggs in the abdomen behind and below the stomach contents, and because they are in the wrong part of the body cavity for their shells to be intact—it is more probable that these eggs were unlaid. As it appeared unlikely that more than two eggs of this size could have been held within the abdomen of this dinosaur, Chen *et al.* speculated that the presences of these eggs demonstrates paired ovulation, as had already been proposed for *Oviraptor* (see Dong and Currie 1996) and *Troodon* (Varrichio, Jackson, Borkowski and Horner 1997*a*, 1997*b*), among other theropods, a delay for ovulation transpiring between the laying of each pair.

Chen *et al.* noted that, in both *Sinosauropteryx* specimens, a dark pigmentation is present over the eyes, with a second region of such pigmentation also in the abdominal region of the holotype. These dark areas, the authors speculated, might represent soft tissues of viscera.

As noted by Chen *et al.*, one of the most amazing features of both *Sinosauropteryx* specimens is the preserved integumentary structures, these structures being observed (more clearly in the referred smaller specimen) along the top of the skull, the dorsal surface of the neck, back and hips, continuing along the upper margin of the tail, with another row of such structures on the underside of the tail. "Small patches" of the structures were also seen on the side of the skull (behind the quadrate and above the articular), behind the right humerus, and in front of the right ulna. A small patch was observed outside the left ribs of the referred specimen, but were not found elsewhere along the sides of the body. The density of the integumentary covering dorsal to the body and by the presences of the random patches seen elsewhere indicated to the authors that these structures were probably present in the living animals.

As observed by Chen *et al.*, in both *Sinosauropteryx* specimens "the distances separating the integumentary structures from the underlying bones are directly proportional to the amount of skin and muscle that would have been present," the integument, as in modern animals, closely adhering to the tops of the skull and hips, and becoming gradually closer to the tail vertebrae near the end of the tail. The structures are more distant from the underlying bones in the posterior part of the neck, above the shoulders, and at the base of the tail; in life, the authors noted, a greater thickness of muscle or other tissues would have further separated the integument from the skeletal elements.

According to Chen *et al.*, the orientation and often sinuous lines of these "structures suggest that they were soft and pliable, and semiindependent of each other," frequently crossing one another and sometimes tangled. As both individuals had been buried under a lake, it was clear to the authors that the integumentary structures were not preserved in their normal orientation. Examining the structures under magnification, Chen *et al.* found them to be relatively coarse for so small an animal, the thickest strands being much thicker than the hairs of most small mammals; furthermore, the structures seem to have been hollow, as the larger structures are darker along the edges and lighter medially. In NIGP 127586, the most anterior of the structures above the skull are about 5.5 millimeters in length, rapidly lengthening to at least 21 millimeters over the distal ends of the scapulae, decreasing quickly to 16 millimeters above the ilium, the longest structures apparently being those above the base of the tail, after which they again decrease in size.

The question was, then, are these integumentary structures evidence for feathers in theropod dinosaurs, as originally proposed by various observers, or are they a record of something else? Chen *et al.* found them to be "extremely interesting regardless of whether they are referred to as feathers, protofeathers, or some other structure," noting that the structures are unfortunately "piled so thick that we have been unable to isolate a single one for examination." Though noncommittal on this issue, the authors stated that the morphological characteristics of these structures suggest that they "seem to resemble most closely the plumules of modern birds, having relatively short quills and long, filamentous barbs." Chen *et al.* admitted that much additional work must be done before the integumentary structures of *Sinosauropteryx* can unequivocally be linked to any structural relationship to feathers, further noting that phylogenetic analysis of the skeleton of this theropod places it far from the ancestry of birds. (In his personal communication to this writer, Molnar noted that, although these structures in *Sinosauropteryx* might not be superficially or obviously similar to feathers, the fibers are branched, which does constitute a similarity.)

Chen *et al.* considered the three main functions have been hypothesized for the origins of feathers — display, aerodynamics, and insulation — and tested them as to their appropriateness regarding *Sinosauropteryx*. The density, distribution, and relatively short lengths of the structures indicated to Chen *et al.* that they were not used for display. The structures present no apparent aerodynamic function, but could represent what covered the ancestral stock of birds, with something as complex as a true feather evolving through various simpler stages. Finally, these dense, pliable structures seem inappropriate as heat shields against the sun's rays, though their presence may suggest that *Sinosauropteryx* was endothermic, the primary function for the evolution of these integumentary structures being the retention of heat to maintain high body temperatures.

Chen *et al.* concluded that none of the integumentary structures seen in *Sinosauropteryx* reveal the fundamental morphological features of modern bird feathers, but agreed that "they could be previously unidentified protofeathers which are not as complex as either down feathers of even the hairlike feathers of secondarily flightless birds."

In a separate article published in that same issue of *Nature*, Unwin (1998) commented upon Chen *et al.*'s opinion that the integumentary structures in *Sinosauropteryx* could indicate some kind of protofeathers. Unwin pointed out that, if this genus indeed possessed protofeathers, then it would follow that at least some theropods more closely related to birds probably also bore similar or even more featherlike structures. However, although exceptionally well-preserved specimens of more birdlike dinosaurs have been found, none of them included evidence of the filament-like structures discovered in *Sinosauropteryx*.

More recently, Currie (1998) stated that reports of a preserved liver in the smallest of the three *Sinosauropteryx* specimens could not be proven, finding it more likely that the so-called "liver" could be a chemical staining resulting from the decomposition of stomach acids. Currie (1998) observed that the "halo of integumentary structures" around the margins of the skeletons of this dinosaur resembles "the coronas of feathers around most of the fossil birds from the same localities." While stating that he strongly believes that the evidence supports them as being "branched structures," Currie (1998) further acknowledged that more work must be done before a final determination as to the true nature of these structures can be made.

In the meantime, debate over whether or not the integumentary structures in this taxon represent feathers, protofeathers, or something else altogether continues.

(For a possible explanation of how protofeathers could exist in an Early Cretaceous taxon, while the Late Jurassic *Archaeopteryx* already possessed fully developed feathers, see Norell, Makovicky and Clark's response to Martin and Feduccia 1998, *Velociraptor* entry. See also Quinn 1998, and "Introduction," "Dinosaurs and Birds," section on "The Feathers Issue."

Key references: Chen, Dong and Zhen (1998); Currie (1997*a*, 1998); Geist, Jones and Ruben (1997); Ji and Ji (1996); Martin (1998); Mohn (1998*b*); Ostrom and Wolberg (1998); Unwin (1998).

SONORASAURUS Ratkevich 1998

Saurischia: Sauropodomorpha: Sauropoda: Eusauropoda: Neosauropoda: Macronaria: Camarasauromorpha: Titanosauriformes: Brachiosauridae.

Name derivation: Hispanicized Opata Indian term "Sonora ['referring to the Sonora River, used here as being part of the greater Sonoran Desert region as a general provenance']" + Greek *sauros* = "lizard."

Type species: *S. thompsoni* Ratkevich 1998.

Other species: [None.]

Occurrence: Turney Ranch Formation, Arizona, United States.

Age: "Middle" [=latest Early] Cretaceous (Albian–?Cenomanian).

Known material: Possibly two partial specimens.

Holotype: ASDM 500, left tibia, proximal end of right ?tibia, left and right radii, left ulna, complete ?left metacarpal I, complete metacarpal II, proximal and distal ends of metacarpal ?III, distal half and marginal elements of left ilium, distal one-third of ischium, acetabulum, medial portions of pubis and ?ischium, distal half of left femur, midshaft of right ulna, left ?tibia, left fibula, partial right ?fibula, metatarsals I, II, IV, and V, phalanges I-I, II-I, IV-I,

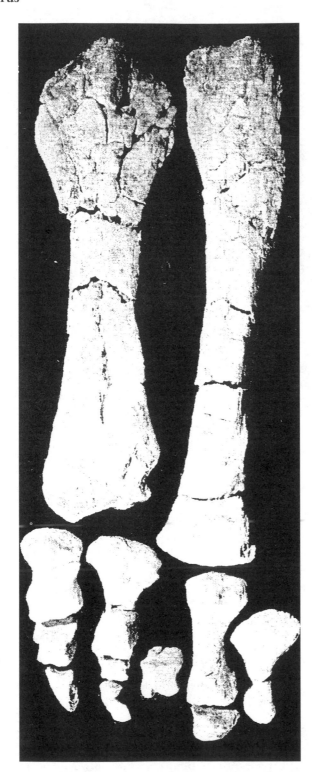

Sonorasaurus thompsoni, ASDM 500, holotype lower left hind limb including tibia, fibula, and almost complete pes, these elements having been found associated but disarticulated. Assembled length = 137 cm. (After Ratkevich 1998.)

phalanx on pedal digits I and II; metacarpals long, slender; tibia with long shaft and broad triangular proximal end; limbs generally hyper-gracile, dorsal centra "brachiosaur-like"; pleurocoels on dorsal vertebrae long, large, caudal vertebrae lacking pleurocoels or neural clefts; caudal vertebrae with transverse processes (caudal ribs) angling posteriorly and flat; neural arches steeply angled; vertebrae having camellate pneumatic structure; hyposphene comparable to that in *Brachiosaurus*; dorsal ribs massive; (second complete dorsal rib, ASDM 807, part of second individual from same horizon as holotype, possibly referable to *S. thompsoni*, "shows a wide curve to create a cavernous abdominal cavity") (Ratkevich 1998.)

Comments: Significant as the first sauropod dinosaur known from the "Middle" Cretaceous (Albian–?Cenomanian) of North America, the genus *Sonorasaurus* was established upon a partial and mostly disarticulated postcranial skeleton (ASDM 500), discovered by Richard Thompson of Tucson in a quarry of the Turney Ranch Formation, Bisbee Group, on the southwestern flanks of the Whetstone Mountains, near the town of Sonoita, Pima County, in southeastern Arizona. Slash marks found on some of the long bones and the absence of some bones (*e.g.*, most of the ribs) indicated that the carcass was scavenged, the discovery of a tooth of the very large carnosaur *Acrocanthosaurus* revealing the identity of at least one of the scavenging animals. A second specimen, ASDM 807, found in the same horizon, may be referable to the type species, *S. thompsoni* (Ratkevich 1998).

According to Ratkevich, the "Middle" Cretaceous, including both Albian and Cenomanian ages, appears from recent studies, based on radioscopic, stratigraphic, and fossil pollen analysis, "to be a distinct transitional period in the history of dinosaurs with a dinosaur population unlike anything directly temporally below or above."

Before the genus was officially named and described, it was informally mentioned (as "Sonorasaurus") in various publications. Thayer and Ratkevich (1995), for example, first briefly described the material as a large "hadrosaurid." Later, Ratkevich (1997) reported on the material in a general review of dinosaur remains collected over the years in southern Arizona. After more of the type specimen was excavated, it was correctly identified as belonging to a sauropod on the basis of metacarpal proportions and the morphology of the radius, ulna, and a caudal vertebra (J. S. McIntosh, personal communication to Ratkevich, 1996).

Ratkevich (1997, 1998) found the erection of a new genus justified by the temporal and geographical isolation of the type material, and because these remains do not favorably conform with specific skeletal

II-III, ungual digits I and II, first, ?second, and ?third dorsal vertebrae, caudal vertebrae approximately 5–12, chevron fragments, dorsal and cervical ribs, gastroliths.

Diagnosis of genus (as for type species): Medium-sized sauropod (approximately 15 meters long, 8 meters tall) having many brachiosaurid characteristics, including the following: diminutive ungual structures of other known brachiosaurids. In addition to listing a suite of diagnostic features linking *Sonorasaurus* with the Brachiosauridae, Ratkevich (1998) also referred, although without giving reasons, this genus to the Brachiosaurinae, a subfamily no longer accepted by most workers. Ratkevich (1998) estimated that the holotype skeleton of *S. thompsoni* was about 30 percent smaller than *Brachiosaurus altithorax*, a brachiosaurid species from the Upper Jurassic of Colorado and Montana (McIntosh 1990*b*).

As pointed out by Ratkevich (1998), an unusual feature of the type specimen of *S. thompsoni* is the retention of only two small claws on phalanx I and II of the pes, this being consistent with the trend in brachiosaurids to lose unguals during their evolution from the Late Jurassic to the Early Cretaceous. The absence of these claws in *Sonorasaurus*, the author noted, seems not to be a bias of collection or preservation, as "the bones of the left pes, though not articulated, were found in a very confined, carefully collected pocket and did not appear to have been transported more than a few inches."

Key references: Ratkevich (1997, 1998); Thayer and Ratkevich (1995).

†SPINOSAURUS

Saurischia: Theropoda: Neotheropoda: Tetanurae: Spinosauroidea: Spinosauridae.

New species: *S. maroccanus* Russell 1996.

Occurrence of *S. maroccanus*: "Grès rouges infracénomaniens" (first of three lithologic entities of the "Trilogie mésocrétacée"; see Choubert 1952), Morocco.

Age of *S. maroccanus*: "Middle" Cretaceous (?Albian).

Diagnosis of *S. maroccanus*: Ratio of approximately 1.5 of length of centrum (excluding anterior articular condyle) to height of posterior articular facet of centrum in midcervical vertebrae (Russell 1996).

Comments: In 1934, Professor Ernst Stromer described some vertebrae, limb bones, and other fragmentary material collected from the Baharija Formation of Baharije, Egypt. Earlier, this same locality had yielded the holotype of Stromer's (1915) type species, *Spinosaurus aegyptiacus*—a giant, poorly understood theropod taxon distinguished by such features as dorsal vertebrae possessing unusually elongated neural spines, these measuring as long as 169 centimeters (more than 5 feet). Stromer (1934) subsequently referred the later-collected remains to the genus as "*Spinosaurus* B," believing that they represented a new species (see "Notes" below). All of this material seems to have been a World War II casualty,

destroyed in Munich by American bomber planes in 1944.

More recently, inhabitants of the Tafilalt (an alluvial plain surrounding the oases of Erfoud and Taouz, lying within a terrain dominated by folded Paleozoic strata ranges [the Anti-Atlas]) in Presahara,

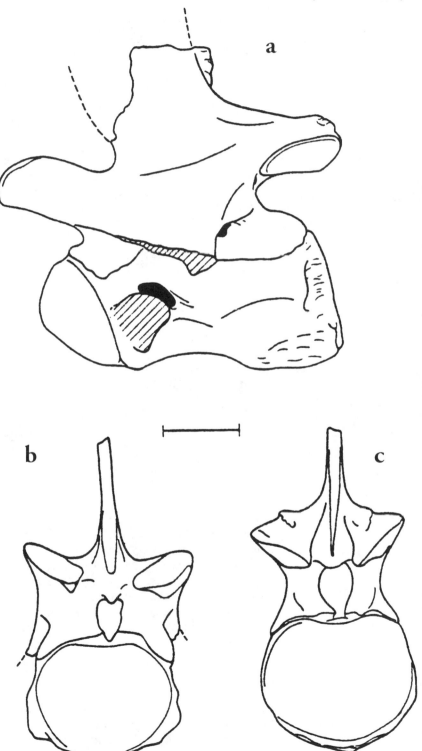

Spinosaurus maroccanus, CMN 50791, holotype median cervical vertebra, a. left lateral, b. anterior, and c. posterior views. Scale = 5 cm. (After Russell 1996.)

Spinosaurus

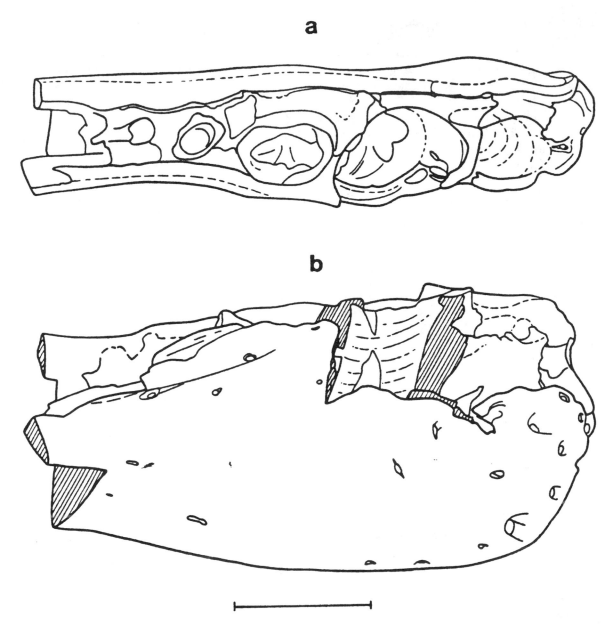

a

b

southern Morocco, "have been encouraged by a grow-ing international market for extinct vertebrates to search adjacent escarpments for fossil teeth and bones." Many of these specimens were then acquired from local sources in the Tafilalt by Brian Eberharde of Moussa Direct, Cambridge, some of them subse-quently obtained by the Canadian Museum of Nature. As the specimens were recovered by nonspecialists, Eberharde could only provide general locality data (Russell 1996).

Included in this new material were a median cau-dal vertebra (CMN 50791), dentary fragments (CMN 50832), median cervical vertebrae (CMN 41768), and a dorsal neural arch (CMN 50813) representing a new longnecked species of *Spinosaurus*, which Russell named *S. maroccanus*, designating CMN 50791 as the holotype.

According to Russell, in the type species the ratio of length of centrum to height of posterior articular facet approaches 1.1, suggesting that in *S. maroccanus* the cervical centra were more slender and the neck was longer. The pedicles of the neural arch are elon-gated, although the vertebrae are otherwise quite sim-ilar in both the new species and *S. aegyptiacus*. The cervical vertebrae differ from those of "*Spinosaurus* B" in possessing much longer spines, and "in that the neck was bowed dorsally, in the manner usual for large theropods."

In the decades following its original description by Professor Stromer, *Spinosaurus*—and also *Oura-nosaurus*, a large ornithopod from Nigeria also having elongated neural spines — has generally been depicted with its long spines supporting a dorsal "fin" or "sail" rather similar to that of certain pelycosaurs (*e.g.*,

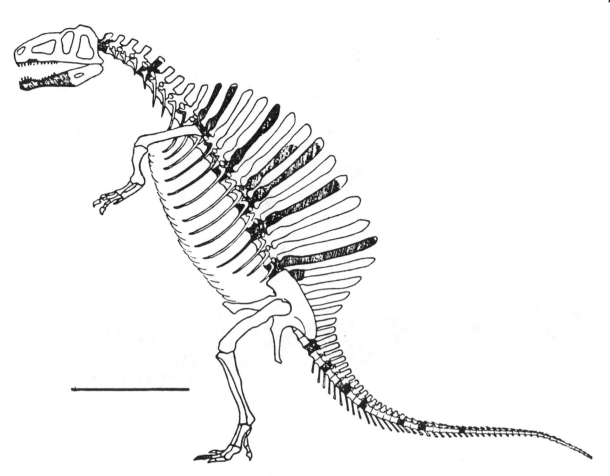

The first attempted skeletal reconstruction of *Spinosaurus aegyptiacus*, this drawing including the now missing IPHG holotype material (shaded), the missing elements hypothetically — and incorrectly — based on those of more typical and "familiar" known theropods. Scale = 2 m. (After Lapparent and Lavocat 1955).

Dimetrodon and *Edaphosaurus*) of the Permian period. As both *Spinosaurus* and *Ouranosaurus* (see respective entries, *D:TE*) both lived in environments with very hot climates, the popular interpretation of these presumed "sails" has been that, possibly like those of pelycosaurs, they served a thermoregulatory function, especially in the dissipation of heat.

Recently, Bailey (1997) proposed another hypothesis regarding the neural spines of *Spinosaurus aegyptiacus* and *Ouranosaurus nigeriensis*, as well as the long dorsal and tail spines possessed by other dinosaurian taxa including the theropods *Acrocanthosaurus atokensis* and *Becklespinax altispinax*, the sauropods *Dicraeosaurus hansemanni*, *D. sattleri*, the stegosaurs *Wuerhosaurus homheni*, *Stegosaurus armatus*, and *S. stenops*, the ornithopod *Tenontosaurus tilletti*, the iguanodontid *Iguanodon atherfieldensis*, the lambeosaurine hadrosaurids *Barsboldia sicinskii*, *Hypacrosaurus altispinus*, *H. stebingeri*, *Parasaurolophus walkeri*, *Corythosaurus casuarius*, and "*Kritosaurus*" *incurvimanus*, and the primitive ceratopsians *Protoceratops andrewsi* and *Montanoceratops cerorhynchus*, among other well-known dinosaurian taxa.

Bailey theorized that such dinosaurs exhibiting long spines were analogous not to "sail-backed" pelycosaurs, but rather to the certain large "hump-backed"

ungulate mammals, including *Bison antiquus antiquus*, a Pleistocene form with very tall neural spines, this taxon exemplified by a composite skeleton (LACM collection) now mounted at the George C. Page Museum of La Brea Discoveries. (*Ouranosaurus* was originally restored by artist William Stout in two versions, one with a sail-back and the other with a hump, based upon then unpublished differing opinions of several paleontologists; see Glut 1982.) In *Spinosaurus* and *Ouranosaurus*, the dorsal neural spines all appear robust in form; they are "laterally compressed but anteroposteriorly broadened into blades that achieve greatest expansion near their distal ends."

It was argued by Bailey that these spines in *Spinosaurus* and the other above mentioned dinosaurian taxa favor the bison-like humps at least in three ways:

1. In functional morphology and relative elongation, these spines are not similar to those of pelycosaurs, but rather homoplastically converge on the spines of high-withered ungulates. For example, the elongated spines of *Dimetrodon* "are very tall, gracile and narrowly cylindrical, distally tapering to a point." However, those of ungulates such as the Pleistocene bison "are broad-beamed, that is, elliptical in cross-section, with the major axis of the ellipse oriented in the anteroposterior plane."

Spinosaurus

Sculpture by Allen A. Debus of *Spinosaurus aegyptiacus*, produced in July 1998, based directly upon the original rendering by artist Robert E. Johnson, which, in turn, was based on Jack Bowman Bailey's (1997) somewhat speculative new interpretation of this dinosaur as a "humpbacked" quadruped. This piece was exhibited in 1998 at the Western Illinois University Geology Department Museum, in Macomb, Illinois.

2. A sail's use in thermoregulation has been exaggerated. It would have been fairly efficient as a thermal amplifier in large tetrapods, but not as a radiator. In dinosaurs as large as *Spinosaurus* and *Ouranosaurus*, size alone would have been sufficient to retard the dissipation of heat acquired externally from the environment, while a dorsal sail would have been neither a necessary adaptation nor a useful one in throwing off body heat.

3. The insulation properties of humps favor gigantothermy—"the inherent thermal inertia of a large body mass" (see Spotila, O'Connor, Dodson and Paladino 1991)—as the most likely thermobiological model for large dinosaurs. Large vertebrates, reptilian and mammalian alike, have similar low metabolic rates while maintaining relatively constant core temperatures. Gigantothermy is best achieved when peripheral insulation (*e.g.*, a hump) aids in the retardation of radiative heat transfer, thereby effectively buffering these animals against extremes in heat and cold.

Concluding that dinosaurs like *Spinosaurus* were hump- instead of sail-backed, Bailey suggested that the fatty humps were probable adaptations serving more than one function, including the following: 1. The storing of energy, maintenance of gigantothermy, and the shielding against heat in unshaded habitats (such as the open, very warm, and at least seasonally dry paleoenvironments of both *Spinosaurus* and *Ouranosaurus*); 2. providing insulation, temperature-shielding, and the storage of energy to be utilized during possible migrations over long distances from feeding to nesting grounds across terrains of variable resource productivity; and 3. conserving additional energy that could be tapped for the physiologically costly production of large clutches of eggs (yolk containing high levels of fat).

Citing the more recent models of some dinosaurs as migrating gigantotherms (which would have benefited from extra weight), Bailey criticized the trend of the past couple decades to restore dinosaurs, regardless of their size, "as emaciated lightweights and anorexic athletes," a trend the author explained as "a predictable corollary of the fashionable 'hot-blooded' image, as large, overweight bodies cannot dissipate metabolic heat efficiently."

Spinosaurus has long been depicted in popular books in largely hypothetical life restorations as a modified *Tyrannosaurus*-type of dinosaur, though one having relatively longer front limbs, a three-fingered (rather than two-fingered) manus, and, of course, its ubiquitous prominent dorsal sail. Many of these illustrations seem to have stemmed from the first skeletal reconstruction of *S. aegyptiacus*, which was offered by Lapparent and Lavocat 1955 in their chapter on dinosaurs in a volume of Pivetau's classic *Traité de Paléontologie* series of books. This reconstruction married the original type material with a typical theropod body plan, posed in an upright stance.

Stokesosaurus

Over the years following the original publication of Lapparent and Lavocat's skeletal reconstruction (and its subsequent reprintings in various other publications, *e.g.*, Glut 1972, 1982), opinions have differed regarding the appearance of *Spinosaurus*. Although some illustrations remained more or less faithful to the tyrannosaur-like Lapparent and Lavocat version for their inspiration (*e.g.*, Stout's life restoration in Glut 1982), others have veered away from that interpretation to depict this dinosaur as having longer forelimbs and as a possible quadruped. Comparisons of *Spinosaurus* with the more recently described, possibly quadrupedal theropod *Baryonyx* (see entries, *D:TE* and this volume; also see Charig and Milner 1986, 1990, 1997) seemed favorable. *Baryonyx* possesses somewhat elongated neural spines (though not to the extreme seen in *Spinosaurus*); both theropods also show similarities in the skull and number of teeth.

Bailey attempted a new life restoration of *Spinosaurus* (drawn by artist R. E. Johnson) that, although speculative in a number of ways, was founded upon sound and logical assumptions and, therefore, may be the closest made to date as conveying how this enigmatic theropod could have appeared in life.

Pointing out that data on the cervical vertebrae of this dinosaur are not clear, Bailey stated that the seven dorsals in the missing remains "strongly argue for a hump that reached its summit near the posterior dorsal region" (see Stromer 1915). If the body proportions of *Spinosaurus* are comparable to those of other known theropods, "the mass of the dorsal hump may have effectively transferred the center of balance in front of the weight-bearing hind limbs, possibly permitting or even requiring a quadrupedal gait."

Bailey's published restoration depicts *Spinosaurus* as a "buffalo-backed dinosaur" down on all fours, this posture inferred from the bulk and forward placement of the hump (ironically reminiscent, in some ways, of the original and highly inaccurate drawings and sculptures made more than a century ago by Benjamin Waterhouse Hawkins of the theropod genus *Megalosaurus*; see *D:TE*). Though hypothetical, the limb and body proportions were based on reconstructions of *Baryonyx walkeri* (see Charig and Milner), and also on a speculative restoration of *Spinosaurus* published by Lambert (1993), which, in turn, had been based on Lapparent and Lavocat's skeletal drawing.

As interpreted by Bailey, *Spinosaurus* was most likely not an agile, catlike sprinter as many short-spined theropods (such as *Allosaurus*) seem to have been, but rather an animal that "perhaps used the huge mass of its bear-like body to overpower young and weak prey, or perhaps to steal the kills of smaller more agile predators." Noting that there is no evidence of tendon ossification in the long neural spines of *Spinosaurus*, Bailey further suggested that, if this theropod were in fact a quadruped, a hump would be a dynamic advantage to this kind of gait, this "through the extra leverage supplied by the elongated spines and the tensile energy loading of the interspinous ligaments when the vertebral column was flexed."

Notes: Isolated remains formerly referred to "*Spinosaurus* B," collected from the same locality that yielded the remains of *S. maroccanus*, as well as the material belonging to this taxon figured by Stromer (1934), were referred by Russell to the new genus *Sigilmassasaurus* (see entry).

As noted by Russell, the most abundant remains found at the "Grès rouges" locality are those of theropods, followed by sauropods. Preserved here are the oldest records of abelisaurid theropods (CMN 41859, a median portion of a right dentary ramus), material referred to *Carcharodontosaurus* and "*Majungasaurus*" [=*Majungatholus*] (see entries), fragmentary remains of various indeterminate theropods, and some of the oldest records of African titanosaurid sauropods.

In 1998, Professor Paul C. Sereno of the University of Chicago returned from Niger with "tons" of fossil material, some of it pertaining to a new genus of spinosaurids. News rapidly appeared in various media, including popular publications (*e.g.*, *Dinosaur World*) and over the Internet, regarding these discoveries, but nothing—to date of this writing—has been officially published identifying or describing the material. Reportedly, the new spinosaurid (to be named *Suchomimus*) has an 18-inch tall "sail," suggesting that the neural spines are not as elongated as those usually associated with *Spinosaurus*.

Key references: Bailey (1997); Charig and Milner (1986, 1990, 1997); Lapparent and Lavocat (1955); Russell (1996); Stromer (1915, 1934).

†STOKESOSAURUS

Saurischia: Theropoda: Neotheropoda: Tetanurae: Avetheropoda; Coelurosauria: Manuraptoriformes: Arctometatarsalia *incertae sedis*.

New material: Basicranium (probably referable).

Comments: The genus *Stokesosaurus*, founded upon an isolated ilium, remains among the rarer of Morrison Formation theropod dinosaurs. A basicranium (UUVP 2455) collected from the Cleveland-Lloyd Dinosaur Quarry (from which some 9,000 theropod bones have already been recovered) in Emory County, Utah, first mentioned in a preliminary report by Chure and Madsen (1993), may be referable to the type species, *S. clevelandi*, thereby constituting the first material representing that part of the skull in this taxon. This well-preserved, only slightly distorted specimen includes the basioccipital, basisphenoid, and part of the parasphenoid (Chure and Madsen 1998).

In describing UUVP 2455, Chure and Madsen (1998) tentatively assigned the specimen to *Stokesosaurus clevelandi* for the following inferential reasons: 1. Only four theropod taxa—*Allosaurus*, *Ceratosaurus*, *Marshosaurus*, and *Stokesosaurus*—are known from the Cleveland-Lloyd Dinosaur Quarry, and this basicranium clearly does not belong either to *Allosaurus* or *Ceratosaurus*; 2. the size range of Cleveland-Lloyd *Allosaurus* specimens includes individuals comparable in size to UUVP 2455, but the latter's distinct morphology separates it from *Allosaurus*; 3. the only known Cleveland-Lloyd *Ceratosaurus* specimen lacks a braincase, although other skeletal elements belong to an animal much too large to accommodate UUVP 2455; also, the morphology of MWC 1.1.1., a *Ceratosaurus* braincase from the Fruita (Colorado) Paleontological Area, is quite different from that of UUVP 2455; 4. two partial skulls of *Marshosaurus* from Dinosaur National Monument, currently under study by Chure and Madsen, possess different and more primitive braincases than UUVP 2455; 5. *Stokesosaurus* was tentatively referred by Madsen (1974) to the Tyrannosauridae based on features of the ilium; 6. *Marshosaurus*, a "megalosaurid," is more primitive than the theropod represented by UUVP 2455, and the former's type ilium is more primitive than that of *Stokesosaurus*; and 7. the premaxilla (premaxillae being known from all four Cleveland-Lloyd theropods) referred to *Stokesosaurus* (see *D:TE*) is small enough for a skull having a basicranium the size of UUVP 2455.

According to Chure and Madsen (1998), UUVP 2455 is the most advanced basicranium of any known Jurassic theropod, combining features regarded as synapomorphies for two Cretaceous theropod families, the "Itemeridae" and Tyrannosauridae, and exhibits "a curious mix of primitive and derived features."

Deep pockets on the lateral surface of the basipterygoid surfaces, one of the most striking features in UUVP 2455, are matched or approached only in the Late Cretaceous Asian species, *Itemerus medullaris*. UUVP 2455 is more derived, however, than *Itemerus* in the following features: Much greater angle degree of shortening of basicranium; almost 180-degree angle between occipital condyle, basal tubera, and basipterygoid processes; flattened basal tubera; and basisphenoidal sinus visible in occipital view. Also, the basicranium of UUVP 2455 is extensively pneumatic (as revealed by CT scanning), while sectioning of the skull of *Itemerus* revealed no sinuses within the basicranial bones (Kurzanov 1976).

The shortening of the braincase of UUVP 2455 is seen only in most advanced members of the Tyrannosauridae, including *Tyrannosaurus rex* and *Alioramus remotus*, although neither are as shortened as in the Cleveland-Lloyd specimen. The latter is more primitive than in tyrannosaurids in that the long, narrow subsellar pit can be seen in ventral view (pit nearly vertical and visible only in anterior view in some carnosaurs and tyrannosaurids).

According to Chure and Madsen (1998), UUVP 2455 could be an early "itemerid," although one that is very advanced over the only other known member of this group which has been found in rocks of considerably younger age. If an early tyrannosaurid, then the closest affinities of UUVP 2455 seem to be with the most derived members of that family, particularly *T. rex*. Unfortunately, the histories of neither "itemirids" nor tyrannosaurids are known well enough for such an assessment to be made. UUVP 2455 might also represent "a theropod lineage that independently achieved an itemerid/tyrannosaurid level of organization (at least in the basicranium) by the Late Jurassic." Given the limited materials presently available for *Stokesosaurus*, the authors were unable to choose between these three alternatives.

As further noted by Chure and Madsen (1998), specimens such as UUVP 2455 attest to the fact that the morphological diversity of Morrison Formation theropods is clearly greater than previously suspected.

Key references: Chure and Madsen (1993, 1998); Madsen (1974).

†**STRUTHIOSAURUS** Bunzel 1870—(=?*Onychosaurus*)

Type species: *S. austriacus* Bunzel 1871 [*nomen dubium*].

Other species: *Struthiosaurus transylvanicus* Nopcsa 1915.

Occurrence: Gosau Formation, Muthmannsdorf, Austria; Sinpetru beds, Szentpeterfalva region, Transylvania, Romania.

Age: Late Cretaceous (early Campanian–late Maastrichtian).

Known material: Fragmentary cranial remains, subadult, fragments of skull roof, subadult to adult, posterior half of skull and partial postcrania, adult; also undescribed postcranial remains belonging to the type species, including vertebrae from the Iberian peninsula (upper Campanian) [Pereda-Suberbiola, in preparation].

Holotype: UWPI 2349/6, fragmentary braincase including posterior part of skull roof, most of occipital region, and posteroventral portion of basicranium, subadult.

Diagnosis of genus: Ventrally projecting shape of basisphenoid; cervical vertebrae elongated; tall dorsal neural arch pedicles and neural canal; scapula with hooklike acromion process; armor distinctive [Pereda-Suberbiola and Galton, in preparation] (Pereda-Suberbiola and Galton 1997).

Diagnosis of *S. austriacus*: Small, estimated adult skull length 20–25 centimeters in length; occiput comparatively high, narrow relative to that of advanced nodosaurids; basisphenoid bone projecting ventrally relative to general posterior level of basicranium; infratemporal fenestra narrow, elongated; armor pattern on skull roof with anteroposteriorly narrow scute along rear edge, probably two rows composed of three or four scutes on orbital region (pattern possibly obliterated in fully adult individuals) (Pereda-Suberbiola and Galton 1994).

Comments: The diminutive European ankylosaur *Struthiosaurus* has been a problematic and controversial genus (see *D:TE*) since it was first announced and named in a preliminary notice by Bunzel (1870), based upon a fragmentary cranium (UWPI 2349/6), discovered in a coal mine of the Gosau Formation (lower Campanian; Brix and Plöchinger 1988), at Muthmannsdorf, near Wiener Neustadt, in Lower Austria. Bunzel, because of the specimen's somewhat birdlike appearance, proposed the generic name *Struthiosaurus* (meaning "ostrich lizard") for it; subsequently, Bunzel (1871) erected the species *Struthiosaurus austriacus*, at the same time describing other fragmentary reptilian remains from the Gosau beds of Muthmannsdorf. (For a more detailed taxonomic history of *Struthiosaurus* and its two proposed species, as well as references to related genera, see Pereda-Suberbiola and Galton 1994).

Seeley (1881), noting that the skull was not really birdlike, was the first author to point out similarities in the skull of *S. austriacus* to that of the armored dinosaur *Acanthopholis* and, therefore, suggested that the specimen belonged to a "scelidosaurian" dinosaur. At the same time, Seeley described two fragments of the supraorbital roof of a skull (UWPI 2349/17 and 2349/no number) as postfrontal bones of a chelonian, apparently with the same occurrence as the holotype (this material regarded as belonging to a subadult to adult *S. austriacus* by Pereda-Suberbiola and Galton 1994).

Later, Nopcsa (1915), who considered *Struthiosaurus* to belong to the family Acanthopholidae (now a junior synonym of Nodosauridae), erected a second species, *S. transylvanicus*, based on a specimen (BMNH R4966) recovered from the Sinpetru beds of the Szentpeterfalva region (upper Maastrichtian; Weishampel, Grigorescu and Norman 1991), Hateg Basin, Judetul Hunedoara, Transylvania, Hungary [now in Romania]. This specimen comprised the posterior half of a skull, including posterodorsal and circumorbital portions of dermal elements of the skull roof, endocranium (occiput and incomplete basicranium), fragments of pterygoids, and ends of quadrates, and also some postcranial bones (including an atlas, a dorsal and a caudal vertebra, caudal centrum, almost complete rib, the right scapula, a partial humerus, and some indeterminate fragments).

Numerous subsequent authors, commencing with Lapparent and Lavocat (1955), have generally classified *Struthiosaurus* with the Ankylosauria. At first, Coombs (1971, 1978*a*) regarded the type species as a probable nodosaurid; subsequently, Coombs (1978*b*) expressed doubts that *S. austriacus* was ankylosaurian or even ornithischian. In their review of the Ankylosauria, Coombs and Maryańska (1990) suggested that the holotype of *S. austriacus* could belong to a saurischian dinosaur, based upon the saurischian-like feature of the large, ventrally projecting basisphenoid, and referred to it as Saurischia *incertae sedis*, the authors further noting that the genus is in need of revision. *S. austriacus* was also listed by Molnar, Kurzanov and Dong (1990) in their review of "carnosaurian" theropods as Carnosauria *incertae sedis*. Consequently, the genus *Struthiosaurus* has, in recent years, been regarded as a questionable ankylosaur, a possible saurischian, and perhaps a theropod, while its second species, accepted as nodosaurid, has usually been cited with its generic name set in quotation marks ("*Struthiosaurus*" *transylvanicus*).

More recently, the genus *Struthiosaurus* was critically reviewed in a series of papers published by Xabier [Javier] Pereda-Suberbiola and Peter M. Galton. Pereda-Suberbiola and Galton (1992) reinterpreted the holotype skull of *S. austriacus* as belonging to the Nodosauridae based upon the following observed nodosaurid characters: Dermal armor co-ossified with skull roof; mostly obliterated skull sutures; occipital condyle hemispherical, formed exclusively by basioccipital, separated from braincase by distinct neck; posteroventrally directed paroccipital processes, visible in dorsal aspect; rugose basipterygoid processes.

Subsequently, Pereda-Suberbiola and Galton (1994) published a detailed description of the type specimen of *S. austriacus*, including its endocranial cast. In their description, the authors noted that the skull piece, though massive in general appearance, is very small, the greatest height from the base of the occipital to the top of the skull roof being only about 55 millimeters.

Again reassessing the systematic status of *Struthiosaurus*, Pereda-Suberbiola and Galton (1994) noted that a ventrally projected basisphenoid (also present in *Gastonia*; K. Carpenter, personal communication

1997)—the feature for which previous authors had recently regarded *S. austriacus* as a theropod—can be more modest in some theropod taxa. This feature is also present in the skull of *S. transylvanicus*, a species exhibiting at least two features (not preserved in *S. austriacus*) diagnostic of the Nodosauridae (quadrate shaft possibly angled anteroventrally, and a narrow, elongated infratemporal fenestra). Also, the braincases of both *S. austriacus* and *S. transylvanicus* share the same cranial construction, indicating a close relationship between the two species.

Furthermore, Pereda-Suberbiola and Galton (1994) listed the following suite of characters observed in the braincases of both *S. austriacus* and *S. transylvanicus*:

1. Absence of prominent sheet or bone or crista passing from ventromedial edge of paroccipital process onto sidewall of braincase, and down onto lateral surface of basisphenoid to basipterygoid process; 2. endocranial cast lacking flocular lobe of cerebellum; 3. ventral part of exoccipital adjacent to foramen magnum is indented to form recess overhung by dorsal border of exoccipital plus supraoccipital, floored by occipital condyle; 4. dermal armor co-ossified with roof of braincase; 5. sutural boundaries between individual cranial bones mostly obliterated, only suture between quadratojugal and quadrate visible in *S. transylvanicus*; 6. supratemporal fenestra closed; 7. occiput low, supraoccipital poorly developed; 8. occipital condyle hemispherical, formed exclusively by basioccipital, set off from ventral braincase by distinct neck; 9. basipterygoid process of basisphenoid comprising pair of rugose stubs; 10. skull roof not overhanging occipital region, so paroccipital processes are visible in dorsal aspect; 11. occipital condyle only slightly wider than greatest diameter of foramen magnum; 12. basisphenoid projecting ventrally below level of basioccipital; and, 13. braincases (with estimated length of 20 to 25 centimeters) smaller than those of most ankylosaurs.

Pereda-Suberbiola and Galton (1994) noted that, of the above characters, all except numbers 12 and 13 are distinctly nonsaurischian, 1 and 2 are typical of the Ornithischia, 3 links Stegosauria plus Ankylosauria, 4 through 7 are diagnostic for the Ankylosauria, 8 to 11 are diagnostic for the Nodosauridae, and 12 and 13 were tentatively interpreted as specialized features that distinguish *Struthiosaurus* from other nodosaurids (except *Minmi* for number 13).

Taphonomic evidence, according to Pereda-Suberbiola and Galton (1994), also reinforces associating *Struthiosaurus* with the Nodosauridae, more than 95 percent of all dinosaurian remains recovered from the Gosau beds of Muthmannsdorf being nodosaurid.

Therefore, the authors concluded that *S. austriacus* is a nodosaurid, and that "the ventrally projecting shape of the basisphenoid bone characterizes both skulls and serves to distinguish *Struthiosaurus* from other ankylosaurs."

The following disparities in the skulls of the two species *S. austriacus* and *S. transylvanicus* were noted by Pereda-Suberbiola and Galton (1994) as growth features: 1. Type specimen of *S. austriacus* smaller than that of *S. transylvanicus*; 2. paroccipital process, dorsal end of quadrate, and squamosal fused together in *S. transylvanicus*; 3. pattern of scutes co-ossified with skull roof is well preserved in type species, poorly exposed in *S. transylvanicus*; 4. exoccipitals plus supraoccipital, in *S. austriacus*, forming border dorsally that overhangs foramen magnum; and 5. cranial armor in type species not overhanging supraoccipital region, unlike condition in *S. transylvanicus*.

Although growth changes in subadult and adult ankylosaurs are not yet clear, Pereda-Suberbiola and Galton (1994) explained, of the above differences, numbers 1, 2, and possibly 3 through 5 as probably the result of ontogeny, with the skull of the type species interpreted as that of a subadult nodosaurid.

The different disposition of the basisphenoid floor in *S. transylvanicus* as compared with the type species was tentatively explained as 1. the result of an artefact of preservation, or 2. that of a specific difference. If the latter, the authors noted, "it is possible to recognize a nodosaurid series on the basis of the increase of the angle between the basisphenoid and the horizontal it follows: *Panoplosaurus mirus* (approximately horizontal) < *S. austriacus* (about 20–25°) < *S. transylvanicus* (40–45°)."

Pereda-Suberbiola and Galton (1994) found that the material of *Struthiosaurus* is not adequate enough to resolve unequivocally the question of the relationship between the two species assigned to this genus, or to allow for an accurate diagnosis of *S. transylvanicus*. Although the different stratigraphic positions of their type specimens suggest the occurrence of two distinct species, no unambiguous character currently supports their taxonomic separation. Pending the future discovery of additional materials that may answer the question of their relationship, the authors favored provisionally regarding *S. transylvanicus* as *Struthiosaurus* cf. *S. austriacus*. This view was sustained in Pereda-Suberbiola and Galton's (1997) subsequent detailed description of *S. transylvanicus*.

Comparing *Struthiosaurus* to other nodosaurids, Pereda-Suberbiola and Galton (1994) noted that this genus retains various conservative features for the Nodosauridae, including a relatively narrow, high occiput and an elongated infratemporal fenestra. The basisphenoid projecting ventrally relative to the general level of the posterior part of the basicranium was regarded by the authors as a character diagnostic for this genus, its significance not yet accurately understood.

Pereda-Suberbiola and Galton (1997) regarded *Struthiosaurus* "as an endemic, small-sized nodosaurid component of the Late Cretaceous dinosaur fauna of Europe."

As pointed out by Pereda-Suberbiola and Galton (1994), Nopcsa (1915) spelled the specific name of the second species of *Struthiosaurus* in more than one way — originally "*transilvanicus*" then, in the same publication, "*S. transylvanicus.*" Later, Nopcsa (1923) himself chose the latter spelling, "*transylvanicus*" stemming from the Latinization of the name Transylvania. Although some authors (see *D:TE*) have used "*S. transilvanicus,*" based upon its page priority, the other spelling is correct according to the Code of Zoological Nomenclature (article 24c).

Erratum: On page 320 of *D:TE*, in the entry for *Crataeomus*, a figure of the referred femur (GIUV collection) of the type species, *C. lepidophorous*—which some workers (*e.g.*, Coombs and Maryańska 1990) believe to be a junior synonym of "*Struthiosaurus transilvanicus*"—was incorrectly identified as a humerus.

Key references: Bunzel (1870, 1871); Coombs (1971, 1978*a*, 1978*b*); Coombs and Maryańska (1990); Lapparent and Lavocat (1955); Molnar, Kurzanov and Dong (1990); Nopcsa (1915, 1923); Pereda-Suberbiola and Galton (1992, 1994, 1997); Seeley (1881).

†STYGIMOLOCH

Diagnosis of genus (as for type species): Intermediate-sized pachycephalosaur characterized by a long, narrow skull having a vaulted frontoparietal dome; squamosal very robust, forming thickened posterior shelf, its posterodorsal surface ornamented with three to four large, low-angle horns and multiple clusters of smaller bony nodes; braincase heavily ossified, with numerous accessory ossifications; occipital region rotated anteroventrally, to lie anterior to squamosal (Goodwin, Buchholtz and Johnson 1998).

Comments: *Stygimoloch spinifer*, a pachycephalosaurid dinosaur having "a high-domed, transversely narrow skull, distinguished by a unique cluster of well-developed horns and bony nodes preserved along the posterodorsal surface of a thickened squamosal shelf," has, until recently, been known only from several very incomplete cranial specimens (see *D:TE*), these not including the still undescribed incomplete skeleton and skull discovered by Michael Triebold and presumably belonging to this type species (see "Notes" below).

Recently, the most complete skull (MPM 8111) yet found — a well-preserved specimen discovered in

Stygimoloch spinifer, referred partial skull (MPM 8111) in right lateral view. Scale = 5 cm. (After Goodwin, Buchholtz and Johnson 1998.)

Stygimoloch

Stygimoloch spinifer, referred partial skull (MPM 8111), ventral view, illustrating the relative size of the robust left squamosal (upper left area) and its participation in overall skull length; the ventral surface of the parietal (upper middle) is dominated by large muscle scars above its contact with the supraorbital (lower middle). (After Goodwin, Buchholtz and Johnson 1998.)

1987 by Jeff Howe, a member of a Milwaukee Public Museum field crew, in the Upper Cretaceous (Maastrichtian) badlands of the Hell Creek Formation surrounding Marmarth, Slope County, North Dakota, first reported by Goodwin and Johnson (1995) — has allowed for a new study of *S. spinifer*. Resulting from this study was the first extensive description of the cranial anatomy of this taxon, and also a confirmation of the diagnostic characters for the genus and species. Also described were a number of other specimens recently collected from different localities [see "Errata," below] (Goodwin, Buchholtz and Johnson 1998).

In reevaluating the various pro and con arguments regarding possible agonistic "head-butting" in *Stygimoloch* as well as other pachycephalosaurs (see *Pachycephalosaurus*, *Stegoceras*, and *Stygimoloch* entries, *D:TE*), Goodwin *et al.* observed that the laterally constricted skull dome slopes dorsally to an acute angle in anterior view, thereby producing a surface unsuitable for head-to-head contact. Thus, contact with its horns during head-to-head or even head-to-flank encounters would have been almost impossible anatomically in this genus, as the horns point posteriorly in the horizontal plane (a suggestion made earlier by Goodwin and Johnson 1995). The authors found it more plausible that the dome and cranial horns in *Stygimoloch* were primarily utilized in 1. broadside displays (as suggested by Galton and Sues 1983), 2. deflecting a blow to the head, or 3. protecting the neck. The dinosaur would have presented a formidable display of its horns and broad squamosal shelf by simply tilting its head downward. If actual agonistic encounters ever took place involving this genus, the authors suggested, they were lateral.

Notes: In *D:TE*, in the "Notes" ending the *Pachycephalosaurus* entry, it was reported that Dale A. Russell (1995) had briefly described a large though still unidentified pachycephalosaur specimen discovered by private fossil collector Michael Triebold in the Sandy Quarry, Hell Creek Formation, near Buffalo, South Dakota.

In that same book, accompanying the *Stygimoloch* entry, was a photograph of a mounted specimen — consisting of an incomplete skeleton reconstructed and cast by Triebold Industries — exhibited at Dinofest™ International, held in 1996 at Arizona State University in Tempe. This specimen, the most complete one of a large pachycephalosaur yet found, includes a skull missing the premaxilla, tip of the dentary, and the dome. It was identified by the present writer in the picture caption as *Stygimoloch spinifer*, mostly because of the prominent spikes of the skull (and also because it was referred to as *Stygimoloch* by a number of Dinofest™ attendees).

Russell's reported-on specimen and the skeleton displayed in Tempe were, of course, one and the same. Some of the confusion leading to regarding them as two separate specimens possibly representing two distinct taxa — *Pachycephalosaurus* and *Stygimoloch* — may have resulted from Triebold's reconstruction of the skull. As pointed out by Tracy L. Ford (1998) in an article on pachycephalosaurs in the popular journal *Dinosaur World*, Triebold (personal communication to Ford) had not yet heard of *Stygimoloch* when he reconstructed and cast the skull of the Sandy Quarry pachycephalosaur specimen. Consequently, Triebold restored the skull of his specimen with the large, thick dome of *Pachycephalosaurus* rather than the smaller, thin dome of *Stygimoloch*.

Indeed, Triebold (1997), in the proceedings volume published following the Dinofest™ International Symposium of 1996, identified this skeleton as simply "Pachycephalosaur skeleton from Sandy site." More recently, in *Dinosaurs Invade Philadelphia* — a one-shot magazine published in 1998 as a souvenir of both the third Dinofest™ (now referred to as "The World's Fair of Dinosaurs") and the opening of the new "Dinosaur Hall" at The Academy of Natural Sciences of Philadelphia — a photograph of the skull of this specimen was identified as "*Pachycephalosaurus*, the largest of the bone-headed dinosaurs."

A cast of this skeleton, which seems to belong to *S. spinifer* but yet awaits a formal referral to that species and a full description, is now mounted at the Academy in Philadelphia.

Errata: On p. 865 of *D:TE*, it was incorrectly stated that Goodwin and Johnson had reported two additional skulls, two domes, and some associated postcranial remains belonging to *Stygimoloch* from the same locality that yielded MPM 8111. Actually, only MPM 8111 was found at that locality. The other specimens, described by Goodwin *et al.*, include the following: UCMP 131163, a partial skull and associated squamosal, discovered by Harley Garbani in 1987 in the Hell Creek Formation, Garfield County, Montana; UCMP 128383, a posterior frontoparietal dome, associated squamosal horn fragments, and postcranial elements (mostly vertebrae and ossified tendons), found in 1983 by Jennifer Woodcock and a field crew of the University of California Museum of Paleontology, in the Hell Creek Formation of Garfield County, Montana; UCMP 147063, a frontoparietal dome (juvenile) from the Hell Creek Formation, Carter County, Montana; UCMP 147258, a squamosal horn from the Lance Formation, Niobrara County, Wyoming; and AMNH 21541, various cranial and postcranial remains collected in 1908 by Barnum Brown from the Hell Creek Formation at Garfield County.

Key reference: Galton and Sues (1983); Goodwin,

Stygimoloch

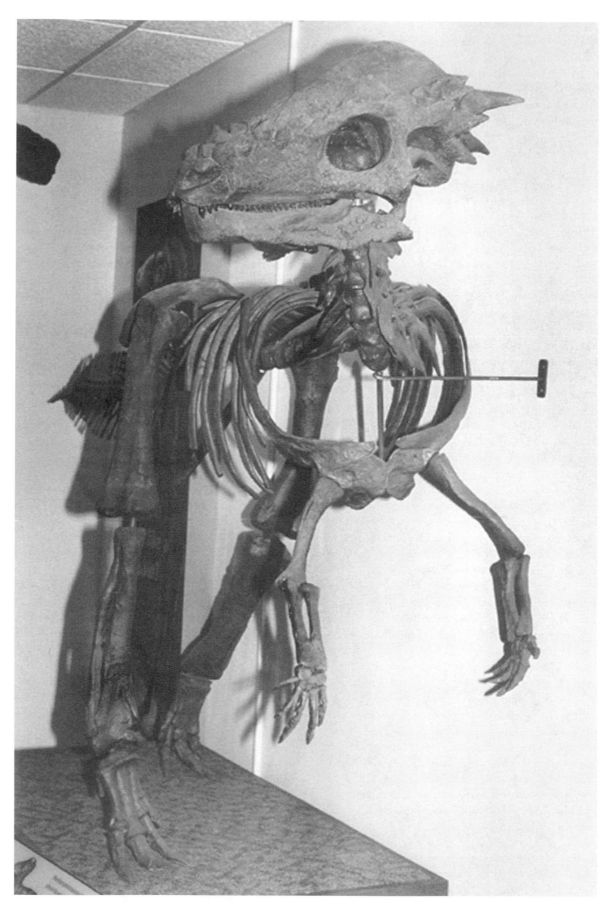

Buchholtz and Johnson (1998); Goodwin and Johnson (1995); Russell (1995); Triebold (1997).

†SUPERSAURUS—(=*Ultrasauros*)

Saurischia: Sauropodomorpha: Sauropoda: Eusauropoda: Neosauropoda: Diplodocoidea: Diplodocidae.

Comments: When first discovered in the early 1970s, the type species of the diplodocid that came to be named *Supersaurus vivianae* (Jensen 1985) was touted as the largest sauropod ever found.

Supersaurus held this distinction until, in 1979, what seemed to be an even bigger sauropod was found by Jensen. For more than half a decade, Jensen, in the popular media, informally referred to this second sauropod as simply "Ultrasaurus." This taxon was primarily based on two specimens — a very large scapulocoracoid (BYU 9462), measuring about 2.6 meters in length, and a dorsal vertebra (BYU 9044), both collected from the Brushy Basin Member of the Morrison Formation, Dry Mesa Dinosaur Quarry, near Mesa County, in western Colorado. Jensen referred to this species two other specimens, a cervical (BYU 9024) and caudal (BYU 9045) vertebra, because of their size.

With "Ultrasaurus" still not formally named, Kim (1983), apparently unaware of Jensen's intentions to use the generic name, gave it to his own species, *Ultrasaurus tabriensis*, a questionable Korean sauropod taxon based upon undiagnostic remains.

Eventually in 1985, Jensen, designating the dorsal vertebra to be the holotype, officially named this second sauropod *Ultrasaurus macintoshi*, presuming that his informal use of the name gave it priority, but actually violating the rules of the International Code of Zoological Nomenclature. Olshevsky (1991), with Jensen's approval, finally renamed this sauropod *Ultrasauros macintoshi* (Olshevsky's earlier suggested "Jensenosaurus macintoshi" not having been accepted by Jensen).

Jensen originally described *U. macintoshi* as a brachiosaurid, believing that its remains represented the largest sauropod yet discovered. Subsequently, Jensen (1987) removed the cervical vertebra from this species, noting that it possessed such diplodocid characters as a bifed neural spine, and referred it to *Supersaurus*.

Although some authors (*e.g.*, Paul 1988*a*; Britt 1991), suggested, over the years, that this sauropod could be synonymous with *Brachiosaurus altithorax*, perhaps representing the largest known individual of that species, others (*e.g.*, McIntosh 1990*b*, Olshevsky 1991), accepted *U. macintoshi* as a valid genus and species. Regardless as to whether or not *Ultrasauros*

was considered to be a distinct genus or a junior synonym of *Brachiosaurus*, its referral to the Brachiosauridae remained generally accepted.

Published suspicion that the affinities of *Ultrasauros* were not with this family surfaced when Miller, Baer, Stadtman and Britt (1991), in commenting on dinosaur remains from the Dry Mesa Quarry, observed that the anatomy of BYU 9044 was similar to that of the anterior sacral vertebra of *Supersaurus*, thereby suggesting possible diplodocid affinity for BYU 9044. Later, Curtice (1995) referred caudal vertebra BYU 9045 to *Supersaurus* because of various diplodocid features (*e.g.*, slight emargination of neural spine, mild pneumatic fossae, procoelous centrum).

More recently, both the remaining holotype dorsal vertebra and referred scapulocoracoid were reexamined by Curtice, Stadtman and Curtice (1996),

James A. ("Dinosaur Jim") Jensen (1918–1998) with the reconstructed forelimb of the giant sauropod originally named *Ultrasaurus macintoshi*. Real elements belonging to this species were recently referred to two different sauropod genera, *Supersaurus* and *Brachiosaurus*.

T

who found that, taken together, the specimens constitute a chimera representing two distinct families, with only BYU 9044 belonging to *U. macintoshi* (see "Note," below).

Curtice *et al.* correctly identified BYU 9044 as a dorsal vertebra having a caudal position within the vertebral column. In fully describing BYU 9044 and comparing it with other brachiosaurid and diplodocid dorsals, Curtice *et al.* (see also Curtice 1996) observed the following in the specimen: Prominent supradiapophysial laminae, lacks transversely expanded supradiapophysial laminae; neural spine twice as tall as centrum, twice length of transverse process; parapophysis located on transverse process next to diapophysis (indicating vertebra is a dorsal); very well-developed hyposphene/hypantrum complex present; large vacuity below hyposphene; postzygapophyses overhanging centrum considerably. According to these authors, this suite of characters is found in diplodocid caudal dorsal vertebrae but are unknown in brachiosaurid caudal dorsals. The size and morphology of BYU 9044 matches sacrals found on a pelvis (BYU 13018) of *Supersaurus vivianae*. Also, maps of the Dry Mesa Quarry show that the holotype of *U. macintoshi* was found upstream from that of *S. vivianae*, between a pair of *Supersaurus* scapulae. For these reasons, Curtice *et al.* referred BYU 9044 to *Supersaurus vivianae*.

According to Curtice *et al.*, *Supersaurus* has the arguable distinction of being the world's largest known diplodocid, now known from a total of six caudal vertebrae, a pelvis with four sacral vertebrae, an ilium, pubis, ischia, a phalanx, and a carpal (Stadtman, White and Curtice, in preparation).

Note: The scapulocoracoid catalogued as BYU 9462 was identified by Curtice *et al.* as that of a brachiosaurid and referred to *Brachiosaurus* sp. (see *Brachiosaurus* entry, this book).

Key references: Britt (1991); Curtice (1995, 1996); Curtice, Stadtman and Curtice (1996); Jensen (1985, 1987); Kim (1983); McIntosh (1990*b*); Miller, Baer, Stadtman and Britt (1991); Olshevsky (1991*0*; Paul (1988*a*).

†TATISAURUS—(See *Scelidosaurus*.)

†TARCHIA

Comments: Skulls of ankylosaurs, as pointed out by Tumanova, Gallagher and Dodson (1998) in a preliminary report, do not retain the diapsid temporal openings present in those of other kinds of dinosaurs, and the internal structure of their skulls is obscured in many places by cranial armor. Study of the internal structure of ankylosaurid ankylosaurs, therefore, requires either destructive sectioning or nondestructive computerized tomography (that is CT scanning).

Subjecting skulls of the Asian ankylosaurid ankylosaurs *Tarchia*, *Saichania*, and *Shamosaurus* to computerized tomography using a GE high-speed neuroscanner, Tumanova *et al.* found no observable trace of vestigial diapsid openings, but did find something unexpected in the *Tarchia* skull. An asymmetrical osteoma or bone growth was discovered on the right side in the sinus of the *Tarchia* specimen, between the right nasal passage and right orbit. As described by the authors, this anomaly possessed "a layered structure, with a dense core of bone surrounded by a spongy outer zone." It was located below a hole in the armored surface of the skull. The hole was 3 centimeters in width and roughly D-shaped [as are the teeth of tyrannosaurid theropods in cross section] on its outer surface, some of dermal bone around it being concave. As the skull was otherwise "in pristine condition, with no other traces of breakage or abrasian," Tumanova *et al.* interpreted the anomaly as not being an artifact of postmortem transport or burial.

Tumanova *et al.* interpreted the hole in the *Tarchia* skull as being a puncture wound resulting from the attack of a large theropod. Comparing the premaxillary teeth of the giant Asian tyrannosaurid *Tyrannosaurus bataar* with the opening in the skull, the authors found them to be of appropriate size and shape to have caused the wound, the angle of the hole relative to the osteoma suggesting an oblique attack. The osteoma was interpreted as probably the repair of the damage caused by the wound, this suggesting that the *Tarchia* individual had lived for some time following the attack. The authors further speculated that the "predisposition of ankylosaurs to generate bone may have also served as a way of repairing injuries."

Additional study of the *Tarchia* skull utilizing computerized tomography revealed the brain to have had a volume of less than 77.1 cubic centimeters (the volume of the brain case), perhaps weighing no more than 2 ounces for an animal measuring some 7 meters (23 feet) in length.

Erratum: In *D:TE*, p. 881, last paragraph, the words "nodosaurid evolution" constitute a typographical error; they should have read "ankylosaurid evolution."

Key reference: Tumanova, Gallagher and Dodson (1998).

†TENONTOSAURUS

Ornithischia: Genasauria: Cerapoda: Ornithopoda: Euornithopoda: "Hypsilophodontidae."

New species: *T. dossi* Winkler, Murry and Jacobs 1997.

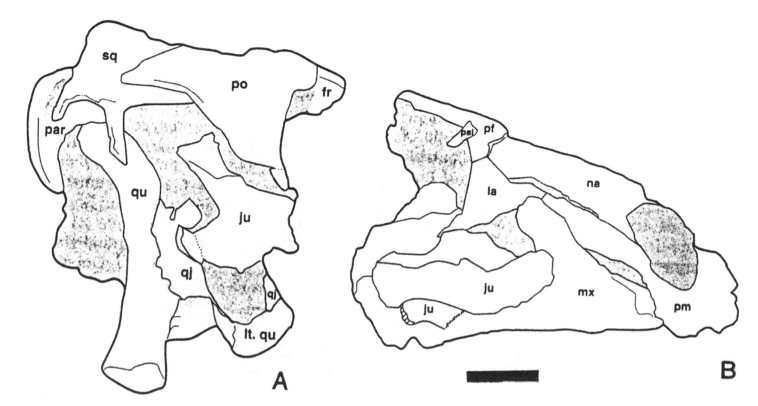

A

B

Tenontosaurus dossi,
FWMSH 93B1, holotype A.
posterior and B. anterior
parts of skull, right lateral
view. Scale = 5 cm. (After
Winkler, Murry and Jacobs
1997.)

Occurrence of *T. dossi*: Twin Mountains Formation, Texas, United States.

Age: Early Cretaceous (late Albian).

Known material: Two skeletons with skulls.

Holotype: FWMSH 93B1, almost complete skeleton with skull.

Diagnosis of *T. tilletti*: External nares large (relative to orbit); orbit subrectangular; maxilla high; antorbital fenestra reniform to slitlike; supraoccipital barely excluded from foramen magnum by thin processes of exoccipital (derived relative to *Hypsilophodon*); postcranial characters (from Ostrom 1970; Forster 1990) including: vertebral count of 12-16-5-60 (autapomorphy); three proximal carpals, ulnare largest, ulnare and intermedium tightly articulated but unfused; phalangeal formula of manus 2-3-3-1-1- (or ?2); ilium having deep, posteriorly raised postacetabular blade, long ventrolaterally curved preacetabular process; prepubic process long, laterally compressed but with no expansion at anterior end (derived relative to *Hypsilophodon*) (Winkler, Murry and Jacobs 1997).

Diagnosis of *T. dossi*: Large adult length of 7–8 meters; one or more prexillary teeth present; scapula having slight anterior flare dorsal to coracoid suture; scapula only 6 percent longer than humerus; ulnare and intermedium tightly interlocked; anterior blade of pubis smoothly convex ventrally; postpubis as long as ischium; ischium with low obturator process having gently sloping attachment to shaft; ilium without bre-

vis shelf; metatarsal V more than 30 percent length of metatarsal III (Winkler *et al.* 1997).

Comments: New insights into the well-known ornithopod genus *Tenontosaurus*, and also reinterpretations of at least two higher taxa within the Ornithopoda, "Hypsilophodontidae" and Iguanodontia, resulted from a study of the second species referred to this genus, *T. dossi*. This new species was based on two mostly articulated skeletons preserved in matrix largely in their original orientation. The specimens were recovered by Fort Worth Museum of Science and History crews from a small area of cross-bedded oyster-bearing sand of the Twin Mountains Formation (Lower Cretaceous, latest Albian; see Winkler, Murry, Jacobs 1989; Jacobs, Winkler and Murry 1991), approximately 17 meters below the marine Glen Rose Limestone, on the Doss Ranch, in the Twin Mountains Formation, Parker County, Texas. The holotype, FWMSH 93B1, consists of an almost complete skeleton with skull discovered by Thad and Ted Williams; the second specimen is a partial skull and skeleton. The material represents fairly old individuals, as evidenced by the completely fused sacral rib yoke and apparent fusion of posteriormost sacrals (Winkler *et al.* 1997).

Also recovered at this site, the authors noted, were fossils of turtles including *Naomichelys*, a possibly dromaeosaurid theropod (having a body size much smaller than either *T. dossi* specimen), the ray *Pseudohypolophus*, bony fish *Lepidotes*, an amiform fish, a

Tenontosaurus

Tenontosaurus dossi, FWMSH 93B2, referred braincase, left lateral view. Scale = 2 cm. (After Winkler, Murry and Jacobs 1997.)

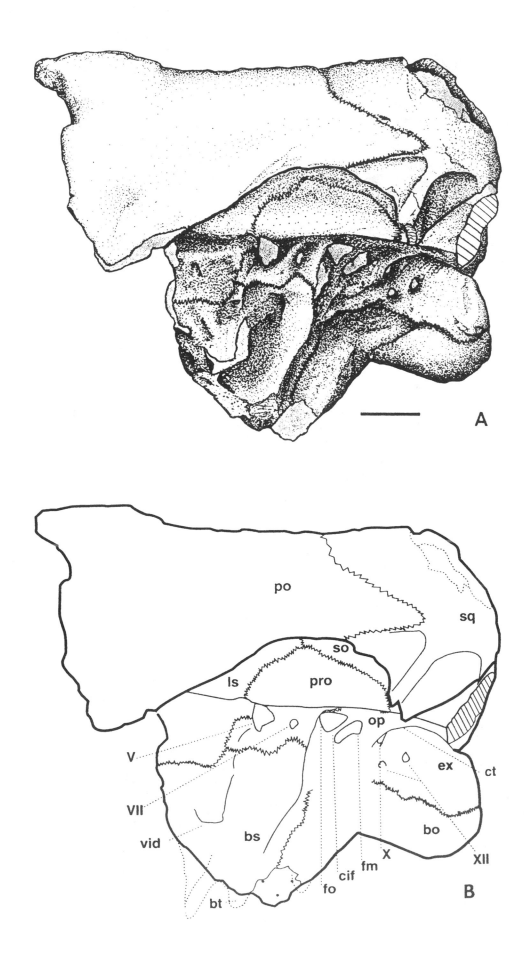

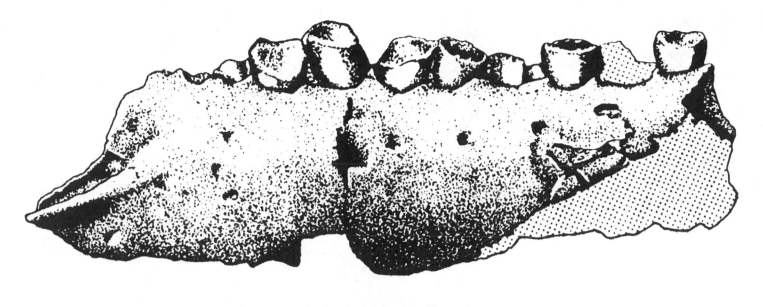

Tenontosaurus dossi,
FWMSH 93B2, referred left
dentary, lateral view. Scale =
2 cm. (After Winkler,
Murry and Jacobs 1997.)

crocodilian, and also various plant material. Both vertical and lateral facies relationships and the fauna at this unit suggest a brackish water lagoonal or estuarine environment. Despite the occurrence of the ?dromaeosaurid teeth, no major bone dislocations were found in either *T. dossi* skeleton; nor were any major signs of scavenging expected from a theropod of such comparatively smaller size.

In comparing *Tenontosaurus* with other ornithopods, Winkler *et al.* observed that this genus may be distinguished from more primitive taxa, like *Hypsilophodon*, by various characters (*e.g.*, ventrally everted premaxilla, smaller and fewer or no premaxillary teeth, at least three denticles on predentary) and more derived forms, like *Iguanodon*, by others (*e.g.*, less everted premaxilla, single anterior maxillary process, small or no brevis shelf).

The two species of *Tenontosaurus* were regarded by the authors as sister taxa to higher iguanodontians, with *T. dossi* identified as the more primitive and temporally older species, as well as being the most primitive of all known iguanodontians.

The differences between the species of *Tenontosaurus* were interpreted as possibly illustrating evolutionary forces, working over a relatively short span of Early Cretaceous time, resulting in important functional changes (*e.g.*, cranially, an increase in tooth packing and transference of cropping functions of the muzzle from toothbased to beak-margin based; postcranially, reduction of long postpubic rods, their muscle attachment areas moved onto the ischium, see Galton 1969, and reduction of metatarsal V). In acquiring such changes, *Tenontosaurus* may parallel more derived iguanodontians in its evolution.

Although the iguanodontian genera *Dryosaurus*

and *Camptosaurus* occur considerably earlier in the fossil record than does *Tenontosaurus*, the former taxa appear to be more derived and possess "the specific functional innovations that are central to the evolutionary transition from Hypsilophodontidae to primitive iguanodontians to hadrosaurids." Winkler *et al.* suggested that *Tenontosaurus* could represent a late offshoot from a relatively primitive ornithopod (see Norman 1998, below), its evolution, therefore, paralleling trends of the phylogenetic series of taxa that eventually led to hadrosaurs. Furthermore, the change in iguanodontians from possessing a premaxilla toward having a more ducklike bill — an important event in the evolution of ornithopods — took place before the loss of premaxillary teeth. As an alternative scenario, character states in *Tenontosaurus*, especially in *T. dossi*, may represent reversals from some earlier iguanodontian lineage.

Features of *T. dossi* led Winkler *et al.* to reevaluate the definitions of higher taxa within Ornithopoda. Based on their interpretation of this species, the authors suggested that some of the characters formerly used to support a monophyletic "Hypsilophodontidae" be removed, as they are also seen in *T. dossi*, and that certain features of *T. dossi* remove several key synapomorphies formerly used to define the Iguanodontia (see section on Iguanadonts, "Introduction"; also, see "Systematics" chapter). In lieu of the data gleaned from *T. dossi*, the genus *Tenontosaurus*, previously generally regarded as a small *Iguanodon* kind of dinosaur, was reinterpreted by Winkler *et al.* as functionally more like a large *Hypsilophodon*.

Winkler *et al.* pointed out that the marked variation among some of the Cloverly Formations specimens of *Tenontosaurus* may indicate species other than

Tenontosaurus dossi,
FWMSH 93B1, holotype
caudal vertebrae numbers
five through eight, right lateral view. Scale = 5 cm.
(After Winkler, Murry and
Jacobs 1997.)

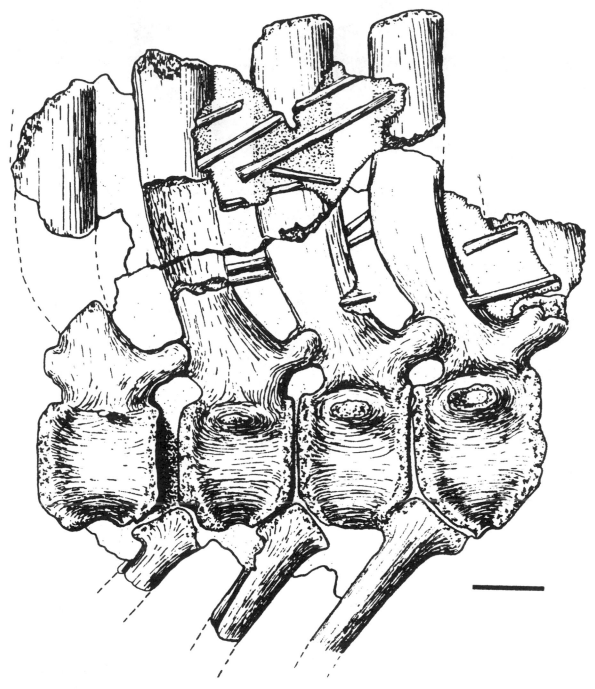

T. tilletti. Also, it is not unlikely that *T. dossi* may someday be found in the Cloverly, while specimens possibly referable to *T. tilletti* have already been collected from higher levels of the Trinity Group in Texas and Oklahoma.

More recently, Norman (1998) regarded *Tenontosaurus* as an unusually large and late member of the "Hypsilophodontia" (see "Systematics" chapter), which independently lost its premaxillary teeth. Norman commented on the following characters that had been used by previous workers (*e.g.*, Sereno 1986; Forster 1990; Coria and Salgado 1996; Winkler *et al.*) to clas-

sify the genus as a basal member of a clade including Dryomorpha plus Camptosauria plus Iguanodontia:

1. Loss of premaxillary teeth (convergent, invalidated by *T. dossi*); 2. oral margin of premaxilla everted, thickened (size-related convergence within Euornithopoda); 3. enlargement of external naris to at least 20 percent of base skull length (size-related convergence within Euornithopoda); 4. circular or oval antorbital fenestra (common within Euornithopoda); 5. denticulations on oral margin of predentary (size-related convergence within Euornithopoda); 6. manus digit III having lost one phalanx

(consistent, but rarely preserved in basal forms); and 7. humerus length equal to, or longer than, that of scapula (variable, probably locomotor-related proportions within Euornithopoda).

Note: Stanford and Stanford (1998) reported a trackway of ornithopod tracks (four-toed pes and five-fingered manus), "conceivably made by *Tenontosaurus*," from the Lower Cretaceous of Maryland.

Key reference: Coria and Salgado (1996); Forster (1990); Norman (1998); Sereno (1986); Stanford and Stanford (1998); Winkler, Murry and Jacobs (1997).

†THESCELOSAURUS

Ornithischia: Genasauria: Cerapoda: Ornithopoda: Euornithopoda: ?"Hypsilophodontidae."

Diagnosis of genus (as for species): Transverse width of frontals at midorbital level greater than their maximum width across posterior end; ventral part of supraoccipital wedge-shaped, almost excluded from dorsal margin of foramen magnum by deep excavation that is Y-shaped in dorsal aspect; low angle (less than 15 degrees) between ventral margin of braincase (occipital condyle, basal tubera, and basipterygoid) process and line drawn through centers of trigeminal foramen and posterodorsal hypoglossal foramen; surangular having prominent lateral process; well-enameled surface of cheek tooth (buccal for maxillary and lingual for dentary teeth) with numerous secondary ridges forming two converging concentric patterns; femur longer than tibia (Galton 1997*a*).

Comments: The cranial morphology of the small, basal "hypsilophodontid" dinosaur *Thescelosaurus neglectus* was redescribed, based upon the following postcranial specimens: The holotype USNM 7757, an almost complete skeleton from the Lance Formation of Niobrara [formerly Converse] County, Wyoming; paratype USNM 7758, a partial skeleton from Lance Creek, Niobrara County; and from the following referred specimens including cranial material: AMNH 5020, a toothless dentary from the Hell Creek Formation east of Lima, Montana; LACM 3354, a partial skull from the Hell Creek Formation, Garfield County, Montana; CMN [formerly NMC] 8537, holotype of *T. edmontonicus* [= *T. neglectus*], a complete skeleton with partial skull from the Scollard [formerly Edmonton] Formation, near Ramsey, Red Deer River, Alberta, Canada; and SMNH P.1225, a partial postcranial skeleton with a fragmentary skull from the Frenchman Formation, Valley of Frenchman River, Saskatchewan, Canada.

According to Galton (1997*a*), homoplastic characters that evolved independently in other "hypsilophodontids" include the following: 1. Transversely wide squamosal (also in *Parksosaurus*); 2. premaxillary

teeth lack marginal denticles (also in *Zephyrosaurus*); and 3. primary vertical ridge of a maxillary tooth is centrally located on the crown (also in *Othnielia*).

Galton also noted that *Thescelosaurus* can be distinguished from the majority of other known "hypsilophodontids" by these nonautapomorphic characters: 1. Frontal-postorbital suture consists of interlocking ridges and grooves, a plesiomorphic ornithischian condition also found in *Lesothosaurus* and *Heterodontosaurus*; 2. raised and rugose area on the anterolateral surface of the postorbital (opposite to the upper half of the squamosal process), this condition also being present in *Orodromeus*, but is probably plesiomorphic for the Ornithischia, also occurring in the primitive ornithischian *Lesothosaurus*; and 3. shallow fossa subarcuata on the medial junction region of the supraoccipital and prootic (for small lobe of cerebellum); fossa arcuata is deep and elongate (for prominent floccular lobe) in *Hypsilophodon*, *Parksosaurus*, and *Zephyrosaurus*, but unknown in other "hypsilophodontids" and *Lesothosaurus*.

Key reference: Galton (1997*a*).

†TITANOSAURUS—(= *Laplatasaurus*)

Saurischia: Sauropodomorpha: Sauropoda: Eusauropoda: Neosauropoda: Macronaria: Camarasauromorpha: Titanosauriformes: Somphospondyli: Titanosauria *incertae sedis*.

Type species: *T. indicus* Lydekker 1877.

Other species: *T. blandfordi* Lydekker 1879, ?*T. nanus* Lydekker 1893, *T. madagascariensis* Depéret 1896, *T. araukanikus* (Huene 1927), (new) *T. colberti* Jain and Bandyopadhyay 1997.

Occurrence: Lameta Formation, Madhya Pradesh, Maharashtra, Aviyalur Group, Tamil Nadu, Pisdura, India; Grès á Reptiles, Var, France; [unnamed formation], Lieda, Spain; Grès de Maevarano, Majunga, Madagascar.

Diagnosis of genus: Large advanced sauropods with strongly procoelous caudal vertebrae throughout series; cervical and dorsal vertebrae opisthocoelous with well-marked pleurocoels; transverse process of cervicals robust, laterally directed, very wide posteriorly in shoulder region; transverse process in dorsals narrow, outwardly directed, slightly upward; neural spine not bifed, posteriorly directed; sacrum with six co-ossified vertebrae and ribs; first and sixth sacral centra convex anteriorly and posteriorly respectively; midcaudal and part of distal caudal vertebrae having prominent variable chevron facets; prezygapophyses robust, extending to anterior margin of caudals; first sacral rib extended outward below iliac blade; preacetabular process of ilium projecting outward, becoming almost horizontal; ischium bladelike, expanded

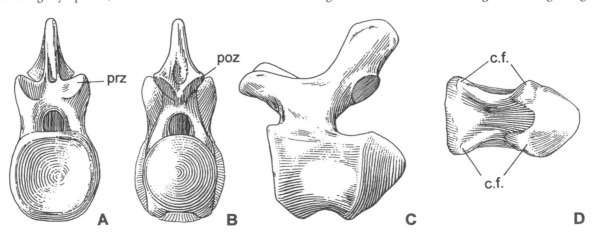

Titanosaurus colberti, A. distribution of the sixty-five elements comprising holo-type ISIR335/1–65) and B. hypothesized orientation of animal at burial. Scale = 2 meters. (After Jain and Bandyopadhyay 1997.)

transversely in middle; radius slender, shaft perpendicular to axis of expanded distal ends; ulna robust, triangular in cross section; humero-femoral ratio 0.74; tibio-femoral ratio 0.65; femur without lateral prominence; moderate development of nuchal crest of braincase; transverse ridge on parietal, high buttress ridge below paroccipital process (Jain and Bandyopadhyay 1997.)

Diagnosis of *T. colberti*: Large, advanced titanosaurid (as diagnosed by McIntosh 1990*a*) with strongly procoelous caudal vertebrae throughout; cervical and dorsal vertebrae strongly opisthocoelous with well-marked pleurocoels; cervical centra small; transverse process of cervicals wide, laterally directed, robust in shoulder region; neural spines of medium height, not bifid, more posteriorly directed laterally, and slightly upward; sacrum with six co-ossified vertebrae and ribs; anterior face of last sacral (sacro-caudal) centrum convex; sacricostal yoke well developed; first sacral rib moderately developed, extending outward; chevron facets on anterior rim of midcaudal vertebrae, located on raised prominent ridges, on posterior rim on low, faint ridges; middle part of caudal centra flat ventrally, without ridge; chevron facets located on very low ridges in distal caudals; scapula broad; preacetabular process of ilium directed strongly outward; ischium flat, bladelike, transversely expanded in middle; pubis robust; ulna robust, triangular in cross section (Jain and Bandyopadhyay 1997.)

Comments: Among all known sauropods, *Titanosaurus* has for decades been one of the least understood, although much material (most of it very incomplete) and numerous species have been referred to this genus. *Titanosaurus*, as had *Megalosaurus* regarding

Titanosaurus colberti, holotype midcaudal vertebrae (ISIR335/44) in A. anterior, B. posterior, C. lateral, and D. ventral views. Scale = 10 cm. (After Jain and Bandyopadhyay 1997.)

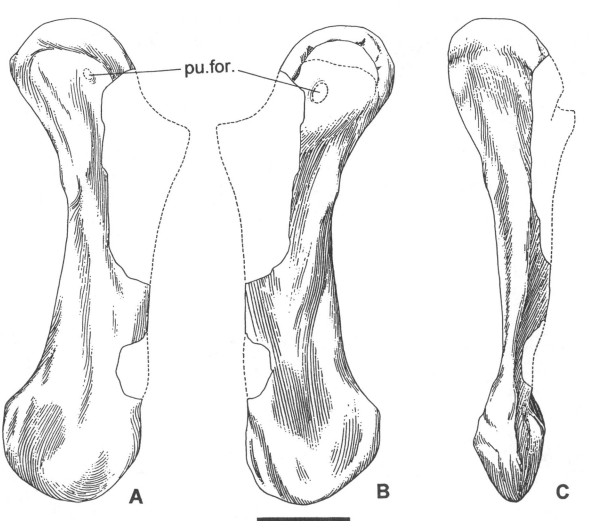

pu.for.

A B C

Titanosaurus colberti, holotype left pubis (ISIR335/63) in A. dorsal, B. medial, and C. lateral views. Scale = 10 cm. (After Jain and Bandyopadhyay 1997.)

European theropods, has been used as a kind of catch basin for sauropod material, primarily remains collected in India and South America, and only in recent years have workers begun to arrive at a clearer understanding of what constitutes this genus.

The most thorough recent study of *Titanosaurus* was that published by Jain and Bandyopadhyay in 1997. In addition to offering a detailed taxonomic history of *Titanosaurus* and its species (and junior synonyms), the authors recognized three previously named species from India — *T. indicus, T. blandfordi,* and *T. madagascariensis*— and introduced a new Indian species, *T. colberti* (see below).

Jain and Bandyopadhyay published a new diagnosis of the genus *Titanosaurus*, largely influenced by the material belonging to *T. colberti*, but excluding the biconvex feature of this specimen's first caudal centrum, a feature also found in several other titanosaur taxa (Gauthier 1986) including *Alamosaurus sanjuanensis, Neuquensaurus australis* [=*Titanosaurus australis* of their usage], and an undescribed titanosaur from the Bauru Formation of Brazil.

T. colberti was based by Jain and Bandyopadhyay on a partial articulated and associated skeleton (ISIR335/1–65) representing a single individual, collected from the green clays of the Lameta Formation (Maastrichtian) of Wardha Valley, village of Dongargaon, Chandrapur district, in Maharashtra, Central India. The type specimen includes nine cervical vertebrae (ISIR335/1–9), seven dorsals (ISIR335/10–16), 14 ribs (ISIR335/17–30), a complete sacrum with co-ossified vertebrae and ribs (ISIR335/35), 16 caudal vertebrae (ISIR335/32–47), nine chevrons (ISIR335/48–56), a left scapula (ISIR335/57), left coracoid (ISIR335/58), left humerus and left ulna (ISIR335/59–60), ilia (ISIR335/61–62), pubes (ISIR335/63–64) and a right ischium (ISIR335/65).

Recently, Bonaparte (1996*b*) accepted Powell's (1986) earlier assessment that the South American taxon *Laplatasaurus araukanikus* should be considered a species of *Titanosaurus*. Huene (1929) had based *L. araukanikus* on various postcranial specimens collected by S. Roth and R. Wichmann from three major titanosaur quarries in the Allen Formation in

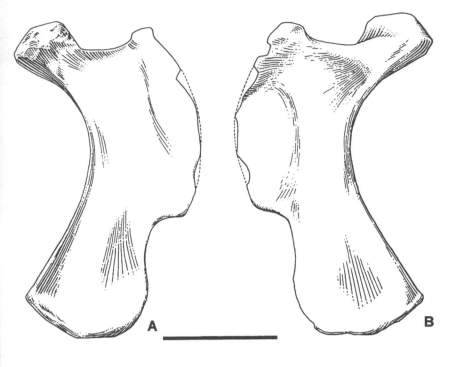

Left: Titanosaurus colberti, holotype right ischium (ISIR335/65) in A. dorsomedial and B. ventrolateral views. Scale = 25 cm. (After Jain and Bandyopadhyay 1997.)

Argentina, and housed at the Museo de La Plata, every piece having its own collection number. According to Bonaparte, the association of these remains is not certain, probably representing more than one individual; also, this species and *T. indicus* "show significant affinities in different parts of the skeleton, with some slight differences in the morphology of the caudal vertebrae." McIntosh (1990*a*), in his review of the Sauropoda, listed *Laplatasaurus* as a valid genus separate from *Titanosaurus*; however, this was done only because Powell's work had not been published, McIntosh accepting Powell's determination (J. S. McIntosh, personal communication 1998).

Chatterjee and Rudra (1996) described a new braincase (ISIR467) referred to the type species, *T. indicus*, from the Lameta Group or Raiholi, India.

Bottom: Titanosaurus indicus, referred braincase (ISIR467), in A. caudal, B. lateral, and C. rostral views. (After Chatterjee and Rudra 1996.)

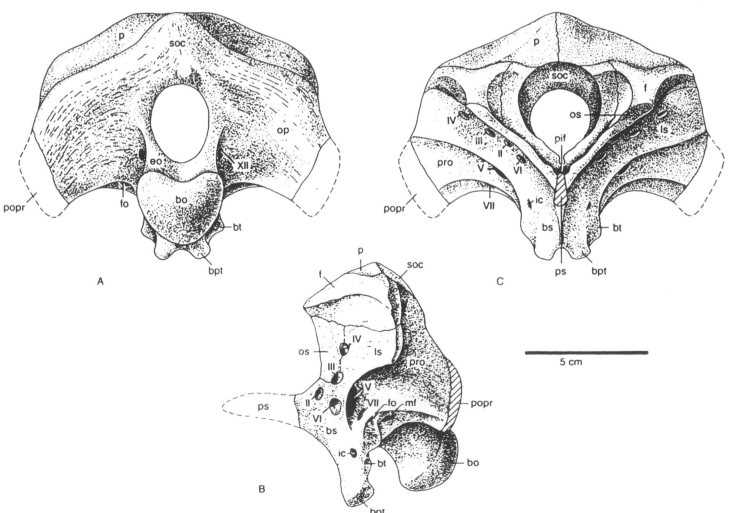

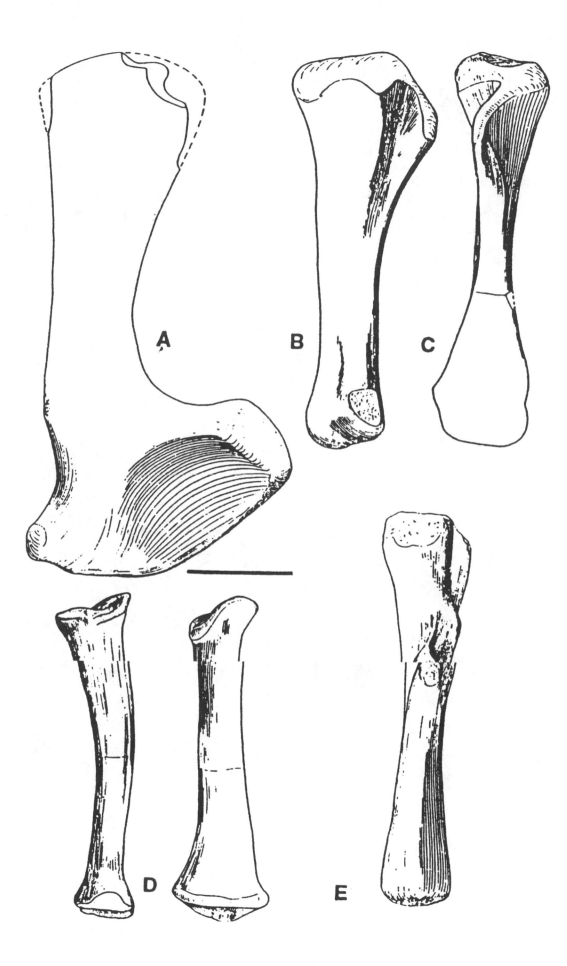

Titanosaurus araukanikus, A. right scapula, B.–C. MLP.CS.1128, lectotype right tibia, lateral and anterior views, D. left radius, anterior and medial views, E. MLP.CS.1127, lectotype right fibula, lateral view, specimens originally referred to *Laplatasaurus araukanikus*. Scale = 200 mm. (After Huene 1929 and Bonaparte 1996b.)

According to the Chatterjee and Rudra, this specimen is quite similar in size and morphology to a rather poorly preserved braincase (ISIR199) referred to this species from the Lameta Group at Dongargon and described by Berman and Jain (1982), and is very different from that of *Antarctosaurus*.

Powell reevaluated the species *T. nanus* Lydekker 1893, based upon a poorly preserved, incomplete cervical and dorsal vertebra (MLP. LY. 18/19 from the Río Colorado Formation (Coniacian), Nequén Province, Argentina, finding that this species cannot be referred with certainty to *Titanosaurus*, and is best regarded at this time as ?*Titanosaurus nanus*.

Key references: Berman and Jain (1982); Bonaparte (1996*b*); Chatterjee and Rudra (1996); Huene (1927, 1929); Lydekker (1893); Jain and Bandyopadhyay (1997); McIntosh (1990*a*); Powell (1986).

†TOROSAURUS

Ornithischia: Genasauria: Cerapoda: Marginocephalia: Ceratopsia: Neoceratopsia: Ceratopsomorpha: Ceratopsidae: Chasmosaurinae.

Torosaurus utahensis, USNM 15875, paratype parietal of *Arrhinoceratops utahensis*.

Diagnosis of *T. utahensis*: Large chasmosaurine with broad triangular squamosals having a smooth border bearing only three subtle anterior undulations, with small elliptical epoccipitals; thick, rounded bar along parietal suture; parietal broad, thin, sheetlike with relatively small subcircular fenestrae and numerous subtle irregular undulations along posterior margin; epoccipitals lacking or low and elliptical; supraorbital horncores relatively straight, smoothly confluent with frill, arising posterior to orbit, tapering distally and having hollow bases; distinguished from *Chasmosaurus mariscalensis* and *Pentaceratops sternbergii* by broad triangular form of squamosal, its smooth lateral margin, and thin sheetlike parietal (Lehman 1996).

Comments: In 1976, Douglas A. Lawson referred some ceratopsian remains found in Utah — originally identified by Gilmore (1946*b*) as *Arrhinoceratops? utahensis* — to the genus *Torosaurus*, a giant chasmosaurine with an enormous skull and frill, as new species *T. utahensis*.

Subsequent to this referral, other workers (*e.g.*, Lehman 1990; Dodson and Currie 1990) concluded

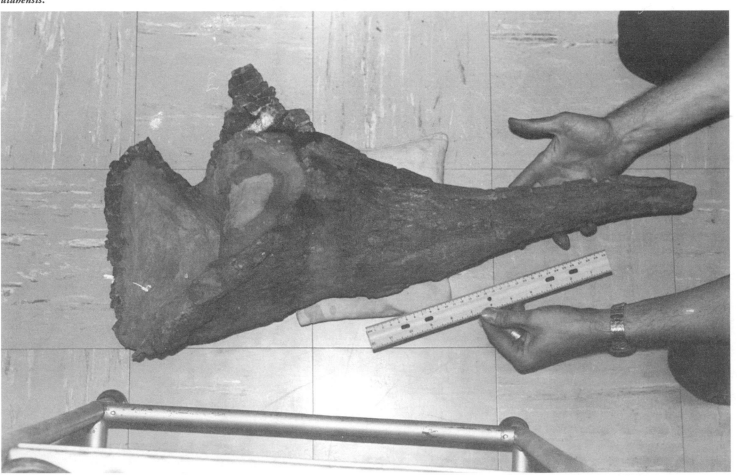

Photograph by Robert A. Long and Samuel P. Welles (neg. #73/200-15), courtesy National Museum of Natural History, Smithsonian Institution.

that there was no justification to differentiate this species from the type species *T. latus*, which is known from Wyoming, Montana, South Dakota, and possibly Saskatchewan (see *D:TE*).

Later, Lehman (1996) reevaluated the status of *T. utahensis*. Lehman (1996) observed that the relatively short and broad squamosal and short parietal of *T. utahensis* suggest that this species had a much shorter frill than did the type species. Also, Lehman (1996) pointed out the geographic separation between this taxon and *T. latus*. Lehman (1996) concluded that, until better specimens are available to resolve the issue unequivocally, *T. utahensis* is best regarded as a distinct species.

More recently, Farke (1998), in a very brief preliminary report, utilized a shape-based morphometric analysis on a sample of eight squamosals and eight parietals from *Torosaurus* specimens in an attempt to determine the number of valid species belonging to this genus. Farke's analysis showed that two species— *T. latus* (known only from Wyoming, Montana, and South Dakota) and *T. utahensis* (known from Utah, New Mexico, Texas, South Dakota, Montana, and Saskatchewan)—are valid. According to Farke, *T. latus*

is characterized by a long, narrow squamosal, while this bone in *T. utahensis* is short and wide.

Note: Lehman will describe a new, very large *Torosaurus* skull measuring about 2.65 (about 9 feet) long (P. Dodson, personal communication 1998).

Key references: Dodson and Currie (1990); Farke (1998); Gilmore (1946*b*); Lawson (1976); Lehman (1990, 1996).

†TRICERATOPS

Ornithischia: Genasauria: Cerapoda: Marginocephalia: Ceratopsia: Neoceratopsia: Ceratopsomorpha: Ceratopsidae: Chasmosaurinae.

Comments: The chasmosaurine genus *Triceratops*, with its nonfenestrated frill, small nasal horn, and two long brow horns, is one of the most famous of all dinosaurs and certainly the best known ceratopsian, with 16 species having been referred to this large genus since it was named by Othniel Charles Marsh in 1889. In 1986, John H. Ostrom and Peter Wellnhofer consolidated all of the species of *Triceratops* into one valid taxon, *T. horridus*, these authors

Skull of *Triceratops horridus* found in sandstone also preserving (right) snail and clam fossils, exhibited at Dinofest™, 1998.

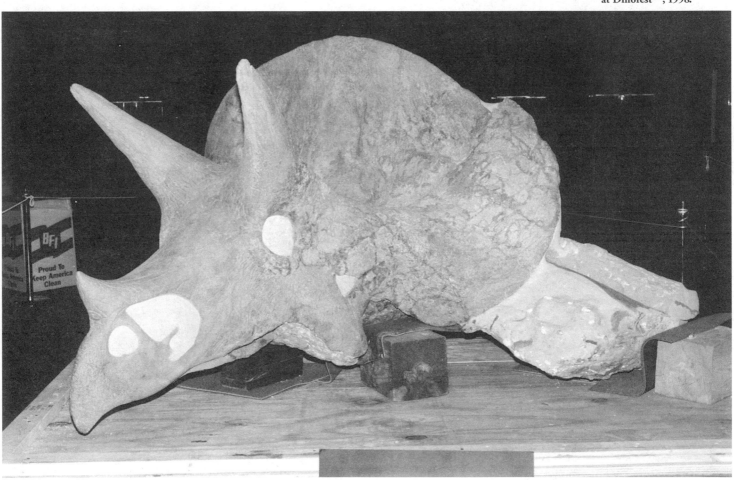

Photograph by the author.

Triceratops

Triceratops horridus, composite skeleton (AMNH 5116, 5039, 5045 and 5033) mounted with the front legs in a sprawling pose (compare with photograph on p. 356).

This study suggested to them that two separate populations, sharply divided by geographic location, of horn angles — narrow horns of 39 degrees ± 8 degrees, found in the Frenchman and Hell Creek Formations, originating from the northern range of *Triceratops*; and broad horns of 76 degrees ± 9 degrees, from the Lance and Laramie Formations and Denver Beds, originating from the southern range. The set of northern narrow horns includes adult, subadult, and juvenile specimens exhibiting positive allometry between basal length and nasal horncore width, although the angle does not change with ontogeny; southern group specimens were previously regarded as sexually dimorphic based upon brown horn analysis. As allometry and sexual dimorphism could not explain divergent nasal horncore angles, Happ and Morrow proposed two distinct species of *Triceratops* to explain the two allopatric populations, with two subgroups within each geographic region possibly attributed to sexual dimorphism.

Yet another independent study was conducted by Farke (1997), utilizing bivariate plot analysis, to examine variation and sexual dimorphism in the genus *Triceratops*. This method — forms of which had previously been used to determine sexual dimorphism in *Protoceratops* (see Dodson 1976) and to clarify the systematics within the ceratopsid subfamily Centrosaurinae (Dodson 1990*b*) — "analyzes a specimen's position on a scatter graph relative to the line of best fit." Farke's study was based upon a variety of specimens collected from both the Hell Creek Formation and Lance Formation.

Farke's findings proved to be consistent with Forster's — that two valid species (*T. horridus* and *T. prorsus*), largely separated by formation (*T. prorsus* most common in the Hell Creek Formation, *T. horridus* most common in the Lance Formation), probably exist within *Triceratops*, although Farke disagreed with several of Forster's species assignments: Farke scored FMNH 12003, YPM 1823, and SVMP P62/1/1 as belonging to the species *T. prorsus*, as opposed to Forster's identification of these specimens as *T. horridus*.

Following this analysis, Farke determined the following differences between the two species: Orbital horncores longer and more erect, and relatively farther apart, in *T. horridus* than in *T. prorsus*; crest longer, wider, and taller in *T. horridus*; generally, nasal horn slightly longer in *T. prorsus*; and rostrum with "reversed S-shaped rostral margin" in *T. horridus*, with "smoothly convex rostral margin" in *T. prorsus* (see Forster), these differences probably reflecting dietary differences (larger individual plant leaves in the Hell Creek Formation suggesting a lusher habitat with more rainfall than the Lance, this, however, based on

emphasizing the great degrees of individual variation within a single species, but not taking into account variations due to sexual dimorphism. Four years later, Thomas H. Lehman (1990) suggested criteria by which chasmosaurine skulls can be differentiated according to sex, after which Catherine A. Forster (1996), utilizing cladistics and morphometrics, divided the genus *Triceratops* into two valid species, *T. horridus* and *T. prorsus* (see *Triceratops* entry, *D:TE*).

In a more recent preliminary report, Happ and Morrow (1996) reached their own conclusions regarding distinction of species in *Triceratops*, based on their analysis of 22 nasal horncores for horn angle.

Triceratops prorsus skeleton (LACM 7207/118118; skull cast of LACM 7207/59049, see *D:TE*), mounted with the front legs posed to reflect a semi-erect stance.

only a relatively small sampling of fossil plant specimens; K. Johnson, personal communication 1996 to Farke).

The posture and stance of *Triceratops*, as well as other ceratopsids, has been a subject of discussion and argument among paleontologists for about a century. During that time, this large horned dinosaur has been reconstructed with its front legs positioned in various ways, including totally erect as in large mammals such as the rhinoceros (an idea first proposed by Marsh 1896; mostly championed in more recent decades by Bakker 1987 and Paul 1991), then sprawled out to the side in lizard fashion (Gilmore 1905; see *D:TE*), and a so-called semi-erect "reptilian high walk" (Farlow and Dodson 1975; Czerkas and Czerkas 1990).

One reason for the uncertainty regarding this posture, as pointed out by Burnham, Garstka and Hebdon (1996), and by Garstka and Burnham (1997), is that *Triceratops*, though known from abundant cranial specimens, had not been known from even partially articulated postcranial skeletons.

Dodson and Farlow (1997) noted that museums have often mounted display skeletons of *Triceratops*

(*e.g.*, composite skeleton AMNH 5116, 5039, 5045, and 5033) in the rather awkward pose of having fully-upright hindlegs and widely sprawling forelegs. However, in recent years, with dinosaurs being "modernized" to conform to new data and speculations, genera like *Triceratops* are often portrayed, in life restorations and some museum skeletal mounts, in an entirely upright rhinoceros-like stance (*e.g.*, cast of AMNH skeleton mounted at the Royal Tyrrell Museum of Palaeontology). For the last couple of decades or more, this mammalian-type interpretation has been advocated and perpetuated by a number of paleontologists and "paleo-artists" (*e.g.*, Mark Hallett and Gregory S. Paul), primarily Robert T. Bakker, who in 1987 predicted that unequivocally ceratopsid trackway evidence would someday show that the manuses of these animals "were placed down under the body very close to the midline during locomotion."

Only a few years later, Bakker's prediction seemed to have been validated, at least in part, by *Ceratopsipes goldenensis*, the name given by Lockley and Hunt (1995) to the first fossil dinosaur tracks (holotype CU-MWC 220.1, plaster cast of a pedal track

Triceratops

Photograph by the author, courtesy Royal Tyrrell Museum/Alberta Community Development.

Triceratops horridus, cast of the American Museum of Natural History's mounted skeleton, posed with its front legs positioned fully upright.

which is part of the trackway figured by Lockley 1986; also, referred specimens, representing both front and hind feet) unequivocally assigned to the Ceratopsidae (possibly *Triceratops* itself), from the Laramie Formation, near Denver, Colorado.

Lockley and Hunt diagnosed the type species of this ichnogenus, *C. goldenensis*, as follows: Large quadrupedal dinosaur track differing from all others in having four blunt pedal impressions and four manual digit impressions; pedal imprint approximately twice size of manual imprint; manual impressions with more concave posterior margins than pedal impressions.

According to Lockley and Hunt, if the hind limb of the *Ceratopsipes* trackmaker was held erect while the forelimbs sprawled, it could be predicted that 1. the manual prints would be somewhat lateral to the pedal prints, and 2. the trackway would be wider (at least relative to the manual impressions) than for other

totally erect-walking dinosaurs (*e.g.,* sauropods). The manual print of *Ceratopsipes* is anterolateral to the pedal impression (not close to the midline, as Bakker believed), and the lateral position of the former lies within the range of variation shown by trackways of dinosaurs known to have undoubtedly erect forelimb posture; the manual prints are located slightly more laterally than in some sauropod and ankylosaur trackways, but more medial than some alleged prosauropod tracks; also, no evidence was found that the manus prints are located further from the midline than are manus prints in the trackways of other large quadrupedal dinosaurs.

Lockley and Hunt were of the opinion that a sprawling forelimb posture during locomotion in large ceratopsids like *Triceratops* was inconsistent with the evidence of the *Ceratopsipes* trackways, leaving the options of 1. a mammalian type posture, with forelimbs entirely erect (*e.g.,* Bakker), and 2. a reptilian or crocodilian high walk posture (*e.g.,* Czerkas and Czerkas 1990). As the relation of the manus prints in *Ceratopsipes* is within the range of variation observed with dinosaurs with fully erect forelimbs, the authors considered it most parsimonious to conclude that the trackmaker held its forelimbs fully erect.

Furthermore, Lockley and Hunt speculated that the osteological evidence, presumably suggesting a sprawling forelimb posture during locomotion (as suggested by Gilmore), might have other significance related to the relatively large size and massiveness of the dinosaur's head. Considerable stresses would have been imposed upon the forelimbs during cranial rotation for display or low browsing (*e.g.,* Farlow and Dodson 1975). Perhaps, the authors further speculated, animals like *Triceratops* spent much of their time feeding with their forelimbs sprawled out to support their heads.

Additional evidence regarding this matter came from recently recovered skeletal remains. Burnham *et al.* reported the collection in 1994, from the Hell Creek Formation of North Dakota, of two well-preserved, remarkably articulated *Triceratops* skeletons. One skeleton, nicknamed "Willy," offers an articulated dorsal view, the vertebral column made rigid by ossified tendons; "Raymond," the other specimen, furnishes an articulated lateral view. According to Burnham *et al.*, a narrow chest and upright forelimbs are indicated by the position of the glenoid, curve of the coracoid, and flattened, almost straight anterior ribs.

Garstka and Burnham regarded both skeletons — "Willy" (WFQ:9309) and "Raymond" (WFQ:WRG 94.014) — as belonging to *T. horridus,* and representing the best articulations known belonging to this species. The "Willy" specimen possesses an articulated pelvis with seven dorsal vertebrae, with the right leg buckled underneath with a set of three articulated metatarsals and an associated ulna. "Raymond" has a disarticulated skull, vertebral column articulated from the syncervical to the pelvis with the right ribcage in place, and the complete and articulated right shoulder and forelimb, and right hind limb.

From their study of these two specimens, Garstka and Burnham reached the following conclusions: 1. Scapulocoracoids of *T. horridus* were oriented almost vertically; shoulders were narrow and set anterior to ribcage; 2. forelimbs were near vertical, but probably slightly splayed to be consistent with narrow shoulder width, and because forelimb prints [in the *C. goldenensis* trackway] are slightly more widely spaced than hind-limb prints; 3. vertebral column was anterior to pelvis in S-shaped cantilever arrangement hung from pelvis by means of ossified tendons (as in hadrosaurs); 4. manus was digitigrade, pes plantigrade (consistent with the *C. goldenensis* trackway and as also in hadrosaurs); 5. ilia and sacrum were level or tipped slightly forward to support cantilever vertebral column; tail possibly curved over the back, but not mobile and not dragged.

Farlow and Dodson offered their own interpretations of the *C. goldenensis* tracks. The authors noted that the width of this trackway is 1.25 meters (almost 4.25 feet) wide, that (*contra* Bakker) the manus prints lie outside the pes prints, and that the axis of the manus prints apparently diverges from the line of travel. As the hips of these dinosaurs are wider than the shoulders, then it should not be expected in an animal with parasagittal posture that the manus prints should fall outside the line of the pes prints, nor that the manus prints should be turned outward. Observing the anatomy of large mammals for comparison, the authors concluded that inferences of posture, based upon ceratopsid skeletal anatomy, offers the more correct basis for the forelimb posture in ceratopsids than do footprints, and that the *C. goldenensis* tracks confirm a complex forelimb posture and contradict a simple upright posture.

Later, Dodson and Farlow (1997) pointed out that examination of the shoulder and upper arm region

A herd of galloping *Triceratops horridus* depicted with upright-positioned front legs. Such rhinoceros-like locomotion in large ceratopsians is a controversial issue among vertebrate paleontologists.

Illustration by Gregory S. Paul (from *Predatory Dinosaurs of the World*). Copyright © 1988 G. S. Paul.

of the ceratopsid forelimb creates a serious anatomical problem — "a large, inward-directed flange of bone on the proximal end of the humerus that would dig uncomfortably into the side of the dinosaur if the humerus had been held vertically. In order for this process to clear the ribcage, at least some outward angling of the humerus was necessary."

Dodson and Farlow quoted at length Sternberg (1927) and Osborn (1933), both of whom had expressed, decades earlier, their frustration over failing to mount large ceratopsid skeletons with entirely upright forelimbs, while at the same time articulating the head of the humerus with its corresponding glenoid cavity (the head being on the outside of the proximal end, rather than on the end, as it is with most other kinds of dinosaurs). Dodson and Farlow simply put it this way: "It is impossible to reconstruct ceratopsid skeletons in rhinoceros-like parasagittal posture with steel pipe and rod, but it is possible to do so on paper and canvas."

Considering the apparently contradictory evidence of the *C. goldenensis* footprints, Dodson and Farlow cautioned that correctly interpreting the trackway requires other detailed information not necessarily offered by the trackway itself, including the overall size and body proportions of the animal that made the tracks. According to Dodson and Farlow, this trackway does not provide conclusive evidence for an erect forelimb, and also may not contradict at least a slight sprawl of the ceratopsid forelimb. However, the degree of the outward angle taken by the trackmaker's humerus depends on various unknown factors including the length of the humerus, width across the hips, and width across the shoulders compared to that across the hips.

Dodson and Farlow further stated that, if the trackmaking animal's hip and shoulder widths were equal, or if the shoulder width was less than that of the hip (as it is in *Triceratops* and other ceratopsids), then manus prints could only be located farther than pes prints from the midline of the trackway in one of three ways: 1. part of the forelimb (probably the humerus) angled away from the trackmaker's the midline; 2. the hind limb angled inward, while the forelimb was directed straight downward, or 3. some compromise of possibilities 1. and 2. However, if shoulder width was greater than hip width (which it is not in ceratopsids), then the manus prints could be positioned farther from the midline than the pes prints, with both front and hind limbs held erect.

Goodwin, Clemens and Horner (1997) briefly discussed sutural contacts, morphological variation, and growth patterns in *Triceratops*, based upon new data observed in the skull (UCMP 154452) of an immature *Triceratops*, found by Harley J. Garbani in the

Hell Creek Formation of Garfield County, Montana, this specimen preserving the basioccipital, exoccipital, dentary, and surangular.

The following was observed by Goodwin *et al.* in UCMP 154452: Skull elements displaying highly vascular matrix of primary, woven bone; parietal and squamosals with overlapping sutures delineated by bony ridge; postorbital with horncore of 4 centimeters in length preserved above orbit; parietal midline marked by four raised prominences radiating posterolaterally from postorbitals and onto squamosals.

From the above specimen, and also two previously undescribed *Triceratops* skulls documenting later ontogenetic stages of development (the intermediate-sized UCMP 136306 and larger UCMP 113697), Goodwin *et al.* observed the following growth-related features: In UCMP 154452, lateral and posterior margins of squamosals and parietals with scalloped edge; each squamosal with minimum of five scallops and parietal with seven, one spanning midline; in UCMP 136306, well-defined scallops along frill margin; scallops much reduced in UCMP 113697; none of these three skulls showing separate ossifications on frill despite pronounced development of scalloped margin in juveniles (see also Goodwin 1998 for a brief follow-up report on this study).

Happ and Morrow (1997) briefly discussed the taphonomic history of a specimen of a subadult (estimated total length of animal to be about 3.3 meters or 11 feet) *Triceratops*, collected from the Hell Creek Formation, near Jordan, Montana. The specimen includes a partial parietal, left squamosal, and a disarticulated postorbital horncore that was found in close proximity to the other elements. Apparently the remains were buried during a flood event in fine-grained sediment that also preserved skin impressions from the left squamosal and parietal areas.

As observed by Happ and Morrow (1997), an epoccipital at the posterior edge of the squamosal reveals, in fine detail, a tooth impression made by a stout, blunt tooth having a dozen regularly spaced vertical ridges and possibly corresponding to a goniopholidid tooth, a rare crocodilian known from the Hell Creek Formation. The horncore shows four to five circular tooth impressions comparing favorably in size and position with those made in soft clay by the left maxillary of a recent *Alligator mississippiensis* skull, the latter belonging to an individual with a skull length of 53 centimeters (21 inches) and body length of 3.3 meters (11 feet). Along the line of the tooth impressions Happ and Morrow (1997) saw evidence of severe bone crushing requiring significant biting force, the most severe of which corresponds to the base of the crocodilian jaw. Happ and Morrow (1997) pointed out that this *Triceratops* specimen is approximately the size as an adult wildebeest, an African mammal known to suffer attacks by crocodilians at sources of drinking water.

Numerous small toothmarks made by small theropod dinosaurs on the parietal surface of the skull suggested to Happ and Morrow (1997) that the specimen had been scavenged before burial — a rather quick burial, as evidenced by the preservation of integument.

Errata: The *Triceratops* skeleton shown in the photograph on p. 14 of *D:TE* belongs to the species *T. prorsus*, not *T. horridus*; the vertebrae of *?Triceratops maximus* figured on p. 927 of that volume was printed inverted.

Key references: Bakker (1986); Burnham, Garstka and Hebdon (1996); Czerkas and Czerkas (1990); Dodson and Farlow (1997); Farke (1997); Farlow and Dodson (1975, 1996); Forster (1996); Garstka and Burnham (1997); Gilmore (1905); Goodwin (1998); Goodwin, Clemens and Horner (1997); Happ and Morrow (1996, 1997); Lehman (1990); Lockley and Hunt (1995); Marsh (1889, 1896); Ostrom and Wellnhofer (1986); Paul (1991).

†TROODON

Saurischia: Theropoda: Neotheropoda: Tetanurae: Avetheropoda: Coelurosauria: Manuraptoriformes: Arctometatarsalia: Bullatosauria: Troodontidae.

Comments: In a preliminary report, Horner and Varrichio (1997) announced that fossil eggs from the Two Medicine Formation of Montana, containing embryonic skeletons originally identified as belonging to the small ornithischian dinosaur *Orodromeus makelai*, have, after further preparation and examination of the material, been correctly identified as belonging to the theropod *Troodon formosus*. The authors explained that the earlier misidentification was influenced by "some unusual tooth morphology including cylindrical tooth roots, and antero-posteriorly symmetrical tooth crowns with no serrations."

Horner and Varrichio observed in these tiny skeletons maxillary, pelvic, and femoral similiarities to *Troodon*, also humeri with distinct deltopectoral crests identical to juvenile and adult specimens of that genus. Contrary to findings resulting from an earlier study, the authors noted that the absence of the fourth trochanter of the femur is not an ontogenetic feature, but instead a normal theropod condition. Also, the metatarsals of the embryonic specimens are distinctive in having proportions similar to those of adults.

Based on these new interpretations, the authors cautioned that all previous writings concerning eggs and embryos from the Egg Mountain and Willow Creek Anticline localities, and referred to *O. makelai*, actually relate to *T. formosus*.

Another early report regarding *Troodon* eggs and nests was presented by Varrichio, Jackson, Borkowski and Horner (1997a, 1997b), who pointed out that crocodilians and birds share several reproductive features ("assembly-line oviducts, hard-shelled eggs, and some parental care"), but also that the reproductive styles of these two groups of animals also differ significantly, providing disparate models for comparison with dinosaurs.

In a statistical analysis of *Troodon* egg clutches, Varrichio *et al.* (1997a, 1997b) confirmed that this theropod laid eggs in a paired arrangement — two simultaneously. This pairing of eggs, and also the size, shape, and microstructure of the eggs, indicated that *Troodon* retained two functional and birdlike oviducts. According to Varrichio *et al.* (1997a, 1997b), the dinosaur laid two eggs at daily or greater intervals, creating a clutch of eggs in days' to weeks' time.

One well-preserved *Troodon* nest, Varrichio *et al.* (1997a) noted, includes "24 half-buried eggs, tightly placed within a shallow open bowl with a raised rim"; another clutch includes "an adult *Troodon* in direct contact with the eggs," this apparently suggesting that *Troodon*, like *Oviraptor* (see entry), "incubated eggs without egg rotation using a combination of soil and direct body contact."

From the evidence derived from this nest, Varrichio *et al.* (1997a) deduced that nonavian coelurosaurian theropods possess several primitive features seen in crocodilians ("hard eggs, lack of egg rotation and chalaza [in an egg, one of two spiral tissue bands, connecting yolk to lining membrane], two functional ovaries/oviducts, some burial of eggs") and several derived features also seen in birds ("large eggs, loss of egg rotation, one egg produced per oviduct per day, brooding").

Key references: Horner and Varrichio (1997); Varrichio, Jackson, Borkowski, and Horner (1997a, 1997b).

†TYRANNOSAURUS — (=*Clevelanotyrannus, Dynamosaurus, Jenghiskan, Maleevosaurus, Manospondylus, Nanotyrannus, Tarbosaurus*)

Saurischia: Theropoda: Neotheropoda: Tetanurae: Avetheropoda; Coelurosauria: Manuraptoriformes: Arctometatarsalia: Tyrannosauridae: Tyrannosaurinae.

Comments: *Tyrannosaurus*, the largest known tyrannosaurid theropod, continues to be a major source of interest among dinosaur paleontologists as well as the public. Its gigantic head, very long teeth, and diminutive, two-fingered forelimbs are familiar images to scientist and layman alike, with the animal itself having taken on mythic status in our collective

Cast of the holotype skull (CMNH 7541) of *Nanotyrannus lancensis*, formerly referred to *Gorgosaurus lancensis*, now believed by many (though not all) paleontologists to represent a juvenile *Tyrannosaurus rex*.

consciousness. For many years represented by only a few reasonably substantial specimens, the type species, *Tyrannosaurus rex*, is now known from at least 23, including some that had previously been described as distinct genera and species.

Both *Nanotyrannus* and *Maleevosaurus*, tyrannosaurid genera formerly regarded as valid (see individual entries, *D:TE*), were recently referred by Carr (1996), in a preliminary report, to *Tyrannosaurus* (although Robert T. Bakker, one of the authors of *Nanotyrannus*, maintains that this is a valid genus and that its holotype represents an adult individual).

Nanotyrannus was named and described by Bakker, Williams and Currie (1988), founded on a well-preserved, almost complete skull (CMNH 7541) collected in 1942 by David H. Dunkle from the Lance Formation at Sand Creek, in Carter County, eastern Montana, this skull having first been described by Gilmore (1946a) as "*Gorgosaurus*" *lancensis*. Bakker *et al.* observed that this skull resembled *Tyrannosaurus* more than it did *Gorgosaurus*. Furthermore, the authors identified the skull as that of a new genus of "pygmy tyrannosaur" (though so small an advanced tyrannosaurid occurring that late in the Cretaceous

was unusual), having a narrow snout and wide posterior region, the orbits being directed forwardly to allow for binocular vision.

Maleevosaurus was named by Carpenter (1992), founded upon an almost complete, relatively small tyrannosaurid skeleton (PIN 552-2) collected from the Nemegt Formation at Tsagan Ula, Mongolian People's Republic, and originally named *Gorgosaurus novojilovi* by Maleev (1955). Rozhdestvensky (1965) believed this species to be a juvenile *Tyrannosaurus* [= *Tarbosaurus* of his usage] *bataar*.

Despite their relatively smaller sizes, both *Nanotyrannus* and *Maleevosaurus* were regarded as adults by Bakker *et al.* and Carpenter, respectively, these authors citing various features apparently attesting to the maturity of the type specimens. However, as pointed out by Carr, adult and juvenile tyrannosaurids can be distinguished by such criteria as the following: 1. Degree of pneumatization by antorbital and basisphenoidal air sacs into surrounding elements; 2. shift from gracile to robust morphotypes; 3. relative width to length ratios of anterior lateral teeth; and 4. degree of development or ornamental excrescences. Carr's assessments of the above taxa were based upon the pattern of ontogenetic changes seen in the well-represented tyrannosaurid species *Gorgosaurus* [=*Albertosaurus* of his usage] *libratus*.

Carr observed a number of features in CMNH 7541 conforming to those observed in juveniles of *G. libratus*, these including: Snout low, elongate; orbit large, round; antorbital fossa shallow, extending anteriorly to maxillary fenestra; basisphenoid pneumatopores reduced, anteroventral; first maxillary tooth incisiform; anterior lateral teeth bladelike; nasal and postorbital rugosities reduced.

According to Carr, the holotype skull of *N. lancensis* shares with adult *Tyrannosaurus* specimens these features: 1. Premaxillary supranarial processes appressed for entire length; 2. antorbital fossa reaching nasal suture; 3. reduced contribution of jugal to antorbital fenestra; and 4. anterior basisphenoid plate posteriorly displaced.

Carr concluded that the type specimen of "*G.*" *lancensis* represents a juvenile *T. rex* (although the authors of *Nanotyrannus*, to date of this writing, remain unconvinced of this synonymy), while, for similar reasons, that of *G. novojilovi* represents a juvenile *Tyrannosaurus* [=*Tarbosaurus* of his usage] *bataar*. Holtz (1997), in a new preliminary analysis of the Tyrannosauridae, agreed that *Nanotyrannus* and *Maleevosaurus* share several derived cranial features with species of *Tyrannosaurus* that are consistent with the proposal that these two taxa are juveniles of, respectively, *T. rex* and *T. bataar*.

Regarding *Nanotyrannus* as a young *T. rex*, Carr and Essner (1997) compared further the morphological disparity between juvenile and adult tyrannosaurids. Thin-plate spline (TPS) analysis resulted in a summary of ontogenetic changes and allowed for the quantifying of the deformation between CMNH 7541 and various adult specimens of *T. rex*.

Carr and Essner observed the following: Though *T. rex* individuals supposedly have short and deep skulls, this effect is really an artifact of the transversely and vertically expanded adductor chamber, which also reorients the orbital region, producing the effect of anteroposterior narrowing in side view; also in side view, the ventral region of the maxilla deepens posteroventrally, further modifying the profile of the skull. In dorsal view, the frontals are short anteriorly and expanded laterally to accommodate the medially encroaching lacrimals. Among changes to the occipital plate were "a dorsoventral shallowing of the occipital condyle and medial resorption of the dorsal process of the supraoccipital by deep and invasive muscle insertions," therefore resulting in a dorsally forked bone.

More information regarding details of the skull of *Tyrannosaurus rex* resulted from the study of the skeleton (BHI 3033) informally called "STAN," a specimen including an almost complete but disarticulated skull. The specimen was collected during the 1990s in South Dakota by the Black Hills Institute of Geological Research, Inc., a commercial fossil-

Photograph by the author, courtesy Natural History Museum of Los Angeles County.

Skeleton (cast) of *Tyrannosaurus bataar* (formerly *Tarbosaurus bataar*), part of the "Great Russian Dinosaurs Exhibition," original specimen collected from the Nemegt Formation, Late Cretaceous (late Campanian–early Maastrichtian), Gobi Desert, southern People's Republic of Mongolia.

Tyrannosaurus

Photograph by the author, courtesy American Museum of Natural History.

Among the most famous of all dinosaur specimens, skeleton (AMNH 5027) of *Tyrannosaurus rex* as reprepared and remounted in a correct horizontal posture. Collected in Montana in 1908 by American Museum of Natural History paleontologist Barnum Brown, this skeleton — the third *T. rex* to be found and one of the only real specimens of this species on exhibit — originally stood upright, with incorrect three-fingered hands and about 3 meters of extra tail vertebrae (see *D:TE*). The skull (the original displayed separately) shows a facial abscess; the skeleton exhibits signs of possible injury or disease (broken then healed ribs, and fused cervical and dorsal vertebrae).

collecting firm. According to the Black Hills Institute's Neal L. Larson (1998), preparation by staff members revealed that the palpebral and "horns," the latter possibly analogous to prefrontals, were really distinct elements, unattached in this specimen, with sutures between them and the underlying bones. ("STAN" was mounted at the Black Hills Institute in a way to facilitate easy dismantling and reassembling for display in other locations.)

Although there has been much speculation offered in technical journals and popular publications about the biology and possible life style of *Tyrannosaurus*, little is actually known concerning these topics. Research, however, continues.

In 1995, Mary Higby Schweitzer reported the discovery of heme-bearing proteins and hemoglobin breakdown products in extracts of *T. rex* bony tissues. Noting that hemoglobin can be an indicator of physiology and metabolic rates, Schweitzer found these compounds and breakdown products after pursuing five different lines of study (see *D:TE*).

Subsequently, Schweitzer, Marshall, Carron, Bohle, Arnold, Buss and Starkey (1996); Marshall,

Barnard and Schweitzer (1996); and Schweitzer, Marshall, Barnard, Bohle, Carron, Arnold and Starkey (1997) reported on a sixth line of evidence, conducted in the spring of 1990, pointing to the presence of heme-containing compounds and breakdown products in *T. rex*. Utilizing a combination of physical chemistry and biomechanical techniques, minute amounts of what may be ancient proteins were found in a very well-preserved, fairly complete articulated *T. rex* specimen (MOR 555) collected in 1990 from the Hell Creek Formation in east-central Montana by personnel from the Museum of the Rockies. Rats were then injected with extracts prepared from trabecular tissues of *T. rex* to stimulate an antibody response. When the antiserum generated by the rats was tested against purified turkey hemoglobins, strong antibody-antigen binding was detected. According to Marshall *et al.*, Schweitzer *et al.* (1996), and Schweitzer *et al.* (1997), this and the other avenues of research suggest the presence of blood-derived hemoglobin compounds preserved in these *T. rex* samples.

The first evidence that tyrannosaurids suffered from the gout — a metabolic disorder resulting in nonarticular, sphere-shaped erosions in bone — was reported by Rothschild, Tanke and Carpenter (1997*a*, 1997*b*). Such evidence, in the form of uniformly excavated erosive lesions characteristic of gout, was observed in two of many examined specimens of *T. rex* — a cast of metacarpal I of the right forearm of the skeleton popularly known as "Sue" (see below), and a partial tyrannosaurid pedal proximal phalanx (I-1) (RTMP 92.36.328) from Dinosaur Provincial Park, Alberta, referable to *Albertosaurus*, *Gorgosaurus*, or *Daspletosaurus* (Rothschild *et al.* 1997*b*).

Rothschild *et al.* (1997*b*) noted that gouty arthritis has been seen rarely in crocodilians, lizards, turtles, and only in 1–5 percent of some birds. Factors contributing to this condition in humans include renal failure, dehydration, and the ingestion of foods with high purine content (*e.g.*, red meat). As envisioned by Rothschild *et al.* (1997*a*), "Caricatures of the aging and ill-temper of those afflicted with gout are magnified by its recognition in *Tyrannosaurus rex*."

Schweitzer, Johnson, Zocco, Horner and Starkey (1997) analyzed some exceptionally well-preserved

bone tissues taken from specimen MOR 555, an almost complete skeleton of *T. rex* collected in spring, 1990, by the Museum of the Rockies from the Hell Creek Formation of McCone County, Montana. The fine condition of this relatively unaltered material seems to be the result of the very dense cortical bone which surrounds the cancellous bone tissues, protecting these tissues from water infiltration and mineral disposition. By studying these cancellous tissues, the authors tested two main hypotheses: 1. Bony tissues of this specimen show only minimal signs of permineralization or replacement, and 2. lack of extreme diagenetic alteration of bony tissues may have allowed for the preservation of some indigenous molecules. The tests performed by Schweitzer *et al.* (1997) did not demonstrate conclusively that either hypothesis is correct, but none showed the contrary, most tests instead supporting each hypothesis.

Analyses by Schweitzer *et al.* (1997) of these tissues for amino acid content produced ratios similar to those found in the bones of modern horses and ostriches. Other analyses found evidence suggesting the

Skeleton of *Tyrannosaurus bataar* mounted at Dinofest™ 1989 so as to portray this giant dinosaur as an active predator, pursuing the large ornithomimid *Gallimimus bullatus*. (In 1992, Kenneth Carpenter referred the Asian species *Tarbosaurus bataar* to *Tyrannosaurus*, a synonymy some workers are now questioning.)

Photograph by the author.

Tyrannosaurus

Two *Tyrannosaurus rex* individuals portrayed as active, rapidly moving animals.

presence of remnants of collagen type I, the primary protein in bone. The analyzed tissues were also found to contain numerous biomolecules — molecules pertaining to life — some of them probably contaminants, although the presence of collagen type I suggests that some of these molecules are of dinosaurian origin.

Studies in molecular paleontology such as the above may yet be in their pioneering stages. As pointed out by Schweitzer *et al.* (1997): "Biomolecules such as DNA and proteins carry abundant information about an organism, and can provide important clues to its evolutionary relationships and physiology."

One question regarding the life style of *Tyrannosaurus* continues to be asked: Was this theropod an active predator, a scavenger, or both? Holtz (1998) addressed this controversy again in a brief report, citing some of the lines of evidence used to support the position that *Tyrannosaurus* was incapable of killing its own prey — 1. eyes of small size, 2. femur longer than tibia, 3. arms too short, and 4. teeth too thick.

Holtz (1998) countered the above arguments as follows: 1. *Tyrannosaurus'* eyes are not unexpectedly small, as (in dinosaurs and other animals) orbital size does not increase as rapidly as the rest of the face as total skull size increases, without apparent loss of visual ability. 2. Tyrannosaurids possess a tibia and metatarsus that are longer and more slender than those of any other large theropod as well as contemporary herbivores (*e.g.*, hadrosaurs and ceratopsians), these proportions and the special stress-absorbing arctometatarsalian condition of the pes suggesting that *Tyrannosaurus* was more specialized for running than its potential prey. 3. Tyrannosaurid arms, though short, were powerful (see *Tyrannosaurus* entry, *D:TE*), though they were probably not primary weapons in

acquiring prey. 4. The thick teeth and well-developed ossified secondary palate suggest that the skulls of *Tyrannosaurus* and other tyrannosaurids were specialized to resist twisting forces.

According to Holtz (1998), comparisons with suites of adaptations among other predators suggest that dinosaurs like *Tyrannosaurus* were not hawklike or catlike hunters, which ambush their prey primarily utilizing their claws, but possibly, as with wolves and hyenas, overtook their prey and killed them primarily with their jaws, the forelimbs, if used at all, being utilized only to stabilize the prey. Interpretating the data as supporting the concept that *Tyrannosaurus* was a predator and finding no data to support this dinosaur's portrayal as an obligate scavenger, Holtz (1998) also found no evidence to contradict the idea that tyrannosaurids were also opportunistic scavengers. "Indeed, particular individuals, growth stages, regional populations, or even species of tyrannosaurid may have obtained more food by scavenging than by predation (although it may be impossible to determine this from the evidence)."

Information relating to the diet and feeding habits of dinosaurs like *T. rex* has resulted from recent studies such as that of fossilized dung by Karen Chin, a specialist in the area of coprolites. Chin (1996*b*) reported a very large coprolite (the largest single phosphatic coprolite known to date) found in a bentonitic mudstone of the Frenchman Formation (Maastrichtian) of Saskatchewan, Canada, within 10 meters of the Cretaceous–Tertiary boundary. As described by Chin, the main body of the coprolite has an irregular morphology, being "an elongated, fractured mass that is approximately $44 \times 16 \times 13$ centimeters. About 200 small associated fragments apparently weathered off the larger mass and contributed to the original volume of the specimen, estimated at over 2 liters." *T. rex* was

"Dueling Dinosaurs"—
skeletons of *Tyrannosaurus
rex* (LACM 7244/23844,
most of postcrania cast from
RTMP specimen) and
Triceratops prorsus (LACM
7207/118118, skull cast of
MCM 7207/59049)—
mounted in a dynamic com-
bat pose.

the only likely candidate in the Frenchman Formation
to have produced such a large mass.

Mineralogical and petrographic analyses of the
specimen by Chin revealed that it contains bone fragments, indicating the consumption of large quantities
of bone not completely dissolved by stomach acids.
Chin noted that the fibro-lamellar microstructure of
the ingested skeletal fragments is characteristic of dinosaurs in general; their seeming lack of secondary
bone suggests a subadult; and the absence of lines of
arrested growth (LAGs) may indicate that the consumed animal was an ornithischian. As interpreted by
Chin, these data seem to indicate that the *T. rex* that
produced this fecal mass apparently possessed bone-
crunching capabilities and had fed upon a juvenile
?ornithischian.

Other studies have resulted in more specific information regarding the probable diet of *Tyrannosaurus*. Erickson and Olson (1996) noted that tooth
marks on carnivorous animals on fossil bones may not
only reveal the identity of the feeding animal, they can
also provide insights into the ecology, behavior, and
functional morphology of those taxa. Relatively un-

common have been reports of tooth marks attributable to *T. rex*: Carpenter (1988) saw healed wounds on
an *Edmontosaurus* caudal vertebra as evidence of a
failed attack by a *T. rex* on this duckbilled dinosaur;
and Horner and Lessem (1993) discussed a *Triceratops*
femur displaying punctures that could be teeth marks
attributable to a *T. rex*.

Erickson and Olson suggested that punctures in
a pelvis (sacrum and left ilium) referred to *Triceratops*
sp., found by Kenneth H. Olson in the Hell Creek
Formation of Montana, and in a proximal pedal phalanx (collected from the same general vicinity as the
Triceratops specimen) referred to *Edmontosaurus* sp.
(UCMP cast 140601, with five bite marks) were made
by *T. rex*.

Erickson and Olson suggested that the punctures
in the *Triceratops* specimen were produced by an adult
T. rex because of the large size of these marks (2.5
centimeters wide and 3.7 centimeters deep), rounded
cross sectional areas (unlike the more elliptical punctures
made by most nontyrannosaurid theropods), wide
spacing (more than 4 centimeters), and because some
bones have coarse serration marks on their periosteal

Skull (right lateral view) of the *Tyrannosaurus rex* specimen (FMNH PR 2081) nicknamed "Sue," before it was packed and shipped to its new permanent home, The Field Museum.

surfaces; because a cast of one of the deeper punctures matches the shape of a lateral tooth of an adult *T. rex*; and because *T. rex* is the only Hell Creek carnivorous animal large enough to have made such marks.

As described by Erickson and Olson, the bite marks on the *Edmontosaurus* specimen are *T. rex*–like, being broad and deep elongate furrows distributed axially on the dorsal and lateral surfaces of the bone, the largest furrow measuring 5.4 centimeters long and 0.9 centimeters deep. As these marks are deeper toward the proximal end of the phalanx, Erickson and Olson deduced that the *T. rex* was pulling away from the carcass when it made the furrows. No tooth-serration marks were seen on this specimen.

From the numerous bite marks on specimens of *Triceratops* and *Edmontosaurus*, Erickson and Olson concluded that, at least on some occasions, *T. rex* fed upon the two predominent large herbivores from the Hell Creek fauna; when feeding on large carcasses, *T. rex*, at least sometimes, produced deep, bone-penetrating bites, usually with its larger anterior lateral

teeth, which produced punctures or furrows, the latter indicative of "puncture and pull" biting; the anterior premaxillary teeth may have been used to nip or strip flesh away from the carcass, although these teeth caused little damage to the bones (as evidenced by shallow furrows on the *Triceratops* specimen); *T. rex* tooth serrations rarely marked impacted bones (unlike smaller theropods, whose more laterally compressed teeth left numerous serration marks; personal observation by Erickson and Olson); and teeth of this taxon were very strong, able to withstand the high forces incurred during bone impacts.

From the concentrated biting that occurred at the anterior portion of the *Triceratops* ilium, Erickson and Olson found it likely that the *T. rex* had ingested some bone while feeding, the consumption of bone — rich in calcium and potassium, nutrients not always available in flesh; see Richardson, Mundy and Plug (1986) — being normal for modern predators.

Erickson and Olson noted that the seeming rarity of *T. rex* bite marks "may be an artifact of collection and publication biases, the absence of systematic surveys for bite marks, a lack of knowledge of their appearance, bone consumption, loss of marks by degradation, and possible taphonomic biases."

The concept that *Tyrannosaurus* was an active predator that preyed upon *Triceratops* was dramatically reflected in a mounted skeletal display in spring, 1996, when the Natural History Museum of Los Angeles County unveiled its new "Dueling Dinosaurs" exhibit (see Harris 1996 for complete details). Some three decades earlier, between 1964 and 1969, museum preparator Harley J. Garbani, working in the Hell Creek Formation of Montana, had excavated, among other dinosaurian remains, a *Triceratops prorsus* skull and partial skeleton (LACM 7207/118118) and a *T. rex* disarticulated skull (then the largest and most complete skull known of this species) and hind foot (LACM 7244/23844), the latter specimen associated with additional limb bone fragments and vertebrae, some of which pertained to another smaller individual. The *T. rex* skull and foot and *T. prorsus* skull were put on exhibit in 1970 (as a preview for a planned Mesozoic hall). In the mid–1980s, the Los Angeles County museum traded a cast of its *T. rex* skull for one of a *T. rex* postcranial skeleton (RTMP 81.6.1, nicknamed "Black Beauty," found in 1981 by high school students near Crows Nest River, southern Alberta, and mounted at the Royal Tyrrell Museum of Palaeontology in 1992, the bones black due to the high concentration of manganese in the rocks where the specimen was found), both institutions thereby possessing a complete skeleton that could be mounted for display. In 1992, when the Los Angeles museum's exhibit of *Allosaurus fragilis* and *Camptosaurus dispar* skeletons (LACM 3719/46030) and 3719/46031, respectively; see *D:TE*) were relocated from its main foyer to another gallery, a large enough open space was released to exhibit both the *Tyrannosaurus* and *Triceratops*.

Museum model maker Michael Stokes suggested that the two skeletons be posed in a combat situation, with *Tyrannosaurus* attacking the horned dinosaur. The "Dueling Dinosaurs" skeletons were subsequently mounted by Research Casting International of Toronto under the direction of Peter May, formerly of the Royal Ontario Museum. Too heavy for the internal armatures supporting these skeletons, the massive skulls were replaced by resin casts of much lighter weight, the original skulls being exhibited, as they had been for more than two and one half decades, in another room where they can be viewed up close and studied. As mounted, the *Tyrannosaurus* skeleton contains approximately 15 percent bone, the *Triceratops* about 60 percent, the remaining percentage consisting of cast material.

As briefly recounted earlier (see *D:TE*) the then largest known and apparently female *T. rex* skeleton (approximately 85 percent complete, lacking the left arm, left foot, some vertebrae, and several dorsal ribs; originally catalogued as BHI 2033; now FMNH PR 2081) nicknamed "Sue" (after the specimen's discoverer, archaeologist and paleontologist Susan Hendrickson of the Black Hills Institute of Geological Research) had been seized by agents of the Federal Bureau of Investigation on May 14, 1992. Peter L. Larson and the Black Hills Institute were charged with violation of the antiquities act, theft of United States Government property, and theft of tribal property.

Since that time, this fine skeleton has remained in storage in government custody, unavailable to scientists, with most of the specimen left unstudied (see Dodson 1997 for a detailed history of the specimen, as well as commentary regarding the commercial collection and sale of vertebrate fossils found on private land).

Henrickson discovered the specimen on August 12, 1990. The controversy over the skeleton involved its collection that same year by the Black Hills Institute on private land belonging to Maurice Williams on his ranch near Faith, South Dakota. The ranch lay within the borders of the Cheyenne River Sioux reservation, Williams being a member of that tribe. The Black Hills Institute paid Williams $5,000, claiming that the fee was to collect, own, and possess full rights pertaining to the specimen. Williams, though, stated that the fee was only to allow the Institute to do fossil reconnaissance work on his land.

Although Black Hills Institute President Larson had claimed that the skeleton would not be sold abroad, but would rather be the centerpiece for his own museum in Hill City, South Dakota, fears and rumors persisted that "Sue" would end up gracing the home of some wealthy Japanese (or other foreign) businessman and be forever inaccessible for study. Also, Larson had contacted various vertebrate paleontologists, Peter Dodson among them, about eventually participating in a thorough monograph detailing all the elements of the specimen, a project that was prematurely terminated by the FBI's seizure of the specimen.

Complicating the situation, Williams' land had been held in trust by the Federal Government at the time of "Sue's" discovery. According to the United States Government, the specimen, under South Dakota law, had to be treated as "land." Therefore, Williams would have to be granted approval by the Secretary of the Interior for sale of any part of his trust land. As he did not seek approval regarding "Sue," Williams' sale to the Black Hills Institute was deemed null and void. Subsequently, Williams was granted permission to auction off parts of his "land." Thus, in

spring of 1997, "Sue" was offered to the highest bidders at Sotheby's Auction House (see [Anonymous] 1997b) in New York. With that, the specimen was in danger of possibly being lost to science forever, perhaps being sold to some wealthy private collector living on some foreign continent.

On the historic Saturday of October 4, 1997, The Field Museum in Chicago, backed with additional funds from both McDonald's restaurants and Disney Enterprises, outbid other museums and private collectors, purchasing the rocklike remains of "Sue" for $8,362,500 (including Sotheby's fees), the highest amount ever paid for a single fossil specimen. The skeleton will be prepared in public at the McDonald's Fossil Preparatory Laboratory, to be set up temporarily in The Field Museum's very spacious Stanley Field Hall (the same hall in which the museum's "*Gorgosaurus*"-*Lambeosaurus* skeletons had previously been displayed; see *Gorgosaurus* and *Daspletosaurus* entries; also, see various photos in *D:TE*) where, in the year 2000, it should be completely mounted. According to a museum spokesperson, "The original 'Sue' skeleton will become a permanent component of The Field Museum's world-class paleontology collections."

McDonald's and Disney will receive casts of the celebrated skeleton for display in their own exhibitions, the latter at Dinoland U.S.A. in Disney's Animal Kingdom, at Walt Disney World, Orlando, Florida.

As observed by Peter L. Larson (1997a) (he being one of the relatively few researchers to have any access to the skeleton before its confiscation), the "Sue" specimen revealed evidence that *T. rex*, on occasion, killed individuals of its own species. "Sue" died as the result of another *T. rex* tearing off the side of her face. "The left postorbital is torn and lies broken to the side. The rear of the lower jaw is pulled away from the skull and there are puncture marks along the crushed squamosal just the right size and positioned properly for the bite of another *T. rex*." Larson further noted that "Steven," a yet more recently collected *T. rex* skeleton (BHI 3033, mounted for display at the Black Hills Museum of Natural History, Hill City, South Dakota), has "the dorsal vertebrae chopped apart. The portions of the vertebrae containing the T-bone and tenderloin steaks were gone and many of the centra were bitten off entirely in half," evidence, according to Larson, of another *T. rex* versus *T. rex* encounter.

Notes: On February 19, 1998, newspapers, including Chicago's *Sun-Times*, published articles stating that a few bones representing other *T. rex* individuals, including "two leg bones of an adult male … a skull bone of a baby … and a skull bone" of a juvenile, had been shipped to The Field Museum along with the "Sue" specimen. Various vertebrate paleontologists (including Larson, Philip J. Currie of the Royal Tyrrell Museum of Palaeontology, and Robert T. Bakker of the Tate Museum of Wyoming's Casper College) were quoted in the article speculating that these additional remains could suggest that the individuals represented by the specimens comprised a family. Paleontologists at The Field Museum, however, remained cautious regarding preliminary assessments of this material. As stated by The Field Museum's William F. Simpson, "Sue's" alleged family consists of "just a couple of isolated bones," and any theory concerning them at this early stage is "very premature."

In 1997, news media reported the discovery on a Montana ranch of apparently the largest *Tyrannosaurus* skull yet known. As in the case of "Sue," ownership of the specimen — which was subsequently damaged by local vandals since its discovery — is, as of this writing, in question. According to these news reports, the specimen might represent a new species, supposedly exhibiting anatomical details differing from those of other *Tyrannosaurus* species. Reportedly its femur is more than one foot longer than that of "Sue." J. Keith Rigby, Jr., the University of Notre Dame vertebrate paleontologist who has seen this specimen, told the fan publication *Prehistoric Times* (issue number 27, 1997–98) that three more *Tyrannosaurus* specimens might be present at the discovery site.

Erratum: In *D:TE*, page 954, the photograph of the mounted skeleton of *T. rex* mounted by Kenneth Carpenter was not taken by the author, but rather supplied by the Ewell Sale Stewart Library, The Academy of Natural Sciences of Philadelphia.

Key references: [Anonymous] (1997b); Bakker, Williams and Currie (1988); Carpenter (1988, 1992); Carr (1996); Chin (1996b); Dodson (1997); Erickson and Olson (1996); Gilmore (1946a); Harris (1996); Holtz (1997, 1998); Horner and Lessem (1993); Larson (1997a); Maleev (1995); Marshall, Barnard and Schweitzer (1996); Rothschild, Tanke and Carpenter (1997a, 1997b); Rozhdestvensky (1965); Schweitzer (1995); Schweitzer, Johnson, Zocco, Horner and Starkey (1997); Schweitzer, Marshall, Barnard, Bohle, Carron, Arnold and Starkey (1997); Schweitzer, Marshall, Carron, Bohle, Arnold, Buss and Starkey (1996).

†ULTRASAUROS—(See *Supersaurus*.)

†UTAHRAPTOR

Saurischia: Theropoda: Neotheropoda: Tetanurae:
    Avetheropoda: Coelurosauria: Manuraptoriformes:

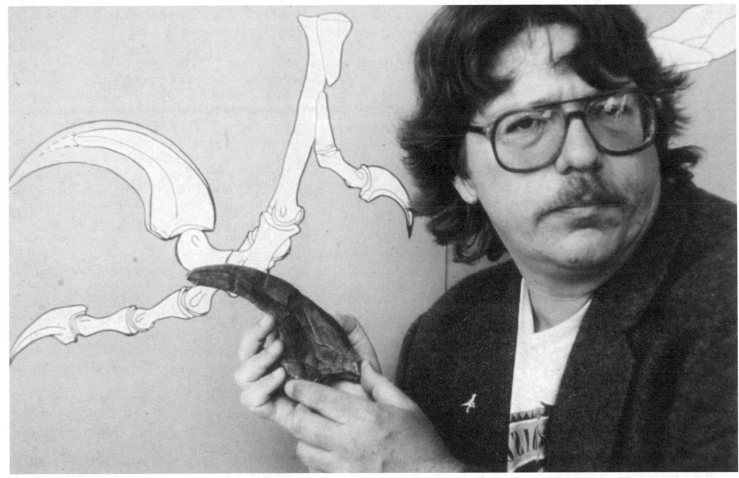

Paleontologist James I. Kirkland with the holotype (CEU 184v.86) second right pedal ungual of *Utahraptor ostrommaysi*, the giant dromaeosaurid theropod that he, Robert Gaston, and Donald Burge described in 1993.

Manuraptora: Eumanuraptora: Dromaeosauridae: Velociraptorinae.

Comments: As of this writing, the genus *Utahraptor* retains the distinction of being the largest known definite dromaeosaurid yet found.

As recounted by George Callison (1997), *Utahraptor*— now informally called the "Super Slasher"™— was discovered in 1992 during a joint research project between Dinamation International Society and the College of Eastern Utah, Prehistoric Museum. Amateur paleontologist Robert Gaston had led Dinamation paleontologist James I. Kirkland to a fossil site in the Cedar Mountain Formation of Utah to inspect some ankylosaur fossils the former had found there. The first remains of this very large dromaeosaurid, a giant claw bone, was found while excavations were underway to extract the armored dinosaur remains. Further digging led to the discovery of more dromaeosaurid material (see *D:TE*), with excavations and more discoveries continuing.

With rumors circulating in 1992 that large dromaeosaurid dinosaurs (inaccurately to be called *Velociraptor*) would be playing prominent roles in the major upcoming motion picture *Jurassic Park*, Dina-

mation International Corporation (see "Introduction," section on "Dinosaurs and the Public")—then the parent company of Dinamation International Society—considered adding a life-sized *Utahraptor* to their group of robotic prehistoric creatures.

As Callison recalled, Kirkland was contacted for his advice, which Dinamation International Corporation utilized in developing their visualization of this dinosaur. Dinamation designers began by comparing the sizes, shapes, and proportions of the known *Utahraptor* remains to those of more completely known dromaeosaurids such as *Deinonychus*, *Dromaeosaurus*, and *Velociraptor*. The shapes of the preserved premaxilla and lacrimal bones of *Utahraptor* aided in guessing what the size and shape of skull profile of this theropod may have been, while the tibiotarsus helped in the reconstruction of the size and segment proportions of the hind limb. With the skeleton of *Deinonychus* serving as a guide, and with the length estimated to be approximately 20 feet (almost 6 meters), Dinamation produced a projected recreation of the possible skeleton of *Utahraptor*. As new bones continued to be found, adjustments were made on the hypothetical skeleton.

Various scenarios were considered in which to place the robotic *Utahraptor*, Dinamation International Corporation's designers finally settling upon one with the dinosaur eating its already dismembered prey, and in the presence of two small mammals. According to Callison, "We proposed to use this basic stance and to then add a base cover of bones and the accent of 2 tiny multituberculate mammals to help develop the educational messages of how death sometimes leads to fossilization and that mammals played persistent roles as tiny terrestrial vertebrates throughout the millennia of the dinosaurs."

Key reference: Callison (1997).

†VELOCIRAPTOR

Saurischia: Theropoda: Neotheropoda: Tetanurae: Avetheropoda: Coelurosauria: Manuraptoriformes: Manuraptora: Eumanuraptora: Dromaeosauridae: Velociraptorinae.

New species: *Velociraptor* cf. *V. langstoni* Burnham, Derstler and Linster 1997.

Occurrence of *Velociraptor* cf. *V. langstoni*: Two Medicine Formation, Montana, United States.

Age: Late Cretaceous (Campanian).

Known material/holotype of *Velociraptor* cf. *V. langstoni*: Nearly complete skeleton, subadult.

Comments: Though a popular theropod in recent years, mostly through exposure in the popular media (particularly its alleged appearance in the 1993 motion picture *Jurassic Park*), fossil specimens belonging to this rather small dromaeosaurid — for over a century, known only from Asia — have been relatively rare. Now, if the tentative identification of a newly recovered specimen proves to be correct, the occurrence of *Velociraptor* will have been extended to include North America.

Burnham, Derstler and Linster (1997) briefly described a small, well-preserved, almost complete and partially articulated dromaeosaurid skeleton (no collection or catalogue designation given; specimen under preparation by David A. Burnham) recovered from a bonebed of partially articulated and closely associated hadrosaur (presumably *Maiasaura*) skeletons, in the upper Two Medicine Formation (Upper Cretaceous, Campanian), near Choteau, Montana. (A hind limb of a medium-sized tyrannosaurid and remains of an adult dromaeosaurid were also found at this site.) This specimen — including about 90 percent of the appendicular elements, much of the vertebral column, a well-preserved furcula (wishbone), sternal plates, shoulder and especially well-preserved pelvic girdles, and much of the rather crushed skull (apparently missing the upper jaws), with possibly more remains yet to be exposed — represents the most complete dromaeosaurid yet found in North America (Burnham, Derstler and Linster 1997).

As Burnham *et al.* observed, preserved in this skeleton are various features typical of the Dromaeosauridae, most significantly the following: 1. Specialized digit II, having a large, retractible "sickle claw" (modified toe bones allowing extreme flexure and retraction of claw); 2. tail enhanced with bony rods (extremely long overlapping chevrons and zygapophyses); and 3. teeth having posterior serrations or denticles larger than anterior ones. Also, the specimen displays enlarged forelimbs, as do other dromaeosaurids.

The skeleton's small size (height estimated to be about 0.5 meters (18 inches) and less than a meter (3 feet) length, and unfused neural arches indicate that this individual is subadult. Because of the immaturity of the specimen, with some characters changing through ontogeny, and because the specimen lacks some diagnostic cranial bones, especially the frontal, the authors took a conservative approach and did not attempt to name it as a new genus.

Comparing the new specimen with other dromaeosaurids (*i.e., Dromaeosaurus, Velociraptor, Deinonychus,* and *Saurornitholestes*), Burnham *et al.* found it to be indistinguishable from *Saurornitholestes langstoni* from Alberta, Canada, but also to be very close to the Mongolian type species, *Velociraptor mongoliensis*. However, although *S. langstoni* could be nearer to the skeleton from Montana in age, locality, and size, the Canadian species had not yet been described adequately enough for the authors to compare the two. Hesitant to refer the specimen to *Saurornitholestes*, Burnham *et al.*, at least for the present, referred it to *Velociraptor* cf. *V. langstoni*.

Velociraptor mongoliensis referred skull (left lateral view) from the Djadokhta Formation, Shabarak Usa, Gobi Desert, southeastern Peoples' Republic of Mongolia, at the "Great Russian Dinosaurs Exhibition" (1996), Mesa Southwest Museum, Mesa, Arizona.

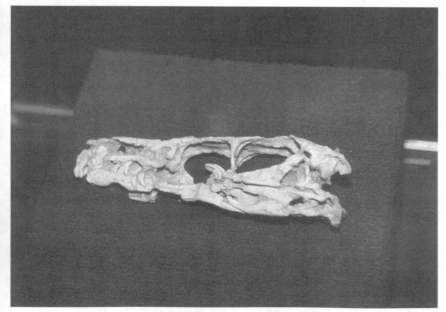

Photograph by the author, courtesy Mesa Southwest Museum.

Burnham *et al.* acknowledged that the Montana specimen is particularly important because of its completeness, beautiful preservation, and the articulated elements that "will lead to a greater understanding of its anatomy (for instance, range of movements of the arms and legs). The authors added that new osteological evidence, such as the presence of a furcula, might help in our understanding more of the relationship between dinosaurs and birds, and also may have a bearing on the evolution of flight mechanisms. Coincidentally (and perhaps ironically), shortly before the publication of Burnham *et al.*'s paper in which the authors expressed this hope, the discovery of a furcula in a *Velociraptor* specimen was reported.

A furcula, consisting of two clavicles fused together, had already been tentatively reported in the celebrated skeleton of *V. mongoliensis* found in 1971 embracing the skeleton of the primitive ceratopsian *Protoceratops* (see *D:TE*), although subsequent examinations of this specimen by various workers resulted only in denials of this claim. However, a *bona fide* furcula (the first found in any dromaeosaurid) was recently reported by Norell, Makovicky and Clark (1997) in a well-preserved, articulated partial skeleton (IGM 100/976) comprising an almost complete skull and anterior postcranium (including sternal plates, posterior cervical vertebrae, proximal ends of left and right humeri, coracoids, and right scapula), discovered at Tugrugeen Shireh, Mongolia during the Mongolian Academy of Sciences–American Museum of Natural History Expedition in 1991. The skeleton is large compared to other collected *Velociraptor* specimens, and the cervical ribs are almost fused to the vertebral centra, these features indicating that this individual was almost fully grown when it died.

Included in their detailed description of this furcula, Norell *et al.* observed that the bone is in articulation between the scapulocoracoids anterior to the sternal plates, the same position as in oviraptorids and birds; "V"-shaped; quite slender; considerably thinner than in oviraptorids and the *Archaeopteryx*; and almost circular in cross section.

Norell *et al.* proposed that the presence of a bird furcula in a broad range of nonavian theropods suggests that the origins of this bone do not relate directly to the origin of flight, and that its use in powered flight, therefore, is "a co-option of a structure already present before flight evolved in the lineage leading to modern birds."

According to Norell *et al.*, the lack of a furcula in previously examined articulated specimens might be attributed to artifacts of preservation or to ontogenetic sampling problems.

In a later criticism of the above study and Norell *et al.*'s interpretation of a "furcula" in *Velociraptor*,

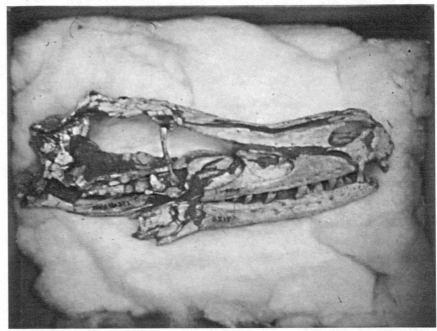

Velociraptor mongoliensis, AMNH 6515, holotype skull in right lateral view.

Alan Feduccia and Larry D. Martin (1998), both specialists in fossil birds (see "Introduction," section on "Dinosaurs and Birds") stated their main objections:

1. *Archaeopteryx*, the earliest known bird, occurred 75 to 80 million years earlier than *Velociraptor* and other theropods possessing "wishbones," with Jurassic examples being from carnosaurs that are considered to be rather distant from birds.

2. The furcula-like structure in the above *Velociraptor* specimen has a round cross section, while that of *Archaeopteryx* and other primitive birds is dissimilar ("grooved postero-dorsally along almost its entire length"); and the articulation of the arms of *Velociraptor*'s furcula-like structure along the margin of the coracoid is different from the articular relationship of the avian furcula, but similar to the coracoids seen in primitive diapsids, this perhaps suggesting that the "furculae" in theropods might be nonhomologous to birds.

3. The furcula in most flightless birds degenerates into two clavicular splints resembling those reported in some dinosaurs, this indicating to the authors "that flight arose as an original function in birds, not as a modification of a structure already present before flight evolved."

4. A furcula-like structure in the primitive Triassic archosaur *Longisquama*, which possessed long feather-like scales and may have been arboreal, indicates that this kind of structure may have developed more than once in archosauromorphs.

That response was followed (same citation) with a reply by Norell, Makovicky and Clark, who stated mainly the following:

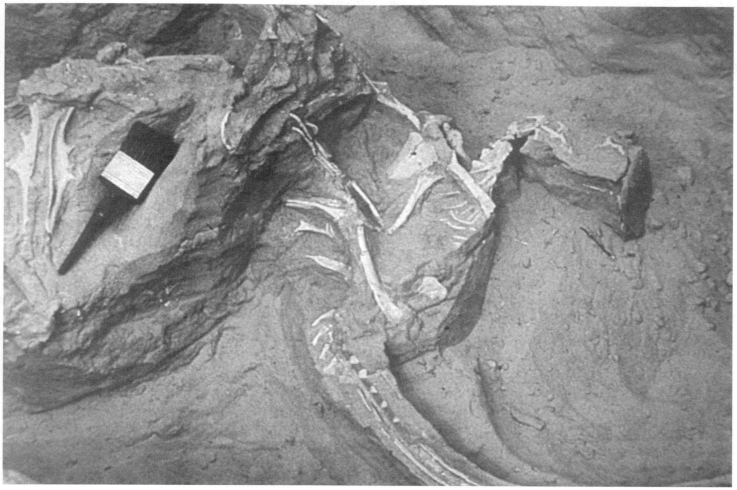

Among the most remarkable dinosaur finds, this specimen (IGM 100/25) from Mongolia shows the skeletons of *Velociraptor mongoliensis* and *Protoceratops andrewsi* literally locked together in combat, preserving a dramatic moment in time.

1. Manuraptoran theropods and theropods with furculae are known from the Late Jurassic; nor had these authors suggested that *Velociraptor* was a direct ancestor, but only that dromaeosaurs were related to birds. (The authors used as an example the existence of primitive mammals, such as monotremes and marsupials, 100 million years after they split from the line leading to man.)

2. Exact similarity is not required for homology (*e.g.,* the variation in the forelimbs of modern bats, whales, and humans). Also, there is much variety in the furculae of living birds and from that of *Archaeopteryx*; and examination of the actual fossil reveals that the furcula in *Velociraptor* attaches to the scapula as it does in modern birds.

3. The fact that nonavian manuraptorans did not fly does not preclude their possessing furculae.

4. *Longisquama* is a fossil of poor quality and interpretation of its single elements is questionable; also, this genus lacks other features that are present in manuraptorans which would ally it with birds; furthermore, regarding *Longisquama* as a close ancestor of birds only increases the time parodox, this genus having lived 80 million years before *Archaeopteryx*.

Note: Norell and Makovicky (1997) discovered important previously unverified features of the dromaeosaur skeleton in two incomplete postcranial specimens collected in 1993 by the Mongolian Academy of Sciences–American Museum of Natural History Joint Expedition to Mongolia. The first specimen (IGM 100/985), and the one offering the most anatomical information, is a three-dimensionally preserved skeleton found at Tugrugeen Shireh in the Gobi Desert. The skeleton represents an immature individual, identified as such by the unclosed sutures between the centra and neural arches. It was identified as belonging to the Dromaeosauridae based upon the presence of a highly modified pedal digit II and the elongate prezygapophyses in the caudal vertebrae (Ostrom 1990). The other specimen (IGM 100/986) was recovered from a locality called Chimney Buttes. Neither of these specimens was referred to any genus.

Among the features observed by Norell and Makovicky, IGM 100/985 possesses paired sternal plates (previously reported only in *V. mongoliensis* among the Dromaeosauridae) having well-developed articular grooves for the coracoids. The articulated

Illustration by Gregory S. Paul (from *Predatory Dinosaurs of the World*). Copyright © 1988 G. S. Paul.

Velociraptor mongoliensis (left) and *Saurornithoides mongoliensis* (right) contest ownership of a dead *Protoceratops andrewsi.* **The feathers are conjectural, although some paleontologists believe some theropods may have possessed such structures.**

gastral basket of this specimen reveals a complex regularly overlapping structure consisting of 12 pairs of gastral segments, with an articular facet configuration that possibly allowed some longitudinal sliding between these segments; the seventh segment on the right side possesses a dorsolaterally directed bifid proximal gastral bone (this element previously unknown in coelurosaurs). The sacrum consists of five co-ossified vertebrae, this apparently being the primitive condition for tetanuran theropods, also found in primitive avialians, primitive ornithomimosaurs (Barsbold 1983), and most likely *Ornitholestes hermanni* (AMNH 619); diagnostic features of the dromaeosaurid sacrum include zygapophyses fused, forming a sinuous ridge on either side of the fused neural spine lamina; possibly diagnostic is the pneumatization of the dorsal vertebrae. The ilium of IGM 100/985 lacks a medial shelf along the antiliac blade, this advanced character being shared with birds but is unknown in other manuraptoran lineages; the pubic peduncle is markedly longer than the iliac peduncle, a feature also seen in *Archaeopteryx litho-*

graphica, the size differences of these processes being less pronounced in other manuraptorans. Other similarities between dromaeosaurs and birds, as revealed by the articulated pelvis of the Tugrugeen specimen, include the reduction of the antiliac hook, the derived character of the absence of a medial shelf along the antiliac blade for the m. cuppedicus, and the distally unfused ischia (this condition seen in most birds). The most significant revelation regarding the pelvis is that the pubis in dromaeosaurs was sharply retroverted at an angle of 155 degrees to the horizontal axis, far more pronounced than shown in reconstructions of *Deinonychus antirrhopus* (Ostrom 1976*b*), and more resembling the condition in the Berlin specimen of *A. lithographica*. The well-preserved feet, found in IGM 100/985 with all but the distal phalanges preserved in articulation in three dimensions, revealed that the hallux (or first digit) was not reversed or semireversed (as in birds and as shown in earlier reconstructions of dromaeosaurs), but articulated in parallel with the other digits. This latter condition is also known in oviraptorids and other theropods; the reversal, as

seen in *A. lithographica*, is found only within the Avialae.

Key references: Burnham, Derstler and Linster (1997); Feduccia and Martin (1998); Norell and Makovicky (1997); Norell, Makovicky and Clark (1997); Ostrom (1976*b*, 1990).

†VELOCISAURUS

Saurischia: Theropoda: Neotheropoda: ?"Ceratosauria"; ?Neoceratosauria: ?Abelisauroidea: ?Abelisauridae.

Comments: Bonaparte (1996*b*), in a preliminary report on tetrapods of the Cretaceous of Argentina, noted that the genus *Velocisaurus*—founded upon postcranial remains (MUCPv 41) collected by O. de Ferrariis in 1985—possesses metatarsals showing characters unknown in other theropods. In most theropods, metatarsals II, III, and IV are of about the same thickness, or III becomes reduced in its proximal half and is anteriorly covered by II and IV. However, in *Velocisaurus*, metatarsal III is the thickest, and II and IV, though of normal length, are very thin except at their distal articulation with unreduced digits.

From the anatomy of the pedal phalanges, Bonaparte deduced that *Velocisaurus* was cursorial, but not predacious, and further hypothesized that this genus was possibly omnivorous.

Based on the morphology of the metatarsals, Bonaparte suggested that this dinosaur "might be part of an adaptive radiation of the Ceratosauria, comprising large predators (*e.g.*, *Abelisaurus*, *Carnotaurus*), small predators (*e.g.*, *Noasaurus*), and not predators types (*e.g.*, *Velocisaurus*)," though acknowledging that the anatomical foundation for this hypothesis is not strong. Furthermore, Bonaparte found *Velocisaurus* to be "as far as known, an endemic theropod for South America, very different to what is known from Laurasia."

Key reference: Bonaparte (1996*b*).

†VULCANODON

Diagnosis of genus (as for type species): Marked dorsoventral flattening of unguals of pedal digits II and III, which have proximal dimensions that are significantly more broad than deep (Wilson and Sereno 1998).

Comments: The genus *Vulcanodon* (type species, *V. karibaensis*) remains distinguished as the most primitive of all known sauropods.

In reviewing this taxon, Wilson and Sereno (1998) noted that the unusually broad proportions of the unguals in pedal digits II and III seem to be unique to this genus among all known sauropodomorphs.

Key reference: Wilson and Sereno (1998).

†XENOTARSOSAURUS

Saurischia: Theropoda: Neotheropoda: "Ceratosauria": Neoceratosauria: Abelisauroidea: Abelisauridae.

Comments: In a preliminary new report, Bonaparte (1996*b*) stated that aspects of the tibia and femur of *Xenotarsosaurus* suggest that this genus was heavier than *Carnotaurus*, but possesses the same diagnostic characters of the hind limb: Femoral head anteromedially projected; lesser trochanter poorly developed dorsally; greater trochanter lower than femoral head; and mediodistal crest well developed. Also, the proximal portion of the tibia closely resemble that of *Carnotaurus*.

The fact that the astragalus and calcaneum are fused to each other, but not to the fibula, suggested to Bonaparte that the foot was still able to rotate.

Key reference: Bonaparte (1996*b*).

†ZIGONGOSAURUS—(See *Mamenchisaurus*.)

ZUNICERATOPS   Wolfe and Kirkland 1998

Ornithischia: Genasauria: Cerapoda: Marginocephalia: Ceratopsia: Neoceratopsia: Ceratopsomorpha.

Name derivation: "Zuni [people whose ancestral homelands include the region where the specimens were found]" + Greek *keratos* = "horn" + Greek *ops* = "face."

Type species: *Z. christopheri* Wolfe and Kirkland 1998.

Other species: [None.]

Occurrence: Moreno Hill Formation, New Mexico, United States.

Age: Late Cretaceous (Turonian).

Known material: Various fragmentary skull and postcranial elements, subadult to adult.

Holotype: MSM P2101, disarticulated skull parts, including a relatively complete portion of the basioccipital, right postorbital horncore, two maxillae, partial right dentary, two caudal centra, much of a coracoid, and distal right humerus, adult.

Diagnosis of genus (as for type species): Intermediate-sized ceratopsian having well-defined, elongate postorbital brow horns arising from immediately above orbit, with flattened lateral margin; low, subrectangular maxilla with large antorbital fenestra; only one single-rooted replacement tooth per file;

dentary teeth exhibiting expanded and reclined crowns, all teeth showing vertical-shear wear pattern; dentary rectangular in profile; coronoid expanded caudally (but not rostrally); elongate, subrectangular process on ventrocaudal margin; ischium decurved; postcranial skeleton gracile (as in "protoceratopsids"); concept of the genus including probable variation in size of brow horns and other cranial elements typical of ontogenetic, morphologic, and sexual variation described for other ceratopsians (Wolfe and Kirkland 1998).

Comments: The genus *Zuniceratops*— the oldest known ceratopsian dinosaur possessing brow horns— was founded upon a partial disarticulated skeleton (MSM P2101) discovered in November 1996 by paleontologist Douglas G. Wolfe and his young son Christopher James Wolfe at Two Rocks Balanced Basin, in the lower part of the Moreno Hill Formation in west-central New Mexico (Anonymous 1997*a*). Casts of the type remain were presented by Wolfe, Kirkland, Denton and Anderson (1997) as a poster at the annual meeting of the Society of Vertebrate Paleontology in 1997 (see also Wolfe, Kirkland, Denton and Anderson 1997).

Paratype specimens of the type species *Zuniceratops christopheri* include various disarticulated cranial and postcranial elements (MSM 98-78, 98-79, and P2110). Other disarticulated but associated fossil material collected at this locality—all from the Haystack Butte bonebed in what is now called the Two Rocks Balanced outcrop area—include remains of a possible tyrannosaurid, a new small dromaeosaurid, hadrosaurine hadrosaurid, several partial chelonid carapaces, crocodilian teeth, dermal scutes, and a partial skeleton, common fish (*Melvius*) teeth, gar (*Lepisosteus*) scales, petrified wood, and leaves (Wolfe and Kirkland 1998).

As noted by Wolfe and Kirkland, *Z. christopheri* is a particularly important ceratopsian find, as it exhibits a combination of characters—both primitive and derived—that are unique among all known horned dinosaurs. Primitive characters retained in this species include a relatively gracile appendicular skeleton and teeth having a single root, with only one replacement tooth per file. Characters allying *Z. christopheri* with the more derived Ceratopsidae include a large skull with an elongate fenestrated frill, prominent postorbital horns, teeth showing a vertical-shear wear pattern, a caudal extension of the tooth row on the maxilla, and a decurved ischium.

The above unique combination of characters suggested to Wolfe *et al.*, and Wolfe and Kirkland, that *Zuniceratops*—a genus more primitive than Asian forms lacking well-developed brow horns but possessing double-rooted teeth (*e.g.*, *Leptoceratops* and

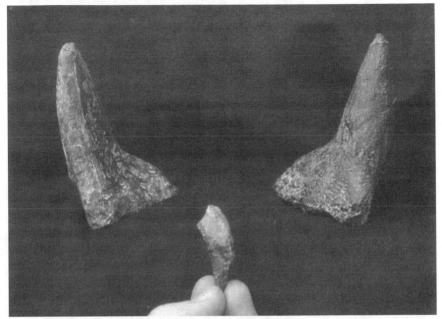

Courtesy James I. Kirkland.

Zuniceratops christopheri, MSM P2101, holotype postorbital horncores and dentary tooth.

Montanoceratops)—lies outside the crown group definition of the Ceratopsidae; for this reason, Wolfe and Kirkland proposed that *Zuniceratops*, along with *Turanoceratops* (see *D:TE*), a primitive genus from central Asia, be placed in their own new ceratopsian clade, Ceratopsomorpha (see "Systematics" chapter).

According to Wolfe and Kirkland, the presence in *Zuniceratops* of prominent brow horns, a large frill, a maxilla with a tooth-bearing extension, a deflected ischium, and single-rooted teeth show that brow horns are, as already suggested by Penkalski (1994), a primitive feature of the Ceratopsidae. Therefore, brow horns developed before the development of dental batteries with double-rooted teeth. This also indicates

Zuniceratops christopheri, MSM P2101, holotype right dentary (lateral view).

Courtesy James I. Kirkland.

Zuniceratops

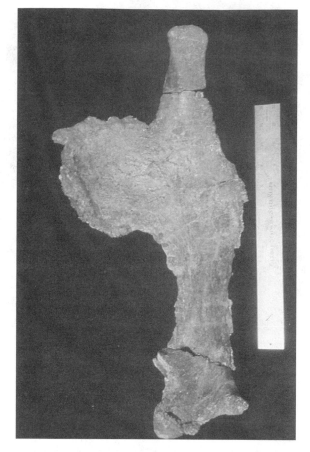

Element (MSM P2106) originally identified by Wolfe and Kirkland (1998) as a squamosal of *Zuniceratops christopheri*; to be reinterpreted by these authors as a nonceratopsian ischium.

***Zuniceratops christopheri*, MSM P2101, holotype single-rooted dentary teeth, caudal views.**

atops in the "Middle" Cretaceous of central Asia indeed suggests an Asian origin for this clade. However, a North American origin is also suggested by the presence of *Zuniceratops*, and also various comparable isolated neoceratopsian teeth from even older strata (Lower Cretaceous) on that continent, with *Turanoceratops* possibly representing a short-lived immigration of the Ceratopsomorpha from North America into Asia.

that relatively advanced ceratopsians were present in North America earlier than previously suspected. Similarities between this dinosaur and *Turanoceratops* reinforce the proposal that a land connection existed between Asia and western North America during the "Middle" Cretaceous.

Notes: As pointed out by Wolfe and Kirkland, the presence of *Zuniceratops* in the Turonian of North America prompts new questions regarding the origins of the Ceratopsidae. The occurrence of *Turanocer-*

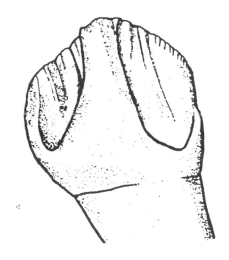

***Zuniceratops christopheri*, MSM P2107, paratype left ischium, lateral view.**

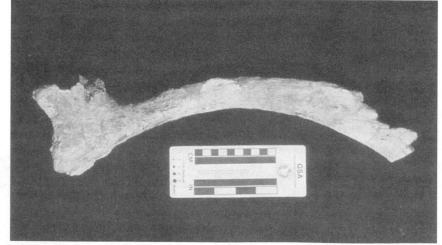

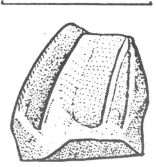

Lateral views of neoceratopsian ?dentary tooth (OMNH 28179) and ?maxillary tooth (MNA v9023) from the Cedar Mountain Formation, Utah. Scale = 1 cm. (After Chinnery, Lipka, Kirkland, Parrish and Brett-Surman 1998.)

Chinnery, Lipka, Kirkland, Parrish and Brett-Surman (1998) described the older neoceratopsian teeth, which were collected from the Mussentuchit Member of the Cedar Mountain Formation (Albian–Cenomanian; see Kirkland, Britt, Burge, Carpenter, Cifelli, DeCourten, Eaton, Hasiotis and Lawton 1997), on the west side of the San Rafael Swell, Emory County, Utah (MNA v9023 and OMNH 28179), and from the Muirkirk clay pit in the Arundel Formation (late Aptian) of the Potomac Group, Prince George's County, Maryland (USNM 337977 and 497708). These teeth, although similar in some ways to ornithopod teeth, were identified by Chinnery *et al.* as belonging to the Neoceratopsia based on a suite of distinguishing characters including "a bulbous, convex nonenameled crown, deep indentations, a well-developed cingulum, and secondary ridges that end within the cingulum."

One of the above teeth, the first collected from the Arundel Formation — USNM 337977, a very small specimen found by Peter M. Krantz in April 1990 in the brick clay pit of the Cherokee Sandford Company, in Muirkirk — was tentatively named (but not formally described) *Magulodon muirkirkensis* [*nomen nudum*] by Krantz (1996). According to Krantz, most paleontologists who had seen this tooth believed it to be that of a "dryosaur," although its double roots imply a ceratopsian, and David B. Weishampel (personal communication to Krantz, 1995) suggested that it could represent a juvenile "tenontosaur." Chinnery *et al.*, while acknowledging that the Utah and Maryland teeth resemble teeth of the ornithopods *Tenontosaurus* and *Dryosaurus*, identified USNM 337977 as a neoceratopsian tooth. Noting the high amount of variability among neoceratopsian teeth, and following the suggestion of Maryańska and Osmólska (1975) "that [due to this variability] isolated protoceratopsid teeth should not be used as a basis for the erection of new taxa," Chinnery *et al.* regarded the name given by Krantz for USNM 337977 as a *nomen dubium*.

Previously known with certainty from only the Early and Late Cretaceous of Asia and the Late Cretaceous of western North America, the above specimens — only a subset of recent North American neoceratopsian discoveries, according to Chinnery *et al.* — now extend the occurrence of the Neoceratopsia to the Early Cretaceous of North America. "The eventual result of these new discoveries," the authors predicted, "will be a more concise understanding of the evolution and biogeography of the clade than was previously possible."

The "squamosal" (MSM P2106) referred to by Wolfe and Kirkland in their description of *Z. christopheri* was misidentified, and is actually a different element belonging to a non-ceratopsian dinosaur (J. I. Kirkland, personal communication 1999).

Key references: Anonymous (1997*a*); Chinnery, Lipka, Kirkland, Parrish and Brett-Surman (1998); Krantz (1996); Maryańska and Osmólska (1975); Penkalski (1994); Wolfe and Kirkland (1998); Wolfe, Kirkland, Denton and Anderson (1997).

Final Note

As already stated elsewhere in the text, much time can pass between a book's going "to press" and its actual publication. In the case of this volume in particular, in which the editorial work is immense, well over a year has elapsed since the point of "no more changes" and the actual release of the book. Consequently, a number of new dinosaurian genera and species were named and described in the paleontological literature too late for inclusion. These (and possibly others), which will be dealt with in "Supplement 2," include the following:

Beipiaosaurus inexpectus (therizinosauroid)
Camposaurus arizonensis (coelophysoid)
Caseosaurus crosbyensis (herrerasaurid)
Cristatusaurus lapparenti (spinosaurid)
Dinheirosaurus lourinhanensis (diplodocoid)
Eucoelophysis baldwini ("ceratosaurian")
Gonxianosaurus shibeiensis (eusauropod)
Lourinhanosaurus antunesi (allosauroid)
Lourinhasaurus alenquerensis (diplodocoid)
Lurdusaurus arenatus (iguanodontid)
Nodocephalosaurus kirtlandensis (ankylosaurid)
Protohadros byrdi (hadrosaurid)
Suchomimus tenerensis (spinosaurid)
Tianzhenosaurus youngi (ankylosaurid)
Variraptor mechinorum (dromaeosaurid)
Yimenosaurus youngi (plateosaurid)

IV. Excluded Genera

*D*inosaurs: The Encyclopedia included a list of genera that were, at one time or more, regarded as dinosaurs, but are now generally believed to belong to other nondinosaurian groups.

The following new list comprises additional genera now considered by most workers to be nondinosaurian, but which were formerly described in the paleontological literature as dinosaurs and were, therefore, treated as dinosaurs in *D:TE* (*e.g.*, *Alvarezsaurus*); were reidentified as dinosaurs subsequent to the publication of that book (*e.g.*, *Patagonykus*); or, although not originally described as dinosaurs, were later reinterpreted as such by workers other than the authors of those genera (*e.g.*, *Rahonavis*).

(For additional older generic names once regarded as dinosaurian — *e.g.*, the crocodilian *Brachytaenius* Meyer 1842, phytosaur *Centemodon* Lea 1856, prolaceritilian *Tribelesodon* Bassani 1886, and others — see the comprehensive list of both valid and invalid published names [excluding taxa based on trace fossils and most birds after *Archaeopteryx*], totaling 806 entries, compiled by George Olshevsky and printed in *Encyclopedia of Dinosaurs* [1997], edited by Philip J. Currie and Kevin Padian, pages 797–806.)

ALVAREZSAURUS   Bonaparte 1991
    Alvarezsaurid bird.
    Note: (See "Introduction" section on "Dinosaurs and Birds").

DRAVIDOSAURUS   Yadagiri and Ayyasami 1979
    Plesiosaur.
    Note: (See "Introduction," "New Discoveries, Ideas and Studies," section on "Thyreophorans").

LISBOASAURUS   Seiffert 1973
    Crocodilian.

PALAEOSAURISCUS   Kuhn 1959 — (=*Palaeosaurus* Riley and Stutchbury 1836)
    "Thecodontian."
    Note: The referred species *P. diagnosticus* is a juvenile of the prosauropod species *Sellosaurus gracilis* (see *D:TE*). All other species referred to this genus, including the type species *P. cylindrodon*, and to the preoccupied *Palaeosaurus*, seem to be nondinosaurian.

PALAEOSAURUS   Riley and Stutchbury 1836 —
    (Preoccupied, Geoffroy Saint-Hillaire 1831; see *Palaeosauriscus*.)

PATAGONYKUS   Novas 1996
    Alvarezsaurid bird.
    Note: This taxon, described as a bird by Novas (1996*c*), was included as a valid dinosaur name on Olshevsky's list.

RAHONA   Forster, Sampson, Chiappe and Krause 1998 — (See *Rahonavis*.)

RAHONAVIS   Forster, Sampson, Chiappe and Krause 1998 — (=*Rahona* Forster *et al.* 1998)
    Mesozoic bird.
    Note: Though described by Forster, Sampson, Chiappe and Krause (1998) as a bird, this genus was regarded by Larry D. Martin as a nonavian theropod (see "Introduction," section on "Dinosaurs and Birds").

SHUVOSAURUS   Chatterjee 1993
    ?Rauisuchian.
    Notes: This genus is tentatively removed from the Dinosauria based on the following:
    In 1993, Sankar Chatterjee described a new type species, *Shuvosaurus inexpectatus*, based upon remains of at least three individuals collected from the Upper Dockum Group (Upper Triassic, early–middle Norian) of western Texas (see *Shuvosaurus* entry, *D:TE*). Chatterjee referred this species to its own family Shuvosauridae, interpreted by him as representing a new clade of primitive yet toothless ornithomimosaurs. However, this identification was controversial, as, until this discovery was made, the Ornithomimosauria had only been known unequivocally from Cretaceous rocks (although other questionable remains from the Late Jurassic of Africa have been reported; see Osmólska's 1997 report on the Ornithomimosauria).
    Recently, in a 1997 report on the Dockum Group, Phillip A. Murry and Robert A. Long, specialists on various Triassic faunas who had not studied the skull of *S. inexpectatus* in detail, tentatively concluded "that Chatterjee's diagnosis of *Shuvosaurus* fails to include it specifically within the Dinosauria." Furthermore, Murry and Long noted that probable remains of *S. inexpectatus* found in Texas and New Mexico are closely associated with postcranial fossils belonging to the rauisuchian archosaur *Chatterjeea elegans* (Long and Murry 1995), both taxa matching in size and preservation. According to these authors, "The morphology of *Chatterjeea* has a number of convergent features with those of ornithomimosaurs, including attenuation of the vertebral column and limbs, development of a synsacrum, and the presence of an ornithomimosaur-like deltopectoral crest on the humerus," these similarities indicating that all of these remains could represent a single rauisuchian taxon, with the generic name *Shuvosaurus* having priority.

UNENLAGIA   Novas and Puerta 1997
    Mesozoic flightless bird.
    Note: (See "Introduction," section on "Dinosaurs and Birds.")

Reconstructed, 30-percent complete *Tyrannosaurus rex* skeleton mounted at the Royal Tyrrell Museum of Palaeontology. This specimen was discovered in 1946 by Charles M. Sternberg imbedded in hard limestone high on a bluff outside the town of Huxley, in central Alberta. Not until 1981, with modern technology available to paleontologists, were the remains collected. Once a rare species, *T. rex* is now known from many good specimens, a testimony as to how dinosaur fossils continue to be discovered, thereby increasing our knowledge of these extinct animals.

A List of Abbreviations

The following is a list of abbreviations that appear in this volume, and which refer to museums and other institutions where fossil specimens are housed:

AC   Pratt Museum of Natural History, Amherst College, Amherst, Massachusetts, United States

AM   Australia Museum, Sydney, Australia

AMNH   American Museum of Natural History, New York, New York, United States

ANSP   The Academy of Natural Sciences of Philadelphia, Philadelphia, Pennsylvania, United States

ASDM   Arizona-Sonora Desert Museum, Tucson, Arizona, United States

AU   University of Arkansas, Fayetteville, Arkansas, United States

BCM   Bristol City Museum, England

BEXHM   Bexhill Museum, East Sussex, England

BHI   Black Hills Institute of Geological Research, Hill City, South Dakota, United States

BMNH   The Natural History Museum, London; formerly British Museum (Natural History), London, England

BSP   Bayerische Staatssammlung für Paläontologic und Historische Geologie, Munich, Germany

BYU   Brigham Young University Vertebrate Paleontology, Provo, Utah, United States

CEUM [also CEU]   College of Eastern Utah, Prehistoric Museum, Price, Utah, United States

CM   Carnegie Museum of Natural History, Pittsburgh, Pennsylvania, United States

CMN   Canadian Museum of Nature (formerly National Museum of Canada [NMC]), Ottawa, Canada

CMNH   Cleveland Museum of Natural History, Cleveland, Ohio, United States

DGM   Museum da Divisao Geologia e Mineralogia, Departmento Nacional da Producao Mineral, Rio de Janeiro, Brazil

DIS   Dinamation International Society, Casper, Wyoming, United States

DMNH   Denver Museum of Natural History, Denver, Colorado, United States

FMNH   The Field Museum (formerly Field Museum of Natural History; Chicago Natural History Museum), Chicago, Illinois, United States

FMSH   Fort Worth Museum of Science and History, Fort Worth, Texas, United States

FUB   Freie Universität, Berlin, Germany

GI   see IGM

GIUV   Geological Institute, University of Vienna, Austria

GMV   see NGMC

GP   Universidade de São Paulo, São Paulo, Brazil

HM   Museum für Naturkunde der Humboldt, Berlin, Germany

IG   Institute of Geology, Beijing, People's Republic of China

IGM   (also GI) Mongolian Museum of Natural History (formerly Geological Institute section of Palaeontology and Stratigraphy), The Academy of Sciences of the Mongolian People's Republic Geological Institute, Ulan Bataar

IRSN   Institut Royal des Sciences Naturelle de Belgique, Brussels, Belgium

ISI   Indian Statistical Institute, Calcutta, India

IST   Institut Superieur Technique, Lisbon, Portugal

IVPP   Institute of Vertebrate Paleontology and Paleoanthropology, Academia Sinica, Beijing, People's Republic of China

IWCMS   Isle of Wight County Museum, Sandown, England

IZ   Institute of Zoology, Academy of Sciences of the Kazakhstan, CLCP, Alma-Ata, Russia

KMV   Kunming Municipal Museum, Kunming, Yunnan Province, People's Republic of China

LACM   Natural History Museum of Los Angeles County (also known as Los Angeles County Museum of Natural History), Los Angeles, California, United States

LH   Museo de Cuenca, Cuenca, Spain

LP   Institut d'Estudis Illerdencs, Lleida, Spain

MACN   Museo Argentino de Ciencias Naturales, Buenos Aires, Argentina

MC   Museo de Cipolleti, Argentina

MCF   Museo Carmen Funes, Paleontologia de Vertebrados, Plaza Huincul, Argentina

MCZ   Museum of Comparative Zoology, Harvard University, Cambridge, Massachusetts, United States

MDE   Musée des Dinosaures, Espéraza, France

MHBR   Muséum d'Historie Naturelle du Havre, Brun Collection, Le Havre, France

MIWG   Museum of the Isle of Wight Geology, Sandown, England

MLP   Museo de La Plata, Buenos Aires, Argentina

MN   Museu Nacional, Rio de Janeiro, Brazil

MNA   Museum of Northern Arizona, Flagstaff, Arizona, United States

A List of Abbreviations

MNEMG Maidstone Museum, Surrey, England

MNHN Muséum National d'Histoire Naturelle, Paris, France

MOR Museum of the Rockies, Bozeman, Montana, United States

MPCA Museo Provincial de "Carlos Ameghino," Cipoletti, Río Negro, Argentina

MPM Milwaukee Public Museum, Milwaukee, Wisconsin, United States

MSGPA Museo Servicos Geologicos de Portugal, Lisboa, Portugal

MSM Mesa Southwest Museum, Mesa, Arizona, United States

MUCP Museo de Ciencias Naturales de la Universidad Nacional del Comahue, Neuquén, Argentina

MUO Stovall Museum of Science and History, University of Oklahoma, Norman, Oklahoma, United States

MWC Museum of Western Colorado, Grand Junction, Colorado, United States

NCSMNS North Carolina State Museum of Natural Sciences, North Carolina State University, Raleigh, North Carolina, United States

NGMC National Geological Museum of China, Beijing, People's Republic of China

NIGP Nanjing Institute of Geology and Paleontology, Academia Sinica, Nanjing, People's Republic of China

NM National Museum, Bloemfontein, South Africa

NMC National Museum of Canada; see CMN

NMMNH New Mexico Museum of Natural History and Science, Albuquerque, New Mexico, United States

OMNH Oklahoma Museum of Natural History, University of Oklahoma, Norman, Oklahoma, United States

OUM Sedgwick Museum, Cambridge University, Cambridge, England

PIN The Paleontological Institute, Academy of Science, Moscow, Russia

POL Musée de Poligny, Poligny, France

PVL Paleontologia de Vertebrados de la Fundación Miguel Lillo, Argentina

QM Queensland Museum, Queensland, Australia

ROM Royal Ontario Museum, Toronto, Canada

RTMP Royal Tyrrell Museum of Palaeontology, Drumheller, Alberta, Canada

SAM South African Museum, Cape Town, South Africa

SC Sierra College, Rocklin, California, United States

SGM Ministère de l'Energie et des Mines Collection, Rabat, Morocco

SMNH Royal Saskatchewan Museum of Natural History, Regina, Saskatchewan, Canada

SMNS Staatliches Museum für Naturkunde, Stuttgart, Germany

SMP State Museum of Pennsylvania, Harrisburg, Pennsylvania, United States

SMU Shuler Museum of Paleontology, Southern Methodist University, Dallas, Texas, United States

SVMP Saint Paul Science Museum Vertebrate Paleontology Collection, Saint Paul, Minnesota, United States

TATE Tate Geological Museum, Casper Community College, Casper, Wyoming, United States

TMM Texas Memorial Museum, The University of Texas, Austin, Texas, United States

TMP Tyrrell Museum of Palaeontology; see RTMP

TTU Texas Tech University Museum, Lubbock, Texas, United States

UA Université d'Antananarivo, Madagascar

UCM University of Colorado Museum, Boulder, Colorado, United States

UCMP University of California Museum of Paleontology, Berkeley, California, United States

UNM University of New Mexico, Albuquerque, New Mexico, United States

UNPSJB Universidad Nacional de la Patagonia "San Juan Bosco," Comodoro, Rivadavia, Chubut, Argentina

UOP University of Portsmouth, Portsmouth, England

USNM National Museum of Natural History, Smithsonian Institution, Washington, D.C., United States

UTEP Centennial Museum of The University of Texas at El Paso, Texas, United States

UUVP Museum of Natural History, University of Utah, Salt Lake City, Utah, United States

UWPI Universität Wien, Paläontologisches Institut, Vienna, Austria

WFQ Warfield Fossils Quarry, North Dakota, United States

WM Warwickshire Museum, Warwick, England

YPM Yale Peabody Museum of Natural History, Yale University, New Haven, Connecticut, United States

ZDM Zigong Dinosaur Museum, Danshanpu, Sichuan, People's Republic of China

ZPAL Paleobiological Institute of the Polish Academy of Sciences, Warsaw, Poland

Appendix One:
Corrected Derivations
of Dinosaur Names

Today, it is the rule among modern paleontologists to reveal and sometimes also explain the etymology of a new genus (and also species) in the scientific paper in which that taxon is named and first described. In the past, however, especially in the earlier days of dinosaur discoveries, such was not always the common practice. Authors of dinosaurian names did not always reveal how or why a certain name was coined. In some cases, the explanation was cryptically included or implied somewhere in the text describing the new dinosaur's fossil remains. Sometimes, in those years past, the name derivation was not given (or implied) until the publication of a paper subsequent to the original description.

Furthermore, some dinosaurs named in foreign-language papers for which English translations have not been provided or are otherwise unavailable have left the real derivations of their names open to mystery.

Consequently, the true meaning of a number of dinosaurian generic names have remained unknown, sometimes for many years. Although some authors (the present writer included) have made attempts to decipher the meaning of these names—utilizing various dictionaries, world atlases, and other sources, plus a knowledge of foreign words (particularly Latin and Greek) and a bit of "educated guesswork"—these deductions have frequently been in error. Benjamin S. Creisler has made a project of extensively researching the correct etymology and the authentic stories behind the scientific names for dinosaurs and other Mesozoic animals, and has compiled comprehensive lists of such names with their correct (or most plausible) derivations. The following compilation of dinosaur names—based upon Creisler's work—comprises those which had their own entries in *D:TE*, but for which their name derivations were not entirely correct.

AEPISAURUS
Greek *aipys* = "high, lofty" + Greek *sauros* = "lizard."

AETONYX—(See *Massospondylus*.)
Greek *aetos* = "eagle" + Greek *onyx* = "claw."

ALECTROSAURUS
Greek *alektros* = "unmarried [loosely meaning 'mateless' or 'alone,' referring to large forelimbs and claws distin-

guishing this genus from other theropods]" + Greek *sauros* = "lizard."

ALLOSAURUS
Greek *allos* = "strange" + Greek *sauros* = "lizard."

ALOCODON
Greek *alox* = "furrow" + Greek *odous* (also *odon*) = "tooth."

ALWALKERIA—(= *Walkeria*, preoccupied, Fleming 1823.) "Alick [D.] Walker."

ANCHICERATOPS
Greek *anchi* = "near" + Greek *keratos* = "horn" + Greek *ops* = "face."

ANCHISAURUS
Greek *anchi* = "near" + Greek *sauros* = "lizard."

ANTRODEMUS—(See *Allosaurus*.)
Greek *antron* (or Latin *antrum*) = "cave [or 'cavity in bone']" + Greek *demas* = body.

BACTROSAURUS
Greek *baktron* = "staff, rod, or club [shape of vertebrae]" + Greek *sauros* = "lizard."

BOROGOVIA
"Borogoves" [fantastic creatures mentioned in Louis Carroll's *Through the Looking Glass*].

CAMPTONOTUS—(See *Camptosaurus*.)
Greek *kamptos* = "flexible" + Greek *notos* = "back."

CAMPTOSAURUS
Greek *kamptos* = "flexible" + Greek *sauros* = "lizard."

CENTROSAURUS
Greek *kentron* = "hook, spur [of frill]" + Greek *sauros* = "lizard."

CETIOSAURUS
Greek *keteios* = "whalelike" + Greek *sauros* = "lizard."

COELURUS
Greek *koilos* = "hollow" + Greek *oura* = "tail."

CRATAEOMUS
Greek *krataios* = "strong" + Greek *omos* = "shoulder, humerus."

CRYPTOSAURUS
Note: This name is not preoccupied (*contra* entry in *D:TE*).

DATOUSAURUS
[Pun combining] Malay *datou* = "chieftain, headman" and Chinese *da* = "big" + Chinese *tou* "head" + Greek *sauros* = "lizard."

DIMODOSAURUS—(See *Plateosaurus*.)
Greek *deimodos* = "terrible" + Greek *sauros* = "lizard."

DIRACODON—(See *Stegosaurus*.)
Greek *deire* = "neck" + Greek *ake* = "point" + Greek *odous* (also *odon*) = "tooth."

DRYOSAURUS
Greek *dryos* = "tree" + Greek *sauros* = "lizard."

ELOSAURUS—(See *Apatosaurus*.)
Greek *helos* (also *elo*) = "marsh" + Greek *sauros* = "lizard."

GONGBUSAURUS
Chinese "Gong Bu [pun meaning 'Ministry of Public Works']" + Greek *sauros* = "lizard."

GRYPOSAURUS
Greek *grypos* = "hook-nosed" + Greek *sauros* = "lizard."

HALTICOSAURUS
Greek *haltikos* = "good at leaping, nimble" + Greek *sauros* = "lizard."

HORTALOTARSUS—(See *Massospondylus*.)
Greek *hortalis* = "young chick" + Greek *tarsos* = "tarsus."

HYPACROSAURUS
Greek *hypakros* = "nearly the highest [approaching in size the giant theropod *Tyrannosaurus*]" + Greek *sauros* = "lizard."

INGENIA
"Ingeni-Khobor [a depression near the fossil site]".

ISCHYROSAURUS
Greek *iskhyros* = "strong" + Greek *sauros* = "lizard."

LABROSAURUS—(See *Allosaurus*.)
Greek *labros* = "rapacious, greedy" + Greek *sauros* = "lizard."

LEIPSANOSAURUS
Greek *leipsanon* = "remnant" + Greek *sauros* = "lizard."

LEXOVISAURUS
"Lexovil [ancient Gallic people from the region where the French specimens were found]" + Greek *sauros* = "lizard."

MASSOSPONDYLUS
Greek *masson* = "longer" + Greek *spondylus* = "vertebra."

MORINOSAURUS
"Morini [ancient people from northern France in the region where the holotype was found]" + Greek *sauros* = "lizard."

NOTOCERATOPS
Greek *notos* = "south [from South America]" + Greek *keratos* = "horn" + Greek *ops* = "face."

OMOSAURUS—(=*Dacentrurus*.)
Greek *omos* = "shoulder, humerus [regarding the development of the muscular crests and processes of the humerus]" + Greek *sauros* = "lizard."

PICRODON
Greek *pikros* = "sharp" + Greek *odous* (also *odon*) = "tooth."

PINACOSAURUS
Greek *pinax* = "board, plank" + Greek *sauros* = "lizard."

POEKILOPLEURON
Greek *poikilos* = "various" + Greek *pleuron* = "rib."

PRICONODON
Greek *prion* = "saw" + Greek *odous* (also *odon*) = "tooth."

RHODANOSAURUS
Greek *Rhodanos* = "Rhone River [in France]" + Greek *sauros* = "lizard."

RHOETOSAURUS
"Rhoetos [a giant in Greek and Roman mythology]" + Greek *sauros* = "lizard."

SCELIDOSAURUS
Greek *skelis* (combining form *skelido*) = "hind limb [more powerful than that of most other then known dinosaurs]" + Greek *sauros* = "lizard."

SHANTUNGOSAURUS
"Shantung [Province, formerly Shandong]" + Greek *sauros* = "lizard."

STENOPELIX
Greek *stenos* = "narrow" + Greek *pelyx* = "pelvis."

VECTISAURUS—(See *Iguanodon*.)
Latin *Vectis* [old name for the Isle of Wight] + Greek *sauros* = "lizard."

WALKERIA [preoccupied, Fleming 1823; renamed *Alwalkeria* by Chatterjee and Creisler 1994.] (See *Alwalkeria*, this appendix.)

XIAOSAURUS
Chinese *xiao* = "early" + Greek *sauros* = "lizard."

YANDUSAURUS
Chinese *Yandu* = "salt capital [old name for Zigong]" + Greek *sauros* = "lizard."

Appendix Two:
Museums Exhibiting Dinosaurs

The following is a list of some of the museums around the world at which dinosaur bones, skeletons, and traces — either as original fossil materials or as cast replicas — are on display for public viewing. (At many museums, a vast amount of fossil specimens are not on exhibit, but are preserved in the collections for purposes of research.)

This partial list was built upon lists compiled from a number of earlier publications (*e.g.*, *Dinosaurs: Their Discovery and Their World*, by Edwin H. Colbert, 1961; *Dinosaurs: An Illustrated History*, Colbert, 1983; *The Illustrated Encyclopedia of Dinosaurs* by David B. Norman, 1985; but mostly on "Museums and Displays," a chapter by Daniel J. Chure in *Encyclopedia of Dinosaurs*, edited by Philip J. Currie and Kevin Padian, 1997).

The list is arranged by continent, and then by country. Museums are then listed in alphabetical order by their current name (*e.g.*, The Field Museum, as opposed to an earlier Chicago Natural History Museum). Addresses are included when available, and, in certain instances, significant displays are noted.

This list is not comprehensive. Given the current popularity of dinosaurs and the desires of the public to see them, exhibits (fossils and skeletal casts, but also miniature dioramas, mechanical figures, paintings, sculptures, motion picture and video presentations, interactive exhibits, *etc.*) relating to these erstwhile creatures are often to be seen in museums that otherwise have little or no connection with paleontology or even natural history in general. The following list is of the more important museums where dinosaur exhibits can be viewed.

AFRICA

Morocco

THE MUSEUM OF EARTH SCIENCES
Université Mohamed V
Avenue Ibn Batouta, BP No. 1014
Rabat

Niger

MUSÉE NATIONAL DU NIGER
B.P. 248
Niamey

South Africa

ALBANY MUSEUM
Grahamston

BERNARD PRICE INSTITUTE OF PALAEONTOLOGY
University of Witwatersrand
1 Jan Smuts Avenue
Johannesburg, 2001

NATIONAL MUSEUM
Bloemfontein

SOUTH AFRICAN MUSEUM
PO Box 61
Cape Town, 8000
    Note: Includes various prosauropods.

Zimbabwe

MUSEUM OF NATURAL HISTORY
Bulawayo

NATIONAL MUSEUM OF ZIMBABWE
Harare
    Note: Mainly includes dinosaurs from Africa (*e.g.*, *Syntarsus*).

ASIA

China

BEIPEI MUSEUM
Beipei, Sichuan
People's Republic of China
    Note: Mainly features dinosaurs from China.

CHENGDU COLLEGE OF GEOLOGY MUSEUM
Chengdu
People's Republic of China

CHONGQING NATURAL HISTORY MUSEUM (also known as THE NATURAL HISTORY MUSEUM OF CHONGQING)
Chongqing, Sichuan
People's Republic of China
    Note: Mounted skeletons of Chinese dinosaurs.

ERENHOT DINOSAUR MUSEUM
Erenhot
Inner Mongolia

INSTITUTE OF VERTEBRATE PALEONTOLOGY AND PALEO-
ANTHROPOLOGY
IVPP Academia Sinica
PO Box 643
Beijing 100044
People's Republic of China
    Note: Mainly features dinosaurian genera from China.

LUFENG DINOSAUR MUSEUM
Lufeng, Yunnan
People's Republic of China

NATIONAL GEOLOGICAL MUSEUM OF CHINA (BEIJING
NATURAL HISTORY MUSEUM)
Beijing
People's Republic of China

ZIGONG DINOSAUR MUSEUM
Dashanpu, Sichuan
People's Republic of China
    Note: The first Asian museum specializing in dinosaurs.

India

GEOLOGY MUSEUM (also known as THE GEOLOGY STUD-
IES UNIT)
Indian Statistical Institute
203 Barrackpore Trunk Road
Calcutta 700035
    Note: Includes a skeleton of the sauropod *Bara-
pasaurus tagorei*, the only mounted dinosaur in India (see
D:TE for photograph).

Japan

GUNMA PREFECTURAL MUSEUM OF HISTORY
Maebashi, Gunma

HIMEJI MUSEUM OF NATURAL HISTORY
Himeji

HISTORICAL MUSEUM OF HOKKAIDO
Sapporo, Hokkaido

HOKKAIDO CENTENNIAL OFFICE
Hokkaido

HYABASHIBARA MUSEUM OF NATURAL HISTORY
700 Shimoishi 1-Chrome
Okayama Shi 700

HYOGO MUSEUM
Hyogo

IBARAKI PREFECTURAL MUSEUM OF NATURAL HISTORY
700 Ozaki
Iwai City, Ibaraki Prefecture

INSTITUTE FOR BREEDING RESEARCH
Tokyo University of Agriculture
Tokyo

IWAKI MUSEUM OF COAL AND FOSSILS
Iwaki, Fukushima

KAGOSHIMA PREFECTURAL MUSEUM
Kagoshima

KANAGAWA PREFECTURE LIVING PLANET AND EARTH MU-
SEUM
499 Iryuda Odawara City
Kanagawa Ken 250

KASAOKA CITY MUSEUM
Kasaoka

KITAKYUSHU MUSEUM OF NATURAL HISTORY
Kitakyushu, Fukuoka

KYOTO MUNICIPAL SCIENCE CENTER FOR YOUTH
Kyoto

NAKASOTO DINOSAUR CENTER
Gunma Prefecture

NATIONAL SCIENCE MUSEUM
Ueno Park 7-20
Taito-ku
Tokyo 110

NATURAL HISTORY MUSEUM
Tokai University
Shimizu, Shikuoka

NIIGATA PREFECTURAL NATURAL SCIENCE MUSEUM
Niigata

OSAKA MUSEUM OF NATURAL HISTORY
Osaka

SAITO HO-ON KAI MUSEUM OF NATURAL HISTORY
Sendai, Miyagi

TAKIKAWA MUSEUM OF ART AND NATURAL HISTORY
Takikawa, Hokkaido

TOCHIGI PREFECTURAL MUSEUM
Utsunomiya, Tochigi

TOYAMA SCIENCE MUSEUM
Toyama

TOYOHASHI MUSEUM OF NATURAL HISTORY
Toyohashi, Aichi

Mongolia

MONGOLIAN MUSEUM OF NATURAL HISTORY (formerly
THE GEOLOGICAL INSTITUTE SECTION OF PALAEON-
TOLOGY AND STRATIGRAPHY)
The Academy of Sciences of the Mongolian People's Re-
public Geological Institute (also known as Mongolian
Academy of Sciences)

Ulan Bataar 46
  Note: Mainly features Mongolian dinosaurs.

South Korea

NATIONAL SCIENCE MUSEUM OF KOREA
Seoul

Taiwan

NATIONAL MUSEUM OF NATURAL SCIENCE
Taichung

AUSTRALIA AND NEW ZEALAND

Australia

AUSTRALIAN MUSEUM
PO Box A285
Sydney, New South Wales 2000

MUSEUM OF VICTORIA
285–321 Russell Street
Melbourne, Victoria 3000

NATIONAL DINOSAUR MUSEUM
Young, New South Wales

QUEENSLAND MUSEUM
Gregory Terrace
Fortitude Valley
Queensland 4996
  Note: Includes dinosaurs indigenous to Australia.

SOUTH AUSTRALIAN MUSEUM
North Terrace
Adelaide, South Australia 5000

WESTERN AUSTRALIAN MUSEUM
Perth, Western Australia

New Zealand

CANTERBURY MUSEUM
Rollenstone Avenue
Christchurch 1

EUROPE

Austria

NATURHISTORISCHES MUSEUM WIEN
Vienna

Belgium

BERNISSART MUSEUM
Bernissart, Hainut

INSTITUT ROYAL DES SCIENCES NATURELLE DE BELGIQUE
Rue Vautier 29
B-1040, Brussels
  Note: Main exhibit is the collection of numerous specimens of *Iguanodon* from Bernissart.

Denmark

GEOLOGIST MUSEUM
Copenhagen

MUSEUM VON GRAM
Gram

England

BIRMINGHAM MUSEUM
Department of Natural History
Chamberlain Square
Birmingham B3 3DH

CITY OF LIVERPOOL MUSEUM
Liverpool

THE DINOSAUR MUSEUM
Icen Way
Dorchester
Dorset DTI 1EW

GEOLOGY MUSEUM (also known as GEOLOGICAL SURVEY AND MUSEUM)
London

THE LEICESTERSHIRE MUSEUM
96 New Walk
Leicester LE1 6TD

THE MANCHESTER MUSEUM
The University of Manchester
Oxford Road
Manchester M13 9PL

MUSEUM OF THE ISLE OF WIGHT GEOLOGY
Sandown Library
High Street
Sandown
Isle of Wight Po36 8af
  Note: Mostly taxa from the Isle of Wight.

THE NATURAL HISTORY MUSEUM, LONDON (formerly THE BRITISH MUSEUM [NATURAL HISTORY])
Cromwell Road
London SW7 5BD
  Note: Includes taxa from England, also dinosaurs from other parts of the world.

SEDGWICK MUSEUM
Cambridge University
Downing Street
Cambridge CB2 3EQ

UNIVERSITY MUSEUM
Oxford University
Parks Road
Oxford OX1 3PW
  Note: Features mostly British taxa.

France

LABORATOIRE DE PALEONTOLOGIE
Faculté des Sciences
Place Eugene-Bataillon
Montpelier 34095
Cedex 05

MUSÉE DES DINOSAURES
Espéraza

MUSÉUM D'HISTOIRE NATURELLE DU HAVRE (NATURAL
  HISTORY MUSEUM)
Le Havre

MUSÉUM GUIMET D'HISTOIRE NATURELLE
(Musée de Lyon)
28 Boulevard des Belges
13004 Marseille

MUSÉUM NATIONAL D'HISTOIRE NATURELLE
8 rue Buffon
F-75005, Paris

MUSEUM OF EARTH SCIENCES
Nancy

NATURAL HISTORY MUSEUM
Aix-en-Provence

NATURAL HISTORY MUSEUM
Nantes

Germany

BAYERISCHE STAATSSAMLUNG FÜR PALÄONTOLOGIE UND
  HISTORISCHE GEOLOGIE (BAVARIAN STATE COLLECTION
  FOR PALEONTOLOGY AND HISTORICAL GEOLOGY; also
  known as INSTITUT FÜR PALÄONTOLOGIE UND HIS-
  TORISCHE GEOLOGIE)
Richard-Wagner-Strasse 10/2
8000 Munich 2

BELDHEIM CASTLE
Hildburghausen

FREILICHTMUSEUM
near Bad regurg-Loccum
Munchenhagen

GEOLOGICAL AND PALAEONTOLOGICAL INSTITUTE
University of Münster
Pferdegasse 3
D4400 Münster

HEIMATMUSEUM
Trössingen

INSTITUT UND MUSEUM FÜR GEOLOGIE UND PALÄOLOGIE
Universität Tübingen
Sigwartstrasse 10
7400 Tübingen 1

JURA MUSEUM
Willibaldsburg
Eichstätt 8078

LANDESMUSUEM FÜR NATURKUND
Münster

LIPPISCHES LANDESMUSEUM
Detmold

MUSEUM AM SCHOLERBERG
Onasbruck

MUSEUM DES GEOLOGISCH-PALÄONTOLOGISCHEN INSTI-
  TUTS DER UNIVERSITÄT
Münster

MUSEUM FÜR NATURKUNDE DER HUMBOLDT–UNIVER-
  SITÄT ZU BERLIN
Paläontologisches Museum
Unter der Linden 6
108 Berlin
  Note: Includes African genera from Tendaguru, in-
cluding the giant mounted composite skeleton of *Bra-
chiosaurus brancai* (See *D:TE* for photograph).

MUSEUM HAUFF
Holzmaden

MUSEUM HEINEANUM
Halberstadt

MUSEUM IM INSTITUT FÜR GEOLOGIE UND PALÄONTOLO-
  GIE DER UNIVERSITÄT
Göttingen

NIEDERSACHISCHES LANDESMUSEUM
Hannover

SCHAUMBURGISCHES HEIMATMUSEUM
Eulenberg
Rintlen

SENCKENBERG NATURMUSEUM
Forschunginstitut Senckenberg
Senckenberg Anlage 25
6000 Frankfurt am Main 1

STAATLICHES MUSEUM FÜR NATURKUNDE
Rosenstein 1, D-7000
Stuttgart 1

STADTMUSEUM
Brilon

STATE MUSEUM FOR NATURAL HISTORY
Arsenalplatz 3
D7140 Ludwigsburg 1

WESTPHALISCHES LANDESMUSEUM FÜR NATURKUNDE
Münster

Hungary

TEMESZETTUDOMANYI MUZEUM
Fold-es Oslenytar
Muzeum korut 14-16
H-1088 Budapest

Ireland

ULSTER MUSEUM
Belfast BT9 5AB

Italy

G. CAPELLO MUSEUM
Bologna

MUSEO CIVICO DI STORIA NATURALE DE MILANO
Corse Venezia 55
20121 Milan

MUSEO CIVICO DI STORIA NATURALE DI VENEZIA
S. Croce 1739
30125 Venice

MUSEO DI SCIENZE NATURALI "E. CAFFI"
74100 Bergamo

Poland

INSTYTUT PALEOBIOLOGII (also known as PALEOBIOLOGY
    INSTITUTE OF THE POLISH ACADEMY OF SCIENCES)
Al Zwirki Wigury 93
02-098 Warsaw
    Note: Includes specimens from the Polish-Mongolian
expeditions.

Portugal

MUSEO SERVICOS GEOLOGICOS DE PORTUGAL
Rua Academia Das Ciencias
Lisbon

Russia

CENTRAL GEOLOGICAL AND PROSPECTING MUSEUM
St. Petersburg

ORLOV MUSEUM OF PALEONTOLOGY (also known as THE
    PALEONTOLOGICAL INSTITUTE)
Paleontological Institute
Russian Academy of Sciences
Profsoyuzanaya 113
Moscow 117321
    Note: Mostly dinosaurs from Mongolia.

Scotland

HUNTERIAN MUSEUM
The University
Glasgow G12 8QQ

ROYAL SCOTTISH MUSEUM
Chambers Street
Edinburgh EH1 1JF

Spain

MUSEO NACIONAL DE CIENCIAS NATURALES
Jose Gutierrez, Abscal 2
Madrid

Sweden

PALAEONTOLOGICAL MUSEUM
Uppsala University
PO Box 256
751 05 Uppsala

Switzerland

GEOLOGISCHE-PALÄONTOLOGISCHES INSTITUT
Universität Basel
Bernoullistrasse 32, Ch 4506
Basel

MUSEUM D'HISTORIE NATURALLE
Route de Malagnou, Case Postale 434
1211 Geneva 6

PALÄONTOLOGISCHES INSTITUT UND MUSEUM DER UNI-
    VERSITÄT ZÜRICH
Karl Schmid-Strasse 4
Ch-8006 Zürich

Turkey

MINERAL RESEARCH AND EXPLORATION INSTITUTE
Ankara

Wales

NATIONAL MUSEUM OF WALES
Cardiff CF1 3NP

NORTH AMERICA ————————

Canada

CANADIAN MUSEUM OF NATURE (formerly NATIONAL MUSEUM OF CANADA)
PO Box 3443, Station D
Ottawa, Ontario K1P 6P4
   Note: Exhibits include dinosaur specimens collected in Canada by members of the Sternberg Family.

DRUMHELLER DINOSAUR AND FOSSIL MUSEUM
Box 2135
Drumheller, Alberta Toj Oyo
   Note: Most Canadian taxa.

MANITOBA MUSEUM OF MAN AND NATURE
190 Rupert Avenue
Winnipeg, Manitoba R3B ON2

MUSEUM OF NATURAL SCIENCES
University of Saskatchewan
Saskatoon, Saskatchewan S7N OWO

PROVINCIAL MUSEUM OF ALBERTA
12845 102 Avenue
Edmonton, Alberta T5N OM6
   Note: Mostly Canadian taxa.

REDPATH MUSEUM
McGill University
859 Sherbrook Street West
Quebec H3A 2K6

ROYAL ONTARIO MUSEUM
100 Queen's Park
Toronto, Ontario M5S 2C6
   Note: Includes mostly Canadian but also some non–Canadian taxa.

ROYAL SASKATCHEWAN MUSEUM OF NATURAL HISTORY
College Avenue and Albert Street, 2445 Albert Street
Regina, Saskatchewan S4P 3V7

ROYAL TYRRELL MUSEUM OF PALAEONTOLOGY (formerly TYRRELL MUSEUM OF PALAEONTOLOGY)
PO Box 7500
Drumheller, Alberta TOJ OYO
   Note: Features the most comprehensive and extensive display of dinosaur skeletons (real fossils and casts) anywhere, representing most of the major dinosaurian groups.

Mexico

NATURAL HISTORY MUSEUM
Mexico City

MUSEO CIVICO NATURALES
Vilahermosa
Tabasco

United States

THE ACADEMY OF NATURAL SCIENCES OF PHILADELPHIA
1900 Benjamin Franklin Parkway
Philadelphia, Pennsylvania 19103-1195
   Note: Includes much of the dinosaur fossil material collected by Edward Drinker Cope.

AMERICAN MUSEUM OF NATURAL HISTORY
Central Park West at 79th Street
New York, New York 10024-5192
   Note: Displays the finest collection of original dinosaur specimens in the world, including most "classic" dinosaurian taxa, some represented by virtually complete skeletons and the famous *Edmontosaurus* "mummy." Much of the dinosaur material having been collected in Canada and the United States by Barnum Brown and in Mongolia by Roy Chapman Andrews.

ANNIE RIGGS MUSEUM
Fort Stockton Historical Society
301 South Main
Fort Stockton, Texas 79735

ANNISTON MUSEUM OF NATURAL HISTORY
Box 1587
Anniston, Alabama 36202

ARIZONA MUSEUM OF SCIENCE AND TECHNOLOGY
147 East Adams
Phoenix, Arizona 85004

ARKANSAS MUSEUM OF SCIENCE AND HISTORY
MacArthur Park
Little Rock, Arkansas 72202

AUDUBON INSTITUTE—PATHWAYS TO THE PAST
6500 Magazine Street
New Orleans, Louisiana 70118

BLACK HILLS MUSEUM OF NATURAL HISTORY
217 Main Street
Hill City, South Dakota 57745

BRAZOSPORT MUSEUM OF NATURAL SCIENCE
400 College Drive
Lake Jackson, Texas 77566

BUFFALO MUSEUM OF SCIENCE
1020 Humboldt Parkway
Buffalo, New York 14211

BURKE MUSEUM
University of Washington
DB-10
Seattle, Washington 98185

C. NASH DINOSAUR MUSEUM
Route 116, Amherst Road
South Hadley, Massachusetts 01075

CALIFORNIA ACADEMY OF SCIENCES
Golden Gate Park
San Francisco, California 94118-4599

CARNEGIE MUSEUM OF NATURAL HISTORY
4400 Forbes Avenue
Pittsburgh, Pennsylvania 15213-4080
 Note: Includes fine and "classic" specimens collected by Earl Douglass from what became Dinosaur National Monument, as well as the mounted holotype skeleton of *Tyrannosaurus rex* (see *D:TE* for photograph).

CARTER COUNTY MUSEUM
100 Main Street
Ekalaka, Montana 59324

CHILDREN'S MUSEUM OF INDIANAPOLIS
Box 3000
Indianapolis, Indiana 46208

CLEVELAND-LLOYD DINOSAUR QUARRY
c/o Bureau of Land Management
PO Drawer A.B.
900 North 700 East
Price, Utah 84501

CLEVELAND MUSEUM OF NATURAL HISTORY
One Wade Oval Drive
University Circle
Cleveland, Ohio 44106
 Note: Late Jurassic, Morrison Formation taxa (*e.g.*, *Allosaurus*).

COLLEGE OF EASTERN UTAH PREHISTORIC MUSEUM (also
 known as the PREHISTORIC MUSEUM)
College of Eastern Utah
155 East Main Street
Price, Utah 84501
 Note: Mostly Morrison Formation taxa.

CONNECTICUT STATE MUSEUM OF HISTORY
University of Connecticut
Route 195
Storrs, Connecticut 06269-3023

CORPUS CHRISTI MUSEUM OF SCIENCE AND HISTORY
1900 North Chaparral
Corpus Christi, Texas 78401

COUNTRY SEAT AND COURTHOUSE TRACKS
421 North Main
Nashville, Arkansas 71852

CRANBROOK INSTITUTE OF SCIENCE
500 Lone Pine Road
Box 801
Bloomfield Hills, Michigan 48013

DAKOTA DINOSAUR MUSEUM
Dickinson, North Dakota 58601

DALLAS MUSEUM OF NATURAL HISTORY
Box 150349
Dallas, Texas 75315

DAN O'LAURIE MUSEUM
118 East Center Street
Moab, Utah 84532

DAYTON PUBLIC LIBRARY MUSEUM
2600 Deweese Parkway
Dayton, Ohio 45414

DENVER MUSEUM OF NATURAL HISTORY
2001 Colorado Boulevard
City Park
Denver, Colorado 80205

DEPARTMENT OF GEOLOGY
University of Alabama
Tuscaloosa, Alabama 35486

DEPARTMENT OF GEOLOGY
University of Wichita
Wichita, Kansas 67213

DEPARTMENT OF GEOLOGY
The University of Texas at El Paso
El Paso, Texas 79968

DEVIL'S CANYON DISCOVERY CENTER
Box 307
Fruita, Colorado 81521
 Note: Late Jurassic taxa.

DICK'S ROCK MUSEUM
490 Moraine Route
Estes Park, Colorado 80517

DINOSAUR DISCOVERY CENTER
Box 313
Canon City, Colorado 81215-0313

THE DINOSAUR MUSEUM
754 South 200 West
Blanding, Utah 83511

DINOSAUR NATIONAL MONUMENT
PO Box 128
Jensen, Utah 84035
 Note: Features a Morrison Formation quarry site where a great number of Late Jurassic dinosaur fossils can be viewed *in situ*, and where excavation of some of these fossils is still in progress.

DINOSAUR STATE PARK
West Street
Rocky Hill, Connecticut 06067
 Note: Large collection of dinosaur footprints.

DINOSAUR VALLEY (a division of THE MUSEUM OF WESTERN COLORADO)
Box 20000-5020
Grand Junction, Colorado 81502
Note: Includes mostly taxa from the Morrison Formation.

DINOSAUR VALLEY STATE PARK
Box 396
Glen Rose, Texas 76043
Note: Dinosaur tracks.

DOROTHY C. PAGE MUSEUM
323 Main Street
Wasilla, Alaska 99687

DUNN-SEILER MUSEUM
Box 5167
Mississippi State University, Mississippi 39762

EARTH AND SCIENCE MUSEUM
Pennsylvania State University
112 Steidle Building
University Park, Pennsylvania 16802

EARTH SCIENCE MUSEUM
Brigham Young University
PO Box 23300
Provo, Utah 84602
Note: Includes dinosaur material collected by ("Dinosaur Jim") James A. Jensen.

EVERHART MUSEUM
Nay Aug Park
Scranton, Pennsylvania 18510

FARMINGTON MUSEUM
302 North Orchard
Farmington, New Mexico 87401

FERNBANK MUSEUM OF NATURAL HISTORY
767 Clifton Road NE
Atlanta, Georgia 30307

THE FIELD MUSEUM (formerly FIELD MUSEUM OF NATURAL HISTORY; CHICAGO NATURAL HISTORY MUSEUM, FIELD MUSEUM)
1400 S. Lake Shore Drive
Chicago, Illinois 60605-2496
Note: Dinosaur fossils include specimens collected by Elmer S. Riggs, including the holotype of *Brachiosaurus altithorax*, and also the celebrated *Tyrannosaurus rex* skeleton known as "Sue" (see *Tyrannosaurus* entry for photograph).

FORT WORTH MUSEUM OF SCIENCE AND HISTORY
1501 Montgomery Street
Fort Worth, Texas 76107

FRANK H. MCCLUNG MUSEUM
University of Tennessee
1327 Circle Park Drive
Knoxville, Tennessee 37919

FRYXELL GEOLOGY MUSEUM
820 38th Street
Rock Island, Illinois 61201

GARFIELD COUNTY MUSEUM
Box 325
Jordan, Montana 59337

GEOLOGY MUSEUM
Western Illinois University
Macomb, Illinois 61455

GREYBULL MUSEUM
325 Greybull Street
Greybull, Wyoming 82462

HOUSTON MUSEUM OF NATURAL SCIENCE
One Hermann Circle Drive
Houston, Texas 77030

IDAHO STATE MUSEUM OF NATURAL HISTORY
Idaho State University
Campus Box 8096
Pocatello, Idaho 83209

JOACHIM REGIONAL MUSEUM
Visitor's Center
314 Third Avenue, West
Dickinson, North Dakota 58601

JOSEPH MOORE MUSEUM
Earlham College
Richmond, Indiana 47374

KINGMAN MUSEUM OF NATURAL HISTORY
175 Limits
Battle Creek, Michigan 49017

LANIER MINERAL MUSEUM
2601 Buford Dam Road
Buford, Georgia 30518

LAS VEGAS MUSEUM OF NATURAL HISTORY
900 Las Vegas Boulevard North
Las Vegas, Nevada 89101

LEONARD HALL
University of North Dakota
Box 8358
Grand Forks, North Dakota 58202

LIFE SCIENCES MUSEUM
Pierce College
1601 Winnetka Avenue
Woodland Hills, California 91371
Note: Includes Upper Jurassic dinosaur bones, gastroliths, tracks, and a skeleton (cast) of a subadult *Allosaurus fragilis* from the Cleveland-Lloyd Dinosaur Quarry.

"The Dueling Dinosaurs"—*Tyrannosaurus rex* and *Triceratops prorsus*—gracing the exterior of the Natural History Museum of Los Angeles County since 1998. This full-scale tableau, based on the skeletal display inside the museum (see pages 355 and 365), was rendered in bronze by Douglas Van Howd of Sierra Sculpture; production artist and engineer was Richard Campbell, consulting paleontologist Kenneth Kirkland.

LONG ISLAND NATURAL HISTORY MUSEUM
Long Island University
Long Island, New York

LSU MUSEUM OF GEOSCIENCE
Louisiana State University
109 Howe — Russell Geoscience Complex
Baton Rouge, Louisiana 70803

MCKINLEY MUSEUM OF HISTORY
800 McKinley Monument Drive NW
Canton, Ohio 44708-4800

MEMPHIS PINK PALACE MUSEUM
3050 Central Avenue
Memphis, Tennessee 38111

MESA SOUTHWEST MUSEUM
53 North MacDonald Street
Mesa, Arizona 85201

MICHIGAN STATE UNIVERSITY MUSEUM
West Circle Drive
East Lansing, Michigan 48824

MILWAUKEE PUBLIC MUSEUM
800 West Wells Street
Milwaukee, Wisconsin 53233

MONTSHIRE MUSEUM OF SCIENCE
Box 770
Montshire Road
Norwich, Vermont 05055

MORRIS MUSEUM
6 Normandy Heights Road
Morristown, New Jersey 07960

MORRISON NATURAL HISTORY MUSEUM
PO Box 564
Morrison, Colorado 80456

MUSEUM OF COMPARATIVE ZOOLOGY
Harvard University
26 Oxford Street
Cambridge, Massachusetts 02138

MUSEUM OF CULPEPER HISTORY
140 East Davis Street
Culpeper, Virginia 22701

MUSEUM OF GEOLOGY
South Dakota School of Mines and Technology
501 East St. Joseph Street
Rapid City, South Dakota 57701-3995

MUSEUM OF NATURAL HISTORY
University of Wisconsin
Stevens Point, Wisconsin

Appendix Two

MUSEUM OF NORTHERN ARIZONA
Box 720
Flagstaff, Arizona 86001

MUSEUM OF PALEONTOLOGY
University of California
Valley Life Sciences Building
Berkeley, California 94720

MUSEUM OF PALEONTOLOGY
University of Michigan
1109 Geddes Avenue
Ann Arbor, Michigan 48109-1079

MUSEUM OF SAN RAFAEL
95 North 100 East
Castle Dale, Utah 84513

MUSEUM OF SCIENCE
Science Park
Boston, Massachusetts 02114

MUSEUM OF SCIENCE AND HISTORY
1025 Museum Circle
Jacksonville, Florida 32207-9854

MUSEUM OF TEXAS TECH UNIVERSITY
Texas Tech University
4th and Indiana Avenue
Lubbock, Texas 79409

MUSEUM OF THE ROCKIES
Montana State University
600 West Kagy Boulevard
Bozeman, Montana 59715
    Note: Includes numerous dinosaur fossils, including eggs and embryos, collected in Montana by John R. Horner.

NATIONAL MUSEUM OF NATURAL HISTORY (formerly UNITED STATES NATIONAL MUSEUM)
Smithsonian Institution
Tenth Street and Constitution Avenue NW
Washington, D.C. 20560
    Note: This fine display includes dinosaurian taxa described by Othniel Charles Marsh and Charles Whitney Gilmore.

NATURAL HISTORY MUSEUM OF LOS ANGELES COUNTY (also known as LOS ANGELES COUNTY MUSEUM OF NATURAL HISTORY)
900 Exposition Boulevard
Los Angeles, California 90007
    Note: Includes the "Dueling Dinosaurs" exhibit, free standing skeletons of *Tyrannosaurus rex* and *Triceratops prorsus* posed as if in combat (photograph page 395).

NATURAL SCIENCE CENTER
4301 Lawndale Drive
Greensboro, North Carolina 27401

NEW JERSEY STATE MUSEUM
CN-530
205 West State Street
Trenton, New Jersey 08625

NEW MEXICO MUSEUM OF NATURAL HISTORY AND SCIENCE
1801 Mountain Road Nw
Albuquerque 87104-1375

NEW YORK STATE MUSEUM
c/o New York Geological Survey
State Educational Center
Albany, New York 12230

NORTH CAROLINA MUSEUM OF LIFE AND SCIENCE
433 Murray Avenue
Durham, North Carolina 27705

NORTH CAROLINA STATE MUSEUM OF NATURAL SCIENCES
Box 27647
Raleigh, North Carolina 27647

OKLAHOMA MUSEUM OF NATURAL HISTORY
University of Oklahoma
1335 Asp Avenue
Norman, Oklahoma 73019-0606

OLD TRAIL MUSEUM
Choteau, Montana 59422

OTTAWA COUNTY HISTORICAL MUSEUM
110 South Concord
Minneapolis, Kansas 67467

PACIFIC SCIENCE CENTER
200 Second Avenue North
Seattle, Washington 98102

PANHANDLE-PLAINS HISTORICAL MUSEUM
Western Texas State University
Box 967
2401 Fourth Avenue
Canyon, Texas 79016

PEABODY MUSEUM OF NATURAL HISTORY
Yale University
Whitney Avenue and S Street
New Haven, Connecticut 06511
    Note: Includes many dinosaur specimens collected and described by Othniel Charles Marsh.

PETRIFIED FOREST NATIONAL PARK
Box 2217
Petrified Forest National Park, Arizona 86028
    Note: Mostly Late Triassic specimens.

PETROLEUM MUSEUM
1500 1-20 West
Midland, Texas 79701

PRATT MUSEUM OF NATURAL HISTORY
Amherst College
Amherst, Massachusetts 01002
   Note: Includes fine collection of dinosaur fossil footprints.

PRINCETON MUSEUM OF NATURAL HISTORY
Princeton University
Guyot Hall
Washington Street
Princeton, New Jersey 08544

R. A. VINES ENVIRONMENTAL SERVICE CENTER
8856 Westview Drive
Houston, Texas 77055

RAYMOND M. ALF MUSEUM
1175 West Baseline Road
Claremont, California 91711
   Note: Highlight being collection of dinosaur footprints.

RED MOUNTAIN MUSEUM
1421 22nd Street South
Birmingham, Alabama 35205

RIVERSIDE MUNICIPAL MUSEUM
3720 Orange Street
Riverside, California 92501

RUTGERS UNIVERSITY COLLEGE MUSEUM
Geology Hall C.A.C.
Rutgers University
New Brunswick, New Jersey 08903

RUTH HALL MUSEUM OF PALEONTOLOGY
Ghost Ranch Conference Center
HC77 Box 11
Abiquiu, New Mexico 87510-9601
   Note: At the sight of the Ghost Ranch *Coelophysis* quarry, exhibits include specimens of this dinosaur.

SAN BERNARDINO MUSEUM OF NATURAL HISTORY
2024 Orange Tree Lane
Redlands, California 92374

SAN DIEGO NATURAL HISTORY MUSEUM (formerly NATURAL HISTORY MUSEUM)
PO Box 1390
Balboa Park
San Diego, California 92112

SCIENCE CENTER
Wesleyan University
Church Street
Middletown, Connecticut 06459

THE SCIENCE MUSEUM OF MINNESOTA
30 East Tenth Street
Saint Paul, Minnesota 55101

SHERIDAN COLLEGE GEOLOGY MUSEUM
3059 Coffeen Avenue
Sheridan, Wyoming 82801

SHULER MUSEUM OF PALEONTOLOGY
Southern Methodist University
Department of Geological Science
Dallas, Texas 75275-0395

SPRINGFIELD SCIENCE MUSEUM
236 State Street
Springfield, Massachusetts 01103

STATE MUSEUM OF PENNSYLVANIA
3rd and North Streets
Harrisburg, Pennsylvania 17108

STERNBERG MUSEUM
Fort Hays State University
Campus Drive
Hays, Kansas 67601

STRECKER MUSEUM
South Fourth and Speight
Box 97154
Waco, Texas 76798

TATE GEOLOGICAL MUSEUM
Casper Community College
Casper, Wyoming 82062

TEXAS MEMORIAL MUSEUM
The University of Texas at Austin
24th and Trinity
Austin, Texas 78705

THERMOPOLIS DINOSAUR MUSEUM
Wyoming Dinosaur Center
Route 3, Box 209
Thermopolis, Wyoming 82443

UNIVERSITY OF ALASKA MUSEUM
907 Yukon Drive
Fairbanks, Alaska 99775

UNIVERSITY OF COLORADO MUSEUM
University of Colorado
Henderson Building, Campus Box 218
Boulder, Colorado 80309-0315

UNIVERSITY OF KANSAS MUSEUM OF NATURAL HISTORY (formerly SYSTEMATICS MUSEUMS–UNIVERSITY OF KANSAS)
University of Kansas
Dyche Hall
14th and Jaybrook Boulevard
Lawrence, Kansas 66045-2454

UNIVERSITY OF MICHIGAN EXHIBIT MUSEUM
Alexander G. Ruthven Museum Building
1109 Geddes Avenue
Ann Arbor, Michigan 48109

UNIVERSITY OF NEBRASKA STATE MUSEUM
University of Nebraska
Morrill Hall
Lincoln, Nebraska 68588

UNIVERSITY OF WYOMING GEOLOGICAL MUSEUM
Box 3254
Laramie, Wyoming 82071

UPPER MUSSELSHELL MUSEUM
11 South Central
Harlowton, Montana 59036

UTAH FIELD HOUSE OF NATURAL HISTORY
446 South 100 West
Vernal, Utah 84078

UTAH MUSEUM OF NATURAL HISTORY
University of Utah
Salt Lake City, Utah 84112
    Note: Mostly dinosaurs from the Upper Jurassic Morrison Formation.

VIRGINIA LIVING MUSEUM
524 Clyde Morris Boulevard
Newport News, Virginia 23601

VIRGINIA MUSEUM OF NATURAL HISTORY
1001 Douglas Avenue
Martinsville, Virginia 24112

WAGNER FREE INSTITUTE OF SCIENCE
17th Street and Montgomery Avenue
Philadelphia, Pennsylvania 19121

WEBER STATE UNIVERSITY MUSEUM OF NATURAL SCIENCE
3750 Harrison Boulevard
Ogden, Utah 84408

WEINMAN MINERAL MUSEUM
PO Box 1255
Cartersville, Georgia 30120

WISTARIAHURST MUSEUM
238 Cabot Street
Holyoke, Massachusetts 01041

WITTE MUSEUM OF HISTORY AND SCIENCE (also known as the WITTE MEMORIAL MUSEUM)
3801 Broadway
San Antonio, Texas 78209

SOUTH AMERICA

Argentina

INSTITUTO MIGUEL LILLO
Falcultad de Ciencias Naturales
Miguel Lillo 205
AR 4000 San Miguel de Tucuman

MUSEO ARGENTINO DE CIENCIAS NATURALES
"Bernardino Rivadavia"
Av. Angel Gallardo 470
Buenos Aires 1405
    Note: Mostly dinosaurian taxa from South America.

MUSEO DE LA PLATA
University La Plata
Paseo de Bosque s/n 1900
La Plata

MUSEO DE CIENCIAS NATURALES DE LA UNIVERSIDAD NACIONAL DEL COMAHUE
Buenos Aires 1400
Neuquén

MUSEO MUNICIPAL "CARMEN FUNES"
8318 Plaza Huincul
Neuquén
    Note: Includes giant dinosaurs recently collected from Argentina, such as the theropod *Giganotosaurus* and the sauropod *Argentinosaurus*.

MUSEO PASEO DEL BOSQUE S/N
Buenos Aires 1900
La Plata

Brazil

MUSEU NACIONAL
20942 Quinta da Boa Vista
São Cristóvão
Rio de Janeiro 20940
    Note: Includes Mostly sauropod material.

Uruguay

MUSEO NACIONAL DE HISTORIA NATURALES
Casilla de Correo 399
1100 Montivedeo

Glossary

The following terms appear in this volume, but are not necessarily defined in the text. Definitions of terms were mostly based upon those published in a number of earlier sources, these including various dictionaries of the English language, and also the following books: A Dictionary of Scientific Terms *(Kenneth 1960),* The Illustrated Encyclopedia of Dinosaurs *(Norman 1985),* The Dinosauria *(Weishampel, Dodson and Osmólska 1990),* Encyclopedia of Dinosaurs *(Currie and Padian 1997), and* The Complete Dinosaur *(Farlow and Brett-Surman 1998).*

A PRIORI   Conclusion reached about a specific instance based upon something generally known.

ABDUCTION   Movement of part of the body away from the midline axis of body (opposite of adduction).

ABDUCTOR   Muscle that brings one bony part away from another.

ABRADED   Worn.

ACETABULUM   Cup-shaped socket in the pelvic girdle for the head of the femur.

ACROMIAL   Artery, process, or ligament pertaining to the acromion.

ACROMION   Ventral prolongation of the scapular spine.

ADAPTATION   Ability of a species or population of organisms to undergo change in response to its environment.

ADDUCTION   Movement of part of the body toward the midline axis of the body (opposite of abduction).

ADDUCTOR   Muscle that brings one bony part towards another.

ALA   Winglike projection or structure.

ALLOMETRY   Study of relative growth; change of proportions relating to growth.

ALTRICIAL BEHAVIOR   Behavior in which a parent or parents care for the newly born.

ALVEOLI   Pits or sockets on the surface of an organ or a bone.

AMBIENS   Thigh muscle.

AMMONITE   Any of various invertebrate organisms of the Mesozoic, belonging to the Cephalopoda, having a flat, coiled, chambered shell.

AMNION   An internal membrane characteristic of the amniote egg.

AMNIOTE   Tetrapod (reptile, bird, and mammal) that reproduces via amniote egg or its derivatives.

AMNIOTIC   Pertaining to amnion (a foetal membrane of reptiles, birds and mammals), applied to a sac, folds, cavity, and fluids.

AMPHIBIAN   Tetrapod adapted to live on both land and in water.

AMPHICOELOUS   Concave on both surfaces of a vertebral centra.

AMPHYPLATYAN   Flat on both ends of a vertebral centra.

ANALAGOUS   Describing structures in different kinds of organisms which serve the same function, without being derived from the same ancestral structure.

ANGIOSPERM   Seed plant in which its seed is enveloped by a seed vessel fruit; the flowering plants.

ANGULAR   In most vertebrates, a dermal bone in the lower jaw, upon which rest the dentary and splenial bones.

ANTERIOR   Toward the front end.

ANTIBODY   Protein produced by the body for attacking foreign bodies such as germs.

ANTITROCHANTER   Articular surface of the ilium of birds, against which the trochanter of the femur plays.

ANTORBITAL   In front of the orbits.

ANTORBITAL FENESTRA   Opening in the skull, behind the external nares and in front of the orbit.

ANTORBITAL FOSSA   Depression surrounding the antorbital fenestra.

APOMORPHIC   In cladistics, the derived state occurring only within members of an ingroup, when a character exhibits two states within that ingroup.

APOMORPHY   In cladistics, a derived character.

APPENDICULAR SKELETON   That part of the skeleton including the pectoral girdles, forelimbs, pelvic girdles, and hind limbs.

AQUATIC   Living in the water.

ARBOREAL   Living mostly or exclusively in trees, bushes, or shrubs.

ARCADE   In anatomy, a bony bridge.

ARCHAEOLOGIST (also **ARCHEOLOGIST**)   Scientist who makes a study of the life and culture of man.

ARCHOSAURIA   Diapsid group including dinosaurs, pterosaurs, thecodontians, and crocodiles, defined primarily by the possession of an antorbital fenestra.

ARCHOSAUROMORPH   One of a group of diapsids including dinosaurs, birds, pterosaurs, crocodilians, and their close relatives.

ARCTOMETATARSALIAN CONDITION   Central metatarsal (III) pinched proximally, therefore obscured from view anteriorly, reduced or excluded from contact with the tibiotarsus.

ARMOR   Bony scutes, plates, shields, horns, spikes, and clubs possessed by some dinosaurs.

ARTHROPOD   Member of the Arthropoda, an invertebrate phylum consisting of animals with a chitinous exoskeleton and jointed appendages.

ARTICULAR   In dinosaurs, the bone toward the rear of the mandible by which the lower jaw articulates with the quadrate bone.

ARTICULATED   Jointed or joined together.

ASSEMBLAGE   Large group of fossils and other items found at the same location, considered to originate from the same time period.

ASTRAGALUS   Larger tarsal bone which mostly articulates with the tibia dorsally and metatarsus ventrally.

ATLAS   First cervical vertebra.

ATLANTAL   Pertaining to the atlas bone.

AUTAPOMORPHY   In cladistics, a character state unique to one taxon.

AVIAN   Having to do with birds.

AXIAL SKELETON   That part of the

skeleton including the vertebral column and ribs.

AXIS Second cervical vertebra.

BADLANDS Area of barren land heavily roughly eroded by water and wind into ridges, mesas and peaks.

BARB Delicate threadlike structure that extends obliquely from a feather rachis, forming the vane.

BASAL Near or at the base of a group; a group outside a more derived clade.

BASI- Prefix meaning "basis."

BASICRANIUM Base of the skull.

BASIOCCIPITAL Median bone in the occipital region of the skull, forming at least part of the occipital condyle.

BASIPTERYGOID Process of the basisphenoid contacting the pterygoid.

BASISPHENOID Cranial bone between the basioccipital and presphenoid.

BATTERY Distinctive tooth pattern wherein a number of small, slender teeth are tightly wedged together along the length of the jaw, with multiple teeth stacked in a single tooth position (as in hadrosaurs).

BAUPLAN General body plan for a group of organisms; literally, a German word meaning an architect's or a building's plan.

BED In geology, distinct layers of sedimentary rock.

BICIPITAL Groove on the upper part of the humerus; crests of the greater and lesser tubercles of the humerus; divided into two parts at one end.

BIFURCATED Forked; having two prongs or branches.

BINOMIAL SYSTEM OF NOMENCLATURE Traditional practice of using two scientific names (for genus and species) in the formal scientific name of a species.

BIOCHRON Short interval of geologic time defined on the basis of fossil evidence.

BIOGEOGRAPHIC Relating to biogeography, the study of the location and distribution of life on Earth.

BIOLOGY Science of life.

BIOMASS Total estimated body mass or weight of all the animals of a population combined; also, the total mass or weight of a single individual.

BIOMECHANICS Study of the motion of a body of a given organism in the context of mechanical laws and principles.

BIOMOLECULE Molecule relating to life.

BIOSTRATIGRAPHY Study of the distribution of fossils in distinct strata.

BIOTA Flora and fauna of a region.

BIPEDALITY Habitually walking on two feet.

BIVALVE Invertabrate organism consisting of two valves or plates, such as a mussel shell.

BIVARIATE Variable condition occurring simultaneously with another variable.

BODY FOSSIL Fossil consisting of an actual part of the organism.

BONEBED (also **BONE BED**) Sedimentary layer having a large concentration of fossil remains.

BOSS Raised ridge or rounded body part, such as the bony mass on the snout of some ceratopsians.

BRAINCASE Part of the skull enclosing the brain.

BRANCH On a cladogram, a line connecting a taxon to a node that joins it to another taxon, representing the divergence of a taxon from its nearest relatives.

BREVIS SHELF Median shelf on the postacetabular section of the ilium for the origin of some of the caudifumoralis brevis muscle.

BROWSER Animal that feeds on high foliage (*e.g.*, bushes, not grasses).

BUCCAL Pertaining to the cheek; the surface of a tooth toward the cheek or lip.

BUTTRESS Bony structure for reinforcement.

CALCANEUM Smaller tarsal bone, lateral to the astragalus and distal to the fibula.

CALCAREOUS Composed of, containing, or characteristic of calceum carbonate, calcium, or limestone.

CANALICULATE Possessing canals.

CANCELLOUS BONE Spongy bone, having tissues that are not closely packed.

CAPITULUM Knoblike swelling at the end of a bone.

CARAPACE Hard outer covering to the body, like the shell of a turtle.

CARCASS Dead body of an animal.

CARINA On some bones and teeth, a keel-like ridge or edge.

CARNIVORE Flesh-eater.

CARNOSAUR In the original (and abandoned) usage, an informal term generally referring to any large theropod; in the modern sense, a member of the Carnosauria, a restricted group of large theropods.

CARPAL Pertaining to the wrist; also, a bone of the wrist.

CARTILAGE Transluscent firm and elastic tissue usually found in connection with bones and on the articular ends of limb bones.

CATASTROPHIC Pertaining to theories and beliefs that mass extinctions were the result of cataclysmic events.

CAUDAL Pertaining to the tail; toward the tail; also used in place of "posterior."

CEMENTUM Substance investing parts of the teeth, chemically and physically allied to bone.

CENTRUM Main body of the vertebra (ventral to the neural chord) from which rise the neural and hemal arches.

CERVICAL Pertaining to the neck.

CHARACTER Distinctive feature or trait of an organism, or any difference among organisms, that can be used in classification or in estimating phylogeny.

CHARACTER STATE Range of expressions or conditions of a character.

CHELONIAN Member of the Chelonia, a reptilian group including turtles and tortoises.

CHEVRON Bone that hangs below a caudal vertebra.

CHOANA Funnel-shaped internal nasal opening.

CHONDROCYTES Cells that produce and maintain the plate, producing a mineralized matrix around themselves.

CINGULUM Girdle-like structure on teeth.

CLADE Monophyletic taxon as diagnosed by synapomorphies.

CLADISTICS Scientific approach in taxonomy to classify groups of organisms in terms of the recency of their last common ancestor.

CLADOGRAM Diagram representing the distribution of shared-derived characters for groupings of organisms.

CLASSIFICATION Process of organizing clades into groups related by common descent.

CLAVICLE Collarbone forming the anterior portion of the shoulder-girdle.

CNEMIAL CREST Crest along the anterior dorsal margin of the tibia.

COCHLEA Part of the labyrinth of the ear.

COELUROSAUR In the original (and abandoned) usage, an informal term generally referring to all small theropods; in the modern sense, a large group of theropods including both small and gigantic forms.

COLD-BLOODED Informal term for "ectothermic."

COLLAGEN Gelatinous protein present in all multicellular organisms, particularly in connective tissue.

COMMON ANCESTOR In cladistics, a taxon exhibiting all synapomorphies of that taxon but neither autapomorphies nor the synapomorphies at higher levels within that taxon.

COMMUNITY Ecological relationships between a local environment and all its fauna and flora.

COMPETITION Simultaneous use of a limited resource by more than one species, resulting in conflicting efforts by them for continued survival.

CONDYLE Process on a bone utilized in articulation.

CONE (See Mammilla.)

CONGENERIC Belonging to the same genus.

CONIFER One of a group of gymnosperms including pines, spruces, larches, firs, and related plants.

CONSERVATIVE Tending to remain unchanged, as in being similar to an ancestral group.

CONSPECIFIC Belonging to the same species.

CONVERGENCE (also **CONVERGENT EVOLUTION; PARALLELISM**) Organisms evolving similar appearances due to responses to similar lifestyle demands, though not sharing direct common ancestors.

COPROLITE Fossilized dung.

CORACOID Bone between the scapula and the sternum, participates in the shoulder joint.

CORONOID PROCESS In reptiles, a prong-shaped bony process on the lower jaw for the attachment of jaw-closing muscles.

COSMOPOLITAN Having a very wide or worldwide distribution.

CRANIAL Toward the head; sometimes used in place of "anterior."

CRANIUM Bones of the skull, particularly the braincase, but excluding those of the lower jaw.

CREST Ridge or rounded area of bone; in hadrosaurids, a rounded area of bone on the upper part of the skull, sometimes containing hollow passages.

CROCODILIAN Member of the Crocodilia, a successful group of Mesozoic and extant archosaurs related to dinosaurs.

CROWN Exposed part of the tooth.

CROWN GROUP All descendants of the closest common ancestor of living forms.

CRUSTACEAN A member of the Crustaceous, a group of mostly aquatic invertebrates having segmented bodies, chitinous skeletons, and paired, jointed limbs.

CRYPTIC Not obvious or clear from the available evidence, ambiguous.

CT SCAN (also **CAT SCAN**) Process by which a computer is used to process data from a tomograph in order to display a reconstructed cross section of an organism's body without physically cutting into it.

CURSORIAL Running.

DEFINITION Meaning of a taxon name, defined by its member taxa or by a statement of ancestry; formerly, sometimes used as a diagnosis.

DELTOPECTORAL CREST Bony flange of the humerus for attachment of the deltoid and pectoralis muscles.

DENTARY Largest bone of the lower jaw, usually bearing teeth.

DENTICLE Small bump-like processes along the edges of teeth.

DENTICULATE Having denticles.

DENTITION Teeth.

DEPOSIT Accumulation of a substance (*e.g.*, sediment, bones).

DERIVED CHARACTER More specialized character evolved from a simpler, more primitive condition.

DERMAL Pertaining to the skin.

DERMAL ARMOR Platelets or small plates of bone that grew in the flesh but were not connected to the skeleton.

DESCRIPTION In paleontology, a detailed verbal representation of material.

DIAGNOSIS Concise statement enumerating the distinctive characters of a particular organism.

DIAPHRAGM In synapsids, a muscle sheet separating the chest cavity from the abdomen.

DIAPOPHYSIS Lateral or transverse process of the neural arch.

DIAPSID Reptiles with a skull having a pair of openings behind the orbit.

DIASTEMA Toothless space in a jaw, generally between two different kinds of teeth (such as the canine and post-canines in mammals).

DIGIT Toe or finger.

DIGITIGRADE Walking with only the digits touching ground.

DIMORPHISM State of having two different forms, usually according to sex.

DISARTICULATED Pulled apart.

DISPERSAL In biogeography, spreading out.

DISPLAY Body feature or behavior pattern that acts as a physical signal or indicator to others of its (or another) species.

DISTAL End of any structure farthest from the midline of an organism, or from the point of attachment; away from the mass of the body; segments of a limb or of elements within a limb; the edge of a tooth away from the symphysis along the tooth row.

DISTRIBUTION (also **GEOGRAPHIC DISTRIBUTION**) Total geographic range in which a taxon occurs.

DIVERGENCE In evolution, moving away from a central group or changing in form.

DIVERTICULUM Sac or tube, "blind" at the distal end, that branches off from a cavity or canal.

DNA Deoxyribonucleic acid, the chemical substance within cells of living organisms containing the organism's genetic information.

DORSAL Relating to the back; toward the back.

ECOSYSTEM Ecological system formed by interaction of organisms and their environment.

ECOLOGY Biological study of the relationship between organisms and their environment.

ECTOPTERYGOID Ventral membrane bone behind the palatine, extending to the quadrate.

ECTOTHERMIC Relying on external sources of heat to maintain body temperature; "cold-blooded."

EDENTULOUS Toothless.

EMBAYMENT A baylike shape or depression in a bone.

EMBRYO Young organism in prebirth stages of development.

ENAMEL Form of calceum phosphate forming the hard outer covering on teeth.

ENDEMIC Relating to an indigenous species or population occurring in a specific geographic range.

ENDOCRANIUM The brain cavity of the skull.

ENDOTHERMIC Able to generate body heat internally by means of chemical reactions; "warm-blooded."

ENVIRONMENT Surroundings in which organisms live.

EOLIAN (also **AEOLIAN**) Caused by the wind.

EPAXIAL Above the axis; dorsal.

EPIDERMIS Outer, nonvascular, and protective layer of the skin.

EPIJUGAL Hornlike projection off the jugal in ceratopsians.

EPIPHYSEAL Pertaining to the part or process of a bone formed from a separate center of ossification, later fusing with the bone.

EPIPODIUM Region of the rear part of the foot, or the bones in that region.

EPOCCIPITAL Small bone located on the edge of the ceratopsian frill.

EPOCH Lesser division of geologic time, part of a period.

ERA Largest division of geologic time.

EROSION   Result of weathering on exposed rocks.

EVOLUTION   Change in the characteristics of a population of organisms, caused by natural selection over time.

EXOCCIPITAL   Bone of the skull on each side of the foramen magnum.

EXOSTOSIS   Growth of bone resulting from partial parietal detachment.

EXPOSURE   In geology, where rock is exposed due to weathering.

EXTENSOR   Muscle that extends a limb or part of a limb; also used to designate surfaces of a limb, manus, or pes.

EXTINCTION   Termination of a species.

FACIES   In geology, one of different types of contemporaneous deposits in a lateral series of deposits; also, the paleontological and lithological makeup of a sedimentary deposit.

FACULTATIVE   Having the ability to live and adapt to certain conditions, while not being restricted to those conditions.

FAMILY   In Linnaean classification, a grouping of similar genera.

FAUNA   All the animals of a particular place and time.

FAUNACHRON   A span of time characterized by a special group or groups of animals.

FEMUR   Thigh-bone.

FENESTRA   Opening in a bone or between bones.

FIBRO-LAMELLAR BONE   Somewhat open hard tissue, filled with blood vessels, indicative of fast-growing bone.

FIBULA   Smaller, outer shin bone.

FLEXOR   Muscle which bends a joint; also used to designate surfaces of a limb, manus, or pes.

FLORA   All the plants of a particular place and time.

FONTANELLE   Opening on the frill in some ceratopsians.

FORAMEN   Opening through a bone or membraneous structure.

FORAMEN MAGNUM   Opening in the occipital area of the skull through which the spinal cord passes.

FORMATION   In geology, a formally defined and mappable unit of sedimentary rock.

FOSSA   Pit or trench-like depression.

FOSSIL   Preserved remains of an animal or plant at least 10,000 years old, usually formed through burial and possibly involving a chemical change; evidence of life in the geologic past.

FOSSILIZED   Having become a fossil.

FRONTAL   Bone of the skull roof in front of the parietal.

FUNCTIONAL MORPHOLOGY   Study of the movements and patterns of locomotion of an organism, mostly relative to its form or structure.

FUSION   In anatomy, the firm joining together of bones, either naturally or abnormally.

GASTRALIA   Belly ribs that help to support the viscera in some dinosaurs.

GASTROLITH   Small "stomach" stone that is swallowed for ballast or to grind up already consumed food.

GENUS   Group of closely related species.

GEOLOGIC TIME   Period of time spanning the formation of the Earth to the beginning of recorded history.

GEOLOGY   Science of the study of the Earth.

GIRDLE   Curved or circular structure, particularly one that encircles another.

GIZZARD   Muscular portion of the stomach utilized in grinding up food.

GLENOID   Socket in the pectoral girdle to which the head of the humerus attaches.

GONDWANA   Southern continent including South America, Africa, India, Madagascar, Australia, and Antarctica.

GRACILE   Having a graceful or slim build of form.

GRADE   Paraphyletic taxon as diagnosed by the absence and presence of synapomorphies, delineated based upon morphologic distance.

GRAVIPORTAL   Slow-moving or lumbering.

GRAZER   Animal that feeds on low-lying vegetation (e.g., grasses).

GREGARIOUS   Animals of the same species living in groups rather than in isolation.

GYMNOSPERM   Seed plant in which the seed is not enveloped by a fruit, including cycadophytes, seed ferns, conifers, and related plants.

HABITAT   Place in which an organism or population of organisms normally lives or occurs.

HALLUX   First digit of the pes.

HATCHLING   Organism newly hatched from an egg.

HAVERSIAN BONE   Kind of secondary bone that replaces primary bone, forming a series of vascular canals called "Haversian canals."

HEAD-BUTTING   Behavior in which two (usually male) individuals of the same species compete for dominance of their group by repeatedly colliding head to head.

HEMAL (or HAEMAL)   Pertaining to blood or blood vessels.

HERBIVORE   Plant-eater.

HERD   Large group of (usually herbivorous) animals of the same species.

HETERO-   Prefix meaning "other" or "different."

HETEROCHRONY   Condition of having a different beginning and ending of growth, or a different growth rate for a different feature, relative to the beginning and end, or the rate of development, of the same feature in an ancestor.

HISTO-   Prefix pertaining to tissue.

HISTOLOGY   Study of the fine structure of body tissues.

HOLOTYPE   Single specimen chosen to designate a new species.

HOMEOTHERMY   Maintaining a fairly constant body temperature regardless of environmental temperature changes.

HOMO-   Prefix meaning "same" or "alike."

HOMOLOGOUS   Similar because of common ancestry.

HOMOPLASY   In cladistics, a shared similarity between taxa explained by character reversal, convergence, or chance, and not a result of common ancestry.

HORIZON   Soil layer formed at a definite time and characterized by definite fossil species.

HUMERUS   Upper arm bone.

HYPANTRUM   In some reptiles, a notch on vertebrae for articulation with the hyposphene.

HYPAXIAL   Below the vertebral column; ventral.

HYPER-   Prefix meaning "more than," "greater than," *etc.*

HYPEREXTENSION   Atypical extension of a body part.

HYPERMORPHOSIS   Evolutionary change wherein sexual maturity takes place later in the descendant than in the ancestor.

HYPERTROPHY   Atypical enlargement or expansion of a body part.

HYPOSPHENE   In some reptiles, a wedge-shaped process on the neural arch of a vertebra, fitting into the hypantrum.

IBERIAN PENINSULA   Region of southwestern Europe, consisting of Spain and Portugal, separated from France by the Pyrenees mountains.

ICHNITE   Fossil footprint.

ICHNO-   Prefix meaning "track" or "footprint."

ICHNOGENUS   Genus name for a trackmaker.

ICHTHYOSAURS   Mesozoic marine reptiles with streamlined, somewhat dolphin-shaped bodies.

ILIUM   Dorsal bone of the pelvic arch; hipbone.

IN SITU   Referring to specimens in place in the ground where they are discovered.

INCISIFORM   Incisor-shaped.

INDETERMINATE   Incapable of being defined or classified.

INDEX TAXON   Taxon known from abundant fossils that are restricted to a particular span of geologic time, and which can, therefore, reliably be used to date the rocks in which its fossils are found.

INFRA-   Prefix meaning "below."

INGROUP   In cladistics, a monophyletic grouping of taxa.

INSTINCT   Unlearned, complex, and normally adaptive innate aspect of behavior.

INTEGUMENT   Outer covering, usually pertaining to skin.

INTERCENTRUM   Second central ring in a vertebra having two vertical rings in each centrum.

INTERMEDIUM   Small bone of the carpus and tarsus.

INTRA-   Prefix meaning "within."

INTRASPECIFIC   Within the same species.

INVERTEBRATE   Animal without a backbone.

ISCHIUM   Ventral and posterior bone of each half of the pelvic girdle.

ISOLATED   Set apart from similar items.

ISOMETRY   Growth of a part at the same rate as the whole.

ISOTOPE   Atom that differs in atomic weight from another atom of the same element.

JUGAL   Skull bone between the maxilla and quadrate.

JUNIOR SYNONYM   Taxon suppressed because another name, pertaining to the same fossil materials, was published previously.

JUVENILE   Young or immature animal.

KERATIN   Matter composed of fibrous protein, the main constituent in vertebrates of such epidermal structures as hair, nails, and horn.

KINETIC   In zoology, bones joined together but capable of movement.

K-T BOUNDARY (also **KT**, or **K/T, Boundary**)   In geologic time, the transition from the end of the Cretaceous (K) period to the beginning of the Tertiary (T), approximately 65 million years ago.

K-T EXTINCTION (also **KT Extinction**)   The termination of numerous (but not all) groups of animals and plants at the end of the Cretaceous period.

LABIAL   Near the lip.

LACRIMAL (also **LACRIMAL BONE, LACHRIMAL**)   Skull bone contributing to the anterior border of the orbit.

LAMELLAR   Referring to a thin, scale- or platelike tissue structure.

LATERAL   At the side externally; away from the midline.

LATEROSPHENOID   One of the bones of the braincase.

LAURASIA   Hypothetical northern supercontinent including North America, Europe, and parts of Asia.

LECTOTYPE   Specimen chosen from syntypes to redesignate the type of a species.

LIGAMENT   Strong fibrous band of tissue that support joints between bones and joins muscles to bones.

LINEAGE   Continuous line of descent, over an evolutionary span of time, from a particular ancestor.

LINEAR-   In a line.

LINES OF ARRESTED GROWTH (also **LAGs**)   Pattern of development wherein there are pauses in the deposition of bone and a related slower growth rate.

LINGUAL   Pertaining to the tongue; the surface of a tooth toward the tongue.

LOCALITY   In geology, named place where specimens have been found.

LOCOMOTION   An organism's ability to move from place to place; also, the manner in which an organism moves.

LONG BONE   Limb bone.

MANDIBLE   Lower jaw.

MANDIBULAR   Relating to the mandible.

MANUS   Part of the forelimb corresponding to the hand, comprising metacarpals and phalanges.

MARINE   Pertaining to the sea.

MARLY   relating to marl (muddy limestone).

MASS EXTINCTION   Death of all members of a number of diverse animal groups apparently due to a common cause.

MATRIX   Fossil-embedded rock.

MAXILLA   Usually tooth-bearing principal bone in the upper jaw.

MAXILLARY   Relating to the maxilla.

MECKEL'S (also **MECKELIAN**) **GROOVE**   Groove inside the jaw for Meckel's cartilage and associated vessels/nerves.

MEDIAL   From the inside or inner; toward the midline.

MEDULLA   Central part of a bone or organ.

MEGA-   Prefix meaning "large."

MEGAPREDATORY   Referring to a large carnivorous animal.

MESIAL   In a middle longitudinal or vertical plane; the edge of a tooth toward the symphysis or premaxillary midline.

METABOLISM   Constructive and destructive chemical changes in the body for maintenance, growth, and repair of an organism.

METACARPAL   Relating to the metacarpus; also, a bone of the metacarpus, generally one per digit.

METACARPUS   Bones of the manus between the wrist and fingers.

METAPODIALS   In tetrapods, bones of the metacarpus and metatarsus.

METATARSAL   Relating to the metatarsus; also, a bone of the metatarsus, generally one per digit.

METATARSUS   Part of the foot between the tarsus and toes.

MICRO-   Prefix meaning "very small."

MICROBE   Minute organism.

MIDLINE   Imaginary line extending dorsally along the length of an animal.

MIGRATION   Behavior pattern whereby a group of animals of the same species move from one location to another on a regular or recurring basis.

MINERALIZED   Formerly organic matter that has been transformed into mineral matter.

MODERN   Living now or recently.

MOLLUSC (also **MOLLUSK**)   Member of the Mollusca, a group of bilaterally symmetrical invertebrates, such as snails, clams, cephalopods, and other forms.

MONOPHYLETIC   Group of taxa including a common ancestor and all of its descendants; derived from a single origin; having the condition of "monophyly."

MORPHOLOGY   Science of form.

MORPHOMETRIC   Regarding the analysis or measurement of an organism's shape or form.

MORPHOTYPE   Type specimen of one form of a polymorphic species.

MULTI-   Prefix meaning "many."

MULTITUBURCULATE   Member of the Multituberculata, a successful group of early mammals that may have been the first herbivorous members of the Mammalia.

MUMMIFICATION   Process by which parts (*e.g.*, soft tissues) of an ancient animal, which would normally not be preserved over time, are preserved.

MUSCULATURE   Arrangement of muscles.

MUZZLE   Anterior part of the head containing the nostrils and jaws.

NARIAL Pertaining to the nostrils.

NARIS Nostril opening.

NASAL Bone near the front of the skull, between the premaxilla and the frontal; also, that which pertains to the nostrils or nose.

NEO- Prefix meaning "new."

NEOCOMIAN Old term used to designate a subdivision of the Early Cretaceous period, equivalent to Hauterivian.

NEONATE Newly born organism.

NEOTENOUS (also **NEOTENIC**) State of being sexually mature while having retained some juvenile characteristic.

NEURAL Closely connected with nerves or nervous tissues.

NEURAL ARCH Bony bridge over the passage of the spinal cord.

NEURAL CANAL Canal formed by the neural arch and centrum.

NEURAL SPINE Spine rising up from the neural arch.

NEUROCENTRAL Having to do with a neurocentrum, a type of centrum in primitive vertebrates.

NICHE Unique place occupied by a particular species within a larger ecological community.

NODE Point on a cladogram where two or more lines meet, this constituting a taxon including all descendant taxa that will meet at that point.

NODE-BASED Defining a taxonomic group as the descendants of the most recent common ancestor of two other groups and all descendants of that ancestor.

NOMEN DUBIUM Taxon founded upon material of questionable diagnostic value.

NOMEN NUDUM Taxon improperly founded without published material, diagnosis, type designation, and figure.

NOMENCLATURE Official naming or system of naming of taxa.

NONAVIAN (also **NON-AVIAN**) Pertaining to dinosaurs other than birds; also, not pertaining to birds.

NUCHAL Pertaining to the neck.

OBLIGATE Limited or restricted to a particular mode of behavior or environmental condition.

OBTURATOR Pertaining to any structure in the area of the obturator foramen.

OBTURATOR FORAMEN Oval foramen within the ischium for the passage of the obturator nerve/vessels.

OCCIPITAL CONDYLE Condyle with which the skull moves on the atlas and axis.

OCCIPUT Back part of the skull.

OCCLUSION Surfaces of the upper and lower teeth making contact with each other when the jaws are closed in a bite.

ODONTOID Toothlike process.

OLECRANON Process for insertion of the triceps muscle at the proximal end of the ulna.

OLFACTORY Pertaining to the sense of smell.

OMNIVORE Animal that eats both plant and animal food.

ONTOGENY Growth and development of an individual.

OPISTHOCOELOUS Having the centrum concave posteriorly.

OPISTHOPUBIC Pubis that is directed rearward.

OPISTHOTIC Inferior posterior bony element of the otic capsule.

OPTIC Pertaining to vision.

OPTIC LOBE Part of the brain connected with vision.

ORBIT Bony cavity in which the eye is housed.

ORBITOSPHENOID Paired elements in the skull located between the presphenoid and frontal.

ORDER In Linnaean classification, a category including related families within a class.

ORGANIC Relating to things alive.

ORGANISM Any individual living being.

ORNAMENTATION Visible external body feature (*e.g.*, horn, frill, *etc.*) that primarily functions in social behavior.

ORNITH- Prefix meaning "bird" or "birdlike."

ORNITHOLOGICAL Regarding ornithology, the study of birds.

OSSEOUS Resembling or composed of bone.

OSSICLE Bony platelets set under the skin, serving as secondary armor.

OSSIFICATION The process by which bone forms.

OSTEO- Prefix meaning "bone" or "relating to bones."

OSTEODERM Bony plates or scutes in the skin.

OSTEOLOGY Part of zoology dealing with the structure and development of bones.

OSTEOMA Bone growth.

OTIC Pertaining to the ear.

OUTGROUP In cladistics, the character state occurring in the nearest relatives of an ingroup.

PAEDOMORPHOSIS Evolutionary change in which adults of a descendant species retain juvenile characteristics of the ancestral species.

PALATE Roof of the mouth.

PALATINE One of the bones of the palate, located near the front of the skull and to the side of the vomer; also, pertaining to the palate.

PALEO- (also **PALAEO-**) Prefix meaning "ancient" or "past," pertaining to something very old or prehistoric.

PALEOBIOLOGY Study of ancient extinct organisms.

PALEOECOLOGICAL Pertaining to paleoecology, the study of the relationships between extinct organisms and their paleoenvironments.

PALEOENVIRONMENT Environmental conditions in the geologic past.

PALEOGEOGRAPHIC Pertaining to paleogeography, the study of the geographic distribution of life forms in the geologic past.

PALEONTOLOGY Scientific study of past life, based on the study of fossil and fossil traces.

PALPEBRAL Small bone located on the rim of the eye socket, often forming a body eyelid.

PALYNOLOGY Study of fossil pollen grains and spores.

PALYNOMORPH Spores, pollen, and cysts of certain algae.

PANGAEA (also **PANGEA**) Hypothetical huge supercontinent formed by the collision of all Earth's continents during the Permian period.

PAPILLA Conical dermal structure constituting the beginning of a feather.

PARA- Prefix meaning "beside."

PARALLELISM (See **CONVERGENCE**)

PARAPHYLETIC In cladistics, relating to a taxonomic group including a hypothetical common ancestor and only some of that ancestor's descendants.

PARASAGITTAL Parallel to the midline of an animal.

PARASPHENOID Membrane bone forming the floor of the braincase.

PARATAXON Taxon classified on the basis of trace fossils, the method of classification parallel to the Linnaean system.

PARATYPE Specimen used along with the holotype in defining a new species.

PARIETAL Bone of the skull roof behind the frontal.

PAROCCIPITAL PROCESS Bony process at the back of the skull.

PARSIMONY In cladistic analysis, a subjective criterion for selecting taxa, usually that which proposes the least number of homoplasies.

PECTINEAL Pertaining to a ridgeline on the femur and the attached pectineus muscle.

PECTORAL   Pertaining to the chest area of the skeleton.

PECTORAL GIRDLE   Bones of the shoulder, including scapula, corocoid, sternum, and clavicle.

PEDICLE   Backward-projecting vertebral process.

PEDUNCLE   Stalk- or stemlike process of a bone.

PELVIC GIRDLE   Hip area of the skeleton, comprising the ilium, ischium, and pubis.

PERAMORPHOSIS   Evolutionary change wherein juveniles of a descendant species exhibit some adult characteristics of the ancestral species.

PERIOD   Division of geologic time, a subdivision of an Era.

PERIOTIC   Skull bone enclosing parts of the membranous labyrinth of the internal ear.

PERMINERALIZATION   Fossil forming process wherein additional mineral materials are deposited in pore spaces of the originally hard parts of animals.

PES   Foot.

PHALANGEAL FORMULA   Formula giving the number of phalanges in the digits of the manus and pes.

PHALANX   Segment of the digits, a bone of the fingers or toes.

PHYLOGENETIC   Concerning the evolutionary relationships within and among groups of organisms.

PHYLOGENY   Evolutionary treelike diagram or "tree" showing the relationships between ancestors and descendants.

PHYSIOLOGY   Biological study dealing with the functions and activities of organisms.

PHYTOSAUR   crocodile-like, semiaquatic "thecodontians" of the Triassic.

PLANKTON   Generally microscopic plant and animal organisms that drift or float in large masses in fresh or salt water.

PLANTIGRADE   Walking with the entire sole of the foot touching the ground.

PLATE (also DERMAL PLATE)   In paleobiology, a piece of bone embedded in the skin.

PLATE TECTONICS   Study of the plates making up the earth's crust.

PLATYCOELOUS   Condition in which the posterior articular end of a vertebral centrum is flat.

PLESIOMORPH   In cladistics, the more primitive character state of two that are exhibited within members of an ingroup while also occurring in the nearest outgroup; a primitive feature.

PLESIOSAUR   One of a group of Mesozoic marine reptiles.

PLEUROCOEL   Cavity in the side of a vertebral centrum.

PLEUROKINETIC HINGE   Hinge between the maxilla and remainder of the skull, allowing the maxillae to swing outward when the mouth is closed.

PLEXIFORM   Having interwoven blood vessels, like a network.

PLUMULACEOUS   Downy feathers.

PNEUMATIC   Bones penetrated by canals and air spaces.

POLLEX   In the manus, the thumb or innermost digit of the normal five.

POLYPHYLETIC   Associated groups that do not share a single common ancestor.

POROUS   Spongelike.

POST-   Prefix meaning "after"; in anatomy, meaning "closer to the rear."

POSTACETABULAR PROCESS   Portion of the ilium posterior to the acetabulum.

POSTCRANIA (or POSTCRANIAL SKELETON)   Skeleton excluding the skull.

POSTER   Research work presented (at a symposium, conference, convention, or other gathering of scientists) in the form of a visual display, sometimes incorporating charts, photographs, maps, *etc.*

POSTERIOR   Toward or at the rear end.

POSTMORTEM   Following the death of an organism.

POSTURE   Walking or standing position.

POSTZYGAPOPHYSIS   Process on the posterior face of the neural arch, for articulation with the vertebra behind it.

PREACETABULAR PROCESS   Portion of the ilium anterior to the acetabulum.

PREARTICULAR   Bone in the lower jaw of primitive tetrapods.

PRECOCIAL   Species in which the young are relatively advanced upon hatching.

PRECURSOR   Earlier form of life from which a later form is descended.

PREDATOR   Organism that hunts and eats other organisms.

PREDENTARY   In ornithischians, a small crescent-shaped bone located at the tip of the lower jaw.

PREHISTORIC   Referring to an era before recorded history.

PREMAXILLA   A usually paired bone at the front of the upper jaw.

PREOCCUPIED   In zoological nomenclature, a taxonomic name identical to one published previously by another author.

PREORBITAL   Anterior to the orbit (=antorbital).

PREPARATION   One or more procedures applied to a fossil specimen so that the specimen can be strengthened, handled, preserved, studied, displayed, *etc.*

PREPARATOR   Person who prepares fossils for study or display.

PRESERVATION   General condition of a fossil specimen, referring to its quality and completeness.

PREY   Creature hunted and caught for food.

PREZYGAPOPHYSIS   Process on the anterior face of the neural arch, for articulation with the vertebra in front of it.

PRIMARY BONE   Bone that is formed as an organism grows.

PRIMITIVE   Characters or features found in the common ancestor of a taxonomic group, which are also found in all members of that group; also (more generally), less developed, earlier.

PRIORITY   Rule in scientific nomenclature stating that, in the case of different taxonomic names given to the same form or groupings of forms, the name published first is valid.

PRO-   Prefix meaning "for."

PROCESS   Outgrowth or projection of bone.

PROGENESIS   Evolutionary change wherein sexual maturity takes place earlier in the descendant species than in the ancestor.

PROOTIC   Anterior bone of the otic capsule.

PROTO-   Prefix signifying "first" or "earliest."

PROTO TAIL CLUB   Incipient club, not as fully developed as in most dinosaurs bearing tail clubs.

PROTOFEATHER   Incipient feather including branching barbs, but lacking the aerodynamic quality of the true avian feather.

PROVENANCE   Place of origin.

PROXIMAL   Nearest to the center of the body; toward the mass of the body; segment of a limb or of elements within a limb.

PTEROSAUR   Flying reptile of the Mesozoic, related to dinosaurs.

PTERYGOID   Winglike posterior bone of the palate.

PUBIC   Relating to the pubis.

PUBIS   Antero-ventral bone of the pelvic girdle.

PUBOISCHIAL   Place where the pubis and ischium meet.

PULMONARY   Pertaining to the lungs.

QUADRATE   In birds, reptiles, and amphibians, the bone with which the lower jaw articulates.

QUADRATOJUGAL Bone connecting or overlying the quadrate and jugal.
QUADRUPEDALITY Habitually walking on four legs.

RACHIS Shaft of a feather.
RADIALE Carpal bone aligned with the radius.
RADIATION Process by which a group of species diverge from a common ancestor, thereby producing an increased biological diversity, usually over a relatively short span of time.
RADIOMETRIC DATING Dating method involving the measurement of decay, at a constant known rate, in various naturally occurring radioactive isotopes.
RADIUS Smaller forelimb bone between the humerus and carpals, lying next to the ulna.
RAMUS Branchlike structure.
RANK In classification, the position of a given level relative to levels above and below it.
RAPTOR One of various modern birds of prey, including falcons and hawks; a suffix used in the names of a number of sometimes rather diverse theropods; more recently, a popular term inaccurately used to designate any dromaeosaur.
RATITE One of a group of flightless birds having an unkeeled sternum.
RECONSTRUCTION Drawn or modeled skeleton or partial skeleton, based upon the original fossil remains, often incorporating extrapolation and knowledge of the more complete remains of other taxa (sometimes used to mean "restoration").
RECTRICES Stiff tail feathers of a bird or some nonavian theropods, used in steering.
RECURVED Curved backward.
RED BEDS Sedimentary beds that are reddish in color.
REMEX (plural: **REMIGES**) Large feather or quill on a bird's wing, consisting of primaries and secondaries.
RESPIRATION Breathing process, accomplished by an exchange of gases between an organism and its surrounding atmosphere.
RESPIRATORY TURBINATE (also **RT**) Thin, complex structure consisting of cartilage or bone in the nasal airway.
RESTORATION In paleontology, a drawn, sculpted, or other representation of a fossil organism as it may have appeared in life (sometimes used as synonymous with "reconstruction").
REVERSAL Transformation of a character in an advanced lineage back to its ancestral state.

RACHIS (also spelled **RHACHIS**) Shaft of a feather.
RHYNCHOSAUR A member of the Rhynchosauria, a group of large, squat, beaked, archosaur-like reptiles of the Triassic.
RIB Elongate and sometimes curved bone of the trunk articulating with vertebrae.
ROBUST Strongly formed or built; also, a method of study or analysis, verified by past results, which will probably result in a correct inference.
ROSTRAL (also **ROSTRUM**) In ceratopsians, median unpaired bone located at the tip of the upper jaw; also, toward the rostrum or tip of the head.
RUGOSE Possessing a rough surface (or "rugosity").

SACRAL Pertaining to the sacrum.
SACRAL RIB Rib that connects the sacral vertebrae to the pelvis.
SACRUM Structure formed by the sacral vertebrae and pelvic girdle.
SAGITTAL Pertaining to the midline on the dorsal aspect of the cranium.
SCALATION Form, arrangement, or pattern of epidermal scales.
SCAPULA Shoulder blade.
SCAVENGER Animal that feeds on dead animal flesh or other decomposing organic matter.
SCLEROTIC RING Ring of a series of overlapping bones around the outside of the eyeball.
SCUTE Horny or bony plate embedded in the skin.
SECONDARY BONE Bone formed during internal reconstruction following the dissolution and reconstitution of preexisting bone.
SEDIMENT Deposit of inorganic or organic particles.
SEDIMENTARY ROCKS Rocks formed from sediments.
SELECTION Principle that organisms having a certain hereditary characteristic will have a tendency to reproduce at a more successful rate than those of the same population not having this characteristic, consequently increasing their numbers in later generations.
SEMILUNATE Having the approximate shape of a half-crescent.
SENIOR SYNONYM Taxon having priority over another identically named taxon and regarded as the valid name, because of the former's earlier publication.
SEPTUM Partition separating spaces.
SERRATED Having a notched cutting edge.
SEXUAL DIMORPHISM Marked differences in shape, color, structure,

etc., between the male and female of the same species.
SIGMOID S-shaped.
SINUS Space within a body.
SISTER GROUP (also **SISTER CLADE, SISTER TAXON**) Group of organisms descended from the same common ancestor as its closest group.
SOCIAL BEHAVIOR Association of two or more individuals of a single species over a period of time other than the usual interaction of males and females for the purpose of reproduction.
SPATULATE Spatulate-shaped.
SPECIALIZED Modified in a particular way in response to certain environmental conditions.
SPECIES In paleontology, a group of animals with a unique shared morphology; in zoology, a group of naturally interbreeding organisms that do not naturally interbreed with another such group.
SPECIMEN Sample for study.
SPHENOID Large, wedge-shaped bone at the base of the skull.
SPINAL Having to do with the backbone or tail.
SPLENIAL Dermal bone in the lower jaw, covering much of Meckel's groove.
SQUAMOSAL In the vertebrate skull, a bone that forms part of the posterior side wall.
STEM-BASED Pertaining to a taxonomic group defined as all those entities that share a more recent common ancestor with one group than with another.
STERNAL Pertaining to the breastbone or chest.
STERNUM Breastbone.
STRATIGRAPHY Study of the pattern of deposition.
STRATUM Layer of sediment.
SUB- Prefix meaning "under."
SUBFAMILY In Linnaean classification, a category smaller than a family, including one genus or more.
SUBGENUS Subtle classification between a genus and a species; a group of related species within a genus.
SUITE Group of characters associated with a particular organism or species.
SULCUS Groove.
SUPER- Prefix meaning "greater" or "above."
SUPERCONTINENT Large structures formed by the joining of various continental areas.
SUPRA- Prefix meaning "above" or "over."
SUPRAORBITAL Small bone along

the upper rim of the orbit of the skull; in ceratopsians, a horn above the eye or brow.

SUPRATEMPORAL FENESTRA Opening in the top of the skull, posterior to the orbit.

SURANGULAR Bone of the upper rear area of the lower jaw, contacting (and posterior to) the dentary, the angular, and the articular.

SUTURE Line where bones contact each other.

SYMPHYSIS Line of junction of two pieces of bone.

SYN- Prefix meaning both "together" and "with"; also "united" or "fused."

SYNAPOMORPHY Shared/derived feature defining a monophyletic group; a unique character shared by two or more taxa.

SYNAPSID Member of the Synapsida, a group of tetrapods having a skull with one opening behind the eye socket, including pelycosaurs, therapsids, and mammals.

SYNCLINE In bedrock, a low, troughlike area in which rocks incline together from opposite sides.

SYNONYM Different names for the same taxon.

SYNSACRUM Single-unit structure formed by the fusion of several vertebrae.

SYSTEMATICS Scientific study that involves the classification and naming of organisms according to specific principles.

TAPHONOMY Study of the processes of burial and fossilization of organisms.

TARSAL Ankle bone.

TARSOMETATARSUS In birds and some dinosaurs, a bone formed by the fusion of the distal row of tarsals with the second to fourth metatarsals.

TARSUS Region where the leg and foot join.

TAXON Definite unite in the classification of animals and plants.

TAXONOMIC Pertaining to or according to the principles of taxonomy.

TAXONOMY Science of naming and classifying biological organisms.

TEMPORAL Bone on either side of the skull that forms part of its lateral surface; also, pertaining to that area of the skull.

TERRESTRIAL Land-dwelling.

TERRITORIAL Displaying a pattern of behavior whereby an organism or group of organisms of one species inhabit a particular area, and defend

that area against intrusion by other individuals of that species.

TETRAPOD Vertebrate with four limbs.

"THECODONTIAN" (also, "THECODONT") One of an obsolete and artificial "order" (Thecodontia) of early archosaurian reptiles of the Late Permian and Early Triassic, some of which may have been ancestral to dinosaurs, pterosaurs, and crocodiles.

THERAPSID Member of the Therapsida, a group of Late Permian and early Mesozoic (Triassic to Middle Jurassic) advanced mammal-like reptiles.

THERMOREGULATION One of various processes by which the body of an organism maintains internal temperature.

THORACIC Pertaining to the thorax; in the chest region.

THORAX Part of the body between the neck and abdomen.

TIBIA Shin bone.

TIBIOTARSUS In birds and some dinosaurs, the tibial bone to which are fused the proximal tarsals.

TOMOGRAPHY Recording internal images in a body via X-rays; a CT (or CAT) scan.

TOOTH BATTERY Set of numerous interlocking teeth arranged to form a grinding or cutting surface.

TRABECULAE Small sheets of bone.

TRACE FOSSIL Not the actual remains of an extinct organism, but rather the fossilized record of something left behind by that organism.

TRACKSITE Location of fossil footprints.

TRACKWAY Series of successive footprints made by a moving animal.

TRANSVERSE PROCESSES Laterally directed process of the vertebral centrum, for attachment of intervertebral muscles.

TRIDACTYL Having three digits.

TRIGEMINAL FORAMEN Opening for the fifth cranial nerve.

TRIPODAL Stance incorporating the hind feet and tail.

TROCHANTER Prominence or process on the femur to which muscles are attached.

TROPHIC Pertaining to food or the feeding process.

TROPICAL Hot and humid area with lush vegetation.

TUBERA Rounded protuberances.

TUBERCLE Small, rounded protuberance.

TUBERCULUM One of the heads of

the rib, attaches to the transverse process of the vertebral centrum.

TYMPANIC Pertaining to the ear or eardrum.

TYPE LOCALITY Geographic site at which a type specimen or type species was found and collected.

TYPE SPECIMEN Specimen used to diagnose a new species.

ULNA In the forearm, the larger long bone on the medial side, parallel with the radius.

ULNARE In the proximal row of carpals, the bone at the distal end of the ulna.

UNCINATE PROCESS In birds and some reptiles, a process on the ribs which overlaps other ribs.

UNGUAL Phalanx bearing a nail or claw.

VACUITY Open space.

VARIATION Range of appearance within a group of organisms.

VARIETY In biology, a taxonomic category below the species level, comprising naturally occurring or selectively bred individuals having varying characteristics.

VASCULAR Of or pertaining to the circulatory system.

VASCULARIZED Possessing blood vessels.

VASCULARIZATION Formation or development of blood vessels.

VENTRAL From beneath, relating to the belly or venter [abdomen or lower abdominal surface]; toward the belly.

VERTEBRA Bony segment of the backbone.

VERTEBRATE Animal with a backbone.

VERTEBRATE PALEONTOLOGY Scientific study of fossil animals having backbones.

VISCERA Internal organs of the body, particularly those of the digestive tract.

VOLCANISM Volcanic activity or force.

VOMER Bone at the front of the palate.

WARM-BLOODED Informal term for "endothermic."

ZONAL BONE Bone material resulting from a development pattern that involves slow to moderate growth during intermittent periods.

ZYGAPOPHYSIS Bony, usually peg-like process on the neural arch of a vertebra, by which it articulates with other vertebrae.

Bibliography

[Anonymous], 1966, *A Great Name in Oil: Sinclair Through Fifty Years*. New York: F. W. Dodge Company/McGraw Hill, 104 pages.

[Anonymous], 1994, *Chicago's Dinosaurs*. Chicago: Field Museum of Natural History, 21 pages ["written and produced by Peter R. Crane, Nina M. Cummings, Marlene H. Donnelly, Ron Dorfman, John J. Flynn, Laura D. Gates, Lori L. Grove, Zbigniew T. Jastrzebski, Olivier C. Rieppel, Clara R. Simpson, William F. Simpson, Nancy E. Walsh, John S. Weinstein"].

[Anonymous], 1997*a*, A ceratopsian resurfaces out West: *Geotimes*, "News Notes," 42 (10), pp. 12–14.

[Anonymous], 1997*b*, *Tyrannosaurus rex*. A highly important and virtually complete fossil skeleton. New York: Sotheby's [illustrated catalogue, unpaginated].

[Anonymous], 1998, Dinamation joins Discover Card in jr. paleontologist award contest: *Paleo Horizons*, 5 (1), p. 5.

Alden, David, 1996, Life restoration of *Acrocanthosaurus atokensis*: *Dinofest^TM International Symposium, April 18–21, 1996, Program and Abstracts*, p. 23.

Alvarez, Luis W., Walter Alvarez, Frank Asaro and Helen V. Michel, 1980, Extraterrestrial cause for the Cretaceous-Tertiary extinction: *Science*, 209 (4448), pp. 1095–1108.

Anderson, J. F., A. Hall-Martin, and Dale A. Russell, 1985, Long-bone circumference and weight in mammals, birds and dinosaurs: *Journal of Zoology, London*, 207, pp. 53–61.

Anderson, J. M., and A. R. I Cruickshank, 1978, The biostratigraphy of the Permian and Triassic, Part 5. A review of the classification and distribution of Permo-Triassic tetrapods: *Palaeontologia Africana*, 21, pp. 15–44.

Archibald, J. David, 1996, Dinosaur extinction and the end of an era: what the fossils say: *Dinofest^TM International Symposium, April 18–21, 1996, Programs and Abstracts*, p. 25.

Archibald, J. David, and L. J. Bryant, 1990, Differential Cretaceous/Tertiary extinctions of nonmarine vertebrates; evidence from northeastern Montana, *in*: V. L. Sharpton and P. D. Ward, editors, *Global Catastrophes in Earth History*, Geological Survey or America Special Paper, 247, pp. 549–562.

Ardévol, L., M. L. Casanovas, and J. V. Santafé, 1995, Restos de dinosaurios del Maastrichtiense de la Conca de Tremp, Lieda (cuenca de antepais Pirenaica meridional): *XI Jornadas Paleont.*, pp. 25–27, Tremp.

Ardolino, A., and D. Delpino, 1987, Senoniano (continental-marino), Comarca Nordpatágonica, Prov. del Chubut, Argentina: *In Congreso Geológico Argentino, No. 10, Actas*, 3, pp. 193–196, Tucumán, Argentina.

Azuma, Yoichi, and Philip J. Currie, 1995, A new giant dromaeosaurid from Japan: *Journal of Vertebrate Paleontology*, 15 (Supplement to Number 3), Abstracts of Papers, Fifty-fifth Annual Meeting, p. 17A.

Bailey, Jack Bowman, 1997, Neural spine elongation in dinosaurs: sailbacks or buffalobacks?: *Journal of Paleontology*, 71 (6), pp. 1124–1146.

Baird, Donald, 1986, Upper Cretaceous reptiles from the Severn Formation of Maryland: *The Mosasaur*, 3, pp. 63–85.

Bakker, Robert T., 1986, *The Dinosaur Heresies: New Theories Unlocking the Mystery of the Dinosaurs and Their Extinction*. New York: William Morrow and Company, 481 pages.

_____, 1987, The return of the dancing dinosaurs, *in*: Sylvia J. Czerkas and Everett C. Olson, editors, *Dinosaurs Past and Present*, Volume 1. Seattle: Natural History Museum of Los Angeles County, in association with University of Washington Press, pp. 38–69.

_____, 1988, Review of the Late Cretaceous nodosaurid Dinosauria, *Denversaurus schlessmania*, a new armor-plated dinosaur from the Latest Cretaceous of South Dakota, the last survivor of the nodosaurians, with comments on stegosaur-nodosaur relationships: *Hunteria*, 1 (3), pp. 3–23.

_____, 1996*a*, Dinosaur feet in three dimensions: *Sixth North American Paleontological Convention (Paleobiology, Smithsonian Institution, Washington, D.C.), Abstracts, The Paleontological Society Special Publication*, 8, p. 20.

_____, 1996*b*, The real Jurassic Park: Dinosaurs and habitats at Como Bluff, Wyoming, *in*: Michael Morales, editor, *Museum of Northern Arizona Bulletin 60*, pp. 35–49.

_____, 1997*a*, Megalosaurian mid-life crisis: Diversity, co-evolution and extinction at the Jurassic-Cretaceous boundary: *Journal of Vertebrate Paleontology*, 17 (Supplement to Number 3), Abstracts of Papers, Fifty-seventh Annual Meeting, p. 30A.

_____, 1997*b*, Raptor family values: Allosaur parents brought giant carcasses into their lair to feed their young, *in*: Donald L. Wolberg, Edmund Stump, and Gary Rosenberg, editors, *Dinofest^TM International: Proceedings of a Symposium Held at Arizona State University*. Philadelphia: Academy of Natural Sciences, pp. 51–63.

_____, 1998, Dinosaur mid-life crisis: The Jurassic-Cretaceous transition in Wyoming and Colorado, *in*: Spencer G. Lucas, James I. Kirkland, and John W. Estep, editors, *Lower and Middle Cretaceous Terrestrial Ecosystems*. Albuquerque: New Mexico Museum of Natural History and Science, Bulletin 14, pp. 67–78.

Bakker, Robert T., and A. Allen, 1996, The Wyoming Morrison, *in*: A. Hunter, editor, *Dino 96 — Paleoenvironments of the Jurassic, Tate Museum Field Conference 1996*, pp. 1–23.

Bakker, Robert T., Michael Williams, and Philip J. Currie, 1988, *Nanotyrannus*, a new genus of pygmy tyrannosaur, from the Latest Cretaceous of Montana: *Hunteria*, 1 (5), pp. 1–30.

Baldoni, A., 1992, Palinología de la Formación Santa Marta, Cretácico superior de la Isla James Ross, Antártida, *in*: C. Rinaldi, editor, *Geología de la Isla James Ross*. Buenos Aires, Argentina: Instituto Antártico Argentino, pp. 359–374.

Barnes, Fran, 1988, *Canyonlands National Park: Early History and First Descriptions*. Moab, Utah: Canyon Country Publications.

Barreto, Claudia, 1997, Dinosaur growth plates and dinosaur bone growth, *in*: Donald L. Wolberg, Edmund Stump, and Gary Rosenberg, editors, *Dinofest^TM International: Proceedings of a Symposium Held at Arizona State University*. Philadelphia: Academy of Natural Sciences, pp. 95–100.

Barrett, Paul M., 1997, Correlated progression and the evolution of herbivory in nonavian dinosaurs: *Journal of Vertebrate Paleontology*, 17 (Supplement to Number 3), Abstracts of Papers, Fifty-seventh Annual Meeting, p. 31A.

Barrett, Paul M., You Hailu, Paul Upchurch, and Alex C. Burton, 1998, A new ankylosaurian dinosaur (Ornithischia: Ankylosauria) from the Upper Cretaceous of Shanxi Province, People's Republic of China: *Journal of Vertebrate Paleontology*, 18 (2), pp. 376–384.

Barsbold, Rinchen, 1983, Carnivorous dinosaurs from the Cretaceous of Mongolia. *The Joint Soviet-Mongolian Palaeontological Expedition: Transactions*, 19, 117 pages.

Barsbold, Rinchen, Teresa Maryańska, and Halszka Osmólska, 1990, Oviraptorosauria, *in*: David B. Weishampel, Peter Dodson, and Osmólska, editors, *The Dinosauria*. Berkeley and Los Angeles: University of California Press, pp. 249–258.

Barsbold, Rinchen, and Halszka Osmólska, 1990, Ornithomimosauria, *in*: David B. Weishampel, Peter Dodson, and Osmólska, editors, *The Dinosauria*. Berkeley and

Bibliography

Los Angeles: University of California Press, pp. 225–244.

Bartholomai, Alan, and Ralph E. Molnar, 1981, *Muttaburrasaurus*, a new iguanodontid (Ornithischia: Ornithopoda) dinosaur from the Lower Cretaceous of Queensland: *Memoirs of the Queensland Museum*, 20 (2), pp. 319–49.

Batten, Mary, 1997, Hey, Stretch!: *Dinosaurus*, Sept.-Oct., pp. 42–47.

Bendukidze, N. S., 1964, Verkhnyaya yura Gruzii [Upper Jurassic of Georgia]: *Geologiya SSSR*, 10, pp. 1–181.

Benton, Michael J., 1990, Origin and Interrelationships of Dinosaurs, *in*: David B. Weishampel, Peter Dodson, and Halszka Osmólska, editors, *The Dinosauria*. Berkeley and Los Angeles: University of California Press, pp. 11–30.

Benton, Michael J., and P. S. Spencer, 1995, *Fossil Reptiles of Great Britain*. London: Chapman and Hall, 386 pages.

Berman, David S., and Sohn L. Jain, 1982, The braincase of a small sauropod dinosaur (Reptilia: Saurischia) from the Upper Cretaceous Lameta Group, central India, with review of Lameta Group localities: *Annals of the Carnegie Museum*, 51, pp. 405–422.

Berman, David S, and John S. McIntosh, 1978, Skull and relationships of the Upper Jurassic sauropod *Apatosaurus* (Reptilia, Saurischia): *Bulletin of Carnegie Museum of Natural History*, 8, 35 pages.

Bigot, Alexandre, 1938, Sauroptérygiens du Jurassique du Calvados: *Bulletin, Société Géologique de France*, 5 (8), pp. 631–637, Paris.

Bird, Roland T., 1941, A dinosaur walks into the musuem: *Natural History*, 43, pp. 254–261.

Bodily, N. M., 1969, An armored dinosaur from the Lower Cretaceous of Utah: *Brigham Young Geology Studies*, 16, pp. 35–60.

Bonaparte, José F., 1978, El Mesozoico de America del Sur y sus tetrapodos: *Tucumán*, 26, pp. 565–573, Argentina.

——, 1985, A Horned Dinosaur from Patagonia: *National Geographic Research*, Winter, pp. 149–151.

——, 1986a, The early radiation and phylogenetic relationships of the Jurassic sauropod dinosaurs, based on vertebral anatomy, *in*: Kevin Padian, editor, *The Beginning of the Age of Dinosaurs: Faunal Change Across the Triassic-Jurassic Boundary*. New York: Cambridge University Press, pp. 247–258.

——, 1986b, Les dinosaures (carnosaures, allosauridés, sauropodes, cétiosauridés) du Jurassic moyen de cerro cóndor (Chubut, Argentine): *Annales de Paléontologie (Vert.-Invert.)*, 72 (3), pp. 247–289.

——, 1991, Los vertebrados fosiles de la Formación Río Colorado, de la ciudad de Neuquén y cercanias, Cretácico Superior, Argentina: *Revista del Museo Argentino de Ciencias Naturales (Bernardino Rivadavia), el Instituto Nacional de Investigación de las Ciencias Naturales*, 4 (3), pp. 68–101.

——, 1995, Dinosaurios de América del Sur: *Museo Argentino de Ciencias Naturales*, 175 pages.

——, 1996a, The presacral vertebra of *Apatosaurus* suggest a different family: Apatosauridae: *Dinofest™ International Symposium, April 18–21, 1996, Program and Abstracts*, p. 30.

——, 1996b, Cretaceous tetrapods of Argentina: *Müncher Geowissenschaftliche Abhandlung*, A (30), pp. 73–130.

——, 1998, An armoured sauropod from the Aptian of northern Patagonia, Argentina, *in*: Yukimitsu Tomida, Thomas R. Rich, and Patricia Vickers-Rich, editors, *Second Symposium Gondwana Dinosaur, 12–13 July, 1998, National Science Museum, Tokyo, Abstracts with Program*, p. 10.

Bonaparte, José F., and G. E. Bossi, 1967, Sobre la presencia de dinosaurios en la Formación Pirgua del Grupo Salta y su significado cronológico: *Acta Geológica Lilloana*, 10 (2), pp. 25–44.

Bonaparte, José F., and Rodolfo Anibal Coria, 1993, Un nuevo y gigantesco saurópodo titanosaurio de la Formación Río Limay (Albiano-Cenomaniano) de la Provincia del Neuquén, Argentina: *Ameghiniana*, 30 (3), pp, 271–282, Buenos Aires.

Bonaparte, José F., and Jorge Ferigolo, 1998, A new and primitive saurischian dinosaur, *Guaibasaurus dandelariai*, gen. et sp. nov., from the Late Triassic Caturrita Formation of southern Brazil, *in*: Yukimitsu Tomida, Thomas R. Rich, and Patricia Vickers-Rich, editors, *Second Symposium Gondwana Dinosaur, 12–13 July, 1998, National Science Museum, Tokyo, Abstracts with Program*, p. 11.

Bonaparte, José F., M. R. Franchi, Jaime E. Powell, and E. G. Sepúlveda, 1984, La Formación Los Alamitos (Campaniano-Maastrichtiano) del sudeste de Río Negro, con descripción de *Kritosaurus australis* n. sp. (Hadrosauridae). Significado paleontográfico de los vertebrados: *Rebista de la Asociación Geológica Argentina*, 39 (3–4), pp. 284–299.

Bonaparte, José F., and Fernando E. Novas, 1985, *Abelisaurus comahuensis*, n.g., n.sp., carnosauria del Cretacio tardo de Patagonia: *Ameghiniana*, 21 (2–4), pp. 259–265.

Bonaparte, José F., Fernando E. Novas, and Rodolfo Anibal Coria, 1990, *Carnotaurus sastrei* Bonaparte, the horned, lightly built carnosaur from the Middle Cretaceous of Patagonia: *Contributions in Science*, 416, pp. 1–42.

Bonaparte, José F., and Jaime E. Powell, 1980, A continental assemblage of tetrapods from the Upper Cretaceous beds of El Brete, northwestern Argentina (Sauropoda-Coelurosauria-Carnosauria-Aves): *Mémoires de la Societé Géologique de France, Nouvelle Serie*, pp. 19–28.

Bonaparte, José F., and J. A. Pumares, (in press), Notas sobre el primer craneo de un Melanorosauridae, *Riojasaurus incertus* (Dinosauria: Prosauropoda), Triasico Superior, La Rioja, Argentina: *Ameghiniana*, Buenos Aires.

Bonnan, Matthew F., 1997, Functional biology of the sauropod manus and pes: Results of a pilot study: *Journal of Vertebrate Paleontology*, 17 (Supplement to Number 3),

Abstracts of Papers, Fifty-seventh Annual Meeting, p. 33A.

Boulenger, G. A., 1881, *Iguanodon bernissartensis*, *in*: P.-J. van Beneden, Sur l'arc pelvien chez les dinosauriens de Bernissart: *Bulletins de l'Académie Royale des Sciences, des Lettres et des Beaux-Arts de Belgique, Classe des Sciences*, (3) 1 (5), pp. 600–608 (in French).

Brandvold, John W., 1996, Breakage and wear patterns in Campanian theropod teeth suggesting hammering to crush bones: *Journal of Vertebrate Paleontology*, 16 (Supplement to Number 3), Abstracts of Papers, Fifty-sixth Annual Meeting, p. 23A.

Brandvold, Marion, and John W. Brandvold, 1996, Taphonomy of the Jones' site, Two Medicine Formation (Campanian) of north-central Montana with evidence of theropod feeding techniques based on bioturbation: *Journal of Vertebrate Paleontology*, 16 (Supplement to Number 3), Abstracts of Papers, Fifty-sixth Annual Meeting, p. 23A.

Bray, Emily S., 1998, Dinosaur eggshell *Boletuoolithus carlyensis*, oogenus nov. from the Lower Cretaceous Cedar Mountain Formation of Utah, *in*: Spencer G. Lucas, James I. Kirkland, and John W. Estep, editors, *Lower and Middle Cretaceous Terrestrial Ecosystems*. Albuquerque: New Mexico Museum of Natural History and Science, Bulletin 14, pp. 221–224.

Breithaupt, Brent H., 1997, Como Bluff, Wyoming Territory, 1868–1877: An initial glimpse of one of the world's premiere dinosaur sites, *in*: Donald L. Wolberg, Edmund Stump, and Gary Rosenberg, editors, *Dinofest™ International: Proceedings of a Symposium Held at Arizona State University*. Philadelphia: Academy of Natural Sciences, pp. 19–29.

——, 1998, The *Allosaurus* "Big Al"; its place in time and space, *in*: Donald L. Wolberg, K. Gittis, S. Miller, and A. Raynor, editors, *The Dinofest™ Symposium* [abstracts], Presented by The Academy of Natural Sciences of Philadelphia, Pennsylvania, pp. 2–3.

Brett-Surman, Michael K., and James O. Farlow, 1997, Some irreverant thoughts about dinosaur metabolic physiology: Jurisphagous food consumption rates of *Tyrannosaurus rex*, *in*: Farlow and Brett-Surman, editors, *The Complete Dinosaur*. Bloomington and Indianapolis: Indiana University Press, pp. 350–351.

Briggs, Derek E. G., Philip R. Wilby, Bernardino P. Pérez-Moreno, José Luis Sanz, and Marian Fregenal Martínez, 1997, The mineralization of dinosaur soft tissue in the Lower Cretaceous of Las Hoyas, Spain: *Journal of the Geological Society, London*, 154, pp. 587–588.

Britt, Brooks B., 1991, The theropods of Dry Mesa Quarry (Morrison Formation, Late Jurassic), Colorado: With an emphasis on the osteology of *Torvosaurus tanneri*: *Brigham Young University Geology Studies*, 37, pp. 1–72.

——, 1995, The nature and distribution of pneumatic vertebrae in the Theropoda: *Journal of Vertebrate Paleontology*, 15

(Supplement to Number 3), Abstracts of Papers, Fifty-fifth Annual Meeting, p. 20A.

Britt, Brooks B., and Kenneth L. Stadtman, 1997, Dalton Well Quarry, *in*: Philip J. Currie and Kevin Padian, editors, *Encyclopedia of Dinosaurs*. San Diego: Academic Press, pp. 165–166.

Britt, Brooks B., Kenneth L. Stadtman, R. D. Scheetz, and John S. McIntosh, 1997, Caramasaurid and titanosaurid sauropods from the Early Cretaceous Dalton Wells Quarry (Cedar Mountain Formation), Utah: *Journal of Vertebrate Paleontology*, 17 (Supplement to Number 3), Abstracts of Papers, Fifty-seventh Annual Meeting, p. 34A.

Brix, P., and B. Plöchinger, 1988, Erläuterungen zu Blatt 76 Wiener Neustadt: *Geologische Karte der Republik Österreich, 1/50000*, 85 pages, Wien (Geologische Bundesanst).

Brown, Barnum, 1914, A complete skull of *Monoclonius* from the Belly River Cretaceous of Alberta: *Bulletin of the American Museum of Natural History*, 33, pp. 549–558.

_____, 1935, Sinclair dinosaur expedition, 1934: *Natural History*, 36, pp. 3–15.

Buatois, L. A., and Alejandro Lopez Angriman, 1992, Evolución de sistemas deposicionales en el Grupo Gustav, Cretácico de Isla James Ross, Antártida, *in*: C. Rinaldi, editor, *Geología de la Isla James Ross*. Buenos Aires: Instituto Antártico Argentino, pp. 263–297.

Buffetaut, Éric, 1984, Une vertebre de dinosaurien sauropodedans le Crétacé du Cap de la Hève (Normandie): *Actes du Museum de Rouen*, pp. 213–221.

_____, 1989, New remains of the enigmatic dinosaur *Spinosaurus* from the Cretaceous of Morocco and the affinities between *Spinosaurus* and *Baryonyx*: *Neus Jahrbuch für Geologie und Paläontologie, Monatshefte*, 1989, 2, pp. 79–87, Stuttgart.

_____, 1992, Remarks on the Cretaceous theropod dinosaurs *Spinosaurus* and *Baryonyx*: *Ibid*, 1992 (2), pp. 88–96.

Buffetaut, Éric, and Jean Le Loeuff, 1996, Late Cretaceous dromaeosaurids from southern France: *Journal of Vertebrate Paleontology*, 16 (Supplement to Number 3), Abstracts of Papers, Fifty-sixth Annual Meeting, p. 48A.

Buffetaut, Éric, Patrick Mechin and Annie Mechin-Salessy, 1988, Un dinosaure théropode d'affinitiés gondwandiennes dans le Crétacé supérieur de Provence: *Comptes Rendus des Séances de l'Académie des Sciences, Paris*, Serie II, pp. 153–158.

Buffetaut, Éric, and Phillipe Taquet, 1977, The giant crocodilian *Sarcosuchus* in the early Cretaceous of Brazil and Niger: *Paleontology*, 20, pp. 203–208.

_____, 1979, An early Cretaceous terrestrial crocodilian and the opening of the South Atlantic: *Nature*, 280 (5722), pp. 486–487.

Bunzel, Emanuel, 1870, Notice of a fragment of a reptilian skull from the Upper Cretaceous of Europe: *Quarterly Journal of the Geological Society, London*, 24, p. 394, London.

_____, 1871, Die Reptilfauna der Gosau-Formation in der neuen Welt bei Wiener-Neustadt: *Abhandlungen der kaiserl. königl. k. k. geolog. Reichsanstalt*, 5, pp. 1–16, Winer-Neustadt.

Burge, Donald L., 1996, New dinosaur discoveries in the Lower Cretaceous of southeastern Utah. *Fossils of Arizona*, volume 4. Mesa, Arizona: Southwest Paleontological Society and Mesa Southwest Museum, pp. 85–105.

Burke, Ann C., and Alan Feduccia, 1997, Developmental patterns and the identification of homologies in the avian hand: *Science*, 278, pp. 666–668.

Burnham, David A., Kraig Derstler, and Cliff L. Linster, 1997, A new specimen of *Velociraptors* (Dinosauria: Theropoda) from the Two Medicine Formation of Montana, *in*: Donald L. Wolberg, Edmund Stump, and Gary Rosenberg, editors, *Dinofest™ International: Proceedings of a Symposium Held at Arizona State University*. Philadelphia: Academy of Natural Sciences, pp. 73–75.

Burnham, David A., William R. Garstka, and Richard Hebdon, 1996, Posture and stance of *Triceratops*: Evidence of digitigrade manus and antilever vertebral column: *Dinofest™ International Symposium, April 18–21, 1996, Programs and Abstracts*, p. 34.

Callison, George, 1997, Robotically animated dinosaurs; how do they do that?, *in*: Donald L. Wolberg, Edmund Stump, and Gary Rosenberg, editors, *Dinofest™ International: Proceedings of a Symposium Held at Arizona State University*. Philadelphia: Academy of Natural Sciences, pp. 569–572.

Calvo, Jorge O., 1991, Huellas de Dinosaurios en la Formación Río Limay (Albiano-Cenomaniano) Picún Leufú, Prov. del Neuquén, Rep. Arg. (Ornithischia, Saurischia: Sauropoda-Theropoda): *Ameghiniana*, 28 (3–4), pp. 241–310, Buenos Aires.

_____, 1994a, Feeding mechanisms in sauropod dinosaurs: Unpublished M.S. thesis, University of Illinois at Chicago.

_____, 1994b, Jaw mechanics in sauropod dinosaurs: *Gaia*, 10, pp. 183–193.

Calvo, Jorge O., and José F. Bonaparte, 1991, *Andesaurus delgadoi* gen et sp. nov. (Saurischia-Sauropoda), Dinosaurio Titanosauridae de la Formación Río Limay (Albiano-Cenomaniano), Neuquén, Argentina: *Ameghiniana*, 28 (3–4), pp. 303–310, Buenos Aires.

Calvo, Jorge O., and C. E. Gazzera, 1989, Paleoecologia en el sector inferior del Miembro Candeleros (Formación Río Limay, Grupo Neuquén, Cretácio) en el área del Largo Ezequiel Ramos Mexia. Pcia. del Neuquén, Patagonia, Argentina: *Actas VI Jornadas Argentinas de Paleontologia de Vertebrados*, San Juan, May, pp. 3–5, Buenos Aires.

Calvo, Jorge O., and Leonardo Salgado, 1991, Posible registro de *Rebbachisaurus* Lavocat (Sauropoda) en el Cretácio medio de Patagonia. VIII Jornadas Argentinas de Paleontologia de Vertebratos, La Roja,

May: *Ameghiniana*, 28, p. 404, Buenos Aires.

_____, 1995, *Rebbachisaurus tessonei* sp. nov. a new Sauropoda from the Albian-Cenomanian of Argentina; new evidence on the origin of the Diplodocidae: *Gaia*, 11, pp. 13–33.

_____, 1996, Sauropod crossing: The Africa/South America connection: *The Dinosaur Report*, summer, 1996, pp. 1, 4–5.

Camp, Charles L., 1936, A new type of small bipedal dinosaur from the Navajo Sandstone of Arizona: *University of California Publications in Geological Sciences*, 24, pp. 39–56.

Camp, Charles L., Samuel P. Welles, and M. Green, 1953, Bibliography of fossil vertebrates 1944–1948: *Geological Society of America, Memoirs*, 57, 456 pages.

Campos, Diogenes de A., and Alexander W. A. Kellner, 1998, Description of titanosaurid (Sauropoda) pelves from the continental Cretaceous of Brazil, *in*: Yukimitsu Tomida, Thomas R. Rich, and Patricia Vickers-Rich, editors, *Second Symposium Gondwana Dinosaur, 12–13 July, 1998, National Science Museum, Tokyo, Abstracts with Program*, p. 14.

Carpenter, Kenneth, 1988, Evidence of predatory behavior by *Tyrannosaurus*, *in*: John R. Horner, editor, *International Symposium on Vertebrate Behavior as Derived from the Fossil Record*. Bozeman, Montana: Museum of the Rockies, Montana State University, [unpaginated].

_____, 1990, Ankylosaur systematics: Example using *Panoplosaurus* and *Edmontonia* (Ankylosauria: Nodosauridae), *in*: Carpenter and Philip J. Currie, editors, *Dinosaur Systematics: Approaches and Perspectives*. Cambridge, New York and Melbourne: Cambridge University Press, pp. 281–299.

_____, 1992, Tyrannosaurids (Dinosauria) of Asia and North America, *in*: Niall J. Mateer and Chen Pei-Ji, editors, *International Symposium on Non-marine Cretaceous Correlation*. Beijing: China Ocean Press, pp. 250–268.

_____, 1996, Evolutionary significance of new ankylosaurs (Dinosauria) from the Upper Jurassic and Lower Cretaceous, Western interior: *Journal of Vertebrate Paleontology*, 16 (Supplement to Number 3), Abstracts of Papers, Fifty-sixth Annual Meeting, p. 25A.

_____, 1997a, A giant coelophysoid (Ceratosauria) theropod from the Upper Triassic of New Mexico, U.S.A.: *Neus Jahrbuch für Geologie und Paläontologie, Abhandlungen*, 205 (2), pp. 189–208.

_____, 1997b, Dinosaurs as museum exhibits, *in*: James O. Farlow and Michael K. Brett-Surman, editors, *The Complete Dinosaur*. Bloomington and Indianapolis: Indiana University Press, pp. 150–164.

_____, 1997c, "The leg bone connects to the knee bone ..." Dinosaur skeletons in the public eye, *in*: Donald L. Wolberg, Edmund Stump, and Gary Rosenberg, editors, *Dinofest™ International: Proceedings of a Symposium Held at Arizona State*

Bibliography

University. Philadelphia: Academy of Natural Sciences, pp. 171–180.

Carpenter, Kenneth, James I. Kirkland, Donald Burge, and John Bird, 1998, Ankylosaurs (Dinosauria: Ornithischia) of the Cedar Mountain Formation, Utah, and their stratigraphic distribution, *in*: David D. Gillette, editor, *Vertebrate Fossils of Utah*. Salt Lake City: Utah Geological Survey.

Carpenter, Kenneth, James I. Kirkland, C. A. Miles, K. Cloward, and Donald Burge, 1996, Evolutionary significance of new ankylosaurs (Dinosauria) from the Upper Jurassic and Lower Cretaceous, Western interior: *Journal of Vertebrate Paleontology*, 16 (Supplement to Number 3), Abstracts of Papers, Fifty-sixth Annual Meeting, p. 25A.

Carpenter, Kenneth, and C. A. Miles, 1997, New, primitive stegosaur (Ornithischia) from the Upper Jurassic: *Journal of Vertebrate Paleontology*, 17 (Supplement to Number 3), Abstracts of Papers, Fifty-seventh Annual Meeting, p. 35A.

Carpenter, Kenneth, Clifford Miles, and Karen Cloward, 1998, Skull of a Jurassic ankylosaur (Dinosauria): *Nature*, 393, pp. 782–783.

Carpenter, Kenneth, and J. Michael Parrish, 1985, Late Triassic vertebrates from Reuvuelto Creek, Quay County, New Mexico: *New Mexico Geological Society Guidebook*, 36, pp. 197–198.

Carpenter, Kenneth, Dale Russell, Donald Baird, and Robert K. Denton, 1997, Redescription of the holotype of *Dryptosaurus aquilunguis* (Dinosauria: Theropoda) from the Upper Cretaceous of New Jersey: *Journal of Vertebrate Paleontology*, 17 (30), pp. 561–573.

Carr, Thomas D., 1995, Towards a systematic revision of the Tyrannosauridae from the Judith River Group (Late Campanian) of Alberta: *Journal of Vertebrate Paleontology*, Abstracts of Papers, Fifty-fifth Annual Meeting, p. 21A.

_____, 1996, Craniofacial ontogeny in tyrannosaurids: taxonomic implications: *Journal of Vertebrate Paleontology*, 16 (Supplement to Number 3), Abstracts of Papers, Fifty-sixth Annual Meeting, p. 25A.

Carr, Thomas D., and Richard L. Essner, Jr., 1997, A quantitative approach to cranial ontogeny in tyrannosaurids (Dinosauria: Theropoda): *Journal of Vertebrate Paleontology*, 17 (Supplement to Number 3), Abstracts of Papers, Fifty-seventh Annual Meeting, p. 35A.

Carroll, Robert L., 1988, *Vertebrate Paleontology and Evolution*. New York: W. H. Freeman and Co., 698 pages.

Casanovas-Cladellas, M. L., X. Pereda-Suberbiola, and J.V. Santafé-Llopis, 1998, Hadrosaurid dinosaurs from the pre-Pyrenees of Catalina, *in*: John W. M. Jagt, Paul H. Lambers, Eric W. A. Mulder, and Anne S. Schulp, editors, *Third European Workshop on Vertebrate Palaeontology*, Maastricht, 6–9, May 1998, Programme and Abstracts Field Guide, [unpaginated].

Casanovas-Cladellas, M. L., J. V. Santafé-Llopis, and A. Isidoro-Llorens 1993, *Pararhabdodon isonense*. n. gen. n. sp. (Dinosauria) Estudio morfológico, radio-tomográfico y consideraciones biomecánicas: *Paleontologia y Evolució*, 26–27, pp. 121–131 (in Spanish).

Chapman, Ralph E., David B. Weishampel, Gene Hunt, and Diego Rasskin-Gutman, 1997, Sexual dimorphism in dinosaurs, *in*: Donald L. Wolberg, Edmund Stump, and Gary Rosenberg, editors, *Dinofest^{TM} International: Proceedings of a Symposium Held at Arizona State University*. Philadelphia: Academy of Natural Sciences, pp. 83–93.

Charig, Alan J., and Angela C. Milner, 1986, *Baryonyx*, a remarkable new theropod dinosaur: *Nature*, 324, pp. 359–361.

_____, 1990, The systematic position of *Baryonyx walkeri*, in the light of Gauthier's reclassification of the Theropoda, *in*: Kenneth Carpenter and Philip J. Currie, editors, *Dinosaur Systematics: Approaches and Perspectives*. Cambridge, New York and Melbourne: Cambridge University Press, pp. 127–140.

_____, 1997, *Baryonyx walkeri*, a fish-eating dinosaur from the Wealden of Surrey: *Bulletin of The Natural History Museum, London*, (Geology) 53 (1), pp. 11–70.

Chatterjee, Sankar, 1978 *Indosuchus* and *Indosaurus*, Cretaceous carnosaurs from India: *Journal of Paleontology*, 52 (3), pp. 570–580.

_____, 1991, Cranial anatomy and relationships of a new Triassic bird from Texas: *Philosophical Transactions of the Royal Society of London*, B, 332, pp. 277–346.

_____, 1992, A kinematic model for the evolution of the Indian plate since the Late Jurassic, *in*: Sankar Chatterjee and Nicholas Hotton, III, editors, *New Concepts in Global Tectonics*. Lubbock, Texas: Texas Tech University Press, pp. 33–62.

_____, 1993, *Procompsognathus* from the Triassic of Germany is not a crocodylomorph: *Journal of Vertebrate Paleontology*, 13 (Supplement to Number 3), Abstracts of Papers, Fifty-third Annual Meeting, p. 29A.

_____, *Shuvosaurus*, a new theropod: *Natural Geographic Research Exploration*, 9 (3), pp. 274–285.

_____, 1995a, The KT impact event: new links between the Chicxulub and the Shiva craters: *Journal of Vertebrate Paleontology*, 15 (Supplement to number 3), Abstracts of Papers, Fifty-fifth Annual Meeting, p. 23A.

_____, 1995b, The last dinosaurs of India: The Dinosaur Report, Fall, 1995, pp. 12–17.

_____, 1995c, The Triassic Bird *Protoavis*: *Archaeopteryx*, 13, pp. 15–31, Eichstätt.

_____, 1997, The beginnings of avian flight, *in*: Donald L. Wolberg, Edmund Stump, and Gary Rosenberg, editors, *Dinofest^{TM} International: Proceedings of a Symposium Held at Arizona State University*. Philadelphia: Academy of Natural Sciences, pp. 311–335.

_____, 1998, Reassessment of *Procompsognathus* skull, *in*: Donald L. Wolberg, K. Gittis, S. Miller, and A. Raynor, editors, *The Dinofest^{TM} Symposium* [abstracts], Presented by The Academy of Natural Sciences of Philadelphia, Pennsylvania, pp. 6–7.

Chatterjee, Sankar, and Dhiraj K. Rudra, 1993, Shiva Crater: A possible K/T boundary impact structure at the India-Seychelles plate margin, *in*: *74th Annual Meeting of the Pacific Division, AAAS, Program with Abstracts*, p 38.

_____, 1996, KT events in India: Impact, rifing, volcanism and dinosaur extinction, *in*: Fernando S. Novas and Ralph E. Molnar, editors, *Proceedings of the Gondwanan Dinosaur Symposium: Memoirs of the Queensland Museum*, 39 (part 3), pp. 489–532.

Chatterjee, Sankar, and Zhong Zheng, 1997, The feeding strategies in sauropods: *Journal of Vertebrate Paleontology*, 17 (Supplement to Number 3), Abstracts of Papers, Fifty-seventh Annual Meeting, p. 37A.

Chen, Pei-Ji, Zhi-ming Dong, and Shuo-nan Zhen, 1998, An exceptionally well-preserved theropod dinosaur from the Yixian Formation of China: *Nature*, 391, pp. 147–152.

Chiappe, Luis M., 1995, The first 85 million years of avian evolution: *Nature*, 378, pp. 349–355.

_____, 1996, Early avian evolution in the southern hemisphere: The fossil record of birds in the Mesozoic of Gondwana, *in*: Fernando S. Novas and Ralph E. Molnar, editors, *Proceedings of the Gondwanan Dinosaur Symposium: Memoirs of the Queensland Museum*, 39 (part 3), pp. 533–555.

Chiappe, Luis M., Mark A. Norell, and James M. Clark, 1995, Is *Mononykus* a bird?: Testing phylogenetic hypotheses: *Journal of Vertebrate Paleontology*, 15 (Supplement to Number 3), Abstracts of Papers, Fifty-fifth Annual Meeting, p. 23A.

_____, 1996, Phylogenetic position of *Mononykus* (Aves: Alvarezsauridae) from the Late Cretaceous of the Gobi Desert, *in*: Fernando S. Novas and Ralph E. Molnar, editors, *Proceedings of the Gondwanan Dinosaur Symposium: Memoirs of the Queensland Museum*, 39 (part 3), pp. 557–582.

_____, 1998, The skull of a relative of the stem-group bird *Mononykus: Nature*, 392, pp. 275–278.

Chin, Karen, 1996a, A coprolitic view of dinosaurian herbivory: *Dinofest^{TM} International Symposium, April 18–21, 1996, Programs and Abstracts*, p. 39.

_____, 1996b, Probable *Tyrannosaurus rex* coprolite from the Maastrichtian Frenchman Formation of Saskatchewan: *Journal of Vertebrate Paleontology*, 16 (Supplement to Number 3), Abstracts of Papers, Fifty-sixth Annual Meeting, p. 27A.

Chinnery, Brenda J., Thomas R. Lipka, James I. Kirkland, J. Michael Parrish, and Michael K. Brett-Surman, 1998, Neoceratopsian teeth from the Lower to Middle Cretaceous of North America, *in*: Spencer G. Lucas, James I. Kirkland, and John W. Estep, editors, *Lower and Middle Cretaceous Terrestrial Ecosystems*. Albuquerque: New Mexico Museum of Natural History and Science, Bulletin 14, pp. 297–292.

Chinnery, Brenda J., and David B. Weishampel, 1996, *Montanoceratops cerorhynchus* and the question of monophyly of the Protoceratopsidae: *Journal of Vertebrate*

Paleontology, 16 (Supplement to Number 3), Abstracts of Papers, Fifty-sixth Annual Meeting, p. 27A.

Chinsamy, Anusuya, Thomas Rich, and Patricia Vickers-Rich, 1998, Polar dinosaur bone histology: *Journal of Vertebrate Paleontology,* 18 (2), pp. 385–390.

Choo, Brian, 1997, Dinosaurs of Oz: A brief review of Australian dinosaurs; Part 2: Victoria: *Dinosaur World,* 1 (3), pp. 35–38.

Chopard, Seraphin, 1883, Le géologie du Jura. Considérations préliminaires sur les environs de Poligny. Rapport de la commission de géologie et de Paléontologie sur une excursion entre Poligny et Saint-Lothian, faite le 23 juin 1862: *Bull. Soc. Agric. Sci. Arts Poligny,* 22 pages, Poligny.

Choubert, G., 1962, Histoire Géologique du domaine de l'Anti-Atlas: Notes *Mémoires du Service Géologique* (Maroc), 100, pp. 75–194.

Christiansen, Per, 1996, The "whiplash" tail of diplodocid sauropods: Was it really a weapon?, *in:* Michael Morales, editor, *Museum of Northern Arizona Bulletin 60,* pp. 51–58.

Chure, Daniel J., 1995, A reassessment of the gigantic theropod *Saurophagus maximus* from the Morrison Formation (Upper Jurassic) of Oklahoma, U.S.A., *in:* A. Sun and Y. Wang, editors, *Sixth Symposium on Mesozoic Terrestrial Ecosystems and Biota, Short Papers.* Bejing: China Ocean Press, pp. 103–106.

Chure, Daniel J., Brooks B. Britt, and James H. Madsen, Jr., 1997, A new specimen of *Marshosaurus bicentesimus* (Theropoda) from the Morrison Formation (Late Jurassic) of Dinosaur National Monument: *Journal of Vertebrate Paleontology,* 17 (Supplement to Number 3), Abstracts of Papers, Fifty-seventh Annual Meeting, p. 38A.

Chure, Daniel J., and Anthony J. Fiorillo, 1997, "'One big Al to go and hold the mayo': evidence of scavenging of a specimen of *Allosaurus* from the Morrison Formation (Late Jurassic) of Wyoming: *Journal of Vertebrate Paleontology,* 17 (Supplement to Number 3), Abstracts of Papers, Fifty-seventh Annual Meeting, p. 38A.

Chure, Daniel J., and James H. Madsen, Jr., 1993, A tyrannosaurid-like braincase from the Cleveland-Lloyd Dinosaur Quarry, Emery County, Utah (Morrison Formation: Late Jurassic): *Journal of Vertebrate Paleontology,* 13 (Supplement to Number 3), Abstracts of Papers, Fifty-third Annual Meeting, p. 30A.

_____, 1996a, Variations in aspects of the tympanic pneumatic system in a population of *Allosaurus fragilis* from the Morrison Formation (Upper Jurassic): *Ibid,* 16 (1), pp. 63–66.

_____, 1996b, The furcula in allosaurid theropods and its implications for determining bird origins: *Ibid,* 16 (Supplement to Number 3), Abstracts of Papers, Fifty-sixth Annual Meeting, p. 28A.

_____, 1998, An unusual braincase (?*Stokesosaurus clevelandi*) from the Cleveland-Lloyd Dinosaur Quarry, Utah (Morrison Formation: Late Jurassic): *Ibid,* 18 (1), pp. 115–125.

Chure, Daniel J., Makoto Manabe, Masahiro Tanimoto, and Yukimitsu Tomida, 1998, An unusual theropod tooth from the Mifune Group (Upper Cenomanian-Turonian), Kumamoto, Japan, *in:* Yukimitsu Tomida, Thomas R. Rich, and Patricia Vickers-Rich, editors, *Second Symposium Gondwana Dinosaur, 12–13 July, 1998, National Science Museum, Tokyo, Abstracts with Program,* p. 24.

Chure, Daniel J., and John S. McIntosh, 1989, *A Bibliography of the Dinosauria (Exclusive of the Aves), 1677–1986.* Grand Junction, Colorado: Museum of Western Colorado, Paleontology Series 1, 226 pages.

Claessens, L. P. A. A., S. F. Perry, and Philip J. Currie, 1998, Reconstructing theropod lung ventilation, *in:* Donald L. Wolberg, K. Gittis, S. Miller, and A. Raynor, editors, *The Dinofest™ Symposium* [abstracts]. Presented by The Academy of Natural Sciences of Philadelphia, Pennsylvania, pp. 8–9.

Clark, Robert, 1997, Uncovering Patagonia's Lost World: *National Geographic,* 192 (6), pp. 120–137.

Colbert, Edwin H., 1947, The little dinosaurs of Ghost Ranch: *Natural History,* 56, pp. 392–399.

_____, 1953, *Dinosaurs.* New York: The American Museum of Natural History, Man and Nature Publications, Science Guide No. 70, 32 pages.

_____, 1961, *Dinosaurs: Their Discovery and Their World.* New York: E. P. Dutton & Co., xiv, 300 pages.

_____, 1989, The Triassic dinosaur *Coelophysis: Museum of Northern Arizona Bulletin,* 57, xv, 160 pages.

_____, 1990, Variation in *Coelophysis bauri, in:* Carpenter and Philip J. Currie, editors, *Dinosaur Systematics: Approaches and Perspectives.* Cambridge, New York and Melbourne: Cambridge University Press, pp. 81–90.

_____, 1995, *The Little Dinosaurs of Ghost Ranch.* New York: Columbia University Press, 250 pages.

_____, 1997, The protean dinosaurs, *in:* Donald L. Wolberg, Edmund Stump, and Gary Rosenberg, editors, *Dinofest™ International: Proceedings of a Symposium Held at Arizona State University.* Philadelphia: Academy of Natural Sciences, pp. 1–5.

Colbert, Edwin H., and Dale A. Russell, 1969, The small Cretaceous dinosaur *Dromaeosaurus: American Museum Novitates,* 2380, pp. 145–162.

Connely, Melissa V., 1997, Analysis of head-neck functions and feeding ecology of common Jurassic sauropod dinosaurs based on a new find from Como Bluff, Wyoming: *Journal of Vertebrate Paleontology,* 17 (Supplement to Number 3), Abstracts of Papers, Fifty-seventh Annual Meeting, pp. 39A–40A.

Connely, Melissa V., and R. Hawley, A study of apatosaurine crania, based on new material at the Tate Museum, (in preparation).

Cooley, Jonathan, 1997, Lost tyrannosaur flock rediscovered in Alberta Badlands: *Paleo Horizons,* 4 (2), pp. 1, 6.

Coombs, Walter P., Jr., 1971, The Ankylosauria: Unpublished Ph.D. thesis, Ann Arbor (Michigan) Microfilms Intern., Columbia University, New York, 487 pages.

_____, 1978a, The families of the ornithischian dinosaur order Ankylosauria: *Paleontology,* 21, part 1, pp. 143–170.

_____, 1978b, An endocranial cast of *Euoplocephalus* (Reptilia, Ornithischia): *Palaeontographica,* 161, pp. 176–182.

Coombs, Walter P., Jr., and Teresa Maryańska, 1990, Ankylosauria, *in:* David B. Weishampel, Peter Dodson, and Halszka Osmólska, editors, *The Dinosauria.* Berkeley and Los Angeles: University of California Press, pp. 456–483.

Coombs, Walter P., Jr., and Ralph E. Molnar, 1981, Sauropoda (Reptilia, Saurischia) from the Cretaceous of Queensland: *Memoirs of the Queensland Museum,* 20, pp. 351–373.

Cope, Edward Drinker, 1866, Remarks on dinosaur remains from New Jersey: *Academy of Natural Sciences of Philadelphia, Proceedings,* June, pp. 275–279.

_____, 1876, Descriptions of some vertebrate remains from the Fort Union beds of Montana: *Ibid,* 28, pp. 248–261.

_____, 1877a, On a gigantic saurian from the Dakota epoch of Colorado: *Paleontology Bulletin,* 27, pp. 5–10.

_____, 1877b, On *Amphicoelias,* a genus of Saurians from the Dakota Epoch of Colorado: *Ibid,* 27, pp. 1–5.

_____, 1877c, On a dinosaurian from the Trias of Utah: *American Philosophical Society, Proceedings,* 16 (99), pp. 579–584.

_____, 1887a, The dinosaurian genus *Coelurus: American Naturalist,* vol. 21, pp. 367–369.

_____, 1887b, A contribution to the history of the Vertebrata of the Trias of North America: *American Philosophical Society, Proceedings,* 24 (126), pp. 209–228.

_____, 1892, Fourth note on the Dinosauria of the Laramie: *American Naturalist,* 26, pp. 756–758.

Coria, Rodolfo A., 1998, Ornithopod dinosaurs from the Neuquén Group, Patagonia, Argentina: Phylogeny and biogeography, *in:* Yukimitsu Tomida, Thomas R. Rich, and Patricia Vickers-Rich, editors, *Second Symposium Gondwana Dinosaur, 12–13 July, 1998, National Science Museum, Tokyo, Abstracts with Program,* pp. 8–9.

Coria, Rodolfo A., and Philip J. Currie, 1997, A new theropod from the Río Limay Formation: *Journal of Vertebrate Paleontology,* 17 (Supplement to Number 3), Abstracts of Papers, Fifty-seventh Annual Meeting, p. 40A.

Coria, Rodolfo A., and Leonardo Salgado, 1995, A new giant carnivorous dinosaur from the Cretaceous of Patagonia: *Nature,* 377, pp. 224–226.

_____, 1996, A basal iguanodontian (Ornithischia: Ornithopoda) from the Late Cretaceous of South America: *Journal of Vertebrate Paleontology,* 16 (3), pp. 445–457.

Cracraft, Joel, 1971, Caenagnathiformes, Cretaceous birds convergent in jaw

Bibliography

mechanism of dicynodont reptiles: *Journal of Paleontology*, 45 (5), pp. 805–809.

Crichton, Michael, 1990, *Jurassic Park*. New York: Alfred A. Knopf, xi, 401 pages.

Cruz, C. F., P. Condat, E. Kozlowski, and R. Manceda, 1989, Análisis estratigráfico secuencial del grupo Neuquén (Cretácio Superior) en el Valle del Río Grande, provincia de Mendoza: *Actas I Congreso Argentino de Hidrocarburos, Mar del Plata*, 2, pp. 689–714.

Cuny, G., and G. Ramboer, 1991, Nouvelles données sur la faune et l'âge de Saint-Nicolas-de-Port: *Revisions in Paleontology*, 10, pp. 69–78, Geneva.

Currie, Philip J., 1989, Long-distance dinosaurs: *Natural History*, 6, pp. 60–65.

_____, 1990, Elmisauridae, *in*: David B. Weishampel, Peter Dodson, and Halszka Osmólska, editors, *The Dinosauria*. Berkeley and Los Angeles: University of California Press, pp. 245–248.

_____, 1992, Saurischian dinosaurs of the Late Cretaceous of Asia and North America, *in*: Niall J. Mateer and Chen Pei-Ji, editors, *Aspects of Nonmarine Cretaceous Geology*. Beijing: China Ocean Press, pp. 237–249.

_____, 1995, Phylogeny and systematics of theropods (Dinosauria): *Journal of Vertebrate Paleontology*, 15 (Supplement to Number 3), Abstracts of Papers, Fifty-fifth Annual Meeting, 25A.

_____, 1997a, "Feathered" dinosaurs, *in*: Currie and Kevin Padian, editors, *Encyclopedia of Dinosaurs*. San Diego: Academic Press, p. 241.

_____, 1997b, Theropods, *in*: James O. Farlow and Michael K. Brett-Surman, editors, *The Complete Dinosaur*. Bloomington and Indianapolis: Indiana University Press, pp. 216–233.

_____, 1998a, "Feathered" dinosaurs: *in*: Donald L. Wolberg, K. Gittis, S. Miller, and A. Raynor, editors, *The Dinofest™ Symposium* [abstracts], Presented by The Academy of Natural Sciences of Philadelphia, Pennsylvania, pp. 9–10.

_____, 1998b, *Caudipteryx* revealed: *National Geographic*, 194 (1), pp. 86–89.

Currie, Philip J., and David A. Eberth, 1993, Palaeontology, sedimentology and paleoecology of the Iren Dabasu Formation (Upper Cretaceous), Inner Mongolia, People's Republic of China: *Cretaceous Research*, 14, pp. 127–144.

Currie, Philip J., Stephen J. Godfrey, and Lev Nessov, 1993, New caenagnathid (Dinosauria: Theropoda) specimens from the Upper Cretaceous of North America and Asia: *Canadian Journal of Earth Sciences*, 30 (10–11), pp. 2255–2272.

Currie, Philip J., and Kevin Padian, 1997, editors, *Encyclopedia of Dinosaurs*. San Diego: Academic Press, xxx, 869 pages.

Currie, Philip J., J. Keith Rigby, Jr., and Robert E. Sloan, 1990, *in*: Carpenter and Philip J. Currie, editors, *Dinosaur Systematics: Approaches and Perspectives*. Cambridge, New York and Melbourne: Cambridge University Press, pp. 107–125.

Currie, Philip J., and Dale A. Russell, 1988, Osteology and relationships of *Chi-*

rostenotes pergracilis (Saurischia, Theropoda) from the Judith River (Oldman) Formation of Alberta, Canada: *Canadian Journal of Earth Sciences*, 25, pp. 972–986.

Currie, Philip J., and Xi-Jin Zhao, 1993, A new carnosaur (Dinosauria, Theropoda) from the Jurassic of Xinjiang, People's Republic of China: *Canadian Journal of Earth Sciences*, 30 (10–11), pp. 2037–2081.

Curry, Kristina A., 1996, Diplodocid osteogenesis: *Journal of Vertebrate Paleontology*, 16 (Supplement to Number 3), Abstracts of Papers, Fifty-sixth Annual Meeting, p. 29A.

Curtice, Brian David, 1995, A description of the anterior caudal vertebrae of *Supersaurus vivianae*: *Journal of Vertebrate Paleontology*, 15 (Supplement to No. 3), Abstracts of Papers, Fifty-fifth Annual Meeting, p. 25A.

_____, 1996, Death of a dinosaur: A reevaluation of *Ultrasauros macintoshi*: *Ibid*, 16 (Supplement to Number 3), Abstracts of Papers, Fifty-sixth Annual Meeting, p. 29A.

Curtice, Brian David, John R. Foster, and D. R. Wilhite, 1997, A statistical analysis of sauropod limb elements: *Journal of Vertebrate Paleontology*, 17 (Supplement to Number 3), Abstracts of Papers, Fifty-seventh Annual Meeting, p. 41A.

Curtice, Brian David, Kenneth L. Stadtman, and Linda J. Curtice, 1996, A reassessment of *Ultrasauros macintoshi* (Jensen, 1985), *in*: Michael Morales, editor, *Museum of Northern Arizona Bulletin 60*, pp. 87–95.

Czerkas, Stephen A., 1992, Discovery of dermal spines reveal a new look for sauropod dinosaurs: *Geology*, 20, pp. 1068–1070.

_____, 1994, The history and interpretation of sauropod skin impressions: *Gaia*, 10, pp. 173–182.

_____, 1997, Skin, *in*: Currie and Kevin Padian, editors, *Encyclopedia of Dinosaurs*. San Diego: Academic Press, p. 669–675.

Czerkas, Stephen A., and Sylvia J. Czerkas, 1997, The integument and life restoration of *Carnotaurus*, *in*: Donald L. Wolberg, Edmund Stump, and Gary Rosenberg, editors, *Dinofest™ International: Proceedings of a Symposium Held at Arizona State University*. Philadelphia: Academy of Natural Sciences, pp. 155–158.

Czerkas, Sylvia J., and Stephen A. Czerkas, 1990, *Dinosaurs: A Global View*. Limpsfield, England: Dragon's World Ltd., 120 pages.

Czerkas, Sylvia Massey, and Donald F. Glut, 1982, *Dinosaurs, Mammoths and Cavemen: The Art of Charles R. Knight*. New York: E. P. Dutton, vii, 120 pages.

Dal Sasso, Cristiano, and Marco Signore, 1998, Exceptional soft-tissue preservation in a theropod dinosaur from Italy: *Nature*, 392, pp. 838–387.

Danis, Gilles, 1997a, Mounting the type specimen of *Parasaurolophus cyrtocristatus*: *Journal of Vertebrate Paleontology*, 17 (Supplement to Number 3), Abstracts of Papers, Fifty-seventh Annual Meeting, pp. 41A–42A.

_____, 1997b, Shuffling old bones, a fresh new

look at the paleontology hall at the Field Museum of Natural History: *Ibid*, p. 42A.

De Broin, F., 1980, Les Tortues de Gadoufaoua (Aptien du Niger); aperçu sur la paléobiogéographie des Pelomedusidae (Pleurodira): *Mémoires de la Societé Géologique de France*, Nouvelle Serie, 59 (139), pp. 39–46.

De Klerk, W. J., Forster, Callum F. Ross, Catherine A., Scott D. Sampson, and Anusuya Chinsamy, 1997, New maniraptoran and iguanodontian dinosaurs from the Early Cretaceous Kirkwood Formation, South Africa: *Journal of Vertebrate Paleontology*, 17 (Supplement to Number 3), Abstracts of Papers, Fifty-seventh Annual Meeting, p. 42A.

Deeming, D. Charles, and David M. Unwin, 1993, Fossil embryos and neonates: Are they what we want them to be?: *Journal of Vertebrate Paleontology*, 15 (Supplement to Number 3), Abstracts of Papers, Fifty-third Annual Meeting, p. 32A.

Denton, Robert K., Jr., 1990, A revision of the theropod *Dryptosaurus* (*Laelaps*) *aquilunguis* (Cope 1869): *Journal of Vertebrate Paleontology*, 3 (Supplement to Number 9), Abstracts of Papers, Fiftieth Annual Meeting, p. 20A.

Depéret, Charles, 1896, Note sur les dinosauriens sauropodes et théropodes du Crétacé supérieur de Madagascar: *Bulletin, Societé Géologique de France*, Series 3, 24, pp. 176–194.

Dilkes, David W., 1996, Ontogeny and locomotion in *Maiasaura peeblesorum* (Dinosauria: Hadrosauridae) from the Upper Cretaceous of Montana: *Journal of Vertebrate Paleontology*, 16 (Supplement to Number 3), Abstracts of Papers, Fiftysixth Annual Meeting, p. 31A.

Dingus, Lowell, 1996, *Next of Kin*. New York: Rizzoli International Publications, 160 pages.

Dingus, Lowell, Eugene S. Gaffney, Mark A. Norell, and Scott D. Sampson, 1996, *The Halls of Dinosaurs: A Guide to Saurischians and Ornithischians*. New York: American Museum of Natural History, 100 pages.

Dodson, Peter, 1976, Quantitative aspects of relative growth and sexual dimorphism in *Protoceratops*: *Journal of Paleontology*, 50, pp. 929–940.

_____, 1980, Comparative osteology of the American ornithopods *Camptosaurus* and *Tenontosaurus*: *Mémoires de la Societé Géologique de France* (ns), 59, pp. 81–85.

_____, 1990a, Counting dinosaurs: How many kinds were there?: *Proceedings of the National Academy of Sciences*, 87, pp. 7608–7612.

_____, 1990b, On the status of the ceratopsids *Monoclonius* and *Centrosaurus*, *in*: Carpenter and Philip J. Currie, editors, *Dinosaur Systematics: Approaches and Perspectives*. Cambridge, New York and Melbourne: Cambridge University Press, pp. 231–243.

_____, 1995, Reviews, *Dinosaur Eggs and Babies*: *Journal of Vertebrate Paleontology*, 15 (4), pp. 863–866.

_____, 1997, *Tyrannosaurus rex*—plus ultra?: *American Paleontologist*, 5 (4), pp. 5–7.

Dodson, Peter, and Philip J. Currie, 1990, Neoceratopsia, *in*: David B. Weishampel, Dodson, and Halszka Osmólska, editors, *The Dinosauria*. Berkeley and Los Angeles: University of California Press, pp. 593–618.

Dodson, Peter, and James O. Farlow, 1997, The forelimb carriage of ceratopsid dinosaurs, *in*: Donald L. Wolberg, Edmund Stump, and Gary Rosenberg, editors, *Dinofest*[TM] *International: Proceedings of a Symposium Held at Arizona State University*. Philadelphia: Academy of Natural Sciences, pp. 393–398.

Dodson, Peter, Catherine A. Forster, Scott D. Sampson, Florent Ravoavy, and David W. Krause, 1998, Continuing discoveries of dinosaurs and associated fauna, Late Cretaceous of Madagascar, *in*: Donald L. Wolberg, K. Gittis, S. Miller, and A. Raynor, editors, *The Dinofest*[TM] *Symposium* [abstracts], Presented by The Academy of Natural Sciences of Philadelphia, Pennsylvania, pp. 11–12.

Dodson, Peter, David W. Krause, Catherine A. Forster, Scott D. Sampson, and F. Ravoavy, 1997, Titanosaur osteoderms in Madagascar confirmed: *Journal of Vertebrate Paleontology*, 17 (Supplement to Number 3), Abstracts of Papers, Fifty-seventh Annual Meeting, p. 43A.

Dodson, Peter, and Allison Tumarkin, 1998, Problematic ceratopsids: Don't throw baby out with the bathwater, *in*: Donald L. Wolberg, K. Gittis, S. Miller, and A. Raynor, editors, *The Dinofest*[TM] *Symposium* [abstracts], Presented by The Academy of Natural Sciences of Philadelphia, Pennsylvania, pp. 12–13.

Dong Zhiming [also spelled Zhi-Ming] 1997*a*, editor, *Sino-Japanese Silk Road Dinosaur Expedition*. Beijing: China Ocean Press, vii, 114 pages.

———, 1997*b*, Introduction, *in*: *Ibid*, pp. 1–2.

———, 1997*c*, On small theropods from Mazongshan Area, Gansu Province, China, *in*: *Ibid*, pp. 18.

———, 1997*d*, On the sauropod from Mazongshan Area, Gansu Province, China, *in*: *Ibid*, pp. 19–23.

———, 1997*e*, A small ornithopod from Mazongshan Area, Gansu Province, China. *in*: *Ibid*, pp. 24–26.

———, 1997*f*, Vertebrates of the Turpan Basin, the Xinjiang Uygur Autonomous Region, China, *Ibid*, pp. 96–101.

———, 1997*g*, A gigantic sauropod (*Hudiesaurus sinojapanorum* gen. et sp. nov.) from the Turpan Basin, China: *Ibid*, pp. 102–110.

———, 1997*h*, On a large claw of sauropod from the Upper Cretaceous in the Turpan Basin, Xinjiang, China: *Ibid*, pp. 111–112.

Dong Zhiming, and Yoichi Azuma, 1997, On a primitive neoceratopsian from the Early Cretaceous of China, *in*: Dong, editor, *Sino-Japanese Silk Road Dinosaur Expedition*. Beijing: China Ocean Press, pp. 68–89.

Dong Zhi-Ming [also Dong Zhiming], and Philip J. Currie, 1995, On the discovery of an oviraptorid skeleton on a nest of eggs: *Journal of Vertebrate Paleontology*, 15 (Supplement to Number 3), Abstracts of Papers, Fifty-fifth Annual Meeting, p. 26A.

———, 1996, On the discovery of an oviraptorid skeleton on a nest of eggs at Bayan Mandahu, Inner Mongolia, People's Republic of China: *Canadian Journal of Earth Sciences*, 33, pp. 631–636.

Dong Zhiming, and Yu Hailu, 1997, A new segnosaur from Mazongshan Area, Gansu Province, China, *in*: Dong, editor, *Sino-Japanese Silk Road Dinosaur Expedition*. Beijing: China Ocean Press, pp. 90–95.

Dong Zhi-Ming, Zhou Shiwu, and Zhang Zicheng, 1983, The dinosaurian remains from Sichuan Basin, China: *Paleontologia Sinica*, whole number 162, New Series C, 23, pp. 1–145.

Eberth, David A., 1993, Depositional environments and facies transitions of dinosaur-bearing Upper Cretaceous redbeds at Bayan Mandahu (Inner Mongolia, People's Republic of China): *Canadian Journal of Earth Sciences*, 30, pp. 2196–2213.

———, 1996, Ceratopsian bonebeds in the Dinosaur Park Formation (Campanian) of southern Alberta: bigger than we thought?: *Journal of Vertebrate Paleontology*, 16 (Supplement to Number 3), Abstracts of Papers, Fifty-sixth Annual Meeting, p. 32A.

Elżanowski, Andrzej, and Peter Wellnhofer, 1996, Cranial morphology of *Archaeopteryx*, evidence from the seventh skeleton: *Journal of Vertebrate Paleontology*, 16 (1), pp. 81–94.

Ensom, P. C., 1989, New scelidosaur remains from the lower Lias of Dorset: *Dorset Natural History and Archaeological Society Proceedings*, 110, 165, 167.

Erickson, Gregory M., and Kenneth H. Olson, 1996, Bite marks attributable to *Tyrannosaurus rex*: Preliminary description and implications: *Journal of Vertebrate Paleontology*, 16 (1), pp. 175–178.

Farke, Andrew A., 1997, The distribution and taxonomy of *Triceratops*, *in*: Donald L. Wolberg, Edmund Stump, and Gary Rosenberg, editors, *Dinofest*[TM] *International: Proceedings of a Symposium Held at Arizona State University*. Philadelphia: Academy of Natural Sciences, pp. 47–49.

———, 1998, A morphometric analysis of *Torosaurus*, *in*: Donald L. Wolberg, K. Gittis, S. Miller, and A. Raynor, editors, *The Dinofest*[TM] *Symposium* [abstracts], Presented by The Academy of Natural Sciences of Philadelphia, Pennsylvania, pp. 13–14.

Farlow, James O., 1997, Dinosaurs and Geologic Time, *in*: Farlow and Michael K. Brett-Surman, editors, *The Complete Dinosaur*. Bloomington and Indianapolis: Indiana University Press, pp. 107–111.

Farlow, James O., and Michael K. Brett-Surman, 1997, editors, *The Complete Dinosaur*. Bloomington and Indianapolis: Indiana University Press, xi, 749 pages.

Farlow, James O., and Peter Dodson, 1975, The behavioral significance of frill and horn morphology in ceratopsian dinosaurs: *Evolution*, 29, pp. 353–361.

———, 1996, Ichnology vs. anatomy? *Ceratopsipes* and the forelimb of ceratopsids: *Journal of Vertebrate Paleontology*, 16 (Supple-ment to Number 3), Abstracts of Papers, Fifty-sixth Annual Meeting, p. 33A.

Farlow, James O., Jeffrey G. Pittman, and J. Michael Hawthorne, 1989, *Brontopodus birdi*, Lower Cretaceous sauropod footprints from the U.S. Gulf Coastal Plain, *in*: David D. Gillette and Martin G. Lockley, editors, *Dinosaur Tracks and Traces*. Cambridge, England: Cambridge University Press, pp. 371–394.

Fastovsky, David Eliot, and Peter M. Sheehan, 1997, Demythicizing dinosaur extinctions at the Cretaceous-Tertiary boundary, *in*: Donald L. Wolberg, Edmund Stump, and Gary Rosenberg, editors. *Dinofest*[TM] *International: Proceedings of a Symposium Held at Arizona State University*. Philadelphia: Academy of Natural Sciences, pp. 527–531.

Feduccia, Alan, 1980, *The Age of Birds*. Cambridge, Massachusetts: Harvard University Press, ix, 196 pages.

Feduccia, Alan, and Larry D. Martin, 1998, Theropod-bird link reconsidered: *Nature*, 391, p. 754.

Filla, B. James, and Pat D. Redman, 1994, *Apatosaurus yahnahpin*: A preliminary description of a new species of diplodocid dinosaur from the Late Jurassic Morrison Formation of southern Wyoming, the first sauropod dinosaur found with a complete set of "belly ribs": *Forty-Fourth Annual Field Conference—1994 Wyoming Geological Association Guidebook*, pp. 159–175.

Fiorillo, Anthony R., 1996, Further comments on the patterns of microwear and resource partitioning in the Morrison Formation sauropods *Diplodocus* and *Camarasaurus*: *Journal of Vertebrate Paleontology*, 16 (Supplement to Number 3), Abstracts of Papers, Fifty-sixth Annual Meeting, p. 33A.

———, 1998, Dental microwear in the sauropod dinosaurs *Camarasaurus* and *Diplodocus* and the role of eating in determining social behavior, *in*: Donald L. Wolberg, K. Gittis, S. Miller, and A. Raynor, editors, *The Dinofest*[TM] *Symposium* [abstracts], Presented by The Academy of Natural Sciences of Philadelphia, Pennsylvania, p. 15.

Fisher, W. L., and P. U. Rodda, 1996, Nomenclature revision of basal Cretaceous rocks between the Colorado and Red Rivers, Texas: *University of Texas Bureau of Economic Geology Report of Investigation*, 58, pp. 1–18.

Ford, Tracy L., 1997, Did theropods have lizard lips?: *Southwest Paleontological Symposium Proceedings, 1997*. Mesa, Arizona: Southwest Paleontological Society and Mesa, pp. 65–78.

———, 1998*a*, A crocodile smile, or a lizard smile, which was it for theropods?, *in*: Donald L. Wolberg, K. Gittis, S. Miller, and A. Raynor, editors, *The Dinofest*[TM] *Symposium* [abstracts], Presented by The Academy of Natural Sciences of Philadelphia, Pennsylvania, pp. 15–16.

———, 1998*b*, The surfing nodosaur or riding up the Pacific Plate, *in*: Donald L. Wolberg, K. Gittis, S. Miller, and A. Raynor, editors, *The Dinofest*[TM] *Symposium* [abstracts], Presented by The Academy of

Bibliography

Natural Sciences of Philadelphia, Pennsylvania, pp. 16–17.

Forster, Catherine A., 1990, The postcranial skeleton of the ornithopod dinosaur *Tenontosaurus tilletti: Journal of Vertebrate Paleontology*, 10 (3), pp. 273–294.

———, 1996, Species resolution in *Triceratops*: Cladistic and morphometric approaches: *Ibid*, 16 (20), pp. 259–270.

———, 1997, Phylogeny of the Iguanodontia and Hadrosauridae: *Ibid*, 17 (Supplement to Number 3), Abstracts of Papers, Fifty-seventh Annual Meeting, p. 47A.

Forster, Catherine A., Paul C. Sereno, Thomas W. Evans, and Timothy Rowe, 1993, A complete skull of *Chasmosaurus mariscalensis* (Dinosauria: Ceratopsidae) from the Aguja Formation (Late Campanian) of West Texas: *Journal of Vertebrate Paleontology*, 13, pp. 161–170.

Forster, Catherine A., Scott D. Sampson, Luis M. Chiappe, and David W. Krause, 1998a, The theropod ancestry of birds: New evidence from the Late Cretaceous of Madagascar: *Science*, 279, pp. 1915–1919.

———, 1998b, Genus correction: *Ibid*, p. 185.

Fraser, Nicholas C., and Kevin Padian, 1995, Possible basal dinosaur remains from Britain and the diagnosis of the Dinosauria: *Journal of Vertebrate Paleontology*, 15 (Supplement to Number 3), Abstracts of Papers, Fifty-fifth Annual Meeting, p. 30A.

Fretz, Phelan R., 1998, Discovering dinosaurs: being true to the exhibition title, *in*: Donald L. Wolberg, K. Gittis, S. Miller, and A. Raynor, editors, *The Dinofest™ Symposium* [abstracts], Presented by The Academy of Natural Sciences of Philadelphia, Pennsylvania, p. 18.

Frey, Eberhard, and David M. Martill, 1995, A possible oviraptorid theropod from the Santana Formation (Lower Cretaceous, ?Albian) of Brazil: *Neus Jahrbuch für Geologie und Paläontologie, Monatshefte*, 1995, 7. pp. 397–412.

Gabunia, Leo K., Guram Mchedlidze, Viacheslav M. Chkhikvadze, and Spencer G. Lucas, 1998, Jurassic sauropod dinosaur from the Republic of Georgia: *Journal of Vertebrate Paleontology*, 18 (1), pp. 233–236.

Gale, Henry H., 1997, Breathing through a long neck: Sauropod lung ventilation: *Journal of Vertebrate Paleontology*, 17 (Supplement to Number 3), Abstracts of Papers, Fifty-seventh Annual Meeting, p. 48A.

Gallagher, William B., 1995, Evidence for juvenile dinosaurs and growth stages in the Late Cretaceous deposits of the Atlantic Coastal Plain: *Bulletin of the New Jersey Academy of Sciences*, 40, pp. 5–8.

———, 1997, New data on old discoveries: Reinvestigating East Coast dinosaurs, *in*: Donald L. Wolberg, Edmund Stump, and Gary Rosenberg, editors, *Dinofest™ International: Proceedings of a Symposium Held at Arizona State University*. Philadelphia: Academy of Natural Sciences, pp. 199–201.

Gallagher, William B., and David C. Parris, 1996, Age determinations for Late Cretaceous dinosaur sites in the New Jersey Coastal Plain, *in*: J. E. Repetski, editor, *Sixth North American Paleontological Convention, Abstracts of Papers*, Smithsonian Institution, Washington, D.C., p. 133.

Gallagher, William B., P. J. Sugarman, and M. D. Feigenson, 1996, Strontium isotope age estimates for East Coast dinosaurs: *Journal of Vertebrate Paleontology*, 16 (Supplement to Number 3), Abstracts of Papers, Fifty-sixth Annual Meeting, p. 36A.

Gallup, Marc R., 1989, Functional morphology of the hindfoot of the Texas sauropod *Pleurocoelus* sp. indet., *in*: James O. Farlow, editor, *Paleobiology of the Dinosaurs*, Geological Society of America Special Paper 238, pp. 71–74.

Galton, Peter M., 1969, The pelvic musculature of the dinosaur *Hypsilophodon* (Reptilia: Ornithischia): *Postilla*, 131, pp. 1–64.

———, 1981, A juvenile stegosaurian dinosaur, "*Astrodon pusillus*," from the Upper Jurassic of Portugal, with comments on Upper Jurassic and Lower Cretaceous biogeography: *Journal of Vertebrate Paleontology*, 1 (3–4), pp. 245–256.

———, 1983, Armored dinosaurs (Ornithischia: Ankylosauria) from the Middle and Upper Jurassic of Europe: *Palaeontographica*, A 182, pp. 1–25.

———, 1985a, The poposaurid thecodontian *Teratosaurus suevicus* v. MEYER, plus referred specimens mostly based on prosauropod dinosaurs, from the Middle Stubensandstein (Upper Triassic of Nordwürttemberg.—*Stuttgarter Beiträge zur Naturkunde*, Serie B (Geologie und Paläontologie), 116, pp. 105–123, Oslo.

———, 1985b, British plated dinosaurs (Ornithischia, Stegosauridae): *Journal of Vertebrate Paleontology*, 5 (3), pp. 211–254.

———, 1985c, Cranial anatomy of the prosauropod dinosaur *Plateosaurus* from the Knollenmergel (Middle Keuper, Upper Triassic) of Germany: *Geologica et Palaeontologica*, 19, pp. 119–159.

———, 1986, Prosauropod dinosaur *Plateosaurus* (=*Gresslyosaurus*) (Saurischia: Sauropodomorpha) from the Upper Triassic of Nordwürttemberg, West Germany: *Stuttgarter Beitr. Naturk*, (B), 116, pp. 1–29.

———, 1990a, A partial skeleton of the stegosaurian *Lexovisaurus* from the uppermost Lower Callovian (Middle Jurassic) of Normandy, France: *Geologica et Palaeontologica*, 24, pp. 185–199.

———, 1990b, Basal Sauropodomorpha—Prosauropoda, *in*: David B. Weishampel, Peter Dodson and Halszka Osmólska, editors, *The Dinosauria*. Berkeley and Los Angeles: University of California Press, pp. 320–344.

———, 1990c, Stegosauria, *Ibid*, pp. 435–455.

———, 1991, Postcranial remains of stegosaurian dinosaur *Dacentrurus* from Upper Jurassic of France and Portugal: *Geologica et Palaeontologica*, 25, pp. 299–327, Marburg.

———, 1994, Notes on Dinosauria and Pterodactylia from the Cretaceous of Portugal: *Neus Jahrbuch für Geologie und Paläontologie, Abhandlungen*, 194, 2/3, pp. 253–267.

———, 1997a, Cranial anatomy of the basal hypsilophodontid dinosaur *Thescelosaurus neglectus* Gilmore (Ornithischia: Ornithopoda) from the Upper Cretaceous of North America: *Revue Paléobiologie, Genève*, 16 (1), pp. 231–258.

———, 1997b, Comments on sexual dimorphism in the prosauropod dinosaur *Plateosaurus engelhardti* (Upper Cretaceous, Trossingen): *Neus Jahrbuch für Geologie und Paläontologie, Monatshefte*, 1997, H. 11, pp. 674–682, Stuttgart.

———, 1998, The prosauropod dinosaur *Plateosaurus* (*Dimodosaurus*) *poligniensis* (Pidancet & Chopard, 1862) (Upper Triassic, Poligny, France): *Neus Jahrbuch für Geologie und Paläontologie, Abhandlungen*, 207 (2), pp. 255–288.

Galton, Peter M., and Gerard Boine, 1980, A stegosaurian dinosaur femur from the Kimmeridgian Beds (Upper Jurassic) of the Cap de la Hève, Normandy: *Bulletin Trimestriel de la Societé Géologique de Normandie et des Amis du Museum du Havre*, 67 (4), pp. 31–35.

Galton, Peter M., Roger Brun, and Michel Riolt, 1980, Skeleton of the stegosaurian dinosaur *Lexovisaurus* from the lower part of Middle Callovian (Middle Jurassic) of Argences (Calvados), Normandy: *Normandy: Bulletin Trimestriel de la Societé Géologique de Normandie et des Amis du Museum du Havre*, 67 (4), pp. 39–53.

Galton, Peter M., and Hans-Dieter Sues, 1983, New data on pachycephalosaurid dinosaurs (Reptilia: Ornithischia) from North America: *Canadian Journal of Earth Science*, 20, pp. 462–472.

Galton, Peter M., and Alick D. Walker, 1996a, *Bromsgroveia* from the Middle Triassic of England, the earliest record of a poposaurid thecodontian reptile (Archosauria: Rauisuchia): *Neus Jahrbuch für Geologie und Paläontologie, Abhandlungen*, 201 (3), pp. 303–325, Stuttgart.

———, 1996b, Supposed prosauropod dinosaurs from Middle Triassic of England referred to Parasuchia and Dinosauriformes: *Neus Jahrbuch für Geologie und Paläontologie, Monatshefte*, H. 12, pp. 727–738, Stuttgart.

Galton, Peter M., and Jacques Van Heerden, 1997, The affinities of *Melanorosaurus*—a Late Triassic prosauropod from South Africa: *Neus Jahrbuch für Geologie und Paläontologie, Monatshefte*, H. 1, pp. 39–55, Stuttgart.

Garstka, William R., and David A. Burnham, 1997, Posture and stance of *Triceratops*: Evidence of digitigrade manus and cantilever vertebral column, *in*: Donald L. Wolberg, Edmund Stump, and Gary Rosenberg, editors, *Dinofest™ International: Proceedings of a Symposium Held at Arizona State University*. Philadelphia: Academy of Natural Sciences, pp. 385–391.

Gasparini, Zumla, E. Olivero, R. Scasco, and C. Rinaldi, 1987, Un Ankylosaurio (Reptilia, Ornithischia) Campanico en el Continente Antartico: *Anais do X Congresso Brasileiro de Paleontologia*, Rio de Janeiro, 19–25 de Julho, 1987, pp. 131–141.

Gasparini, Zumla, Xabier Pereda-Suberbiola,

and Ralph E. Molnar, 1996, New data on the ankylosaurian dinosaur from the Late Cretaceous of the Antarctic Peninsula, *in*: Fernando S. Novas and Ralph E. Molnar, editors, *Proceedings of the Gondwanan Dinosaur Symposium: Memoirs of the Queensland Museum*, 39 (part 3), pp. 583–594.

Gatesy, Stephen M., and K. P. Dial, 1996, Saurischian monophyly and the evolution of avian flight: *Evolution*, 50, pp. 331–340.

Gatesy, Stephen M., and Kevin M. Middleton, 1997, Bipedalism, flight, and the evolution of theropod locomotor diversity: *Journal of Vertebrate Paleontology*, 17 (2), pp. 308–309.

Gauffre, Francois Xavier, 1993*a*, The prosauropod dinosaur *Azendohsaurus laaroussii* from the Upper Triassic of Morocco: *Palaeontology*, 36 (4), pp. 897–908.

_____, 1993*b*, Biochronostratigraphy of the Lower Elliot Formation (Southern Africa) and preliminary results on the Maphutseng dinosaur (Saurischia: Prosauropoda) from the same formation of Lesotho: *Bulletin of the New Mexico Museum of Natural History and Science*, 3, pp. 147–149.

_____, 1995, Phylogeny of prosauropod dinosaurs: *Journal of Vertebrate Paleontology*, 15 (Supplement to Number 3), Abstracts of Papers, Fifty-fifth Annual Meeting, p. 31A.

Gauthier, Jacques A., 1984, A cladistic analysis of the higher systematic categories of the Diapsida: Ph.D. thesis, Department of Paleontology, University of California, Berkeley, 565 pages (no. 85-12825, University Microfilms, Ann Arbor, Michigan).

_____, 1986, Saurischian monophyly and the origin of birds, *in*: Kevin Padian, editor, The Origin of Birds and the Evolution of Flight. *Memoirs of the California Academy of Sciences*, 8, pp. 1–55.

Gauthier, Jacques A., and Kevin Padian, 1985, Phylogenetic, functional, and aerodynamic analyses of the origin of birds and their flight, *in*: Max K. Hecht, John H. Ostrom, G. Viohl and Peter Wellnhoffer, editors, *The Beginnings of Birds*. Eichstätt: Freunde des Jura-Museums, pp. 185–197.

Geist, Nicholas R., Terry D. Jones, and John A. Ruben, 1997, Implications of soft tissue preservation in the compsognathid dinosaur, *Sinosauropteryx: Journal of Vertebrate Paleontology*, 17 (Supplement to Number 3), Abstracts of Papers, Fifty-seventh Annual Meeting, p. 48A.

_____, 1998, Implications of soft tissue preservation in the compsognathid dinosaur, *Sinosauropteryx*, *in*: Donald L. Wolberg, K. Gittis, S. Miller, and A. Raynor, editors, *The Dinofest™ Symposium* [abstracts], Presented by The Academy of Natural Sciences of Philadelphia, Pennsylvania, pp. 19–20.

Gemellaro, M., 1921, Rettili maëstrichtiani de Egitto: *Gionarle di Scienze Naturali ed Economiche, Palermo*, 32, pp. 339–351.

Getty, M., David A. Eberth, David B. Brinkman, Darren Tanke, Michael J. Ryan, and M. Vickaryous, 1997, Taphonomy of two *Centrosaurus* bonebeds in the Dinosaur Park Formation, Alberta, Canada: *Journal of Vertebrate Paleontology*, 17 (Supplement to Number 3), Abstracts of Papers, Fifty-seventh Annual Meeting, pp. 48A–49A.

Gibbons, Ann, 1998, Missing link times birds, dinosaurs: *Science*, 279, pp. 1851–1852.

Gierlinski, Gerard, 1991, New dinosaur ichnites from the Early Jurassic of the Holy Cross Mountains, Poland: *Palaeogeography, Palaeoclimatology, Palaeoecology*, 85, pp. 137–148.

_____, 1996, Feather-like impressions in a theropod resting trace from the Lower Jurassic of Massachusetts, *in*: Michael Morales, editor, "The Continental Jurassic": *Museum of Northern Arizona Bulletin*, 60, pp. 179–184.

_____, 1997, What type of feathers could nonavian dinosaurs have, according to an Early Jurassic evidence from Massachusetts?: *Przeglad Geologiczny*, 45 (4), pp. 419–422.

_____, 1998, The furry dino: *Dinosaur World*, 4, pp. 3–5.

Gierlinski, Gerhard, and A. Ahlberg, 1994, Late Triassic and Early Jurassic dinosaur footprints in the Hoganas Formation of southern Sweden: *Ichnos*, 3, pp. 99–105.

Gillette, David D., 1993, Type locality and stratigraphic position of *Dystrophaeus viaemalae* Cope 1879, the earliest sauropod dinosaur in North America: *Journal of Vertebrate Paleontology*, 15 (Supplement to Number 3), Abstracts of Papers, Fifty-third Annual Meeting, p. 37A.

_____, 1996*a*, Stratigraphic position of the sauropod *Dystrophaeus viaemalae* Cope 1877 and its evolutionary implications, *in*: Michael Morales, editor, *Museum of Northern Arizona Bulletin*, 60, pp. 59–68.

_____, in press, Origin and early evolution of the sauropod dinosaurs of North America: the type locality and stratigraphic position of *Dystrophaeus viaemalae* Cope 1877: *Paradox Basin Symposium*.

Gillette, J. Lynette, Francis A. Barnes, David D. Gillette, and John S. McIntosh, 1989, The type locality and stratigraphic position of *Dystrophaeus viaemalae* Cope 1877 (Dinosauria, Sauropoda), *in*: Jeffrey G. Eaton, Grace V. Irby, and Michael Morales, editors, *Abstracts of the Symposium on Southwestern Geology and Paleontology, 1989*, p. 11.

Gilmore, Charles Whitney, 1905, The mounted skeleton of *Triceratops prorsus: Proceedings of the United States National Museum*, 29 (1426), pp. 433–435.

_____, 1914, Osteology of the armored Dinosauria in the United States National Museum, with special reference to the genus *Stegosaurus: Memoirs of the United States National Museum*, 89, pp. 1–316.

_____, 1920, Osteology of the carnivorous dinosauria in the United States National Museum, with special reference to the genera *Antrodemus* (*Allosaurus*) and *Ceratosaurus: Bulletin of the United States National Museum*, 110, pp. 1–154.

_____, 1924, A new coelurid dinosaur from the Belly River Cretaceous of Alberta: *Geo-* *logical Survey of Canada, Department of Mines*, Bulletin 38, Geological Series, 43, pp. 1–12.

_____, 1925, A nearly complete articulated skeleton of *Camarasaurus*, a saurischian dinosaur from the Dinosaur National Monument: *Memoirs of the Carnegie Museum*, 10, pp. 347–384.

_____, 1933, Two new dinosaurian reptiles from Mongolia with notes on some fragmentary specimens: *American Museum Novitates*, 679, pp. 1–20.

_____, 1946*a*, A new carnivorous dinosaur from the Lance Formation of Montana: *Smithsonian Miscellaneous Collections*, 106 (13), 19 pages.

_____, 1946*b*, Reptilian fauna of the North Horn Formation of Central Utah: *United States Geological Survey Professional Paper*, 210-C, pp. 29–53.

Glut, Donald F., 1972, *The Dinosaur Dictionary*. Secaucus, New Jersey: Citadel Press, 218 pages.

_____, 1980, *The Dinosaur Scrapbook*. Secaucus, New Jersey: Citadel Press, 320 pages.

_____, 1982, *The New Dinosaur Dictionary*. Secaucus, New Jersey: Citadel Press, 288 pages.

_____, 1997, *Dinosaurs: The Encyclopedia*. Jefferson, North Carolina: McFarland & Company, xi, 1076 pages.

Godefroit, P., Dong Z.-M., P. Bultynck, Li H., and Feng L., 1998, Cretaceous dinosaurs and mammals from Inner Mongolia, Part 1: New *Bactrosaurus* (Dinosauria: Euhadrosauria) material from Iren Dabasu (Inner Mongolia, P. R. China): *The Sino-Belgian Dinosaur Expedition in Inner Mongolia, Bulletin, Institut Royal des Sciences Naturelles de Belgique*, Suppl. 68, pp. 1–70.

Gomani, Elizabeth M., 1996, New sauropod remains from the Early Cretaceous of Malawi, Africa: *Dinofest™ International Symposium, April 18–21, 1996, Programs and Abstracts*, p. 54.

_____, 1998*a*, The skeleton of *Malawisaurus*, an Early Cretaceous titanosaurid (Sauropoda) from Africa, *in*: Donald L. Wolberg, K. Gittis, S. Miller, and A. Raynor, editors, *The Dinofest™ Symposium* [abstracts], Presented by The Academy of Natural Sciences of Philadelphia, Pennsylvania, p. 21.

_____, 1998*b*, *Malawisaurus* and a summary of titanosaurian phylogeny, *in*: Yukimitsu Tomida, Thomas R. Rich, and Patricia Vickers-Rich, editors, *Second Symposium Gondwana Dinosaur, 12–13 July, 1998, National Science Museum, Tokyo, Abstracts with Program*, p. 19.

Gomani, Elizabeth M., Louis L. Jacobs, and Dale A. Winkler, 1998, Comments on vertebral structure in African titanosaurian sauropods, *in*: Yukimitsu Tomida, Thomas R. Rich, and Patricia Vickers-Rich, editors, *Second Symposium Gondwana Dinosaur, 12–13 July, 1998, National Science Museum, Tokyo, Abstracts with Program*, p. 20.

Gonzales-Leon, C. M., and Spencer G. Lucas, 1996, Late Cretaceous dinosaurs and other fossils from the Cabullona Basin,

Bibliography

Northeastern Sonora, Mexico: *Dinofest™ International Symposium, April 18–21, 1996, Programs and Abstracts*, p. 55.

Goodwin, Mark B., 1998, Cranial ontogeny in *Triceratops*: New records from the Upper Cretaceous Hell Creek Formation (Maastrichtian) of Montana, *in*: John W. M. Jagt, Paul H. Lambers, Eric W. A. Mulder, and Anne S. Schulp, editors, *Third European Workshop on Vertebrate Palaeontology*, Maastricht, 6–9 May 1998, Programme and Abstracts Field Guide, [unpaginated].

Goodwin, Mark B., Emily A. Buchholtz, and Rolfe E. Johnson, 1998, Cranial anatomy and diagnosis of *Stygimoloch spinifer* (Ornithischia: Pachycephalosauria) with comments on cranial display structures in agonistic behavior: *Journal of Vertebrate Paleontology*, 18 (2), pp. 363–375.

Goodwin, Mark B., William A. Clemens, and John R. Horner, 1997, Morphological variation and ontogeny in the skull of *Triceratops*: *Journal of Vertebrate Paleontology*, 17 (Supplement to Number 3), Abstracts of Papers, Fifty-seventh Annual Meeting, p. 49A.

Goodwin, Mark B., and Rolfe E. Johnson, 1995, A new skull of the pachycephalosaur *Stygimoloch* casts doubt on head butting behavior: *Journal of Vertebrate Paleontology*, 15 (Supplement to Number 3), Abstracts of Papers, Fifty-fifth Annual Meeting, p. 32A.

Gow, Christopher E., J. W. Kitching, and Michael A. Raath, 1990, Skulls of the prosauropod dinosaur *Massospondylus carinatus* Owen in the collections of the Bernard Price Institute for Palaeontological Research: *Palaeontologia Africana*, 27, pp. 45–58, Johannesburg.

Gradstein, F. M., F. P. Agterberg, J. G. Ogg, J. Hardenbol, P. van Veen, J. Thierry, and Z. Huang, 1994, A Mesozoic time scale: *Journal of Geophysical Research*, 99 (B12), 24,051–24,074.

Gradziński, R., and T. Jerzykiewicz, 1972, Additional geographical and geological data from the Polish-Mongolian Palaeontological Expeditions. Results of the Polish-Mongolian Expeditions, Part IV: *Palaeontologia Polonica*, 7, pp. 17–32.

Griffiths, P., 1993, The question of *Compsognathus* eggs: *Revisions in Paleobiology*, Special Issue 7, pp. 85–94.

Hammer, William R., 1996, Jurassic dinosaurs from Antarctica, *in*: Donald L. Wolberg, Edmund Stump, and Gary Rosenberg, editors. *Dinofest™ International: Proceedings of a Symposium Held at Arizona State University*. Philadelphia: Academy of Natural Sciences, pp. 249–251.

———, 1998, Searching for dinosaurs in Antarctica: Why are they so rare?, *in*: Donald L. Wolberg, K. Gittis, S. Miller, and A. Raynor, editors, *The Dinofest™ Symposium* [abstracts], Presented by The Academy of Natural Sciences of Philadelphia, Pennsylvania, pp. 24–25.

Hammer, William R., and William J. Hickerson, 1993, A new Jurassic dinosaur fauna from Antarctica: *Journal of Vertebrate Paleontology*, 13 (Supplement to Number 3),

Abstracts of Papers, Fifty-third Annual Meeting, p. 40A.

———, 1994, A crested theropod dinosaur from Antarctica: *Science*, 264, pp. 828–830.

———, 1998, Gondwana dinosaurs from the Jurassic of Antarctica, *in*: Yukimitsu Tomida, Thomas R. Rich, and Patricia Vickers-Rich, editors, *Second Symposium Gondwana Dinosaur, 12–13 July, 1998, National Science Museum, Tokyo, Abstracts with Program*, p. 18.

Happ, John W., and Christopher M. Morrow, 1996, Separation of *Triceratops* (Dinosauria: Ceratopsidae) into two allopatric species by cranial morphology: *Journal of Vertebrate Paleontology*, 16 (Supplement to Number 3), Abstracts of Papers, Fifty-sixth Annual Meeting, p. 40A.

———, 1997, Bone modification of subadult *Triceratops* (Dinosauria: Ceratopsidae) by crocodilian and theropod dining: *Ibid*, 17 (Supplement to Number 3), Abstracts of Papers, Fifty-seventh Annual Meeting, p. 51A.

Harland, Walter Brian, A. V. Cox, P. G. Llewellyn, A. G. Smith, and R. Walters, 1989, *A Geologic Time Scale 1989*. Cambridge, England: Cambridge University Press, xv, 263 pages.

Harris, Jerald David, 1998, A reanalysis of *Acrocanthosaurus atokensis*, its phylogenetic status, and paleobiogeographic implications, based on a new specimen from Texas: *New Mexico Museum of Natural History and Science, Bulletin 13*, 75 pages.

Harris, John M., 1996, Dueling dinosaurs: *Terra*, 33 (5), pp. 2–5.

Hatcher, John Bell, 1901, *Diplodocus* (Marsh): its osteology, taxonomy, and probable habits, with a restoration of the skeleton: *Memoirs of the Carnegie Museum*, 1 (1), pp. 1–61.

———, 1903, A new sauropod dinosaur from the Jurassic of Colorado: *Proceedings of the Biological Society of Washington*, 16, pp. 1–2.

Haughton, Sidney H., 1924, The fauna and stratigraphy of the Stormberg Series: *Annals of the South African Museum*, 12, pp. 323–497.

He Xinlu, Li Kui, and Cai Kaiji, 1988, *The Middle Jurassic dinosaur fauna from Dashanpu, Zigong, Sichuan*, volume IV, The Sauropod Dinosaurs (II): Sichuan Publishing House of Science and Technology, Chengdu, pp. 114–113.

He Xinlu, Li Kui, Cai Kaiji, and Gao Yuhui, 1984, *Omeisaurus tianfuensis*—A new species of *Omeisaurus* from Dashanpu, Zigong, Sichuan: *Journal of Chengdu College of Geology*, 2, pp. 15–32.

Head, Jason J., 1996, A primitive hadrosaur (Dinosauria: Ornithischia) from the Cenomanian of Texas and its implications for hadrosaurian phylogenetic and biogeographic histories: *Journal of Vertebrate Paleontology*, 16 (Supplement to Number 3), Abstracts of Papers, Fifty-sixth Annual Meeting, p. 40A.

Heckert, Andrew B., and Spencer G. Lucas, 1995, Synchronous Pangea-wide diversification of Late Triassic dinosaurs and the importance of western North America in early dinosaur evolution: *Geological Society of America, Abstracts*, p. A–60.

Heckert, Andrew B., Spencer G. Lucas, and Adrian P. Hunt, 1997, Biostratigraphic significance of ornithischian dinosaur teeth in the Upper Triassic Chinle Group, Southwestern U.S.A.: *Journal of Vertebrate Paleontology*, 17 (Supplement to Number 3), Abstracts of Papers, Fifty-seventh Annual Meeting, p. 52A.

Heilmann, Gerhard, 1926, *The Origin of Birds*. London: Witherby, 208 pages.

Hengst, Richard A., 1998, Mesozoic breathing: Comparing the progress of North and South American theropods, *in*: Donald L. Wolberg, K. Gittis, S. Miller, and A. Raynor, editors, *The Dinofest™ Symposium* [abstracts], Presented by The Academy of Natural Sciences of Philadelphia, Pennsylvania, p. 25.

Hengst, Richard A., Mitchell Alix, and J. Keith Rigby, 1996, Did dinosaur breathing affect the evolution of dinosaur activity?: *Dinofest™ International Symposium, April 18–21, 1996, Programs and Abstracts*, p. 59.

Hildebrand, A. R., G. T. Penfield, D. A. King, M. Pilkington, A. Z. Camaro, S. B. Jacobson, and W. B. Boynton, 1991, Chicxulub Crater: A possible Cretaceous/Tertiary boundary impact crater on the Yucatán Peninsula, Mexico: *Geology*, 19, pp. 867–871.

Hillenius, Willem J., 1996, Criteria used to determine the presence or absence of respiratory turbinates in extinct taxa: *Journal of Vertebrate Paleontology*, 16 (Supplement to Number 3), Abstracts of Papers, Fifty-sixth Annual Meeting, p. 41A.

Hilton, Richard P., Frank L. DeCourten, Michael A. Murphy, Peter U. Rodda, and Patrick G. Embree, 1997, An Early Cretaceous ornithopod dinosaur from California: *Journal of Vertebrate Paleontology*, 17 (3), pp. 557–560.

Hitchcock, Edward, 1844, Report on ichnolithology, or fossil footmarks, with a description of several new species, and the coprolites of birds, from the valley of Connecticut River, and of a supposed footmark from the valley of Hudson River: *American Journal of Science*, 47, pp. 292–322.

Hoffstetter, Robert, 1957, Quelques observations sur les stegosaurines: *Bulletin du Muséum National d'Historie Naturelle, Paris*, 2 (29), pp. 537–547.

Hoffstetter, Robert, and Roger Brun, 1956, Un dinosaurien stegosaurine dans le Callovien du Calvados: *Comptes Rendus des Séances de l'Académie des Sciences*, 243, pp. 1651–1653.

———, 1958, Note complementaire sur la decouverte d'un dinosaurien stegosaurine dans le Callovien d'Argences (Calvados): *Revue des Societés Savantes de Haute-Normandie, (Sci.)*, 9, pp. 69–78.

Holl, Friedrich, 1829, *Handbuch der Petrefactenkunde*, part 1. Dresden, Germany: Hilscher, 115 pages (in German).

Holland, William J., 1915, Heads and tails: A few notes relating to the structure of the sauropod dinosaurs: *Annals of the Carnegie Museum*, 9, pp. 273–278.

Holmes, Thom, and Peter Dodson, 1997, Counting more dinosaurs — How many kinds are there (1996)?, *in*: Donald L. Wolberg, Edmund Stump, and Gary Rosenberg, editors, *Dinofest™ International: Proceedings of a Symposium Held at Arizona State University*. Philadelphia: Academy of Natural Sciences, pp. 125–128.

Holtz, Thomas R., Jr., 1994a, The phylogenetic position of the Tyrannosauridae: implications for theropod systematics: *Journal of Paleontology*, 68 (5), pp. 1100–1117.

_____, 1994b, The arctometatarsalian pes, an unusual structure of the metatarsus of Cretaceous Theropoda (Dinosauria: Saurischia): *Journal of Vertebrate Paleontology*, 14 (4), pp. 480–519.

_____, 1995a, Adaptive trends in major subgroups of theropods and related taxa: *Journal of Vertebrate Paleontology*, 15 (Supplement to Number 3), Abstracts of Papers, Fifty-fifth Annual Meeting, p. 35A.

_____, 1995b, A new phylogeny of the Theropoda: *Ibid*, p. 35A.

_____, 1996, Phylogenetic taxonomy of the Coelurosauria (Dinosauria: Theropoda): *Journal of Paleontology*, 70, pp. 536–538.

_____, 1997, Preliminary phylogenetic analysis of the Tyrannosauridae (Theropoda: Coelurosauria): *Journal of Vertebrate Paleontology*, 17 (Supplement to Number 3), Abstracts of Papers, Fifty-seventh Annual Meeting, p. 53A.

_____, 1998, Evidence for the predatory nature of *Tyrannosaurus rex* and other tyrant dinosaurs, *in*: Donald L. Wolberg, K. Gittis, S. Miller, and A. Raynor, editors, *The Dinofest™ Symposium* [abstracts], Presented by The Academy of Natural Sciences of Philadelphia, Pennsylvania, pp. 26–27.

Holtz, Thomas R., Jr., and Kevin Padian, 1995, Definition and diagnosis of Theropoda and related taxa: *Journal of Vertebrate Paleontology*, 15 (Supplement to Number 3), Abstracts of Papers, Fifty-fifth Annual Meeting, p. 35A.

Hopp, Thomas, and Mark Orsen, 1998, Dinosaur brooding behavior and the origin of flight feathers, *in*: Donald L. Wolberg, K. Gittis, S. Miller, and A. Raynor, editors, *The Dinofest™ Symposium* [abstracts], Presented by The Academy of Natural Sciences of Philadelphia, Pennsylvania, pp. 27–28.

Horner, John R., 1982, Evidence of colonial nesting and 'site fidelity' among ornithischian dinosaurs: *Nature*, 297 (5868), pp. 675–676.

_____, 1996, New evidence for post-eclosion parental attention in *Maiasaura peeblesorum*: *Journal of Vertebrate Paleontology*, 16 (Supplement to Number 3), Abstracts of Papers, Fifty-sixth Annual Meeting, p. 42A.

_____, 1998, Cold-blooded, warm-blooded or both? Let's have another look at dinosaur bone histology, *in*: Donald L. Wolberg, K. Gittis, S. Miller, and A. Raynor, editors, *The Dinofest™ Symposium* [abstracts], Presented by The Academy of Natural Sciences of Philadelphia, Pennsylvania, p. 28.

Horner, John R., and Philip J. Currie, 1994, Embryonic and neonatal morphology and ontogeny of a new species of *Hypacrosaurus* (Ornithischia: Lambeosauridae) from Montana and Alberta, *in*: Kenneth Carpenter, Karl F. Hirsch, and John R. Horner, editors, *Dinosaur Eggs and Babies*. New York: Cambridge University Press, pp. 312–336.

Horner, John R., and James Gorman, 1988, *Digging Dinosaurs*. New York: Workman Publishing, 210 pages.

Horner, John R., and Don Lessem, 1993, *The Complete T. rex*. New York: Simon and Schuster, 239 pages.

Horner, John R., and Robert Makela, 1979, Nest of juveniles provides evidence of family structure among dinosaurs: *Nature*, 282 (5736), pp. 296–298.

Horner, John R., and David J. Varrichio, 1997, Embryonic remains of *Troodon formosus* from the Two Medicine Formation of Montana: *Journal of Vertebrate Paleontology*, 17 (Supplement to Number 3), Abstracts of Papers, Fifty-seventh Annual Meeting, pp. 53A–54A.

Horner, John R., and David B. Weishampel, 1988, An embryological study of two ornithischian dinosaurs: *Nature*, 332, pp. 256–257.

Hou L. H., Chao [Zhou] S. W., and Chu [Chao] S.C., 1976, New discovery of sauropod dinosaurs from Szechuan: *VertebrataPalasiatica*, XIV, 3, pp. 160–165.

Hu S. J., 1993, A new Theropoda (*Dilophosaurus sinensis*, sp.n.) from Yunnan, China: *Vertebrata PalAsiatica*, 31, pp. 56–69.

Huene, Frederich von, 1901, Der vermutliche Hautpanzer des *Compsognathus longipes* Wagner: *Neus Jahrbuch für Mineralologie, Geologie und Paläontologie*, 1901, 1 (1), pp. 157–160.

_____, 1904, *Dystrophaeus viamalae* Cope in neuer Beleuchtung: *Neus Jahrbuch für Mineralogie, Geologie und Paläontologie, Abhandlugen*, 19, pp. 319–333, Stuttgart.

_____, 1905, Über die Trias-Dinosaurier Europas: *Z. Deutsch. Geol. Ges., Mh.*, 57, pp. 345–349, Berlin.

_____, 1907–08, Die Dinosaurier der europäischen Triasformation mit Berucksichtigung der europaischen Vorkommisse: *Geologische und Paläontologische Adhandlungen, Jena*, Supplement 1, 419 pages.

_____, 1927, Short review of the present knowledge of the Sauropoda: *Memoirs of the Queensland Museum*, 9, pp. 121–126.

_____, 1929, Los Saurisquios y Ornitisquios del Cretaceo Argentina: *Annales Museo de La Plata*, 3, Serie 2a., 196 pages.

_____, 1932, Die fossile Reptil-Ordnung Saurischia, ihre Entwicklung und Geschichte: *Monographien zur Geologie und Palaeontologie*, Series 1, 4, 361 pages.

Huene, Frederich von, and Charles Alfred Matley, 1933, The Cretaceous Saurischia and Ornithischia of the Central Provinces of India: *Paleontologica Indica*, 21 (1), pp. 1–74.

Hulke, James W., 1887, Note on some dinosaurian remains in the collection of A. Leeds, Esq. of Eyebury, Northamptonshire: *Quarterly Journal of the Geological Society, London*, 43, pp. 695–702.

Hunt, Adrian P., 1991, The early diversification of the dinosaurs in the Late Triassic: *Modern Geology*, 16, pp. 43–60.

_____, 1996, A new clade of herrerasaur-like theropods from the Late Triassic of western North America: *Journal of Vertebrate Paleontology*, 16 (Supplement to Number 3), Abstracts of Papers, Fifty-sixth Annual Meeting, p. 43A.

Hunt, Adrian P., Martin G. Lockley, Spencer G. Lucas, and Christian A. Meyer, 1994. The global sauropod fossil record: *Gaia*, 10, pp. 261–279.

Hunt, Adrian P., and Spencer G. Lucas, 1987, J. W. Stovall and the Mesozoic of the Cimarron Valley, Oklahoma and New Mexico, *in*: Spencer G. Lucas and Adrian P. Hunt, editors, *Northwestern New Mexico. New Mexico Geological Society Guidebook, 38th Field Conference, Northwestern New Mexico*, pp. 139–151.

_____, 1989, Late Triassic vertebrate localities in New Mexico, *in*: Lucas and Hunt, editors, *Dawn of the Age of Dinosaurs in the American Southwest*. Albuquerque: New Mexico Museum of Natural History, pp. 72–101.

_____, 1991, *Rioarribasaurus*, a new name for a Late Triassic dinosaur from New Mexico (USA): *Paläontraphica Zeitschrift*, 65 (1/2), pp. 191–198.

Hunt, Adrian P., Robert M. Sullivan, Spencer J. Lucas, and Andrew B. Heckert, 1995, Herrerasaur and theropod diversity in the Late Triassic of Western United States: *Journal of Vertebrate Paleontology*, 15 (Supplement to Number 3), Abstracts of Papers, Fifty-fifth Annual Meeting, p. 36A.

Hutt, Steve, David M. Martill, and Michael J. Barker, 1996, The first European allosaurid dinosaur (Lower Cretaceous, Wealden Group, England): *Neus Jahrbuch für Geologie und Paläontologie, Monatshefte*, 1996, H. 10, pp. 635–644.

Huxley, Thomas Henry, 1868, On the animals which are most nearly intermediate between the birds and reptiles: *Annals and Magazine of Natural History*, 2, pp. 66–75.

Jacobs, Louis, 1995, *Lone Star Dinosaurs*. College Station, Texas: Texas A&M Press, Number 22: Louise Lindsey Merrick Natural Environment Series, xiv, 160 pages.

Jacobs, Louis L., Dale A. Winkler, William R. Downs, and Elizabeth M. Gomani, 1993, New material of an Early Cretaceous titanosaurid sauropod dinosaur from Malawi: *Palaeontology*, 36 (3), pp. 523–534.

Jacobs, Louis L., Dale A. Winkler, and Phillip A. Murry, 1991, On the age and correlation of the Trinity mammals, Early Cretaceous of Texas, U.S.A.: *Newsletters on Stratigraphy*, 24, pp. 35–43.

Jacobsen, Aase Roland, 1996, Wear patterns on tyrannosaurid teeth: an indication of biting strategy: *Journal of Vertebrate Paleontology*, 16 (Supplement to Number 3), Abstracts of Papers, Fifty-sixth Annual Meeting, p. 43A.

Jain, Sohan, and Saswati Bandyopadhyay, 1997, New titanosaurid (Dinosauria: Sauropoda) from the Late Cretaceous of central India: *Journal of Vertebrate Paleontology*, 17 (1), pp. 114–136.

Jain, Sohan L., T. S. Kutty, Tapan Row-Chowdbury, and Sankar Chatterjee, 1979, Some characteristics of *Barapasaurus tagorei*, a sauropod dinosaur from the Lower Jurassic of Deccan, India: *Proceedings of the IV International Gondwana Symposium, Calcutta*, 1, pp. 204–216.

Jensen, James A., 1970, Fossil eggs from the Lower Cretaceous of Utah: *Brigham Young University Geology Studies*, 17, pp. 51–66.

_____, 1985, Three new sauropod dinosaurs from the Upper Jurassic of Colorado: *Great Basin Naturalist*, 45 (4), pp. 697–709.

_____, 1987, New brachiosaur material from the Late Jurassic of Utah and Colorado: *Ibid*, 47 (4), pp. 592–608.

_____, 1988, A fourth new sauropod dinosaur from the Upper Jurassic of the Colorado Plateau and sauropod bipedalism: *Great Basin Naturalist*, 48 (2), pp. 121–145.

Jerzykiewicz, T., and Dale A. Russell, 1991, Late Mesozoic stratigraphy and vertebrates of the Gobi Basin: *Cretaceous Research*, 12, pp. 345–377.

Jerzykiewicz, T., Philip J. Currie, David A. Eberth, P. A. Johnson, E. H. Koster, and J. J. Zheng, 1993, Djadokhta Formation correlative strata in Chinese Inner Mongolia: An overview of the stratigraphy, sedimentary geology, and paleontology and comparisons with the type locality in the pre–Altai Gobi: *Canadian Journal of Earth Sciences*, 30, pp. 2180–2195.

Ji Qiang, Philip J. Currie, Mark A. Norell, and Ji Shu-An, 1998, Two feathered dinosaurs from northeastern China: *Nature*, 393, pp. 753–761.

Ji Qiang and Ji S., 1996a, On discovery of the earliest bird fossil in China and the origin of birds: *Chinese Geology*, 10 (233), pp. 30–34 (in Chinese).

_____, 1996b, *Protoarchaeopteryx*, a new genus of Archaeopteryygidae in China: *Ibid*, pp. 38–42 (in Chinese).

_____, 1997, A proarchaeopterygid bird (*Proarchaeopteryx* gen. nov.) — Fossil remains of archaeopterygids from China: *Ibid*, 238, pp. 38–41.

Jianu, Coralia-Maria, and David B. Weishampel, 1998, The smallest of the largest: A new look at possible dwarfing in sauropods, *in*: John W. M. Jagt, Paul H. Lambers, Eric W. A. Mulder, and Anne S. Schulp, editors, *Third European Workshop on Vertebrate Palaeontology*, Maastricht, 6–9, May 1998, Programme and Abstracts Field Guide, [unpaginated].

Jones, Ramal, and Donald L. Burge, 1995, Radiological surveying as a method for mapping dinosaur bone sites: *Journal of Vertebrate Paleontology*, 15 (Supplement to Number 3), Abstracts of Papers, Fifty-fifth Annual Meeting, p. 38A.

Jones, Terry D., John A. Ruben, and Nicholas R. Geist, 1998, Lung structure in theropod dinosaurs and early birds: Implications for physiology and phylogeny, *in*: Donald L. Wolberg, K. Gittis, S. Miller, and A. Raynor, editors, *The Dinofest™ Symposium* [abstracts], Presented by The Academy of Natural Sciences of Philadelphia, Pennsylvania, p 29.

Kaye, Tom, 1998, A new theory on mid caudal fusion in sauropods, *in*: Donald L. Wolberg, K. Gittis, S. Miller, and A. Raynor, editors, *The Dinofest™ Symposium* [abstracts], Presented by The Academy of Natural Sciences of Philadelphia, Pennsylvania, pp. 29–30.

Keller, Gerta, 1998, The K/T boundary mass extinction: Theories and facts, *in*: Donald L. Wolberg, K. Gittis, S. Miller, and A. Raynor, editors, *The Dinofest™ Symposium* [abstracts], Presented by The Academy of Natural Sciences of Philadelphia, Pennsylvania, p. 30.

Kellner, Alexander W. A., 1996, Remarks on Brazilian dinosaurs, *in*: Fernando S. Novas and Ralph E. Molnar, editors, *Proceedings of the Gondwanan Dinosaur Symposium: Memoirs of the Queensland Museum*, 39 (part 3), pp. 611–626.

Kellner, Alexander W. A., and Sergio A. K. Azevedo, 1998, A new titanosaurid sauropod from the Late Cretaceous Bauru Group, São Paulo, Brazil, *in*: Yukimitsu Tomida, Thomas R. Rich, and Patricia Vickers-Rich, editors, *Second Symposium Gondwana Dinosaur, 12–13 July, 1998, National Science Museum, Tokyo, Abstracts with Program*, pp. 12–13.

Kellner, Alexander W. A., and Diogenes de A. Campos, 1996, First Early Cretaceous theropod dinosaur from Brazil with comments on Spinosauridae: *Neus Jahrbuch für Geologie und Paläontologie Abhandlungen*, 199, pp. 151–166.

_____, 1997, The Titanosauridae (Sauropoda) of the Bauru Group, Late Cretaceous of Brazil: *Journal of Vertebrate Paleontology*, 17 (Supplement to Number 3), Abstracts of Papers, Fifty-seventh Annual Meeting, p. 56A.

Kenneth, J. H., 1960, *A Dictionary of Scientific Terms* [seventh edition], by I. F. Henderson and W. D. Henderson. Edinburgh: Oliver and Boyd, xv, 595 pages.

Kim, Haang Mook, 1983, [Cretaceous dinosaurs from Korea]: *Journal of the Geological Society of Korea*, 19 (3), pp. 115–126. [Note: There are two versions of this paper: the first, apparently an offprint, does not give specific name; the second, the published version, does.]

Kirkland, James Ian, 1996, Reconstruction of polacanthid ankylosaurs based on new discoveries from the Late Jurassic and Early Cretaceous: *Dinofest™ International Symposium, April 18–21, 1996, Programs and Abstracts*, p. 67.

_____, 1997a, Carrion bugs found in Gobi Desert fossils: *Paleo Horizons*, 4 (2), p. 3.

_____, 1997b, Cedar Mountain Formation, *in*: Philip J. Currie and Kevin Padian, editors, *Encyclopedia of Dinosaurs*. San Diego: Academic Press, pp. 98–99.

_____, 1998a, A polacanthine ankylosaur (Ornithischia: Dinosauria) from the Early Cretaceous (Barremian) of eastern Utah, *in*: Spencer G. Lucas, James I. Kirkland, and John W. Estep, editors, *Lower and Middle Cretaceous Terrestrial Ecosystems*. Albuquerque: New Mexico Museum of Natural History and Science, Bulletin 14, pp. 271–282.

_____, 1998b, A new hadrosaurid from the Upper Cedar Mountain Formation (Albian-Cenomanian: Cretaceous) of eastern Utah — the oldest known hadrosaurid (lambeosaurine?), *Ibid*, pp. 283–296.

Kirkland, James I., Brooks B. Britt, Donald L. Burge, Kenneth Carpenter, Richard L. Cifelli, Frank L. DeCourten, Jeffrey G. Eaton, Stephen Hasiotis, and Tim F. Lawton, 1997, Lower to Middle Cretaceous dinosaur faunas of the central Colorado Plateau: A Key to understanding 35 million years of tectonics, sedimentology, evolution, and biogeography: *Brigham Young University Geology Studies*, 42, Part II, pp. 69–103.

Kirkland, James I., Brooks B. Britt, Christopher H. Whittle, Scott K. Madsen, and Donald L. Burge, 1998, A small coelurosaurian theropod from the Yellow Cat Member of the Cedar Mountain Formation (Lower Cretaceous, Barremian) of Eastern Utah, *in*: Spencer G. Lucas, James I. Kirkland, and John W. Estep, editors, *Lower and Middle Cretaceous Terrestrial Ecosystems*. Albuquerque: New Mexico Museum of Natural History and Science, Bulletin 14, pp. 239–249.

Kirkland, James Ian, and Kenneth Carpenter, 1994, North America's first pre–Cretaceous ankylosaur (Dinosauria) from the Upper Jurassic Morrison Formation of Western Colorado: *BYU Geology Studies 1994*, 40, pp. 25–42.

Koppelhus, E. B., 1997, Palynological data reveal clues to understand the paleoenvironments of the monogeneric *Centrosaurus* bonebeds in Dinosaur Park Formation, Alberta, Canada: *Journal of Vertebrate Paleontology*, 17 (Supplement to Number 3), Abstracts of Papers, Fifty-seventh Annual Meeting, p. 58A.

Krantz, Peter M., 1996, Notes on the sedimentary iron ores of Maryland and their dinosaurian fauna, *in*: David K. Brezinski and James P. Reger, editors, *Studies in Maryland Geology — In Commemoration of the Centennial of the Maryland Geological Survey*, pp. 87–115.

_____, 1998, *Astrodon* rediscovered: America's first sauropod, *in*: Donald L. Wolberg, K. Gittis, S. Miller, and A. Raynor, editors, *The Dinofest™ Symposium* [abstracts], Presented by The Academy of Natural Sciences of Philadelphia, Pennsylvania, pp. 33–34.

Kuhn, Oskar, 1964, Ornithischia (Supplementum I), *in*: F. C. Westphal, editor, *Fossilium Catalogus I: Animalia 105*. Uitgeverij. 's.-Gravenhage, 80 pages.

Kurzanov, Seriozha [Sergei] M., 1976, Braincase structure in the carnosaur *Itemerus* n. gen. and some aspects of the cranial anatomy of dinosaurs: *Palaeontological Journal*, 10, pp. 361–369.

Kurzanov, Seriozha [Sergei] M., and A. F. Banikov, 1983, A new sauropod from the Upper Cretaceous of Mongolia: *Paleontologiche Zhurnal*, 2, pp. 90–96 (in Russian), English translation pp. 91–97, Moscow.

Lamb, James P., Jr., 1996, Ankylosauria from the Upper Cretaceous of Alabama: *Journal of Vertebrate Paleontology*, 16 (Supplement to Number 3), Abstracts of Papers, Fifty-sixth Annual Meeting, p. 47A.

Lambe, Lawrence M., 1903, The lower jaw of *Dryptosaurus incrassatus* (Cope): Ottawa Naturalist, 17, pp. 133–139.

_____, 1904, On *Dryptosaurus incrassatus* (Cope), from the Edmonton Series of the North West Territory: *Geological Survey of Canada, Contributions to Canadian Paleontology*, 3, pp. 1–27.

_____, 1914a, On the fore limb of a carnivorous dinosaur from the Belly River Formation of Alberta, and a new genus of Ceratopsia from the same horizon, with remarks on the integument of some Cretaceous herbivorous dinosaurs: *Ottawa Naturalist*, 27 (10), pp. 129–135.

_____, 1914b, On a new genus and species of carnivorous dinosaur from the Belly River Formation of Alberta, with a description of the skull of *Stephanosaurus marginatus* from the same horizon: *Ibid*, 28, pp. 13–20.

Lambert, David, 1993, *The Ultimate Dinosaur Book*. London: Dorling Kindersley Ltd., p. 127.

Langston, Wann A., Jr., 1974, Non-mammalian Comanchean tetrapods: *Geoscience and Man*, 3, pp. 77–102.

_____, 1989, A history of vertebrate paleontology at the University of Oklahoma. Unpublished Report to the Oklahoma Museum of Natural History.

Lapparent, Albert F. de, and René Lavocat, 1955, Dinosauriens, *in*: Jean Piveteau, editor, *Traité de Paléontologie*. Paris: Masson et. Cie, pp. 785–962.

Lapparent, Albert F. de, and Georges Zbyszewski, 1957, Les dinosauriens du Portugal: *Mémoires des Services Géologiques du Portugal* (n.s.) 2, 63 pages.

Larson, Neal L., Robert A. Farrar, and Larry Shaffer, 1998, New information on the osteology of the skull of *Tyrannosaurus rex* [poster], *in*: Donald L. Wolberg, K. Gittis, S. Miller, and A. Raynor, editors, *The Dinofest™ Symposium* [abstracts], Presented by The Academy of Natural Sciences of Philadelphia, Pennsylvania, pp. 68–69.

Larson, Peter L., 1997a, The King's new clothes: A fresh look at *Tyrannosaurus rex*: *in*: Donald L. Wolberg, Edmund Stump, and Gary Rosenberg, editors, *Dinofest™ International: Proceedings of a Symposium Held at Arizona State University*. Philadelphia: Academy of Natural Sciences, pp. 65–71.

_____, 1997b, Do dinosaurs have class? Implications of the avian respiratory system, *Ibid*. Pp. 105–111.

Laurent, Yves, Jean Le Loeuff, and Eric Buffetaut, 1997, Les Hadrosauridae (Dinosauria, Ornithopoda) du Maastrichtien supérieur des Corbières orientales (Aude, France): *Revue Paléobiol., Genève*, 16 (2), pp. 411–423 (in French).

Lavocat, René, 1954, Sur les Dinosauriens du continental intercalaire des Kem-Kemm de la Daoura: *Comptes Rendus 19th International Géological Congress, 1952*, Part 15 (3), pp. 65–68.

_____, 1955, Sur une portion de mandibule de théropode provenant du Crétacé Supérieur de Madagascar: *Bulletin du Muséum National d'Historie Naturelle*, 2, pp. 256–259.

Laws, Rebecca R., 1997, Allosaur trauma and infection: Paleopathological analysis as a tool for lifestyle reconstruction: *Journal of Vertebrate Paleontology*, 17 (Supplement to Number 3), Abstracts of Papers, Fifty-seventh Annual Meeting, pp. 59A–60A.

Lawson, Douglas A., 1972, Paleoecology of the Tornillo Formation, Big Bend National Park, Brewster County, Texas: Unpublished M. A. thesis, University of Texas at Austin, 182 pages.

_____, 1976, *Tyrannosaurus* and *Torosaurus*, Maastrichtian dinosaurs from Trans-Pecos, Texas: *Journal of Paleontology*, 50 (1), pp. 158–164.

Legarreta, L., and C. Gulisano, 1989, Análisis estratigráfico secuencial de la Cuenca Neuquina (Triásico Superior-Terciario Inferior), *in*: C. Chebli and L. Spalleti, editors, *Cuencas Sedimentarias Argentinas, Serie Correlacion Geológica*, 6, pp. 221–243.

Lehman, Thomas M., 1989, *Chasmosaurus mariscalensis*, sp. nov., a new ceratopsian dinosaur from Texas: *Journal of Vertebrate Paleontology*, 9 (2), pp. 137–162.

_____, 1990, The ceratopsian subfamily Chasmosaurinae: Sexual dimorphism and systematics, *in*: Kenneth Carpenter and Philip J. Currie, editors, *Dinosaur Systematics: Approaches and Perspectives*. Cambridge, New York and Melbourne: Cambridge University Press, pp. 211–229.

_____, 1993, New data on the ceratopsian dinosaur *Pentaceratops sternbergii* Osborn from New Mexico: *Journal of Paleontology*, 67 (2), pp. 279–288.

_____, 1996, A horned dinosaur from the El Picacho Formation of West Texas, and review of ceratopsian dinosaurs from the American Southwest: *Ibid*, 70 (30), pp. 494–508.

_____, 1998, Population age structure and preferred habitat in the horned dinosaur *Chasmosaurus*, *in*: Donald L. Wolberg, K. Gittis, S. Miller, and A. Raynor, editors, *The Dinofest™ Symposium* [abstracts], Presented by The Academy of Natural Sciences of Philadelphia, Pennsylvania, pp. 35–36.

Leidy, Joseph, 1865, Memoir on the extinct reptiles of the Cretaceous Formations of the United States: *Smithsonian Contributions to Knowledge*, 14 (6), pp. 1–135.

Le Loeuff, Jean, 1995, *Ampelosaurus atacis* (nov. gen. nov. sp.) un nouveau Titanosauridae (Dinosauria, Sauropoda) du Crétacé supérieur de la Haute Vallée de l'Aude (France): *Comptes Rendus de l'Académie des Sciences de Paris* (sér. IIa), 321, pp. 693–699.

_____, 1998, New data on Late Cretaceous titanosaurid diversity in western European island, *in*: John W. M. Jagt, Paul H. Lambers, Eric W. A. Mulder, and Anne S. Schulp, editors, *Third European Workshop on Vertebrate Palaeontology*, Maastricht, 6–9 May 1998, Programme and Abstracts Field Guide, [unpaginated].

Lemonick, Michael D., 1996, Big, fast and vicious: *Time*, May 27, p. 45.

Lessem, Don, 1997, Dinosaur Society, *in*: Philip J. Currie and Kevin Padian, editors, *Encyclopedia of Dinosaurs*. San Diego: Academic Press, p. 185.

Lockley, Martin G., 1986, *Dinosaur Tracksites: University of Colorado at Denver Geology Department Magazine*, Special Issue 1, 56 pages.

Lockley, Martin G., and Adrian P. Hunt, 1995, Ceratopsid tracks and associated ichnofauna from the Laramie Formation (Upper Cretaceous: Maastrichtian) of Colorado: *Journal of Vertebrate Paleontology*, 15 (3), pp. 592–614.

Long, John A., and Kenneth J. McNamara, 1997, Heterochrony: The key to dinosaur evolution, *in*: Donald L. Wolberg, Edmund Stump, and Gary Rosenberg, editors. *Dinofest™ International: Proceedings of a Symposium Held at Arizona State University*. Philadelphia: Academy of Natural Sciences, pp. 113–123.

Long, Robert A., and Phillip A. Murry, 1995, Late Triassic (Carnian and Norian) tetrapods from the southwestern United States: *New Mexico Museum of Natural History Bulletin*, 4, pp. 1–254.

López-Martinez, Nieves, Lluis Ardévol, M. E. Arribas, J. C. Civis, and J. A. Gonzalez-Delgado, 1998, The last European dinosaurs, *in*: John W. M. Jagt, Paul H. Lambers, Eric W. A. Mulder, and Anne S. Schulp, editors, *Third European Workshop on Vertebrate Palaeontology*, Maastricht, 6–9 May 1998, Programme and Abstracts Field Guide, [unpaginated].

Lu Junchang, 1997, A new Iguanodontidae (*Probactrosaurus mazongshanensis* sp. nov.) from Mazongshan Area, Gansu Province, China, *in*: Dong Zhiming, editor, *Sino-Japanese Silk Road Dinosaur Expedition*. Beijing: China Ocean Press, pp. 27–47.

Lucas, Spencer G., 1996, The thyreophoran dinosaur *Scelidosaurus* from the Lower Jurassic Lufeng Formation, Yunnan, China: *in*: Michael Morales, editor, *Museum of Northern Arizona Bulletin*, 60, pp. 81–85.

Lucas, Spencer G., and Adrian P. Hunt, 1989, Revised Triassic stratigraphy in the Tucumcari Basin, East-Central New Mexico, *in*: S. G. Lucas and A. P. Hunt, editors, *Dawn of the Age of Dinosaurs in the American Southwest*. Albuquerque: New Mexico Museum of Natural History, pp. 150–170.

Lull, Richard Swann, 1919, The sauropod dinosaur *Barosaurus* Marsh: Redescription of the type specimen in the Peabody Museum, Yale University: *Memoirs of the Connecticut Academy of Arts and Sciences*, 6, 42 pages.

Lydekker, Richard, 1888, *Catalogue of the fossil Reptilia and Amphibia in the British Museum (Natural History). Part I. Containing the Ornithodira, Crocodilia, Dinosauria, Squamata, Rhyncocephalia, and Pterosauria*: London, 309 pages.

_____, 1893, Contributions to a knowledge of the fossil vertebrates of Argentina. I. The dinosaurs of Patagonia: *Annales del Museo de La Plata, Palaeontologia Argentina*, 2, pp. 1–14.

Bibliography

Makovicky, Peter J., 1995, Phylogenetic aspects of coelurosaurian vertebral morphology: *Journal of Vertebrate Paleontology*, 15 (Supplement to Number 3), Abstracts of Papers, Fifty-fifth Annual Meeting, p. 43A.

———, 1996, Discovery of a furcula in tyrannosaurid theropods: *Ibid*, 16 (Supplement to Number 3), Abstracts of Papers, Fifty-sixth Annual Meeting, p. 50A.

———, 1997, A new small theropod from the Morrison Formation of Como Bluff, Wyoming: *Journal of Vertebrate Paleontology*, 17 (4), pp. 755–757.

Makovicky, Peter J., and Philip J. Currie, 1998, The presence of a furcula in tyrannosaurid theropods, and its phylogenetic and functional implications: *Journal of Vertebrate Paleontology*, 18 (1), pp. 143–149.

Makovicky, Peter J., and Hans-Dieter Sues, 1997, A reappraisal of the phylogenetic affinities of *Microvenator celer* (Theropoda: Dinosauria) from the Cloverly Formation: *Journal of Vertebrate Paleontology*, 17 (Supplement to Number 3), Abstracts of Papers, Fifty-seventh Annual Meeting, p. 62A.

Madsen, James H., Jr., 1974, A new theropod dinosaur from the Upper Jurassic of Utah: *Journal of Paleontology*, 48 (1), pp. 41–55.

———, 1976, *Allosaurus fragilis*: A revised Osteology: *Utah Geological and Mineral Survey, a division of the Utah Department of Natural Resources*, 109, xii, 163 pages.

Maleev, Evgeny [Eugene] Alexandrovich, 1955, [Gigantic carnivorous dinosaurs of Mongolia]: *Dokladi Akademii Nauk S.S.S.R.*, 104 (4), pp. 634–637.

———, 1974, Giant carnosaurs of the family Tyrannosauridae, *in*: N. N. Kramarenko, et al., editors, *Mesozoic and Cenozoic Faunas and Biostratigraphy of Mongolia. Joint Soviet-Mongolian Paleontological Expedition, Transactions*, 1, pp. 132–191.

———, 1974, Giant carnosaurs of the family Tyrannosauridae: *Trudy Sovmestnaya Sovetsko-Mongol'skaya Paleontologicheskaya Ekspeditsiya*, 1, pp. 132–191.

Manning, T. W., K. A. Joysey, and A. R. I. Cruickshank, 1997, Observations of microstructures within dinosaur eggs from Henan Province, People's Republic of China, *in*: Donald L. Wolberg, Edmund Stump, and Gary Rosenberg, editors. *Dinofest™ International: Proceedings of a Symposium Held at Arizona State University*. Philadelphia: Academy of Natural Sciences, pp. 287–290.

Mantell, Gideon Algernon, 1825, Notice on the *Iguanodon*, a newly discovered fossil reptile, from the sandstone of Tilgate Forest, in Sussex: *Philosophical Transactions of the Royal Society*, 115 (1), pp. 179–186.

Marsh, Othniel Charles, 1879, Notice of new Jurassic reptiles: *American Journal of Science*, 18, pp. 501–505.

———, 1882, Classification of the Dinosauria: *Ibid*, 4 (23), pp. 81–86.

———, 1889, Notice of gigantic horned Dinosauria from the Cretaceous: *American Journal of Science*, 38, pp. 173–175.

———, 1890*a*, Description of new dinosaurian reptiles: *Ibid*, 39, pp. 81–86.

———, 1890*b*, Additional characters of the Ceratopsidae, with notice of new Cretaceous dinosaurs: *Ibid*, 39, pp. 418–426.

———, 1896, The Dinosaurs of North America: *Sixteenth Annual Report of the U. S. Geological Survey*, 1, pp. 133–415.

Marshall, M., D. Barnard, and M. H. Schweitzer, 1996, Detection of bone proteins in trabecular bone of a *Tyrannosaurus rex* by a novel immunological method: *Journal of Vertebrate Paleontology*, 16 (Supplement to Number 3), Abstracts of Papers, Fifty-sixth Annual Meeting, p. 50A.

Martill, D. M., A. R. I. Cruickshank, E. Frey, P. G. Small, and M. Clarke, 1996, A new crested maniraptoran dinosaur from the Santana Formation (Lower Cretaceous) of Brazil: *Journal of the Geological Society, London*, 153, pp. 5–8.

Martill, D. M., and S. Hutt, 1996, Possible baryonychid dinosaur teeth from the Wessex Formation (Lower Cretaceous, Barremian) of the Isle of Wight, England: *Proceedings of the Geologists' Association*, 107, pp. 81–84, Bath.

Martill, D. M., D. K. Loydell, and D. J. Batten, 1997, A thyreophoran dinosaur with oganically preserved skin and dermal ossifications from the ?Lower Jurasic of England: *Journal of Vertebrate Paleontology*, 17 (Supplement to Number 3), Abstracts of Papers, Fifty-seventh Annual Meeting, p. 62A.

Martin, Larry D., 1995, The relationship of *Mononykus* to ornithopod dinosaurs: *Journal of Vertebrate Paleontology*, 15 (Supplement to Number 3), Abstracts of Papers, Fifty-fifth Annual Meeting, p. 43A.

———, 1997, The difference between dinosaurs and birds as applied to *Mononykus*, *in*: Donald L. Wolberg, Edmund Stump, and Gary Rosenberg, editors. *Dinofest™ International: Proceedings of a Symposium Held at Arizona State University*. Philadelphia: Academy of Natural Sciences, pp. 337–343.

———, 1998. Information on the soft tissues of dinosaurs, *in*: Donald L. Wolberg, K. Gittis, S. Miller, and A. Raynor, editors, *The Dinofest™ Symposium* [abstracts], Presented by The Academy of Natural Sciences of Philadelphia, Pennsylvania, p. 38.

Martin, Larry D., and C. Rinaldi, 1994, How to tell a bird from a dinosaur: *Maps Digest*, 17 (4), pp. 190–196.

Martin, Larry D., and John Simmons, 1998, Theropod dinosaur nesting behavior, *in*: Donald L. Wolberg, K. Gittis, S. Miller, and A. Raynor, editors, *The Dinofest™ Symposium* [abstracts], Presented by The Academy of Natural Sciences of Philadelphia, Pennsylvania, p. 39.

Martínez, Rubén Dario, O. Giménez, J. Rodriguez and M. Luna 1990, Un titanosaurio articulado de género *Epachthosaurus* de la Formación Bajo Barreal, Cretácio del Chubut: *Ameghiniana*, 26 (3–4), p. 246, Buenos Aires.

Maryańska, Teresa, and Halszka Osmólska, 1975, Results of the Polish-Mongolian palaeontological expeditions, Part VI. Protoceratopsidae (Dinosauria) of Asia: *Palaeontologica Polonica*, 33, pp. 133–182.

Mathur, U. B., and S. Srivastava, 1987, Dinosaur teeth from Lameta Group (Upper Cretaceous) of Kheda District, Gujarat: *Journal of the Geological Society of India*, 29, pp. 554–566.

Matthew, William Diller, and Barnum Brown, 1923, Preliminary notices of skeletons and skulls of Deinodontidae from the Cretaceous of Alberta: *American Museum Novitates*, 30, pp. 1–10.

Maxwell, W. Desmond, Brian M. Hallas, and John R. Horner, 1997, Further neonate dinosaurian remains and dinosaurian eggshell from the Cloverly Formation of Montana: *Journal of Vertebrate Paleontology*, 17 (Supplement to Number 3), Abstracts of Papers, Fifty-seventh Annual Meeting, p. 63A.

Maxwell, W. Desmond, and Lawrence M. Witmer, 1996, New material of *Deinonychus* (Dinosauria, Theropoda): *Journal of Vertebrate Paleontology*, 16 (Supplement to Number 3), Abstracts of Papers, Fifty-sixth Annual Meeting, p. 51A.

McCarthy, Steve, and Mick Gilbert, 1994, *The Crystal Palace Dinosaurs: The Story of the World's First Prehistoric Sculptures*. London: The Crystal Palace Foundation, 99 pages.

McIntosh, John S., 1990*a*, Species determination in sauropod dinosaurs with tentative suggestions for their classification, *in*: Carpenter and Philip J. Currie, editors, *Dinosaur Systematics: Approaches and Perspectives*. Cambridge, New York and Melbourne: Cambridge University Press, pp. 53–69.

———, 1990*b*, Sauropoda, *in*: David B. Weishampel, Peter Dodson, and Halszka Osmólska, editors, *The Dinosauria*. Berkeley and Los Angeles: University of California Press, pp. 345–401.

———, 1992, Sauropoda, *in*: David B. Weishampel, Peter Dodson, and Halszka Osmólska, editors, *The Dinosauria* (revised paperback edition). Berkeley: University of California Press, pp. 345–401.

———, 1997, The saga of a forgotten sauropod dinosaur: *in*: Donald L. Wolberg, Edmund Stump, and Gary Rosenberg, editors. *Dinofest™ International: Proceedings of a Symposium Held at Arizona State University*. Philadelphia: Academy of Natural Sciences, pp. 7–12.

McIntosh, John S., Walter P. Coombs, and Dale A. Russell, 1992, A new diplodocid sauropod (Dinosauria) from Wyoming, U.S.A.: *Journal of Vertebrate Paleontology*, 12 (2), pp. 1558–1567.

McIntosh, John S., Wade E. Miller, Kenneth L. Stadtman, and David D. Gillette, 1996, The osteology of *Camarasaurus lewisi* (Jensen, 1988): *BYU Geology Studies*, 41, pp. 73–115.

McIntosh, John S., and Michael E. Williams, 1988, A new species of sauropod dinosaur, *Haplocanthosaurus delfsi* sp. nov., from the Upper Jurassic Morrison Fm. of Colorado: *Kirtlandia*, 43, p. 2–26.

McNeil, Lana S., 1998, The mystery of *Mononykus*: A functional approach, *in*: Donald L. Wolberg, K. Gittis, S. Miller, and

A. Raynor, editors, *The Dinofest^(TM) Symposium* [abstracts], Presented by The Academy of Natural Sciences of Philadelphia, Pennsylvania, pp. 39–40.

Meyer, Hermann von, 1832, *Palaeologica zur Geschichte der Erde und ihrer Geschöpfe*, xii, 560 pages, Schmerber, Frankfurt-am-Main.

Mikhailov, Konstantin E., 1991, Classification of fossil eggshells of amniotic vertebrates: *Acta Palaeontologica*, 36 (2), pp. 193–238, Warsaw.

Mikhailov, Konstantin E., K. Sabath, and Seriozha [Sergei] M. Kurzanov, 1994, Eggs and nests from the Cretaceous of Mongolia, *in*: Kenneth Carpenter, Karl F. Hirsch, and John R. Horner, editors, *Dinosaur Eggs and Babies*. Cambridge: Cambridge University Press, pp. 88–115.

Miller, Wade E., 1996, The Cleveland-Lloyd Dinosaur Quarry, Emery County, Utah: *Dinofest^(TM) International Symposium, April 18–21, 1996, Programs and Abstracts*, p. 84.

Miller, Wade E., J. L. Baer, Kenneth L. Stadtman, and Brooks B. Britt, 1991, The Dry Mesa Dinosaur Quarry, Mesa County, Colorado, *in*: *Guidebook for Dinosaur Quarries and Tracksites Tour: Western Colorado and Eastern Utah*. Grand Junction, Colorado: Grand Junction Geological Society, pp. 31–46.

Miller, Wade E., Rodney D. Horrocks, and James H. Madsen, Jr., 1996, The Cleveland-Lloyd Dinosaur Quarry, Emery County, Utah: A U.S. natural landmark (including history and quarry map): *BYU Geology Studies*, 41, pp. 3–24.

Milner, Angela C., 1996, Morphology, relationships and ecology of spinosaurs, aberrant long-snouted Cretaceous theropods: *Journal of Vertebrate Paleontology*, 16 (Supplement to Number 3), Abstracts of Papers, Fifty-sixth Annual Meeting, p. 53A.

Mohn, Bruce J., 1996, First three dimensional skeletal mount of *Compsognathus longipes*: *Journal of Vertebrate Paleontology*, 16 (Supplement to Number 3), Abstracts of Papers, Fifty-sixth Annual Meeting, p. 54A.

———, 1998a, A three dimensional reconstruction of *Compsognathus longipes*, *in*: Donald L. Wolberg, K. Gittis, S. Miller, and A. Raynor, editors, *The Dinofest^(TM) Symposium* [abstracts], Presented by The Academy of Natural Sciences of Philadelphia, Pennsylvania, p. 41.

———, 1998b, Observations on the possible lifestyles of compsognathids, *in*: Donald L. Wolberg, K. Gittis, S. Miller, and A. Raynor, editors, *The Dinofest^(TM) Symposium* [abstracts], Presented by The Academy of Natural Sciences of Philadelphia, Pennsylvania, p. 41.

Molnar, Ralph E., 1974, A distinctive theropod dinosaur from the Upper Cretaceous of Baja California (Mexico): *Journal of Paleontology*, 48 (5), pp. 1009–1017.

———, 1980, An ankylosaur (Ornithischia: Reptilia) from the Lower Cretaceous of southern Queensland: *Memoirs of the Queensland Museum*, 20 (1), pp. 77–87.

———, 1990, Problematic Theropoda: "Carnosaurs," *in*: David B. Weishampel, Peter Dodson, and Halszka Osmólska, editors,

The Dinosauria. Berkeley and Los Angeles: University of California Press, pp. 306–317.

———, 1994, A dragon of the south: *Kyoryugaku Saizensen*, 8, pp. 102–111 (in Japanese).

———, 1996a, Observartions on the Australian ornithopod *Muttaburrasaurus*, *in*: Fernando S. Novas and Ralph E. Molnar, editors, *Proceedings of the Gondwanan Dinosaur Symposium: Memoirs of the Queensland Museum*, 39 (part 3), pp. 639–652.

———, 1996b, Preliminary report on a new ankylosaur from the Early Cretaceous of Queensland, Australia: *Ibid*, pp. 653–668.

Molnar, Ralph E., Alejandro Lopez Angriman, and Zulma Gasparini, 1996, An Antarctic Cretaceous theropod, *in*: Fernando S. Novas and Ralph E. Molnar, editors, *Proceedings of the Gondwanan Dinosaur Symposium: Memoirs of the Queensland Museum*, 39 (part 3), pp. 669–674.

Molnar, Ralph E., Seriozha M. Kurzanov, and Dong Zhi-Ming [Zhiming], 1990, Carnosauria, *in*: David B. Weishampel, Peter Dodson, and Halszka Osmólska, editors, *The Dinosauria*. Berkeley and Los Angeles: University of California Press, pp. 169–209.

Molnar, Ralph E., and Joan Wiffen, 1994, A Late Cretaceous polar dinosaur fauna from New Zealand: *Cretaceous Research*, 15, pp. 689–706.

Morales, Michael, 1969, Unresolved controversies in the study of dinosaurs: *Dinofest^(TM) International Symposium, April 18–21, 1996, Programs and Abstracts*, p. 85.

Moratalla, José J., José Luis Sanz, and Santiago Jiménez, 1994, Dinosaur tracks from the Lower Cretaceous of Regumiel de la Sierra (province of Burgos, Spain): Inferences on a new quadrupedal ornithopod trackway: *Ichnos*, 3, pp. 89–97.

Morris, William J., 1973, A review of Pacific Coast hadrosaurs: *Journal of Paleontology*, 47, pp. 551–561.

Murphy, Michael A., G. L. Peterson, and Peter U. Rodda, 1964, Revision of Cretaceous lithostratigraphic nomenclature, northwest Sacramento Valley, California: *American Association of Petroleum Geologists Bulletin*, 40, pp. 496–502.

Murphy, Michael A., Peter U. Rodda, and D. M. Morton, 1969, Geology of the Ono Quadrangle, Shasta and Tehama counties, California: *California Division of Mines and Geology Bulletin*, 19, pp. 1–28.

Murry, Phillip A., and Robert A. Long, 1997, Dockum Group, *in*: Philip J. Currie and Kevin Padian, editors, *Encyclopedia of Dinosaurs*. San Diego: Academic Press, pp. 191–193.

Myhrvold, Nathan P., and Philip J. Currie, 1998, Supersonic sauropods? Tail dynamics in the diplodocids, *in*: Donald L. Wolberg, K. Gittis, S. Miller, and A. Raynor, editors, *The Dinofest^(TM) Symposium* [abstracts], Presented by The Academy of Natural Sciences of Philadelphia, Pennsylvania, p. 41.

Naish, Darren, 1998a, Theropods eating theropods in the Wealden Group fauna of

England: Evidence from a previously undescribed tibia, *in*: John W. M. Jagt, Paul H. Lambers, Eric W. A. Mulder, and Anne S. Schulp, editors, *Third European Workshop on Vertebrate Palaeontology*, Maastricht, 6–9 May 1998, Programme and Abstracts Field Guide, [unpaginated].

———, 1998b, A small Wealden theropod, represented only by a femur, *in*: Gary Aillud and Mark Hylton, editors, *Progressive Palaeontology 1998*, Department of Geological Sciences, University of Plymouth, Wednesday, 27 May, Programme and Abstracts, [unpaginated].

———, Predatory dinosaurs in England's Lower Cretaceous: Crocodile heads, puffin snouts and the odd lizards taxon: *European Palaeontological Association & The Palaeontological Association, 1998 Summer Workshop, July 11–12, Cretaceous Biodiversity*, University of Portsmouth, Palaeobiology Research Group, [unpaginated].

Nessov, Lev A., 1995, Dinosaurs of Northern Eurasia: New data about assemblages, ecology and palaebiogeography [translation], 156 pages.

Newman, Barney H., 1968, The Jurassic dinosaur *Scelidosaurus harrisoni*, Owen: *Paleontology*, 11, Part 1, pp. 40–43.

Nopcsa, Baron Franz [also Ferencz, Francis] (von Felsö-Szilva's), 1902a, Notizen über Cretacische Dinosaurier. Pt. 3. Wirbel eines sudamerikanischen Sauropoden: *Sitzungsberichte Berlin Klasse Akademie Wissenschaften*, 3, pp. 108–114, Vienna.

———, 1902b, Dinosaurierreste aus Siebenbürgen III (weitere Schädelreste von Mochlodon). Mit einem Anhange: Zur Phylogenie der Ornithopodiden: *Denkschriften der Akademie der Wissenschaften*, 72, pp. 149–175, Vienna.

———, 1911a, *Omosaurus lennieri*, un nouveau Dinosaurien du Cap de la Hève: *Bulletin Trimestriel de la Societé Géologique de Normandie et des Amis du Museum du Havre (1910)*, 30, pp. 23–42.

———, 1911b, Notes on British dinosaurs, Part IV: *Stegosaurus priscus* sp. nov.: *Geological Magazine*, (new series), 8, pp. 109–115, 143–153.

———, 1914, Die Lebensbedingungen der obercretacischen Dinosaurier Siebenbürgens: *Centralblatt für Mineralogie, Geologie und Paläontologie*, 18, pp. 564–567.

———, 1915, Die Dinosaurier der Siebenbürgischen Landesteile Ungarns: *Mitteilungen Des Jahrbuch Ungarischen Geologischen Reichsforschungsanstalt*, 1 (23), pp. 14–15, Budapest.

———, 1918, *Leipsanosaurus* n. gen. ein neurer Thyreophore aus der Gosau: *Földragzi Közlemenyck, Uj Folyam* [New Series], 48, pp. 324–328.

———, 1923, On the geological importance of the primitive reptilian fauna in the Uppermost Cretaceous of Hungary: *Quarterly Journal of the Geological Society, London*, 79, pp. 100–116.

———, 1934, The influence of geological and climatological factors on the distribution of non-marine fossil reptiles and Stegocephalia: *Quarterly Journal of the Geological Society of London*, 90, pp. 76–140.

Bibliography

Norell, Mark A., James M. Clark, Luis M. Chiappe, and Demberelyin Dashzeveg, 1995, A nesting dinosaur: *Nature*, 378, pp. 774–776.

Norell, Mark A., James M. Clark, Demberelyin Dashzeveg, Rinchen Barsbold, Luis M. Chiappe, Amy R. Davidson, Malcolm C. McKenna, Altangerel Perle, and Michael J. Novacek, 1994, A theropod dinosaur embryo and the affinities of the Flaming Cliffs dinosaur eggs: *Science*, 266, pp. 779–882.

Norell, Mark A., and Peter J. Makovicky, 1997, Important features of the dromaeosaur skeleton: Information from a new specimen: *American Museum Novitates*, 3215, 28 pages.

Norell, Mark A., Peter J. Makovicy, and James M. Clark, 1991, A *Velociraptor* wishbone: *Nature*, 389, p. 447.

Norman, David B., 1980, On the ornithischian dinosaur *Iguanodon bernissartensis* from Belgium: *Mémoires de l'Institut Royal des Sciences Naturelles de Belgique*, 178, pp. 1–105.

_____, 1985, *The Illustrated Encyclopedia of Dinosaurs: An Original and Compelling Insight into Life in the Dinosaur Kingdom*. New York: Crescent Books (Crown Publishing, Inc.), 208 pages.

_____, 1986, On the anatomy of *Iguanodon atherfieldensis* (Ornithischia: Ornithopoda): *Bulletin, Institut Royal des Sciences Naturelle de Belgique*, 56, pp. 281–372.

_____, 1996, On Mongolian ornithopods (Dinosauria: Ornithischia). 1. *Iguanodon orientalis* Rozhdestvensky 1952: *Zoological Journal of the Linnean Society*, 116 (3), pp. 303–315.

_____, 1998, On Asian ornithopods (Dinosauria: Ornithischia). 3. A new species of iguanodontid dinosaur: *Ibid*, 122, pp. 291–348.

Norman, David B., and Sergei M. Kurzanov, 1997, New ornithopod dinosaurs from Asia and their evolution: *Journal of Vertebrate Paleontology*, 17 (Supplement to Number 3), Abstracts of Papers, Fifty-seventh Annual Meeting, p. 67A.n.

Norman, David B., and David B. Weishampel, 1990, Iguanodontidae and related ornithopods, *in*: Weishampel, Peter Dodson, and Halszka Osmólska, editors, *The Dinosauria*. Berkeley and Los Angeles: University of California Press, pp. 510–533.

Novas, Fernando E., 1992a, Phylogenetic relationships of the basal dinosaurs, the Herrerasauridae: Palaeontology, 35, Part 1, pp. 51–62.

_____, 1992b, La Evolución de los dinosaurios carnívoros, *in*: José Luis Sanz and Angela D. Buscalioni, editors, *Los Dinosaurios y su Entorno Biótico. Actas II Curso de Paleontologica en Cuenca*. Spain: Instituto "Juan de Valdés," Ayuntamiento de Cuenca, pp. 123–163.

_____, 1993a, Diagnosis y filogenia de los Dinosauria: *Ameghiniana*, 30, p. 110 (abstract), Buenos Aires.

_____, 1993b, New information on the systematics and postcranial skeleton of *Herrerasaurus ischigualastensis* (Theropoda: Herrerasauridae) from the Ischigualasto Formation (Upper Triassic) of Argentina: *Journal of Vertebrate Paleontology*, 13 (4), pp. 400–423.

_____, 1996a, New theropods from the Late Cretaceous of Patagonia: *Journal of Vertebrate Paleontology*, 16 (Supplement to Number 3), Abstracts of Papers, Fifty-sixth Annual Meeting, p. 56A.

_____, 1996b, Dinosaur monophyly: *Journal of Vertebrate Paleontology*, 16 (4), pp. 723–741.

_____, 1996c, Alvarezsauridae, Cretaceous basal birds from Patagonia and Mongolia, *in*: Fernando S. Novas and Ralph E. Molnar, editors, *Proceedings of the Gondwanan Dinosaur Symposium: Memoirs of the Queensland Museum*, 39 (part 3), pp. 675–702.

_____, 1998, *Megaraptor namunhuaiiquii*, gen. et sp. nov., a large-clawed, Late Cretaceous theropod from Patagonia: *Journal of Vertebrate Paleontology*, 18 (1), pp. 4–9.

Novas, Fernando E., Gerardo Cladera, and Pablo Puerta, 1996, New theropods from the Late Cretaceous of Patagonia: *Journal of Vertebrate Paleontology*, 16 (Supplement to Number 3), Abstracts of Papers, Fifty-sixth Annual Meeting, p. 56A.

Novas, Fernando E., and Pablo F. Puerta, 1997, New evidence concerning avian origins from the Late Cretaceous of Patagonia: *Nature*, 387, pp. 390–92.

Nowiński, Aleksander, 1979, *Nemegtosaurus mongoliensis* n. gen., n. sp. (Sauropoda) from the Uppermost Cretaceous of Mongolia. Results of the Polish-Mongolian Palaeontological Expeditions — Part III: *Palaeontologia Polonica*, 25, pp. 57–81, Warsaw.

Olivero, E., Z. Gasparini, C. Rinaldi, and R. Scasso, 1991, First record of dinosaurs in Antarctica (Upper Cretaceous, James Ross Island): Palaeogeographical implications, *in*: M. R. A. Thomson, J. A. Crame, and J. W. Thomson, editors, *Geological Evolution of Antarctica*. Cambridge: Cambridge University Press, pp. 617–622.

Olsen, Paul E., and Peter M. Galton, 1984, A review of the reptile and amphibian assemblages from the Stormberg Series of southern Africa, with special emphasis on the footprints and the age of the Stormberg: *Paleont. Afr.*, Johannesburg, 25, pp. 87–109.

Olshevsky, George, 1978, The Archosauria (excluding the Crocodylia): *Mesozoic Meanderings*, 1, 49 pages.

_____, 1991, *A Revision of the Parainfraclass Archosauria Cope 1869, Excluding the Advanced Crocodylia*. Buffalo, New York: Publications Requiring Research, iv, 196 pages.

_____, 1992, *A revision of the parainfraclass Archosauria Cope, 1869, Excluding the advanced Crocodylia*. Ibid, 2, iv, 268 pages.

_____, 1993, The origin and evolution of the brontosaurs: *Kyoryugaki Saizensen (Dino-Frontline)*, 2, 90–115.

Orsen, Mark J., and Thomas P. Hopp, 1998, Was brooding a selective pressure in the evolution of flight feathers? [poster], *in*: Donald L. Wolberg, K. Gittis, S. Miller, and A. Raynor, editors, *The Dinofest* TM Symposium [abstracts], Presented by The Academy of Natural Sciences of Philadelphia, Pennsylvania, p. 70.

Osborn, Henry Fairfield, 1899, A skeleton of *Diplodocus*: *Memoirs of the American Museum of Natural History*, 1, pp. 191–214.

_____, 1905, *Tyrannosaurus* and other Cretaceous carnivorous dinosaurs: *Bulletin of the American Museum of Natural History*, 21, p. 261.

_____, 1923, Two Lower Cretaceous dinosaurs of Mongolia: *Ibid*, 95, 10 pages.

_____, 1924, Three new Theropoda, *Protoceratops* zone, central Mongolia: *American Museum Novitates*, 144, pp. 1–12.

_____, 1933, Mounted skeleton of *Triceratops elatus*. *American Museum Novitates*, 654, pp. 1–14.

Ostrom, John H., 1964, *The Strange World of Dinosaurs*. New York: G. P. Putnam's Sons, 127 pages.

_____, 1969a, A new theropod dinosaur from the Lower Cretaceous of Montana: *Postilla, Peabody Museum of Natural History*, 128, pp. 1–17.

_____, 1969b, Osteology of *Deinonychus antirrhopus*, an unusual theropod from the Lower Cretaceous of Montana: *Bulletin of the Peabody Museum of Natural History*, 30, pp. 1–165.

_____, 1970, Stratigraphy and paleontology of the Cloverly Formation (Lower Cretaceous) of the Bighorn Basin area, Wyoming and Montana: *Peabody Museum of Natural History, Yale University*, 35, 234 pages.

_____, 1976a, Archaeopteryx and the origin of birds: *Biological Journal of the Linnean Society*: 8, pp. 91–182.

_____, 1976b, On a new specimen of the Lower Cretaceous theropod dinosaur *Deinonychus antirrhopus*: *Breviora*, 439, pp. 1–21.

_____, 1976c, Some hypothetical anatomical stages in the evolution of avian flight: *Smithsonian Contributions to Paleobiology*, 27, pp. 1–21.

_____, 1986, The cursorial origin of avian flight: *Memoirs of the California Academy of Sciences*, 8, pp. 73–81.

_____, 1990, The Dromaeosauria, *in*: David B. Weishampel, Peter Dodson, and Osmólska, editors, *The Dinosauria*. Berkeley and Los Angeles: University of California Press, pp. 269–279.

_____, 1991, The bird in the bush: *Nature*, 353, p. 212.

_____, 1996, The questionable validity of *Protoavis*: *Archaeopteryx*, 14, pp. 39–42, Eichstätt.

_____, 1997, How bird flight might have come about: *in*: Donald L. Wolberg, Edmund Stump, and Gary Rosenberg, editors, *Dinofest* TM *International: Proceedings of a Symposium Held at Arizona State University*. Philadelphia: Academy of Natural Sciences, pp. 301–310.

Ostrom, John H., and Peter Wellnhofer, 1986, The Munich specimen of *Triceratops* with a revision of the genus: *Zitteliana Abandlungen der Bayerischen Staatssammlung für Paläontologie und historische Geologie*, 14, pp. 111–158.

Ostrom, John H., and Donald L. Wolberg, 1998, New insights — Feathers, sex and gender: *Dinosaurs Invade Philadelphia*, pp. 33–36.

Osmólska, Halszka, 1980, The Late Cretaceous vertebrate assemblage of the Gobi Desert (Mongolia): *Mémoires de la Societé Géologique de France* (Nouvelle série), 59 (139), pp. 145–150.

———, 1981, Coossified tarsometatarsi in theropod dinosaurs and their bearing on the problem of bird origins: *Palaeontologia Polonica*, 42, pp. 79–95.

———, 1996, An unusual theropod dinosaur from the Late Cretaceous Nemegt Formation of Mongolia: *Acta Palaeontologica Polonica*, 41 (1), pp. 1–38.

———, 1997, Ornithomimosauria, *in*: Philip J. Currie and Kevin Padian, editors, *Encyclopedia of Dinosaurs*. San Diego: Academic Press, pp. 499–505.

Osmólska, Halszka, and Rinchen Barsbold, 1990, Troodontidae, *in*: David B. Weishampel, Peter Dodson, and Osmólska, editors, *The Dinosauria*. Berkeley and Los Angeles: University of California Press, pp. 259–268.

Ouyang, H., 1986, A new sauropod (*Abrosaurus gigantorhinus*) from the Middle Jurassic of Dashanpu, Zigong, Sichuan; Unpublished Ph.D. dissertation in Geology, Chengdu College.

Owen, Richard, 1861, The Fossil Reptilia of the Liassic Formations: Supplement (No. II) to the Monograph on the fossil Reptilia of the Wealden and Purbeck Formations, *Palaeontographical Society*, 1, pp. 1–14, London.

———, 1875, Monographs on the British fossil Reptilia of the Mesozoic Formations, Part II (Genera *Bothriospondylus, Cetiosaurus, Omosaurus*): *Palaeontographical Society (Monograph)*, pp. 1–93, London.

Padian, Kevin, 1986, On the type material of *Coelophysis* Cope (Saurischia: Theropoda) and a new specimen from the Petrified Forest of Arizona (Late Triassic: Chinle Formation), *in*: Kevin Padian, editor, *The Beginning of the Age of Dinosaurs: Faunal Change Across the Triassic-Jurassic Boundary*. New York: Cambridge University Press, pp. 45–60.

———, 1989, Presence of the dinosaur *Scelidosaurus* indicates Jurassic age for the Kayenta Formation (Glen Canyon Group, northern Arizona): *Geology*, 17, pp. 438–441.

———, 1998a, Problems in avian origins and the evolution of flight, *in*: Donald L. Wolberg, K. Gittis, S. Miller, and A. Raynor, editors, *The Dinofest™ Symposium* [abstracts], Presented by The Academy of Natural Sciences of Philadelphia, Pennsylvania, pp. 44–45.

———, 1998b, When is a bird not a bird?: *Nature*, 393, pp. 729–730.

Padian, Kevin, John R. Hutchinson, and Thomas R. Holtz, 1997, Phylogenetic definitions and nomenclature of the major taxonomic categories of the theropod dinosaurs: *Journal of Vertebrate Paleontology*, 17 (Supplement to Number 3), Abstracts of Papers, Fifty-seventh Annual Meeting, p. 68A.

Pagnac, Darrin, and Daniel J. Chure, 1997, Rare sauropod elements from the Carnegie Quarry (Morrison Formation), Dinosaur National Park, Utah: *Journal of Vertebrate Paleontology*, 17 (Supplement to Number 3), Abstracts of Papers, Fifty-seventh Annual Meeting, p. 68A.

Papp, Michael J., 1997, Assessment of the status of cheeks in ornithischian dinosaurs: *Journal of Vertebrate Paleontology*, 17 (Supplement to Number 3), Abstracts of Papers, Fifty-seventh Annual Meeting, pp. 68A–69A.

Parks, William A., 1933, New species of dinosaurs and turtles from the Upper Cretaceous formations of Alberta: *University of Toronto Studies, Geological Series*, 34, pp. 3–33.

Parrish, J. Michael, and Kenneth Carpenter, 1986, A new vertebrate fauna from the Dockum Formation (Late Triassic) of eastern New Mexico, *in*: Kevin Padian, editor, *The Beginning of the Age of Dinosaurs*. New York: Cambridge University Press, pp. 151–160.

Pasch, Anne D., 1997, A Turonian hadrosaur emerges from the Talkeetna Mountains in southcentral Alaska: *The Dinosaur Report*, summer, pp. 14–15.

———, 1998, Youngest paleontologist in Alaska helps recover its oldest dinosaur: *Dinosaur World*, 4, pp. 15–16.

Paul, Gregory S., 1985, The segnosaurian dinosaurs: Relics of the prosauropod-ornithischian transition?: *Journal of Vertebrate Paleontology*, 4 (4), pp. 507–515.

———, 1988a, The brachiosaur giants of the Morrison and Tendaguru with a description of a new subgenus, *Giraffatitan*, and a comparison of the world's largest dinosaurs: *Hunteria*, 3 (3), pp. 1–14.

———, 1988b, *Predatory Dinosaurs of the World*. New York: Simon and Schuster, 403 pages.

———, 1991, Giant horned dinosaurs did have fully erect forelimbs: *Journal of Vertebrate Paleontology*, 11 (Supplement to Number 3), Abstracts of Papers, Fifty-first Annual Meeting, p. 50A.

———, 1995, Can nasal turbinates be used to diagnose paleometabolics?: *Journal of Vertebrate Paleontology*, Abstracts of Papers, 15 (Supplement to Number 3), Fifty-fifth Annual Meeting, p. 48A.

———, 1997, Dinosaur models: the good, the bad, and using them to estimate the mass of dinosaurs, *in*: Donald L. Wolberg, Edmund Stump, and Gary Rosenberg, editors. *Dinofest™ International: Proceedings of a Symposium Held at Arizona State University*. Philadelphia: Academy of Natural Sciences, pp. 129–154.

Peng Guangzhao, 1990, A new small ornithopod (*Agilisaurus louderbacki* gen. et. sp. nov.) from Zigong, Sichuan, China: *Newaleters Zigong Dinosaur Museum*, 2, pp. 19–27. [In Chinese.]

———, 1997, Fabrosauridae, *in*: Philip J. Currie and Kevin Padian, editors, *Encyclopedia of Dinosaurs*. San Diego: Academic Press, pp. 237–240.

Penkalski, Paul G., 1994, The morphology of *Avaceratops lammersi*, a primitive ceratopsid from the Judith River Formation (late Campanian) of Montana: Unpublished M. S. thesis, University of Pennsylvania, Philadelphia, 55 pages.

Pereda-Suberbiola, Xabier [Javier], 1993, *Hylaeosaurus, Polacanthus*, and the systematics and stratigraphy of Wealden armoured dinosaurs: *Geological Magazine*, 130, pp. 767–781.

———, 1994, *Polacanthus* (Ornithischia, Ankylosauria), a Transatlantic armoured dinosaur from the Early Cretaceous of Europe and North America: *Palaeontographica*, A, 323, pp. 133–159.

Pereda-Suberbiola, Xabier [Javier], and Peter M. Galton, 1992, On the taxonomic status of the dinosaur *Struthiosaurus austriacus* Bunzel from the Late Cretaceous of Austria: *Comtes Rendu des Seances de l'Académie des Sciences, Paris*, 315, pp. 4275–4280, Paris.

———, 1994, A revision of the cranial features of the dinosaur *Struthiosaurus austriacus* BUNZEL (Ornithischia: Ankylosauria) from the Late Cretaceous of Europe: *Neus Jahrbuch für Geologie und Paläontologie, Abhandlungen*, 191 (2), pp. 173–200.

———, 1997, Armoured dinosaurs from the Late Cretaceous of Transylvania: *Sargetia, Serie Scienta Naturae*, 17, pp. 203–217.

Pérez-Moreno, Bernardo P., José Luis Sanz, Angéla D. Buscalioni, José J. Moratalla, Francisco Ortega, and Diego Rasskin-Gutman, 1994, A unique multitoothed ornithomimosaur dinosaur from the Lower Cretaceous of Spain: *Nature*, 370, pp. 363–367.

Perle, Altangerel, 1979, Segnosauridae — A new family of theropods from the Late Cretaceous of Mongolia: *Joint Soviet-Mongolian Paleontological Expedition, Transactions*, 8, pp. 45–55.

Perle, Altangerel, Luis M. Chiappe, Rinchen Barsbold, James M. Clark, and Mark A. Norell, 1994, Skeletal morphology of *Mononykus olecrans* (Theropoda: Aviale) from the Late Cretaceous of Mongolia: *American Musuem Novitates*, 3105, pp. 1–29.

Perle, Altangerel, Mark A. Norell, Luis M. Chiappe, and James M. Clark, 1993, Flightless bird from the Cretaceous of Mongolia: *Nature*, 362, pp. 623–626.

Pidancet, J., 1863, Sur un réptile dinosaurien découvert à Poligny, dans les Marnes irisées de la formation du Trias: *Bull. Soc. Agric. Sci. Arts Poligny*, 4, 118 pages, Poligny.

Pidancet, J., and S. Chopard, 1862, Note sur un saurien gigantesque aux Marnes irisées: *Comptes Rendus des Seances de l'Académie des Sciences, Paris*, 54, pp. 1259–1262, Paris.

Pillmore, C. L., 1998a, The Cretaceous-Tertiary boundary in continental rocks: Evidence for asteroid impact and mass extinction, *in*: Donald L. Wolberg, K. Gittis, S. Miller, and A. Raynor, editors, *The Dinofest™ Symposium* [abstracts], Presented by The Academy of Natural Sciences of Philadelphia, Pennsylvania, p. 47.

———, 1998b, Dinosaur tracks near the K/T boundary — How close are they?, *ibid*, p. 47.

Bibliography

Pipiringos, G. N., and R. B. O'Sullivan, 1978, Principal unconformities in Triassic and Jurassic rocks, western interior United States — A preliminary survey: *U. S. Geological Survey Professional Paper 1035-A*, pp. A1–A29.

Pons, D., P. Y. Berthou, and D. A. Campos, 1990, Quelques observations sur la palynologie de l'Aptien Supérieur et de l'Albien du bassin d'Araripe (N. E. du Brésil), *in*: D. A. Campos, M. S. S. Viana, P. M. Brito, and G. Beurlen, editors, *Atlas 1 Simpósio sobre a Bacia do Araripe e Bacias Interiores do Nordeste, Crato, 1990*, pp. 241–252.

Powell, Jaime Eduardo, 1979, Sobre una asociación de dinosaurios y otras evidencias de vertebrados del cretacico superior de la region de la Candelaria, Prov. de Salta, Argentina: *Ameghiniana*, 16 (1–2), pp. 191–204, Buenos Aires.

_____, 1986, Revisión de los Titanosauridos de América del Sur. Tésis Doctoral inédita Fac. de Ciencias Exactas y Naturales, Universidad Nacional de Tucumán, Argentina, 472 pages (unpublished).

_____, 1990, *Epachthosaurus sciuttoi* (gen. et sp. nov.) un dinosaurio sauropodo del Cretacico de Patagonia (Provincia de Chubut, Argentina): *V Congreso Argentino de Paleontologia y Bioestratigrafia*, Tucumán, 1990, Actas 1, pp. 123–128.

Quinn, J. H., 1973, Arkansas dinosaur: *Geological Society of America Abstracts with Program*, 5 (3), pp. 276–277.

Quinn, Thomas, 1998, The informational origin of feathers: An overview, *in*: Donald L. Wolberg, K. Gittis, S. Miller, and A. Raynor, editors, *The Dinofest™ Symposium* [abstracts], Presented by The Academy of Natural Sciences of Philadelphia, Pennsylvania, pp. 47–48.

Raath, Michael A., 1996, Earliest evidence of dinosaurs from central Gondwana, *in*: Fernando S. Novas and Ralph E. Molnar, editors, *Proceedings of the Gondwanan Dinosaur Symposium: Memoirs of the Queensland Museum*, 39 (part 3), pp. 703–709.

Rasmussen, Mette E., 1998, Phylogenetic relationships of hadrosaurs and related ornithopods — Based on forelimb morphology: *in*: John W. M. Jagt, Paul H. Lambers, Eric W. A. Mulder, and Anne S. Schulp, editors, *Third European Workshop on Vertebrate Palaeontology*, Maastricht, 6–9 May 1998, Programme and Abstracts Field Guide, [unpaginated].

Ratkevich, Ronald P., 1997, Dinosaur remains of southern Arizona, *in*: Donald L. Wolberg, Edmund Stump, and Gary Rosenberg, editors. *Dinofest™ International: Proceedings of a Symposium Held at Arizona State University*. Philadelphia: Academy of Natural Sciences, pp. 213–221.

_____, 1998, New Cretaceous brachiosaurid dinosaur, *Sonorasaurus thompsoni* gen. et sp. nov. from Arizona: *Journal of the Arizona-Nevada Academy of Science*, 31 (1), pp. 71–82.

Rauhut, Oliver W. M., 1995, Zur systematischen Stellung der afrikanischen Theropoden *Carcharodontosaurus* Stromer 1931 und *Bahariasaurus* Stromer 1934: *Berliner geowissenschaftliche Abhandlung*, E 16, pp. 357–375.

Ray, G. R., 1941, Big for his day: *Natural History*, 48 (1), pp. 36–39.

Reid, Robin E. H., 1981, Lamellar-zonal bone with zones and annuli in the pelvis of a sauropod dinosaur: *Nature*, 292, pp. 49–51.

_____, 1984, The histology of dinosaurian bone, and its possible bearing on dinosaurian physiology: *Symposium of the Zoological Society of London*, 52, pp. 629–663.

_____, 1987, Bone and dinosaurian "endothermy": *Modern Geology*, 11, pp. 133–154.

_____, 1990, Zonal "growth rings" in dinosaurs: *Ibid*, 15, pp. 19–48.

_____, 1996, Bone histology of the Cleveland-Lloyd dinosaurs and of dinosaurs in general, Part I: Introduction: Introduction to bone tissues: *BYU Geology Studies*, 41, pp. 25–71.

Reuben, J. A., Andrew Leitch, and Willem J. Hillenius, 1995, Respiratory turbinates and the metabolic status of some theropod dinosaurs and *Archaeopteryx*: *Journal of Vertebrate Paleontology*, 15 (Supplement to Number 3), Abstracts of Papers, Fifty-fifth Annual Meeting, p. 50A.

Reyes, F. C., and J. Salfity, 1973, Consideraciones sobre la estratigrafia del Cretácico (SubGrupo Pirgua) del Noroestes Argentino: *In Congreso Geológico Exactas, Universidad Nacional de Buenos Aires*, 720 pages, Buenos Aires.

Rich, Thomas H., 1998, The Hypsilophodontidae from southeastern Australia, *in*: Yukimitsu Tomida, Thomas R. Rich, and Patricia Vickers-Rich, editors, *Second Symposium Gondwana Dinosaur, 12–13 July, 1998, National Science Museum, Tokyo, Abstracts with Program*, p. 15.

Richardson, P. R. K., P. J. Mundy, and I. Plug, 1986, Bone crushing carnivores and their significance to osteodystrophy in griffon vulture chicks: *Journal of the Zoological Society of London*, A, 210, pp. 23–43.

Ricqlès, Armand J. de, 1983, Cyclical growth in the long limb bones of sauropod dinosaurs: *Acta Palaeontologia Polonica*, 18, pp. 225–232.

Riggs, Elmer S., 1903a, *Brachiosaurus altithorax*, the largest known dinosaur: *American Journal of Science*, Series 4, 15, pp. 299–306.

_____, 1903b, Structure and relationships of opisthocoelian dinosaurs. Part I, *Apatosaurus* Marsh: *Field Columbian Museum*, Geological Series 2, 4, pp. 165–196.

Rodriguez de la Rosa, Rubén Armando, 1996, Vertebrate remains from a Late Cretaceous locality (Campanian, Cerro del Pueblo Formation), Coahuila, Mexico: *Journal of Vertebrate Paleontology*, 16 (Supplement to Number 3), Abstracts of Papers, Fifty-sixth Annual Meeting, p. 60A.

Romer, Alfred Sherwood, 1956, *Osteology of the Reptiles*. Chicago: University of Chicago Press, 772 pages.

Ross, A. J., and E. Cook, 1995, The stratigraphy and palaeontology of the Upper Weald Clay (Barremian) at Smokejack's Brickworks, Ockley, Surrey, England: *Cretaceous Research*, 16, pp. 705–716, London.

Rothschild, Bruce M., and Darren Tanke, 1997, Thunder in the Cretaceous: Interspecies conflict as evidence for ceratopsian migration?, *in*: Donald L. Wolberg, Edmund Stump, and Gary Rosenberg, editors, *Dinofest™ International: Proceedings of a Symposium Held at Arizona State University*. Philadelphia: Academy of Natural Sciences, pp. 77–81.

Rothschild, Bruce M., Darren Tanke, and Kenneth Carpenter, 1997a, Tyrannosaurs suffered from gout: *Nature*, 22, p. 357.

_____, 1997b, Spheroid erosions in tyrannosaurids: Mesozoic gout: *Journal of Vertebrate Paleontology*, 17 (Supplement to Number 3), Abstracts of Papers, Fifty-seventh Annual Meeting, p. 72A.

Rowe, Timothy, 1989, A new species of theropod dinosaur *Syntarsus* from the Early Jurassic Kayenta Formation of Arizona: *Journal of Vertebrate Paleontology*, 9 (2), pp. 125–136.

Rozhestvensky, Anatoly Konstantinovich, 1952, Otkritiye igvanodonta v Mongolii [Discovery of iguanodonts in Mongolia]: *Doklady Akademiya Nauk CCCP*, 84 (6), pp. 1243–146.

Ruben, John A., Terry D. Jones, Nicholas R. Geist, and W. Jaap Hillenius, 1997, Lung structure and ventilation in theropod dinosaurs and early birds: *Science*, 278, pp. 1267–1270.

Ruben, John A., Andrew Leitch, and Willem J. Hillenius, 1995, Respiratory turbinates and the metabolic status of some theropod dinosaurs and *Archaeopteryx*: *Journal of Vertebrate Paleontology*, 15 (Supplement to Number 3), Abstracts of Papers, Fifty-fifth Annual Meeting, p. 50A.

Russell, Dale A., 1970, Tyrannosaurs from the Late Cretaceous of western Canada: *National Museum of Natural Sciences, Publications in Paleontology*, 1, viii, 34 pages.

_____, 1972, Ostrich dinosaurs from the Late Cretaceous of western Canada: *Canadian Journal of Earth Sciences*, 9 (375), pp. 375–402.

_____, 1984, A check list of the families and genera of North American dinosaurs: *Syllogeus*, 53, National Museums of Canada, National Museum of Natural Science, 35 pages.

_____, 1995, An associated skeleton of a large pachycephalosaur from the Hell Creek Formation: *Journal of Vertebrate Paleontology*, 15 (Supplement to Number 3), Abstracts of Papers, Fifty-fifth Annual Meeting, p. 51A.

_____, 1996, Isolated dinosaur bones from the Middle Cretaceous of the Tafilalt, Morocco: *Bulletin du Muséum National d'Historie Naturelle, Paris*, sér. 4 (18), Section C, nᵒˢ 2–3, pp. 3409–402.

_____, 1998, The context of *Acrocanthosaurus*, *in*: Donald L. Wolberg, K. Gittis, S. Miller, and A. Raynor, editors, *The Dinofest™ Symposium* [abstracts], Presented by The Academy of Natural Sciences of Philadelphia, Pennsylvania, pp. 50–51.

Russell, Dale A., and Dong Zhi-Ming, 1993a, The affinities of a new theropod from the

Alxa Desert, Inner Mongolia, People's Republic of China: *Canadian Journal of Earth Sciences*, 30 (10–11), pp. 2107–2127.

Russell, Dale A., Philippe Taquet, and H. Thomas, 1976, Nouvelles récoltes de vértebre's dans les terrains continentaux du Crétacé supérieur de la région de Majunga (Madagascar): *Compte Rendus Sommaire des Seances et Bulletin de la Societé Géologique de France*, 5, pp. 205–208.

Russell, Dale A., and Zhong Zheng, 1993, A large mamenchisaurid from the Junggar Basin, Xinjiang, People's Republic of China: *Canadian Journal of Earth Sciences*, 30 (10–11), pp. 2082–2095.

Ryan, Michael J., and Philip J. Currie, 1996, First report of Protoceratopsidae (Neoceratopsia) from the late Campanian, Judith River Group, Alberta, Canada: *Journal of Vertebrate Paleontology*, 16 (Supplement to Number 3), Abstracts of Papers, Fifty-sixth Annual Meeting, p. 61A.

Ryan, Michael J., Philip J. Currie, James D. Gardner, and J. M. Lavigne, 1997, Baby hadrosaurid material associated with an unusually high abundance of *Troodon* teeth from the Horseshoe Canyon Formation (Early Maastrichtian), Alberta, Canada: *Journal of Vertebrate Paleontology*, 17 (Supplement to Number 3), Abstracts of Papers, Fifty-seventh Annual Meeting, p. 72A.

Sabath, K., 1991, Upper Cretaceous amniotic eggs from the Gobi Desert: *Paleontologica Polonica*, 36, pp. 151–192.

Salgado, Leonardo, 1996, *Pellegrinisaurus powelli* nov. gen. et sp. (Sauropoda, Titanosauridae) from the Upper Cretaceous of Lago Pellegrini, northwestern Patagonia, Argentina: *Ameghiniana*, 33 (4), pp. 355–365, Buenos Aires.

Salgado, Leonardo, and José F. Bonaparte, 1991, Un nuevo sauropodo Dicraeosauridae, *Amargasaurus cazui* gen. et sp. nov., de la Formación la Amarga, Neocomiano de la Provincia del Neuquén, Argentina: *Ameghiniana*, 28 (3–4), pp. 333–346, Buenos Aires.

Salgado, Leonardo, and Jorge Orlando Calvo, 1992, Cranial osteology of *Amargasaurus cazaui* Salgado and Bonaparte (Sauropoda-Dicraeosauridae) from the Neocomanian of Patagonia: *Ameghiniana*, 29 (4), pp. 337–346, Buenos Aires.

_____, 1997, Evolution of titanosaurid sauropods. II. The cranial evidence: *Ibid*, 34 (1), pp. 33–48.

Salgado, Leonardo, Jorge Orlando Calvo, and Rodolfo Aníbal Coria, 1995, Relaciones filogenéticas de *Pleurocoelus* Marsh (Sauropoda): *Resúmes II, Journadas Argentinas de Paleontologia de Vertebrados*, Tucumán.

Salgado, Leonardo, and Rodolfo Aníbal Coria, 1993, El género *Aeolosaurus* (Sauropoda, Titanosauridae) en la Formación Allen (Campanian-Maastrichtian) de la Provincia de Río Negro, Argentina: *Ameghiniana*, 30, pp. 119–128, Buenos Aires.

_____, 1996, First evidence of an ankylosaur (Dinosauria, Ornithischia) in South America: *Ameghiniana*, 33 (4), pp. 367–371, Buenos Aires.

Salgado, Leonardo, Rodolfo Aníbal Coria, and

Jorge Orlando Calvo, 1997, Evolution of titanosaurid sauropods. I: Phylogenetic analysis based on the postcranial evidence: *Ameghiniana*, 34 (1), pp. 3–32.

Salgado, Leonardo, Rodolfo Aníbal Coria, and Susana E. Heredia, 1997, New materials of *Gasparinisaura cincosaltensis* (Ornithischia, Ornithopoda) from the Upper Cretaceous of Argentina: *Journal of Paleontology*, 71 (5), pp. 933–940.

Salgado, Leonardo, and Ruben Dario Martínez, 1993, Relaciones filogenéticas de los titanosáuridos basales *Andesaurus y Epachthosaurus* sp.: *Ameghiniana*, 3, pp. 673–711.

Sampson, Scott D., David W. Krause, Peter Dodson, and Catherine A. Forster, 1996, The premaxilla of *Majungasaurus* (Dinosauria: Theropoda), with implications for Gondwanan paleobiogeography: *Journal of Vertebrate Paleontology*, 16 (4), pp. 601–605.

Sampson, Scott D., David W. Krause, Catherine A. Forster, and Peter Dodson, 1996, Non-avian theropod dinosaurs from the Late Cretaceous of Madagascar and their paleobiogeographic implications: *Journal of Vertebrate Paleontology*, 16 (Supplement to Number 3), Abstracts of Papers, Fifty-sixth Annual Meeting, p. 62A.

Sampson, Scott D., Michael J. Ryan, and Darren H. Tanke, 1997, Cranofacial ontogeny in centrosaurine dinosaurs: Taxonomic and behavorial implications: *Zoological Journal of the Linnean Society*, pp. 293–337.

Sampson, Scott D., Lawrence M. Witmer, Catherine A. Forster, David W. Krause, and Patrick M. O'Connor, 1997, Discovery of a complete theropod skull from the Late Cretaceous of Madagascar yields new information on *Majungasaurus*, *Majungatholus*, and Abelisauridae: *Journal of Vertebrate Paleontology*, 17 (Supplement to Number 3), Abstracts of Papers, Fifty-seventh Annual Meeting, p. 73A.

Sampson, Scott D., Lawrence M. Witmer, Catherine A. Forster, David W. Krause, Patrick M. O'Connor, Peter Dodson, and Florent Ravoavy, 1998, Predatory dinosaur remains from Madagascar: Implications for the Cretaceous biogeography of Gondwana: *Science*, 280, pp. 1048–1051.

Sanz, José Luis, and José F. Bonaparte, 1992, A new order of birds (class Aves) from the Early Cretaceous of Spain, *in*: K. E. Campbell, editor, *Papers in Avian Paleontology. Honoring Pierce Brodkorb*. Science Series, 36. Los Angeles: Natural History Museum of Los Angeles County, pp. 39–49.

Sanz, José Luis, José F. Bonaparte, and A. Lacasa, 1998, Unusual Lower Cretaceous birds from Spain: *Nature*, 331, pp. 433–435.

Sanz, José Luis, Ángela D. Buscalioni, 1992, A new bird from the Early Cretaceous of Las Hoyas, Spain, and the early radiation of birds: *Palaeontology*, 35, pp. 829–845.

Sanz, José Luis, J. J. Moratalla, M. Diaz-Molina, N. López-Martínez, O. Kälin, and M. Vianey-Liaud, 1995, Dinosaur nests at the sea shore: *Nature*, 376, pp. 731–732.

Sattler, Helen Roney, 1983, *The Illustrated Dinosaur Dictionary*. New York: Lothrop, Lee & Shepard Books, 316 pages.

Savalle, Emile, and Gustave Lennieri, 1899, Note sur des ossements de dinosaurien dicouvérts a Octeville par M. M. Savalle et G. Lennieri: *Bulletin of the Geological Society of Normandie*, 18, pp. 59–51, Le Havre.

Schweitzer, Mary Higby, 1995, Preservartion of heme-bearing proteins in unpermineralized dinosaur tissues: *Journal of Vertebrate Paleontology*, 15 (Supplement to Number 3), Abstracts of Papers, Fifty-fifth Annual Meeting, p. 52A.

_____, 1998, Claws, beaks, scales and feathers: The evolutionary implications of keratin preservation in the fossil record, *in*: Donald L. Wolberg, K. Gittis, S. Miller, and A. Raynor, editors, *The Dinofest™ Symposium* [abstracts], Presented by The Academy of Natural Sciences of Philadelphia, Pennsylvania, p. 52.

Schweitzer, Mary Higby, Craig Johnson, Thomas G. Zocco, John R. Horner, and Jean R. Starkey, 1997, Preservation of biomolecules in cancellous bone of *Tyrannosaurus rex*: *Journal of Vertebrate Paleontology*, 17 (2), pp. 349–359.

Schweitzer, Mary Higby, Mark Marshall, Darlene Barnard, Scott Bohle, Keith Carron, Ernst Arnold, and J. R. Starkey, 1997, Blood from a Stone?, *in*: Donald L. Wolberg, Edmund Stump, and Gary Rosenberg, editors, *Dinofest™ International: Proceedings of a Symposium Held at Arizona State University*. Philadelphia: Academy of Natural Sciences, pp. 101–104.

Schweitzer, Mary Higby, Mark Marshall, Keith Carron, Scott Bohle, Ernst Arnold, S. Buss, and J. R. Starkey, 1996, Identification of possible blood-derived heme compounds in *Tyrannosaurus rex* trabecular tissues: *Dinofest™ International Symposium, April 18–21, 1996, Programs and Abstracts*, p. 99.

Seeley, Harry Govier, 1881, On the reptile fauna of the Gosau Formation preserved in the Geological Museum of the University of Vienna: *Quarterly Journal of the Geological Society of London*, 37, pp. 619–707.

Senter, Phil, 1998, Tyrannosaurid jaw adductor configuration and biting style, *in*: Donald L. Wolberg, K. Gittis, S. Miller, and A. Raynor, editors, *The Dinofest™ Symposium* [abstracts], Presented by The Academy of Natural Sciences of Philadelphia, Pennsylvania, p. 54.

Sereno, Paul C., 1986, Phylogeny of the bird-hipped dinosaurs (order Ornithischia): *National Geographic Research*, 2, pp. 234–256.

_____, 1989, Prosauropod monophyly and basal sauropodomorph phylogeny: *Journal of Vertebrate Paleontology*, 10 (Supplement to Number 3), Abstracts of Papers, Fiftieth Annual Meeting, p. 38A.

_____, 1991, Basal archosaurs: Phylogenetic relationships and functional implications: *Society of Vertebrate Paleontology Memoir*, 2, pp. 1–53.

_____, 1993, The skull and neck of the basal

theropod *Herrerasaurus ischigualastensis*: *Journal of Vertebrate Paleontology*, 13 (4), pp. 451–476.

———, 1995, Theropoda early evolution and major patterns of diversification: *Journal of Vertebrate Paleontology, 15* (Supplement to Number 3), Abstracts of Papers, Fifty-fifth Annual Meeting, p. 52A–53A.

———, 1996, Dinosaur descent: Phylogenetic structure and evolutionary implications: *Journal of Vertebrate Paleontology*, 16 (Supplement to Number 3), Abstracts of Papers, Fifty-sixth Annual Meeting, p. 64A.

———, 1997, The origin and evolution of dinosaurs: *Annual Review of Earth Planet Science*, 25, pp. 435–489.

Sereno, Paul C., and Andrea Beatriz Arcucci, 1994*a*, Dinosaurian precursors from the Middle Triassic of Argentina: *Lagerpeton chanarensis: Journal of Vertebrate Paleontology*, 13, pp. 385–399.

———, 1994*b*, Dinosaurian precursors from the Middle Triassic of Argentina: *Marasuchus lilloensis*, gen. nov.: *Ibid*, 14, pp. 53–73.

Sereno, Paul C., and Chao Shichin [Zhao Xijin], 1988, *Psittacosaurus xinjiangensis* (Ornithischia: Ceratopsia), a new psittacosaur from the Lower Cretaceous of Northwestern China: *Journal of Vertebrate Paleontology*, 8 (4), pp. 353–356.

Sereno, Paul C., Didier B. Dutheil, M. Iarochene, Hans C. E. Larsson, Gabrielle H. Lyon, Paul M. Magwene, Christian A. Sidor, David J. Varracchio, and Jeffrey A. Wilson, 1996, Predatory dinosaurs from the Sahara and Late Cretaceous faunal differentiation: *Science*, 272, pp. 986–990.

Sereno, Paul C., Catherine A. Forster, Raymond R. Rogers, and Alfredo M. Monetta, 1993, *Nature*, 361, p.64.

Sereno, Paul C., and Fernando E. Novas, 1990, Dinosaur origins and the phylogenetic position of pterosaurs: *Journal of Vertebrate Paleontology*, 10 (Supplement to Number 3), Abstracts of Papers, Fiftieth Annual Meeting, p. 42A.

———, 1992, The complete skull and skeleton of an early dinosaur: *Science*, 258, November 13, pp. 1137–1140.

———, 1994, The skull and neck of the basal theropod *Herrerasaurus ischigualastensis*: *Journal of Vertebrate Paleontology*, 13, pp. 451–476.

Sereno, Paul C., and Rupert Wild, 1992, *Procompsognathus*: Theropod, "thecodont" or both?: *Journal of Vertebrate Paleontology*, 12 (4), pp. 435–458.

Sereno, Paul C., Jeffrey A. Wilson, Hans C. E. Larsson, Didier B. Dutheil, and Hans-Dieter Sues, 1994, Early Cretaceous dinosaurs from the Sahara: *Science*, 266, pp. 267–271.

Signor, P. W., III, and J. H. Lipps, 1982, Sampling bias, gradual extinction patterns and catastrophes in the fossil record, *in*: L. T. Silver and P. H. Shultz, editors, *Geological Implications of Large Asteroids and Comets on the Earth*, Geological Society of America Special Paper, 190, pp. 291–296.

Simmons, David J., 1965, The non-therapsid reptiles of the Lufeng Basin, Yunnan, China: *Fieldiana*, 15 (1), 93 pages.

Skrepnick, Michael W., 1998, *Sinosauropteryx*: Some cry "fowl" over feathers, *in*: Donald L. Wolberg, K. Gittis, S. Miller, and A. Raynor, editors, *The Dinofest*™ *Symposium* [abstracts], Presented by The Academy of Natural Sciences of Philadelphia, Pennsylvania, p. 55.

Sloan, Robert E., 1997, Plate tectonics and the radiations/extinctions of dinosaurs, the Pele hypothesis, *in*: Donald L. Wolberg, Edmund Stump, and Gary Rosenberg, editors, *Dinofest*™ *International: Proceedings of a Symposium Held at Arizona State University*. Philadelphia: Academy of Natural Sciences, pp. 533–539.

Smith, David K., 1996, A discriminant analysis of *Allosaurus* population using quarries as the operational units, *in*: Michael Morales, editor, *Museum of Northern Arizona Bulletin*, 60, pp. 69–72.

———, 1998, A morphometric analysis of *Allosaurus: Journal of Vertebrate Paleontology*, 18 (1), pp. 126–142.

Smith, Joshua B., You Hailu, and Peter Dodson, 1998, On the age and geologic context of the *Sinosauropteryx* quarry and other sites in the Jehol Group, Liaoning Province, northeastern China, *in*: Donald L. Wolberg, K. Gittis, S. Miller, and A. Raynor, editors, *The Dinofest*™ *Symposium* [abstracts], Presented by The Academy of Natural Sciences of Philadelphia, pp. 55–56.

Spotila, James R., Michael P. O'Connor, Peter Dodson, and Frank V. Paladino, 1991, Hot and cold running dinosaurs: Body size, metabolism and migration: *Modern Biology*, 16, pp. 203–227.

Stadtman, Kenneth L., D. R. White, and Brian D. Curtice, in preparation, Osteology of *Supersaurus vivianae* Jensen 1985.

Stanford, Ray, 1998, Sauropod hatchling tracks from the Lower Cretaceous of Texas, *in*: Donald L. Wolberg, K. Gittis, S. Miller, and A. Raynor, editors, *The Dinofest*™ *Symposium* [abstracts], Presented by The Academy of Natural Sciences of Philadelphia, Pennsylvania, p. 56.

Stanford, Ray, and Sheila M. Stanford, 1998, … And the sauropods wore sneakers!, *in*: Donald L. Wolberg, K. Gittis, S. Miller, and A. Raynor, editors, *The Dinofest*™ *Symposium* [abstracts], Presented by The Academy of Natural Sciences of Philadelphia, Pennsylvania, p. 57.

Steel, Rodney, 1969, Ornithischia, *in*: Oskar Kuhn, editor, *Handbuch der Palaeoherpetologie*, Part 15. Stuttgart: Gustav Fischer Verlag, 87 pages.

Steinbock, R. T., 1989, Ichnology of the Connecticut Valley: A vignette of American science in the early nineteenth century, *in*: David D. Gillette and Martin G. Lockley, editors, *Dinosaur Tracks and Traces*. Cambridge, United Kingdom: Cambridge University Press, pp. 27–32.

Sternberg, Charles M., 1927, Horned dinosaur group in the National Museum of Canada: *Canadian Field-Naturalist*, 41, pp. 67–73.

———, 1932, Two new theropod dinosaurs from the Belly River Formation of Alberta: *Ibid*, 46, pp. 99–105.

———, 1934, Notes on certain recently described dinosaurs: *Ibid*, 48, pp. 7–8.

———, 1938, *Monoclonius*, from southeastern Alberta, compared with *Centrosaurus*: *Journal of Paleontology*, 12, pp. 284–286.

———, 1940, Ceratopsidae from Alberta: *Journal of Paleontology*, 14, pp. 468–480.

Stevens, Kent A., and J. Michael Parrish, 1997, Comparisons of neck form and function in the Diplodocidae: *Journal of Vertebrate Paleontology*, 17 (Supplement to Number 3), Abstracts of Papers, Fifty-seventh Annual Meeting, p. 79A.

Stewart, D. J., 1981, A field guide to the Wealden Group of the Hastings area and the Isle of Wight, *in*: T. Elliott, editor, *Field Guides to Modern and Ancient Fluvial Systems in Britain and Spain*. Keele, United Kingdom: University of Keele.

Storey, B. C., 1995: *Nature*, 337, p. 301.

Stovall, J. Willis, and Wann Langston, Jr., 1950, *Acrocanthosaurus atokensis*, a new genus and species of Lower Cretaceous Theropoda from Oklahoma: *The American Midland Naturalist*, 43 (3), pp. 696–728.

Stromer, Ernst, 1915, Ergebnisse der Forschungsreisen Prof. E. Stromers in den Wüsten Ägyptens. II. Wirbeltierreste der Baharije-Stufe (unterstes Cenoman). III. Das Original des Theropoden *Spinosaurus aegyptiacus* n. g. n. sp.: *Abhandlungen der Bayerischen Akademie der Wissenschaften*, 18 (3), pp. 1–32.

———, 1931, Wirbeltierreste de Baharijestufe (unterstes Cenoman). 10. Ein Skelettrest von *Carcharodontosaurus* nov. gen: *Ibid*, 9, pp. 1–23.

———, 1934, Ergebnisse der Forschungsreisen Prof. E. Stromer in den Wüsten Ägyptens. II: Wirbeltier-Reste der Baharije-Stufe unterestes (Cenoman). 13. Dinosauria: *Ibid*, 22, pp. 1–79.

Stromer, Ernst, and W. Weiler, 1930, Beschreibung von Wirbeltier-Resten aus dem nubischen Sandteine Oberägyptens und aus ägyptischen Phosphaten nebst Bemerkungen über die Geologie der Umgegend von Mahamid in Oberägypten: *Abhandlugen der Bayerischen Akademie Wissenschaften Mathemathisch-naturwissenschaft Diche Abteilung*, 7, pp. 1–42.

Sues, Hans-Dieter, 1997, On *Chirostenotes*, a Late Cretaceous oviraptorosaur (Dinosauria: Theropoda) from Western North America: *Journal of Vertebrate Paleontology*, 17 (4), pp. 698–716.

———, 1998, New data on oviraptorosaurian theropods from the Cretaceous of western North America, *in*: Donald L. Wolberg, K. Gittis, S. Miller, and A. Raynor, editors, *The Dinofest*™ *Symposium* [abstracts], Presented by The Academy of Natural Sciences of Philadelphia, Pennsylvania, p. 58.

Sues, Hans-Dieter, and Philippe Taquet, 1979, A pachycephalosaurid dinosaur from Madagascar and a Laurasia-Gondwanaland connection in the Cretaceous: *Nature*, 279, pp. 633–635.

Sullivan, Robert M., 1996*a*, The little dinosaurs of Ghost Ranch (book review): *Journal of Vertebrate Paleontology*, 16 (2), pp. 363–365.

_____, 1996b, The many myths of dinosaur extinction: Decoupling dinosaur extinction from the asteroid impact: _Dinofest^TM International Symposium, April 18–21, 1996, Programs and Abstracts_, p. 105.

_____, 1997, A juvenile _Ornithomimus antiquus_ (Dinosauria: Theropoda: Ornithomosauria), from the Upper Cretaceous Kirtland Formation (De-na-zin Member), San Juan Basin, New Mexico: _New Mexico Geological Society Guidebook, 48th Field Conference, Mesozoic Geology and Paleontology of the Four Corners Region_, pp. 249–253.

_____, 1998, The many myths of dinosaur extinction: Decoupling dinosaur extinction from the asteroid impact, _in_: Donald L. Wolberg, K. Gittis, S. Miller, and A. Raynor, editors, _The Dinofest^TM Symposium_ [abstracts], Presented by The Academy of Natural Sciences of Philadelphia, Pennsylvania, pp. 58–59.

Sullivan, Robert M., and Thomas E. Williamson, 1996c, A new skull of _Parasaurolophus_ (long-crested form) from New Mexico: external and internal (CT scans) features and their functional implications: _Journal of Vertebrate Paleontology_, 16 (Supplement to Number 3), Abstracts of Papers, Fifty-sixth Annual Meeting, p. 68A.

Taggert, Ralph E., and Aureal T. Cross, 1996, The relationship between land plant diversity and productivity and patterns of dinosaur herbivory: _Dinofest^TM International Symposium, April 18–21, 1996, Programs and Abstracts_, p. 106.

Taquet, Philippe, 1984, Une curieuse spécialisation du crâne de certains dinosauriens carnivores du Crétacé le meseau long et étroit des Spinosauridés: _Comptes Rendus des Séances de l'Académie des Sciences_, 299 II (5), pp. 217–222.

Tedesco, Lenore P., Hal E. Halvorsen, and Kent Cooper, 1998, Mass mortality of a herd of hadrosaurs: Lance Creek Formation, east-central Wyoming, _in_: Donald L. Wolberg, K. Gittis, S. Miller, and A. Raynor, editors, _The Dinofest^TM Symposium_ [abstracts], Presented by The Academy of Natural Sciences of Philadelphia, Pennsylvania, p. 60.

Thayer, D. W., and R. P. Ratkevich, 1995, In progress excavation in the Mid–Cretaceous Turney Ranch Formation in southeastern Arizona: _Fossils of Arizona_, volume 3. Mesa, Arizona: Southwest Paleonteological Society.

Thomas, David A., 1996, Dancing predators: Modern predators pick up prey's rhythm to facilitate attacks: _Journal of Vertebrate Paleontology_, 16 (Supplement to Number 3), Abstracts of Papers, Fifty-sixth Annual Meeting, pp. 68A–69A.

Thomas, David A., and James O. Farlow, 1997, Tracking a dinosaur attack: _Scientific American_, 277 (6), pp. 48–53.

Thulborn, Richard A., 1984, The avian relationships of _Archaeopteryx_ and the origin of birds: _Zoological Society of London_, 82, pp. 191–218.

_____, 1985, Birds as neotenous dinosaurs: _Records of the New Zealand Geological Survey_, 9, pp. 90–92.

_____, 1990, _Dinosaur Tracks_. London and New York: Chapman and Hall, xvii, 410 pages.

_____, 1992, A nest of the dinosaur _Protoceratops_: _Lethaia_, 25, pp. 145–149.

Tidwell, Virginia A., and Kenneth Carpenter, 1997, Rediscovery of E. D. Cope locality yields new material of _Camarasaurus supremus_: _Journal of Vertebrate Paleontology_, 17 (Supplement to Number 3), Abstracts of Papers, Fifty-seventh Annual Meeting, p. 81A.

Tkach, J. S., 1996, Multi-element osteohistological analysis of _Dilophosaurus wetherilli_: _Journal of Vertebrate Paleontology_, 16 (Supplement to Number 3), Abstracts of Papers, Fifty-sixth Annual Meeting, p. 69A.

Todria, V. A., 1976, Stratigrafiya verkhneyurskikh otlozheniy Severo-Zapanoi Abkhazil po mikrofaune [Stratigraphy of the Upper Jurassic of northwestern Abkhaziya based on microfauna]: _Fondy Geologicheskogo Instituta im. A. I. Dzhanelidze Akademiya Nauk Gruzii, Tbilisi_, 66 pages (in Georgian).

Trexler, David, 1997, Hadrosaurid dinosaur nest from the upper Two Medicine Formation, Montana, suggests unusual nest building strategy: _Journal of Vertebrate Paleontology_, 17 (Supplement to Number 3), Abstracts of Papers, Fifty-seventh Annual Meeting, p. 81A.

Triebold, Michael, 1997, The Sandy Site: Small dinosaurs from the Hell Creek Formation of South Dakota, _in_: Donald L. Wolberg, Edmund Stump, and Gary Rosenberg, editors. _Dinofest^TM International: Proceedings of a Symposium Held at Arizona State University_. Philadelphia: Academy of Natural Sciences, pp. 245–248.

Triebold, Michael, and Dale A. Russell, 1995, A new small dinosaur locality in the Hell Creek Formation: _Journal of Vertebrate Paleontology_, 15 (Supplement to Number 3), Abstracts of Papers, Fifty-seventh Annual Meeting, p. 57A.

Tumanova, Tatyana A., 1983, The first ankylosaurs from the Lower Cretaceous of Mongolia: _Transactions of the Joint Soviet-Mongolian Palaeontological Expedition_, 24, pp. 110–118 (in Russian).

_____, 1987, The armoured dinosaurs of Mongolia: _Ibid_, 32, pp. 1–80 (in Russian).

Tumanova, Tatyana, William B. Gallagher, and Peter Dodson, 1998, Computerized tomography of Asian ankylosaur skulls: Damage and repair in a _Tarchia_ skull, _in_: Donald L. Wolberg, K. Gittis, S. Miller, and A. Raynor, editors, _The Dinofest^TM Symposium_ [abstracts], Presented by The Academy of Natural Sciences of Philadelphia, Pennsylvania, pp. 60–61.

Tykoski, Ronald S., A new ceratosurid theropod from the Early Jurassic Kayenta Formation of Northern Arizona: _Journal of Vertebrate Paleontology_, 17 (Supplement to Number 3), Abstracts of Papers, Fifty-seventh Annual Meeting, pp. 81A–82A.

Tyson, Amanda R., and Stephen M. Gatesy, 1997, The evolution of tail flexibility in theropods: _Journal of Vertebrate Paleontology_, 17 (Supplement to Number 3), Ab-

stracts of Papers, Fifty-seventh Annual Meeting, p. 82A.

Unwin, David M., 1998, Feathers, filaments and theropod dinosaurs: _Nature_, 391 (8), pp. 119–120.

Upchurch, Paul, 1994, Sauropod phylogeny and palaeoecology: _Gaio_, 10.

_____, 1995, The evolutionary history of sauropod dinosaurs: _Philosophical Transactions of the Royal Society of London_, B 349, pp. 365–390.

_____, 1997, A cladistic analysis of sauropod dinosaur phylogeny: _Journal of Vertebrate Paleontology_, 17 (Supplement to Number 3), Abstracts of Papers, Fifty-seventh Annual Meeting, p. 82A.

Van Heerden, Jacques, 1997, Prosauropods, _in_: James O. Farlow and Michael K. Brett-Surman, editors, _The Complete Dinosaur_. Bloomington and Indianapolis: Indiana University Press, pp. 242–263.

Varricchio, David J., F. Jackson, J. J. Borkowski, and John R. Horner, 1997a, Coelurosaurian eggs: Between a rock and a soft place: _Journal of Vertebrate Paleontology_, 17 (Supplement to Number 3), Abstracts of Papers, Fifty-seventh Annual Meeting, p. 82A.

_____, 1997b, Nest and egg clutches of the dinosaur _Troodon formosus_ and the evolution of avian reproductive traits: _Nature_, 385, pp. 247–250.

Vickaryous, Matthew K., and Michael J. Ryan, 1997, Ornamentation, _in_: Philip J. Currie and Kevin Padian, editors, _Encyclopedia of Dinosaurs_. San Diego: Academic Press, pp. 488–493.

Vickers-Rich, Patricia, 1998, Environment and adaptations of the polar dinosaurs from southeastern Australia, _in_: Yukimitsu Tomida, Thomas R. Rich, and Patricia Vickers-Rich, editors, _Second Symposium Gondwana Dinosaur, 12–13 July, 1998, National Science Museum, Tokyo, Abstracts with Program_, pp. 16–17.

Vickers-Rich, Patricia, Anusuya Chinsamy, and Thomas R. Rich, 1998, Adaptations of S. E. Australian dinosaurs to a polar environment, _in_: Donald L. Wolberg, K. Gittis, S. Miller, and A. Raynor, editors, _The Dinofest^TM Symposium_ [abstracts], Presented by The Academy of Natural Sciences of Philadelphia, Pennsylvania, pp. 61–62.

Vickers-Rich, Patricia, and Thomas H. Rich, 1993, _The ICI Australia Catalogue of The Great Russian Dinosaurs Exhibition 1993–1995_. Clayton, Australia: Monash Science Centre, 80 pages.

_____, 1997, The polar dinosaurs of southeastern Australia, _in_: Donald L. Wolberg, Edmund Stump, and Gary Rosenberg, editors. _Dinofest^TM International: Proceedings of a Symposium Held at Arizona State University_. Philadelphia: Academy of Natural Sciences, pp. 253–257.

Viera, L. I., and J. A. Torres, 1995, Presencia de _Baryonyx walkeri_ (Saurischia, Theropoda) en el Weald de La Rioja (España). Nota previa: _Munibe. Ciencias Naturales_, 47, pp. 57–61, San Sebastian.

Walker, Alick D., 1964, Triassic reptiles from the Elgin area, _Ornithosuchus_ and the origin

Bibliography

of carnosaurs: *Philosophical Transactions from the Royal Society of London, Series B,* 248, pp. 53–134.

———, 1969, The reptile fauna of the "Lower Keuper" Sandstone: *Geological Magazine,* 106, pp. 470–476, London.

Walters, Robert F., 1996, Life restoration of *Giganotosaurus carolinii,* a large theropod dinosaur from the Cretaceous of Argentina: *Journal of Vertebrate Paleontology,* 16 (Supplement to Number 3), Abstracts of Papers, Fifty-sixth Annual Meeting, p. 71A.

Ward, Peter D., 1996, The anatomy of the K/T extinctions: *Dinofest™ International Symposium, April 18–21, 1996, Programs and Abstracts,* p. 112.

———, 1997, On the Cretaceous extinction of the ammonites, *in*: Donald L. Wolberg, Edmund Stump, and Gary Rosenberg, editors. *Dinofest™ International: Proceedings of a Symposium Held at Arizona State University.* Philadelphia: Academy of Natural Sciences, pp. 519–525.

Watabe, Mahito, Shigeru Suzuki, Khishigjaw Tsogtbaatar, Rinchen Barsbold, and David B. Weishampel, 1996, Hatchlings of the dinosaur *Protoceratops* (Ornithischia: Ceratopsia) from the Upper Cretaceous locality Tugrikin Shire, Gobi Desert, Mongolia: *Journal of Vertebrate Paleontology,* 16 (Supplement to Number 3), Abstracts of Papers, Fifty-sixth Annual Meeting, p. 71A.

Weishampel, David B., and Ralph Chapman, 1990, Morphometric study of *Plateosaurus* from Trössingen (Baden-Wurttemberg, Federal Republic of Germany), *in*: Kenneth Carpenter and Philip J. Currie, editors, *Dinosaur Systematic: Approaches and Perspectives.* New York: Cambridge University Press, pp. 43–52.

Weishampel, David B., Peter Dodson, and Halszka Osmólska, editors, 1990, *The Dinosauria.* Berkeley and Los Angeles: University of California Press, xiii, 733 pages.

Weishampel, David B., Dan Grigorescu, and David B. Norman, 1991, The dinosaurs of Translyvania: island biogeography in the Late Cretaceous: *National Geographic Research & Exploration,* 7 (2), pp. 196–215.

Weishampel, David B., and John R. Horner, 1990, Hadrosauridae, *in*: Weishampel, Peter Dodson, and Halszka Osmólska, editors, *The Dinosauria.* Berkeley and Los Angeles: University of California Press, pp. 534–561.

Weishampel, David B., and James A. Jensen, 1979, *Parasaurolophus* (Reptilia: Hadrosauridae) from Utah: *Journal of Paleontology,* 53 (6), pp. 1422–1427.

Weishampel, David B., David B. Norman, and Dan Grigorescu, 1993, *Telmatosaurus transsylvanicus* from the Late Cretaceous of Romania: the most basal hadrosaurid dinosaur: *Paleontology,* 36 (2), pp. 361–385.

Weishampel, David B., and Lawrence M. Witmer, 1990, *Lesothosaurus, Pisanosaurus,* and *Technosaurus, in*: Weishampel, Peter Dodson, and Halszka Osmólska, editors, *The Dinosauria.* Berkeley and Los Angeles: University of California Press, pp. 416–426.

Welles, Samuel P., 1954, New Jurassic dinosaur from the Kayenta Formation of Arizona: *Bulletin of the Geological Society of America,* 65, pp. 591–598.

———, 1971, Dinosaur footprints from the Kayenta Formation of northern Arizona: *Plateau,* 44, pp. 27–38.

Wellnhofer, Peter, 1993, Das siebte Exemplar von *Archaeopteryx* aus den Solnhofener Schichten: *Archaeopteryx,* 11, pp.1–47.

———, 1994, Prosauropod dinosaurs from the Feurletten (Middle Norian) of Ellingen near Weissenburg in Bavaria: *Revisions in Paleobiology,* Special Issue 7, pp. 263–271, Geneva.

Wenz, Sylvie, 1980, A propos du genre *Mawsonia,* Coelacanthe géant du Crétacé inférieur d'Africa et du Brésil: *Mémoires de la Societé Géologique de France,* Nouvelle Serie, 59 (139), pp. 187–190.

Wieland, G. R., 1911, Notes on the armored Dinosauria: *American Journal of Sciences,* 4 (36), pp. 112–124.

Wilby, P. R., D. E. G. Briggs, P. Bernier, and C. Gaillard, 1996, the role of microbial mats in the fossilization of soft-tissues: *Geology,* 24, pp. 787–790.

Williamson, Thomas E., 1996, A centrosaurine ceratopsian dinosaur from the Upper Cretaceous (early Campanian) Menefee Formation, San Juan Basin, New Mexico: *Journal of Vertebrate Paleontology,* 16 (Supplement to Number 3), Abstracts of Papers, Fifty-sixth Annual Meeting, p. 73A.

Williamson, Thomas E., and Daniel J. Chure, 1996, A large allosaurid from the Upper Jurassic Morrison Formation (Brushy Basin Member), west-central New Mexico, *in*: Michael Morales, editor, *Museum of Northern Arizona Bulletin,* 60, pp. 73–79.

Williamson, Thomas E., and Robert M. Sullivan, 1997, Reinterpretation of a *Parasaurolophus* skull from the Upper Cretaceous (Campanian) Kaiparowits Formation, Utah: *Journal of Vertebrate Paleontology,* 17 (Supplement to Number 3), Abstracts of Papers, Fifty-seventh Annual Meeting, p. 84A.

Wilson, Jeffrey A., 1997, A reevaluation of Mongolian sauropods: Implications for sauropod biogeography: *Journal of Vertebrate Paleontology,* 17 (Supplement to Number 3), Abstracts of Papers, Fifty-seventh Annual Meeting, pp. 84A–85A.

Wilson, Jeffrey A., and Paul C. Sereno, 1998, Early evolution and higher-level phylogeny of sauropod dinosaurs: *Journal of Vertebrate Paleontology,* 15 (Supplement to Number 2), Society of Vertebrate Paleontology Memoir 5, 68 pages.

Wilson, Jeffrey A., and Matt B. Smith, 1996, New remains of *Amphicoelias* Cope (Dinosauria: Sauropoda) from the Upper Jurassic of Montana and diplodocid phylogeny: *Journal of Vertebrate Paleontology,* 16 (Supplement to Number 3), Abstracts of Papers, Fifty-sixth Annual Meeting, p. 73A.

Winkler, Dale A., Phillip A. Murry, and Louis L. Jacobs, 1997, A new species of *Tenontosaurus* (Dinosauria: Ornithopoda) from the Early Cretaceous of Texas: *Journal of Vertebrate Paleontology,* 17 (2), pp. 330–348.

———, editors, 1989, *Field Guide to the Vertebrate Paleontology of the Trinity Group, Lower Cretaceous of Central Texas. Society of Vertebrate Paleontology 49th Annual Meeting Field Trip.* Dallas: Institute for the Study of Earth and Man, Southern Methodist University, 33 pages.

Winkler, Dale A., Louis L. Jacobs, and Phillip A. Murry, 1997, Jones Ranch: an Early Cretaceous sauropod bone-bed in Texas: *Journal of Vertebrate Paleontology,* 17 (Supplement to Number 3), Abstracts of Papers, Fifty-seventh Annual Meeting, p. 85A.

Witmer, Lawrence M., and W. Desmond Maxwell, 1996, The skull of *Deinonychus* (Dinosauria: Theropoda): new insights and implications: *Journal of Vertebrate Paleontology,* 16 (Supplement to Number 3), Abstracts of Papers, Fifty-sixth Annual Meeting, p. 73A.

Wolberg, Donald L., Edmund Stump, and Gary Rosenberg, editors, 1997, *Dinofest™ International: Proceedings of a Symposium Held at Arizona State University.* Philadelphia: Academy of Natural Science, ix, 587 pages.

Wolf, Linda, 1998, Discovering dinosaurs in the new Dinosaur Hall: *Dinosaurs Invade Philadelphia,* pp. 9–12.

Wolfe, Douglas G., and James I. Kirkland, 1998, *Zuniceratops christopheri* n. gen. & n. sp., a ceratopsian dinosaur from the Moreno Hill Formation (Cretaceous, Turonian) of west-central New Mexico, *in*: Spencer G. Lucas, James I. Kirkland, and John W. Estep, editors, *Lower and Middle Cretaceous Terrestrial Ecosystems.* Albuquerque: New Mexico Museum of Natural History and Science, Bulletin 14, pp. 303–318.

Wolfe, Douglas G., James, I. Kirkland, Robert Denton, and Brian G. Anderson, 1997, A new terrestrial vertebrate record from the Moreno Hill Formation (Turonian: Cretaceous), west-central New Mexico: *Journal of Vertebrate Paleontology,* 17 (Supplement to Number 3), Abstracts of Papers, Fifty-seventh Annual Meeting, pp. 85A–86A.

Woodward, Arthur A. Smith, 1901, On some extinct reptiles from Patagonia of the genera *Miolina, Dinilysia* and *Genyodectes*: *Proclamations of the Zoological Society of London,* pp. 179–182.

Wroblewski, Anton F.-J., 1996, New perspectives on terminal Cretaceous marine regression and dinosaurian extinction: *Journal of Vertebrate Paleontology,* 16 (Supplement to Number 3), Abstracts of Papers, Fifty-sixth Annual Meeting, p. 74A.

Xikin, and Xing Zu, 1998, The oldest coelurosaurian: *Nature,* 394, pp. 234–35.

Xu Xing, 1997, A new psittacosaur (*Psittacosaurus mazonghanensis* sp. nov.) from Mazongshan Area, Gansu Province, China, *in*: Dong Zhiming, editor, *Sino-Japanese Silk Road Dinosaur Expedition.* Beijing: China Ocean Press, pp. 48–67.

Yadagiri, P., and K. Ayyasami, 1979, A new stegosaurian dinosaur from the Upper Cretaceous sediments of south India: *Journal of the Geological Society of India,* 20, pp. 521–530.

Yang Cai, Li Kui, and He Xinli, 1996, New find of *Mamenchisaurus* (Sauropod Dinosaur): *Geological Science Study Paper*, China Economy Press, Beijing, pp. 83–86 (in Chinese).

Yang, Zhungjian [Young Chung-Chien], 1939, On a new Sauropoda, with notes on other fragmentary reptiles from Szechuan: *Bulletin of the Geological Survey of China*, 19 (3), pp. 299–315.

_____, 1951, The Lufeng saurischian fauna of China: *Palaeontologica Sinica*, Peking, 134, pp. 1–96.

_____, 1954, On a new sauropod from Yiping, Szechuan, China: *Scientia Sinica*, 3, pp. 491–504.

_____, 1958, New sauropods from China: *Vertebrata PalAsiatica*, 2 (4), pp. 231–236.

Yang, Zhungjian [Young Chung-Chien] and Chao, H. C., 1972, *Mamenchisaurus hochuanensis* sp. nov., *Institute of Vertebrate Paleontology and Paleoanthropology Monograph*, series A, 8, pp. 1–30.

Young, Chung-Chien. *See* Yang, Zhungjian.

Yu, C., 1993, Reconstruction of the skull of *Diplodocus* and the phylogeny of the Diplodocidae (Dinosauria-Sauropoda). Ph.D. Thesis, University of Chicago, 143 pages.

Zangerl, Rainer, 1956, *Dinosaurs, Predator and Prey*. Chicago: Chicago Natural History Museum Press, 13 pages.

Zhang Yihong, and Chen Wei, 1996, Preliminary research on the classification of sauropods from Sichuan Basin, China: *in*: Michael Morales, editor, *Museum of Northern Arizona Bulletin 60*, pp. 97–108.

Zhang Yihong, Li Kui, and Zeng Qinghua, 1998, A new species of Sauropod dinosaur from the Upper Jurassic of Sichuan Basin, China: *Journal of Chengdu University of Technology*, 25 (1), pp. 68–70 (in Chinese).

Zhang Yihong, and Yang Zhaolong, 1995, *Jingshanosaurus*. Kunming, China: Yunnan Publishing House of Science and Technology, 100 pages.

Zhao, Xijin, and Xu Xing, 1998, The oldest coelurosaurian: *Nature*, 394, pp. 234–235.

Zhao, Xin Jin [formerly Zhao Xijin], 1975, [The microstructure of the dinosaurian eggshells of Nanshiung, Kwangtung]: *Vertebrata PalAsiatica*, 13 (2), pp. 105–117.

Ziegler, A. M., C. R. Scotese, and S. F. Barrett, 1982, *in*: P. Brosche and J. Sundermann, editors, *Tidal Friction and the Earth's Rotation II*. Berlin: Springer-Verlag, pp. 240–252.

Zimmer, Carl, Dinosaurs in motion: 1997, *Discover*, 18 (11), pp. 96–104, 109.

Zinsmeister, William J., 1987, Cretaceous paleogeography of Antarctica: *Palaeogeography, Palaeoclimatology, Palaeoecology*, 59, pp. 197–206.

_____, 1997, Did the world of the dinosaurs end with a bang or a pop?, *in*: Donald L. Wolberg, Edmund Stump, and Gary Rosenberg, editors. *Dinofest™ International: Proceedings of a Symposium Held at Arizona State University*. Philadelphia: Academy of Natural Sciences, pp. 541–557.

Index

Indexed herein are genera and species; selected authors, discoverers, and other persons; selected institutions, organizations, stratigraphic horizons, localities, sites, symposia, and miscellaneous places; and also relevant general topics that are discussed or appear in the text as well as in picture captions. Junior synonyms are cross-referenced to the currently and most widely accepted senior synonym. Page numbers set in *italics* indicate subjects shown or implied in illustrations, or names and topics mentioned or implied in picture captions or credits. Not indexed: dinosaurian taxa above genus level, most published misspelled taxa, and institutions referred to only as abbreviations used to designate catalogue numbers for fossil specimens.

Index

Index

Index